Wales

Anglesey & the
North Coast
(p259)

Snowdonia &
the Llŷn
(p209)

Aberystwyth &
Mid-Wales
(p178)

Swansea,
the Gower &
Carmarthenshire
(p109)

St Davids &
Pembrokeshire
(p142)

Brecon Beacons &
Southeast Wales
(p71)

Cardiff ☆
(p38)

THIS EDITION WRITTEN AND RESEARCHED BY

Peter Dragicevich
Etain O'Carroll, Helena Smith

PLAN YOUR TRIP

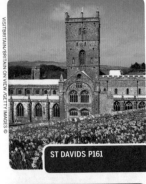

ST DAVIDS P161

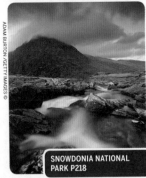

SNOWDONIA NATIONAL PARK P218

ON THE ROAD

VISITBRITAIN/BRITAIN ON VIEW /GETTY IMAGES ©

ADAM BURTON /GETTY IMAGES ©

Contents

SPECIAL FEATURES

Welcome to Wales

The phrase 'good things come in small packages' may be a cliché, but in the case of Wales it's undeniably true

Wilderness

Compact but geologically diverse, Wales offers myriad opportunities for escaping into nature. It may not be wild in the classic sense – humans have been shaping this land for millennia – but there are plenty of lonely corners to explore, lurking behind mountains, within river valleys and along surf-battered cliffs. An extensive network of paths makes Wales a hiker's paradise – and thousands of people duck across the border from England each year for that reason alone. Things are even more untamed on the islands scattered just off the coast, some of which are important wildlife sanctuaries.

Stones with Stories

Castles are an inescapable part of the Welsh landscape. They're absolutely everywhere. You could visit a different one every day for a year and still not see them all. Some watch over mountain passes, while others keep an eye on the city traffic whizzing by; some lie in enigmatic ruins, while others still have families living in them. There's also an altogether more inscrutable and far older set of stones to discover – the stone circles, dolmens and standing stones erected long before castles were ever dreamt up, before even histories were written.

Beaches

Just because it's not exactly tropical doesn't detract from Wales being a superb beach-holiday destination – and the melanoma risk is considerably lower here! The beauty of the British coast is cruelly underrated, and Wales has some of the very best bits. When the sun is shining the beaches fill up with kids building sandcastles and splashing about in the shallows. And when it's not? How about a bracing walk instead.

Hospitality & Hiraeth

Beyond the scenery and the castles, it's interactions with Welsh people that will remain in your memory the longest. Perhaps you'll recall the moment when you were sitting in a Caernarfon cafe, listening to the banter in the ancient British tongue dancing around you. Or that time when you were in the pub, screaming along to the rugby with a red-shirted mob. They talk a lot in Wales about *hiraeth*. A typically Welsh word, it refers to a sense of longing for the green, green grass of home. Even if you're not from Wales, a feeling of *hiraeth* may well hit you when you leave, only to be sated when you return.

Why I Love Wales

By Peter Dragicevich, Author

I remember my first time in Wales – a short trip to Cardiff with a fellow Kiwi living in Lon- We were so impressed with the castle that we took the train to Caerphilly the following for an extra serving. I returned shortly afterwards to walk the extraordinarily beautiful brokeshire Coast Path, and since then I've been back numerous times and explored y corner of the country. I've met lots of interesting people, been repeatedly surprised by beauty of the scenery and I've seen an awful lot of castles. What's not to love?

more about our authors, see p352

Above: Conwy Castle (p269)

Wales

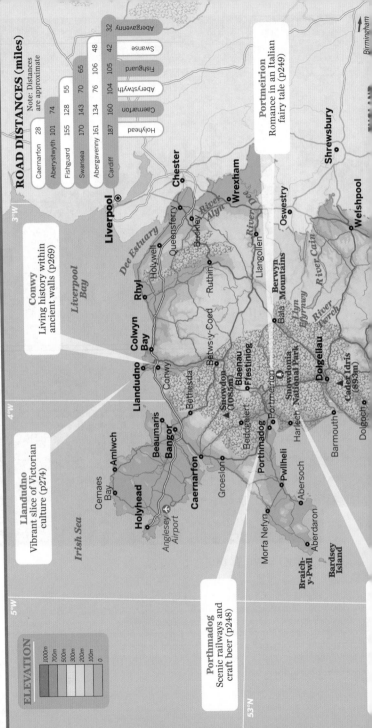

ELEVATION
- 1000m
- 700m
- 500m
- 300m
- 200m
- 100m
- 0

ROAD DISTANCES (miles)
Note: Distances are approximate

	Holyhead	Caernarfon	Aberystwyth	Fishguard	Swansea	Abergavenny
Caernarfon	28					
Aberystwyth	101	74				
Fishguard	155	128	55			
Swansea	170	143	70	65		
Abergavenny	161	134	76	106	48	
Cardiff	187	160	104	105	42	32

Llandudno
Vibrant slice of Victorian culture (p274)

Conwy
Living history within ancient walls (p269)

Portmeirion
Romance in an Italian fairy tale (p249)

Porthmadog
Scenic railways and craft beer (p248)

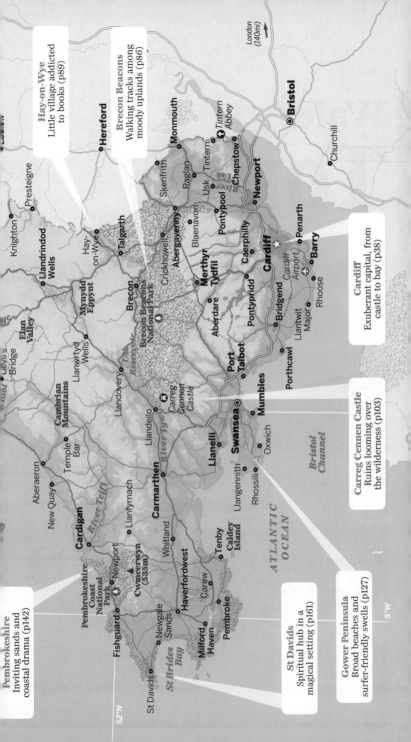

Hay-on-Wye
Little village addicted to books (p89)

Brecon Beacons
Walking tracks among moody uplands (p86)

Cardiff
Exuberant capital, from castle to bay (p38)

Carreg Cennen Castle
Ruins looming over the wilderness (p103)

St Davids
Spiritual hub in a magical setting (p161)

Gower Peninsula
Broad beaches and surfer-friendly swells (p127)

Pembrokeshire
Inviting sands and coastal drama (p142)

London (140mi)

Bristol

Churchill

Hereford

Presteigne
Knighton
Llandrindod Wells

Monmouth
Tintern Abbey
Tintern
Chepstow
Newport

Skenfrith
Raglan
Usk
River Usk
Pontypool

Hay-on-Wye
Talgarth

Crickhowell
Abergavenny
Blaenavon

Mynydd Epynt

Brecon
Brecon Beacons National Park

Merthyr Tydfil
Caerphilly
Cardiff
Penarth
Barry

Elan Valley
Devil's Bridge

Llanwrtyd Wells

Cambrian Mountains

Llandovery

River Tywi
Carreg Cennen Castle

Aberdare
Pontypridd
Bridgend
Cardiff Airport
Rhoose

Llantwit Major

Port Talbot
Porthcawl

Aberaeron
Temple Bar
New Quay

River Teifi

Cardigan

Llanfyrnach
Newport
Cwmcerwyn (535m)

Whitland
Carmarthen

Llandeilo

River Tywi

Llanelli

Swansea
Mumbles
Oxwich

Bristol Channel

ATLANTIC OCEAN

Llangennith
Rhossili

Gower Peninsula

Pembrokeshire Coast National Park
Fishguard
Newgale Sands

St Brides Bay

St Davids

Haverfordwest
Carew
Tenby
Caldey Island

Milford Haven
Pembroke

52°N

5°W

Wales'
Top 16

Wales Coast Path

1 Since 2012 all of Wales' famously beautiful coastal paths have been linked up in one continuous 870-mile route (p128). Walk for two months or walk for two days – there's no rule that you have to do it all in one go. The best stretches take in the Gower's beautiful beaches, Pembrokeshire's multicoloured cliffs and limestone arches, the remote edges of the Llŷn Peninsula and the ancient vistas of Anglesey. And if you link it up with Offa's Dyke Path, you can circle the entire country! Below: Broad Haven (p150)

Snowdonia

2 The rugged northwest corner of the country has rocky mountain peaks, glacier-hewn valleys and lakes, sinuous ridges, sparkling rivers and charm-infused villages. The busiest part is around Snowdon itself, where hordes hike to the summit and many more take the less strenuous cog railway from Llanberis. Elsewhere in Snowdonia's rugged mountains are rarely trodden areas perfect for off-the-beaten-track exploration. Glorious under the summer sun and even better under a blanket of snow, Snowdonia (p218) is one of Wales' absolute treasures. Below: Snowdon (p244)

SLOW IMAGES / GETTY IMAGES ©

JAMES OSMOND / GETTY IMAGES ©

St Davids

3 Some places have a presence all of their own, and that's certainly true of St Davids (p161). Officially a city but more like a large village, the peaceful home of Wales' patron saint has attracted the spiritually minded for centuries. Whether you come seeking salvation in the surf, or hope to commune with the whales in the Celtic Deep, or whether you genuinely wish to embrace the grace of Wales' patron saint, St Davids is a strangely affecting place.

Below: St Davids Cathedral (p161)

Conwy Castle

4 The golden age of castle building happened to coincide with the gold age of 'let's show the Welsh what's wha There's barely a town in Wales of any ne that doesn't have a castle towering over it. None has a more symbiotic relationship with its settlement than Conwy. Th castle (p269) still stretches out its enfo ing arms to enclose the historic town in a stony embrace, originally designed to keep a tiny English colony safe from the populace they displaced. Even today it's awe-inspiring sight.

HUW JONES / GETTY IMAGES ©

VISITBRITAIN/BRITAIN ON VIEW / GETTY IMAGES ©

ood & Drink

In a world obsessed with celebrity chefs d televised cooking tests, new buzzwords e entered the food nacular like 'local', stainable' and 'organic'. in the provision of top-tch produce (p308) that les has found its niche. ny fine restaurants have ung up in the Welsh untryside, namedrop-g their local farmers d butchers as if they re rock stars. Local craft eweries supply the better al pubs, while Penderyn s brought whisky, that ctar of the Celts, back to s once teetotalled land. me classics have never ne away – pass us an-er Welsh cake, will you?

Pembrokeshire

6 Whether you come armed with hiking boots, a bucket and spade, or a surfboard, Wales' western extremity won't disappoint. Famous in Britain for its beaches and coastal walks, Pembro-keshire (p143) is a small sampler of all that Wales has to offer. Pembroke has one of Britain's finest Nor-man castles, and there are smaller versions at nearby Tenby, Manorbier, Carew and Haverfordwest. The Preseli Hills offer upland walking and ancient stand-ing stones. Add to that wildlife reserves, cute vil-lages and an ancient ca-thedral, and all bases are covered. Above: North Beach, Tenby (p143)

Ffestiniog & Welsh Highland Railways

7 Once you could only get views this good if you were a hunk of slate on your way to the port. This twin-set of narrow-gauge train lines now shuttles rail enthusiasts from Porthma-dog up into the mountains of Snowdonia, with the Welsh Highland Railway (p250) slicing right past Snowdon to the coast at Caernarfon. The Ffestiniog Railway (p250) heads to the former industrial heartland of Blaenau Ffes-tiniog, where you can delve into the depths of the slate caverns. Above: Ffestiniog Railway

ADAM BURTON / GETTY IMAGES ©

Brecon Beacons

8 Not as wild as Snowdonia nor as spectacular as the Pembrokeshire Coast, Wales' third national park (p86) manages quite a feat – and that's to be simultaneously bleak and beautiful. Walkers will delight in its unpopulated moors and bald hills, while history buffs can seek out hill forts and barrows, and the enigmatic ruins of abbeys and castles. The towns within the park's confines are some of Wales' most endearingly idiosyncratic, including Hay-on-Wye and Abergavenny – hallowed names for book lovers and food fans respectively. Above: Powys (p191)

Hay-on-Wye

9 When a former US president describes your annual festival as the 'Woodstock of the mind', you know you're doing something right. This unselfconsciously pretty border town (p89) has assumed near mythic proportions among both the worldwide literati and lit-loving Brits as the most book-imbued place in the world. It's like a Bizarro World version of tabloid culture, where intellectuals are admired, poets are praised and librarians are the new Kardashians. Oh, and there's good beer and food to be had, too.

Rugby

10 Take 30 men with maybe 20 necks between them, divide them into two teams and have them chase an odd-shaped pigskin down a field and what do you have? A national obsession? A thing of beauty? A good excuse to sing and drink beer? All of the above. That this product of the English public school system should become such a force of working-class cohesion across the border remains a mystery. For a glimpse into the very soul of Wales catch a live match (p307). Next page, top: Millennium Stadium (p43)

rtmeirion

One man's devotion to the power of itecture to enhance nvironment is encapted in this fanciful slice roque Italy clinging e North Welsh coast -9). Immerse yourself e fantasy by booking one of the scaledn mansions or cutesy ages facing the piazza. unreal might shift s into the surreal if happen upon a *Pris-* convention, where of the cult television es, filmed here in the Os, indulge in dress and human chess naments.

PAUL THOMPSON / GETTY IMAGES ©

ANDY STOTHERT / GETTY IMAGES ©

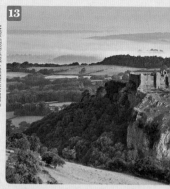

Gower Peninsula

12 It seems like you're barely out of Swansea when the Gower's beauty starts to assert itself. The roads narrow, the houses fall away and suddenly you're in verdant farmland, edged between windswept hills and the glittering sea. It's this strange combination of accessibility and remoteness that makes the Gower Peninsula (p127) unique, but it's the gorgeous beaches that make it truly special. It comes to a worthy coda with the long sandy miles abutting Rhossili Bay, affording blissful solitude for surfers and beach strollers alike.

Carreg Cennen Castle

13 Artfully decaying ruins in remote locations have been attracting romantic souls to Wales for hundreds of years, and it's in places like Carreg Cennen (p103) that they reach their apotheosis. The hilltop setting, within the western reaches of Brecon Beacons National Park, is bleak and barren, moody and mysterious. As you edge nearer along country lanes and the castle looms into view in the distance, it's easy to make the mental trade-in of your rental car for a fine steed, galloping bravely towards unknown danger.

Llandudno

14 Oh the Victorian, they really did li[ke] to be beside the seasid[e], and Llandudno (p274) is one of the few places where you can still stro[ll] along the prom and hav[e a] reasonable chance of h[ear]ing a brass band playin[g] 'tiddely-om-pom-pom'. [It's] not Wales' most beauti[ful] beach but Llandudno h[as] lashings of old-fashione[d] charm. Where else can [you] still watch Mr Punch sq[ua]bbling with fellow puppe[ts] over sausages, and the[n] head into a chintzy hote[l] for high tea. When it all [gets] too genteel, escape up [the] Orme for a wilderness f[ix].

Above: LLandudno Pier (p27[4])

⸺rdiff Bay

⸺ The transformation of stinky Cardiff
Bay (p44) into the shiny archi-
⸺ural showcase of today is a textbook
⸺mple of urban renewal at its best. Yes,
⸺ut off from the city centre and there
⸺bandoned buildings on its fringes, but
⸺iff Bay is a testament to the rebirth of
⸺ncient nation as a modern democratic
⸺try, increasingly in control of its own
⸺ny. And the transformation is ongo-
⸺with the recent opening of the Doctor
⸺ Experience, next to BBC Wales' flash
⸺ studio complex. Top: Pierhead (p45)

Eisteddfods

16 The eisteddfod is the way in which
the nation hooks into its ancient
past. Fundamentally, it's a chance for the
Welsh to simply sit *(eistedd)* and be *(bod)*.
Sure, the long robes and stone-circle ceremonies can seem silly, but if anyone has
a claim to the traditions of ancient Britain,
it's the Welsh. Both the National Eisteddfod and the youth version ping-pong
between North and South Wales annually,
but Llangollen's International Musical
Eisteddfod (p217) is a permanent fixture.
Bottom: Llangollen International Musical Eisteddfod

Need to Know

For more information, see Survival Guide (p316)

Currency
Pound, also called 'pound sterling' (£)

Language
English, Welsh

Money
ATMs widely available. Credit cards accepted in most hotels and restaurants.

Visas
Not required for most citizens of Europe, Australia, New Zealand, Canada and the USA.

Mobile Phones
Phones from most other countries operate in Wales, but roaming charges apply. Local SIM cards are easy to obtain and cost from £10.

Time
Greenwich Mean Time (GMT)

When to Go

Mild to warm summers, cold winters

Caernarfon GO Apr–Sep

Llangollen GO Apr–Sep

Aberystwyth GO Apr–Aug

St Davids GO Mar–Sep

Cardiff GO Mar–Dec

High Season
(Jul & Aug)

➡ Weather is at its warmest; lots of festivals and events.

➡ Accommodation prices increase in coastal areas and national parks, but not in cities.

➡ The absolute peak is the August school holidays.

Shoulder
(Apr–Jun, Sep & Oct)

➡ The season doesn't kick off until Easter, which can be in March or April.

➡ Prices rise to peak levels on bank holidays.

➡ April to June are the driest months; October is one of the wettest.

Low Season
(Nov–Mar)

➡ Prices rise to peak levels over Christmas and New Year.

➡ Snow can close roads, particularly in the mountains.

➡ January and February are the coldest months.

Websites

Visit Wales (www.visitwales.co.uk) Official resource for tourist information.

BBC Wales (www.bbc.co.uk/wales/) The national broadcaster's portal on Wales.

WalesOnline (www.walesonline.co.uk) News and views concerning Welsh life.

Traveline Cymru (www.traveline-cymru.info) Essential public transport information.

Lonely Planet (www.lonelyplanet.com/wales) Traveller forum and more.

Important Numbers

Emergency	☏999
Wales (& UK) country code	☏44
International access code	☏00
Traveline Cymru (public transport)	☏0871 200 2233
Visit Wales (tourist information)	☏08708 300 306

Exchange Rates

Australia	A$1	£0.63
Canada	C$1	£0.63
Euro zone	€1	£0.86
Japan	¥100	£0.66
New Zealand	NZ$1	£0.52
USA	US$1	£0.66

For current exchange rates see www.xe.com.

Daily Costs

Budget up to £50

➡ Dorm bed: £14-23

➡ Cheap meal in cafe or pub: £3-10

➡ Coach ticket (less than 100 miles): up to £18

Midrange £50-120

➡ Double room in hotel/B&B: £60-130

➡ Main course in midrange restaurant: £9-18

➡ Castle admission: £4-11

➡ Car rental: from £30 per day

➡ Train journey: Cardiff–London £41, Cardiff–Holyhead £85

Top End more than £120

➡ Luxury hotel or boutique B&B room: from £130

➡ Three-course meal in top restaurant: £20-50

Opening Hours

Opening hours tend to be fairly standard throughout the year, except venues with an outdoor component (castles, gardens, beach cafes etc), which close earlier in winter.

Banks 9.30am–5pm Monday to Friday, 9.30am–1pm Saturday

Post offices 9am–5pm Monday to Friday, 9am-12.30pm Saturday

Cafes 9am–5pm Monday to Saturday, 11am–4pm Sunday

Restaurants noon–2pm and 6pm–10pm

Pubs 11am–11pm

Shops 9am–6pm Monday to Saturday, 11am–4pm Sunday

Arriving in Wales

London Heathrow Airport Has connecting flights to Cardiff Airport and direct coaches to Chepstow (£37, two hours), Newport (£37, 2½ hours), Cardiff (£43, three hours) and Swansea (£44, 4¼ hours). For train connections, catch the Heathrow Express to Paddington Station.

Cardiff Airport Bus X91 heads to central Cardiff (£3.90, 30 minutes, every two hours). Shuttle buses (£1) head to Rhoose train station, where trains continue to Cardiff Central (£4, 30 minutes, hourly). Allow £30 for a taxi.

Holyhead Ferry Terminal Trains head to Rhosneigr (£4.10, 12 minutes), Llanfair PG (£7.70, 29 minutes), Bangor (£8.70, 30 minutes) and Conwy (£13.50, one hour).

Fishguard Harbour Trains head to Cardiff (£24, 2½ hours) via Carmarthen (£8.60, 52 minutes).

Getting Around

Car Driving will get you to remote corners of Wales not connected to public transport. Cars can be hired from the main cities and the airports.

Bus The most useful form of public transport, with routes connecting most towns and villages. Many services don't run on Sundays. National Express coaches only stop in major destinations.

Train The network isn't extensive, but it's handy for those towns connected to it. Trains are comfortable and reliable, but more expensive than the buses.

For much more on **getting around**, see p326

If You Like...

Industrial Heritage

Blaenavon A World Heritage Site of well-preserved ironworks and the fascinating Big Pit Coal Mine. (p106)

Pontcysyllte Aqueduct & Canal Yet another World Heritage Site, this one focusing on Thomas Telford's ingenious canal system. (p215)

National Slate Museum This fascinating complex is a testimony to the workers who put a roof over the heads of most of Britain. (p241)

Rhondda Heritage Park Descend into the Lewis Merthyr coal mine with guides who once worked the black seam. (p108)

Porthgain An exquisite stretch of coast, made arguably more picturesque by the decaying detritus of the slate industry.

National Waterfront Museum Examine industrial heritage without setting foot anywhere damp, dirty or dark. (p113)

Shopping

The Hayes Cardiff's main shopping strip is a pedestrian-friendly avenue with the giant St David's shopping centre on one side, and a network of dainty Victorian arcades on the other.

Hay-on-Wye A nirvana for book lovers but also rich pickings for admirers of antiques, art and antiquarian maps.

Melin Tregwynt Traditional woollen goods created by a family with 100 years of experience under their belt. (p170)

Craft in the Bay Wales' finest artisans showcase their work in this Cardiff Bay store. (p62)

Narberth If pottering around independent shops in a village-like atmosphere is your thing, Narberth is your place.

Ruthin Craft Centre Buy directly from the craftspeople, at the Centre for the Applied Arts. (p213)

Castles

Caerphilly The most fairy-tale-like of Wales' castles, with a pretty lake serving as its moat. (p66)

Caernarfon Part of an imposing set (including nearby Conwy, Beaumaris and Harlech), which share a World Heritage listing. (p262)

Conwy This one still has its town walls intact, built to protect an exclusive English enclave in the heart of Gwynedd. (p269)

Carreg Cennen The most dramatically positioned fortress in Wales, standing guard over a lonely stretch of Brecon Beacons National Park. (p103)

Cardiff A decadent layer cake comprising a Roman fort, a Norman keep, a Plantagenet manor house and a Victorian fantasy. (p39)

Chepstow You couldn't design a more threatening 'Keep Out' sign than these battlements on the English–Welsh border. (p74)

Pembroke Walk all along the watchtowers at the birthplace of the Tudor dynasty. (p152)

IF YOU LIKE... STATELY HOMES

Set within a large estate and beautiful gardens, Erddig has fascinating displays highlighting the relationships between the grand house's former masters and their servants. (p214)

ve) Cycling, Snowdonia National Park
w) Colliery pit, Rhondda Heritage Park

Mountains & Moors

Snowdon Wales' loftiest mountain has one of the most visited peaks of any in the world. (p244)

Cader Idris Another of Snowdonia's giants but a much more peaceful one. (p224)

Black Mountains The eastern reaches of Brecon Beacons National Park have a desolateness that's utterly appealing. (p87)

Great Orme A real wild child, looming above the most genteel of seaside resorts. (p274)

Cefn Bryn The windblown spine of the Gower Peninsula is made even more mysterious by the ancient dolmen at its crest. (p132)

Preseli Hills Ponder the improbable in these ancient hills where the blue stones of Stonehenge were sourced. (p175)

Cambrian Mountains Wander the empty expanses that form the Desert of Wales. (p207)

Beaches

Rhossili This long stretch of golden sand is so precious it's guarded by a dragon. (p131)

Three Cliffs Bay Another spectacularly beautiful Gower beach, accessible only by foot. (p130)

Barafundle Bay This Pembrokeshire gem hides within the National Trust–managed Stackpole Estate. (p150)

Mwnt A small arc of golden sand watched over by a lonely church, tucked away on the Ceredigion Coast. (p182)

Porth Oer Remote and gorgeous, with 'whispering sands' that squeak as you walk. (p256)

Newport Sands The kind of broad sandy beach where family holiday memories are minted. (p173)

Penbryn A cute little Ceredigion beach surrounded by lush green hills. (p184)

Ruins

Tintern Abbey Riverside ruins that inspired generations of poets and artists. (p77)

Llanthony Priory Just as picturesque as its much bigger sister at Tintern, and even more isolated. (p88)

Caerleon The Romans came, saw, conquered and bathed – and left behind ruins of barracks, baths and an amphitheatre. (p70)

Bishop's Palace The wealth and power of the medieval church are on display in this impressive complex attached to St Davids Cathedral. (p163)

Castell Dinas Brân This decaying Welsh castle provides a dramatic backdrop to the already postcard-worthy town of Llangollen. (p216)

Bryn Celli Ddu Burial Chamber For a truly ancient experience, skip the johnny-come-lately castles, abbeys and Roman baths and enter the Neolithic. (p281)

Tre'r Ceiri Hike up the hill for wonderful views and one of the best-preserved Iron Age sites in Europe. (p258)

Parks & Gardens

Bodnant Garden A breathtaking ensemble of formal gardens and woodlands attached to a gracious manor. (p273)

National Botanic Garden This vast complex is a botanical monument in the making. (p140)

Aberglasney Gardens History is on display in this beautiful set of 400-year-old walled gardens. (p138)

Powis Castle & Garden A baroque masterpiece of manicured yews, terraces, formal gardens and orchards. (p199)

Gregynog Hall The exquisite product of considerable time and space – 500 years and 300 hectares, to be exact. (p197)

Roath Park Cardiff's favourite park, with a lake, lighthouse, rose gardens, sports fields, playgrounds and lots of shady picnic spots. (p48)

Bute Park Another stunner, bounded by Cardiff Castle and the River Taff, and full of mature trees and daffodils in bloom. (p42)

Pubs & Bars

Black Boy Inn Roaring fires, real ales, hearty meals, 500-year-old walls and a resident ghost – what more could you want in a pub. (p266)

Tŷ Coch Inn The walk along the sand to this isolated beachfront pub is all part of the package. (p257)

Albion Ale House A rare gem solely devoted to ale, whisky, wine and conversation. (p274)

Old Black Lion Serving thirsty and hungry punters since the 13th century, and still going strong. (p92)

Gwdihw Young and hip without being remotely irritating, this is Cardiff's countercultural capital. (p58)

Buffalo Bar The edgy head of an ever-expanding Cardiff empire (four venues and counting), with live bands upstairs and cocktails down. (p58)

Y Ffarmers A village pub par excellence, tucked away in the undulating hills south of Aberystwyth. (p189)

Outdoor Activities

Gower Peninsula There are some good spots on the Llŷn Peninsula and in Pembrokeshire but the Gower is Wales' premier surf destination. (p127)

Plas Menai The National Watersports Centre offers sailing, powerboating, sea kayaking, windsurfing and stand-up paddleboarding. (p264)

National Whitewater Centre Near Bala, this is Wales' premier destination for whitewater rafting, kayaking and canoeing. (p219)

Plas y Brenin National Mountain Sport Centre Take a course in rock climbing, mountaineering, kayaking or canoeing. (p240)

Month by Month

January

Rug up warm for one of Wales' coldest months, with temperatures in single digits (Celsius) throughout the country. Spare a thought for the hardcore surfers braving the swells in Pembrokeshire.

Saturnalia

Llanwrtyd Wells' wacky Roman-themed beer-drinking, bull testicle-eating and mountain-bike chariot-racing festival warms spirits in mid-January. (p206)

February

The cold doesn't let up in February. In fact, it can even be slightly worse than January. Snowdonia looks glorious in its gleaming white coat.

Six Nations Championship

The highlight of the Welsh rugby calendar with home matches played at Cardiff's Millennium Stadium in February and March. (p51)

March

Temperatures rise slightly, maybe scraping into double digits in Cardiff, although the Six Nations rugby heats things up. Daffodils pop up in time for their name-saint's feast day.

St David's Day

Wales honours its patron saint on March 1, with black-and-gold St David's Cross flags draped throughout the country.

April

Spring finally starts to kick in properly, with temperatures breaking the two-digit mark throughout the country. April's also the driest month in Mid-Wales and much of the north.

Laugharne Weekend

Musicians, comedians and writers take to various stages in Dylan Thomas' favourite town for a long weekend in April. (p135)

May

Head to the north coast, where May is both the driest and the sunniest month. There might still be snow on the paths heading up Snowdon though.

Urdd National Eisteddfod

One of Europe's biggest youth events, this performing arts competition alternates between North and South Wales in early May.

Hay Festival

Arguably Britain's most important cultural event, this ever-expanding festival of literature and arts is held over 10 days in late May, bringing an intellectual influx to Hay-on-Wye. (p91)

June

Early summer is the prime time to head out walking, with a winning combination of higher temperatures, lower rainfall and lower winds. Cardiff celebrates its driest month.

�✨ Cardiff Festival

The capital's summer-long celebrations kick off, with Cardiff Festival acting as an umbrella to dozens of events. In June it includes the Unity arts festival, the Tafwyl Welsh-language festival and the Mela multicultural festival. (p51)

July

The best bet for beach weather. July is one of the warmest and driest months for most of the country – although there are no guarantees.

☆ International Musical Eisteddfod

A week-long festival of international music, including big-name evening concerts, held at Llangollen's Royal International Pavilion during the second week of July. (p217)

�✨ Royal Welsh Agricultural Show

Prize bullocks and local produce feature at Wales' biggest farm and livestock show at Builth Well's Royal Welsh Showground. (p204)

August

The good weather continues into August, which is officially the warmest month in Cardiff. It couldn't be described as tropical though; average temperatures only just sneak into the 20s.

☆ National Eisteddfod of Wales

Held alternately in North and South Wales in the first week of August, this is the largest celebration of Welsh culture, music and poetry, steeped in history, pageantry and pomp.

☆ Brecon Jazz Festival

Head to Brecon in August for the smoky sounds of one of Europe's leading jazz festivals. (p99)

September

Summer comes to an end with more of a fizzle rather a jolt, but temperatures start to creep down. Grab your surfboard and head to Pembrokeshire before the chill really sets in.

☆ Tenby Arts Festival

A week-long festival of autumnal music, literary and theatre events and sandcastle competitions in the seaside town of Tenby. (p146)

✕ Abergavenny Food Festival

This is the mother of all Welsh food festivals and the champion of the burgeoning local produce scene. (p84)

☆ Festival No 6

The arcane streets of Portmeirion resound with rock music, dance music and comedy over the course of this long weekender. (p251)

October

Here comes the rain again: October is Aberystwyth's wettest month. The mountains of Snowdonia set about living up to their name, with the earliest falls on the higher peaks.

�✨ Dylan Thomas Festival

A celebration of the man's work with readings and events at Swansea's Dylan Thomas Centre. (p114)

✕ Gwledd Conwy Feast

Feast on fine food and digital art over a weekend in late October in the historic walled town. (p270)

November

It's the rest of the country's turn to get properly soggy, with the wettest month on both the north and south coasts. It's back to single digits temperature-wise, too.

🍷 Mid-Wales Beer Festival

Held in Llanwrtyd Wells (where else), this 10-day festival includes the Real Ale Wobble & Ramble cycling, walking and supping event.

December

There's no point dreaming of a white Christmas – for many in Wales it's a given. Christmas cheer helps combat the gloomiest month, sunshine-wise.

☆ Cardiff Winter Wonderland

Festive fun for families at the heart of Cardiff's Civic Centre, with an ice-skating rink and Santa's grotto. (p52)

Itineraries

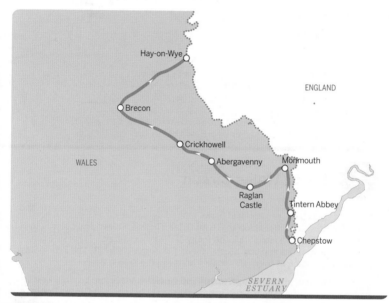

 The Southeastern Marches

This short itinerary explores the historic borderlands between Wales and England, which were once ruled by the Marcher lords, powerful French Norman families who pushed into Wales in the wake of their conquest of England. It's a particularly lush and picturesque landscape, well suited to walkers. Medieval history and architecture buffs will find the numerous castles and ruined abbeys fascinating. In fact, every single place we mention in this itinerary has its own castle.

Start in **Chepstow**, where there's a particularly hefty castle, and head north up the gorgeous Wye Valley to the famous ruins of **Tintern Abbey**. Continue following the river to **Monmouth**, the ancient county town and birthplace of both Henry V and one half of Rolls-Royce. From here, head west along the A40 to the magnificent ruins of **Raglan Castle** before continuing on to **Abergavenny**, Wales' foodie capital. The A40 then leaves Monmouthshire and crosses into Powys and the eastern fringes of Brecon Beacons National Park. Stop for the night in quiet little **Crickhowell** and then head to the sturdy stone town of **Brecon**. From here, cut northeast towards the English border to **Hay-on-Wye**, the most book-loving place on the planet.

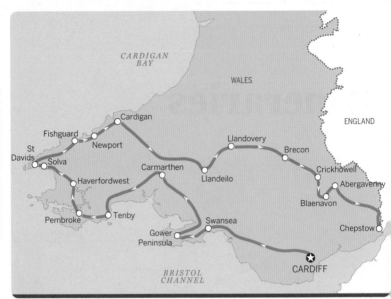

South Wales Circuit

9 DAYS

Taking in the capital, two national parks, numerous castles, many beautiful beaches, industrial sites, and cities associated with Dylan Thomas, St David and Merlin the Magician, this South Welsh circuit ticks off many of the icons of Wales. Make sure you allow time for coastal walks and lazy beach days on the Gower Peninsula and Pembrokeshire (weather dependent, of course), as well as hiking in the Brecon Beacons.

Start by thoroughly exploring **Cardiff** and its surrounds before heading west to **Swansea** for a Dylan Thomas fix. Spend a day on the beach-lined **Gower Peninsula** before proceeding to ancient **Carmarthen**, Merlin's town. Settle in to the seaside vibe at candy-striped **Tenby**, Wales' most appealing resort town and the gateway to Pembrokeshire Coast National Park. Check out the mighty castle at **Pembroke** and head on through **Haverfordwest** and the pretty port of **Solva** to beguiling **St Davids**, a sweet little city in a magical setting. Visit **Fishguard** on your way to food and beach loving **Newport**, where Neolithic and Iron Age sites await discovery in the surrounding hills.

From **Cardigan**, follow the lush Teifi Valley along the border of Ceredigion, stopping at the cute village of Cenarth and the National Woollen Museum. The Cambrian Mountains stand between here and lovely **Llandeilo**, so cut south towards Carmarthen before heading east. Do your homework first, as there are gardens, manor houses and castles to explore in this part of the Carmarthenshire countryside. Head on to the market town of **Llandovery**, with its fine Georgian buildings, and then skirt the northern edge of Brecon Beacons National Park on your way to **Brecon**. The Beacons spread south from here, offering ample opportunities for walking, horse riding and canal trips. Peaceful **Crickhowell** is another good walking base. Cross the River Usk and cut down towards **Blaenavon**, a small town that wears the legacy of its coal-mining and iron-smelting history on its sleeve, and has been inscribed on the World Heritage list as a result. Backtrack towards **Abergavenny**, home to some of Wales' best country restaurants and gastropubs. Finish with a saunter down the Wye Valley, past romantic Tintern Abbey, to **Chepstow**.

Top: River Usk, Powys (p191)

Bottom: Pembroke Castle (p152)

JORGE DUARTE ESTEVAO / GETTY IMAGES ©

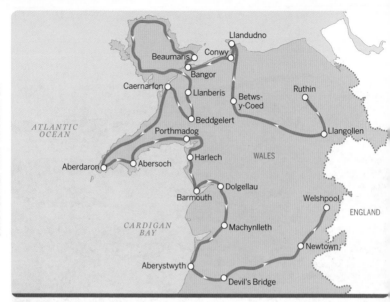

North & Mid-Wales

10 DAYS

The scenic highlights of North and Mid-Wales include river valleys, spectacular mountains and a widely varied coastline. This itinerary cuts a broad arc through the Welsh-speaking heartland, taking in still more castles, industrial sites and beaches – these things are clichés of Wales for a reason.

Start in **Ruthin** and take the beautiful back road which cuts through the bottom of the Clwydian Range to **Llangollen**, a small riverside town famous for outdoor pursuits and its World Heritage–listed canal and aqueduct. From here head west on the A5, swapping Denbighshire for the eastern reaches of Snowdonia National Park. **Betws-y-Coed** makes a pretty base for forest and river walks and mountain biking.

Put Snowdonia behind you for a few days as you head north on the A470, shadowing the River Conwy. Stop along the way at Bodnant Estate before heading north to the beach at **Llandudno**. Hop down to **Conwy** to immerse yourself in the medieval world between its town walls and tick off castle number one of the Castles of Edward I in Gwynedd World Heritage Site. The A55 hugs the coast as it heads southwest towards **Bangor**. Stop for a quick look at the pier and the cathedral before crossing the Menai Strait to the Isle of Anglesey. Base yourself at **Beaumaris** (where you'll find castle number two) and circle the sacred island of the druids.

Cross the Menai Strait again and head to **Llanberis**, where you can plan your assault on Snowdon, either on foot or by train. Circle the mighty mountain, stopping at **Beddgelert**, before heading back to the coast at **Caernarfon** for castle number three. Circle the remote Llŷn Peninsula, stopping at the beaches and pubs of **Aberdaron** and **Abersoch**. Continue through **Porthmadog**, **Harlech** (castle number four) and beachy **Barmouth** before following the Mawddach Estuary to stony faced, heritage-filled **Dolgellau**. Head south to visit the greenies at **Machynlleth** before rejoining the coast at the buzzy student town of **Aberystwyth**. Stop at the **Devil's Bridge** waterfalls and the gallery at **Newtown**, before finishing at **Welshpool** with a visit to sumptuous Powis Castle.

18 DAYS Full Welsh Circuit

This itinerary has been designed for travellers who have got the time and inclination to pack in as many of Wales' highlights as possible into one big loop.

Start at **Cardiff** and head north to see the fairy-tale castle at **Caerphilly**, before cutting west to **Swansea**. Head out along the Gower Peninsula to spectacular **Rhossili Bay**, and then continue north to remote **Carreg Cennen** in Brecon Beacons National Park. Base yourself in **Llandeilo** for a day of gardens and manor houses.

Head west to the seaside resort town of **Tenby**, within Pembrokeshire Coast National Park, before continuing on to the ancient city of **St Davids**. Head up the coast to **Newport** for a day at the beach and a night of good food. Stop at Pentre Ifan and Castell Henllys on the long, leisurely drive up the coast to studenty **Aberystwyth**.

Continue on through ecofriendly **Machynlleth** and historic **Dolgellau** to **Harlech** and its World Heritage castle. At **Porthmadog**, take a steam train ride on the narrow-gauge Ffestiniog Railway to **Blaenau Ffestiniog** and stop to tour the slate caverns. Head along the Llŷn Peninsula to **Aberdaron** for surf-battered views over Bardsey Island from Braich-y-Pwll.

Follow the coast to Caernarfon, and then continue on to **Llanberis**, when you can visit the National Slate Museum and base yourself to tackle Snowdon. Double back to the Menai Strait and cross over to Anglesey to visit **Beaumaris**, **Rhosneigr** and **Plas Newydd**.

Proceed along the north coast to walled **Conwy** and beachy **Llandudno** before turning south to forest-dwelling **Betws-y-Coed**. Head to genteel **Llangollen**, stop at Powis Castle in **Welshpool**, then continue down through Powys to kooky **Llanwrtyd Wells** and on to the market town of **Llandovery**. Head east to **Brecon**, which is a good base for tackling Pen-y-Fan, and then cut down through **Crickhowell** to food-focussed **Abergavenny**. Visit **Blaenavon**, then skirt Monmouth and follow the peaceful Wye Valley to **Tintern Abbey**.

Plan Your Trip

Outdoor Activities

Need a dose of the great outdoors? Simple: head to Wales. The terrain lends itself to all manner of activities, from relaxing to rigorous. The landscape is stunning, access is easy and there's always a cosy pub with a warm fire nearby when you need to dry out – which you almost certainly will.

Don't Miss Experiences

Birdwatching
Some of the best twitching in Wales can be found around South Stack in Holyhead.

Ancient Stones
The most mythology-rich standing stones are in Pembrokeshire's Preseli Hills.

Footsteps of Greatness
Explore the Taf Estuary around Laugharne, the 'heron-priested shore', that inspired Dylan Thomas.

Industrial History
Follow the canal path from Llangollen to Trevor, then take a boat trip over the Pontcysyllte Aqueduct.

Wildlife Encounters
Get close to grey seals, porpoises and dolphins on boat trips around Pembrokeshire's Skomer, Skokholm and Grassholm Islands.

Walking

Whether you're an ambler or a rambler, Wales is a walker's dream. There are some 25,500 miles of footpaths, bridleways and byways – all public rights of way.

For challenging walks, head for Snowdonia National Park, home to the highest mountain in England and Wales, impressive peaks and dramatic valleys, or for the craggy terrain of the Brecon Beacons, where, in the western end of the park, you can walk in almost total isolation.

One of the growing activities for walkers is geocaching, a kind of treasure hunt with the advantages of satellite navigation GPS units, combined with all the resources of the internet; for more information visit www.geocachingwales.com.

Walking can be enjoyed year-round, but be prepared for crowds in July and August, short days in winter and rain at any time. Guard against the weather with decent warm clothing, footwear and waterproofs. A map, compass, first-aid kit, food and water are musts for more adventurous hikes. It's advisable to let someone know your intended route and planned return time and to check the weather forecast with the **Met Office** (www.metoffice.gov.uk/loutdoor/mountainsafety) or the local tourist information centre before setting off.

For more information, visit www.walking.visitwales.com; the Events section includes details of walking festivals throughout Wales, generally between June and October.

Top Walks

The three national trails are open to walkers and horse riders, and are waymarked with an acorn symbol:

Glyndŵr's Way (www.nationaltrail.co.uk/glyndwrsway; 132 miles) Connecting sites associated with the rebellion led by Owain Glyndŵr in the early 15th century.

Offa's Dyke Path (www.offas-dyke.co.uk; 177 miles) Skirting the Wales–England border through an astonishing range of scenery and vegetation.

Pembrokeshire Coast Path (PCP; www.pembrokeshirecoast.org.uk; 186 miles) Hugging the sea cliffs of the Pembrokeshire Coast National Park, this is one of the UK's most beautiful coastal walks.

Cycling

There are 1197 miles of National Cycle Network, 331 miles of traffic-free rides and 11 cycle-hub destinations around the country, all of them chosen for their access to day-cycling routes and for their cycling infrastructure. Local cycling operators can advise on regional routes, while a handful also offer pan-Wales packages for a country-wide adventure. Look out, too, for local cycling events and festivals.

> ### BEST COASTAL PATHS
>
> The 850-mile Wales Coast Path enables ramblers to walk around the whole of the country. These are our favourite sections:
>
> → **Carmarthen Bay Coastal & Estuaries Way** 55 miles; Amroth to Gower
>
> → **Ceredigion Coastal Path** 63 miles; Ynyslas to Cardigan
>
> → **Llŷn Coastal Path** 95 miles; Caernarfon to Porthmadog
>
> → **Pembrokeshire Coast Path** 186 miles; Poppit Sands to Amroth

The traffic-free section of the **National Cycle Network** (NCN; www.sustrans.org.uk) North Wales Coastal Route, running along the seaside promenade from Colwyn Bay to Prestatyn, is one of the best in the UK for cyclists of all abilities.

Take your own bike or rent one from many outlets across the country. Be aware it's best to stick to tracks marked as bridleways on Ordnance Survey (OS) maps and cycling lanes. Avoid footpaths that haven't been split to incorporate cycling lanes. With the exception of July and August when tourism peaks, the unnumbered roads and lanes are quiet and cyclist friendly.

For mountain biking, Wales offers some of the best facilities in the world – it boasts six purpose-built centres throughout the country. The centres offer a mixture of routes to suit all abilities, and all have one trail designed especially for families. Coed y Brenin Forest near Dolgellau is the premier centre, boasting the rockiest, most technically advanced trails and a dual slalom course.

For more information, check out the cycling page at www.visitwales.co.uk and www.mbwales.com.

Water Sports

For canoeing and sea kayaking, head to Pembrokeshire or Anglesey to explore coves and sea caves while paddling the flat waters below the towering cliffs. Inland, Llyn Tegid (Bala Lake) and Llyn Gwynant in North Wales are worth exploring, while slow-moving rivers include River Teifi, near Cardigan, and North Wales' River Dee. Powerful tidal currents create huge standing waves between the Pembrokeshire coast and offshore islands, making the Pembrokeshire Coast National Park (the only coastal park in Britain), one of the UK's finest sea-kayaking areas. Freshwater and Newgale Sands are favourite kayaking spots. The **Welsh Canoeing Association** (www.canoewales.com/paddling-in-wales.aspx) lists the waterways that permit kayaking and canoeing.

An incredible variety of sea life and a seabed littered with shipwrecks make diving in Wales an exciting prospect. Pembrokeshire, again, is the diving hot spot, and is the access point for the Smalls, a group of rocks famous for marine life, including a large colony of seals and pods of dolphins. Visibility here can reach up to 25m, although diving is restricted by the weather and tides. In North Wales, plump for Bardsey Island, the Skerries or the Menai Strait. Be aware that tidal currents rage dangerously at many of Wales' best dive sites, so seek advice locally before taking the plunge.

Surrounded by sea on three sides and netting some of the highest tidal ranges in the world – the Severn Estuary has the second-biggest tidal range anywhere – Wales has no shortage of surfing opportunities. Popular beaches can become crowded between April and September but with a little effort, you're sure to find your own space. Sea temperatures are often warmer than you might imagine thanks to the North Atlantic Drift, but you'll always need a wetsuit, and possibly boots, a hood and gloves in winter.

> ### LONG-DISTANCE CYCLE RIDES
>
> Two of Wales' most popular long-distance rides come under the auspices of the National Cycle Network (NCN; p29):
>
> **Lôn Las Cymru** (Greenways of Wales/Welsh National Route; NCN routes 8 & 42) This 254-mile route runs from Holyhead, through to Hay-on-Wye, then on to Cardiff via Brecon or Chepstow via Abergavenny. Encompassing three mountain ranges – Snowdonia, the Brecon Beacons and the Cambrian Mountains – there's a fair amount of uphill, low-gear huffing and puffing to endure along the way. But each peak promises fantastic views and plenty of downhill, freewheeling delights.
>
> **Lôn Geltaidd** (Celtic Trail; NCN routes 4 & 47) A 337-mile route snaking from Fishguard through the West Wales hills, the Pembrokeshire Coast, the former coalfields of South Wales and ending at Chepstow Castle. The glorious, ever-changing landscape provides a superb backdrop.
>
> End points are linked with the rail network so you can make your way back to the start by train.

The Gower Peninsula is home to the Welsh surfing industry, cramming in a wide choice of breaks and plenty of post-surf activity. Hot spots include Caswell Bay, the Mumbles, Langland Bay, Oxwich Bay and Llangennith. The best breaks in Pembrokeshire are to be found at Tenby South Beach, Manorbier, Freshwater West and West Dale Bay. St Davids' immense Whitesands Bay is good for beginners, although it's often busy. You'll find surf schools at most surf beaches. For more information, check the Welsh Surfing Federation Surf School (p130) website.

There's great potential for windsurfing all around Wales' coast and on many inland lakes. Many surf beaches are also suitable for windsurfing and have gear hire and lessons available. Rhosneigr, on the Isle of Anglesey, is growing as a centre for windsurfing and other water sports. Check out www.ukwindsurfing.com.

The high-energy sport of coasteering originated in Wales: it involves a combination of wild swimming, climbing, canyoning, jumping and diving to negotiate a rocky coastline. Pembrokeshire, the Gower and Anglesey are particular hotspots.

Opportunities for white-water rafting are limited. One of the few Welsh rivers with big and fairly predictable summertime white water (grade three to four) is the dam-released Tryweryn near Bala. Moderate rapids (grade two to four) are found on the River Usk and between Corwen and Llangollen on the River Dee.

For more information about water sports, visit www.waleswatersports.co.uk.

Golf

The staging of the prestigious Ryder Cup tournament at the **Celtic Manor** (www.celtic-manor.com) in Newport in 2010 cemented Wales' reputation as a golfing hub. Some 200 well-crafted and scenery-rich golf courses take in snow-coated mountain valleys and wind-swept coastal stretches.

Other Activities

South Wales harbours a cave area stretching from Crickhowell to Carreg Cennen Castle. Caves are also found in North

Top: Hikers, Snowdonia National Park (p218)

Bottom: Cwmtydu (p184)

COLIN WESTON / GETTY IMAGES ©

TOP PLACES TO PLAY A ROUND

West Monmouthshire Golf Club (www.westmongolfclub.co.uk; Nantyglo, Ebbw Vale) The highest golf course in Britain.

Llanymynech Golf Club (www.llany-mynechgolfclub.co.uk; Pant, Oswestry) Has 15 holes in Wales and three in England. On the fourth, tee off in Wales, putt in England and return to Wales three holes later.

Machynys Peninsula Golf & Country Club (www.machynys.com; Machynys, Llanelli) Designed by Gary Nicklaus, son of golf legend Jack; located in Machynys, Llanelli.

Dewstow Golf Club (www.dewstow. co.uk; Caerwent, Monmouthshire) The Park Course has the UK's only par 6 hole – a monster 630m; located in Caerwent, Monmouthshire.

Tenby Golf Club (www.tenbygolf. co.uk; Tenby, Dyfed) Wales' oldest golf club – established in 1888.

Wales, on the Gower Peninsula and in Pembrokeshire. Highlights for the more experienced caver include the UK's second-longest cave, Ogof Draenen, and the deepest, Ogof Ffynnon Ddu. Porth-yr-Ogof in the Brecon Beacons and Paviland Cave on the Gower Peninsula are better suited to beginners. For more information, contact the **British Caving Association** (www.british-caving.org.uk).

Wales also features some of the best climbing sites in the UK. It's hardest to get a foothold during summer when rock faces are particularly crowded. In winter, ice-climbing is popular in Snowdonia. Equip yourself for emergencies, check the **Met Office** (www.metoffice.gov.uk) weather forecast and seek advice from local climbing shops, climbers' cafes and tourist-information points before making your ascent.

To get a feel for the rock face, have a trial climb at the ProAdventure Activity Centre in Llangollen or take a course at the Plas y Brenin National Mountain Sport Centre in Capel Curig. For more information, contact the **British Mountaineering Council** (www.thebmc.co.uk).

Wales' abundant rivers and lakes, long and winding coastline, and numerous fisheries offer many opportunities for game, sea and coarse fishing. Many species are found here: brown trout are among the catches on the Rivers Usk, Teifi, Wye, Dee, Seiont and Taff in spring. Reel in Welsh shy sewin (sea trout) on the banks of the River Towy, Teifi, Rheidol, Dyfi, Mawddach and Conwy in spring and summer. Chances of salmon improve in autumn in the River Usk. During winter catch grayling in the Rivers Wye, Dee and upper Severn.

To angle for sea fish, you don't necessarily need to charter a boat; cast off from any number of spots along the rocky coastline. For advice on likely catches at various locations throughout the year and a comprehensive list of fisheries, see the **Environment Agency** (www.environment-agency.gov. uk/fish) website. This is your first port of call for details on how to obtain a fishing licence. For more information on fishing in Wales, visit www.fishing.visitwales.com.

Wales has much to offer the equestrian set, thanks to its mix of sandy beaches, rolling hills and dense forest. The horseback vantage point is best exploited in Mid-Wales and the national parks. Riding schools catering for all levels of proficiency are found throughout the country. You can hire a horse or bring your own steed (guest horses are offered B&B at some riding centres); check out www.ridingwales.com.

National Parks

The wonderfully varied landscapes of Wales' three national parks offer spectacular hikes, from coastal cliffs to jagged peaks.

Snowdonia (www.eryri-npa.gov.uk) Designated in 1951, this North Wales stalwart is also home to the highest mountain in England and Wales and is great for off-season walking.

Pembrokeshire Coast (www.pembrokeshire coast.org.uk) Coastal walking plus boat trips to a scattering of nearby islands lends an ozone-blown frisson to a walk. Designated in 1952.

Brecon Beacons (www.breconbeacons.org) A rural haven for flora and fauna amid the rugged landscape of the history-carved mountains. Designated in 1957.

Plan Your Trip
Travel with Children

With glorious beaches, monumental castles, thrilling adventure sports, hands-on museums and trails to hike, bike, ride and wander, Wales is a kid's dream destination. The whole country is very family friendly and we've flagged the best places for kids throughout the book so you can just roll up and let loose.

Wales for Kids

Wales is well geared towards family travel. Children are generally made to feel welcome, facilities are uniformly good and there are discounts at many attractions or family tickets, plus under fives often go free. Public transport is easy to negotiate and baby-changing facilities are widespread.

Most hotels and B&Bs can rustle up a cot or heat a bottle, cafes and restaurants usually have high chairs and offer children's menus, and pubs serving food often have gardens with playgrounds. If you're travelling with small children, your biggest difficulty may be finding a family room as B&Bs and hotels have a limited supply, so it's worth checking self-catering options as well.

Children's Highlights

Beaches

➤ **Whitesands Bay** A wide, sandy Blue Flag beach with excellent swimming, surfing and rock pooling.

Best Regions for Kids

Cardiff & Around
The best museums and hands-on exploration in the country.

Brecon Beacons & Southeast Wales
Explore moody landscapes in the Black Mountains, Brecon Beacons and along the meandering Wye.

Swansea, Gower & Carmarthenshire
Surf the Gower and explore Wales' most dramatic castle.

St Davids & Pembrokeshire
Home to fantastic clifftop walking and some of Wales' best beaches.

Aberystwyth & Mid-Wales
Discover hidden valleys, gen up on all things green, and take the plunge and try coasteering.

Snowdonia & the Llŷn
Hike, bike, sail and kayak in the shadow of the country's highest peaks.

PLANNING

Apart from booking some accommodation and packing your wetsuits, wellies, buckets and spades, a trip to Wales requires very little forward planning. The best time to visit with children is undoubtedly during the summer months when the weather is warmer and you can enjoy endless hours on the beach. Not all beaches have lifeguards, however, so it's a good idea to check locally if the water is safe for swimming. You'll find loads of practical information on visiting wales with children on www.visit-wales.co.uk/uk-family-holidays and in Visit Wales' free brochure *Wales View*.

➡ **Barafundle Bay** Follow the cliff path over dunes and through stone archways and you'll discover a superb hidden beach.

➡ **Tresaith** Golden sands, rock pools, a cascading waterfall and if you're lucky, dolphins visible from the shore.

➡ **Oxwich Bay** Miles of golden sand backed by dunes, salt marshes and woodland.

➡ **South Beach, Tenby** A velvety-soft beach perfect for sandcastles, ball games and kite flying.

Castles

➡ **Beaumaris Castle** The largest of Edward I's great castles with sturdy concentric walls and a wide moat. (p283)

➡ **Conwy Castle** A stunning fortress set on a rocky outcrop with panoramic views from the battlements. (p269)

➡ **Pembroke Castle** A forbidding but family-friendly castle with walks along the walls and passages from tower to tower. (p152)

➡ **Carreg Cennen** Atmospheric 13th-century ruins with a clifftop passage down to an eerie natural cave. (p103)

➡ **Caernarfon Castle** A massive and intimidating stronghold with huge polygonal towers. (p262)

Outdoor Activities

➡ **Surfing** Pick up a board, take a lesson and get out on the waves on one of the Gower's sandy beaches. (p130)

➡ **Narrow-gauge railways** Enjoy some of Wales best scenery at a hypnotic pace. (p225)

➡ **Coasteering** Fling yourself off a cliff into the sea, ride the waves, explore caves and scramble back up the rocks to do it all again. (p167)

➡ **Pony trekking** Explore the coast, the hills or the valleys on horseback at your own pace. (p101)

➡ **Cycling** Wales has 331 miles of traffic-free trails meandering all over the country. Try the Yr Afon forest trail for family fun. (p224)

➡ **Whale watching** Head to the edge of the Celtic Deep to spot whales, porpoises and dolphins. (p163)

Rainy-day Activities

➡ **Techniquest** Whizz-pop science adventures for all. (p44)

➡ **Centre for Alternative Technology** Educational, fun and truly green, CAT offers plenty of interactive displays and a great adventure playground for curious kids. (p191)

➡ **Doctor Who Experience** Don't hide behind the sofa. This exhibition charts the adventures of every family's favourite time lord. (p47)

➡ **National Waterfront Museum** For a hands-on family visit, Swansea's landmark museum is hard to beat. (p113)

➡ **Dan-yr-Ogof** Eerie caves, dinosaurs, shire horses and a petting farm should keep everyone entertained. (p103)

Festivals

➡ **Urdd National Eisteddfod** (http://www.urdd.org) One of Europe's largest youth festivals.

➡ **Croissant Neuf Summer Party** (www.croissantneuf.co.uk) A rip-roaring family festival of music and arts events near Usk, Monmouthshire.

➡ **Hay Fever** Part of the famous Hay Festival dedicated to children. (p91)

➡ **Big Cheese** A fantastic free weekend of historical re-enactments, folk dancing, music and fire-eating. (p66)

➡ **Victorian Extravaganza** Good old-fashioned family fun with fancy dress, parades, funfairs and special events. (p277)

➡ **World Bog Snorkelling Championships** Stand by and watch competitors as they submerge themselves in boggy water for a 110m swim.

Regions at a Glance

Cardiff (Caerdydd)

Architecture
Sport
Nightlife

Civic Showcases

From the neoclassical glory of the Civic Centre, to Victorian shopping arcades, to Cardiff Bay's cutting-edge waterfront, the Welsh capital has plenty to keep building buffs occupied.

Rugby & More

Cardiff is the home of Welsh sport, with the Millennium Stadium completely dominating the city centre and three other major stadia nearby. The city is never more alive than during a rugby international, when the singing from the stands resonates through the streets. And now the Cardiff City football team has been promoted to the premier league, things can only get more interesting.

Cardiff's Bars

An edgy live music scene, some swish bars and a swathe of old-fashioned pubs attract hordes of revellers every weekend.

p38

Brecon Beacons & Southeast Wales

Walks
Castles
Industrial Heritage

River & Mountain Paths

From the lush riverside of the Wye Valley to the wild uplands of the Brecon Beacons, there are plenty of paths to explore here.

Carreg Cennen

The south has some of Wales' most interesting castles, including Chepstow and remote Carreg Cennen, which is perhaps the most romantically positioned of them all.

Blaenavon

Victorian Britain was built on Welsh coal and iron, and the legacy of those industries is preserved in the Blaenavon World Heritage Site and other locations in the industrial heartland of the valleys.

p71

Swansea, the Gower & Carmarthenshire

Beaches
Gardens
Market Towns

The Gower

Sitting right on Swansea's doorstep, the Gower peninsula harbours Wales' most beautiful beaches.

Horticultural Showpieces

Green-fingered travellers will find plenty of inspiration in the showpiece gardens scattered around the green and blissful Carmarthenshire countryside.

Carmarthen Market

The small towns of the countryside are full of genteel charm, Georgian architecture and friendly pubs. The market at Carmarthen remains a centre for the finest Welsh agricultural products.

p109

St Davids & Pembrokeshire

Coastal Scenery
Castles
Wildlife

Pembrokeshire Coast

One of Britain's most beautiful stretches of coast, Pembrokeshire offers clifftop walks, family-friendly beaches, surfing hot spots and watery adventures galore.

Norman Fortresses

Southern Pembrokeshire is littered with castles, built by the Normans to consolidate their conquests. The kids won't be short on inspiration when they start their own building projects in the sands later.

Island Sanctuaries

Take a boat trip to one of the offshore islands for close encounters with seals, porpoises, dolphins, whales, sharks and sunfish. The cliffs are home to millions of seabirds.

p142

Aberystwyth & Mid-Wales

Wildlife
Market Towns
Food

Varying Habitats

The once-rare red kite is now the very symbol of Powys. Coastal Ceredigion shelters important wetland habitats, while Cardigan Bay is home to bottlenose dolphins, harbour porpoises, Atlantic grey seals, sunfish, basking sharks, leatherback turtles and an array of bird life.

Agricultural Powys

The heart of the Powys countryside is scattered with quaint market towns, many of which still serve as agricultural hubs.

Local Produce

The new Welsh gastronomy focuses on the finest fresh, locally grown ingredients. Where better to enjoy them than the Powys countryside.

p178

Snowdonia & the Llŷn

Mountains
Industrial Heritage
Beaches

Snowdonia

Home to Britain's finest mountain scenery south of the Scottish Highlands, Snowdonia's imposing peaks provide a scenic backdrop for innumerable outdoor pursuits.

Slate Quarries

Welsh slate once roofed much of the world and Snowdonia's quarries and caverns bear witness to the toil of generations of workers, while former freight railways now shunt travellers through spectacular terrain.

Surf & Sand

From the family-friendly sands of Barmouth and Tywyn to the surf spots and isolated bays of the Llŷn Peninsula, Northwest Wales has plenty of beach to go round.

p209

Anglesey & the North Coast

Castles
Coastal Scenery
Stately Homes

Edward I's Legacy

While there are castles all over Wales, the fortresses created by Edward I in North Wales are the only ones to be recognised as World Heritage Sites. They truly are exemplars of the castlemakers' craft.

Isle of Anglesey

At times wild and rugged, at times gentle and restrained, this stretch of coast is hugely diverse and rates among the nation's most beautiful.

Menai Mansions

Barons, marquesses and slate magnates all chose to build grand testimonies to their good fortune along the Menai Strait – many of which are now open for the hoi polloi to enjoy.

p259

On the Road

Cardiff (Caerdydd)

POP 346,000

Best Places to Eat

➡ Purple Poppadom (p57)

➡ Mint & Mustard (p57)

➡ Cafe Città (p57)

➡ Woods Bar & Brasserie (p57)

➡ Riverside Market (p55)

Best Places to Stay

➡ Park Plaza (p52)

➡ Lincoln House (p53)

➡ Tŷ Rosa (p53)

➡ River House Backpackers (p52)

➡ Cathedral House (p53)

Why Go?

The capital of Wales since only 1955, Cardiff has embrace the role with vigour, emerging in the new millennium a one of Britain's leading urban centres. Caught between a ancient fort and an ultramodern waterfront, compact Car diff seems to have surprised even itself with how interestin it has become.

The city has entered the 21st century pumped up on ster oids, flexing its recently acquired architectural muscles as i it's still astonished to have them. This newfound confidenc is infectious, and these days it's not just the rugby that draw crowds into the city. Come the weekend, a buzz reverberate through the streets as swarms of shoppers hit the Hayes followed by waves of revellers descending on the capital' thriving pubs, bars and live-music venues.

When to Go

January and February are the coldest months, althoug Wales' home matches in the Six Nations Rugby Champion ship warm spirits in February and March.

June is the driest month and in July the summer-lon Cardiff Festival kicks off, incorporating theatre, comed music and a food festival. In August, the warmest month knights storm the castle, classic cars converge and gay prid takes over the streets.

Making the most of the December chill, Cardiff Winte Wonderland brings ice-skating and Santa's grotto to th Civic Centre.

In AD 75 the Romans built a fort where Cardiff Castle now stands. The name Cardiff probably derives from the Welsh Caer Tâf (Fort on the River Taff) or Caer Didi (Didius' fort), referring to Roman general Aulus Didius. After the Romans left Britain the site remained unoccupied until the Norman Conquest. In 1093 a Norman knight named Robert Fitzhamon (conqueror of Glamorgan and later earl of Gloucester) built himself a castle within the Roman walls and a small town grew up around it. Both were damaged in a Welsh revolt in 1183 and the town was sacked in 1404 by Owain Glyndŵr during his ill-fated rebellion against English domination.

The first of the Tudor Acts of Union in 1536 put the English stamp on Cardiff and brought some stability. But despite its importance as a port, market town and bishopric, only 1000 people were living here in 1801.

The city owes its present stature to iron and coal mining in the valleys to the north. Coal was first exported from Cardiff on a small scale as early as 1600. In 1794 the Bute family – which owned much of the land from which Welsh coal was mined – built the Glamorganshire Canal for the shipment of iron from Merthyr Tydfil down to Cardiff.

In 1840 this was supplanted by the new Taff Vale Railway. A year earlier the second marquess of Bute had completed the first locks at Butetown, just south of Cardiff, getting the jump on other South Wales ports. By the time it dawned on everyone what immense reserves of coal there were in the valleys – setting off a kind of black gold rush – the Butes were in a position to insist that it be shipped from Butetown. Cardiff was off and running.

The docklands expanded rapidly, the Butes grew staggeringly rich and the city boomed, its population mushrooming to 170,000 by the end of the 19th century and to 227,000 by 1931. A large, multiracial workers' community known as Tiger Bay grew up in the harbourside area of Butetown. In 1905 Cardiff was officially designated a city, and a year later its elegant Civic Centre was inaugurated. In 1913 Cardiff became the world's top coal port, exporting some 13 million tonnes of the stuff.

The post-WWI slump in the coal trade and the Great Depression of the 1930s slowed this expansion. The city was badly damaged by WWII bombing, which claimed over 350 lives. Shortly afterwards the coal industry was nationalised, which led to the Butes packing their bags and leaving town in 1947, donating the castle and a large chunk of land to the city.

Wales had no official capital and the need for one was seen as an important focus for Welsh nationhood. Cardiff had the advantage of being Wales' biggest city and boast the architectural riches of the Civic Centre. It was proclaimed the first ever capital of Wales in 1955, chosen via a ballot of the members of the Welsh authorities. Cardiff received 36 votes to Caernarfon's 11 and Aberystwyth's four.

⊙ Sights

◎ Central Cardiff

★**Cardiff Castle** CASTLE

(Map p54; www.cardiffcastle.com; Castle St; adult/child £11/8.50, incl guided tour £14/11; ⊗9am-5pm) The grafting of Victorian mock-Gothic extravagance onto Cardiff's most important historical relics makes Cardiff Castle, quite rightly, the city's leading attraction. Until it was donated to the city in 1947, this was the private domain of the Butes, the family who transformed Cardiff from a small town into the world's biggest coal port.

It's far from a traditional Welsh castle, more a collection of disparate castles scattered around a central green, encompassing practically the whole history of Cardiff. The most conventionally castle-like bits are the motte-and-bailey **Norman shell keep** at its centre (built in wood in around 1081 and re-built in stone in 1135) and the 13th-century **Black Tower** that forms the entrance gate. William the Conqueror's eldest son Robert, Duke of Normandy, was imprisoned in the wooden fort by his brother, England's King Henry I, until his death at the age of 83.

A grand house was built into the western wall in the 1420s by the Earl of Warwick and was extended in the 17th century by the Herbert family (the earls of Pembroke), but by the time the Butes acquired it a century later it had fallen into disrepair. The first marquess of Bute hired architect Henry Holland and Holland's father-in-law, the famous landscape-architect Lancelot 'Capability' Brown, to get the house and grounds into shape.

It was only in the 19th century that it was discovered that the Normans had built

Cardiff Highlights

❶ Marvelling at the over-the-top Victorian interiors of **Cardiff Castle** (p39), the city's ancient citadel

❷ Getting swept away by the exhilaration of a fired-up rugby test at **Millennium Stadium** (p43)

❸ Taking an engrossing journey via the big bang, natural history and fine art at the **National Museum Cardiff** (p42)

❹ Traipsing around the transplanted historical buildings and beautiful gardens of **St Fagans National History Museum** (p50)

❺ Joining the night-time revellers hopping between central-city bars such as **Clwb Ifor Bach** (p60) as the streets thrum with live music

❻ Admiring the architectural showpieces that make up the glitzy entertainment precinct at **Cardiff Bay** (p44)

❼ Crossing the moat at **Caerphilly Castle** (p66) and wandering into a fairy tale

their fortifications on top of Cardiff's original 1st-century Roman fort. The high walls that surround the castle now are largely a Victorian reproduction of the 3rd-century 3m-thick **Roman walls**. A line of red bricks, clearly visible from the city frontage, marks the point where the original Roman section ends and the reconstruction commences.

Also from the 19th century are the towers and turrets on the west side, dominated by the colourful 40m **clock tower**. This faux-Gothic extravaganza was dreamed up by the mind-bendingly rich third marquess of Bute and his architect William Burges, a passionate eccentric who used to dress in medieval costume and was often seen with a parrot on his shoulder. Both were obsessed with Gothic architecture, religious symbolism and astrology, influences that were incorporated into the designs both here and at the Butes' second Welsh home at Castell Coch. Yet along with the focus on the past, the plans included all of the mod cons of the Victorian era, such as electric lighting (it was the second house in Wales to feature this newfangled wizardry) and running water in the en suite attached to the upper-floor bedroom.

A 50-minute guided tour takes you through the interiors of this flamboyant fantasy world, from the **winter smoking room** in the clocktower with decor expounding on the theme of time (zodiac symbols grouped into seasons, Norse gods representing the days of the week, and a fright for anyone who dares listen at the door – look up as you pass through the doorway), to the mahogany-and-mirrors narcissism of **Lord Bute's bedroom**, with a gilded statue of St John the Evangelist (the marquess' name saint) and 189 bevelled mirrors on the ceiling, which reflect the name 'John' in Greek.

The **banqueting hall** boasts Bute family heraldic shields and a fantastically over-the-top fireplace (look for the image of the imprisoned Duke of Normandy) and is overlooked by that medieval must-have, a minstrels' gallery. Marble, sandalwood, parrots and acres of gold leaf create an elaborate Moorish look in the **Arab room**. The neighbouring **nursery** is decorated with fairy-tale and nursery-rhyme characters, while the **small dining room** has an ingenious table, designed so that a living vine could be slotted through it, allowing diners to pluck fresh grapes as they ate. The Roman-style **roof garden** seems to underline how much of a fantasy all this really was – designed with southern Italy in mind, rather than Wales.

Some, but not all, of these rooms can be accessed with a regular castle entry, which includes an excellent audio guide (available in a children's edition and in a range of languages). Start your visit by viewing the short film, screened in a room above the gift shop which provides a wordless representation of the castle's journey through history. Leading off from here is a **WWII air raid shelter** preserved in a long cold corridor within the castle walls.

Housed below the ticket office is **Firing Line**, a small but well-organised museum devoted to the Welsh soldier.

★ **Bute Park**   PARK

(Map p54; ⊘ 7.30am-sunset) Flanked by the castle and the River Taff, Bute Park was donated to the city along with the castle in 1947. With Sophia Gardens, Pontcanna Fields and Llandaff Fields, it forms a green corridor that stretches northwest for 1½ miles to Llandaff. All were once part of the Bute's vast holdings.

Forming the park's southern edge, the **Animal Wall** (Map p54) is topped with stone figures of lions, seals, bears and other creatures. It was designed by castle architect William Burges but only completed in 1892 after his death, with more animals added in the 1920s. In the 1930s they were the subject of a newspaper cartoon strip and many Cardiff kids grew up thinking the animals came alive at night.

In Cooper's Field, the part of the park just west of the castle, is a stone circle, erected in 1978 when Cardiff hosted the National Eisteddfod. Such so-called **gorsedd stones** (Map p54) are found all over Wales where eisteddfods have been held.

Nearby are the foundations of the 13th-century **Blackfriars Priory** (Map p54), which was destroyed in 1404 when Owain Glyndŵr attacked Cardiff, and later rebuilt, only to be finally vacated in 1538 when the monasteries were dissolved.

★ **National Museum Cardiff**   MUSEUM

(Map p54; www.museumwales.ac.uk; Gorsedd Gardens Rd; ⊘ 10am-5pm Tue-Sun) **FREE** Devoted mainly to natural history and art, this grand neoclassical building is the centrepiece of the seven institutions dotted around the country that together form the Welsh National Museum. It's one of Britain's best museums; you'll need at least three hours to do it justice, but it could easily consume the best part of a rainy day.

The *Evolution of Wales* exhibit whizzes onlookers through 4600 million years of geological history, its rollicking multimedia display placing Wales into a global context. Films of volcanic eruptions and aerial footage of the Welsh landscape explain how its scenery was formed, while model dinosaurs and woolly mammoths help keep the kids interested.

The natural-history displays range from brightly coloured insects to the 9m-long skeleton of a humpback whale that washed up near Aberthaw in 1982. The world's largest turtle (2.88m by 2.74m), a leatherback which was found on Harlech beach, is also here, suspended on wires from the ceiling.

The art gallery houses an excellent collection, with a large new space devoted to contemporary exhibitions. Older works include portraits dating as far back as the Tudor era, and paintings by El Greco and Poussin. Welsh artists such as Gwen and Augustus John, Richard Wilson, Thomas Jones, David Jones and Ceri Richards are well represented, along with famous names from across the border such as Francis Bacon, David Hockney and Rachel Whiteread.

Many impressionist and post-impressionist pieces were bequeathed to the museum in 1952 and 1963 by the Davies sisters, Gwendoline and Margaret, granddaughters of 19th-century coal and shipping magnate David Davies. One room is devoted to their collection of seven paintings by British master JMW Turner, which were dismissed as fakes in the 1950s but recently reappraised to have been genuine all along. Other treasures include luminous works by Pissaro; a trio of Monet's *Water Lilies*, alongside his scenes of London, Rouen and Venice; Sisley's *The Cliff at Penarth* (the artist was married in Cardiff); and portraits by Renoir, including the shimmering *La Parisienne*. The sisters' favourite was Cézanne, but there are also works by Matisse and the anguished *Rain: Auvers* by Van Gogh, who killed himself just a few days after finishing the painting. The Pre-Raphaelites are well represented, as is Rodin, with a cast of *The Kiss*.

One of the large upstairs galleries is devoted to Welsh ceramics, while others are set aside for temporary exhibitions. The museum also hosts regular classical and jazz concerts – check the website for information.

★ **Millennium Stadium**   STADIUM
(Map p54; ☎ 029-2082 2228; www.millenniumstadium.com; Westgate St; tours adult/child £8.50/5)
This spectacular stadium squats like a stranded spaceship on the River Taff's east bank. Attendance at international rugby and football matches has increased dramatically since this 74,500-seat, £168 million, three-tiered stadium with sliding roof was completed in time to host the 1999 Rugby World Cup. Cardiff Arms Park (p61), its famous predecessor and home to the Cardiff Blues rugby team, lies literally in its shadow.

Rugby is the national game and when the crowd begins to sing at Millennium, the whole of Cardiff resonates. To watch a test match here is to catch a glimpse of the Welsh psyche, especially when the Six Nations tournament (contested annually in February and March between Wales, England, Scotland, Ireland, France and Italy) is in full swing. Tickets for international

CARDIFF (CAERDYDD) SIGHTS

CARDIFF IN...

Two Days
Start with our Historic Cardiff walking tour, stopping to explore **National Museum Cardiff** and **Cardiff Castle** along the way. Lunch could be a picnic in **Bute Park** with treats acquired at **Cardiff Market** or, if the weather's not cooperating, a meal at any of the reasonably priced central-city eateries. Spend your second day heading back to the future at **Cardiff Bay**, where you can immerse yourself in forward-thinking architecture and have a **Doctor Who Experience**.

Four Days
Spend your third morning steeped in history at **St Fagans National History Museum**, then check out **Barry Island**. On your last day, head north to explore **Llandaff Cathedral**, then continue on to **Castell Coch** and **Caerphilly Castle**. For your last night in the Welsh capital, blast away the cobwebs in one of the city's live-music venues.

fixtures are difficult for mere mortals to get hold of; other matches are easier.

Outside of the rugby season the stadium is used for mammoth events such as Monster Trucks and concerts by the likes of Bruce Springsteen and Madonna. The British Speedway Grand Prix is held here every June.

If you can't get tickets to an event, it's well worth taking a tour – you get to hang out in the dressing rooms (alas *sans* players), run through the tunnel to the recorded cheering of a game-day crowd and sit in the VIP box. Tours last about an hour and are held several times a day, except for event days. Book online or at the **WRU Store** (Map p54; 8 Westgate St; ⊘10am-5.30pm Mon-Sat, 11am-4pm Sun), where you can also stock up on rugby ball key rings and 'lucky' Welsh Rugby Union–branded underwear.

Cardiff Story
MUSEUM

(Map p54; www.cardiffstory.com; Old Library, The Hayes; ⊘10am-5pm Mon-Sat, 11am-4pm Sun) This excellent little museum uses interactive displays, video footage and everyday objects to tell the story of Cardiff's transformation from a small market town into the world's biggest coal port and then into the capital city of today. While you're here, check out the original entrance to the Old Library, lined with beautiful Victorian tiles, and head upstairs for temporary art exhibitions.

St John the Baptist Church
CHURCH

(Map p54; Working St; ⊘10am-3pm Mon-Sat) A graceful Gothic tower rises from this 15th-century church, its delicate stonework looking almost like filigree. Along with the castle keep, this is one of the few remnants of medieval Cardiff. A church has stood on this site since at least 1180. Inside there are regimental flags, elegant pointed arches and a spectacular Elizabethan-era tomb. Free half-hour organ concerts are held here at 1.15pm on the second Friday of each month.

◉ Cardiff Bay

Lined with important national institutions, Cardiff Bay is where the modern Welsh nation is put on display in an architect's playground of interesting buildings, large open spaces and public art. The bay's main commercial centre is Mermaid Quay, packed with bars, restaurants and shops.

It wasn't always this way. By 1913 more than 13 million tonnes of coal were being shipped from Cardiff docks. Following the post-WWII slump the docklands deteriorated into a wasteland of empty basins, cut off from the city by the railway embankment. The bay outside the docks, which has one of the highest tidal ranges in the world (more than 12m between high and low water), was ringed for up to 14 hours a day by smelly sewage-contaminated mudflats. The nearby residential area of Butetown became a neglected slum.

Since 1987 the area has been radically redeveloped. The turning point came with the completion of a state-of-the-art tidal barrage in 1999.

Butetown
NEIGHBOURHOOD

(Map p46) Victorian Butetown, immediately north of Mermaid Quay, was the heart of Cardiff's coal trade – a multiethnic community that propelled the city to world fame. The semi-derelict **Coal Exchange building** (Map p46; www.coalexchange.co.uk; Mount Stuart Sq) was the place where international coal prices were set. It was here in March 1908 that a coal merchant wrote the world's first-ever £1 million cheque. It now houses a function and performance venue, but large parts of the building are boarded up.

Butetown History & Arts Centre
GALLERY

(Map p46; www.bhac.org; Bute St; ⊘10am-5pm Tue-Fri, 11am-4.30pm Sat & Sun) **FREE** This centre is devoted to preserving oral histories, documents and images of the docklands. The displays put the area into both a historical and present-day context, and there's a gallery devoted to temporary exhibitions.

Techniquest
MUSEUM

(Map p46; www.techniquest.org; Stuart St; adult/child £7/5; ⊘9.30am-4.30pm Tue-Fri, 10am-5pm Sat & Sun, 10am-5pm daily school holidays) With the aim of introducing kids to science, Techniquest is jam-packed with engrossing, hands-on exhibits that are equally enjoyable for under-fives and inquisitive adults. The planetarium stages night-sky demonstrations and science shows.

★ Wales Millennium Centre
ARTS CENTRE

(Map p46; ☏029-2063 6464; www.wmc.org.uk; Bute Pl; tour adult/child £5.50/4.50; ⊘tours 11am & 2.30pm) **FREE** The centrepiece and symbol of Cardiff Bay's regeneration is the superb Wales Millennium Centre, an architectural masterpiece of stacked Welsh slate in shades

THE BEAUT BUTES

In Cardiff, the Bute name is inescapable. No family has had a bigger impact on the city. An aristocratic Scottish family related to the Stuart monarchy, the Butes arrived in Cardiff in 1766 in the shape of John, Lord Mount Stuart. He married a local heiress, Charlotte Hickman-Windsor, acquiring vast estates and mineral rights in South Wales in the process. Like his father of the same name (a prime minister under George III), he entered politics and became a Tory MP, privy councillor, ambassador to Spain and, eventually, was awarded the title Marquess of Bute.

Their grandson, the second Marquess of Bute, grew fabulously wealthy from coal mining and then in 1839 gambled his fortune to create a large complex of docks in Cardiff. The gamble paid off. The coal-export business boomed, and his son, John Patrick Crichton-Stuart, the third Marquess of Bute, became one of the richest people on the planet. He was not your conventional Victorian aristocrat; an intense, scholarly man with a passion for history, architecture, ritual and religion (Catholic), he neither hunted nor fished but instead supported the antivivisection movement and campaigned for a woman's right to a university education. In 1887 he gifted Roath Park to the town. His architectural legacy ranges from the colourful kitsch of Cardiff Castle and Castell Coch, to the neoclassical elegance of the Civic Centre.

The Butes had interests all over Britain and never spent more than about six weeks at a time in Cardiff. By the end of WWII they had sold or given away all their Cardiff assets, the fifth Marquess gifting Cardiff Castle and Bute Park to the city in 1947. The present marquess, the seventh, lives in the family seat at Mount Stuart House on the Isle of Bute in Scotland's Firth of Clyde; another maverick, he's better known as Johnny Dumfries, the former Formula One racing driver.

of purple, green and grey topped with an overarching bronzed steel shell. Designed by Welsh architect Jonathan Adams, it opened in 2004 as Wales' premier arts complex, housing major cultural organisations such as the Welsh National Opera, National Dance Company, National Orchestra, Literature Wales, HiJinx Theatre and Ty Cerdd (Music Centre of Wales).

The roof above the main entrance is pierced by 2m-high letter-shaped windows, spectacularly backlit at night, that spell out phrases from poet Gwyneth Lewis: *'Creu Gwir fel Gwydr o Ffwrnais Awen'* (Creating truth like glass from inspiration's furnace) and 'In these stones horizons sing'.

You can wander through the large public lobby at will; the Cardiff Bay tourist information centre is here and there's a stage which is often used for free performances. Guided tours lead visitors behind the giant letters, onto the main stage and into the dressing rooms, depending on what shows are on.

★ **Senedd** NOTABLE BUILDING
(National Assembly Building; Map p46; ☑ 0845 010 5500; www.assemblywales.org; ⊘ 9.30am-4.30pm Mon-Fri, 10.30am-4.30pm Sat & Sun) **FREE** Designed by Lord Richard Rogers (the archi-

tect behind London's Lloyd's Building and Millennium Dome and Paris' Pompidou Centre), the Senedd is a striking structure of concrete, slate, glass and steel, with an undulating canopy roof lined with red cedar. It has won awards for its environmentally friendly design, which includes a huge rotating cowl on the roof for power-free ventilation and a gutter system that collects rainwater for flushing the toilets. The lobby and surrounding area is littered with public artworks, including the 'meeting place', a curved bench made of 3-tonne slate blocks from Blaenau Ffestiniog, thoughtfully provided as a place for protesters to rest their legs.

When they're not on recess, the National Assembly for Wales usually meets in a plenary session from 1.30pm on Tuesday and Wednesday. Seats in the public gallery may be prebooked, although there's usually space if you turn up on the day. Free tours take place at 11am, 2pm and 3pm, except for sitting days when only the 11am tour is held.

Pierhead MUSEUM
(Map p46; www.pierhead.org; ⊘ 10.30am-4.30pm) **FREE** One of the waterfront's few Victorian remnants, Pierhead is a red-brick and

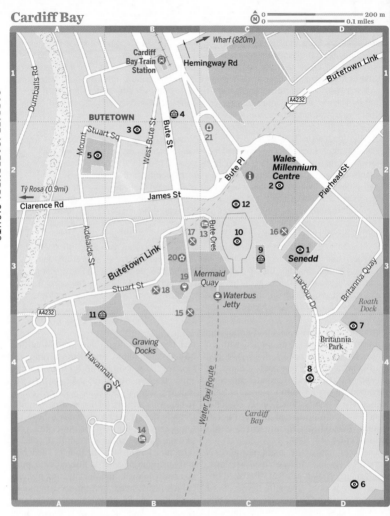

glazed-terracotta French Gothic confection, built in 1897 with Bute family money in order to impress the maritime traffic. Its ornate clocktower earned it the nickname 'Wales' Big Ben'. Inside there's an interesting little display on the history of the bay (including a short film and a slideshow), some important historical documents and a gallery.

Roald Dahl Plass SQUARE
(Map p46) The unusual shape of this large public space is due to its past life as the basin of the West Bute Dock. A large rectangular dock once extended from here all the way up what is now Lloyd George Ave, right to the foot of the city centre, berthing up to 300 ships at a time. Reborn as a square, it was renamed in honour of the Cardiff-born writer. The bowl shape lends it to open-air performances, but it more often serves as a space for kids to run around. The whole thing is overseen by a soaring, stainless-steel water sculpture, which fans of the *Doctor Who* spin-off series will recognise as the location of the secret entrance to *Torchwood's* underground headquarters.

Cardiff Bay

Norwegian Church Arts Centre
ARTS CENTRE

(Map p46; ☎029-2087 7959; www.norwegian-churchcardiff.com; Harbour Dr; ☺9.30am-6pm Easter-Oct, 10am-4pm Nov-Easter) **FREE** Looking like it's popped out of the pages of a story book, this white-slatted wooden church with a black witch's-hat spire was modelled on a traditional Norwegian village church. It was built in 1868 to minister to Norwegian sailors and remained a place of worship until 1974. Roald Dahl, whose parents were from Norway, was christened here and served as president of the preservation trust that restored and renovated the church. It has now been reincarnated as an arts centre with a cafe downstairs and a gallery upstairs, hosting interesting exhibitions, concerts, markets and arts courses.

Goleulong 2000 Lightship
BOAT

(Map p46; ☎029-2048 7609; www.lightship2000.co.uk; Britannia Park, Harbour Dr; ☺10am-4.30pm) **FREE** Bright red and with a lighthouse grafted onto it, this lightship was last stationed off Rhossili, warning sailors away from the Helwick Swatch, a treacherous sandbank. It now houses a Christian centre and a cafe, but you can wander around and check out the neat little cabins and floating chapel. Just ask and staff will unlock the tower for you to climb to the top.

Doctor Who Experience
EXHIBITION

(Map p46; ☎0844 801 2279; www.doctorwhoexperience.com; Porth Teigr; adult/child £15/11; ☺10am-5pm (last admission 3.30pm) Wed-Mon, daily school holidays) The huge success of the reinvented classic TV series *Doctor Who,* produced by BBC Wales, has brought Cardiff to the attention of sci-fi fans worldwide. City locations have featured in many episodes and the first two series of the spin-off *Torchwood* were set in Cardiff Bay.

Capitalising on Timelord tourism, this interactive exhibition is located right next to the BBC studios where the series is filmed – look out for the Tardis hovering outside. Perhaps appropriately, given the show's theme, tickets are booked for specific timeslots.

Visitors find themselves sucked through a crack in time and thrown into the role of the Doctor's companion. It's great fun – especially when you come face to face with full-size Daleks in full 'ex-ter-min-ate' mode. But don't blink – there are weeping angels about. The 'experience' only takes about 20 minutes but afterwards you're transported into a large two-level warehouse, where you can wander at your leisure around the displays of sets, costumes and props spanning the show's 50-year run.

Cardiff Bay Barrage
WATERFRONT

Completed in 1999, this large dam plugs the gap between Penarth and Porth Teigr, containing the waters flowing out from the mouths of the Rivers Taff and Ely, and transforming stinky Cardiff Bay into a freshwater lake. It was a controversial project, as its construction flooded 200 hectares of intertidal mudflats which, despite their unpleasant aspects, were an important habitat for waterfowl. The barrage includes sluice gates to control the water flow, three lock gates to allow passage for boats, and a fish pass that lets migrating salmon and sea trout pass between the river and the sea.

The **Cardiff Bay Trail** heads out over the barrage, allowing walkers and cyclists easy access to Penarth (allow 40 minutes if you're walking). Along the way there's a skate park, a playground, some giant boulders of coal, and a series of display boards telling the story of Captain Robert Scott's expedition to the Antarctic, which set sail from Cardiff in 1910; two years later Scott and his men were dead, having been pipped to the pole by a Norwegian team led by Roald Amundsen.

◉ Cathays & Roath

The bohemian heart of Cardiff lies in the suburbs immediately to the east of the city centre. Proximity to the university makes Cathays' tightly packed Victorian terrace houses popular with students, and while parts of Roath are more well-heeled, the City Rd strip is a little gritty and fabulously multicultural. Few tourists make their way here, but if you want to get a broader taste of Cardiff life, take a stroll along the narrow thoroughfare that starts as City Rd and then morphs into Crwys Rd and then Whitchurch Rd.

Roath Park   PARK

(www.cardiff.gov.uk/parks; Lake Rd) Long and narrow Roath Park rivals Bute Park as Cardiff's favourite green space. The third Marquess of Bute gifted the land in 1887, and the boggy marsh at its northern end was transformed into a large lake by the erection of a dam. The rest was laid out in the Victorian style, with rose gardens, tree-lined paths, lawns and wild nooks. A dinky lighthouse was later added to the lake as a memorial to Captain Scott.

It's a lovely spot for a stroll and a picnic, but if you fancy something a little more diverting, there are playgrounds, bowling greens, tennis courts and basketball courts, along with boating and fishing opportunities on the lake.

◉ Llandaff

Llandaff is a peaceful suburb 2 miles northwest of the castle – a former village clustered around a green that has been swallowed up by the expanding city. Buses 25 and 62 run

City Walk
Historic Cardiff

START CIVIC CENTRE
END THE HAYES
LENGTH 1.5 MILES; ONE HOUR

One of the most elegant administrative quarters in Britain, Cardiff's Civic Centre encompasses formal parks and a grand array of early 20th-century buildings, all dressed in gleaming white Portland stone. Start outside the neoclassical ❶ **Cardiff Crown Court**, continue past the baroquestyle ❷ **City Hall** and turn right and into ❸ **Gorsedd Gardens**. Here you'll find a sweet little statue simply titled *Girl* and a gorsedd stone circle, raised for the National Eisteddfod in 1899.

Head towards the classical facade of the ❹ **National Museum Cardiff** (p42) and then turn the corner into Park Place. Next is the imposing main building of ❺ **Cardiff University**. Head through its black gates and enter via the central door into the short corridor which leads to the foyer (if it's after hours you'll need to circle around the building). In the centre is a white marble statue of John Viriamu Jones the first principal of the university college.

Head through the door on the other side, curve to the left, cross the road and enter ❻ **Alexandra Gardens**. Amid the formal lawns and colourful flowerbeds is an interesting set of war memorials. The standing stone mounted on a pedestal to your left was taken from the battlefield at Mt Harriet in the Falkland Islands, and remembers the Britons killed in the 1982 war. A little further, another standing stone is dedicated to the Welsh volunteers who fought against fascism in the Spanish Civil War. In the centre of the park is the Welsh National War Memorial, erected in 1928 in memory of WWI's dead. A circular colonnade of white Corinthian columns surrounds a statue of a naked angel with a sword, flanked by three servicemen (representing the army, navy and air force) holding aloft wreathes.

Exit the gardens onto King Edward VII Ave. Straight ahead is the old ❼ **Glamorgan County Council Building** (now part of Cardiff University), fronted with more Corinthian columns

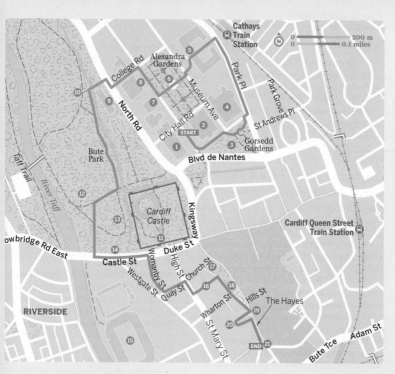

and elaborate statuary (Minerva, to the left, represents mining; Neptune, on the right, navigation). The **8 Bute Building**, to the right, also belongs to the university and features Doric columns and a red dragon on its roof.

When you turn left onto College Rd you'll see, straight ahead of you, the very impressive new home of the **9 Royal Welsh College of Music & Drama** (p61). Cross towards it, turn right and then left past the curved timber-clad end of the building and enter **10 Bute Park** (p42). Cross the little bridge, turn left and follow the canal towards the rear of **11 Cardiff Castle** (p39). At the next bridge take the path to the right; you'll shortly come to the remains of **12 Blackfriars Priory** (p42) and another circle of **13 gorsedd stones** (p42).

Veer left and exit through the West Lodge gate. On Castle St, take a look at the creatures perched on top of the **14 Animal Wall** (p42). Originally positioned by the castle's main gate, the animals were moved here after WWI. Turn right on Womanby St, which is lined with warehouses, many of which have been converted into bars. Its unusual name is either derived from Old German meaning 'the strangers'

quarter' or a Viking word meaning 'quarter of the houndsman'. As you head down the street you will see the **15 Millennium Stadium** (p43) on your right.

Take a left on Quay St; Cardiff's original quay stood here before the River Taff was realigned to make way for the railway in 1860. Turn right on High St and then left to enter **16 Cardiff Central Market** (p62). This cast-iron market hall has been selling fresh produce and hardware since 1891. There's an old market office and a clock tower in the centre. Exit on the far side on Trinity St and you'll see **17 St John the Baptist Church** (p44). Next up is the beautiful sandstone **18 Old Library**, which houses the tourist office and the Cardiff Story museum.

Continue down the street and into the heart of the Hayes. The name is derived from a Norman-French word relating to the small garden enclosures that would have once stood here. It's now Cardiff's main shopping strip, and deliciously car-free. **19 St David's** (p61) mall occupies the entire left-hand flank, but duck into the Victorian-era **20 Morgan Arcade** (p62) on your right. Finish back on the Hayes under the giant hoop and arrow of the sculpture **21 Alliance**.

OFF THE BEATEN TRACK

TAFF TRAIL

Following canal towpaths, country lanes and disused railway routes, the 55-mile Taff Trail walking and cycling route connects Cardiff's Mermaid Quay with Brecon, passing Castell Coch and Merthyr Tydfil on the way. Starting from Brecon will ensure more downhill runs.

along Cathedral Rd to Llandaff every 10 minutes (twice hourly on Sundays).

Llandaff Cathedral CHURCH
(☑ 029-2056 4554; www.llandaffcathedral.org.uk; Cathedral Green; ⊙ 9am-6.30pm Mon-Sat, 7am-6.30pm Sun) Set in a hollow on the west bank of the River Taff, this imposing cathedral is built on the site of a 6th-century monastery founded by St Teilo. His tomb is on the south side of the sanctuary and an ancient stone Celtic cross stands nearby.

The present cathedral was begun in 1120, but it crumbled throughout the Middle Ages, and during the Reformation and Civil War it was used as an alehouse and then an animal shelter. Derelict by the 18th century, it was largely rebuilt in the 19th century and extensively restored after being damaged by a German bomb in 1941. The towers at the western end epitomise the cathedral's fragmented history – one was built in the 15th century, the other in the 19th.

Inside, a giant arch supports Sir Jacob Epstein's huge aluminium sculpture *Majestas* – its modern style a bold contrast in this gracious, vaulted space. Pre-Raphaelite fans will appreciate the Burne-Jones reredos (screens) in St Dyfrig's chapel and the stained glass by Rossetti and William Morris' company.

⊙ St Fagans

Historic buildings from all over the country have been dismantled and re-erected in a beautiful semirural setting at St Fagans National History Museum (☑ 029-2057 3500; www.museumwales.ac.uk; admission free, car park £3.50; ⊙10am-5pm). More than 40 buildings are on show, including furnished thatched farmhouses, barns, a watermill, a school, an 18th-century Unitarian chapel and shops stocked with period-appropriate goods. You'll need half a day to do the whole

complex justice and you could easily spend longer, picnicking in the grounds.

It's a great place for kids, with special events in summer, tractor-and-trailer rides (£1) and an old-time funfair. Craftspeople work in many of the buildings, showing how blankets, clogs, barrels, tools and cider were once made. In winter, fires are stoked by people in period clothes

Highlights include a 16th-century farmhouse imbued with the smell of old timber, beeswax and wood smoke, and a row of six miners' cottages from Merthyr Tydfil, each one restored and furnished to represent different periods in the town's history, from the austere minimalism of 1805 to all the mod cons of 1985. It took 20 years to move St Teilo's church here (built 1150 to 1530), stone by stone. It's been restored to its original look, before Protestant whitewash covered the vividly painted interior.

St Fagans Castle is no johnny-come-lately to this site; it was built by the Normans in 1091 as a motte-and-bailey castle before being rebuilt in stone. The manor house at its heart was grafted on in 1580 and is recognised as one of the finest Elizabethan houses in Wales. The property was donated by the earl of Plymouth in 1948, along with its extensive formal gardens, forming the basis of the museum.

The museum is in the midst of a multi-million-pound redevelopment, which isn't due to be completed until 2018. Until that time the reproduction Celtic village and indoor galleries are likely to remain closed.

St Fagans is 5 miles west of central Cardiff; take bus 32A, 320 or 322 (£3.40 return, 20 minutes, at least hourly until 2.15pm) from the Central bus station. By car, it's reached from the continuation of Cathedral Rd.

⛎ Tours

Cardiff History & Hauntings WALKING TOUR
(☑ 07538 878609; www.cardiffhistory.co.uk; ⊙7.30pm Thu & Sat) Runs a selection of guided history walks, the most acclaimed of which is the Llandaff Ghost Walk, a two-hour torch-lit stroll through the ruins, lanes and graveyards of old Llandaff (£7.50). The Margam Ghost Walk (£8.50) takes in a ruined abbey, Tudor castle and creepy woodland. Private tours start from £25 and include Cardiff's Forgotten Past, Parkland Palace (focussing on the Civic Centre) and Castell Coch.

Where When Wales BUS TOUR
(07773 786228; www.wherewhenwales.com; adult/child from £45/25) Operates a range of one-day itineraries: South Wales Valleys, Wye Valley, the Gower, Wales Border Explorer, West Wales, Mid-Wales. Overnight tours head to Pembrokeshire and Ceredigion, while three-day trips travel all the way to Anglesey.

See Wales BUS TOUR
(029-2022 7227; www.seewales.com; adult/child £45/25) Themed day tours include Mines & Mountains, Romans & Ruins, Golden Gower and Welcome to Cardiff.

City Sightseeing BUS TOUR
(029-2047 3432; www.city-sightseeing.com; adult/child £11/5.50) Open-top double-decker tours, departing every 30 to 60 minutes from outside Cardiff Castle and making a short circuit of the city. Tickets last 24 hours, and you can hop on and off at any of the stops.

⚡ Festivals & Events

Six Nations SPORT
(www.rbs6nations.com; ⊘Feb & Mar) The premier European rugby championship, with Wales taking on England, Scotland, Ireland, Italy and France. Cardiff normally hosts two home games – the atmosphere is supercharged. Book accommodation well in advance.

Cardiff Children's Lit Fest LITERATURE
(www.cardiffchildrenslitfest.com; ⊘Mar) Six days of story telling, reading and activities.

Diffusion: Cardiff International Festival of Photography PHOTOGRAPHY
(www.diffusionfestival.org; ⊘May) A month-long festival of exhibitions, screenings, performance and events, held in various venues every May.

Cardiff Festival SUMMER FESTIVAL
(www.cardiff-festival.com; ⊘Jun-Aug) Acts as an umbrella for most of Cardiff's regular summertime festivals, and includes crazy one-offs and lots of free events, such as the Cardiff Carnival street parade, held in the Hayes in August.

Cardiff International Food & Drink Festival FOOD
(www.cardiff-festival.com; ⊘early Jul) Held over a long weekend (Friday to Sunday) in Roald Dahl Plass.

DON'T MISS

CASTELL COCH

Cardiff Castle's little brother is perched atop a thickly wooded crag on the northern fringes of the city. Fanciful **Castell Coch** (Cadw; 029-2081 0101; www.cadw.wales.gov.uk; adult/child £4.50/3.40; ⊘10am-4pm) was the summer retreat of the third marquess of Bute and, like Cardiff Castle, it was redesigned by William Burges in a gaudy Victorian Gothic style, complete with a working drawbridge and portcullis.

Raised on the ruins of Gilbert de Clare's 13th-century Castell Coch (Red Castle), the Butes' Disneyesque holiday home is a monument to high camp. Lady Bute's huge, circular bedroom is pure fantasy: her bed, with crystal globes on the bedposts, sits in the middle beneath an extravagantly decorated and mirrored cupola, with 28 painted panels around the walls depicting monkeys (fashionable at the time, apparently; just plain weird now). The corbels are carved with images of birds nesting or feeding their young, and the washbasin is framed between two castle towers.

Lord Bute's bedroom is small and plain in comparison but the octagonal drawing room is another hallucinogenic tour de force. Its walls are painted with scenes from *Aesop's Fables*, the domed ceiling is a flurry of birds and stars, and the fireplace is topped with figures depicting the three ages of man.

The tower to the right of the entrance has exhibits explaining the castle's history.

Bus 26A (£3.60 return, 30 minutes, three daily Monday to Friday) stops right at the castle gates. Bus 26 (hourly Monday to Saturday) and bus 132 (four hourly Monday to Saturday, hourly Sunday) stop at Tongwynlais, a 10-minute walk from the castle. Bus 26 continues to Caerphilly Castle, and the two can be combined in a day trip with a Stagecoach Explorer ticket (£7).

Everyman Open Air
Theatre Festival   THEATRE
(www.everymanfestival.co.uk; ⊘ Jul) Three weeks
of theatre, held in Sophia Gardens.

Welsh Proms   MUSIC
(www.stdavidshallcardiff.co.uk; ⊘ mid-Jul) A week
of classical concerts at St David's Hall.

Grand Medieval Melee   MEDIEVAL
(www.cardiffcastle.com; ⊘ mid-Aug) A weekend
of armoured knights engaging in drills,
swordplay, mass battles and general medieval mayhem in Cardiff Castle.

Classic Boat Rally   BOATS
(Cardiff Harbour; ⊘ mid-Aug) A one-day convergence of racy boats in Roald Dahl Plass.

Mardi Gras   GAY & LESBIAN
(www.cardiffmardigras.co.uk; ⊘ late Aug or early
Sep) Cardiff's lesbian, gay, bisexual and trans-
gender pride festival includes a street parade
and a ticketed day-long celebration, which
moved to Millennium Stadium in 2013.

Great British Cheese Festival   FOOD
(www.greatbritishcheesefestival.co.uk; ⊘ late Sep)
A weekend-long opportunity to brush shoul-
ders with the big cheeses in Cardiff Castle.

Cardiff Winter Wonderland   WINTER FESTIVAL
(www.cardiffswinterwonderland.com; ⊘ late Nov–
early Jan) Makes the most of the cold weather
with an outdoor ice-skating rink, Santa's
grotto and family-friendly activities, pre-
ceded by the switching on of the Christmas
lights.

🛏 Sleeping

Cardiff has Wales' broadest range of accommodation, including luxury hotels, personable guesthouses and some great hostels. If
you get stuck, the tourist office can help you
find a room for a small fee.

Most places have higher rates on Friday
and Saturday nights. It can be almost impos-
sible to find a bed anywhere near the city on
big sporting weekends, especially rugby internationals, so keep an eye on the fixtures and
choose another date or book well in advance.
It's sometimes so bad that hotels as far away
as Swansea get swamped with the overflow.

A Space in the City (☑ 0845 260 7050;
www.aspaceinthecity.co.uk) is an agency that
lets out high-quality, short-stay apartments
in the city centre, Atlantic Wharf and Cardiff Bay; rates begin at around £70 per
night for a week-long booking in a studio
apartment.

🛏 Central Cardiff

The central city has the best of both the
budget and the upmarket accommodation.
It's the perfect locale if you're planning a
few nights on the tiles, but if you're a light
sleeper it can be noisy.

★ River House Backpackers   HOSTEL £
(Map p54; ☑ 029-2039 9810; www.riverhouseback-
packers.com; 59 Fitzhamon Embankment; dm/r
from £18/35; @🛜) Professionally run by a
young brother-and-sister team and a pair
of fluffy cats, the River House has a well-
equipped kitchen, small garden and cosy
TV lounge. The private rooms are basically
small dorm rooms and share the same bathrooms. A free breakfast of cereal and toast
is provided.

Premier Inn Cardiff City Centre   HOTEL £
(Map p54; ☑ 0871 527 8196; www.premierinn.com;
10 Churchill Way; r from £45; 🛜) The Cardiff
branch of Britain's biggest chain has 200
beds in a squat mirror-clad former office
tower, right in the city centre. It's not flash,
but it's comfortable, clean and terrific value –
although you'll need to book early and pay
in advance to secure the cheapest rates. Request a higher floor for a quieter room.

NosDa   HOSTEL £
(Map p54; ☑ 029-2037 8866; www.nosda.co.uk;
53-59 Despenser St; dm/s/tw from £21/32/46;
ⓟ@🛜) Directly across the river from the
Millennium Stadium, NosDa is starting to
look a little scuffed – which is a shame, as
it was impressively schmick when it first
opened. Still, for private budget rooms in a
fab location, it's hard to beat. The cheaper
twins share bathrooms.

★ Park Plaza   HOTEL ££
(Map p54; ☑ 029-2011 1111; www.parkplazacardiff.
com; Greyfriars Rd; r from £92; 🛜🏊) Luxurious
without being remotely stuffy, the Plaza has
all the five-star facilities you'd expect from
an upmarket business-orientated hotel. The
snug reception sets the scene, with a gas fire
blazing along one wall and comfy wingback
chairs. The rear rooms have leafy views over
the Civic Centre.

🛏 Cardiff Bay

Jolyons Boutique Hotel   HOTEL ££
(Map p46; ☑ 029-2048 8775; www.jolyons.co.uk; 5
Bute Cres; s/d from £76/82; 🛜) A touch of Geor-

gian elegance in the heart of Cardiff Bay, Jolyons has six individually designed rooms combining antique furniture with contemporary colours and crisp cotton sheets. The front rooms face out over Roald Dahl Plass to the Millennium Centre, while one of the rear rooms has its own terrace.

St David's Hotel & Spa HOTEL **££**

(Map p46; ☏ 029-2045 4045; www.thestdavids hotel.com; Havannah St; r from £95; @ 🛜 🏊) A glittering, glassy tower topped with a sail-like flourish, St David's epitomises Cardiff Bay's transformation from wasteland to desirable address. Almost every room has a small private balcony with a bay view. The exterior is already showing signs of wear and tear, but the rooms have been recently renovated.

🍴 Cathays & Roath

Hotel One Hundred HOTEL **££**

(☏ 07916 888423; www.hotelonehundred.com; 100 Newport Rd; s/d £50/60; ℗ 🛜) Patterned metallic wallpaper and chandeliers add a touch of glam to the rooms of this small B&B-like hotel. It's on a busy arterial road, so expect some street noise in the front rooms. A continental breakfast is included in the rates.

🛏 Pontcanna & Canton

Long, leafy Cathedral Rd is lined with B&Bs and small hotels, nearly all of them in restored Victorian town houses. It's only a 15- to 20-minute walk from the city centre, or a £6 taxi ride from the train or bus stations. Street parking is unrestricted but can be tricky to find during working hours.

★ Lincoln House HOTEL **££**

(Map p56; ☏ 029-2039 5558; www.lincolnhotel. co.uk; 118 Cathedral Rd; s/d from £70/90; ℗ 🛜) Walking a middle line between a large B&B and a small hotel, Lincoln House is a generously proportioned Victorian property with heraldic emblems in the stained-glass windows of its sitting room, and a separate bar. For added romance, book a four-poster room.

★ Cathedral House B&B **££**

(Map p56; ☏ 029-2023 2872; www.cathedralhouse-cardiff.co.uk; 146 Cathedral Rd; s/d from £45/65; 🛜) A recent renovation at this friendly B&B has left neutral tones and modern bathrooms in its wake. The proportions of the

front rooms, while not strictly cathedral-like, certainly are generous.

Number 62 GUESTHOUSE **££**

(Map p56; ☏ 029-2041 2765; www.number62.com; 62 Cathedral Rd; r from £65) The only thing stopping us calling Number 62 a B&B is that breakfast is only offered as an add-on. In all other respects it's very similar to the other converted town houses on this strip, although it does have one of the most lovingly tended front gardens. The cosy rooms are simply decorated in demure colours.

Beaufort Guest House B&B **££**

(Map p56; ☏ 029-2023 7003; www.beauforthouse-cardiff.co.uk; 65 Cathedral Rd; s/d from £57/82; 🛜) Despite a thorough refurbishment, the Beaufort retains an old-fashioned Victorian atmosphere, with period-style furniture, gilt mirrors, heavy drapes and even a portrait of the old queen herself. The breakfast room is ready for royalty, with candlesticks and blue-and-white china adding a touch of grandeur.

Town House B&B **££**

(Map p56; ☏ 029-2023 9399; www.thetownhouse-cardiff.co.uk; 70 Cathedral Rd; s/d £45/70; ℗ 🛜) Succinctly named, this elegant Victorian town house on the Cathedral Rd strip has welcoming owners and a relaxed vibe. It retains lots of period features, including original fireplaces, stained-glass windows and a tiled hallway with busy wallpaper. The rooms are more restrained.

Saco House APARTMENT **£££**

(Map p56; ☏ 0845 122 0405; www.sacoapartments. co.uk; 74-76 Cathedral Rd; apt from £138; ℗) This large town house has been given a contemporary makeover and converted into serviced apartments, complete with comfortable lounges and fitted kitchens. They're set up for longer visits but one-day stays are possible midweek. The two-bedroom apartments are good value for families with kids; there's an extra sofa bed in the lounge.

🛏 Grangetown

★ Tŷ Rosa B&B **££**

(☏ 0845 643 9962; www.tyrosa.com; 118 Clive St; s/d from £49/69, without bathroom £45/59; 🛜) Half an hour's walk from either the bay or Central Cardiff (follow the river south, turn right on to Penarth Rd and then left after 650m), this gay-friendly B&B is noted for its

Central Cardiff

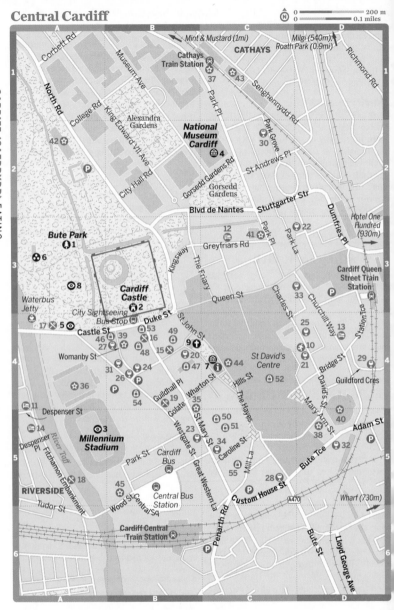

sumptuous breakfasts and affable hosts. The thoughtfully equipped rooms are split between the main house and an annexe across the road. Some rooms share bathrooms.

✕ Eating

As Cardiff has become more glossy, cosmopolitan and multicultural, so has its food scene. A diverse array of restaurants is scattered around the city, with a particularly ritzy batch lining Cardiff Bay. Burger joints

Central Cardiff

and kebab shops cater to the central city's throngs of young drinkers, well into the small hours.

Perhaps the most dynamic segment of the city's food scene belongs to its Indian community, where a select group of restaurants has been confounding expectations and accumulating plaudits.

✕ Central Cardiff

Riverside Market MARKET £
(Map p54; www.riversidemarket.org.uk; Fitzhamon Embankment; ⊗10am-2pm Sun; 🖉) What it lacks in size, Riverside Market makes up for in sheer yumminess, its stalls heaving with cooked meals, cakes, cheese, organic meat, charcuterie, bread, apple juice and real ale. There are plenty of options for vegetarians and the Welsh cakes, hot off the griddle, are exceptional.

Pettigrew Tea Rooms CAFE £
(Map p54; www.pettigrew-tearooms.com; West Lodge, Castle St; mains £5-7; ⊗9am-4pm) Waitresses in white aprons serve cuppas and cakes on delicate china at this perfectly dahling little tea room within the crenulated confines of Bute Park's 1863 gatehouse. Cucumber sandwiches and cream scones are the customary accompaniment to the extensive range of tea on offer – or try the ploughman's platter if you're after something more hearty.

Pontcanna & Canton

Pontcanna & Canton

Sleeping

Eating

Drinking & Nightlife

Entertainment

Coffee Barker CAFE £
(Map p54; Castle Arcade; mains £4-6; ⊙8.30am-5.30pm Mon-Sat, 11am-4.30pm Sun; 🕾🕼) Slink into an armchair, sip on a silky coffee and snack on salmon scrambled eggs or a sandwich in what is Cardiff's coolest cafe. There are plenty of magazines and toys to keep everyone amused.

Restaurant Minuet ITALIAN £
(Map p54; www.restaurantminuet.co.uk; 42 Castle Arcade; mains £4-11; ⊙11am-4.30pm Mon-Sat; 🌶) It may look humble, but this little eatery has a reputation for cheap and cheerful, simple Italian food. The menu has a good vegetarian selection, including plenty of meat-free pasta options.

Goat Major PUB £
(Map p54; www.sabrain.com/goatmajor; 33 High St; pies £7.50; ⊙food noon-6pm Mon-Sat, noon-4pm Sun) A solidly traditional wood-lined pub with armchairs, a fireplace and Brains Dark real ale on tap, the Goat Major's gastronomic contribution comes in the form of its selection of homemade savoury pot pies served with chips. Try the Wye Valley pie, a mixture of buttered chicken, leek, asparagus and Tintern Abbey cheese.

Madame Fromage DELI, CAFE £
(Map p54; www.madamefromage.co.uk; 18 Castle Arcade; mains £4-9; ⊙10am-5.30pm Mon-Sat, noon-5pm Sun) One of Cardiff's best delicatessens, with a wide range of charcuterie and French and Welsh cheese, the Madame also has a cafe with tables spilling into the arcade. Here you can read French newspapers and eat a mixture of Breton and Welsh dish-

es, including rarebit, lamb *cawl* (a stewlike soup) and *bara brith* (fruitcake).

Plan
CAFE **£**

(Map p54; 28 Morgan Arcade; mains £4-9; ⊗ 9am-5pm Mon-Sat, 10am-4pm Sun) Serving quite possibly Wales' best coffee, this appealing cafe also delivers tasty lunch fare, such as homemade pies and salads. Grab a window seat and a copy of the *Guardian* newspaper and caffeinate to your racing heart's content.

★ Cafe Cittá
ITALIAN **££**

(Map p54; ☑ 029-2022 4040; 4 Church St; mains £8-11; ⊗ 11am-9pm Tue-Sat, noon-6pm Sun) Once you're lured through the door by the delicious scents wafting out of the wood-fired oven, you won't want to escape this little slice of *la dolce vita*. The authentic linguine puttanesca is perfect proof that some traditions shouldn't be messed with. There is only a handful of tables, so book ahead.

Zerodegrees
ITALIAN **££**

(Map p54; www.zerodegrees.co.uk; 27 Westgate St; mains £8-16; ⊗ noon-midnight Mon-Sat, noon-11pm Sun; 🐡) Within the factory-like setting of an art nouveau garage this microbrewery and restaurant combines all-day dining with artisan-crafted beers. The excellent food options include a United Nations of pizza toppings (Thai, Mexican, Chinese), pasta, salads and 1kg pots of mussels (the house speciality).

✖ Cardiff Bay

Woods Bar & Brasserie
MODERN WELSH **££**

(Map p46; ☑ 029-2049 2400; www.knifeandforkfood.co.uk; Stuart St; mains £9-17, 2-/3-course menu £17/20; ⊗ noon-2pm & 5.30-11pm Mon-Sat, noon-3pm Sun) Rather like the contemporary makeover of the historic Pilotage Building, which it inhabits, this restaurant delivers a modern take on the classics, highlighting iconic Welsh products such as cockles, black beef, Glamorgan sausages and Perl Las cheese. The service is also exemplary.

Moksh
INDIAN **££**

(Map p46; ☑ 029-2049 8120; www.moksh.co.uk; Mermaid Quay; mains £6-18; ⊗ noon-2.30pm & 6-11pm; ⤢) Moksh's tangerine walls and Buddhist imagery provide ample warning that this is not your typical Indian restaurant. A Goan influence pervades but an adventurous approach incorporates snatches of Chinese, Thai, and even Italian cuisine.

Ffresh
MODERN WELSH **££**

(Map p46; ☑ 029-2063 6465; www.ffresh.org.uk; Wales Millennium Centre; mains £12-17; ⊗ noon-9.30pm Mon-Sat, to 5pm Sun) 🕭 Overlooking the Senedd from the glassed-in end of the Millennium Centre, Ffresh has the Welshiest of settings and a menu to match. Local, seasonal produce features heavily in a creative menu that includes some traditional favourites, such as lamb rack with faggots.

Bosphorus
TURKISH **££**

(Map p46; ☑ 029-2048 7477; www.bosphorus.co.uk; 31 Mermaid Quay; mains £12-18, express lunch £11; ⊗ noon-11.30pm Mon-Sat, to 10pm Sun; ⤢) While the food is good, it's the setting that really distinguishes this upmarket Turkish restaurant. Jutting out over the water on its own private pier, Bosphorus enjoys wonderful all-round views; the best are from the outdoor tables at the end.

✖ Cathays & Roath

★ Mint & Mustard
INDIAN **££**

(☑ 029-2062 0333; www.mintandmustard.com; 134 Whitchurch Rd; mains £8-16, 1-/2-course lunch £6/9; ⊗ noon-2pm & 6-11pm; ⤢) Specialising in seafood dishes from India's southern state of Kerala, this excellent restaurant combines an upmarket ambience with attentive service and delicious, beautifully presented food. If you're not enticed by the lobster, crab, prawn and fish dishes, there are plenty of vegetarian options and an excellent crusted lamb biryani.

Milgi
VEGETARIAN **££**

(☑ 029-2047 3150; www.milgilounge.com; 213 City Rd; mains £9; ⊗ 11am-midnight; ⤢) 🕭 A kooky-chic haven for the city's vegerati, Milgi serves a seasonally affected menu of meat-free pasta, burgers and curries, including options for the discerning gluten-free vegan. Acoustic sessions and storytelling nights are held in the sofa-filled yurt in the back garden.

✖ Pontcanna & Canton

★ Purple Poppadom
INDIAN **££**

(Map p56; ☑ 029-2022 0026; www.purplepoppadom.com; 185A Cowbridge Rd East; mains £11-17, 2-course lunch £12; ⊗ noon-2.30pm & 6-10.30pm Sun-Fri, 6-11pm Sat) Trailblazing a path for 'nouvelle Indian' cuisine, chef Anand George's kitchen offers its own unique take on regional dishes from all over the subcontinent – from Kashmir to Kerala. Whether it's a succulent piece of Moghul-style tandoori chicken or a rich Syrian Christian beef curry, meals are thoughtfully constructed and artfully presented. Don't expect huge portions, though.

Brava
CAFE **££**

(Map p56; www.bravacardiff.co.uk; 71 Pontcanna St; breakfast £4-8, lunch £6-9, dinner £9-11; ⏰8am-4pm Mon, 8am-10pm Tue-Sat, 9am-4pm Sun) With local art on the walls and an informal vibe, this cool cafe is our favourite brunch spot on the strength of its eggs Benedict, silky white coffee and attentive service. Tables spill out onto the pavement in summer and in the evening it morphs into a licensed bistro. Brava indeed.

Drinking & Nightlife

Cardiff is a prodigiously boozy city. Friday and Saturday nights see the city centre invaded by hordes of generally good-humoured, beered-up lads and ladettes tottering from bar to club to kebab shop, whatever the weather (someone fetch that young woman a coat!). It's not as tacky as it sounds – a lively alternative scene, some swish bars and a swathe of old-fashioned pubs keep things interesting.

Try the local Brains SA (meaning Special Ale, Same Again or Skull Attack, depending on how many you've had), brewed by the same family since 1882.

Central Cardiff

Gwdihw
BAR

(Map p54; www.gwdihw.co.uk; 6 Guildford Cres; ⏰3pm-midnight Sun-Wed, noon-2am Thu-Sat) The last word in Cardiff hipsterdom, this cute little bar has an eclectic line-up of entertainment (comedy nights, markets and lots of live music, including microfestivals that spill over into the car park), but it's a completely charming place to stop for a drink at any time.

Buffalo Bar
BAR

(Map p54; www.buffalocardiff.co.uk; 11 Windsor Pl; ⏰noon-3am) A haven for cool kids about town, the laid-back Buffalo features retro furniture, tasty food, life-affirming cocktails and alternative tunes. There's a small beer garden at the rear, while upstairs a roster of cutting-edge indie bands takes to the stage.

Fire Island
BAR

(Map p54; www.fireislandcardiff.co.uk; 25 Westgate St; ⏰9am-1.30am) Craft beer, cocktails and BBQ food collide beautifully in this large industro-chic corner bar. Beer lovers can work their way through a blackboard menu that lists the provenance of each of the brews flowing through the venue's 24 hand pumps.

10 Feet Tall
BAR

(Map p54; www.10feettallcardiff.com; 12 Church St; ⏰noon-3am) Part of a hip quartet of related venues that includes Buffalo Bar, Fire Island and Undertone (downstairs), this three-storey venue merges a cafe, cocktail and tapas bar, and live-music venue. Handsome bartenders swish together two-for-one cocktails between 5pm and 10pm, and all day Sundays.

Porter's
BAR

(Map p54; www.porterscardiff.com; Bute Tce; ⏰noon-midnight Sun-Thu, to 3am Fri & Sat) There's something on most nights at this friendly attitude-free bar, whether it's live music, comedy, a quiz, a movie screening (there's a little cinema attached) or 'bandaoke' – karaoke supported by a live band.

City Arms
PUB

(Map p54; www.thecityarmscardiff.com; 10-12 Quay St; ⏰11am-11pm Mon-Wed, 11am-2am Thu-Sun; 🛜) What's affectionately known in these parts as an 'old man's pub' – despite it attracting just as many young geezers – the City Arms is an unpretentious, old-fashioned kind of place, its walls lined with rugby memorabilia and beer labels. It gets predictably packed out on rugby weekends (Millennium Stadium is right across the road), but on weekday afternoons it's a quiet place for a pint.

Bunk House
BAR

(Map p54; www.bunkhousecardiff.co.uk; 93 St Mary St) Strewn with fairy lights, pennants, candles and tiny bells that tinkle as you brush past them, this bar attached to a hostel manages to be simultaneously cosy, kooky and cool – a rare combination. There's even a made-up bed, should you need a lie down.

Pen & Wig
PUB

(Map p54; www.penandwigcardiff.co.uk; 1 Park Grove; ⏰11am-midnight Sun-Thu, 11am-1am Fri & Sat) Latin legal phrases are printed on the walls of this solidly traditional pub, but there's nothing stuffy about the large beer garden or the entertainment roster (open

BARTENDER TAG

We asked the bartenders at some of our favourite Cardiff bars for their expert tips on the city's best venues (aside from their own, of course).

Cocktail conjurer at 10 Feet Tall 'The Welsh Club (Clwb Ifor Bach), of course. Buffalo, and not just because it's our sister bar; some great bands play upstairs. Moon Bar (Full Moon) is good for live music too. Oh, and try Gwdihw. The name is the Welsh version of an owl's call – you know, "to-whit-to-woo".'

Dreadhead and Tatts at Full Moon 'The Club (Clwb Ifor Bach) – that place is legendary. Everyone starts out at Pen & Wig for a cheap beer in the beer garden.'

Hip lasses at Gwdihw 'If we head out after work, we head to Buffalo – it's open really late. Otherwise, there are some great old pubs along City Rd, east of the city centre.'

mic Mondays, quiz Tuesdays, live music Saturdays). *Caveat emptor*: the impressive range of ales may induce *mens rea* the morning after.

Full Moon BAR
(Map p54; www.thefullmooncardiff.com; 1/3 Womanby St; ⊙5pm-late) There are no pretences at this friendly, grungy rock bar, directly opposite Clwb Ifor Bach. Sample from the large selection of rum, whisky and vodka, or try the 'jar of green shit' if you dare. Upstairs, the Moon Club thrums to live bands.

Pica Pica BAR
(Map p54; www.picapicacardiff.com; 15-23 Westgate St; ⊙noon-midnight; ⊚) Housed in a series of low-ceiling brick vaults, this cool bar serves tapas, mezze and two-for-one cocktails before 8pm.

Yard BAR
(Map p54; ☑029-2022 7577; www.yardbarkitchen.co.uk; 42-43 St Mary St; ⊙10am-11pm Sun-Thu, 10am-1am Fri & Sat; ⊛) Occupying the site of an 18th-century brewery, Yard sports an industrial-chic decor of stainless steel, polished copper pipes and zinc ducting, with clubby sofas and plenty of tables. Outdoor seating, food and a child-friendly policy pull in families during the day, while live bands entertain from 9pm Thursday to Saturday. Upstairs, at the Jam Jar, DJs kick on until 3am on weekends.

Atlantic Wharf

Wharf PUB
(☑029-2040 5092; www.thewharfcardiff.co.uk; 121 Schooner Way; ⊙noon-11pm; ⊚⊛) The expanse of old brick warehouses and brand-new apartments that fill the former docklands

between the city and Cardiff Bay still feels a little desolate. The exception is this large, family-friendly pub inhabiting a striking Victorian industrial building on East Bute Dock. On sunny days the tables by the water are some of Cardiff's prime drinking spots. Entertainment includes regular quiz nights.

Cardiff Bay

Cwtch BAR
(Map p46; www.jolyons.co.uk; 5 Bute Cres; ⊙5.30-11pm Mon-Thu, to 1am Fri & Sat) A '*cwtch*' is either a warm, safe place or a cuddle. This little bar, below Jolyons Hotel, is certainly the former and it imparts a cosy feeling that's almost as good as the latter. Sink into a sofa and slip into Cwtch's warm embrace. In summer, head through the Tardis door to the beer garden.

Salt BAR
(Map p46; www.saltcardiff.com; Mermaid Quay; ⊙10am-midnight Sun-Thu, 10am-2am Fri & Sat; ⊚) A large bar with an open, breezy feel and a 1st-floor terrace with a view of the bay. DJs spin on weekends and there's occasionally live music on Fridays.

Pontcanna & Canton

Y Mochyn Du PUB
(Map p56; www.ymochyndu.com; Sophia Close; ⊙noon-11pm) Right by SWALEC Stadium, 'The Black Pig' is both the de facto cricketer's pub and one of the few places in Cardiff where you might hear Welsh spoken. There's a big variety of beer on tap, including a range of craft ales. Once you've checked out the cricket memorabilia in the wood-lined

GAY & LESBIAN CARDIFF

Cardiff's small gay and lesbian scene is focussed on a cluster of venues on Churchill Way and Charles St (for listings and general information check www.gaycardiff.co.uk). The big event is the annual Mardi Gras (p52), held as part of the Cardiff Festival in late August or early September.

Eagle (Map p54; www.eaglecardiff.com; 39 Charles St; ⊙5pm-2.30am Sun-Thu, to 5am Fri & Sat) A bastion for blokiness, the Eagle has a gay men-only policy after 9pm on the weekends, enabled by a membership system (£3 annually). There's no DJ, drag or back room, just a friendly little basement bar open until the wee smalls, with a smoking deck at the rear. Special events cover the spectrum from rubber, leather and bear nights to Monday-night karaoke.

Golden Cross (Map p54; www.sabrain.com/golden-cross; 282 Hayes Bridge Rd; ⊙noon-11pm Mon & Tue, to 2am Wed-Sat, to 1am Sun; 🐾) One of the oldest pubs in the city and a long-standing gay venue, this Victorian bar retains its handsome stained glass, polished wood and ceramic tiles. It hosts drag, cabaret, quiz and karaoke nights, and there's a little dance floor.

WOW (Map p54; www.wow-cardiff.com; 4A Churchill Way; ⊙9am-3am) A strange mix of industrial and camp (fringed curtains, chandeliers, exposed ducting and an excess of orange), WOW is the most consistently busy of the bunch. 'Cheeky hour' drink specials run from 4pm to 8pm daily and there's a busy roster of drag, DJs and quizzes. The WOW Club lurks beneath.

Bar Icon (Map p54; www.bariconcardiff.co.uk; 60 Charles St; ⊙noon-midnight Mon-Thu, to 3am Fri & Sat; 🐾) Cocktail bar with comfy sofas that attracts a mixed crowd.

Locker Room (Map p54; www.lockerroomcardiff.co.uk; 50 Charles St; admission £14; ⊙noon-11pm Mon-Fri, nonstop noon Sat-10pm Sun) Gay men's sauna.

pub, head outside to the garden to catch the rays.

☆ Entertainment

Pick up a copy of **Buzz** (www.buzzmag.co.uk), a free monthly magazine with up-to-date entertainment listings, available from the tourist office, bars, theatres and the like. The staff at tourist offices can also help out with recommendations.

Live Music & Comedy

Massive rock and pop concerts are staged at Millennium Stadium. If you're after a more intimate experience, try one of the many bars hosting live bands, such as Gwdihw, Buffalo Bar, 10 Feet Tall and Full Moon.

Most major arts companies are now based at the Wales Millennium Centre. Occasional classical concerts are held in Cardiff Castle, Llandaff Cathedral and St John's Church.

Clwb Ifor Bach   LIVE MUSIC
(Map p54; ☎029-2023 2199; www.clwb.net; 11 Womanby St) Truly an independent music great, Y Clwb has broken many a Welsh band since the early 1980s. It started as a venue for Welsh-language music in Anglo-

phone Cardiff and has built a reputation as Cardiff's most eclectic and important venue. It now hosts bands performing in many tongues and it's the best place to catch gigs by up-and-coming new acts as well as by more established artists.

St David's Hall   CLASSICAL MUSIC
(Map p54; ☎029-2087 8444; www.stdavidshall-cardiff.co.uk; The Hayes) The National Concert Hall of Wales, this is the home of the Welsh Proms in July and a full roster of classical music performances and comedy throughout the year.

Cardiff University
Students' Union   LIVE MUSIC
(Map p54; ☎029-2078 1400; www.cardiffstudents.com; Park Pl) The students' union hosts regular live gigs by big-name bands, usually of an alternative bent, in its four venues. It also hosts regular comedy, club and quiz nights.

Motorpoint Arena   LIVE MUSIC
(Map p54; ☎029-2022 4488; www.livenation.co.uk/cardiff; Mary Ann St) A 7500-capacity indoor arena staging concerts, big-time comedians, *Celebrities on Ice* and *Cage Warriors*.

Glee Club
COMEDY

(Map p46; ☑ 0871 472 0400; www.glee.co.uk; Mermaid Quay; ⊗ Thu-Sat) Hosts touring and local comics.

Cafe Jazz
JAZZ

(Map p54; ☑ 029-2038 7026; www.cafejazzcardiff.com; Sandringham Hotel, 21 St Mary St) It's not exactly your traditional smoky basement, but this cafe-bar is the city's main jazz venue, with live jazz from Monday to Thursday, and blues on Friday (Saturdays are disco nights).

Theatre & Cinema

Other companies are based at the Wales Millennium Centre.

Chapter
THEATRE, CINEMA

(Map p56; ☑ 029-2030 4400; www.chapter.org; Market Rd, Canton) The city's edgiest arts venue, Chapter has a varied rota of contemporary drama, as well as art exhibitions, arthouse cinema, workshops, alternative theatre and dance performances. There's also a good cafe-bar, with Cardiff's biggest range of European beers.

Sherman Cymru
THEATRE

(Map p54; ☑ 029-2064 6900; www.shermancymru.co.uk; Senghennydd Rd, Cathays) South Wales' leading theatre company, Sherman stages a wide range of material, from classics and children's theatre to works by new playwrights.

Royal Welsh College of Music & Drama
MUSIC, THEATRE

(Map p54; ☑ 029-2039 1391; www.rwcmd.ac.uk; Bute Park) All manner of performances are staged in this impressive building's state-of-the-art venues, including theatre from the college's inhouse Richard Burton Company.

New Theatre
THEATRE

(Map p54; ☑ 029-2087 8889; www.newtheatrecardiff.co.uk; Park Pl) This restored Edwardian playhouse hosts various touring productions, including musicals and pantomime.

Vue
CINEMA

(Map p54; ☑ 08712 240 240; www.myvue.com; Stadium Plaza, Wood St) Huge 13-screen multiplex seating nearly 3000 people.

Cineworld
CINEMA

(Map p54; ☑ 0871 200 2000; www.cineworld.com; Mary Ann St) Fifteen-screen multiplex at the rear of the St David's complex.

Sport

Cardiff Arms Park
SPECTATOR SPORT

(Map p54; www.cardiffrfc.com; Westgate St) Rugby union is this city's favourite sport and while the big test matches held at Millennium Stadium provide a more thrilling spectacle, you're more likely to be able to score tickets to a game here in its historic neighbour. It's home to both the Cardiff Rugby Football Club, aka the Blue & Blacks, founded in 1876, and the Cardiff Blues (www.cardiffblues.com), the professional regional side. It's Wales' richest, most star-studded club. Tickets to Blues matches will set you back around £20 to £25.

Cardiff City Stadium
SPECTATOR SPORT

(☑ 0845 345 1400; Leckwith Rd, Canton) Greedy Cardiff couldn't stop with one new stadium – this 26,800-seater opened in 2009. It's home to Cardiff City Football Club (www.cardiff-fcityfc.co.uk), a team that's riding high after winning the Championship League in 2013 and being promoted to the English Premier League. Local football fans still hark back to 1927 when the Bluebirds took the English FA Cup out of England for the first (and only) time – Welsh football's equivalent of Owain Glyndŵr's rebellion.

SWALEC Stadium
SPECTATOR SPORT

(Map p56; www.swalecstadium.co.uk; Sophia Gardens) This is the home of the Glamorgan Cricket Club (www.glamorgancricket.com), the only Welsh club belonging to the England and Wales Cricket Board.

🔒 Shopping

If you thought Cardiff's 21st-century makeover was all about political edifices, arts centres and sports stadia, think again. One of the most dramatic developments in the central city is the transformation of the Hayes shopping strip, with the giant, glitzy extension of the St David's shopping centre now eating up its entire eastern flank. Balancing this modern mall is a historic network of Victorian and Edwardian shopping arcades spreading their dainty tentacles either side of St Mary St.

St David's
MALL

(Map p54; www.stdavidscardiff.com; The Hayes; ⊗ 9.30am-8pm Mon-Sat, 11am-5pm Sun; 🔊) One of Britain's largest shopping centres (the equivalent of 30 football pitches), the redeveloped and greatly extended St David's was completed in 2009 at a cost of £675 million.

All of the high street chains you could name have a home here, along with a smorgasbord of eateries, a cinema multiplex and a large branch of the John Lewis department store, which dominates its south end.

Craft in the Bay
ARTS & CRAFTS
(Map p46; www.makersguildinwales.org.uk; Lloyd George Ave; ⊙10.30am-5.30pm) This retail showcase for the Welsh Makers Guild co-operative sells work by its members, including a wide range of ceramics, textiles, woodwork, jewellery, glassware and iron-work.

Royal & Morgan Arcades
SHOPPING ARCADE
(Map p54; www.royalandmorganarcades.co.uk; btwn St Mary St & The Hayes) Cardiff's oldest arcade (1858), the Royal connects up with the Morgan Arcade via a series of covered lanes, forming a ritzy shopping precinct called the Morgan Quarter. Along with name-brand fashion, there are shops selling skateboards, vintage books and antiques. Look out for Spillers Records, the excellent Wally's Delicatessen and Liam Gallagher's pricy menswear boutique, Pretty Green.

Spillers Records
MUSIC
(Map p54; www.spillersrecords.co.uk; Morgan Arcade; ⊙11am-4pm Sun, 10am-6pm Mon-Sat) The world's oldest record shop, founded in 1894 (when it sold wax phonograph cylinders), Spillers stocks a large range of CDs and vinyl, and prides itself on catering to the non-mainstream end of the market (it's especially good on punk). In-store gigs promote local talent.

Castle Arcade
SHOPPING ARCADE
(Map p54; www.cardiffcastlearcade.co.uk; btwn Castle & High Sts) The most decorative of the city's arcades, it houses Troutmark Books (secondhand and Welsh-language books), Claire Grove Buttons (beads and buttons of every description), Madame Fromage, Coffee Barker and Cafe Minuet.

High St Arcade
SHOPPING ARCADE
(Map p54; www.cardiffhighstreetarcade.co.uk; btwn High St & St John Sts) Stop into the NY Deli for a burger or sandwich, then head on to Hobo's for secondhand 1960s and '70s clothing, or to Hubbards for a very cool mixture of vintage and locally designed womenswear. Dance-music gurus Catapult keep Cardiff's DJs up to date.

Cardiff Market
MARKET
(Map p54; www.cardiff-market.co.uk; btwn St Mary & Trinity Sts; ⊙8am-5.30pm Mon-Sat) For an age-old shopping experience, head to this Victorian covered market, which is packed with stalls selling everything from fresh fish to mobile phones. Stock up here for a picnic in Bute Park with goodies such as fresh bread, cheese, cold meats, barbecued chicken, cakes and pastries.

Cardiff Fashion Quarter
MARKET
(CFQ; Map p54; www.facebook.com/cardifffashionquarter; Womanby St; ⊙10am-6pm Tue-Sat, 11am-5pm Sun) Oddball graffiti heralds this kooky collection of independent stalls, selling everything from vintage clothes to antiques.

Wales Centre & Things Welsh
SOUVENIRS
(Map p54; www.castlewelshcrafts.co.uk; 1 Castle St; ⊙9am-5.30pm) If you're after stuffed dragons, lovespoons or Cardiff T-shirts, this is the city's biggest souvenir shop, conveniently located across the street from the castle.

Wyndham Arcade
SHOPPING ARCADE
(Map p54; btwn St Mary St & Mill Lane) An historic arcade (1887), the Wyndham is a little run-down but it is home to the gloriously old-fashioned Havana House, a specialist cigar merchant from a bygone era. It's known locally as the 'bear shop', thanks to a prominently displayed 200-year-old piece of taxidermy called Bruno.

ⓘ Information

Head to **Lonely Planet** (www.lonelyplanet.com/wales/cardiff-caerdydd) for planning advice, author recommendations, traveller reviews and insider tips.

Cardiff Bay Tourist Office (Map p46; ⌨029-2087 7927; www.visitcardiffbay.info; Wales Millennium Centre; ⊙10am-6pm, extended on show nights) Information, advice, accommodation bookings and souvenirs.

Cardiff Tourist Office (Map p54; ⌨029-2087 3573; www.visitcardiff.com; Old Library, The Hayes; internet per 30min £1; ⊙9.30am-5.30pm Mon-Sat, 10am-4pm Sun; @) Cardiff's main tourist office stocks Ordnance Survey maps and Welsh books, and offers an accommodation booking service and internet access.

Police (⌨101; www.south-wales.police.uk; King Edward VII Ave)

University Hospital of Wales (⌨029-2074 8047; www.cardiffandvaleuhb.wales.nhs.uk; Heath Park) Cardiff's main accident and emergency department, located 2 miles north of the Civic Centre.

ℹ Getting There & Away

AIR

Cardiff Airport (☎ 01446-711111; www.tbi-cardiffairport.com) is mainly used by budget operators. Aside from summer-only services and charters, following are the airlines flying into Cardiff and the destinations they serve:

Aer Lingus (www.aerlingus.com) Dublin.

Citywing (www.citywing.com) Anglesey.

Eastern Airways (www.easternairways.com) Aberdeen and Newcastle.

Flybe (www.flybe.com) Glasgow, Edinburgh, Belfast, Jersey and Paris.

KLM (www.klm.com) Amsterdam.

Thomson (www.thomson.co.uk) Malaga, Alicante, Gran Canaria, Tenerife and Lanzarote.

BUS

Cardiff's **Central bus station** (Map p54; Wood St) is next to the train station.

National Express (www.nationalexpress.com) coach destinations include Tenby (£18, three hours), Chepstow (£5.40, 55 minutes), Bristol (£9, 1¼ hours), Birmingham (£26, 2¾ hours) and London (£22, 3½ hours).

Greyhound (www.greyhounduk.com) coaches head to Newport (£3, 25 minutes), Swansea (£3, one hour) and Bristol Airport (£6, 1¾ hours).

Arriva (www.arrivabus.co.uk) has buses to Carmarthen (1½ hours) and Aberystwyth (3½ hours).

Stagecoach (www.stagecoachbus.com) destinations include Caerphilly (45 minutes), Abergavenny (1½ hours), Brecon (1½ hours), Llandrindod Wells (2¾ hours) and Newtown (3½ hours).

CAR

Cardiff is easily reached from the M4 (which runs from London to northwest of Swansea). All major car-rental companies have branches in the capital.

TRAIN

Trains from major British cities arrive at Cardiff Central station, on the southern edge of the city centre. Direct services from Cardiff include London Paddington (£41, 2¼ hours), Abergavenny (£13, 40 minutes), Swansea (£9.90, one hour), Fishguard Harbour (£24, three hours) and Holyhead (£85, five hours).

ℹ Getting Around

TO/FROM THE AIRPORT

➺ Cardiff Airport is 12 miles southwest of Cardiff, past Barry.

➺ The X91 bus (£3.90, 30 minutes, two hourly) heads between the airport and the Central bus station.

➺ The 905 shuttle bus (£1, seven minutes) links the airport terminal to nearby Rhoose Cardiff Airport train station. Trains to Cardiff Central station (£4, 30 minutes) run hourly Monday to Saturday and two hourly on Sunday.

➺ A taxi from the airport to the city centre takes 20 to 30 minutes, depending on traffic, and costs about £28.

BIKE

Cardiff City Council (www.cardiff.gov.uk) has a dedicated cycling officer and its website has lots of information including lists of bike shops and route maps; click on Environment, then Cycling.

CAR & MOTORCYCLE

Cardiff doesn't pose many difficulties for drivers, although most of the central city streets between Westgate St, Castle St and St David's are closed to traffic.

If you're prepared to walk, it's often possible to find free street parking in the suburbs. Pontcanna's Cathedral Rd has unrestricted parking but it's difficult to find an empty spot during working hours. St David's has 2000 parking spaces above the shopping centre, with an additional 550 below John Lewis. The main car park is open 24 hours (per three/six/24 hours £4/9/18), with £2 overnight parking (5pm to 6am). In Cardiff Bay, there's a car park on Havannah St (per hour/day 50p/£5).

PUBLIC TRANSPORT

Local buses are operated by **Cardiff Bus** (Map p54; ☎ 029-2066 6444; www.cardiffbus.com; trip/day pass £1.70/3.40); buy your ticket from the driver (no change given). Free route maps and timetables are available from its Wood St office. Generally the buses are more convenient for short trips than the trains, although there are a handful of stations scattered around the city.

Two boats run alternating waterbus services along the River Taff from Bute Park to Mermaid Quay, departing every half-hour from 10.30am to 5pm. The journey takes about 25 minutes and costs £3 each way.

TAXI

Cabs can be hailed in the street, ordered by phone, or picked up at taxi ranks outside the train station, in Duke St opposite the castle, and on the corner of Greyfriars Rd and Park Pl. Reliable companies include **Capital Cabs** (☎ 029-2077 7777; www.capitalcabs.co.uk) and **Dragon Taxis** (☎ 029-2033 3333; www.dragontaxis.com). **Checker Cars** (☎ 01446 711747; www.checkercars.com) has the airport concession.

AROUND CARDIFF

If you're basing yourself in Cardiff there is a diverting selection of day trips to choose between – from the peculiar time-warped traditions of the British seaside, on display at Penarth and Barry, to the hills and valleys of the hinterland, peppered with ancient ruins, castles and manor houses.

Penarth

POP 22,100

Well-heeled Penarth is slowly transforming from an old-fashioned seaside resort to a virtual suburb of Cardiff, despite it being in the neighbouring county, the Vale of Glamorgan. It's connected to Cardiff Bay by the freshwater lake formed by the construction of the barrage and it now sports a busy marina on the lakefront.

⊙ Sights & Activities

Penarth Pavilion   ARTS CENTRE

(www.penarthpavilion.co.uk; Penarth Pier) Penarth's rock-strewn shoreline may not be particularly attractive, but it is the closest beach to Cardiff. In 1894 it was graced with that icon of the Victorian seaside, a pier. An elegant art deco pavilion followed in 1927 but it inevitably went into decline and for decades it was left to decay. By the time you're reading this, a major restoration will have taken place and the pavilion should have reopened, complete with a brand-new gallery, marine history exhibition, cinema, cafe and shops.

Alexandra Gardens   PARK

This pretty Edwardian-era park slopes from Penarth's bustling town centre down to the esplanade. Its formal gardens are filled with topiary and colourful flowerbeds.

Around Cardiff

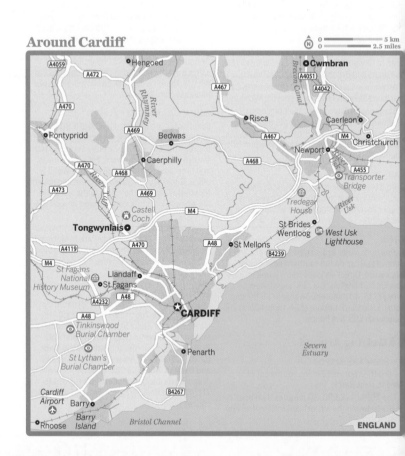

Ffotogallery GALLERY

(☎ 029-2034 1667; www.ffotogallery.org; Plymouth Rd; ☺11am-5pm Tue-Sat) **FREE** Also known as the Turner House Gallery, this red-brick building near the train station hosts edgy photographic, video and multimedia exhibitions, and runs summer workshops where kids can learn stuff such as printmaking and pinhole photography. It's at its busiest during the month-long Diffusion international photography festival in May.

Waverley Excursions CRUISE

(☎ 0845 130 4647; www.waverleyexcursions.co.uk; adult/child from £23/12) In June the Waverley, the world's last seagoing paddle steamer, departs from Penarth Pier for trips across the Bristol Channel to Holm Island, Clevedon, Weston-super-Mare, Minehead, Ilfracombe and Lundy Island.

✗ Eating

Fig Tree WELSH **££**

(☎ 029-2070 2512; www.thefigtreepenarth.co.uk; The Esplanade; mains £11-19, 1-/2-/3-course lunch £7.50/11/14; ☺noon-3pm & 6.30-9.30pm Tue-Fri, 5.30-9.30pm Sat) The name might sound like it has Mediterranean delusions but this Fig Tree is a Welsh affair, with a commitment to sourcing most of its products from within 30 miles of the restaurant. It's a great place to tuck into Welsh lamb, turkey, mussels and cheese, and the waterfront location and reasonably priced lunch menu gears it perfectly towards day-trippers.

❶ Getting There & Away

➡ Cardiff buses 92, 93 and 94 (£1.70, 20 minutes, every 15 minutes Monday to Saturday, hourly Sunday and evenings) run to Penarth, and there are frequent trains from Cardiff Central (one way/return £2.50/3.50, 20 minutes).

➡ **Cardiff Aquabus** (☎ 029-2034 5163; www.cardiffaquabus.com) departs Penarth Marina for Mermaid Quay at 10.20am, returning from Mermaid Quay at 5.30pm.

➡ You can walk or cycle along the barrage from Cardiff Bay to Penarth Marina (allow 40 minutes on foot). From here it's a steep but short walk up to the town centre and down again to the pier.

Barry (Y Barri)

POP 51,500

Nowhere have the recent triumphs of the BBC Wales television department been more keenly felt than in Barry, a seaside town 8 miles southwest of Cardiff. If you watch *Doctor Who* or *Being Human*, you'll no doubt be aware that the town is infested with aliens, zombies, ghosts, werewolves and vampires. Yet it's the massive popularity of the altogether more down-to-earth comedy *Gavin & Stacey* that has given the town a new caché. The staff at Island Leisure (on the Promenade) are used to fans of the show making a pilgrimage to the booth where Nessa (played in the show by co-writer Ruth Jones) worked. Other sites include nearby Marco's Cafe, where Stacey worked, and Trinity St, where Stacey's mum and Uncle Bryn lived.

The real attraction here is Barry Island, which is well signposted at the south end of the town. It stopped being a real island in the 1880s when it was joined to the mainland by a causeway. Amusement arcades and fun parks line the waterfront at sandy Whitmore Bay, which is easily the best beach this side of the Gower.

❶ Getting There & Away

➡ Frequent trains head to the Barry and Barry Island train stations from Cardiff Central (one way/return £3.10/4.70, 30 minutes).

➡ Cardiff bus services depart every 15 minutes during the day (routes 92-96, £2.40, one hour), but hourly in the evening and on Sundays.

Tinkinswood & St Lythan's Burial Chambers

Neolithic standing stones, stone circles and burial chambers are a dime a dozen in Wales – so much so that many of them don't even make it into tourist brochures and maps. That's the case with this mysterious duo, each standing in a forlorn field 7 miles west of Cardiff, orientated towards the rising sun.

The 6000-year-old Tinkinswood chamber consists of a wall of stones supporting a mammoth 7.4m-long, 36-tonne limestone capstone, thought to be the largest of its kind in Britain. It was once covered in an earth mound, but excavations in 1914 left one half of it open after pottery and the bones of 50 people were removed. A brick pillar was then added to prop up the capstone. The entrance to the mound is approached by a curving avenue of stones, and other stones have been arranged nearby. The site was once known as Castell Carreg – the fairy castle.

Dating from a similar age, the St Lythan's cromlech is considerably smaller, consisting of three supporting stones capped with a large, flat stone, forming a chamber nearly 2m high. It too was probably once covered with a mound that is now long gone. As with many such pre-Christian/pre-Celtic sites, St Lythan's has many local legends attached to it. It was once thought to be a druid's altar and on midsummer's eve the capstone supposedly spins around three times. The field it stands in is known as the Accursed Field.

While located on private farmland, both sites are freely accessible to the public and each has an information post with a wind-up device that plays a recorded commentary.

❶ Getting There & Away

You'll need your own car to get here and preferably a detailed road map. Head west of the city to Culverhouse Cross and continue west on the A48 to St Nicholas, where the sites are signposted. Turn left at the lights and look for a parking area to the right of the road where you can walk across the field to the Tinkinswood chamber. Continue down this road for a further mile and turn left at the end to find St Lythan's.

Caerphilly (Caerffili)

POP 30,400

The town of Caerphilly, with its fairy-tale castle, guards the entrance to the Rhymney Valley to the north of the capital. Its name is synonymous with a popular variety of mild, slightly crumbly, hard white cheese that originated in the surrounding area.

◎ Sights

★Caerphilly Castle   CASTLE
(Cadw; ☑ 029-2088 3143; www.cadw.wales.gov.uk; adult/child £4.75/3.60; ⊙ 9.30am-5pm Mar-Oct,

10am-4pm Nov-Feb) You could be forgiven for thinking that Caerphilly Castle – with its profusion of towers and crenellations reflected in a duck-filled lake – was a film set rather than an ancient monument. While it is often used as a film set, it is also one of Britain's finest examples of a 13th-century fortress with water defences.

Most of the construction was completed between 1268 and 1271 by the powerful English baron Gilbert de Clare (1243–95), Lord Marcher of Glamorgan, in response to the threat of attack by Prince Llewelyn ap Gruffydd, Prince of Gwynedd (and the last Welsh Prince of Wales), who had already united most of the country under his control. Edward I's subsequent campaign against the Welsh princes put an end to Llewelyn's ambitions, and Caerphilly's short-lived spell on the front line came to an end. The leaning tower at the southeast corner is a result of subsidence rather than battle.

In the 13th century Caerphilly was state-of-the-art, being one of the earliest castles to use lakes, bridges and a series of concentric fortifications for defence. To reach the inner court you had to overcome no fewer than three drawbridges, six portcullises and five sets of double gates. In the early 14th century it was remodelled as a grand residence and the magnificent great hall was adapted for entertaining, but from the mid-14th century onward the castle began to fall into ruin.

Much of what you see today is the result of restoration by the castle-loving Bute family. The third Marquess of Bute purchased and demolished houses built up against the walls, and in 1870 the great hall was given a magnificent wooden ceiling (the Gothic windows were added in 1968 and the hall is now used to host special events). The fourth

---

THE BIG CHEESE

Any festival that includes a Cheese Olympics and a Tommy Cooper Tent has got to be worth a look. On the last weekend of July, Caerphilly welcomes more than 70,000 people to the **Big Cheese** (www.caerphilly.gov.uk/bigcheese; admission free; ⊙ Jul), three days of family-oriented fun and games that offers everything from fireworks to falconry, comedy acts to cheese tasting, and medieval battle re-enactments, food and craft stalls, archery demonstrations, live music and a traditional funfair.

The Cheese Olympics are held on the Friday evening, and include cheese throwing, rolling and stacking. The Tommy Cooper Tent – named after the much-loved British comedian, who was born in Caerphilly and died in 1984 – stages comedy acts, including a Tommy Cooper tribute act. A statue to Cooper, in his trademark fez and with a rabbit at his feet, overlooks the castle near the tourist office.

marquess instituted a major restoration from 1928 to 1939, giving jobs to many Great Depression–affected locals in the process. Work continued after 1950, when the fifth marquess gifted the castle to the state. In 1958 the dams were reflooded, creating its current fairy-tale appearance.

You can enter through the outside gate and into the first tower before reaching the ticket office. Upstairs, there are detailed displays about the castle's history. A cartoonish film projected onto the walls of one of the inner towers tells a truncated version of the same story.

On the south dam platform you can see reconstructions of medieval siege weapons; they are working models and lob stone projectiles into the lake during battle re-enactments. Fans of toilet humour should seek out the communal latrine in a small tower nearby.

ℹ️ Information

Caerphilly Tourist Office (☎029-2088 0011; www.visitcaerphilly.com; The Twyn; ⏰10am-5.30pm) Not only is this friendly office a good place to stock up on information, it's also the only place in town selling Caerphilly cheese – along with Penderyn spirits and locally made chocolates. There's a small cafe attached.

ℹ️ Getting There & Away

➳ The easiest way to reach Caerphilly from Cardiff is by train (single/return £4/6.40, 19 minutes).

➳ Buses 26, A and B each depart hourly from Cardiff's Central bus station between about 9am and 4pm, Monday to Saturday (£3.70 return, 45 minutes). Bus 26 also has limited Sunday services.

➳ Bus 26 stops near Castell Coch en route, making it possible to visit both castles in one day.

Newport (Casnewydd)

POP 146,000

Sitting at the muddy mouth of the River Usk and flanked by the detritus of heavy industry, Newport is never going to win any awards for beauty. Despite its grim appearance and gritty undercurrents, Wales' third-largest city does have some fascinating things to see. It's well worth a day trip, although you're unlikely to be tempted to stay over.

Newport takes its name from the fact that it was built after the 'old port' at Caerleon, further upstream, following the construction of Newport Castle in Norman times. The Welsh name, Casnewydd, actually means 'new castle' for much the same reason. Like many harbour towns in South Wales, it grew rich on the back of the iron and coal industries in the 19th and early 20th centuries.

In the second half of the 20th century, Newport's shipbuilding industry disappeared, and the docks declined in importance as coal exports shifted to Barry and iron-ore imports to Port Talbot. In 2001 the huge Llanwern steelworks closed down. Today the city is busy trying to reinvent itself as a centre for the service sector and technology industries.

⊙ Sights

★**Tredegar House**　　HISTORIC BUILDING
(NT; ☎01633-815880; www.nationaltrust.org.uk; house adult/child £6.75/3.60, parking £2; ⏰park 9am-dusk year-round, house 11am-5pm Feb-Oct) The seat of the Morgan family for more than 500 years, Tredegar House is a stone and red-brick 17th-century country house set amid extensive gardens. It is one of the finest examples of a Restoration mansion in Britain, the oldest parts dating to the 1670s. The Morgans, once one of the richest families in Wales, were an interesting lot – Sir Henry was a 17th-century pirate (Captain Morgan's Rum is named after him); Godfrey, the second Lord Tredegar, survived the Charge of the Light Brigade; and Viscount Evan was an occultist, a Catholic convert and a twice-married homosexual who kept a boxing kangaroo.

The National Trust took over management of the property in late 2011 and has done a great job bringing the fascinating stories of its owners to life. The grand dining room has been set up as if for a wedding feast, complete with fake hog's heads and suckling pigs. The adjoining 'gilt room' is blanketed in gold leaf and paintings of barebreasted mythological figures; you're invited to recline on the day bed in order to get a better look. In another parlour there are period costumes to try on and board games to play. The decor of the upstairs bedrooms jumps forward in time to the 1930s, when Evan Morgan was hosting his fabulous parties at Tredegar.

Tredegar House is 2 miles west of Newport city centre. Buses 30 and 36 stop nearby.

THE NEWPORT RISING

Chartism, a parliamentary reform movement that arose during the early years of Queen Victoria's reign, was particularly strong in Wales. It argued for a charter of reforms, most of which we would consider to be essential to democracy today: a vote for every man in a secret ballot (up until this time only male landowners could vote); no property requirement for Members of Parliament (MPs); equal-sized electorates; and payment for MPs (making it possible for poor men to serve).

On 4 November 1839 some 5000 men from the Usk, Ebbw and Rhymney Valleys converged on Newport, intent on taking control of the town and sparking off a national uprising. They tried to storm the Westgate Hotel on Commercial St, where several Chartists were being held; police and infantrymen inside fired into the crowd, killing at least 20 people. Five men were subsequently imprisoned and three were transported to Australia. The bodies of 10 rioters were surreptitiously recovered and buried secretly in the churchyard in unmarked graves.

The rising is remembered in several plaques and monuments around town, notably the Westgate Hotel, where the masonry is still bullet-scarred. Outside, among the hurrying shoppers, is an ensemble of determined bronze figures.

Property requirements for male voters weren't completely removed until 1918. Landless women had to wait another decade.

St Woolos Cathedral — CHURCH

(www.churchinwales.org.uk/monmouth/people/cathedral/; Stow Hill) Newport's ancient cathedral provides a fascinating walk through history. First you enter into the oldest part of the building, a 9th-century stone chapel built to replace a wooden church built here in 500 on the burial site of Welsh king-turned-monk St Gwynllyw (Woolos is an English corruption of his name).

The Normans came next, represented by the magnificent Romanesque arch leading into their grand nave (look up to the curved timbers of the medieval 'wagon roof'). You can see the transition from the Romanesque to the Gothic style in the pointy windows of the outside aisles, which were grafted on later. The mutilations to the stone statues in this part of the church are the handiwork of Puritans in the 1650s. Newport's prosperous Victorian period is evident in the chancel, while the very end of the building is pure 1960s, including the painted marble effect behind the altar.

This cathedral is a steep 10-minute walk uphill from the main shopping strip.

Newport Museum & Art Gallery — MUSEUM

(☑ 01633-656656; www.newport.gov.uk/museum; John Frost Sq; ⊙ 9.30am-4.30pm Mon-Sat) **FREE** Sharing the same building as the tourist office, Newport Museum covers the town's history from the prehistoric to the Romans at Caerleon, to the rise of the coal and iron industries.

Newport Castle — CASTLE

Not much remains of Newport's pre-industrial past apart from the cathedral and the litter-strewn ruins of Newport Castle squeezed between traffic-clogged Kings Way and the river. It was soundly trashed by Owain Glyndŵr in 1402 and never properly recovered. Only the section facing the river is still standing; it's not possible to enter the site.

Riverfront — ARTS CENTRE

(☑ 01633-656757; www.newport.gov.uk/riverfront; Kingsway; ⊙ 10am-6pm Mon-Sat) Opened in 2004, the city's swish cultural centre takes a prominent position by the river. Temporary exhibitions are held in its gallery and it also stages theatre, opera, classical music and dance, as well as cinema, comedy and pantomime.

Nearby is the huge red circle of Steel Wave (1990) by Peter Fink, now almost a civic trademark, and the striking Usk Footbridge (opened in 2006).

Transporter Bridge — BRIDGE

(www.newport.gov.uk/transporterbridge; Usk Way vehicle/passenger £1/50p; ⊙ 10am-5pm Wed-Sun Easter-Sep) The spidery towers of the 1906 Transporter Bridge rise over the river, about a mile south of the city centre. A remarkable piece of Edwardian engineering, it can carry up to six cars across the river in a gondola suspended beneath the high-level track while still allowing high-masted ships to pass beneath. It's the largest of eight such bridges remaining in the world.

If you're planning on driving across and straight back again, you may as well consider paying the day visitor rate (adult/child £2.50/1.50) which includes access to the motor house and high-level walkway.

🛏 Sleeping

West Usk Lighthouse B&B £££

(📞 01633-810126; www.westusklighthouse.co.uk; St Brides Wentloog; r £145-160; 🅿🛜) Quirky doesn't even begin to describe this restored 19th-century lighthouse offering views over the Severn Estuary. It's a little worn around the edges but filled with endearingly eccentric details, such as a full-size Dalek in the lobby. It's at the end of a potholed private road off the B4239, 6 miles southwest of Newport.

ℹ Information

Tourist Office (📞 01633-656656; www.newport.gov.uk/tourism; John Frost Sq; ⊙9am-6pm Mon-Fri, 9am-4pm Sat)

ℹ Getting There & Around

BUS

➡ Newport's bus station is on Kings Way, across from the river, but it can also be accessed from John Frost Sq.

➡ **National Express** (www.nationalexpress.com) coach destinations include Swansea (£9.10, 1½ hours), Cardiff (£3, 30 minutes), Chepstow (£3.80, 25 minutes), Bristol (£8.10, 35 minutes) and London (£22, three hours).

➡ **Greyhound** (www.greyhounduk.com) coaches stop at the train station en route between Cardiff (£3, 25 minutes) and Bristol Airport (£6, 1¼ hours).

➡ **Newport Bus** (www.newportbus.co.uk) covers the local routes, and has services to Cardiff (bus X30; £2, 35 minutes), Caerleon (buses 27 and 28; £1.60, 15 minutes) and Chepstow (bus 73; £2, 50 minutes).

Other operators run buses to Caerphilly (bus 50; 38 minutes), Raglan (bus 60; 39 minutes), Blaenavon (bus X24; 51 minutes) and Monmouth (bus 60; one hour).

TRAIN

➡ Newport train station is on Queensway, immediately north of the High St.

➡ The fastest and easiest connection with Cardiff is by train (£4.60, 16 minutes, six hourly). Direct trains also head to Chepstow (£6.80, 15 minutes), Abergavenny (£8.20, 23 minutes),

Swansea (£15, 1¼ hours) and London Paddington (£38, two hours).

Caerleon

POP 8100

Hidden in plain view beneath the small, genteel town of Caerleon is one of the largest and most important Roman settlements in Britain. After the Romans invaded in AD 43, they controlled their new territory through a network of forts and military garrisons. The top tier of military organisation was the legionary fort, of which there were only three in Britain – at Eboracum (York), Deva (Chester) and Isca (Caerleon).

Caerleon ('Fort of the Legion') was the headquarters of the elite 2nd Augustan Legion for more than 200 years, from AD 75 until the end of the 3rd century. It wasn't just a military camp but a purpose-built township some 9 miles in circumference, complete with a 6000-seat amphitheatre and a state-of-the-art Roman baths complex.

⊙ Sights

National Roman Legion Museum MUSEUM

(www.museumwales.ac.uk/en/roman; High St; ⊙10am-5pm Mon-Sat, 2-5pm Sun) FREE Put your Caerleon explorations into context at this excellent museum, which paints a vivid picture of what life was like for soldiers in one of the most remote corners of the

---

THE NEWPORT SHIP

In 2002 construction work for the new Riverfront Art Centre uncovered the remains of the most complete medieval ship ever found. Buried in the mud on the west bank of the River Usk, the 25m-long **Newport Ship** (www.thenewportship.com) dates from around 1450 and was probably built in France (archaeologists discovered a French silver coin that had been placed in one of the ship's timbers by the boat builder). Some 2000 individual timbers have been recovered, and are currently undergoing conservation so that the ship's remains can be reassembled and put on display in a purpose-built museum. In the meantime, the ship can be viewed on monthly open days; enquire at the tourist office or check the website for details.

Empire. It displays a host of intriguing Roman artefacts uncovered locally, from jewellery to armour and from teeth to tombstones.

Caerleon Roman Fortress Baths RUIN

(www.cadw.wales.gov.uk; High St; ⊘ 9.30am-5pm Apr-Oct, 9.30am-5pm Mon-Sat, 11am-4pm Sun Nov-Mar; **P**) **FREE** Like any good Roman town, Caerleon had a grand public baths complex. Parts of the outdoor swimming pool, apodyterium (changing room) and frigidarium (cold room) remain under a protective roof, and give some idea of the scale of the place. Projections of bathers splashing through shimmering water help bring it to life.

Roman Amphitheatre RUIN

(The Broadway; ⊘ 9.30am-5pm) **FREE** The side street opposite the museum leads to a park on the left where you'll find the turf-covered terraces of the only fully excavated Roman amphitheatre in Britain; it lay just outside the old Roman fortress walls. Follow the signs on the other side of the Broadway to see the foundations of the Barracks.

🛏 Sleeping & Eating

Old Rectory B&B ££

(☏ 01633-430700; www.the-oldrectory.co.uk; Christchurch Rd; s/d £50/75; **P** 🛜) One mile south of Caerleon, in the village of Christchurch, the Old Rectory offers a warm welcome and three luxurious rooms with views over the Severn Estuary to England.

The Stuffed Dormouse BRASSERIE ££

(☏ 01633-430142; www.thestuffeddormouse.co.uk; Ponthir Rd; mains £13-16; ⊘ noon-2pm & 6-9pm Mon-Sat, noon-2pm Sun) While its name references a Roman delicacy, you won't find any dormice on the menu – but you will find ostrich, kangaroo, crocodile, llama, squirrel, snake and zebra. It's located about a mile north of the main part of Caerleon in the Roman Lodge Hotel.

ⓘ Getting There & Away

Caerleon is 3 miles northeast of central Newport. Buses 27 and 28 (£1.60, 15 minutes, six hourly) run from Newport bus station to Caerleon High St.

Brecon Beacons & Southeast Wales

Why Go?

Wales' southeast corner, where the River Wye meanders along the border with England, is the birthplace of British tourism. For over 200 years travellers have visited this tranquil waterway and its winding, wooded vale, where the ruins of Tintern Abbey inspired poets and artists such as Wordsworth and Turner. But there's more to the region than the market towns and rural byways of the Lower Wye. To the west, the dramatically serried South Wales valleys tell the story of the industrial revolution through heritage sites and still close-knit communities. Move north and the landscape opens out to the magnificent upland scenery of Brecon Beacons National Park, where high mountain roads dip down to remote hamlets and whitewashed ancient churches. The hiking and mountain-biking terrain here is superb.

Best Places to Eat

➡ Walnut Tree (p86)

➡ Hardwick (p86)

➡ Old Black Lion (p92)

➡ Felin Fach Griffin (p102)

➡ Nantyffin Cider Mill (p94)

When to Go

Outdoor types should head for the Brecon Beacons in late spring or early autumn in what should be reasonable weather (though there's no guarantee); the narrow country roads may be impassable in winter, and become congested during school summer holidays. And note that many hostels and campgrounds don't open till after Easter.

The literary extravaganza of the Hay Festival occurs in May, the world-famous Brecon Jazz Festival is in August, while foodies should focus a trip around Abergavenny's food festival in September.

Best Places to Stay

➡ Llanddeusant Youth Hostel (p104)

➡ Bear (p91)

➡ Start (p91)

➡ Bell at Skenfrith (p81)

➡ Cantre Selyf (p99)

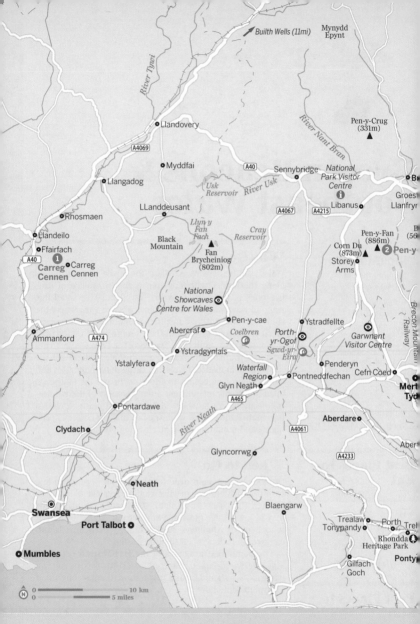

Brecon Beacons & Southeast Wales Highlights

1 Gaze up at **Carreg Cennen** (p103), Wales' most dramatically positioned fortress

2 Stretch your legs to the max by climbing the region's

highest mountain, **Pen-y-Fan** (p86)

3 Wander the elegant streets of **Hay-on-Wye** (p89), discovering your literary side at the umpteen bookshops

4 Grit your teeth for a spectacular drive through the chapel-dotted **Vale of Ewyas** (p88)

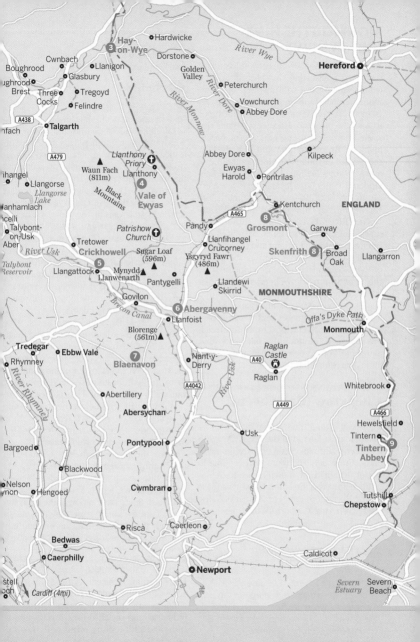

Map labels:

Hardwicke, Hay-on-Wye, Dorstone, River Wye, Hereford, Cwnbach, Boughrood, Llanigon, Golden Valley, Peterchurch, ughrood, Glasbury, Brest, Three Cocks, Tregoyd, Felindre, Vowchurch, Abbey Dore, Kilpeck, A438, Talgarth, Abbey Dore, Ewyas Harold, Pontrilas, A479, Llanthony Priory, Llanthony, ihangel, Llangorse, Llangorse Lake, Waun Fach (811m), Vale of Ewyas, Kentchurch, ENGLAND, anhamlach, Black Mountains, A465, Grosmont, ncelli, Talybont-on-Usk, Aber, River Usk, Patrishow Church, Pandy, Garway, Tretower, Crickhowell, Sugar Loaf (596m), Llanfihangel Crucorney, Skenfrith, Broad Oak, Talybont Reservoir, Llangattock, Mynydd, Llanwenarth, Ysgyryd Fawr (486m), Llangarron, Pantygelli, Llandewi Skirrid, MONMOUTHSHIRE, Govilon, Abergavenny, Brecon Canal, Llanfoist, Offa's Dyke Path, Monmouth, Blorenge (561m), Raglan Castle, Tredegar, Ebbw Vale, Blaenavon, Nant-y-Derry, A40, Raglan, Whitebrook, Rhymney, A4042, River Usk, A449, Hewelsfield, River Rhymney, Abertillery, A466, Tintern, Bargoed, Abersychan, Tintern Abbey, Pontypool, Usk, Blackwood, Nelson, ynon, Hengoed, Cwmbran, Tutshill, Chepstow, astell, och, Bedwas, Risca, Caerleon, Caldicot, Caerphilly, Cardiff (4mi), Newport, Severn Estuary, Severn Beach

5 Consider the sedately pretty village of **Crickhowell** (p94) as a base in the area

6 Eat to your heart's content in the fine **gastropubs** (p82) in and around Abergavenny

7 Take a mine tour in rugged **Blaenavon** (p106) and eat award-winning cheese

8 Head to the hills to explore the rugged hamlets

of **Grosmont** (p81) and **Skenfrith** (p81)

9 Take time out at the ultimate Romantic ruin: graceful **Tintern Abbey** (p77)

MONMOUTHSHIRE (SIR FYNWY)

You need only ponder the preponderance of castles to realise that this pleasantly rural county was once a wild frontier. The Norman marcher lords kept stonemasons extremely busy, erecting mighty fortifications to keep the unruly Welsh at bay. Despite this stone line marking out a very clear border along the Rivers Monnow and Wye, the 1543 second Act of Union left Monmouthshire in a kind of jurisdictional limbo between England and Wales. This legal ambiguity wasn't put to rest until 1974 when Monmouthshire was definitively confirmed as part of Wales.

The River Wye, Britain's fifth-longest, flows from the mountains of Mid-Wales, tootles its way into England and then returns to the middle ground – forming the border of the two countries – before emptying into the River Severn below Chepstow. Much of it is designated an area of outstanding natural beauty (www.wyevalleyaonb.org.uk), famous for its limestone gorges and dense broad-leaved woodland. The most beautiful stretch lies between Monmouth and Chepstow, along the border between Monmouthshire and Gloucestershire.

Chepstow (Cas-Gwent)

POP 14,200

Chepstow is an attractive market town nestled in a great S-bend in the River Wye, with a splendid Norman castle perched on a cliff above the water. The town is also home to one of Britain's best known racecourses.

Chepstow was first developed as a base for the Norman conquest of southeast Wales, later prospering as a port for the timber and wine trades. As river-borne commerce gave way to the railways, Chepstow's importance diminished to reflect its name, which means 'market place' in Old English.

◉ Sights

★ **Chepstow Castle** CASTLE
(www.cadw.wales.gov.uk; Bridge St; adult/child £4.50/3.40; ⊙ 9.30am-5pm) Run by Cadw (the Welsh historic monuments agency), magnificent Chepstow Castle perches atop a limestone cliff overhanging the river, guarding the main river crossing from England into South Wales. The best view is from the far bank – cross the 1816 Old Wye Bridge and turn left. It is one of the oldest castles in Britain – building began in 1067, less than a year after William the Conqueror invaded England – and the impressive Great Tower retains its original Norman architecture.

The castle's history is explained in an exhibition in the Lower Bailey, where you can see the oldest surviving castle door in Europe, a massive wooden barrier dating to before 1190. Nearby, beside the stairs down to the wine cellar, take a peek into the latrine and imagine baring your backside over this draughty stone box with a giddy drop straight down to the river. Kids will enjoy the castle grounds – there are plenty of staircases, battlements and wall walks to explore, and lots of green space.

A cave in the cliff below the castle is one of many places where legend says King Arthur and his knights are napping until the day they're needed to save Britain.

Once the entire town was enclosed in fortifications, fastening it to the castle. Parts of the 13th-century **Port Wall** edge the west side of the town centre. You can see it from the Welsh St car park and near the train station. Chepstow's main street, High St, passes through the **Gate House**, the original city gate, which was restored in the 16th century.

Chepstow Museum MUSEUM
(Bridge St; ⊙ 11am-5pm Mon-Sat, 2-5pm Sun) FREE Housed in an 18th-century town house just across the road from the castle, this small, child-friendly museum covers Chepstow's industrial and social history. A collection of 18th- and 19th-century prints and drawings reflects the area's importance to early tourists and students of the picturesque.

🏃 Activities

The classic Tintern and Return walk begins at the tourist office and heads upriver along

---

WYE VALLEY WALK

The **Wye Valley Walk** (www.wyevalley walk.org) is a 136-mile riverside trail running from the river's source on the slopes of Plynlimon (Pumlumon Fawr) to Chepstow. The section downstream from Monmouth, past Tintern, is particularly beautiful.

Following the lush borderland between Wales and England, the route passes through some magical places: as well as Tintern, you'll encounter Ross-on-Wye, Symonds Yat and Hay-on-Wye.

Chepstow

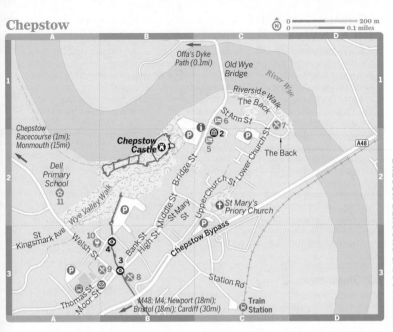

the Wye Valley path to Tintern Abbey, returning via Offa's Dyke Path on the eastern bank. The total distance is around 13 miles; allow a full day, with lunch at Tintern. The tourist office sells various guides, but Ordnance Survey (OS) *Explorer Map OL14* is recommended. You can cut the walk short at Tintern and return to Chepstow (or continue to Monmouth) by bus.

✿✿ Festivals & Events

Chepstow Farmers Market FOOD
Held on the morning of the 2nd and 4th Saturdays of the month.

Chepstow Festival HISTORY
(www.chepstowfestival.co.uk; ☺ Jul) Month-long festival held in even-numbered years, with medieval pageantry, drama and music, outdoor art exhibits, comedy, street entertainment and Shakespeare in the castle.

Two Rivers Folk Festival MUSIC
(www.tworiversfolkfestival.com; ☺ Jul) Three days of traditional music, morris dancers and concerts held in the castle in early July, which happily coincides with a beer and cider festival at the Coach & Horses Inn.

Chepstow

◉ **Top Sights**
1 Chepstow Castle...................................B2

◉ **Sights**
2 Chepstow Museum..............................C2
3 Gate House B3
4 Port Wall..B3

🛏 **Sleeping**
5 Castle View Hotel.................................C2
6 Three Tuns Chepstow C1

🍴 **Eating**
7 Boat Inn C1
Castle View Hotel........................ (see 5)
8 Chepstow Farmers Market..................B3
9 Mythos!...B3

🍷 **Drinking & Nightlife**
10 Coach & Horses Inn.............................A3

✪ **Entertainment**
11 Chepstow Male Voice Choir A2

Chepstow Show AGRICULTURE, CRAFTS
(www.chepstowshow.co.uk; ☺ Aug) An agricultural one-dayer, with the usual array of livestock, craft and kennel-club competitions.

THE WYE TOUR

The Wye Valley has a valid claim to be the birthplace of British tourism. Boat trips along the River Wye began commercially in 1760, but a best-selling book – in fact, one of the first ever travel guidebooks – William Gilpin's *Observations on the River Wye and Several Parts of South Wales* (1771), inspired hundreds of people to take the boat trip down the river from Ross-on-Wye (in England) to Chepstow, visiting the various beauty spots and historical sites en route. Early tourists included many famous figures, from poets William Wordsworth and Samuel Taylor Coleridge and painter JMW Turner, to celebrities such as Admiral Lord Nelson, who made the tour in 1802. Doing the Wye Tour soon became *de rigueur* among English high society.

Local people made good money providing crewed rowing boats for hire, which were equipped with canopies and comfortable chairs and tables where their clients could paint or write, while inns and taverns cashed in on the trade by providing food, drink and accommodation. It was normally a two-day trip, with an overnight stay in Monmouth and stops at Tintern Abbey and Chepstow Castle, among others. In the second half of the 19th century, with the arrival of the railways, the hundreds increased to thousands, and the tour became so commercialised that it was no longer fashionable.

You can still do the Wye Tour, but these days it's a less glamorous, more DIY affair.

🛏 Sleeping

Three Tuns Chepstow   PUB **££**
(☎ 01291-645797; threetunschepstow.co.uk; 32 Bridge St; r from £70) This early 17th-century pub by the castle has had a beautiful boho makeover, with attractive pine furniture, rugs and antiques alongside the more rugged features of the ancient building. The three rooms feature a glamorous combination of French and Welsh furniture. The pub has a good live music program, but the noise winds down at 11pm. Breakfast on Gloucester old spot sausage or homemade veggie leek and Caerphilly sausage.

Castle View Hotel   HOTEL **££**
(☎ 01291-620349; www.hotelchepstow.co.uk; 16 Bridge St; s/d from £45/72) The 300-year-old Castle View has intriguing historic details, including 18th-century wall paintings in two of the bedrooms and hand-painted glass in the back door. Most rooms are small and the floors are creaky, but there's plenty of atmosphere.

🍴 Eating & Drinking

Boat Inn   PUB **£**
(☎ 01291-628192; The Back; mains £3-6) A great riverside pub strewn with nautical knick-knacks and a particularly snug 'snug', the Boat dishes up better-than-average pub grub and a good menu of daily specials. The three best tables are upstairs, beside the windows overlooking the river.

Castle View Hotel   GASTROPUB **££**
(☎ 01291-620349; 16 Bridge St; mains £9-17) Serving solid, meaty, country fare (much of it sozzled in vodka or wine-based sauces), this historic, castle-gazing gastropub isn't short on atmosphere. It's heightened in the evening when candles flicker in moody corners and the young owner is in host-with-the-most mode.

Mythos!   GREEK **££**
(☎ 01291-627222; Welsh St; mains £9-19; ☺ noon-2am Mon-Sat, 5pm-midnight Sun) Exposed beams, stone walls and dramatic lighting make this lively Greek bar and restaurant memorable, but it's the authentic, delicious food that justifies that pretentious exclamation mark in the name: tzatziki, grilled haloumi, spanakopita, lamb and chicken souvlaki, moussaka – served as meze or main-sized portions.

Coach & Horses Inn   PUB
(☎ 01291-622626; www.sabrain.com/coach-and-horses; Welsh St) The owners of this welcoming pub, housed in a 16th-century coaching inn, are from South Africa, so they understand the Welsh passion for rugby. It gets packed to the rafters during games. Sunday night is quiz night, and they play host to the annual Chepstow Beer, Cider & Perry Festival (July) and the Chepstow Beer & Sausage Festival (October).

☆ Entertainment

Chepstow Male Voice Choir   MUSIC
(☏01291-641675; www.chepstowmvc.co.uk; Dell Primary School, Welsh St) Chepstow's equivalent of the cast of *Glee* (albeit a considerably older, exclusively male, much more Welsh version) rehearses every Monday and Thursday from 7pm to 9pm at a local primary school. All fans of booming Welsh manhood are welcome.

Chepstow Racecourse   HORSE RACING
(☏01291-622260; www.chepstow-racecourse.co.uk) Set in rolling parkland alongside the River Wye, north of the town centre, Chepstow Racecourse is one of Britain's most famous horse-racing venues. It's home to Wales' most prestigious race meeting, the Welsh National – a roughly 3-mile steeplechase held between Christmas and New Year, which has been run here since 1949.

ⓘ Orientation

Chepstow sits on the west bank of the River Wye, at the north end of the old Severn Road Bridge. The train station is 250m southeast of the compact town centre (follow Station Rd); the bus station is 250m west. There are convenient car parks off Welsh St and next to the castle.

ⓘ Information

Tourist Office (☏01291-623772; www.chepstowtowncrier.org.uk; Castle car park, Bridge St; ◷9.30am-5pm Apr-Oct, 9.30am-3.30pm Nov-Mar) Ask about local walking trails, such as the Tintern and Return path.

ⓘ Getting There & Around

BIKE

Lôn Las Cymru, the Welsh National Cycle Route (Sustrans route 8), starts at Chepstow, heading north to Abergavenny.

BUS

Bus route 69 links Chepstow with Monmouth (40 minutes) via Tintern (15 minutes), while route 74 heads to Newport (55 minutes).

National Express (www.nationalexpress.com) destinations include London (£22, three hours), Cardiff (£5.50, one hour), Swansea (£12, two hours), Carmarthen (£20.80, 2¼ hours), Tenby (£19.10, three hours) and Pembroke (£19.10, 3¼ hours).

CAR & MOTORCYCLE

Short-term pay-and-display parking is available in large lots by the castle, off Welsh St, off Lower Church St and off Upper Church St. All except the latest offer long-stay rates.

TRAIN

There are direct **Arriva Trains Wales** (www.arrivatrainswales.co.uk) services to Chepstow from Cardiff (£9, 40 minutes) via Newport (£6.80, 23 minutes), and from Gloucester (£9.10, 30 minutes).

Chepstow to Monmouth

The A466 road follows the snaking, steep-sided valley of the River Wye from Monmouth all the way to Chepstow, passing through the straggling village of Tintern with its famous abbey. This is a beautiful drive, rendered particularly mysterious when a twilight mist rises from the river and shrouds the illuminated ruins.

◉ Sights

Tintern Abbey   HISTORIC BUILDING
(Cadw; ☏01291-689251; www.cadw.wales.gov.uk; adult/child £4.50/3.40; ◷9am-5pm Apr-Oct, 9.30am-4pm Mon-Sat, 11am-4pm Sun Nov-Mar; P) The spectral ruins of Tintern Abbey sit by the River Wye, the worn stone scabbed with lichen and mottled grey, purple, pink and gold. Founded in 1131 by the Cistercian order, this sprawling monastic complex is one of the most intact medieval abbeys in Britain, its soaring Gothic arches and ornate tracery a testament to Cistercian wealth and power.

The haunting ruins and their riverside setting have inspired poets and artists through the centuries, including William Wordsworth, who penned *Lines Composed a Few Miles Above Tintern Abbey* during a visit in 1798, and JMW Turner, who made many paintings and drawings of the ruins.

The huge abbey church was built between 1269 and 1301, and the stone shell remains surprisingly intact; the finest feature is tracery that once contained the magnificent west windows. Spreading to the north are the remains of the cloisters, the infirmary, the chapter house, the refectory, the latrines, and a complex system of drains and sewers.

The site is clearly visible from the road, but if you want to explore it properly you'll need at least two hours to do it justice. It's best visited towards the end of the day after the coach-tour crowds have dispersed.

There are plenty of options for riverside walks around Tintern. One of the best begins at the old railway bridge just upstream from the abbey, and leads up to the Devil's Pulpit, a limestone crag on the east side of the river with a spectacular view over the abbey (2.5 miles round trip).

Bus 69 stops here, en route between Chepstow (15 minutes) and Monmouth (30 minutes).

Old Station Tintern   NOTABLE BUILDING
(☑ 01291-689566; http://www.tinternvillage.co.uk/seedo/tintern-old-station/; parking per 3/5hr 50p/£1; ⊙ 10am-5.30pm Apr-Oct) **FREE** Just over 1 mile upstream from Tintern Abbey is Old Station Tintern, a Victorian train station with old railway coaches that house a tourist information desk, temporary exhibitions and a cafe. There's a large grassy play area for kids, picnic spots and easy riverside walks.

🛏 Sleeping

Parva Farmhouse   B&B **££**
(☑ 01291-689411; www.parvafarmhouse.co.uk; s/d from £58/72) This cosy 17th-century farmhouse has low oak-beamed ceilings, leather Chesterfield sofas and a wood-burning stove in the lounge, and a garden with beautiful views across the valley. The bedrooms are chintzy and appealingly old-fashioned; one has a four-poster.

Monmouth (Trefynwy)

POP 10,500

Against a background of pastel-painted Georgian prosperity, the compact market town of Monmouth bustles and thrives. It sits at the confluence of the Rivers Wye and Monnow, and has hopped in and out of Wales over the centuries as the border shifted back and forth. Today it feels more English than Welsh.

The town is famous as the birthplace of King Henry V, victor at the Battle of Agincourt in 1415 and immortalised by Shakespeare. Other locals who have passed into history include the 12th-century historian Geoffrey of Monmouth and Charles Stewart Rolls, co-founder of Rolls-Royce.

In modern times Monmouth's main claim to fame is the Rockfield recording studio, a few miles to the northwest. Established in the 1960s, the studio has produced a string of hit albums, including Queen's *A Night at the Opera*, Oasis' *(What's the Story) Morning Glory?* and Super Furry Animals' *Rings Around the World*, and has been used by artists from Iggy Pop to Coldplay. It's not unknown for rock stars to be spotted in Monmouth's pubs and restaurants.

SOUTHEAST WALES IN...

One Day

Spend the first part of the day exploring the lower Wye Valley, starting at the impressive castle at Chepstow. Head upstream to the ghostly remains of Tintern Abbey and then continue through the wooded gorge, crossing in and out of England, until you reach Monmouth. Follow the River Monnow to either Skenfrith or Grosmont: they're both wonderfully isolated hamlets, each with an ancient church, castle, good place to sleep and, of course, a village pub.

Two Days

Continuing on roads less travelled, take the A465 to Llanfihangel Crucorney and journey through the heart of the Black Mountains on the lonely road traversing the Vale of Ewyas. Llanthony Priory's photogenic ruins are worth a visit. Continue over Gospel Pass, soaking up the moody moorland vistas. Drop anchor in charming Hay-on-Wye, spending the afternoon rummaging through secondhand bookshops and antique shops. Have dinner at one of the excellent pubs, then check out the funky Globe at Hay.

Three Days

Have a quick wander around Brecon in the morning, then continue towards Abergavenny. Some of Wales' best eating places lurk in country lanes along this route, so book for lunch and dinner. Either spend the afternoon walking off the calories, or head up to World Heritage–rated Blaenavon, a former mining town. Consider pretty Crickhowell as a place to spend the night.

Monmouth

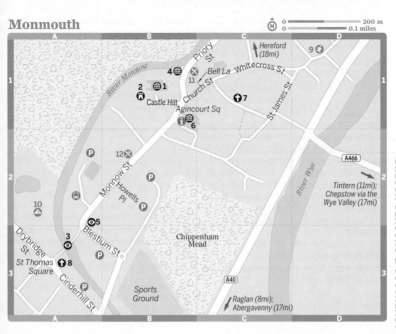

◉ Sights & Activities

Monnow Street   STREET

Monmouth's main drag, such that it is, starts at car-free Monnow Bridge, the UK's only complete example of a medieval fortified bridge. It was built in 1270, although much of what you see now was restored in 1705. Before you cross into town, it's worth poking your head into **St Thomas the Martyr's Church**. Parts of it date from around 1180 – there's an impressive Norman Romanesque arch, and pews and a gallery fashioned out of dark wood.

When Catholicism was banned in Britain, Monmouthshire was a pocket of resistance. In the 16th century, secret Masses were held at the **Robin Hood Inn** (☑ 01600-715423; 124 Monnow St), which still stands at the foot of Morrow St; apart from its historic connections, it's a great place for a pint or pub meal, with a big beer garden. In 1679 a Catholic priest, Fr (later St) David Lewis, was discovered, tried in Monmouth and hung, drawn and quartered in nearby Usk. In 1793, after the Catholic suppression ended, the first new Catholic church in Wales was built in Monmouth. Even then, **St Mary's Church** (St Mary's St) needed to be discreet and hidden behind a line of cottages; they're now removed, explaining why it's set back from the road.

At the top end of Monnow St is Agincourt Sq, dominated by the arcade of the 1724 **Shire Hall** and a statue of former Monmouth resident Charles Stewart Rolls (1877–1910). One half of the team that founded Rolls-Royce, Rolls was not only a pioneering motorist and aviator, he was the first British citizen to die in an air accident (his statue is clutching a model of the Wright biplane in which he died).

Nelson Museum & Local History Centre   MUSEUM

(☑ 01600-710630; www.culture24.org.uk/am22451; Priory St; ⊙ 10am-1pm & 2-5pm Mon-Sat, 2-5pm Sun) **FREE** Admiral Horatio Nelson visited Monmouth twice in 1802, officially en route to inspect Pembrokeshire forests for ship timber (though it may have had more to do with his affair with local heiress Lady Emma Hamilton). Despite this tenuous connection, Lady Llangattock, local aristocrat and mother of Charles Stewart Rolls, became an obsessive collector of 'Nelsoniana', and the results of her obsession can be seen in this endearing museum. It's fascinating to see how fanatical Nelson-worship was in 19th-century Britain, with forged items, such as locks of his hair, displayed alongside banal relics of the great man himself (his first attempt at left-handed writing being a case in point). Monmouth history is also covered, including a display on Rolls, naturally, and some interesting old photographs.

Monmouth Castle   CASTLE

(Castle Hill) **FREE** The meagre remains of Monmouth Castle, where in 1397 Henry V was born, are set back from Monnow St. Except for the great tower (no public access), it was dismantled in the 17th century and the stone used to build **Great Castle House** next door, now headquarters of the Royal Monmouthshire Regiment. Inside is the volunteer-run **Castle & Regimental Museum** (☑ 1600-772175; www.monmouthcastlemuseum. org.uk; admission free; ⊙ 2-5pm Easter-Oct), a labour of love squeezed into a cupboard-sized space, tracing the regiment's history from the 16th century.

Monmouth Canoe & Activity Centre   WATER SPORTS

(☑ 01600-716083; www.monmouthcanoe.co.uk; Old Dixton Rd, Castle Yard) If you're keen to do your own version of the Wye Tour you can hire a two-person Canadian canoe (half-day/day/five days £26/35/135), single kayak (£20/25/115) or double kayak (£26/35/165) from this centre; transport and guides/instructors cost extra (guided trips £45 to £95). You'll need a guide to navigate the tidal section of the river downstream from Bigsweir Bridge, near Tintern. Beginners can opt for a half-day trip through the gorge at Symonds Yat (near the Welsh–English bor-

der), or an evening's leisurely paddle from Monmouth down to Redbrook.

⛄ Festivals & Events

Wye Valley Chamber Music Festival   MUSIC

(www.wyevalleyfestival.com; ⊙ Jan) A week of warming chamber music, held in early January at Treowen Manor (when it's not cut off by the snow, as it was in 2010).

Monmouth Women's Festival   POLITICS

(www.monmouthwomensfestival.org.uk; ⊙ Mar) Interesting speakers, films and exhibitions, held over two weeks in early March.

Monmouth Festival   MUSIC

(www.monmouthfestival.co.uk; ⊙ Jul) Nine days of free music held in late July. It's a mixed bag of mainly obscure acts with the occasional nearly there or past-their-prime performer.

Monmouth Show   AGRICULTURE

(www.monmouthshow.co.uk; ⊙ Aug) A one-day agricultural show, held in late August, with entertainment, livestock competitions and skurry (horse and carriage) races.

🛏 Sleeping

Monnow Bridge Camping   CAMPGROUND

(☑ 01600-714004; Drybridge St; sites £11) Just across the Monnow Bridge from central Monmouth, this tiny campground has a quiet riverside location and friendly owners; it's a 10-minute walk into town.

🍴 Eating

Thyme Out   CAFE £

(☑ 01600-719339; 31-33 Monnow St; mains £4-7; ⊙ 9am-5pm Mon-Sat, 10am-4pm Sun) An excellent little place for breakfasts (croissants, eggs or a fry-up) and snack lunches (soup, quiche, baked potatoes, salads and wraps), this little gem has a sunny patio and an equally sunny disposition. It's located upstairs from the Salt & Pepper kitchenware shop, and the neighbouring clothes boutique is part of the same group.

Misbah Tandoori   INDIAN ££

(☑ 01600-714940; 9 Priory St; mains £6-14; ⊙ noon-2.30pm & 5.30-11pm) One of Wales' top curry houses (check out the Welsh Curry House of the Year Awards if you don't believe us), the Misbah is an authentic Bangladeshi family restaurant with a large, loyal and sometimes famous following. Paul

Weller, REM, Oasis and Arthur Scargill have all dined here.

❶ Information

Tourist Office (☎ 01600-775257; www.shire-hallmonmouth.org.uk; Shire Hall, Agincourt Sq; ⊙ 10am-4pm)

❶ Getting There & Around

Bus route 69 runs along the Wye Valley from Monmouth to Chepstow (40 minutes) via Tintern (35 minutes); route 83 heads to Abergavenny (45 minutes) via Raglan (20 minutes); and route 60 heads to Newport (55 minutes) via Raglan.

National Express (www.nationalexpress.com) coaches head from Monmouth to Birmingham (£19.50, 1½ hours), Newport (£8.20, 35 minutes) and Cardiff (£10.70, 1¼ hours).

There's free parking on Cinderhill St, near St Thomas the Martyr's Church.

Around Monmouth

Raglan

The last great medieval castle to be built in Wales was the magnificent **Raglan Castle** (Cadw; ☎ 01291-690228; www.cadw.wales.gov.uk; adult/child £3/2.60; ⊙ 9am-5pm Apr-Oct, 9.30am-4pm Mon-Sat, 11am-4pm Sun Nov-Mar; P). Designed more as a swaggering declaration of wealth and power than a defensive fortress, it was built in the 15th and 16th centuries by Sir William ap Thomas and his son, the Earl of Pembroke.

A sprawling complex built of dusky pink sandstone, its centrepiece is the lavish Great Tower, a hexagonal keep ringed by a moat. It bears a savage wound from the civil wars of the 1640s, when it was besieged by Cromwell's soldiers – after its surrender the tower was undermined, until eventually two of the six walls collapsed.

The impressive courtyards beyond the Great Tower display the transition from fortress to grandiose palace, with ornate windows and fireplaces, gargoyle-studded crenellations and heraldic carvings.

Raglan is 8 miles southwest of Monmouth and 9 miles southeast of Abergavenny. Bus 83 from Monmouth (20 minutes) and Abergavenny (25 minutes), and bus 60 from Monmouth and Newport (36 minutes) stop here; it's a five-minute walk to the castle.

MOVING ON?

For tips, recommendations and reviews, head to shop.lonelyplanet.com to purchase a downloadable PDF of the Oxford, Cotswolds & Around chapter from Lonely Planet's *England* guide.

Skenfrith

A chocolate-box village of stone buildings set around a hefty castle and ancient church and skirted by the River Monnow, Skenfrith encapsulates the essence of the Monmouthshire countryside. **Skenfrith Castle** (admission free; ⊙ 24hr) was built around 1228 by Hubert de Burgh on the site of earlier Norman fortifications. Its keep and walls remain reasonably intact and there are no barriers to prevent you entering and picnicking on the central lawn. Nearby, a squat tower announces 750-year-old **St Bridget's Church**, accessed by a low wooden door with a foot-high step.

The riverside village pub, the Bell at Skenfrith, has had a gastro makeover and is now an esteemed restaurant serving upmarket country fare (mains £15 to £19), with lots of the produce coming from its organic garden. The pub produces its own walk pamphlets (50p) – one route leads over the English border to **Garway Church**, which is adorned with swastikas and mason's marks from its Knights Templar past.

Skenfrith is 8 miles northwest of Monmouth via the B4233, B4347 and B4521. There's no public transport to these parts.

🛏 Sleeping

Bell at Skenfrith INN **£££**
(☎ 01600-750235; www.skenfrith.co.uk; r £110-220; P 🖗) A picturesque village getaway, the Bell has an acclaimed restaurant and elegant rooms, all named after fishing flies. Some have four-posters but all marry an antique feel with contemporary comfort. Be sure to book in for lunch or dinner at the pub.

Grosmont

Pressed from a similar mould to Skenfrith, although its contours are a little more rugged, Grosmont is another charming and character-filled village set amid the classically beautiful Monmouthshire countryside. Its **castle** (admission free) has the same history as Skenfrith's, although de Burgh completed this one 24 years earlier. The ruins are very picturesque, set behind a deep moat with an elegant 14th-century chimney jutting out.

Two protected species of bats live in the belfry of ancient **St Nicholas Church**. Its churchyard is well worth an idle wander, while the **Angel Inn** (☑ 01981-240646; www.grosmont.org/group/the-angel-inn; The Street; ⊙ 6-11pm Mon & Wed, noon-11pm Tue, Thur, Fri & Sat, noon-10pm Sun) is the centrepiece of the village and is never short of good beer and friendly locals. If you feel like stopping, there are excellent rooms above Gentle Jane tearooms.

Grosmont is 5 miles northwest of Skenfrith along the B4347.

🛏 Sleeping

★ **Gentle Jane**　　　　　　　　B&B **££**
(☑ 01981-241655; www.gentlejane.com; s/d £65/90) At the heart of a tiny village this genteel tearoom and B&B offers three classy rooms with creamy marble bathrooms and contemporary furnishings. One has an ancient staircase leading to its en suite bathroom.

Abergavenny (Y-Fenni)

POP 10,000

Bustling, workaday Abergavenny is set amid shapely, tree-fringed hills in the northwest corner of Monmouthshire, on the eastern edge of Brecon Beacons National Park. While not the most immediately attractive town, it's well worth getting under its skin.

Abergavenny was traditionally best known as a place for outdoor pursuits (it makes a fine base for walks, cycling and paragliding in the surrounding hills), but it's as the capital of a burgeoning food scene that the town has really come into its own. Its position at the heart of Wales' new cuisine, which celebrates the best in fresh, local and organic produce, is generating international interest in both its food festival and its acclaimed eateries, the best of which are actually just out of town in the surrounding countryside.

Its ancient name, Y-Fenni (uh-*ven*-ni; Welsh for 'place of the smiths'), was given to a stream that empties into the River Usk here, and later anglicised to Gavenny (Abergavenny means 'mouth of the Gavenny'). The Romans established Gobannium Fort here, exactly a day's march from their garrison at Caerleon, which they maintained from AD 57 to 400. In around 1100 a marcher lord, Hamelin de Ballon, built the castle and the town's regional importance grew.

⊙ Sights

★ **St Mary's Priory Church**　　　　CHURCH
(www.stmarys-priory.org; Monk St; ⊙ 9am-5pm Mon-Sat) The relatively modest-looking St Mary's Priory Church has been described as the 'Westminster Abbey of South Wales' because of the remarkable treasury of aristocratic tombs that lies within. During the official opening hours there's usually a volunteer warden around to answer questions; outside of these times, ask at the neighbouring Tithe Barn to have the doors unlocked.

St Mary's was founded at the same time as the castle (1087) as part of a Benedictine priory, but the present building dates mainly from the 14th century, with 15th- and 19th-century additions and alterations. A graceful, worn, carved-oak effigy (1325) in the north transept commemorates Sir John de Hastings, who was responsible for the church's 14th-century transformation. It survived Henry VIII's dissolution of the monasteries by being converted into a parish church, making it an interesting counterpoint to the ruins of nearby Tintern and Llanthony abbeys.

The oldest memorial (1256) is the stone figure near the sanctuary of Eva de Braose, Lady Abergavenny, portrayed holding a shield. Her husband William was hanged after being found in the bedchamber of Prince Llywelyn the Great's wife, daughter of England's King John; the family tradition of royal adultery and execution continued with their direct descendant, Anne Boleyn.

In the northern transept is one of the most important medieval carvings in Europe – a monumental 15th-century wooden representation of the biblical figure of Jesse. It was the base of what must have been a mighty altarpiece showing the lineage of Jesus and the only such figure to survive the Reformation.

The Herbert Chapel is packed with recumbent effigies. Most depict members of the Herbert family, starting with Sir William ap Thomas, founder of Raglan Castle, and his wife Gwladys – Sir William's feet rest on a lion that looks like it was modelled on a sheep. The oak choir stalls were carved in

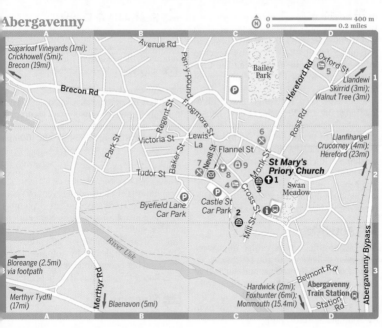

Abergavenny

he 15th century (note the lively misericords
and the little dragons at the ends).

Tithe Barn HISTORIC BUILDING
(www.stmarys-priory.org; Monk St; ⏱9am-5pm
Mon-Sat) FREE The large blocky building
next to the church is the former abbey's
13th-century tithe barn, the place where
people brought their obligatory contributions to the church, usually 10% of whatever
they produced. This particular one has had a
chequered history (it was a 17th-century theatre and a 20th-century disco, among other
things) but has recently been fully restored
and converted into an excellent heritage
centre and a **food hall** focusing on locally
sourced Welsh products.

Pride of place goes to the **Abergavenny
Tapestry**, produced by 60 local volunteers
over six years to mark the new millennium.
Within its 8m width it depicts the history of
the town; look for faint messages from the
stitchers in the borders. Elsewhere on this
floor, a combination of artefacts and touch-
screen monitors tell the story of the town
and the abbey in an excellent interactive
display.

Abergavenny Castle & Museum MUSEUM
(www.abergavennymuseum.co.uk; Castle St;
⏱11am-5pm Mon-Sat, 2-5pm Sun Mar-Oct, 11am-

Abergavenny

◎ Top Sights
1 St Mary's Priory Church C2

◎ Sights
2 Abergavenny Castle & Museum C2
3 Tithe Barn C2

⌂ Sleeping
4 Angel..C2
5 Guest House D1

⊗ Eating
Angel Hotel ....(see 4)
6 Cwtch Cafe C2
7 King's Arms C2

◎ Drinking & Nightlife
8 Hen & Chickens.......................................C2

◎ Entertainment
Borough Theatre...........................(see 9)

⊙ Shopping
9 Abergavenny Market C2

4pm Mon-Sat Nov-Feb) FREE Not much remains of Abergavenny Castle except for an
impressive stretch of curtain wall on either
side of the gatehouse on the northwest
side. It was the site of a notorious event

in 1175 when the Norman lord invited his Welsh rivals for a Christmas dinner and had them massacred. Frequently besieged but never taken, the castle was wrecked by royalist forces in 1645 during the Civil War in order to keep it out of parliamentary hands.

The castle keep, converted into a hunting lodge by the Victorians, now houses the small Abergavenny Museum. It tells the history of the castle and the town, and includes re-creations of a Victorian Welsh farmhouse kitchen, a saddlery workshop and Basil Jones' grocery shop. The latter was transferred when it closed in the 1980s and makes a fascinating display, with many items dating back to the 1930s and '40s.

🏃 Activities

Abergavenny sits between three impressive protrusions: Blorenge to the southwest, Ysgyryd Fawr to the northeast and Sugar Loaf to the northwest. Each has rewarding walks and fine views of the Usk Valley and the Black Mountains, of which the last two form the southernmost summits.

For more leisurely walks, you can follow easy paths along the banks of the River Usk or explore the towpath of the Monmouthshire and Brecon Canal, which passes 1 mile southwest of the town.

You can buy national park walk cards from the tourist office.

Culinary Cottage COOKING COURSE
(📞 01873-890125; www.theculinarycottage.co.uk; Rose Cottage, Pandy) Extend the gastronomic offerings of the Abergavenny countryside with themed cooking courses.

OFF THE BEATEN TRACK

BEACONS WAY

The 100-mile, eight-day Beacons Way trail wends its way across the national park from Abergavenny to Llangadog, knocking off all the highest summits.

Needless to say, this is a stretching walk and requires proper walking gear as well as a good Ordnance Survey (OS) map – the moorland sections can be hard to navigate. The route is manageable in eight days, but you may want to take a little longer to make it more enjoyable and less of an endurance test

---

🎊 Festivals & Events

South Wales Three Peaks Trial WALKING
(www.threepeakstrial.co.uk; ⊙ Mar) An annual walking challenge held in March to test your endurance and map-reading skills.

Abergavenny Festival of Cycling CYCLING
(www.abergavennyfestivalofcycling.co.uk; ⊙ Jul) A mid-July lycra-enthusiasts' meet incorporating the Iron Mountain Sportif, a participatory event with 25-mile, 50-mile and 100-mile courses.

Abergavenny Food Festival FOOD
(www.abergavennyfoodfestival.co.uk; ⊙ Sep) The most important gastronomic event in Wales, held on the third weekend in September, with demonstrations, debates, competitions, courses, stalls and the odd celebrity. But the real drawcard is that this is an enthusiastically local festival, run by volunteers, and not some big-budget food producer's showcase. Kooky things can and do happen.

🛏 Sleeping

Angel HOTEL **££**
(📞 01873-857121; www.angelhotelabergavenny.com; 15 Cross St; r from £79; P 🛜) Abergavenny's top hotel was housed in a fine Georgian building that was once a famous coaching inn. The upgraded communal areas downstairs feel sleek and sophisticated, while the comfortable rooms feature designer bathrooms. The Angel offers similarly tasteful accommodation in mews rooms adjoining the hotel, in a Victorian lodge near the castle and in the 17th-century Castle Cottage, which has room for four.

Guest House B&B **££**
(📞 01873-854823; www.theguesthouseabergavenny.co.uk; 2 Oxford St; s/d from £45/70; 🛜) This family-friendly B&B with cheerful, flouncy rooms (not all en suite) has a minimenagerie of pigs, rabbits, chickens and ducks – and parrots that can match the gregarious owners in colourful language. It's certainly not lacking in character.

🍴 Eating

Cwtch Cafe CAFE
(📞 01873-855466; 58 Cross St; ⊙ 8.30am-5pm Mon-Sat) For coffee and a homemade cake in the heart of town, the stylish little Cwtch (Welsh for 'hug') Cafe is a nice option. It also provides heartier cooked meals, such as cheese and potato pie and lasagne.

Angel Hotel
HOTEL **££**

(☑ 01873-857121; www.angelhotelabergavenny. com; 15 Cross St; mains £8-22) The Angel offers a choice of eating options, from an informal meal in front of the log fire in the bar to the sophisticated restaurant with its crisp, white linen and attentive service, to a romantic dinner in the candle-lit courtyard. The menu makes the most of local produce – the roast lamb is tender and succulent – and there's an excellent wine list.

King's Arms
GASTROPUB **££**

(☑ 01873-855074; 29 Nevill St; mains £10-17; ﬔ) The King's Arms is a 16th-century tavern, where you can down a pint accompanied by lamb's liver and bubble 'n' squeak. It has undergone a rather drastic makeover – an oil painting of Martin Scorsese is an incongruous touch – but the restaurant menu (loin of Gloucester old spot pork, beer-battered cod) takes things to the next level of sophistication, while still keeping a rustic edge.

🍷 Drinking & Entertainment

Hen & Chickens
PUB

(☑ 01873-853613; 7 Flannel St; ⬤) A traditional real-ale pub tucked down a pedestrian alley, the Hen & Chickens hosts live jazz sessions on Sunday afternoons (outside when it's sunny) and occasional folk music sessions. The pub grub's good too.

Borough Theatre
THEATRE

(☑ 01873-850805; www.boroughtheatreabergavenny.co.uk; Cross St) It's strange now to think that the Beatles played this small theatre in Abergavenny Town Hall in 1963. It stages a varied program of drama, opera, dance, comedy and music.

🛍 Shopping

Abergavenny Market
MARKET

(☑ 01873-735811; www.abergavennymarket.co.uk; Cross St; ⊙ 6am-5pm market days) The 19th-century Market Hall is a lively place, hosting a general market (food, drink, clothes, household goods) on Tuesday, Friday and Saturday, a flea market (bric-a-brac, collectables, secondhand goods) on Wednesday, regular weekend craft and antiques fairs, and a farmers market on the fourth Thursday of each month.

Sugarloaf Vineyards
WINE

(☑ 01873-853066; www.sugarloafvineyard.co.uk; ⊙ 10.30am-5pm Tue-Sat, noon-5pm Sun & Mon Easter-Oct) Established in 1992, these vineyards on the western edge of town produce a variety of wines, including an award-winning sparkling. You can take a self-guided tour before sampling the goods at the cafe and gift shop.

ℹ Orientation

The tourist office is next to the bus station, a few minutes' walk southeast of the town centre; the train station is a further half-mile walk along Monmouth Rd and Station Rd.

ℹ Information

Nevill Hall Hospital (☑ 01873-732732; Brecon Rd; ⊙ 24hr) Emergency service.

Police Station (☑ 01873-852273; Tudor St)

Tourist Office (☑ 01873-853254; www.visitabergavenny.co.uk; Swan Meadow, Cross St; ⊙ 10am-4pm) Information on where to eat, drink and stay, plus the lowdown on local events.

ℹ Getting There & Around

BIKE

Lôn Las Cymru passes through Abergavenny, heading north to Builth Wells and south to Chepstow.

BUS

Bus routes include 83 to Monmouth (45 minutes) via Raglan (20 minutes); X3 to Cardiff (1½ hours); X4 to Merthyr Tydfil (1½ hours); and X43 to Brecon (50 minutes) via Crickhowell (15 minutes).

National Express (www.nationalexpress.com) coaches head to Birmingham (£12.70, three hours) and Merthyr Tydfil (£8.60, 50 minutes).

CAR & MOTORCYCLE

There's free parking at a large lot on Byefield Lane, daily except Tuesday. Otherwise the Bailey Park and Castle St lots are cheap.

TAXI

Local companies include **Abergavenny Taxis** (☑ 01873-854140; www.abergavennytaxis. co.uk).

TRAIN

There are direct trains from Cardiff (£12.20, 40 minutes), Newport (£8.20, 25 minutes), Shrewsbury (£26.10, 1¼ hours), Wrexham (£38.70, three hours), Bangor (£64.80, 3½ hours) and Holyhead (£70.70, four hours).

Around Abergavenny

Eating

★**Walnut Tree** MODERN WELSH £££
(☑ 01873-852797; www.thewalnuttreeinn.com;
Llandewi Skirrid; mains £15-25, 2-/3-course lunch
£22/27.50; ☺ noon-2.30pm & 6.30-10pm Tue-Sat)
Established in 1963, the legendary Walnut
Tree remains one of Wales' finest restaurants,
with a Michelin star to prove it. Fresh, local
produce dominates, with saddle of rabbit,
rack of lamb and veal kidneys on the menu.
If you're too full to move far after dinner,
try its elegant cottage accommodation. The
Walnut Tree is 3 miles northeast of Abergavenny on the B4521.

★**Hardwick** MODERN WELSH £££
(☑ 01873-854220; www.thehardwick.co.uk; Old
Raglan Rd, Abergavenny; mains £15-25, 2-/3-course
lunch £18/23; ☺ noon-3pm & 6.30-10pm) The
Hardwick is a traditional pub-style restaurant with an old stone fireplace, low ceiling
beams and terracotta floor tiles. Ex-Walnut
Tree alumnus Stephen Terry has created a
gloriously unpretentious menu that celebrates the best of country cooking; save
room for the homemade ice cream. There
are also plain but elegant rooms (from
£155). The Hardwick is 2 miles south of Abergavenny on the B4598.

Foxhunter MODERN BRITISH £££
(☑ 01873-881101; www.thefoxhunter.com; Nant-y-
Derry; mains £19.25-24.50; ☺ lunch Tue-Sun, dinner
Tue-Sat) A Victorian stationmaster's house
with flagstone floors and wood-burning
stoves that's had an elegant contemporary
makeover, the Foxhunter brings an adventurous approach to fresh, seasonal produce,
which might include slow-roasted goose
leg or wild elvers (baby eels from the River
Wye). The Foxhunter is 7 miles south of Abergavenny, just east of the A4042.

BRECON BEACONS NATIONAL PARK

Rippling dramatically for 45 miles from
Llandeilo in the west all the way to the English border, Brecon Beacons National Park
(Parc Cenedlaethol Bannau Brycheiniog)
encompasses some of the finest scenery
in South Wales. High mountain plateaus
of grass and heather, their northern rims
scalloped with glacier-scoured hollows,
rise above wooded, waterfall-splashed valleys and green, rural landscapes. It couldn't
be more different than rock-strewn Snowdonia to the north, but it offers comparable
thrills.

There are four distinct regions within the
park, neatly bounded by main roads: the
wild, lonely Black Mountain (Mynydd Du)
in the west, with its high moors and glacial
lakes; Fforest Fawr (Great Forest), which
lies between the A4067 and A470, whose
rushing streams and spectacular waterfalls
form the headwaters of the Rivers Tawe
and Neath; the Brecon Beacons (Bannau
Brycheiniog) proper, a group of very distinctive, flat-topped hills that includes Pen-y-Fan
(886m), the park's (and southern Britain's)
highest peak; and, from the A40 northeast
to the English border, the rolling heathland
ridges of the Black Mountains (Y Mynyd-
doedd Duon) – don't confuse them with the
Black Mountain (singular) in the west.

In 2005 the western half of the national
park was given geopark recognition by
Unesco. The Fforest Fawr Geopark (www.
fforestfawrgeopark.org.uk) stretches from Black
Mountain in the west to Pen-y-Fan in the
east, and it takes in important landscape
features such as the ice-sculpted northern
faces of the Brecon Beacons, the gorges and
waterfalls around Ystradfellte, and the caves
and limestone pavements of the southern
Black Mountain.

There are hundreds of walking routes
in the park, ranging from gentle strolls to
strenuous climbs. The park's staff organ-
ise guided walks and other active events
throughout summer. A set of six Walk
Cards (£1 each) is available from the town
tourist offices in and around the park, as
well as the national park visitor centre near
Libanus.

Likewise, there are many excellent off-
road mountain-biking routes, including a
series of 14 graded and waymarked trails detailed in a map and guidebook pack (£7.50);
see also www.mtbbreconbeacons.co.uk.

Ordnance Survey (OS) Landranger maps
160 and 161 cover most of the park, and have
walking and cycling trails marked.

❶ Getting There & Away

There is no public transport other than the Beacons Buses.

Black Mountains (Y Mynyddoedd Duon)

The hills that stretch northward from Abergavenny to Hay-on-Wye, bordered by the A479 road to the west and the English border to the east, are known as the Black Mountains (not to be confused with the Black Mountain, singular, at the western end of the national park). The hills are bleak, wild and largely uninhabited, making them a popular walking area; the highest summit is Waun Fach (811m). The Offa's Dyke Path runs along the easternmost ridge between Pandy and Hay-on-Wye.

Sugar Loaf

The cone-shaped pinnacle of Sugar Loaf (596m) is a 9-mile return trip from the centre of Abergavenny via heath, woodland and the superb viewpoint of Mynydd Llanwenarth. You can cheat by driving to a car park about halfway up on Mynydd Llanwenarth; from here it's a 4-mile round trip. Head west on the A40, and at the edge of town turn right for Sugarloaf Vineyards, then go left at the next two junctions.

Ysgyryd Fawr (Skirrid)

Of the glacially sculpted hills that surround Abergavenny, Skirrid (486m) is the most dramatic looking and has a history to match. A cleft in the rock near the top was believed to have split open at the exact time of Christ's death and a chapel was built here on what was considered a particularly holy place (a couple of upright stones remain). During the Catholic persecutions, as many as 100 people at a time would attend illegal Masses at this remote spot.

Begin your trek from Abergavenny, or take the B4521 to the car park at the base of the hill. It's a steep climb from here through the woods on a track that can be muddy; wear sensible shoes. Once you clear the tree line the walk is less steep, with a final climb right at the end to the summit where you'll be rewarded with extravagant views. From here you can return the way you came or continue down the other side to Llanfihangel Crucorney.

Llanfihangel Crucorney

The name of this little village, 4.5 miles north of Abergavenny, means 'Church of St

RED KITES

Even the least diligent bird watcher is sure to spot red kites in the Brecon Beacons. The birds are magnificent, and pleasingly easy to identify, with their rust-red plumage, forked tails, 2m wingspan and easy gliding motion. Red kites have a small body in relation to their long wings, meaning they can stay airborne for long periods.

The birds were eradicated from England, Scotland and most of Wales by landowners who thought them responsible for preying on livestock; in fact, the kites are primarily scavengers. Their reintroduction across the UK has been a great success, with separate populations spreading and breeding with each other, thus strengthening the gene pool.

Wales alone now has more than 600 breeding pairs, whose great presence and grace will enhance your visit to the Brecon Beacons. You can watch them close up during feeding time at the Red Kite Centre (p103).

Michael at the Corner of the Rock'. It's famous as the home of the Skirrid Inn, said to be the oldest pub in Wales and thoroughly haunted by the many people who were hanged here (it doubled as an assizes court). Although the Hammer House of Horror dummy at the door and 'ancient' scrolls on the walls are a drag, it serves decent pub grub and makes a good base camp or finishing point for an ascent of Ysgyryd Fawr; it's a 4-mile round trip from pub to summit.

🛏 Sleeping

Skirrid Inn   PUB ££
(☑ 01873-890258; www.skirridmountaininn.co.uk; Llanfihangel Crucorney; d £90) Those with a taste for the macabre and ghostly will love this place. Wales' oldest inn (dating prior to 1110) once doubled as a court and over 180 people were hanged here. Just so you don't forget, a noose dangles from the well-worn hanging beam directly outside the doors to the bedrooms.

Partrishow Church

Halfway up a hillside on a narrow country lane, 5 miles northwest of Llanfihangel Cru-

BEACONS BUSES

The **Beacons Buses** (☑ 01873-853254; www.travelbreconbeacons.info) only run on Sundays and bank holidays from April to September, but during that time they successfully shunt visitors both into and around the national park. With a day ticket (£9, buy it on the first bus you board) and a careful analysis of the online timetable you can plan a full day of sightseeing and activities. On the B16 and B17 circular routes you can get on and off at any point (adult/child £5.50/3.50). Some services allow bikes to be transported. Useful routes include the following:

B1 Cardiff, Merthyr Tydfil, Storey Arms, Libanus, Brecon

B2 Storey Arms, Libanus, Brecon

B3 Penderyn, Storey Arms, Libanus, Brecon

B4 Newport, Abergavenny, Crickhowell, Tretower, Brecon

B5 Cardiff, Caerphilly, Merthyr Tydfil, Libanus, Brecon

B6 Swansea, National Showcaves Centre for Wales, Brecon

B10 Carmarthen, National Botanic Garden, Llandeilo, Llandovery, Brecon

B11 Brecon, National Park Visitor Centre

B12 Brecon, Llangorse Lake, Hay-on-Wye

B13 (Geopark Circular) Brecon, National Park Visitor Centre, Storey Arms, National Showcaves Centre for Wales, Penderyn

B15 Brecon, Tretower, Crickhowell, Big Pit, Blaenavon

B16 (Taff Trail Roundabout) Brecon, National Park Visitor Centre, Storey Arms, Brecon Mountain Railway, Llanfrynach

B17 (Offa's Dyke Flyer) Hay-on-Wye, Llanthony Priory, Llanfihangel Crucorney, Pandy

corney, is this tiny part-Norman and part-medieval church. It contains a remarkable, finely carved wooden rood screen and loft, dating from around 1500. On the walls are medieval frescoes of biblical texts, coats of arms, and a red-ochre skeleton (once believed to have been painted with human blood) bearing hourglass and scythe – the figure of Death. The church is usually open; leave a donation in the box.

Down the hill from the church at the corner of the road is a spring, with flowers, toys and other offerings strewn about and ribbons tied in an overhanging tree. Known as the **Holy Well of St Issui**, it is believed to have healing powers and has long been a pilgrimage site: near the spring is a pilgrim stone carved with a Maltese Cross.

Vale of Ewyas

The scenic and secluded valley of the River Honddu runs through the heart of the Black Mountains from Llanfihangel Crucorney to the 542m-high Gospel Pass, which leads down to Hay-on-Wye. It's a magical place, with only a very narrow, single-track road running along it, best explored on foot, bike or horseback.

The first place you encounter descending from the Black Mountains is Capel-y-Ffin – a hamlet with monastic ruins and two churches, including the picturesque whitewashed 18th-century church of Mary the Virgin.

Halfway along the valley lie the atmospheric ruins of the 13th-century **Llanthony Priory**, set among grasslands and wooded hills by the River Honddu. Though not as grand as Tintern Abbey, the setting is even more romantic; JMW Turner painted the scene in 1794. The tiny stone-vaulted bar of the hotel (p89), adjoining the abbey, makes an atmospheric drink stop. **Llanthony Riding and Trekking** (☑ 01873-890359; www.llanthony.co.uk; Court Farm; half-/full day beginners £30/55, experienced £40/65), next door to Llanthony Priory and the Abbey Hotel, has horses available for pony trekking and hacking. Half-day rides begin at 10am and 2pm. It also offers basic campsites (per person £3) and rents self-catering cottages.

There are lots of walking possibilities. From Llanthony, several paths lead up to the top of the Hatterall Ridge to the east; it's a stiff climb, but straightforward (2 to 3 miles round trip). For a more ambitious hike, follow the ridge north for 4 miles then descend to Vision Farm, then walk back along the valley road to Llanthony (9 miles round trip).

🛏 Sleeping

Llanthony Priory Hotel　　　　INN ££

(☑ 01873-890487; www.llanthonyprioryhotel.co.uk; from £80) Seemingly growing out of the priory ruins, and incorporating some of the original medieval buildings, the Priory Hotel is wonderfully atmospheric, with four-poster beds, stone spiral staircases and rooms squeezed into turrets; there are only five rooms and no en suites.

Hay-On-Wye (Y Gelli Gandryll)

POP 1600

Hay-on-Wye, a pretty little town on the banks of the River Wye, just inside the Welsh border, has developed a reputation disproportionate to its size. First came the explosion in secondhand bookshops, a charge led by the charismatic and forthright local maverick Richard Booth. Booth opened his eponymous bookshop in the 1960s, stocking it with cast-off libraries from various national institutions and country houses. He went on to proclaim himself the King of Hay, among other elaborate publicity stunts, while campaigning for an international network of book towns to support failing rural economies.

With Hay becoming the world's secondhand book capital, a festival of literature and culture was established in 1988, growing in stature each year to take in all aspects of the creative arts. Today the Hay Festival is a major attraction in its own right, famously endorsed by former US president Bill Clinton, a high-profile guest in 2001, as 'the Woodstock of the mind'.

But Hay is not all about book browsing and celebrity spotting – it also makes an excellent base for active pursuits, with the Black Mountains, River Wye and Offa's Dyke Path all within easy access of the town's superb facilities.

BROWSING FOR BOOKS IN HAY

There are 26 secondhand and antiquarian bookshops in Hay, with hundreds of thousands of tomes stacked floor to ceiling across town – 500,000 in Booth's alone. Each shop is profiled on a free map, available from the tourist office and from venues around town. However, Hay's shopping potential doesn't stop at books. There are also excellent stores selling antiques, craft, art and historic maps. Lonely Planet has reviewed its top picks.

Addyman Books (☑ 01497-821136; www.hay-on-wyebooks.com; 39 Lion St) Stocks books on all sorts of subjects, has a sitting room upstairs and a sci-fi room.

Booth Books (www.boothbooks.co.uk; 44 Lion St) The most famous, and still the best; has a sizeable Anglo-Welsh literature section and a Wales travel section. There's also a great little cafe, and regular film screenings.

Hay Castle Books (☑ 01497-820503; Hay Castle, Oxford Rd) Booth's primary domain these days, with a suitably eclectic stock and an honesty bookshop (50p per book) in the castle grounds.

Hay Cinema Bookshop (☑ 01497-820071; www.haycinemabookshop.co.uk; Castle St) Huge collection of books about filmmaking and cinema, in a converted cinema.

Mostly Maps (☑ 01497-820539; www.mostlymaps.com; 2 Castle St) Exquisite antiquarian maps, many hand-coloured.

Murder & Mayhem (☑ 01497-821613; 5 Lion St) Filled to the brim with detective fiction, true crime and horror.

Rose's Books (☑ 01497-820013; www.rosesbooks.com; 14 Broad St) Rare children's and illustrated books.

Tom's Record Shop (☑ 01497-821590; 13 Castle St) Some books alongside new and secondhand records and CDs.

Hay-on-Wye

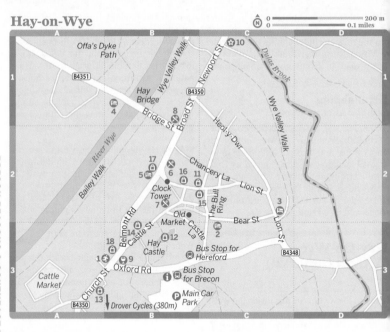

Hay-on-Wye

☺ Activities, Courses & Tours
1 Paddles & Pedals B3

🛏 Sleeping
2 Bear C3
3 Old Black Lion.......................................C2
4 Start...B1
5 Tinto House B2

🍽 Eating
6 Granary B2
Old Black Lion................................ (see 3)
7 Shepherds Ice Cream Parlour B2
8 Three Tuns B1

🍷 Drinking & Nightlife
9 Blue Boar B3

🎭 Entertainment
10 Globe at Hay C1

🛍 Shopping
11 Addyman Books.....................................B2
12 Hay Castle Books...................................B3
13 Hay Cinema Bookshop A3
14 Mostly Maps B3
15 Murder & Mayhem.................................C2
16 Richard Booth's Bookshop...................B2
17 Rose's Books B2
18 Tom's Record Shop B3

The small town centre is made up of narrow sloping lanes, peppered by interesting shops and peopled by the differing types that such individuality and so many books tend to attract. Even outside of festival time, it has a vaguely alternative ambience.

Hay has had a tempestuous history, due to its borderlands position. In fact, at the time of the Norman Conquest it was administered separately as English Hay (the town proper) and Welsh Hay (the countryside to the south and west).

Around 1200 William de Braose II, one of the Norman barons (marcher lords), built a castle here on the site of an earlier one (Richard Booth became king of this castle, buying the dilapidated remains in 1961). For the next three-and-a-half centuries Hay changed hands many times. Following the Tudor Acts of Union it settled down as a market town, and by the 18th century it had become a centre of the flannel trade.

🏃 Activities

Drover Holidays HIKING
(☎01497-821134; droverholidays.co.uk; 🚲) Tackle a long-distance cycling or walking route anywhere in Wales and this Hay-based crowd will take care of the logistics (transfers, bags, bikes and accommodation).

Paddles & Pedals   CANOEING, KAYAKING

(☎ 01497-820604; www.canoehire.co.uk; 15 Castle St; half-/full day £17.50/25) Take to the Wye waters at Hay and get collected further downstream.

✿ Festivals & Events

Hay Festival   LITERARY

(☎ 01497-822629; www.hayfestival.com; ⊙ May) The 10-day Hay Festival in late May has become Britain's leading festival of literature and the arts – a kind of bookworms' Glastonbury or, according to a former American president, 'the Woodstock of the mind'. Like those legendary music festivals, it pulls more than its fair share of the leading exponents of its genre.

As well as Bill Clinton, past speakers have included famous writers (Ian McEwan, Zadie Smith, Stephen Fry, Bill Bryson), priests (Rowan Williams, Desmond Tutu) and politicians (Rhodri Morgan, Gordon Brown, Al Gore). It's proved such a popular formula that there are now Hay Festivals in Segovia, Alhambra, Cartagena, Zacatecas and Nairobi.

As well as readings, workshops, book signings, concerts and club nights, there's also a very successful children's festival called Hay Fever. There are shuttle buses from Hay-on-Wye and surrounding towns to the site, in fields on Hay's southwest fringe

HowtheLightGetsIn   MUSIC, PHILOSOPHY

(http://howthelightgetsin.org; ⊙ Jun) Hay is upping its festival credentials with HowtheLightGetsIn, a high-powered philosophy and music event at the end of June.

Hay Bike Fest   CYCLING

(http://haycycling.org; ⊙ Apr) The new Hay Bike Fest in April includes skills sessions, demos and a thigh-crunching ride in the nearby mountains.

🛏 Sleeping

★**Bear**   B&B ££

(☎ 01497-821302; www.thebearhay.com; 2 Bear St; r £90, s/d £50/70; P 🛜) Homey and rustic with exposed stone walls and original beams, plus a liberal sprinkling of books, this former coaching inn (1590) is an excellent choice. It has three rooms, all beautifully decorated with bright Welsh blankets and retro furniture.

★**Start**   B&B ££

(☎ 01497-821391; www.the-start.net; Bridge St; r from £70; P 🛜) Peacefully set on the fringes of town, this little place boasts an unbeatable riverside setting, homey rooms in a renovated 18th-century house and a flagstone-floored breakfast room. The owner can advise on activities and walks.

BRECON BEACONS & SOUTHEAST WALES HAY-ON-WYE (Y GELLI GANDRYLL)

RICHARD BOOTH, KING OF HAY

Richard Booth is a larger-than-life character and the dynamic force behind Hay's metamorphosis from declining border town into eminent book capital. A provocative character, he's been called a monarchist, anarchist, socialist and separatist. All of which have some element of truth, and he's definitely a superb self-publicist. After graduating from Oxford he bought Hay's old fire station and turned it into a secondhand bookshop. He bought whole libraries from all over the world and sold in bulk to new universities. He's had setbacks, becoming bankrupt in 1984, but never lost his instinct for a good story. He first hit the headlines when he offered books for burning at £1.50 a car-boot load.

Booth established the world's largest bookshop in the old cinema before opening Booth Books and Hay Castle Books. His success attracted other booksellers and nowadays there are over two dozen bookshops in tiny Hay-on-Wye.

The idea for a separate state blossomed during a liquid lunch in 1976. Booth announced that Hay would declare independence on 1 April (April Fools' Day). Breconshire Council fiercely dismissed the idea as a Booth publicity stunt, which only fuelled the media hype. On declaration day, three TV stations, eight national newspapers and the world's press covered the event. Booth was crowned king (King Richard, Coeur de Livre) and the Hay navy sent a gunboat (a rowing boat) up the Wye, firing blanks from a drainpipe. Many of the king's drinking pals gained cabinet posts.

All this comedy has a serious undercurrent, and Booth continues to campaign against the causes of rural decline – with particular contempt reserved for rural development boards, supermarkets and factory farming.

★ **Old Black Lion**   PUB **££**
(☑ 01497-820841; www.oldblacklion.co.uk; Lion St; d £90, s with/without bathroom £53/45; **P**) As traditional and atmospheric as they come, this inn looks 17th century but parts of it date from the 13th; expect low ceilings and uneven floors. The accumulated weight of centuries of hospitality is cheerfully carried by the current staff.

Tinto House   B&B **££**
(☑ 01497-821556; www.tinto-house.co.uk; 13 Broad St; s/d from £60/85) Centrally located in a picture-book Regency town house, Tinto House features three beautiful bedrooms (one twin) and is furnished with French antiques and Turkish carpets. There's a secluded garden, and the owners have an intriguing art collection. Ingredients for breakfast are locally sourced and mostly organic.

✕ Eating

Shepherds Ice Cream Parlour   ICE CREAM **£**
(www.shepherdsicecream.co.uk; 9 High Town; single scoop £1.50; ☉ 9.30am-5.30pm) Nobody should leave Hay without trying the homemade ice cream from Shepherds. It's made from sheep's milk for a lighter, smoother taste.

★ **Old Black Lion**   GASTROPUB **££**
(☑ 01497-820841; Lion St; mains £12-18) Walkers, book browsers and the literary glitterati all flock to this creaky, part-13th-century inn, with heavy black beams and warm red walls. The atmosphere is as cosy as you'd hope such a pub would be, but the food is many leagues beyond pub grub: think stuffed guinea fowl or pork loin with black pudding.

Granary   CAFE **££**
(☑ 01497-820790; Broad St; mains £6-11; ☉ 9am-5.30pm; 🛜) Popular and welcoming, this bustling country-kitchen cafe is a reliable choice for breakfasts and snack lunches. Vegetarians and families are well catered for, with menus for all, and you can check your email over a coffee using the free wi-fi.

Three Tuns   PUB **££**
(☑ 01497-821855; www.three-tuns.com; Broad St; mains £12-18) Rebuilt and expanded after a fire partially destroyed the 16th-century building, this smart gastropub is a welcoming place. It has a large garden area for al fresco food and a fancier restaurant upstairs. The international menu follows that increasingly common mantra: local, organic and sustainable.

🍷 Drinking & Entertainment

Blue Boar   PUB
(Oxford Rd) This cosy, traditional pub with log fires and trad decor serves Timothy Taylor's ale and hearty pub food such as game pie and lamb chops.

Globe at Hay   CLUB, CAFE
(☑ 01497-821762; www.globeathay.org; Newport St; ☉ 9.30am-5pm, till 11pm Tue, Fri & Sat; 🛜) Finally there's something to do in Hay at night other than reading all those books. Converted from a Methodist chapel and filled with artistically mismatched chairs and sofas, this very cool venue is part cafe, part bar, part club, part theatre and all-round community hub – hosting DJs, live music, comedy, theatre, film, kids' events, chess clubs and political talks.

ℹ Information

Tourist Office (☑ 01497-820144; www.hay-on-wye.co.uk; Oxford Rd; ☉ 10am-1pm & 2-5pm) The professional tourist office stocks a free guide and map showing all of Hay's bookshops (most bookshops have the map, too). You can also access the internet here (around £1 per 30 minutes).

ℹ Getting There & Around

Drover Cycles (☑ 01497-821134; www.drover-cycles.co.uk; Forest Rd) rents mountain and touring bikes.

Bus 39 heads to Brecon (41 minutes). Beacons Buses routes 12 and B17 are also options.

There's a large car park on Oxford Rd (per hour 50p, over four hours £2.50, free 6pm to 8am).

Abergavenny to Brecon

Blorenge

Of the three mountains encircling Abergavenny, the summit of the Blorenge (561m) is the closest to town – the round trip is only 5 miles – but it is a steep and strenuous outing, and good walking boots are recommended. Cross the bridge over the River Usk on Merthyr Rd and immediately turn right and follow the lane past the cemetery and under the main road. Cross the B4246 road in Llanfoist and follow the lane beside the church until it bends left; continue through a tunnel under the canal and then follow a steep path straight uphill (a former tram road that carried coal down to the canal). When you emerge from the woods, there is

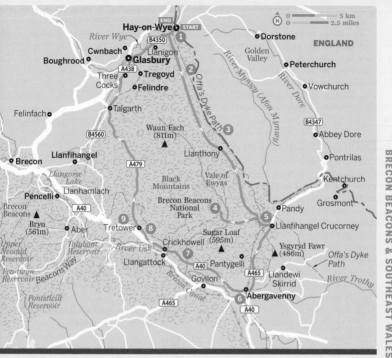

🏃 Driving Tour
Black Mountain Roads

START HAY-ON-WYE
END HAY-ON-WYE
LENGTH 49 MILES; ONE DAY

This slow-paced 49-mile drive takes you through a remote section of the Black Mountains on a narrow back road, climbing to dizzying heights (don't attempt it in winter weather!) and descending into a lush valley. You return via a much easier route, visiting the delightful village of Crickhowell and an intriguing stately home.

Start at the handsome little border town of **1 Hay-on-Wye**, which plays host to a famous literary festival as well as umpteen secondhand bookshops. Head south on the B4350, but turn sharp left onto Forest Rd at the edge of town. The road narrows to a single lane (you'll need to pull over if you encounter another car) and quickly leads upon to desolate moors as it crosses the **2 Gospel Pass**: views of the forbidding Black Mountains are epic. The country gets greener as you head down the other side into

the Vale of Ewyas, via couple of remote little churches and on to the elegant ruins of **3 Llanthony Priory**. With time, you might want to detour from the road to the even narrower country lanes that run to **4 Partrishow Church**, with its intricate oak rood screen, medieval wall paintings and associated holy spring.

Consider a pause at the unfeasibly ancient Skirrid Inn at **5 Llanfihangel Crucorney**. Beyond the village, turn right onto the A465, the main road into **6 Abergavenny**, where the sights include a priory church with graceful effigies. Take the A40 west out of town and stop to have a look around **7 Crickhowell**, one of the Brecon Beacons' most attractive settlements. Continue along the A40 and turn right at the acclaimed **8 Nantyffin Cider Mill** (p94) onto the A479. After a short while you'll come to **9 Tretower Court & Castle.** (p95) Head back onto the A479 and turn right at the edge of the national park onto the A438 and then the B4350 and take it back to Hay-on-Wye.

a final steep climb up an obvious path to the summit.

This is one of Britain's finest paragliding and hang-gliding sites. In fact, it is so good that the South East Wales Hang Gliding and Paragliding Club (www.sewhgpgc. co.uk) purchased the mountain in 1998. Several records have been set from here, and the mountain regularly hosts competition events.

Crickhowell (Crughywel)

This prosperous, picturesque, flower-bedecked village on the Abergavenny–Brecon road is named after the distinctive flat-topped Crug Hywel (Hywel's Rock; 451m), better known as Table Mountain, which rises to the north. You can make a steep but satisfying hike to the impressive remains of an Iron Age fort at the top (3 miles round trip); the tourist office (☑ 01873-811970; www.visitcrickhowell.co.uk; Beaufort St; ☉ 10am-5pm Mon-Sat, 10am-1.30pm Sun; ☎), which incorporates the attractive Oriel Gallery, has a leaflet showing the route.

There's not a lot to see in Crickhowell itself, but it's a pleasant place for an overnight stop. Every Friday and Saturday there's an arts and craft market held in the old market hall (High St); the building also houses the high-ceilinged Courtroom Café (☑ 01873-812497; ☉ 9am-5pm Mon-Fri, 10am-4pm Sun).

The town grew up around the Norman motte (mound) and bailey castle and the nearby ford on the River Usk. All that remains of the castle is a few tumbledown towers, and the ford was superseded by an elegant 17th-century stone bridge, leading to the neighbouring village of Llangattock; it's famous for having 12 arches on one side, and 13 on the other. Try counting them from the riverside beer garden at the Bridge End Inn (☑ 01873-810338; Bridge St). The inn serves a range of real ales, including Hancocks and Speckled Hen, and inside it's all timber beams and angling paraphernalia.

The best of several eateries in the town centre is the Bear Hotel, a fine old coaching inn with low-ceilinged rooms, stone fireplaces, blackened timber beams and antique furniture. The menu (mains £9 to £19) ranges from hearty, meaty country fare (roast venison; slow-roasted pork belly) to more exotic dishes (Moroccan lemon chicken; salmon marinated in chilli, lime and coriander).

One of South Wales' gastronomic pioneers, the 16th-century Nantyffin Cider Mill (☑ 01873-810775; www.cidermill.co.uk; lunch £6-20, dinner £16-20; ☉ lunch Tue-Sun, dinner Tue-Sat) uses local produce to create simple dishes that allow the quality of the ingredients to shine through. The dining room is set around the original 19th-century cider press. The Nantyffin is 1 mile northwest of Crickhowell on the A40, at the turning for Tretower Castle.

Staged in late August in Glanusk Park, 2 miles west of Crickhowell via the B4558, Green Man (www.greenman.net; Glanusk Park; adult/child £145/5) sits proudly at the forefront of Britain's summer music festival circuit as an event with a strong green ethos that caters well for children and people with disabilities. Yet that would all count for naught if the line-up wasn't any good, and here's where Green Man excels. Despite its relatively small size (around 10,000 people) it consistently attracts the current 'it' bands of the alternative music firmament – acts like Animal Collective, Joanna Newsom, Flaming Lips and Wilco, and dead-set legends such as Jarvis Cocker and Robert Plant. Unsurprisingly, it sells out early. Tickets include the weekend's camping.

🛏 Sleeping

Riverside CAMPGROUND £
(☑ 01873-810397; www.riversidecaravanscrickhowell.co.uk; New Rd; sites £10; ☉ Mar-Oct) Well kept and very central, next to the Crickhowell bridge, but it can get crowded in high summer; no under 18 year olds and no single-sex groups.

Britannia Inn INN £
(☑ 01873-812547; www.britanniabunkhouse.co.uk; 20 High St; bed per person £15, d £40) A basic but welcoming bunkroom in a pub in the heart of Crickhowell, which also offers a couple of doubles. There's a kitchenette and a big beer garden out the back.

★ Bear Hotel PUB ££
(☑ 01873-810408; www.bearhotel.co.uk; Beaufort St; s/d from £77/95; P ☎) The Bear is a local institution, a fine old coaching inn with a range of chintzy, old-fashioned rooms, the more expensive ones with four-posters and Jacuzzis. Some renovated rooms have a fresher look.

★ Gwyn Deri B&B ££
(☑ 01873-812494; www.gwynderibedandbreakfast. co.uk; Mill St; s/d £40/65; P ☎) The friendly couple who run this homey B&B keep the

modern rooms immaculately clean. Bonuses include iPod docks, fresh fruit in the rooms and an excellent breakfast selection.

Dragon Inn INN **££**

(☑ 01873-810362; www.dragoncrickhowell.co.uk; 47 High St; s/d from £50/70; P ⓡ) Though set in an 18th-century listed building, the pretty-in-pink Dragon has a modern feel. The 15 bedrooms, while not super flash, boast crisp, clean design with pine furniture and bold colours.

Tŷ Gwyn B&B **££**

(☑ 01873-811625; www.tygwyn.com; Brecon Rd; s/d from £40/66; P @) Once the home of Regency architect John Nash, Tŷ Gwyn is a lovely old Georgian house with four spacious en suite rooms. It's only two minutes' walk from the town centre.

Llangattock (Llangatwg)

Across the oddly arched bridge from Crickhowell, Llangattock's old stone houses are clustered around a castle-like 12th-century church. A late-afternoon stroll is rewarded by views back to Crug Hywel bathed in golden light, its fort looking like one of the magical fairy circles of Welsh myth.

The surrounding countryside is perfect horse-riding country. **Golden Castle Riding Stables** (☑ 01873-812649; www.golden-castle. co.uk; per 30min/day from £30/55) offers pony trekking, hacking, trail riding and children's activity days.

🛏 Sleeping

Old Rectory HOTEL **££**

(☑ 01873-810373; www.rectoryhotel.co.uk; Llangattock; s/d from £55/85; P ⓡ) Surprisingly grand for the price, this partly 16th-century stone mansion was once the home of poet Henry Vaughan. Now it has its own golf course and a clubby atmosphere pervades the downstairs bar and restaurant. Rooms are chic and comfortable.

Tretower Court & Castle

Originally the home of the Vaughan family, **Tretower** (www.cadw.wales.gov.uk; Tretower; adult/child £4.75/3.60; ⊙10am-5pm Apr-Oct, 11am-4pm Fri-Sun Nov-Mar) gives you two historic buildings for the price of one – the sturdy circular tower of a Norman motte-and-bailey castle, and a 15th-century manor house with a fine medieval garden. Together they illustrate the transition from military stronghold to country house that took place in late medieval times. Some domestic clutter has been added to bring the kitchens and banqueting hall to vivid and surprisingly colourful life, but otherwise the rugged authenticity of the place is left intact. Film buffs may like to know that Tretower featured in *The Restoration* starring Robert Downey Jnr, and the Johnny Depp vehicle *The Libertine*.

Tretower is 3 miles northwest of Crickhowell on the A479.

🛏 Sleeping

Gliffaes Hotel HOTEL **£££**

(☑ 01874-730371; www.gliffaeshotel.com; s/d from £95/108; P ⓡ) This Victorian mansion makes quite an impression with its Romanesque towers rising through its thickly wooded grounds on the banks of the Usk. Standard doubles start from £160, but the considerably cheaper 'small doubles' have the same facilities. It's about 4 miles northwest of Crickhowell, off the A40.

Talybont-on-Usk

Tiny Talybont-on-Usk has a venerable transport heritage for its size: an aqueduct takes the canal over the Caerfanell River here, and a disused railway bridge cuts dramatically across the village. Just to the south is the epic Talybont Reservoir. A hostel and a handful of decent pubs make the village a pleasant – if uneventful – holiday base.

🛏 Sleeping

★ **Danywenallt Youth Hostel** HOSTEL **£**

(☑ 0845 371 9548; www.yha.org.uk; Talybont-on-Usk; dm/r from £18/36) Handsome converted farmhouse located beneath the dam of Talybont Reservoir, just outside Talybont. Self-catering facilities are limited, but a pukka restaurant provides terrific and affordable food, including three-course dinners.

Llangorse Lake

Reed-fringed Llangorse Lake (Llyn Syfaddan), to the east of Brecon, may be Wales' second-largest natural lake (after Llyn Tegid), but it's barely more than a mile long and half a mile wide. Close to the northern shore is a **crannog**, a lake dwelling built on an artificial island. Such dwellings or refuges were used from the late Bronze Age until early medieval times. Tree-ring dating shows that this one (of which only the base remains) was built around AD 900, probably by the royal house of Brycheiniog. Among the artefacts found here was a dugout canoe, now on display in Brecon's Brecknock Museum; other finds can be seen at the National Museum Cardiff. There's a reconstruction of a crannog house on the shore.

The lake is the national park's main water sports location, used for sailing, windsurfing, canoeing and water-skiing. **Lakeside Caravan Park** (☎01874-658226; www.llangorselake.co.uk), on the north shore, rents rowing boats (per hour/day £14/32), Canadian canoes (per hour/day £14/45) and Wayfarer sailing dinghies (per hour £28; you'll need to know how to rig them yourself).

Set on a hillside above the eastern end of Llangorse Lake is the **Llangorse Multi Activity Centre** (☎01874-658272; www.activityuk.com; Gilfach Farm; ⊙9am-10pm Mon-Sat, 9am-5pm Sun). It offers a range of adventure activities, including an outdoor aerial assault course that involves clambering up cargo nets, balancing along logs, swinging on tyres and using Indian rope bridges. You can whizz through the air on linked zipwires which stretch for 3km (£25/45 half-/full day). There's also an indoor facility with artificial rock-climbing walls, a log climb, an abseil area, a rope bridge and even an artificial caving area.

Sleeping

Peterstone Court MANOR ££
(☎01874-665387; www.peterstone-court.com; A40, Llanhamlach; s/d from £105/125; P 🛜 ☰) An elegant Georgian manor house overlooking the River Usk, Peterstone enjoys views across the valley to the peaks of Cribyn and Pen-y-Fan. Despite the country-house setting the atmosphere is relaxed. The bedrooms are large, mixing antiques with modern designer furniture and crisp linen. Llanhamlach is 3 miles southeast of Brecon, just off the A40.

Eating

White Swan PUB ££
(☎01874-665276; www.white-swan-brecon.co.uk; Llanfrynach; mains £14-19; ⊙Wed-Sun; 🛜) A traditional village inn that offers a candle-lit dining room with a beautiful garden terrace. The White Swan is a great place to relax after a walk along the canal or a hike in the Brecon Beacons. It changed hands recently, but the menu still emphasises Welsh lamb, beef and venison, with daily fish and vegetarian specials. Llanfrynach is 3.5 miles southeast of Brecon off the B4558.

CLIMBING PEN-Y-FAN

One of the most popular hikes in the national park is the ascent of Pen-y-Fan (886m), the highest peak in the Brecon Beacons (around 120,000 people each year make the climb, giving it the nickname 'the motorway'). The shortest route to the summit begins at the Pont ar Daf car park on the A470, 10 miles southwest of Brecon. It's a steep but straightforward slog up a deeply eroded path (now paved with natural stone) to the summit of Corn Du (873m), followed by a short dip and final ascent to Pen-y-Fan (4.5 miles round trip; allow three hours). A slightly longer (5.5 miles round trip), but just as crowded, path starts at the Storey Arms outdoor centre, 1 mile to the north. The X43 and various Beacons Buses stop at the Storey Arms. (Note: the Storey Arms is not a pub!)

You can avoid the crowds by choosing one of the longer routes on the north side of the mountain, which also have the advantage of more interesting views on the way up. The best starting point is the Cwm Gwdi car park, at the end of a minor road 3.5 miles southwest of Brecon. From here, you follow a path along the crest of the Cefn Cwm Llwch ridge, with great views of the neighbouring peaks, with a final steep scramble up to the summit. The round trip from the car park is 7 miles; allow three to four hours. Starting and finishing in Brecon, the total distance is 14 miles.

Remember that Pen-y-Fan is a serious mountain – the weather can change rapidly and people have to be rescued here every year. Wear hiking boots and take warm clothes, waterproofs, and a map and compass. You can get advice and weather forecasts at the National Park Visitor Centre or from the **Met Office** (☎0870 900 0100; www.metoffice.gov.uk).

Peterstone Court　　　MODERN BRITISH **£££**
(☑ 01874-665387; www.peterstone-court.com; A40, Llanhamlach; mains £17-19; ⊗ 8am-10pm) The genteel environment of a Georgian manor house is a very good starting point for a memorable dining experience. Peterstone Court has the added advantage of serving produce from its own farm, turned out by a Ritz-trained chef who won the Welsh International Culinary Championships in 2010.

❶ Getting There & Away

Bus X43 connects Crickhowell with Abergavenny (17 minutes), Brecon (26 minutes), Merthyr Tydfil (1½ hours) and Cardiff (2¼ hours).

Brecon (Aberhonddu)

POP 8250

The handsome stone market town of Brecon stands at the meeting of the Rivers Usk and Honddu. For centuries the town thrived as a centre of wool production and weaving; today it's the main hub of the national park and a natural base for exploring the surrounding countryside.

An Iron Age hill fort on Pen-y-Crug (331m), northwest of town, and the remains of a Roman camp at Y Gaer, to the west, testify to the site's antiquity. After the Romans, the area was ruled by the Irish-born king Brychan, who married into a Welsh royal house in the 5th century. The town takes its name from him, and his kingdom, Brycheiniog (anglicised to Brecknock), gave its name to the old county of Brecknockshire. Merthyr Tydfil was named for Brychan's daughter, St Tudful.

It was not until Norman times that Brecon began to burgeon. The local Welsh prince, Rhys ap Tewdwr, was defeated in 1093 by Bernard de Neufmarché, a Norman lord, who then built the town's castle and church (which is now a cathedral). The scant remains of the castle have been incorporated into the Castle of Brecon Hotel. Across the road from the hotel is the original Norman motte, capped by the ivy-clad **Ely Tower** (not open to the public).

◉ Sights

★ **Brecon Cathedral**　　　CHURCH
(www.breconcathedral.org.uk; Cathedral Close) Perched on a hill above the River Honddu, Brecon Cathedral was founded as part of a Benedictine monastery in 1093, though little remains of the Norman structure except the vividly carved font and parts of the nave. It's a lovely church and very visitor-friendly; seven information points provide information about key features.

At the western end of the nave, just inside the door, is a stone cresset (an ancient lighting device), the only one in Wales; the 30 cups were filled with oil and lit to illuminate dark corners or steps. To the north is the Harvard Chapel, the regimental chapel of the South Wales Borderers, draped with banners from the Zulu wars.

In the cathedral grounds is a **Heritage Centre** (admission free; ⊗ 10am-4.30pm Mon-Sat), cafe and gift shop housed in a restored 15th-century tithe barn. The cathedral hosts regular choral concerts.

Brecknock Museum & Art Gallery　　　MUSEUM
(www.powys.gov.uk; Captain's Walk) Behind the stolid neoclassical exterior of the former shire hall is the town's museum, currently undergoing a significant restoration and due to reopen in 2015. When it reopens, you'll be able to see a 1200-year-old dugout canoe found at Llangorse Lake, alongside exhibits on the archaeology, history and natural history of the Brecon area. There's also a strong collection of local art.

South Wales Borderers Museum　　　MUSEUM
(☑ 01874-613310; http://royalwelsh.org.uk; The Barracks, The Watton; adult/child £4/free; ⊗ 10am-5pm Mon-Fri year-round, 10am-4pm Sat Easter-Sep) This regimental museum commemorates the history of the Royal Regiment of Wales, which is based in Brecon. Many of the soldiers are Gurkhas, often to be seen in their civvies around the town. The highlight is the Zulu War Room – the regiment's predecessor fought in the 1879 Anglo–Zulu war in South Africa, inspiration for the 1964 film *Zulu* starring Michael Caine. The collection of artefacts recalls the defence of Rorke's Drift, when 150 Welsh soldiers held out against 4000 Zulu warriors.

🏃 Activities

Brecon is the northern terminus of the Monmouthshire and Brecon Canal, built between 1799 and 1812 for the movement of coal, iron ore, limestone and agricultural goods. The 33 miles from Brecon to Pontypool is back in business, transporting a generally less grimy cargo of holidaymakers and river dwellers. The busiest section is around Brecon, with

Brecon

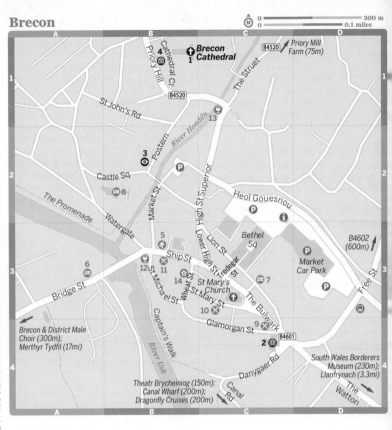

Brecon

◉ Top Sights
1 Brecon Cathedral.....................................B1

◉ Sights
Brecknock Castle............................(see 8)
2 Brecknock Museum & Art
   Gallery C4
3 Ely Tower..B2
4 Heritage Centre.......................................B1

◔ Activities, Courses & Tours
5 Biped Cycles...B3

▦ Sleeping
6 Bridge Cafe...A3

7 Cantre Selyf C3
8 Castle of Brecon Hotel...........................B2

⊗ Eating
Bridge Cafe.......................................(see 6)
9 Gurkha Corner C4
10 Roberto's...C3
11 The Hours..B3

◔ Drinking & Nightlife
12 Boar's Head...B3
13 Bull's Head C1

◉ Entertainment
14 Coliseum Cinema B3

craft departing from the canal basin, 400m south of the town centre.

You can take to the water with **Beacon Park Boats** (☏ 01873-858277; www.beaconparkboats.com), which rents out four- or six-seater electric-powered boats (per hour/half-day/day from £16/35/50; up to six people) and three-seater Canadian canoes (per hour/half-day/day from £10/20/30). It also has a fleet of luxury narrowboats for longer live-in voyages, as does **Cambrian Cruisers** (☎01874-665315; www.cambriancruisers.co.uk; Ty Newydd, Pencelli). **Backwaters Adventure Equipment Ltd** (☎01873-831825; www.backwatershire.co.uk; per day kayak/canoe £27.50/45) also rents kayaks and canoes, including buoyancy aids and waterproof barrels.

Dragonfly Cruises (☎01874-685222; www.dragonfly-cruises.co.uk; adult/child £7.20/4.50; ⌚Mar-Oct) runs 2½-hour narrowboat trips; there are departures once or twice daily on Wednesday, Saturday and Sunday, and on additional days from June to August.

Brecon Beacons' classic off-road mountain-biking route is The Gap, following a 24-mile loop from Brecon that takes in a high pass close to Pen-y-Fan and an easy return along the canal.

Biped Cycles (☎01874-622296; www.bipedcycles.co.uk; 10 Ship St; per half-/full day £18/20) rents bikes and can arrange guided rides. The Taff Trail heads south from here to Cardiff. This forms part of Lôn Las Cymru, which also heads north to Builth Wells.

A peaceful 8.5-mile walk along the towpath leads to the picturesque village of Talybont-on-Usk. You can return on the X43 bus or, on summer Sundays, the Beacons Bus B4 or B16.

Kevin Walker Mountain Activities HIKING
(☎01874-658784; http://mountain-activities.com) Small group hikes and navigational skills courses, with a focus on ecology and community.

Festivals & Events

Brecon Jazz Festival MUSIC
(www.breconjazz.co.uk; ⌚Aug) Organised by the team behind the Hay Festival, one of Europe's leading jazz events is held in Brecon in the second weekend in August. Emerging British talent and big-name internationals, such as 2010 headliners the Buena Vista Social Club, perform.

Brecon Beast CYCLING
(www.breconbeast.co.uk; ⌚Sep) A gruelling mountain-bike challenge over 44 or 68 miles, held in mid-September. The entry fee (£35) covers camping, refreshments on the route, a 'pasta party' and a T-shirt.

Sleeping

Priory Mill Farm CAMPGROUND £
(www.priorymillfarm.co.uk; The Struet; sites per person £7.50; ⌚Easter-Oct) With a cobbled courtyard, ancient mill building, free-range chickens and a lush camping meadow, this small ecofriendly campground is pretty much camping heaven, and it's just a five-minute riverside walk from Brecon. It supplies local wood and charcoal so you can have your very own campfire. Note, Hay Road is called The Struet.

★**Cantre Selyf** B&B ££
(☎01874-622904; www.cantreselyf.co.uk; 5 Lion St; s £50, d £80-90; P wi-fi) This wonderfully elegant 17th-century town house, right in the middle of Brecon, has atmospheric period decor and furnishings, including plaster mouldings, original fireplaces and cast-iron bedsteads.

Bridge Cafe B&B ££
(☎01874-622024; www.bridgecafe.co.uk; 7 Bridge St; s/d from £45/55) Owned by keen mountain bikers and hill walkers who can advise on local activities, the Bridge has three plain but attractive and comfortable bedrooms, with down-filled duvets and crisp cotton sheets.

Castle of Brecon Hotel HOTEL ££
(☎01874-624611; www.breconcastle.co.uk; Castle Sq; s/d from £65/80; P) Built into the ruined walls of Brecknock Castle, this grand and welcoming old-style hotel features 40 comfortable, refurbished rooms, including four-posters.

Eating

Like Abergavenny, many of the best options are a little out of town, such as Peterstone Court, the White Swan and the Felin Fach Griffin.

★**Bridge Cafe** BISTRO ££
(☎01874-622024; 7 Bridge St; mains £8; ⌚6.30-10pm Thu-Sat, 9am-noon Sun; wi-fi) With a particular focus on refuelling weary walkers and mountain bikers, Bridge Cafe offers home-cooked meals such as hearty casseroles in cosy surrounds, with rough-hewn white-washed walls and wooden furniture. Local, organic ingredients are used wherever possible. Be sure to book ahead.

The Hours CAFE £
(☎01874-622800; www.breconbeaconstourism.co.uk/eating/item/67695/The_Hours_Cafe_Bookshop.html#; 15 Ship St; ⌚10am-5pm Tue-Sat; wi-fi) This cute combined bookshop and cafe serves the best coffee in town, plus excellent home baking, soup and snacks. It's located in an endearingly wonky pistachio-coloured cottage.

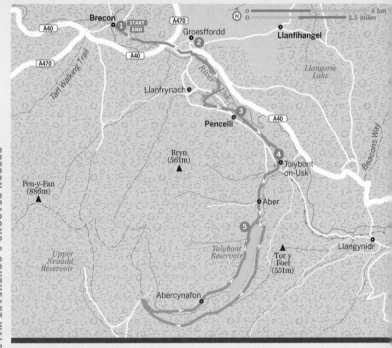

🚶 Cycling Tour
Cycling Round the Talybont Reservoir

START BRECON
END BRECON
LENGTH 26 MILES; ONE DAY

This is very much a cycling route of two halves. The first leg takes you along the canal to the little village of Talybont-on-Usk, where there's a choice of refreshment stops. This is the easy part... Beyond Talybont, a much more stretching circular loop takes you round the vast Talybont Reservoir.

Bike hire is available in **①** **Brecon** at Biped Cycles. The cycle route proper starts near Theatr Brycheiniog with its cluster of canal boats. You leave town past a dwindling number of houses, and the scene grows increasingly rural.

At the first lock at **②** **Groesffordd**, ignore cycle-route signs and continue on the canal towpath – note that the signed Taf Trail follows a similar route, but that it's nicer to stick to the **③** **canal**. For the next few miles you simply follow the left-hand bank of the tranquil tree-lined waterway, which at points offers a view of the sinuous and rushing River Usk. You pass the small settlements of Llanfrynach, Pencelli and Cross Oak, but these are barely perceptible from the path.

Eventually you come to **④** **Talybont-on-Usk**; opposite the village shop you should leave the path and join the lane over the drawbridge. There are a number of eating and drinking options at Talybont, from the handy little Talybont Stores with its cafe to a cluster of pubs: the best is the Star Inn.

Follow the country road through Aber, beyond which is the **⑤** **Talybont Reservoir**. Follow the signs left off the road towards Danywenallt YHA; once you have crossed the water take the lane to the right, which makes a loop right round the reservoir. At the furthest point you're on the fringes of the Taf Fechan Forest – a very steep incline takes you back to the west bank of the reservoir.

The return route – back along the canal the way you came – is easy. Nearing home, at the bridge numbered 162, just remember to cross the canal, following the signs to Brecon.

Roberto's
ITALIAN **££**

(☑ 01874-611880; www.robertos-brecon.co.uk; St Mary St; mains £9-15; ☺ 6-11pm Mon-Sat) They may be plastic vines hanging from the trellis on the ceiling, but everything else about Roberto's is authentically Italian, from the relaxed atmosphere to the free olives and crostini, to the puttanesca sauce. Though, of course, that's Welsh beef lurking underneath the gorgonzola.

Gurkha Corner
NEPALESE

(www.gurkhacorner.co.uk; 12 Glamorgan St; ☺ noon-2.30 & 5.30-11pm) Slightly dingy but agreeable Nepalese restaurant, decorated with rustic scenes of the Himalayas. The food – lightly spiced curries and rich veg side dishes – is delicious.

🍷 Drinking & Nightlife

Boar's Head
PUB

(☑ 01874-622856; Ship St) The Boar's Head is a lively local pub, with sofas in the back room and the full range of Breconshire Brewery real ales on tap. It has a sunny beer garden overlooking the river, and regular live music.

Bull's Head
PUB

(☑ 01874-623900; 86 The Struet) Arguably the best real-ale pub in town, with Evan Evans beer from Llandeilo and a range of guest ales, the riverside Bull's Head is cosy, quiet and friendly. At the time of writing it was being refurbished, with plans to add a bunkhouse.

☆ Entertainment

Coliseum Cinema
CINEMA

(☑ 01874-622501; www.coliseumbrecon.co.uk; Wheat St; tickets £7) Dating back to 1925, the two-screen Coliseum is a wonderful combination of high-tech comfort – digital screening and Italian chairs – and glamorous vintage touches, with old-style usherettes, plush curtain drapes and deco doorhandles. In addition to its mainstream offerings, the local film society shows arthouse films on Monday evenings.

Brecon & District Male Choir
TRADITIONAL MUSIC

(www.breconchoir.co.uk; Llanfaes Primary School, Orchard St; ☺ 7.30-9.30pm Fri) For a few booming harmonies, head to the practice sessions of the local men's choir; visitors are welcome. Since its formation in 1937 it has performed at London's Royal Albert Hall eight times and has even released its own CD.

Theatr Brycheiniog
THEATRE

(☑ 01874-611622; www.brycheiniog.co.uk; Canal Wharf) This attractive canalside theatre complex is the town's main venue for drama, dance, comedy and music. It's worth checking the program, as it sometimes hosts surprisingly big-name touring acts. Its restaurant, Tipple'n'Tiffin, serves good tapas-style food and more substantial dishes.

ℹ Information

Brecon War Memorial Hospital (☑ 01874-622443; Cerrigcochion Rd)

Police Station (☑ 0845 330 2000)

Tourist Office (☑ 01874-622485; Market car park; ☺ 9.30am-5.30pm Mon-Sat, 10am-4pm Sun)

ℹ Getting There & Away

Bus X43 heads to Abergavenny (50 minutes), Crickhowell (26 minutes), Merthyr Tydfil (37 minutes) and Cardiff (1½ hours); bus X63 to Swansea (two hours); bus 39 to Hay-on-Wye (40 minutes); and bus 704 to Newtown (two hours) via Builth Wells (40 minutes) and Llandrindod Wells (55 minutes). Most Beacons Buses routes converge on Brecon.

The Market car park offers short-stay pay-and-display parking. There are long-stay lots on Heol Gouesnou and near the canal basin.

Ride & Hike (☑ 07989-242550; www.rideandhike.co.uk) offers regular taxi services as well as a walkers' shuttle. Indicative fares for the six-seater shuttle: National Park Visitor Centre (£20), Merthyr Tydfil (£45), Cardiff (£100).

Around Brecon

The conical hill of Pen-y-Crug (331m), capped by an Iron Age hill fort, rises to the northwest of the town, and is a good option for a short hike (2.5 miles round trip). There's a superb view of the Brecon Beacons from the summit. The tourist office sells national park walk cards.

🏃 Activities

Cantref Adventure Farm & Riding Centre
HORSE RIDING

(☑ 01874-665223; www.cantref.com; Llanfrynach, Upper Cantref Farm; height over/under 93cm £8.25/free; ☺ 10.30am-5.30pm Easter-Oct, weekends & school holidays only Nov-Easter) In the countryside south of Brecon, Cantref operates a child-focused fun farm, complete with pig races, lamb feeding and people dressed as horses, dancing for the little troops. More interesting for adults are the pony trekking and hacking (per hour/half-/full day £18/27/50), heading out into the Brecon Beacons.

It's reached by a set of narrow country lanes; follow the horseshoe signs from the A40, southeast of town. Bunkhouse accommodation (from £14) and basic camping is available.

🛏 Sleeping

Beacons Backpackers HOSTEL £
(☑ 01874-730215; www.beaconsbackpackers.co.uk; The New Inn, Brecon Road, Bwlch; per person £20 incl tea/coffee & toast) This small but lively hostel between Brecon and Crickhowell is sited in the former New Inn pub, which is still licensed. As well as booze and live music nights, the hostel also provides lunch and dinner, and you can order in stone-baked pizza. It has great hand-outs on local walks, and you can hike with the hostel staff, who will also help out if you want to go canoeing or ice-climbing.

Llwyn-y-Celyn Youth Hostel HOSTEL £
(☑ 0845 371 9029; www.yha.org.uk; dm/r from £18/36) An 18th-century farmhouse in 6 hectares of woodland, 6 miles south of Brecon on the A470. With flagstone floors, rough stone walls and sparse furnishings, this is a a spartan option, but ideal for walking – particularly ascents of Pen-y-Fan.

STARGAZING IN THE BRECON BEACONS

In 2013 the Brecon Beacons became only the fifth place in the world to win dark sky status. The Brecon Beacons Park Society and the National Park Authority combined forces to campaign for the rare accolade, with the help of the community: Talybont-on-Usk staged a light switch off and star party.

Light pollution is now closely monitored in the region, which is one of the UK's best for stargazing. Meteor showers, nebula, strings of constellations and even the Milky Way can be seen in the night sky above the national park. Visitor centres throughout the park can give you information about the stargazing events held year-round, or see www.breconbeacons.org.

Pencelli Castle Caravan & Camping Park CAMPGROUND £
(☑ 01874-665451; www.pencelli-castle.com; Pencelli; tent per person £11.50, caravans £23.80) An award-winning site near the canal in Pencelli near Brecon, whose plaudits include Loo of the Year. There's a well-stocked shop, a pub down the road, a nature trail and a playground.

Felin Fach Griffin HOTEL ££
(☑ 01874-620111; www.felinfachgriffin.co.uk; s/c from £85/115; ☑) There are no chintz or floral patterns here, just neutral decor with a splash of colour to set off antique four-poster beds equipped with goose-down pillows and duvets, plus Roberts Radios and homemade biscuits. It also offers a dinner with B&B rate. The Griffin is 5 miles northeast of Brecon, just off the A470.

🍴 Eating

★ Talgarth Mill CAFE £
(☑ 01874-711125; www.talgarthmill.com; The Mill House, The Sq, Talgarth; ⊙11am-4pm Tue-Sun) Situated in Talgarth, between Brecon and Hay-on-Wye, 18th-century Talgarth Mill produces stone-ground flour, which you can buy in its cooperative craft shop. The bakery sells beautiful olive and apricot breads, cinnamon buns and almond twists, while the attractive cafe supplements baked goods with soups, salads, local cheese and meat and excellent puddings.

★ Felin Fach Griffin GASTROPUB ££
(☑01874-620111; www.felinfachgriffin.co.uk; Felinfach; mains £18-19, s/d from £85/115; ⊙noon-2.30pm & 6-10pm) With a string of awards as lengthy as its wine list, the Griffin offers gourmet dining in a relaxed and unpretentious setting. Open fires, leather sofas and timber beams create a comfortable atmosphere, while the chef makes the most of local fish, meat and game. The Griffin is situated 5 miles northeast of Brecon on the A470.

ℹ Information

National Park Visitor Centre (☑ 01874-623366; www.breconbeacons.org; Libanus; ⊙9.30am-5pm) Set high on a ridge with fine views of Pen-y-Fan and Corn Du is the park's main visitor centre, with full details of walks, hiking and biking trails, outdoor activities, wildlife and geology. It has easy wheelchair access, as well as a book and gift shop, a tearoom and picnic tables. During school holidays there are kids' activities, organised farm visits, guided walks and themed minibus tours.

The centre is off the A470 road, 5 miles southwest of Brecon and 15 miles north of Merthyr Tydfil. Some of the Beacons Buses stop here; otherwise, any of the buses on the Merthyr Tydfil–Brecon route stop at Libanus village, a 1.25-mile walk away.

Fforest Fawr & Black Mountain

West of the A470, this entire half of the national park is sparsely inhabited, without any towns of note. **Fforest Fawr** (Great Forest), once a Norman hunting ground, is now a Unesco geopark famous for its varied landscapes, ranging from bleak moorland to flower-flecked limestone pavement and lush wooded ravines choked with moss and greenery. Rather confusingly, the **Black Mountain** is the collective name for the range of barren peaks. Carreg Cennen castle, in the far southwestern corner of the national park, is a wonderful place to explore; the easiest approach is from Llandeilo.

⊙ Sights & Activities

The Forestry Commission's **Garwnant Visitor Centre** (☑ 01685-723060; www.forestry.gov.uk/garwnant; ⊙ 10am-5pm), at the head of Llwyn Onn Reservoir (5 miles north of Merthyr on the A470), is the starting point for a couple of easy forest walks and a cycle trail, and it also has a cafe, an adventure play area and a rope-swing 'assault course' for kids.

Between the villages of **Pontneddfechan** and **Ystradfellte** is a series of dramatic waterfalls, where the Rivers Mellte, Hepste and Pyrddin pass through steep forested gorges. The finest is **Sgwd-yr-Eira** (Waterfall of the Snow), where you can actually walk behind the torrent. At one point the River Mellte disappears into **Porth-yr-Ogof** (Door to the Cave), the biggest cave entrance in Britain (3m high and 20m wide), only to reappear 100m further south.

Walks in the area are outlined on the national park's Wood of the Waterfalls walk card (£1), which is available from visitor centres, including the **Waterfalls Centre** (☑ 01639-721795; Pontneathvaughan Rd, Pontneddfechan; ⊙ 9.30am-5pm Apr-Oct, 9.30am-3pm Sat & Sun Nov-Mar). Take special care – the footpaths can be slippery, and there are several steep, stony sections.

Black Mountain (Mynydd Du), the western section of the national park, contains the wildest, loneliest and least-visited walking country. Its finest feature is the sweeping escarpment of **Fan Brycheiniog** (802m), which rises steeply above the scenic glacial lakes of Llyn y Fan Fach and Llyn y Fan Fawr. It can be climbed from Llanddeusant; the round trip is 12 miles.

Carreg Cennen   CASTLE
(www.carregcennencastle.com; adult/child £4/3.50; ⊙ 9.30am-6.30pm Apr-Oct, to 4pm Nov-Mar) Perched atop a steep limestone crag high above the River Cennen is Wales' ultimate romantic ruined castle, visible for miles in every direction. The current structure was built at the end of the 13th century in the course of Edward I's conquest of Wales. It was partially dismantled in 1462 during the Wars of the Roses. The most unusual feature is a stone-vaulted passage running along the top of the sheer southern cliff, which leads down to a long, narrow, natural cave; bring a torch or hire one from the ticket office (£1.50).

Carreg Cennen is signposted from the A483, heading south from Llandeilo.

Garn Goch   FORT
(near Bethlehem village) FREE You're likely to have the impressive remains of 4000-year-old Garn Goch (Red Fort) to yourself, despite their splendour. It's the largest Iron Age hill fort in Wales – two distinct circular stone ramparts can be discerned as you wander the site, as well as Bronze Age burial mounds.

Red Kite Centre   WILDLIFE RESERVE
(☑ 01550-740617; www.redkiteswales.co.uk; Llanddeusant; admission £3; ⊙ feeding summer 3pm, winter 2pm) A former pub, now the beautiful Red Kite Cafe, is also a feeding centre for the beautiful kites themselves, who swoop in daily. You may see around 50 of the birds, alongside buzzards and ravens.

National Showcaves
Centre for Wales   CAVE
(☑ 01639-730284; www.showcaves.co.uk; adult/child £13.75/8; ⊙ 10am-4pm Apr-Oct) The limestone plateau of the southern Fforest Fawr, around the upper reaches of the River Tawe, is riddled with some of the largest and most complex cave systems in Britain. Most can only be visited by experienced cavers, but the **National Showcaves Centre for Wales** is a set of three caves that are well lit, spacious and easily accessible, even to children.

The highlight of the 1.5-mile self-guided tour is the **Cathedral Cave**, a high-domed chamber with a lake fed by two waterfalls that pour from openings in the rock. Nearby is the **Bone Cave**, where 42 Bronze Age skeletons were discovered. **Dan-yr-Ogof Cave**, part of a 10-mile complex, has interesting limestone formations.

The admission fee also gives entry to various other attractions on-site, including a museum, a reconstructed Iron Age farm, a prehistoric theme park filled with life-sized fibreglass dinosaurs, a shire-horse centre and a children's playground. The complex is just off the A4067 north of Abercraf.

Beneath the hillside to the east lies the twisting maze of subterranean chambers known as **Ogof Ffynnon Ddu** (Cave of the Black Spring), the deepest and third-longest cave system in the UK (308m deep, with 30 miles of passages). This one is for expert potholers only, but you can explore it virtually at www.ogof.net.

Penderyn Distillery   DISTILLERY
(☎01685-813300; www.welsh-whisky.co.uk; Penderyn; tours adult/child £6/4; ☺9.30am-5pm) Before the ascendency of the chapels in the 19th century, the Welsh were as fond of their whisky as their Gaelic cousins in Scotland and Ireland. Penderyn Distillery marks the resurgence of Welsh whisky-making after an absence of more than

100 years (the Frongoch Distillery in Bala closed in the late 1800s).

This boutique, independently owned distillery released its first malt whisky in 2004. It's distilled with fresh spring water drawn from directly beneath the distillery, then matured in bourbon casks and finished in rich Madeira wine casks to create a golden-hued drop of liquid fire. It also produces Brecon Gin, Brecon Five Vodka and Merlyn Cream Liqueur.

From the imposing black visitors centre you can watch the spirits being made and adult tickets include tastings of two products. If the weather's a bit cold and wet, it's a great way to warm up. Enthusiasts can take a 2½-hour Master Class (per person £45, bookings essential), which includes a guided tour and tastings.

🛏 Sleeping

★**Llanddeusant
Youth Hostel**   HOSTEL, CAMPGROUND £
(☎0845 371 9750; www.yha.org.uk; Old Red Lion; dm/r from £18/60) A former inn nestled in the western fringes of Black Mountain, with wonderful walks from the doorstep up to the glacial valley, including to Lyn y Fan Fach. It's self-catering only, but there's a large kitchen and you can contact the manager in advance to arrange food deliveries from local organic shops. He also does cycling tours, station pick-ups and can even book

---

THE PHYSICIANS OF MYDDFAI

About 8 miles southeast of Llandovery, nestled beneath the high escarpment of the Black Mountain, is a tiny lake called **Llyn y Fan Fach** (Lake of the Little Peak); it's accessible from a car park just beyond the Llanddeusant Youth Hostel). In the mid-13th century, a young man grazing his cattle beside the lake saw a woman, the loveliest he had ever seen, sitting on the surface of the water, combing her hair. He fell madly in love with her, coaxed her to shore with some bread and begged her to marry him. Her fairy father agreed, on the condition that if the young man struck her three times she would return to the fairy world. As dowry she brought a herd of magical cows and for years the couple lived happily near Myddfai, raising three healthy sons.

Naturally the three-strikes-and-you're-out story ends badly. After three abusive incidents, she and her cattle returned forever to the lake. Her sons often visited the lake and one day their mother appeared. She handed the eldest, Rhiwallon, a leather bag containing the secrets of the lake's medicinal plants, and informed him that he should heal the sick.

From this point, legend merges with fact. Historical records confirm that Rhiwallon was a well-known 13th-century physician, and his descendants continued the tradition until the 18th century.

The Pant-y-Meddygon (Physicians' Valley) on Mynydd Myddfai is still rich in bog plants, herbs and lichens, and is well worth visiting for the scenery alone; ask at Llandovery tourist office for details of walks.

storytelling sessions at the hostel. Camping is permitted here.

Dan-yr-Ogof CAMPGROUND £
(☎ 01639-730284; www.showcaves.co.uk; Abercraf; sites per person £7; caravans & motorhomes £15; ☺ Easter-Oct) Part of the Dan-yr-Ogof (p104) cave attraction, this is a verdant family-friendly site with a playbarn for kids. It's also a great spot for walkers, and includes riverside woodland pitches as well as space for motorhomes.

Mandinam CAMPGROUND ££
(☎ 01550-777368; www.mandinam.com; Llangadog; van or hut per night £70) This wonderfully remote estate just west of the national park – the nearest village is Llangadog – offers a great glamping (glamour camping) experience in a Romany van or a shepherd's hut, complete with ecofriendly hot tubs for a spot of romantic stargazing. Both the van and hut are decorated in tasteful bohemian style, and feature tiny kitchens.

🍴 Eating & Drinking

Carreg Cennen Tearoom WELSH £
(☎ 01558-822291; www.carregcennencastle.com; Carreg Cennen Castle; cawl £3.95; ☺ 9.30am-6.30pm Apr-Oct, to 4pm Nov-Mar) Possibly the best castle tearoom anywhere – Carreg Cennen is, unusually, in private hands due to a legal anomaly, which perhaps accounts for the pride with which the tearoom is run. The farmer/owner's longhorn beef is on the menu in the form of cottage pie and beef salad, plus it serves warming *cawl* (traditional Welsh dish) and excellent homemade cakes. The location is an impressive barn, which sits below the castle.

ℹ️ Getting There & Away

Bus 63 between Swansea and Brecon stops at the National Showcaves Centre.

SOUTH WALES VALLEYS

The valleys fanning northwards from Cardiff and Newport were once the heart of industrial Wales. Although the coal, iron and steel industries have withered, the valley names – Rhondda, Cynon, Rhymney, Ebbw – still evoke a world of tight-knit working-class communities, male voice choirs and rows of neat terraced houses set amid a coal-blackened landscape. Today the region is fighting back against its decline by creating a tourist

industry based on industrial heritage – places such as Rhondda Heritage Park, Big Pit and Blaenavon Ironworks are among Wales' most impressive tourist attractions.

The valleys' industrial economy emerged in the 18th century, based on the exploitation of the region's rich deposits of coal, limestone and iron ore. At first the iron trade dictated the need for coal, but by the 1830s coal was finding its own worldwide markets and people poured in from the countryside looking for work. The harsh and dangerous working conditions provided fertile ground for political radicalism – Merthyr Tydfil elected Britain's first ever Labour Party MP in 1900, and many locals went to fight in the Spanish Civil War in the 1930s.

Blaenavon (Blaenafon)
POP 6050

Of all the valley towns that were decimated by the demise of heavy industry, the one-time coal and iron town of Blaenavon shows the greenest shoots of regrowth. This rejuvenation is helped to a large part by the awarding of Unesco World Heritage status in 2000 to its unique conglomeration of industrial sites. Its proximity to Brecon Beacons National Park and Abergavenny doesn't do it any harm either.

Blaenavon is an interesting town to visit, but not necessarily to stay in; the nearest recommended accommodation is in Abergavenny.

🔘 Sights

Blaenavon World Heritage Centre INTERPRETATION CENTRE
(☎ 01495-742333; visitblaenavon.co.uk; Church Rd; ☺ 9am-4pm Tue-Sun) FREE Housed in an artfully converted old school, this centre houses a cafe, tourist office, gallery, gift shop and, more importantly, excellent interactive, audiovisual displays that explore the industrial heritage of the region.

Big Pit: National Coal Museum MINE, MUSEUM
(☎ 029-2057 3650; www.museumwales.ac.uk; ☺ 9.30am-5pm, guided tours 10am-3.30pm) FREE The atmospheric Big Pit provides an opportunity to explore a real coal mine and get a taste of what life was like for the miners who worked here up until 1980. Visitors descend 90m into the mine and explore the tunnels and coalfaces in the company of an ex-miner

guide. It's sobering to experience something of the dark, dank working conditions, particularly considering that children once worked here by candlelight.

Above ground, you can see the pithead baths, blacksmith's workshop and other colliery buildings, filled with displays on the industry and the evocative reminiscences of ex-miners.

You'll be decked out in hard hat, power pack and other safety gear weighing some 5kg, and won't be allowed to bring matches or anything electrical (including photo equipment and watches) down with you. It's cold underground, so take extra layers and wear sturdy shoes. Children must be at least 1m tall. Disabled visitors can arrange tours in advance.

Blaenavon Ironworks HISTORIC SITE
(www.visitblaenavon.co.uk; North St; ☺10am-5pm Apr-Oct, 9.30am-4pm Fri & Sat, 11am-4pm Sun Nov-Mar) FREE When it was completed in 1788, Blaenavon Ironworks was one of the most advanced of its kind in the world. Its three huge coal-fired blast furnaces were provided with air that was powered by a steam engine, making them much more powerful than older, smaller furnaces fired with charcoal and blasted with air from waterwheel-powered bellows. Within a few years it was the world's second-biggest ironworks, after Cyfarthfa at Merthyr Tydfil. Innovation and development continued here until 1904, when the last furnace was finally shut down.

Today the site is one of the best-preserved of all the Industrial Revolution ironworks. You can follow the whole process of production, from the charging of the furnaces to the casting of molten iron in the casting sheds. Also on display are the ironworkers' tiny terraced cottages. The surrounding hillsides are pitted with old tramlines, mines, tunnels and 'scouring' sites, where water was released from holding ponds to wash away topsoil and expose ore seams.

Pontypool & Blaenavon Railway HERITAGE RAILWAY
(www.pontypool-and-blaenavon.co.uk; adult/child £6/3.50; ☺check online for timetables) Built to haul coal and passengers up and down the valley, this railway stopped taking passengers in 1941, and coal haulage ceased when the Big Pit was closed. Since then a section has been restored by local volunteers, allowing you to catch a steam train from the town centre to Big Pit and on to Whistle Halt, the highest train station in England and Wales (396m). The Whistle Inn Pub, beside the station, has a huge collection of miners' lamps.

🏃 Activities

The Blaenavon Cheddar Company crew arranges guided walking and mountain-biking tours for all abilities (walks per person from £2.50) and hires bikes (half-/full day £10/20).

Paraventure Airsports ADVENTURE SPORTS
(☎07775-865095; www.paraventure.co.uk) Learn how to paraglide (two-/four-/eight-day course £300/600/1200) or take a tandem flight off the Blorenge (£85, 20 to 30 minutes) and enjoy a red kite's perspective of the Brecon Beacons.

🍴 Eating

Butterflies Restaurant GASTROPUB ££
(☎01495-791044; www.butterflies-restaurant.co.uk; 31-33 Queen St; mains £12-18; ☺6-9.30pm Tue-Sat, 12.30-2.30pm Sun) As they succinctly put it themselves: 'an oasis in a culinary desert'. This bistro-style place has a good menu of meaty mains: Butterflies Beef Wellington and Welsh lamb cutlets for example, as well as a few fish and veggie options. Friendly service, and pretty puddings to finish.

🛍 Shopping

Blaenavon Cheddar Company FOOD
(☎01495-793123; www.chunkofcheese.co.uk; 80 Broad St; ☺10am-5pm Mon-Sat) On the main drag, Blaenavon Cheddar Company is both a champion for the town and evidence of its gradual resurgence. The shop stocks the company's range of multi award-winning handmade cheese, some of which are matured down in the Big Pit mine shaft. The Pwll Mawr is particularly good, but for extra kick try the chilli- and ale-laced Dragon's Breath. It also stocks a range of Welsh speciality ales, wines and whisky.

ℹ Orientation

Blaenavon is situated at the head of the Llwyd Valley, 16 miles north of Newport. Most buses stop in High St, in the centre of town. Broad St, with its bookshops, is a block to the east. Blaenavon Ironworks is 400m west of High St: walk uphill to the top of High St, turn left on Upper Waun St, then left again on North St. Big Pit: National Coal Museum is another mile west of the ironworks.

Getting There & Away

you're on a bike, a branch of Lôn Las Cymru
nnects to Abergavenny, before heading north
Builth Wells and south to Chepstow.

uses X24 and 30 head here from Newport (50
inutes).

Merthyr Tydfil

OP 55,000

lerthyr Tydfil (*mur*-thir *tid*-vil) occupies
spectacular site, sprawled across a bowl
: the head of the Taff Valley, ringed and
ocked with quarries and spoil heaps. It was
ven more spectacular 200 years ago when
ne town was at the heart of the Industrial
evolution, and this bowl was a crucible
lled with the fire and smoke of the world's
iggest ironworks.

Today all the industry has gone and un-
mployment runs at 27% more than the na-
onal average – it's said to be the toughest
own in Britain for jobseekers. But Merthyr
endeavouring to turn itself around, rede-
eloping former industrial sites and turning
s past into a tourist attraction.

Perhaps unusually for such an indus-
ial town, Merthyr Tydfil has produced two
nternationally famous fashion designers –
aura Ashley (famed for her flowery, femi-
ine designs in the 1970s) and Julien Mac-
onald (he of the shimmery, figure-hugging
resses favoured by Kylie and Britney).

Merthyr Tydfil means 'the place of Tyd-
l's martyrdom' – the town was named in
onour of a Welsh princess who, according
legend, was murdered for her Christian
eliefs in the 5th century. St Tydfil's Church
said to mark the spot where she died.

Merthyr remained a minor village until
ne late 18th century, when its proximity
iron ore, limestone, water and wood led
it becoming a centre of iron production.
he discovery of coal reserves upped the
nte, and by 1801 a string of settlements,
ach growing around its own ironworks –
yfarthfa, Penydarren, Dowlais, Pentrebach
nd others – merged to become the biggest
own in Wales (population 10,000, eight
imes the size of Cardiff at that time). Im-
nigrants came from all over Europe, and the
opulation peaked at 81,000 in the mid-19th
entury.

By 1803 Cyfarthfa was the world's big-
est ironworks. Ever more efficient ways
o make iron were pioneered, on the backs
f overworked labourers (including, until

1842, women and children as young as six)
who lived in appalling, disease-ridden conditions. By the 19th century Merthyr was a
centre of political radicalism. The Merthyr
Rising of 1831 was the most violent uprising
in Britain's history – 10,000 ironworkers,
angry over pay cuts and lack of representation, faced off against a handful of armed
soldiers, and rioting continued for a month.

As demand for iron and steel dwindled in
the early 20th century, one by one the ironworks closed down. Unemployment soared,
reaching as high as 60% in 1935. In 1939 a
Royal Commission even suggested that the
whole town should be abandoned. But community ties were strong and people stayed on.

The Taff Trail runs along the river on the
western edge of town, crossing the handsome railway viaducts of Cefn Coed (the
third biggest in Wales) and Pontsarn, both
completed in 1866, as it heads up to Pontsticill Reservoir.

◉ Sights & Activities

Cyfarthfa Castle   CASTLE

(☑01685-723112; Brecon Rd; ⊙10am-5.30pm Apr-
Sep, 10am-4pm Tue-Fri, noon-4pm Sat & Sun Oct-
Mar; P) FREE For a measure of the wealth
that accumulated at the top of the industrial
pile, check out this castle, built in 1824 by
William Crawshay II, overlooking his ironworks. Across the river from the castle are
the Cyfarthfa Blast Furnaces, all that remains
of them. The house is packed with stuff, from

THE ABERFAN DISASTER

On 21 October 1966 Wales experienced
one of its worst disasters. Heavy rain
loosened an already dangerously
unstable spoil heap above Aberfan, 4
miles south of Merthyr Tydfil, and sent
a 500,000-tonne mudslide of lique-
fied coal slurry down onto the village. It
wiped out a row of terraced houses and
ploughed into Pantglas primary school,
killing 144 people, most of them children.

Today the A470 Cardiff–Merthyr
Tydfil road cuts right through the spot
where the spoil heap once stood. The
site of the school has been turned into
a memorial garden, while the village
cemetery contains a long, double row
of matching headstones, a mute and
moving memorial to those who died.

DON'T MISS

RHONDDA VALLEY

Northwest of Cardiff, the Rhondda Valley – the most famous of the South Wales valleys – was once synonymous with coal mining. The closure of the last pit in 1990 left the valley bereft, but since then Rhondda has succeeded in converting an abandoned colliery into an interesting exploration of the region's industrial heritage.

Rhondda Heritage Park (☑ 01443-682036; www.rhonddaheritagepark.com; Trehafod; admission free; ☺ 9am-4.30pm, closed Mon Oct-Easter) brings new life to the old colliery buildings of the Lewis Merthyr coal mine (closed in 1983). The displays are fascinating. The one on the Tynewydd Colliery Disaster makes for sobering reading.

The highlight is the 40-minute underground Black Gold Tour (adult/child £3.50/2.50; ☺ 10am, noon & 2pm, bookings advised), where you don a miner's helmet and lamp and, accompanied by a guide (all are ex-miners), experience a simulated descent to the coalface. The compelling commentary vividly re-creates the experience of mine workers in the 1950s, and hammers home the social impact of the coal industry. Back at the surface, a multimedia show explores the story of coal mining in South Wales.

The park is 13 miles northwest of Cardiff, between Pontypridd and Porth; take the A470 and then the A4058. There are frequent trains from Cardiff Central station to Trehafod (£4, 35 minutes, half-hourly); the station's a 10-minute walk from the heritage park.

Egyptian and Roman artefacts to Wedgwood porcelain to a George Best tie rack.

Joseph Parry's Cottage   HISTORIC BUILDING
(☑ 01685-723112; 4 Chapel Row; ☺ 2-5pm Thu-Sun Apr-Sep) FREE To the south of the castle a row of 19th-century ironworkers' houses stands in bald contrast to Cyfarthfa Castle. At No 4 is Joseph Parry's Cottage, furnished in 1840s style and birthplace of Welsh composer and songwriter Joseph Parry (1841–1903).

Ynysfach Engine House   HISTORIC BUILDING
Across the river from the bus station is Ynysfach Engine House, a distinctive landmark that housed the huge beam engines that created the blast of hot air for the iron furnaces.

Trevithick's Tunnel   HISTORIC SITE
Trainspotters will love Trevithick's Tunnel, site of the first test of Richard Trevithick's steam-powered locomotive. In 1804 it was the first in the world to haul a load on rails – 10 tonnes of iron for 9.5 miles, at a speed of 4mph. It's off the A470 in Pentrebach.

Brecon Mountain Railway   HERITAGE RAILWAY
(☑ 01685-722988; www.breconmountainrailway.co.uk; adult/child £11/5.50) Between 1859 and 1964 this narrow-gauge railway hauled coal and people between Merthyr and Brecon. A 5.5-mile section of track, between Pant Station and Torpantau at the head of Pontsticill Reservoir, has been restored and operates steam locomotive trips. From April to October there are five departures. It takes 65 minutes with 20 minutes at Pontsticill (you can stay longer and return on a later train).

Pant Station is 3.5 miles north of Merthyr bus station; take bus 35 (20 minutes, four hourly Monday to Saturday) to Pant Cemetery stop, from where it's a five-minute walk.

✖ Eating

The Old Barn Tea Room   CAFE
(☑ 01685-383358; Ystradgynwyn; ☺ 11am-5pm May-Nov) A beautiful 18th-century barn, decked out with vintage furniture, that serves great cream teas and a fine Sunday lunch. To find it, head north out of town on the back road that leads through the national park and towards the Talybont Reservoir.

ⓘ Orientation

Merthyr sprawls across the head of the Taff Valley, and you'll need to do a bit of walking or cycling to see the sights. The train and bus stations are close together at the south end of town.

ⓘ Information

Tourist Office (☑ 01685-727474; www.merthyr.gov.uk; 14 Glebeland St; ☺ 9.30am-4pm Mon-Sat) Near the bus station.

ⓘ Getting There & Away

For cyclists, the Taff Trail heads south from here to Cardiff and north to Brecon.

Bus X43 connects Merthyr Tydfil with Cardiff (45 minutes), Brecon (37 minutes), Crickhowel (1½ hours) and Abergavenny (1½ hours). Bus X4 also heads to Abergavenny (1½ hours) and Cardiff (55 minutes).

Regular trains head to/from Cardiff (£5.30, one hour).

Swansea, the Gower & Carmarthenshire

Best Places to Eat

➡ Slice (p124)

➡ Joe's Ice Cream Parlour (p127)

➡ King's Head (p134)

➡ Angel Vaults (p137)

➡ Heavenly (p138)

Best Places to Stay

➡ Tides Reach Guest House (p127)

➡ King's Head (p134)

➡ Fronlas (p138)

➡ New White Lion (p139)

➡ Port Eynon YHA (p131)

Why Go?

This little slice of Wales sits between the Cambrian Mountains to the north, the Brecon Beacons to the east and attention-hogging Pembrokeshire to the west. But it has its own distinct attractions, the greatest of which is the craggy coastline and epic sand beaches of the Gower, which offers surfing, water sports of all sorts and undulating hikes. Swansea has something approaching big-city sophistication, with a glorious stretch of sand arcing between it and attractive little Mumbles. Inland, the fecund heartland of rural Carmarthenshire is little travelled, but is home to some intriguing prehistoric sights and enticing pubs, where you can enjoy the regional specialities of salt-marsh lamb and Penclawdd Cockles, harvested on the edge of the Gower since at least Roman times and a key ingredient in the iconic Welsh breakfast, laver bread.

When to Go

Water sports fans might want to brave high summer on the Gower to make the most of the golden beaches, though be aware that the narrow country roads – and the B&Bs and campgrounds – are likely to be crammed during this time.

Many hostels and campgrounds don't open till after Easter, and the winter period is pretty quiet. If you're hiking you might prefer to aim for late spring/early summer or the autumn. Come prepared for rain showers whatever time of year you visit.

The Gower Festival in July hosts classical music recitals in ancient churches, and Swansea holds a similarly high-powered music and arts festival in October.

Swansea, the Gower & Carmarthenshire Highlights

1 Watching the surf break at the Worms Head, or walking along the sand at dramatic **Rhossili Bay** (p131)

2 Marvelling at Norman Foster's intriguing glasshouse dome at the **National Botanic Garden of Wales** (p140), which harbours rare and endangered plants

3 Channeling your inner Jane Austen within the walled gardens and yew tunnels of the **Aberglasney Gardens** (p138)

4 Wandering expansive **Dinefwr Park & Castle** (p137) where you can go below stairs in the gracious manor house as well as explore the castle ruins

5 Exploring handsome **Llandovery** (p139), which has all the key ingredients of a fine Carmarthenshire town: Georgian architecture, castle ruins and a whole lot of pubs

6 Reliving a life of poetry and tragedy laid bare at the **Dylan Thomas Centre** (p113) in Swansea

7 Tracing Wales' industrial heritage inside the **National Waterfront Museum** (p113)

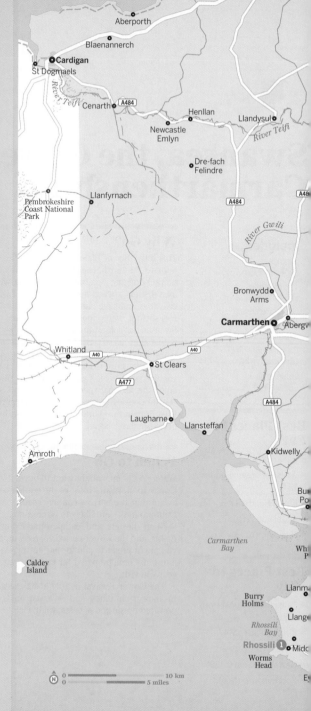

SWANSEA (ABERTAWE)

POP 239,000

Dylan Thomas called Swansea an 'ugly, lovely town', and that remains a fair description today. Though an arrival at the station is unlikely to set your pulse racing, Wales' second-largest city is set along the wonderful 5-mile sweep of Swansea Bay, ending to the southwest in the smart seaside suburb of Mumbles at the foot of the Gower Peninsula. Painted by Turner and compared by the poet Walter Savage Landor with the Bay of Naples, the golden arc of Swansea Bay is undeniably stunning. And the city itself is currently in the grip of a Cardiff-esque bout of regeneration, slowly transforming the drab, post-war centre into something worthy of its natural assets. A new marina, a national museum, a water park, an architecturally tricksy footbridge and a transport centre have already opened, and once-shabby Oystermouth Rd now has more the feel of a seaside boulevard.

Swansea makes up for some visual shortcomings with a visceral charm. A hefty student population takes to the city's bars with enthusiasm and a newly minted restaurant scene has emerged from among all the Chinese and Indian takeaways.

Swansea's Welsh name, Abertawe, describes its location at the mouth of the Tawe, where the river empties into Swansea Bay. The Vikings named the area Sveins Ey (Swein's Island), probably referring to the sandbank in the river mouth.

The Normans built a castle here, but Swansea didn't really get into its stride until the Industrial Revolution, when it developed into an important copper-smelting centre. Ore was first shipped in from Cornwall, across the Bristol Channel, but by the 19th century it was arriving from Chile, Cuba and the USA in return for Welsh coal.

By the 20th century the city's industrial base had declined, although Swansea's oil refinery and smaller factories were still judged a worthy target by the Luftwaffe, which devastated the city centre in 1941. It was rebuilt as a rather drab retail development in the 1960s, '70s and '80s, but gradual regeneration is slowly imbuing it with more soul.

A small pocket around Wind St and Castle Sq escaped the wartime bombing and retains a remnant of Georgian and Victorian Swansea as well as the ruins of 14th-century Swansea Castle (closed to the public). The castle was mostly destroyed by Cromwell in

SWANSEA IN...

One Day

Potter around Swansea's Maritime Quarter in the morning, splitting your time between the Dylan Thomas Centre and the National Waterfront Museum. Devote your afternoon to exploring the Gower: scoot down to Three Cliffs Bay, hike up to Arthur's Stone and wander along Rhossili Bay. Cap it off with a pint at the Joiners Arms before heading back to Mumbles. Stroll along the promenade before dinner, and a end with nightcap at Jones.

Two Days

Take a long, leisurely drive into the Carmarthenshire countryside. Take a gander at a Canadian goose at the National Wetland Centre (p138), storm **Kidwelly Castle** (Cadw; ☑ 01554-890104; www.cadw.wales.gov.uk; Castle St; adult/child £3/2.60; ☉ 9am-5pm Apr-Oct, 9.30am-4pm Mon-Sat & 11am-4pm Sun Nov-Mar) or get green-fingered at the National Botanic Garden of Wales (p140). Call into Carmarthen Market (p136) for some ham, then follow the A484 along the River Gwili and then the Teifi as far as pretty little Cenarth. If you've got time, call into the National Wool Museum (p140), before pressing on to Llandeilo for the night.

Three Days

After yesterday's driving, spend today within a few miles' radius of Llandeilo. Carreg Cennen Castle (p103) is a highlight of any Carmarthenshire trip. Spend the morning among the battlements before heading back to Llandeilo for lunch. Divide your afternoon between Dinefwr Park & Castle (p137) and Aberglasney Gardens (p138) or, if you didn't make it there yesterday, the National Botanic Garden.

1647, but had a brief lease of life as a prison in the 19th century.

Sights & Activities

National Waterfront Museum
MUSEUM
(www.museumwales.ac.uk/en/swansea; South Dock Marina, Oystermouth Rd, South Dock Marina; ⊙10am-5pm) FREE The Maritime Quarter's flagship attraction is the National Waterfront Museum, housed in a 1901 dockside warehouse with a striking glass and slate extension. The 15 hands-on galleries explore Wales' industrial history and the impact of industrialisation on its people from 1750 to the present day, making much use of interactive computer screens and audiovisual presentations. The effect can be a bit overwhelming but there is enough interesting stuff here to occupy several hours.

The museum's Waterfront Cafe has outside seats on the quay and is good for coffee and snacks.

Swansea Museum
MUSEUM
(www.swansea.gov.uk/swanseamuseum; Victoria Rd; ⊙10am-5pm Tue-Sun) FREE It would be hard to find a more complete contrast to the Waterfront Museum than the gloriously old-fashioned Swansea Museum – Dylan Thomas referred to it as 'the museum which should have *been* in a museum'. Founded in 1834, it remains charmingly low-tech, from the eccentric Cabinet of Curiosities and multi-handled wassail cups to the glass cases of archaeological finds from Gower caves. Pride of place goes to the Mummy of Hor at the top of the stairs, which has been here since 1887 – a video in the display room explains the process of its repair and conservation.

Dylan Thomas Centre
MUSEUM
(www.swansea.gov.uk/dtc; Somerset Pl; ⊙10am-4.30pm) FREE Housed in the former guildhall, the Dylan Thomas Centre contains an absorbing exhibition on the poet's life and work. Entitled *Man and Myth,* it pulls no punches in examining the propensity of 'the most quoted author after Shakespeare' for puffing up his own myth; he was eventually trapped in the legend of his own excessive drinking. Aside from the collection of memorabilia and a video documentary, what really brings his work to life is a series of recordings, including the booming baritone of Richard Burton performing *Under Milk Wood* and Thomas himself reading *Do Not Go Gentle into That Good Night,* the celebrated paean to his dying father. The cen-

tre runs a high-powered program of talks, drama and workshops.

Mission Gallery
GALLERY
(www.missiongallery.co.uk; Gloucester Pl; ⊙11am-5pm Tue-Sun) FREE Set in a beautifully converted 19th-century seamen's chapel, the modestly sized Mission Gallery stages some of Swansea's most striking exhibitions of contemporary art. It is also sells glassware, ceramics, jewellery, and art books and magazines.

Glynn Vivian Art Gallery
GALLERY
(www.swansea.gov.uk/glynnvivian; Alexandra Rd; ⊙10am-5pm Tue-Sun) FREE Housed in an elegant Italianate building (closed for major refurbishment till August 2014), the city's main art gallery displays a wide range of Welsh art – Richard Wilson, Gwen John, Ceri Richards, Shani Rhys James – alongside works by Claude Monet and Lucien Freud and a large ceramics collection.

Plantasia
ZOO
(www.plantasia.org; Parc Tawe Link; adult/child £3.95/2.95; ⊙10am-5pm) The name may conjure up images of Disney's hippos in tutus, but it's smaller critters that feature in this glass pyramid, parked between the Parc Tawe Shopping Centre and the river. Plantasia contains hundreds of species of exotic plants, plus attendant insects, reptiles, snakes, tropical fish (including piranhas), birds and tamarin monkeys. A coffee shop and range of kids' activities make it a popular rainy-day retreat.

Egypt Centre
MUSEUM
(www.egypt.swan.ac.uk; Swansea University, Mumbles Rd; ⊙10am-4pm Tue-Sat) FREE Swansea University is in the suburb of Sketty, halfway between the city centre and Mumbles, and the museum, adjoining the Taliesin Arts Centre (p125), displays a fascinating collection of everyday ancient Egyptian artefacts, ranging from a 4000-year-old razor to a mummified crocodile. Kids can try their hand at Muppet mummification.

LC2
SWIMMING
(www.thelcswansea.com; Oystermouth Rd; waterpark adult/child £7/4; ⊙4-8pm Mon-Fri, 9am-8pm Sat & Sun) The Marine Quarter's flash £32-million leisure centre includes a gym and a 10m indoor climbing wall, but best of all is the water park, complete with a wave pool, water slides and the world's first indoor surfing ride.

Swansea

Swansea Bay Rider TOY TRAIN
(adult/child £2.20/1.60) On weekends from May to August the *Swansea Bay Rider*, a toy-town road train, runs along the promenade between Blackpill Lido and the Mumbles.

✨ Festivals & Events

Swansea Bay
Summer Festival SUMMER FESTIVAL
(www.swanseabayfestival.co.uk) From May to September, the waterfront from the city round to the Mumbles is taken over by a smorgasbord of shows, fun fairs, carnivals, music, exhibitions, children's events and smaller festivals. Listen out for the legendary Morriston Orpheus Choir.

Swansea Festival of
Music & the Arts ARTS
(www.swanseafestival.org; ⊙ Oct) Concerts, drama, lectures and exhibitions are staged in five city venues during the first three weeks of October. The Welsh National Opera and the BBC National Orchestra of Wales may feature, as well as international companies.

Dylan Thomas Festival LITERATURE
(www.dylanthomas.com; ⊙ Oct-Nov) This celebrates Swansea's most famous son with poetry readings, talks, films and performances from 27 October (his birthday) to 9 November (the date he died); 2014 is the centenary year.

The Gower
Walking Festival WALKING
(www.gowerwalkingfestival.org; ⊙ Jun) A rich variety of volunteer-led walks are hosted in June. You could start the day with a dawn chorus walk and a study of resident and migrant birds, and end it with a Rhossili sunset stomp.

Swansea

⊙ Sights

⊛ Activities, Courses & Tours

⊜ Sleeping

⊗ Eating

⊙ Drinking & Nightlife

⊛ Entertainment

🛏 Sleeping

Leonardo's
GUESTHOUSE £

(☎01792-470163; www.leonardosguesthouse.co.uk; 380 Oystermouth Rd; s/d £40/50, without bathroom £28/45; 🤶) Leonardo's is the best in the long strip of budget seafront guesthouses on Oystermouth Rd, with small rooms in bright, sunny colours. Five of the nine bedrooms enjoy views over Swansea Bay and some have en suites.

Morgans
HOTEL ££

(☎01792-484848; www.morganshotel.co.uk; Somerset Pl; r £65-250; P) The city's first boutique hotel, set in the gorgeous red-brick and Portland stone former Ports Authority building, Morgans combines historic elegance with contemporary design and a high pamper factor – Egyptian cotton bed linen, suede curtains, big bathrobes and flat-screen TVs. An annexe across the road has lower ceilings but similar standards.

Christmas Pie B&B
B&B ££

(☎01792-480266; www.christmaspie.co.uk; 2 Mirador Cres, Uplands; s/d £49/78; P) The name suggests something warm and comforting, and this suburban villa does not disappoint – three tastefully decorated en suite bedrooms come with power showers and Egyptian cotton sheets, plus fresh fruit and an out-of-the-ordinary, vegetarian-friendly breakfast selection.

Mirador Town House
B&B ££

(☎01792-466976; www.themirador.co.uk; 14 Mirador Cres, Uplands; s/d from £69/95; 🤶) Kooky and kitsch in the extreme, all seven B&B rooms here are elaborately themed – Roman, Mediterranean, African, Spanish, Egyptian, Oriental and French – with murals on the walls and sometimes the ceilings as well.

(Continued on page 124)

CHRIS HEPBURN / GETTY IMAGES ©

Cardiff

1. Cardiff Bay (p44)
Cardiff Bay is lined with important institutions, including the Pierhead.

2. Cardiff Castle (p39)
The castle's Arab Room creates an elaborate Moorish look.

3. Royal Arcade (p62)
Cardiff's oldest arcade is a shopper's delight.

4. National Museum Cardiff (p42)
One of Britain's best museums.

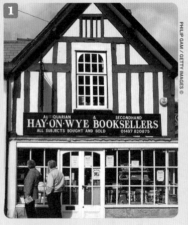

PHILIP GAM / GETTY IMAGES ©

Brecon Beacons & Southeast Wales

1. Hay-On-Wye (p89)
This picturesque little town is known as the second-hand book capital of the world.

2. Food
Seafood dishes dominate the local dining scene.

3. Tintern Abbey (p77)
These haunting ruins have inspired poets and artists for centuries.

4. Big Pit: National Coal Museum (p105)
Visitors can descend 90m to explore the dank, dark conditions of this old mine.

IMAGE SOURCE / GETTY IMAGES ©

wansea,
e Gower &
rmarthenshire

National Botanic Garden Wales (p140)
the size of London's Kew Gardens,
arden has a broad range of plant
ats.

Rhossili Down (p131)
93m Rhossili Down stands above
is considered Britain's best beach.

**National Waterfront
seum (p113)**
wer than 15 hands-on galleries
re Wales' industrial history.

JAMES OSMOND / GETTY IMAGES ©

GRAHAM BELL / GETTY IMAGES ©

mbrokeshire

astell Henllys (p176)
created Iron Age fort where young and old
ravel back in time.

embrokeshire Coast National
k (p152)
lished in 1952, this huge national park spans
st the entire Pembrokeshire coast.

t Davids (p161)
n's smallest city, St Davids has a mystical
ence.

kokholm Island (p158)
ugged island contains an abundance of bird
ncluding puffins.

GREENWALES / ALAMY / GETTY IMAGES ©

(Continued from page 115)

Crescent
B&B **££**

(☑ 01792-465782; www.thecrescentswansea. co.uk; 132 Eaton Cres, Uplands; s £40, d £65-99, family suite from £90; ☎) This jaunty, blue-painted Edwardian house has a great location, perched on a slope with great views across the rooftops to Swansea Bay. The bedrooms are immaculate with an antique feel (in keeping with the house) without being chintzy.

Dragon Hotel
HOTEL **££**

(☑ 01792-657141; www.dragon-hotel.co.uk; The Kingsway; r from £69; P ✳ ☎ ☱) This 1960s city-centre hotel has been given an expensive upgrade, with dragon-red carpets, orange backlighting and well-turned-out bedrooms. It may be a bit bland for some but it's well equipped, with a good-sized gym and a pool.

Eating

The main eat streets are Wind St and St Helen St in the centre, with a range of pubs, cafes and restaurants to cater to all budgets and appetites.

360 Cafe Bar
CAFE **£**

(www.360swansea.co.uk; Mumbles Rd; ⊘ 9am-7.30pm; ☎) This bright and breezy option sits on the beach, a half-hour walk from town. It serves burgers, salads and snacks (from £6) and there's a kids' menu. Tide tables are posted and daily activities such as beach tennis add to the fun – the cafe is part of 360 Beach and Watersports where you can learn paddleboarding, kayaking and kite surfing.

★ Slice
MODERN WELSH **££**

(☑ 01792-290929; www.sliceswansea.co.uk; 73-75 Eversley Rd; three-course dinner £35; ⊘ 6.30-9pm Thu-Sun) A simple and pleasing little restaurant with wooden floors and furniture and pale walls. The elegantly presented food is terrific: locally sourced meat, fish, cheese and beer, plus homemade bread and home-grown herbs.

Hanson at the Chelsea Restaurant
MODERN BRITISH **££**

(☑ 01792-464068; www.hansonatthechelsea.co.uk; 17 St Mary's St; mains £12-20, 2-/3-course lunch £13/17; ⊘ noon-2.15pm & 7-9.30pm Mon-Sat, noon-2.15pm Sun) Perfect for a romantic liaison, this elegant little dining room is discreetly

---

DYLAN THOMAS

Dylan Thomas is a towering figure in Welsh literature, one of those poets who seemed to embody what a poet should be: chaotic, dramatic, drunk, tragic and comic. His work, although written in English, is of the bardic tradition – written to be read aloud, thunderous, often humorous, with a lyrical sense that echoes the sound of the Welsh voice.

Born in Swansea in 1914, he lived an itinerant life, shifting from town to town in search of cheap accommodation and to escape debt. He married Caitlin Macnamara (a former dancer, and lover of Augustus John) in 1936, but had numerous infamous affairs. Margaret Thomas, who was married to the historian AJP Taylor, was one of his admirers and paid his Boathouse rent (mysteriously enough, AJP detested him). His dramatic inclinations sometimes spilt over into real life: during a stay in New Quay he was shot at by a jealous local captain.

Thomas was also a promiscuous pub-goer, honing the habit that eventually killed him in an astonishing number of taverns. By 1946 he had become an immense commercial success, making regular book tours to America, but his marriage was suffering. In December 1952 his father died – his failing health had inspired one of Thomas' most resonant poems *Do Not Go Gentle into That Good Night*. Less than a year later, a period of depression while in New York ended in a heavy drinking spell, and he died shortly after his 39th birthday.

Whether you're a fan, or whether you're just interested to know what all the fuss is about, you'll find plenty of sites in Swansea to stalk the shade of the maverick poet and writer. When you've exhausted them all, you can always head on to Laugharne.

Start at the Dylan Thomas Centre and then check out his statue gazing across the marina outside the Dylan Thomas Theatre. In Uplands, a plaque marks his birthplace, an unassuming terraced house where he wrote two-thirds of his poetry.

Perhaps the places where you're most likely to feel his presence are his beloved drinking haunts, which include No Sign Bar, Queen's Hotel and Uplands Tavern.

tucked away behind the frenzy of Wind St. Seafood's the focus and blackboard specials are chalked up daily. While the name sounds flash, the prices aren't too bad; a £20 three-course set dinner is offered from Monday to Thursday.

Didier & Stephanie
FRENCH £££

(📞 01792-655603; 56 St Helen's Rd; mains £16-19; ⏱ noon-2pm & 7-9pm Tue-Sat) The city centre's top restaurant is an intimate and relaxed place, run by the Gallic duo with their names on the door. It's well regarded for its French cooking, refined setting and attentive service, and offers good-value set menus at lunch (two/three courses £14/17).

🍷 Drinking & Nightlife

In a city synonymous with Dylan Thomas you'd expect some hard drinking to take place...and you'd be right. Swansea's main boozing strip is Wind St (pronounced to rhyme with 'blind', as in drunk), and on weekends it can be a bit of a zoo, full of generally good-natured alcopop-fuelled teens teetering around on high heels. *Buzz* magazine (free from the tourist office and bars around town) has its finger on the pulse of the local scene.

Monkey
CAFE, BAR

(www.monkeycafe.co.uk; 13 Castle St; ⏱ 10am-late) An organic, veggie-friendly cafe-bar by day, with chunky tables, big sofas, modern art and cool tunes, this funky little venue transforms after dark into Swansea's best alternative club, hosting DJs, live musicians, burlesque and salsa upstairs.

No Sign Bar
BAR

(www.nosignbar.co.uk; 56 Wind St) Once frequented by Dylan Thomas (it appears as the Wine Vaults in his story *The Followers*), the No Sign stands out as the only vaguely traditional bar left on Wind St. It's a long, narrow haven of dark-wood panelling, friendly staff, good pub grub and a seasonal beer selection; on weekends there's live music downstairs in the Vault. The window seats, looking out over the hectares of goose-bumped flesh on the street outside, offer a frisson of *schadenfreude*.

Queen's Hotel
PUB

(📞 01792-521531; Gloucester Pl) An old-fashioned corner pub with polished mahogany and brass bar, Victorian tiles and a range of cask-conditioned beers on tap, including Theakston's Old Peculier. Thomas propped up the bar here when he was a cub reporter around the corner at the *South Wales Evening Post*.

Uplands Tavern
PUB

(📞 01792-458242; 42 Uplands Cres) Yet another Thomas hang-out, Uplands still serves a quiet daytime pint in the Dylan Thomas snug. Come nightfall, it turns into a different beast altogether as the hub of the city's live-music scene. It's big and brassy with reasonably priced beer (Greene King Abbott real ale), pool tables and bands playing most nights to a mixed crowd of students and locals.

☆ Entertainment

Dylan Thomas Theatre
THEATRE

(📞 01792-473238; www.dylanthomastheatre.org. uk; Gloucester Pl) Home to Swansea Little Theatre, an amateur dramatic group of which Dylan Thomas was once a member. This company stages a wide repertoire of plays, including regular performances of your man's *Under Milk Wood*.

Swansea Grand Theatre
THEATRE

(📞 01792-475715; www.swanseagrand.co.uk; Singleton St) The city's largest theatre stages a mixed program of ballet, opera, musicals, theatre and pantomimes, plus a regular comedy club.

Taliesin Arts Centre
PERFORMING ARTS

(📞 01792-602060; www.taliesinartscentre.co.uk; Swansea University, Mumbles Rd) Part of the University of Wales, Swansea, this vibrant arts centre named after a 6th-century bard sits next door to the Egypt Centre (p113) and has a program of live music, theatre, dance and film.

🛈 Orientation

The compact city centre clusters around Castle Sq and pedestrianised Oxford St on the west bank of the River Tawe. To its south and east are the redeveloped docklands of the Maritime Quarter, linked to the new SA1 district on the Tawe's east bank by the graceful Sail Bridge (2003). The bus station and tourist office are on the western edge of the city centre, by the Quadrant shopping centre. The train station is 600m north of Castle Sq along Castle St and High St.

Uplands, where many guesthouses are found, is 1 mile west of the centre, on Mansel St and Walter Rd. From the south edge of the centre, Oystermouth Rd runs for 5 miles west, then south along Swansea Bay, becoming Mumbles Rd.

ℹ Information

Morriston Hospital (☎ 01792-702222; Heol Maes Eglwys, Morriston) Accident and emergency department, 5 miles north of the city centre.

Police Station (☎ 101; Grove Pl)

Swansea Tourist Office (☎ 01792-468321; www.visitswanseabay.com; Plymouth St; ⊙ 9.30am-5.30pm Mon-Sat year-round, plus 10am-4pm Sun school holidays)

ℹ Getting There & Away

BUS

Bus X63 links Swansea with Brecon (two hours); X40 with Carmarthen (45 minutes) and Aberystwyth (3¼ hours); and X13 with Llandeilo (1½ hours).

National Express destinations include London (£26, five hours), Chepstow (£12, two hours), Cardiff (£7.30, one hour), Carmarthen (£6, 45 minutes), Tenby (£8, 1½ hours) and Pembroke (£8, 1¾ hours).

TRAIN

Arriva Trains Wales (www.arrivatrainswales. co.uk) has direct services to Swansea from London Paddington (£28, three hours), Cardiff (£8.40, one hour), Carmarthen (£6.10, 45 minutes), Tenby (£13.70, 1½ hours), Llandeilo (£5.60, 57 minutes) and Llandrindod Wells (£11.70, 2½ hours).

ℹ Getting Around

BIKE

Part of the Celtic Trail (Sustrans National Route 4) hugs the bay for the lovely stretch from downtown Swansea to Mumbles; **Action Bikes** (☎ 01792-464640; www.actionbikesswansea. co.uk; 5 St David's Sq; half-/full day £12/18) rents bicycles.

BUS

First Cymru (www.firstgroup.com) runs local services; buses 2, 3 and 37 head to Newton Rd in Mumbles (20 minutes), departing from Oxford St. A Swansea Bay Day Ticket offers all-day bus travel in the Swansea and Mumbles area for £4.50; buy tickets from the driver.

PARKING

Outside of the main commercial strips you should be able to find free street parking; check signs carefully. In the centre, the car park near the intersection of Princess Way and Oystermouth Rd offers two hours free between 10am and 5pm, Monday to Saturday (unlimited at other times).

TAXI

Yellow Cabs (☎ 01792-644446)

LOVE SPOONS

All over Wales, craft shops turn out wooden spoons with contorted handles in a variety of different designs at a speed that would have left their original makers – village lads with their eyes on a lady – gawking in astonishment. The carving of these spoons seems to date back to the 17th century, when they were made by men to give to women to mark the start of a courtship. If you want to see carving in progress, the St Fagans National History Museum can usually oblige. Any number of shops will be happy to sell you the finished product.

Various symbols were carved; the meanings of a few of them are as follows:

Anchor I'm home to stay; you can count on me.

Balls in a cage, links in a chain Captured love, together forever; the number of balls or links may correspond to the number of children desired, or the number of years already spent together.

Bell Marriage.

Celtic cross Faith; marriage.

Double spoon Side by side forever.

Flowers Love and affection; courtship.

Horseshoe Good luck; happiness.

Key, lock, little house My house is yours.

One heart My heart is yours.

Two hearts We feel the same way about one another.

Vines, trees, leaves Our love is growing.

Wheel I will work for you.

THE MUMBLES (Y MWMBWLS)

Strung out along the shoreline at the southern end of Swansea Bay, Mumbles has been Swansea's seaside retreat since 1807, when the Oystermouth Railway was opened. Built for transporting coal, the horse-drawn carriages were soon converted for paying customers, and the now defunct Mumbles train became the first passenger railway service in the world.

Once again fashionable, with bars and restaurants vying for trade along the promenade, Mumbles received a boost to its reputation when its most famous daughter, Hollywood actress Catherine Zeta-Jones, built a £2 million luxury mansion at Limeslade, on the south side of the peninsula. Singer Bonnie Tyler also has a home here.

The origin of Mumbles' unusual name is uncertain, although one theory is that it's a legacy of French seamen who nicknamed the twin rounded rocks at the tip of the headland *Les Mamelles* – 'the breasts'.

◎ Sights

Mumbles Pier PIER
(☑ 01792-365220; www.mumbles-pier.co.uk; Mumbles Rd) At the end of a mile-long strip of pastel-painted houses, pubs and restaurants is a rocky headland abutted by a Victorian pier with a sandy beach below. Built in 1898, it houses the usual amusement arcade and a once-grand cafe festooned with chandeliers.

Oystermouth Castle CASTLE
(www.abertawe.gov.uk/oystermouthcastle; Castle Ave; adult/child £2.50/1.50; ☺11am-5pm mid-June–Sep) It wouldn't be Wales without a castle, hence the trendy shops and bars of Newton Rd are guarded by a majestic ruin. Once the stronghold of the Norman lords of Gower, it's now the focus of summer Shakespeare performances. There's a fine view over Swansea Bay from the battlements.

⌑ Sleeping

★ Tides Reach Guest House B&B ££
(☑01792-404877; www.tidesreachguesthouse.com; 388 Mumbles Rd; s £50, d £70-100; @ ⚆) Delicious ecoconscious breakfasts and stacks of local info are served with a smile at this waterfront guesthouse. Some rooms have sea views; our favourite is room 9, where the dormer windows open out to create a virtual deck from within the sloping roof.

Patricks with Rooms BOUTIQUE HOTEL £££
(☑ 01792-360199; www.patrickswithrooms.com; 638 Mumbles Rd; r £115-175) Patricks has 16 individually styled designer bedrooms in bold contemporary colours, with art on the walls, fluffy robes and, in some of the rooms, roll-top baths and sea views. The restaurant serves well-presented modern British food.

✗ Eating & Drinking

The famous Mumbles Mile – a pub crawl along Mumbles Rd – is not what it once was; many of the old faithful inns have succumbed to the gastropub trend. Newton Rd does have some rather nice wine bars, though, which aren't too bad for a spot of celebrity spotting.

★ Joe's Ice Cream Parlour ICE CREAM £
(☑ 01792-368212; www.joes-icecream.com; 524 Mumbles Rd; sweet snacks £2; ☺10.30am-5.30pm Mon, 9.30am-5.30pm Tue-Fri, 9.30am-6.30pm Sat, 11am-6.30pm Sun)

Jones WINE BAR
(☑ 01792-361764; www.jonesbar.co.uk; 61 Newton Rd) The best of the Newton Rd wine bars, Jones buzzes with 40-somethings giving the chandeliers a run for their money in the bling stakes. There's no chance Dylan Thomas ever did hang out here, or would if he still could, but there's a good wine list and a friendly vibe.

❶ Information

Mumbles Tourist Information (☑ 01792-361302; www.mumbleshead.info; Methodist Church, Mumbles Rd; ☺10am-5pm Mon-Sat, noon-5pm Sun Jul & Aug; 10am-4pm Mon-Sat Sep-Jun) It publishes the free *Mumbles Times* magazine.

❶ Getting There & Away

Buses 1, 2, 3 and 37 head between Swansea and Mumbles (20 minutes).

GOWER PENINSULA (Y GŴYR)

With its broad butterscotch beaches, pounding surf, precipitous clifftop walks and rugged, untamed uplands, the Gower Peninsula feels a million miles from Swansea's urban bustle – yet it's just on the doorstep. This 15-mile-long thumb of land stretching west from Mumbles was designated the UK's

QUENTIN GRIMLEY, WALES COAST PATH

Fancy a stroll? We asked Quentin Grimley, Coastal Access Project Officer for the Countryside Council of Wales, to tell us about the Wales Coast Path (www.walescoastpath.gov.uk), the first walking track to encompass a country's entire coastline.

Tell us about the path. The project started in 2007 with the intention to create a continuous coastal path around all of Wales. It opened in 2012, linking up existing coastal paths like Pembrokeshire, which has been around since 1970, and others such as Ceredigion and Anglesea. If you then walk the Offa's Dyke Path you can circle the whole of Wales.

How long does it take to walk the whole thing? It's 870 miles long. Walking every day for an average of 13 miles, it would take two months to complete – plus an additional two weeks if you finish with Offa's Dyke Path.

Are there any sections that you'd recommend for travellers with only a day or two to spare? Well, places like Pembrokeshire are already well known, so for somewhere a little less obvious, try the Gower Peninsula by Swansea. It's an Area of Outstanding Natural Beauty, it's easy to get to and it's never had a continuous coastal path before now.

first official Area of Outstanding Natural Beauty (AONB) in 1956. The National Trust (NT) owns about three-quarters of the coast and though there is no continuously way-marked path, you can hike almost the entire length of the coastline. The peninsula also has the best surfing in Wales outside Pembrokeshire.

The main family beaches, patrolled by lifeguards during the summer, are Langland Bay, Caswell Bay and Port Eynon. The most impressive, and most popular with surfers, is the magnificent 3-mile sweep of Rhossili Bay at the far end of the peninsula. Much of Gower's northern coast is salt marsh that faces the Burry Inlet, an important area for wading birds and wildfowl.

ℹ Information

Rhossili Visitor Centre (☏ 01792-390707; www.nationaltrust.org.uk/gower; Coastguard Cottages, Rhossili; ⊙ 10.30am-5pm mid-Feb–Dec, 10.30am-4pm Wed-Sun Jan–mid-Feb) The National Trust's centre has information on local walks and wildlife, and an audiovisual display upstairs.

ℹ Getting There & Around

Swansea's First Cymru buses head as far as Limeslade, Langland, Bishopston and Pennard Cliffs, and in summer to Caswell Bay, Parkmill, Oxwich Bay, Port Eynon and Rhossili. The Gower Explorer (day ticket adult/child £4.50/3.10) has year-round services looping the peninsula: 115 Llangennith–Reynoldston–Port Eynon; 117 Port Eynon–Oxwich–Parkmill; and 118 Rhossili–Port Eynon–Reynoldston–Swansea.

Carry coins if you're hoping to park anywhere near a beach. For Three Cliffs Bay, the Gower Heritage Centre always charges, whereas the NT car park at Southgate only charges at weekends and in summer. At Port Eynon they charge between April and September. The NT car park at Rhossili always charges, or you can park a five-minute walk up the road at the church (donation requested).

Mumbles Head to Three Cliffs Bay

Going west from Mumbles Head there are two small bays, Langland Bay and Caswell Bay, which are shingly at high tide but expose hectares of golden sand at low water. Both are easily reached from Swansea and are popular with families and surfers. About 500m west of Caswell, along the coast path, is beautiful Brandy Cove, a tiny secluded beach away from the crowds. West again is Pwlldu Bay, a shingle beach backed by a wooded ravine known as Bishopston Valley; you can walk there from Bishopston village (1.5 miles).

From Pwlldu Head the limestone Pennard Cliffs, honeycombed with caves, stretch westwards for 2 miles to Three Cliffs Bay. Halfway along is the National Trust's Pennard Cliffs car park (a little confusingly, it's in the village of Southgate, not Pennard; the Pennard Cliffs bus stop is also here). The car park is the starting point for scenic coastal walks east to Pwlldu (1.5 miles) and west to Three Cliffs Bay (1 mile).

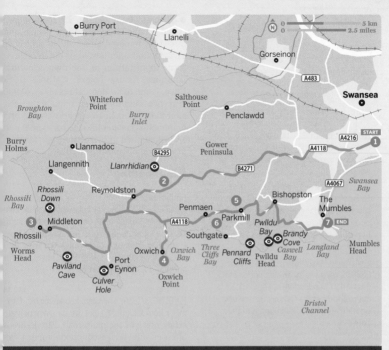

🏃 Driving Tour
Cairns, Castles & Cliffs on the Gower

START SWANSEA
END MUMBLES
LENGTH 40 MILES; 1 DAY

This drive takes you onto the Gower's back roads, which are crowded in holiday season but otherwise have an enjoyably remote feel. The itinerary explores the area's ancient past, taking in a Neolithic tomb and cairn, and brings you to two sweeping sandy beaches and a Tudor castle, winding up in picture-perfect Mumbles.

Take the A4118 west from **1 Swansea** and turn right onto the B4271, the secondary road running through the centre of the Gower Peninsula. Turn left on the back road signposted to Reynoldston, stopping above the village to walk across the heath to the Neolithic tomb known as **2 Arthur's Stone**, with its mighty capstone. The King Arthur Hotel (p134) down the hill in Reynoldston makes for a great pub lunch stop: as well as real ales it serves home-cooked Welsh specialities.

Continue down to the dramatic beach at **3 Rhossili**, where the wide sand beach is a haven for surfers, perhaps taking time to walk down to the undulating headland of the Worms Head, which is cut off at high tide. Backtrack to **4 Oxwich** and visit its romantically ruined Tudor castle. Turn off at Parkmill to view another mesmerising prehistoric monument: the Long Cairn at **5 Parc-le-Breos**. The meadow here, enclosed by trees, also features an early lime kiln and a cave that once sheltered Mesolithic hunters. Then walk down to nearby **6 Three Cliffs Bay**, one of the area's iconic beaches, only accessible on foot and punctuated by an arched cliff.

After a dip or a stroll, meander along to the **7 Mumbles**, a gorgeously picturesque little place: the Mumbles Mile was once known as an inn-crawl, but there's more of a sedate gastropub feel these days. The long promenade features enticing cafes, a long-established ice-cream parlour and an attractive backdrop of green cliffs.

OUTDOORS IN THE GOWER

Gower Coast Adventures (☏07866-250440; www.gowercoastadventures.co.uk) Speedboat trips to Worms Head from Port Eynon (adult/child £30/20) or Mumbles (adult/child £38/24).

Parc-Le-Breos Pony Trekking (☏01792-371636; www.parc-le-breos.co.uk; Parkmill; half-/full day £35/48) The rural byways and bridleways of Gower are ideal territory for exploring on horseback.

Welsh Surfing Federation Surf School (☏01792-386426; www.wsfsurf-school.co.uk; Llangennith) The governing body for surfing in Wales offers initial two-hour surfing lessons for £25 and subsequent lessons for £20.

Swansea Watersports (☏07989-839878; www.swanseawatersports.com; Pilot Wharf; windsurfing per hr £20) An accredited centre for sailing, power boating, jet skiing, kayaking and theory courses.

Three Cliffs Bay is named for the triple-pointed crag, pierced by a natural arch, that guards its eastern point. It is regularly voted one of the most beautiful beaches in Britain, even though the sand disappears completely at high tide.

The only way to get there is on foot. The most scenic approach is along the Pennard Cliffs, but you can also walk in from Parkmill village (1 mile), either along the valley of Pennard Pill or along the edge of the golf course to the east via the imposing ruins of 13th/14th-century Pennard Castle. It is dangerous to swim here at high tide, because of river currents, but safe at low water. The triple-pointed crag is a popular rock-climbing site.

The village of **Parkmill** is home to the garish but enjoyable Gower Heritage Centre, housed in a restored watermill, which features a cafe, puppet theatre, craft workshop, mill race, farm and fish pond. It's a good place to entertain kids when the weather drives you off the beaches.

Continue past the heritage centre and you'll reach bucolic **Parc-le-Breos**, nestled in a tiny valley between wooded hills. Just inside the park is the **Long Cairn**, a 5500-year-old burial chamber consisting of a stone entry-

way, a passageway and two chambers. It once contained the skeletons of 40 people, but these were removed, along with its protective earth mound, after it was dug out in 1869.

Some 100m further on the right, a natural limestone fissure houses **Cathole Rock Cave**, home to hunter gathers up to 20,000 years ago. Flint tools were found in the cave, alongside the bones of bears, hyenas and mammoths. Further into the park you'll find a limekiln, used until a century ago for the production of quicklime fertiliser.

🛏 Sleeping

Nicholaston Farm   CAMPGROUND £
(☏01792-371209; www.nicholastonfarm.co.uk; Penmaen; sites £16-27; hMar-Oct) A working farm that's a short walk from Tor Bay and Three Cliffs Bay. You can pick-your-own fruit and seasonal vegetables, plus they have a farm shop and a peak-season cafe.

Parc-le-Breos House   B&B ££
(☏01792-371636; www.parc-le-breos.co.uk; Parkmill; r from £80; P ⛱) Set in its own private estate north of the main road, Parc-le-Breos offers en suite B&B accommodation in a Victorian hunting lodge. The majestic lounge and dining room downstairs have log fires in winter, and woodland walks abound.

🍴 Eating & Drinking

Joiners Arms   PUB
(☏01792-232658; 50 Bishopston Rd, Bishopston) Pop into the slate-floored Joiners for a pint from the pub's own on-site microbrewery. A drop of the hoppy Three Cliffs Gold Ale is *the* one to try; they also do decent pub food.

Oxwich Bay

Oxwich Bay is a windy, 2.5-mile-long curve of sand backed by dunes. Road access and a large car park (£2) make it popular with families and water-sports enthusiasts (there's no lifeguard, but otherwise it's good for beginner surfers). Behind the beach lies **Oxwich Nature Reserve**, an area of salt and freshwater marshes, oak and ash woodlands and dunes; it is home to a variety of bird life and dune plants.

Set on a hillside above the beach, the stately grey ruin of **Oxwich Castle** (☏01792-390359; www.cadw.wales.gov.uk; Oxwich Castle Farm; adult/child £2.60/2.25; ⊙10am-5pm Apr-Sep), run by Cadw (the Welsh historic monuments agency), is less a castle and more a sumptuous 16th-century, mock-military Tudor mansion.

🛏 Sleeping

Oxwich Camping Park CAMPGROUND £
(☎ 07926-166096; Oxwich; ☺ Easter to Sept) A tree-fringed campground on the edge of Oxwich within easy reach of the beach. They don't allow caravans or motorhomes.

Port Eynon

The three-quarter-mile stretch of dunes at Port Eynon is Gower's busiest beach (in summer, at least), with half a dozen camping and caravan sites nearby.

Around the southern point of the bay is **Culver Hole**, a curious stone structure built into a gash in the cliff. Legend has it that it was a smugglers' hiding place, but the mundane truth is that it served as a dovecote (pigeons were a valuable food source in medieval times; the name comes from Old English *culufre*, meaning 'dove'). It's quite tricky to find – the easiest route is signposted from the youth hostel – and is only accessible for three hours either side of low tide; make sure you don't get caught out by the rising waters.

The coastal walk between Port Eynon and Rhossili (7 miles) is along the wildest and most dramatic part of the Gower coast, and is fairly rough going. Halfway along is **Paviland Cave**.

🛏 Sleeping

★ **Port Eynon YHA** HOSTEL £
(☎ 0845 371 9135; www.yha.org.uk; dm/r from £10/32) Worth special mention for its spec-

tacular location, this former lifeboat station is as close as you can get to the sea without sleeping on the beach itself. Cosier than your average youth hostel, its attractive lounge has sea views and is well stocked with board games.

Culver House APARTMENT ££
(☎ 01792-720300; www.culverhousehotel.co.uk; Port Eynon; apt from £99; @ ☎) A welcome change from B&Bs, this 19th-century house offers eight modern self-contained apartments with TVs that double as computers, plus dishwashers, laundry facilities and continental breakfasts delivered daily to your fridge.

Rhossili

Saving the best for last, the Gower Peninsula ends spectacularly with the 3 miles of golden sand that edges **Rhossili Bay**. Facing nearly due west towards the very bottom of Ireland, this is one of Wales' best and most popular surfing beaches. Indeed, it was recently voted Britain's Best Beach and 10th best in the world. Access to the beach is via a path next to the Worms Head Hotel, across from the NT car park in Rhossili village. When the surf's up, swimming can be dangerous.

The beach is backed by the steep slopes of **Rhossili Down** (193m), a humpbacked, heather-covered ridge whose updraughts create perfect soaring conditions for hanggliders and paragliders. On the summit are numerous Iron Age earthworks, a burial chamber called Sweyne's Howe and the remains of a WWII radar station. At its foot, behind the beach, is the Warren, the sand-buried remains of an old village. At low tide

SWANSEA, THE GOWER & CARMARTHENSHIRE PORT EYNON

THE RED LADY OF PAVILAND

Halfway along the Gower coast between Port Eynon and Rhossili is Paviland Cave, where in 1823 the Reverend William Buckland discovered a Stone Age human skeleton dyed with red ochre. As he also found jewellery buried along with the bones, the good Reverend assumed the deceased must be a woman. Being a devout Christian, he believed she must date from the Roman era, as she could not be older than the biblical flood. The 'Red Lady', as the skeleton became known, was therefore a Roman prostitute or witch, according to Buckland.

Modern analysis shows that the Red Lady was actually a man – possibly a tribal chief – who died, aged around 21, some 29,000 years ago. Dating from before Britain was abandoned during the last Ice Age, his are the oldest human remains found in the UK, and are recognised as the oldest known ritual burial in Western Europe. The Red Lady's peaceful seaside slumber is no more – he's now on display in the National Museum Cardiff.

the stark, ghostly ribs of the *Helvetica,* a Norwegian barque wrecked in a storm in 1887, protrude from the sand in the middle of the beach.

The southern extremity of the bay is guarded by Worms Head (from the Old English *wurm,* meaning 'dragon' – the rocks present a snaking, Loch Ness monster profile). There is a four-hour window of opportunity (two hours either side of low tide) when you can walk out across a causeway and along the narrow crest of the Outer Head to the furthest point of land. There are seals around the rocks, and the cliffs are thick with razorbills, guillemots, kittiwakes, fulmars and puffins during nesting season (April to July).

Pay close attention to the tides – tide tables are posted at the Rhossili Visitor Centre – as people are regularly rescued after being cut off by the rising waters. Among those who have spent a cold, nervous half-night trapped there was the young Dylan Thomas, as he relates in the story 'Who Do You Wish Was With Us?', from *Portrait of the Artist as a Young Dog.* If you do get stuck, do not try to wade or swim back. The currents are fierce and the rocks treacherous.

South of the village is the Viel (pronounced 'vile'), a rare surviving example of a patchwork of strip-fields first laid out in medieval times.

� Activities

Sam's Surf Shack   SURFING
(☑ 01792-390519; www.samssurfshack.com; Rhossili; board & wetsuit hire per day £22, bodyboard & wetsuit £20) Hire surfie gear at the Gower's most beautiful beach; they'll give you dryland instructions but they don't do lessons. Try bodyboarding to get a taste for the thrills of surfing.

✕ Eating

The Worms Head Hotel, which dominates Rhossili, is recommended for its epic beach views.

Bay Bistro & Coffee House   BISTRO £
(☑ 01792-390519; mains £5-8; ⊙ 10am-5.30pm daily summer, weekends & sunny days only in winter; ☑) A buzzy beach cafe with a sunny terrace, good surfy vibrations and the kind of drop-your-panini views that would make anything taste good – although the roster of burgers, sandwiches, cakes and coffee stands up well regardless. Summer nights are given over to al fresco meals (mains £10 to £14).

🛏 Sleeping

Pitton Cross Park   CAMPGROUND £
(☑ 01792-390593; www.pittoncross.co.uk; Rhossili; per pitch from £9 ; ℗) A site with a sea view: Pitton Cross has an idyllic location, plus approachable staff, good loos and a good shop.

Rhossili Bunkhouse   HOSTEL £
(☑ 01792-391509; www.rhossilibunkhouse.com; Rhossili Village Hall, Middleton; per dm bed £19; ℗ 🛜) Located in the village of Middleton within easy walking distance of Rhossili, this community-run bunkhouse is smarter than the name suggests: it's very well equipped, clean and comfortable. There's no food on site, but the kitchen is excellent and the friendly manager can arrange for the Bay Bistro to cook for you.

West Pilton House   B&B ££
(☑ 01792-391364; www.the-gower.com/bandb/westpilton/westpilton.htm; Rhossili; d £65; ℗) Two double rooms in a cream-painted Georgian house with views of the Bristol Channel and the lush surrounding farmland. It's near the coastal path, and well set up for walkers with OS maps and drying facilities.

Reynoldston

At the heart of the peninsula above the village of Reynoldston is Cefn Bryn, a ruggedly beautiful expanse of moorland that rises to a height of 186m. On a fittingly desolate ridge stands a mysterious Neolithic burial chamber capped by the 25-tonne quartz boulder known as Arthur's Stone (Coeten Arthur). In legend it's a pebble that Arthur removed from his boot; the deep cut in the rock was either made by Arthur's Excalibur or by St David; and the muddy spring beneath the stone grants wishes. Local lore also says that a woman who crawls around the stone at midnight during the full moon will be joined by her lover – if he is faithful.

The view from here is fantastic: you can see out to the edges of the Gower in every direction, and on a clear day you can see south to Lundy Island and the Devon and Somerset coast. It's a great spot to watch the sunset.

To find it, turn right on the road leaving the King Arthur Hotel in Reynoldston and look out for a rough parking area on your left. Looking north, you can see the stone on the horizon.

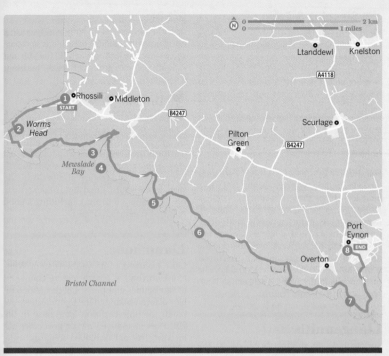

Walking Tour
A Wild Stretch of Coast

START RHOSSILI
FINISH PORT EYNON
LENGTH 7 MILES; 3 HOURS

This wonderful walk takes in a precipitate stretch of Gower coastline, topped with ancient hill forts and punctuated by beautiful sandy coves. It runs from Rhossili in the west to the quaintly touristy village of Port Eynon in the east; there's no refreshment en route so take food and water.

The walk starts at ❶ **Rhossili**, a high vantage point overlooking a beach that's been voted one of the best in the world. You might want to fuel up here at the Bay Bistro and Coffee House (p132). Follow the path down to the ❷ **Worms Head** – it is possible to walk out to the headland, but only at low tide or it will be partly submerged. On the high point facing the head is a Victorian coastguard station, still very much in use.

The route follows the coast above the golden beaches of Fall and ❸ **Mewslade** bays. Beyond, ❹ **Thurba Head** has been in Na-

tional Trust hands since 1933. More ancient history is evident at the ❺ **Knave Promontory Fort**, the largest of several Iron Age structures you'll see on the walk. Built 10,000 years ago, it would originally have been edged by a fence constructed from wooden stakes. Beyond is the fossil-rich Horse Cliff. And then you pass above the ❻ **Goats Hole**, a cave in the cliff (only accessible from the water) that was the site of a hugely significant prehistoric burial: the Red Lady of Paviland.

Beyond this point the cliffs descend and the going is easier for a long stretch. Then you begin to climb upwards to Port Eynon Point. There's an interesting detour near the summit – a steep descent to ❼ **Culver Hole**, a ruined medieval dovecote crammed into a fissure in the cliff. Bear in mind though that it's unsigned, a little hard to find, and the descent is steep.

On the fringes of ❽ **Port Eynon** you pass the Salt House, a salt-extraction unit built in the 16th century. At the village itself, you can catch the Gower Explorer bus back to Rhossili.

🛏 Sleeping & Eating

⭐ King Arthur Hotel
PUB ££

(☑ 01792-390775; www.kingarthurhotel.co.uk;
Higher Green, Reynoldston; s/d from £75/85; ℗)
Downstairs there's a lovely, old-fashioned,
wood-panelled bar with open fires that
serves real ales and good pub grub (mains
£6 to £17). The bedrooms above are less atmospheric but clean and comfortable. For
true romance, ask for stone-walled 18th-
century Guinevere's Cottage (self-catering
or B&B).

Fairyhill
HOTEL £££

(☑ 01792-390139; www.fairyhill.net; s/d from
£160/180; ℗ 🕾) An 18th-century country
house set in extensive grounds, Fairyhill
lives up to its name in terms of its location, aesthetics and holistic treatments.
Dinner-inclusive rates are available for the
acclaimed on-site restaurant (two-/three-
course lunch £20/25, mains £15 to £25). The
menu is pleasantly Welsh – salt-marsh lamb
and bay lobsters both feature.

Llangennith

Surfers head to this pretty village at the
northern end of Rhossili Bay where there's a
good local pub and a large camping ground
right by the beach. At the heart of the village is a Norman church with a blunt stone
tower containing a 13th-century limestone
effigy of a local knight. Right by the church,
PJ's Surf Shop (☑ 01792-386669; www.pjsurf-
shop.co.uk; wetsuits/surfboards/bodyboards per
day £10/10/5), owned by former European
surf champion Pete Jones, stocks all the
gear you'll need; it also operates a 24-hour
surfline (☑ 0901 603 1603; calls per min 60p).
There's a similar (but free) service online at
www.gowerlive.co.uk.

🛏 Sleeping

Hillend
CAMPGROUND £

(☑ 01792-386204; www.hillendcamping.com; Llangennith; sites around £20; ⊙ Easter-Oct) As close
to the beach as you can get, this large camping ground can accommodate 300 tents and
motor homes. On-site surfy-style Eddy's
Restaurant has brilliant views, and rustles
up breakfast for under a fiver, plus burgers,
curries and scampi (around £8).

⭐ King's Head
PUB ££

(☑ 01792-386212; www.kingsheadgower.co.uk;
Llangennith; from £85; ℗ 🕾) Up the hill be-

hind the pub of the same name, these two
stone blocks have been simply but stylishly
fitted out with modern bathrooms and pale
stone tiles. The location, behind the pub and
walking distance from the beach, makes it
a winner.

🍺 Drinking & Nightlife

King's Head
PUB

(☑ 01792-386212; www.kingsheadgower.co.uk;
Llangennith) The centre of Llangennith's social life is the King's Head, which serves real
ales – some courtesy of the new and award-
winning Gower Brewery a mile down the
road in Oldwalls – and home-cooked bar
meals (mains £6 to £12), including a good
range of vegetarian dishes.

Llanmadoc

Little Llanmadoc sits on the edge of Whit-
eford Burrows, a nature reserve composed
of sand dunes and pines. Check the tide tables before walking to the lighthouse on the
point, the only cast-iron lighthouse in the
UK. The cooperatively owned post office has
an attractive old fashioned shop and cafe,
selling tea and cake for walkers.

🍴 Eating & Drinking

Brittania
PUB ££

(☑ 01792-386 624; www.britanniainngower.co.uk;
Llanmadoc; mains £13-20) This plain 18th-cen-
tury inn may not be the most picturesque on
the Gower, but the food is a cut well above
average pub grub: their steak and ale pie is
sublime.

CARMARTHENSHIRE (SIR GAERFYRDDIN)

Castle-dotted Carmarthenshire has gentle valleys, deep-green woods and a small,
partly sandy coast. Caught between dramatic
neighbours – Pembrokeshire to the west and
the Brecon Beacons to the east – it remains
much quieter and less explored. Yet the appeal of its tranquil countryside hasn't gone
entirely unnoticed and charming places like
Llandeilo are starting to sprout upmarket
eateries, galleries and shops. If your interests stretch to gardens, stately homes and all
things green, add this quiet county to your
itinerary.

Laugharne (Talacharn)

POP 1200

Handsome little Laugharne (pronounced 'larn') sits above the tide-washed shores of the Taf Estuary, overlooked by a Norman castle. Dylan Thomas, one of Wales' greatest writers, spent the last four years of his life here, during which he produced some of his most inspired work, including *Under Milk Wood;* the town is one of the inspirations for the play's fictional village of Llareggub (spell it backwards and you will get the gist).

On Thomas' first visit to Laugharne he described it as the 'strangest town in Wales', but returned repeatedly throughout his restless life. Many Thomas fans make a pilgrimage here to see the Boathouse where he lived, the shed where he wrote and (drastically made-over) Brown's Hotel where he drank – he used to give the pub telephone number as his contact number.

Dylan and Caitlin Thomas are buried in a grave marked by a simple white, wooden cross in the churchyard of St Martin's Church, on the northern edge of the town. **Dylan's Walk** is a scenic 2-mile loop that continues north along the shore beyond the Boathouse, then turns inland past a 17th-century farm and back via St Martin's Church. It's clearly signposted.

◉ Sights

Dylan Thomas Boathouse　　　MUSEUM
(www.dylanthomasboathouse.com; Dylan's Walk; adult/child £4.20/3.20; ◷10am-5.30pm May-Oct, 10.30am-3.30pm Nov-Apr) Except at high tide, you can follow a path along the shoreline below the castle, then up some stairs to a lane that leads to the boathouse where the poet lived from 1949 to 1953 with his wife Caitlin and their three children. It's a beautiful setting, looking out over the estuary with its 'heron-priested shore', silent except for the long, liquid call of the curlew and the urgent 'pleep pleep pleep' of the oystercatcher, birds that appear in Thomas' poetry of that time.

The parlour of the Boathouse has been restored to its 1950s appearance, with the desk that once belonged to Thomas' schoolmaster father and recordings of the poet reading his own works. Upstairs are photographs, manuscripts, a short video about his life, and his death mask, which once belonged to Richard Burton; downstairs is a coffee shop.

Along the lane from the Boathouse is the old shed where Thomas did most of his writing. It looks as if he has just popped out, with screwed-up pieces of paper littered around, a curiously prominent copy of *Lives of the Great Poisoners* and, facing out to sea, the table where he wrote *Under Milk Wood* and poems such as *Over Sir John's Hill* (which describes the view).

Laugharne Castle　　　CASTLE
(www.cadw.wales.gov.uk; Laugharne; adult/child £3.20/2.80; ◷10am-5pm Apr-Oct) Built in the 13th century, Laugharne Castle was converted into a mansion in the 16th century for John Perrot, thought to be the illegitimate son of Henry VIII. It was landscaped with lawns and gardens in Victorian times, and the adjoining Castle House was leased by Richard Hughes, author of *High Wind in Jamaica*. Hughes was a friend of Dylan Thomas, who sometimes wrote in the little gazebo looking out over the estuary.

★ Festivals & Events

Laugharne Weekend　　　LITERATURE
(s452743659.websitehome.co.uk) This vibrant small-scale festival held in April concentrates on music and writing by artists with a Welsh connection.

⊨ Sleeping

Boat House　　　B&B ££
(☑01994-427263; www.theboathousebnb.co.uk; 1 Gosport St; £80; @🕾) Friendly, homey and tastefully decorated, the blue-painted Boat House is the smartest B&B in town, with four superior rooms. The building was formerly the Corporation Arms pub, where Dylan Thomas told stories in exchange for free drinks. The great home-cooked breakfasts would assuage even Thomas' legendary hangovers.

Keepers Cottage　　　B&B ££
(☑01994-427404; www.keepers-cottage.com; s/d £60/80; Ⓟ🕾) Sitting on the top of the hill by the main approach to town, this pretty cottage has simply decorated but very comfortable rooms. Complimentary bottled water and glasses of wine are a nice touch.

Corran　　　HOTEL £££
(☑01994-427417; www.thecorran.com; East Marsh; from £225; Ⓟ🕾🏊) Having had a £5 million makeover, you would expect this converted Georgian farm on the salt-marsh flats south of Laugharne to be luxurious. And it is. Rooms have big beds, bold colours and roll-top baths; there's also massage therapy on

WORTH A TRIP

KIDWELLY CASTLE

The small town of Kidwelly, at the mouth of the River Gwendraeth Fach, is dominated by the impressive pigeon-inhabited remains of Kidwelly Castle, a forbidding grey eminence that rises above a narrow waterway dotted with gliding swans. It was founded by the Normans in 1106, but most of the system of towers and curtain walls was built in the 13th century in reaction to Welsh uprisings. If it looks at all familiar, that may be because it featured in the opening scene of Monty Python and the Holy Grail.

Trains head to Kidwelly from Carmarthen (£3.60, 16 minutes) and Swansea (£6.60, 34 minutes).

tap, and a convivial, clubbish lounge bar and restaurant.

Eating

Cors Restaurant MODERN WELSH £££
(☑ 01994-427219; www.thecors.co.uk; Newbridge Road; mains £19-24; ⊙ 7pm-midnight Thu-Sat, noon-3pm Sun; ℗) A colourful, stylish and pleasantly eccentric restaurant that serves excellent local seasonal food such as salt marsh lamb. They are just off the main street, and have a beautiful bog garden ('cors' means bog). Just be aware of the limited opening hours.

ℹ Getting There & Away

Bus 222 runs from Carmarthen to Laugharne (30 minutes).

Carmarthen (Caerfyrddin)

POP 14,200

Carmarthenshire's county town is a place of legend and ancient provenance, but it's not the kind of place you'll feel inclined to linger in. It's a handy transport and shopping hub, but there's not a lot to see. The Romans built a town here, complete with a fort and amphitheatre. A couple of solid walls and a few crumbling towers are all that remains of Carmarthen's Norman castle, which was largely destroyed in the Civil War.

Most intriguingly, Carmarthen is reputed to be the birthplace of the most famous wizard of them all (no, not Harry Potter) –

Myrddin of the Arthurian legends, better known in English as Merlin. An oak tree planted in 1660 for Charles II's coronation came to be called 'Merlin's Tree' and was linked to a prophecy that its death would mean curtains for the town. The tree died in the 1970s and the town, while a little down at heel, is still standing. Pieces of the tree are kept under glass at the Carmarthenshire County Museum.

◉ Sights & Activities

Carmarthen Market MARKET
(www.carmarthenmarket.co.uk; Market Way; ⊙ 9.30am-4.30pm Mon-Sat) There's been a market here since Roman times and in 1180 it was given a royal charter. The main indoor market has an edgy modern feel and sells a bit of everything, from produce to antiques. On Wednesday and Saturday the general market spills out onto Red St, while on Friday there's a farmers market.

Oriel Myrddin GALLERY
(Merlin Gallery; ☑ 222775; www.orielmyrddingallery.co.uk; Church Lane; ⊙ 10am-5pm Mon-Sat) FREE Housed in a former art college, stylish little Oriel Myrddin stages changing exhibitions of contemporary art. The shop sells a nice range of crafts and art books.

King Street Gallery GALLERY
(www.kingstreetgallery.co.uk; King St; ⊙ 10am-5pm Mon-Sat) FREE Opposite Oriel Myrddin is the King Street Gallery, which sells interesting works by a cooperative of 29 local painters, sculptors, ceramicists and printmakers.

Carmarthenshire County Museum MUSEUM
(☑ 01267-228696; www.carmarthenmuseum.org.uk; Abergwili; ⊙ 10am-4.30pm Mon-Sat) FREE Located in the country-house setting of a 13th-century bishop's palace, this museum is a musty emporium of archaeology, Egyptology, pottery and paintings, with re-creations of a Victorian schoolroom and a collection of prehistoric standing stones. The museum is 2 miles east of Carmarthen on the A40; take bus 280 or 281 (11 minutes).

Gwili Steam Railway STEAM TRAIN
(☑ 01267-238213; www.gwili-railway.co.uk; adult/child £9/3) The standard-gauge Gwili Steam Railway runs along the lovely Gwili Valley, departing from Bronwydd Arms, 3.5 miles north of Carmarthen on the A484. It runs nearly daily in August; check the website or Carmarthen tourist office for a full timeta-

ble. Bus 460 between Carmarthen (16 minutes) and Cardigan (one hour and 10 minutes) stops at Bronwydd Arms.

✗ Eating

Carmarthen's contribution to Welsh gastronomy is a salt-cured, air-dried ham. Local legend has it that the Romans liked the recipe so much that they took it back to Italy with them. Look for it at the market.

Cafe at No 4 Queen St   CAFE £
(☑ 01267-220461; 4 Queen St; mains £4-8; ☺ 9am-5pm Mon-Sat) This chic and friendly little corner cafe right in the middle of Carmarthen brews the best coffee in town and serves fantastic homemade cakes and scones, as well as soups, salads, sandwiches and daily specials.

★ Angel Vaults   MODERN WELSH ££
(☑ 01267-238305; www.angelvaultsrestaurant.co.uk; 3 Nott Sq; 2-/3-course lunch £12/16, dinner £25/30; ☺ Tue-Sat 11am-late) For a swanky night out, locals head to Angel Vaults for heavenly food and then finish off across the square at Diablo's for devilish cocktails. The decor marries the modern and ancient, with a beautiful 15th-century limestone window linking the two halves of the upstairs dining room. A locally focused menu features Pembrokeshire salmon and scallops, Gower salt marsh lamb, and Welsh beef and cheeses.

❶ Information

Tourist Office (☑ 01267-231557; www.discovercarmarthenshire.com; Old Castle House; ☺ 9.30am-4.30pm Mon-Sat)

❶ Getting There & Away

The main bus stop is on Blue St. Bus X40 links Carmarthen with Cardiff (two hours), Swansea (45 minutes) and Aberystwyth (2¼ hours). Take bus 280 or 281 for Llandeilo (40 minutes) and Llandovery (1½ hours), 322 for Haverfordwest (one hour) and 460 for Cardigan (1½ hours).

National Express (www.nationalexpress.com) destinations include London (£26, 5¾ hours), Chepstow (£19, 2¼ hours), Swansea (£6, 45 minutes), Tenby (£5.50, 40 minutes), Pembroke (£5.50, one hour) and Haverfordwest (£7, 1½ hours).

The train station is 300m south of town across the river. There are direct trains to Cardiff (£17.60, 1¾ hours), Swansea (£8.60, 45 minutes), Fishguard Harbour (£8.80, 49 minutes), Tenby (£8.70, 41 minutes) and Pembroke (£8.70, 1¼ hours).

Llandeilo

POP 2900

Set on a hill encircled by the greenest of fields, Llandeilo is little more than a handful of narrow streets lined with grand Georgian and Victorian buildings and centred on a picturesque church and graveyard. The surrounding region was once dominated by large country estates, and though they have long gone, the deer, parkland trees and agricultural character of the landscape are their legacy. The genteel appeal of such a place can't be denied, so it's small wonder that Llandeilo's little high street is studded with fashionable shops and eateries.

Used by many travellers as a springboard for the wilder terrain of the Brecon Beacons, it's within a short drive of iconic Carreg Cennen castle (p103).

◉ Sights

Dinefwr Park & Castle   HISTORIC BUILDING
(NT; www.nationaltrust.org.uk; adult/child £3.20/1.80; ☺ 11am-5pm) National Trust–run Dinefwr is a large, landscaped estate just to the west of Llandeilo, home to fallow deer and a herd of rare White Park cattle. Recent archaeological digs uncovered remains of a roman fort here. At the estate's heart is a wonderful 17th-century manor, **Newton House**, made over with a Victorian facade in the 19th century. It's presented as it was in Edwardian times, focusing particularly on the experience of servants in their downstairs domain; recordings start as you enter each room. Other rooms recall Newton's WWII incarnation as a hospital. The **tearoom** serves Welsh set teas, sarnies, Welsh cakes and Bara Brith.

The castle is set on a hilltop in the southern corner of the estate and has fantastic views across the Tywi to the foothills of the Black Mountain. In the 17th century it suffered the indignity of being converted into a picturesque garden feature. There are several marked walking routes around the grounds, some of which are accessible to disabled visitors.

Bus 280 between Carmarthen and Llandeilo stops here.

Aberglasney Gardens   GARDENS
(www.aberglasney.org; Llangathen; adult/child £8/4; ☺ 10am-6pm Apr-Sep, 10.30am-4pm Oct-Mar) Wandering through the formal walled

DON'T MISS

NATIONAL WETLAND CENTRE

Covering 97 hectares on the northern shore of the Burry Inlet, across from the Gower Peninsula, the **National Wetland Centre** (☑ 01554-741087; www.wwt.org.uk/llanelli; Llanelli; adult/child £7.05/3.86; ⊗ 9.30am-5pm Apr-Sep, 9.30am-4.30pm Oct-Mar; ℗) is one of Wales' most important habitats for waders and waterfowl. The big attraction for birdwatchers is the resident population of little egret, whose numbers have increased from a solitary pair in 1995 to around 400. Winter is the most spectacular season, when up to 60,000 birds converge on the salt marsh and mudflats; species include oystercatchers, greylag geese, gadwalls, widgeons, teals and black-tailed godwits. Flashiest of all are the resident flock of nearly fluorescent pink Caribbean flamingos.

There's always plenty on for the little 'uns during the school holidays. Late spring's Duckling Days are filled with downy cuteness, while in the summer months there are canoes and bikes to borrow. There are plenty of hides and observation points, and you can hire binoculars (£5) if you don't have your own.

Approaching from the southeast, take the A484 and turn left onto the B4304. Trains head to Llanelli from Carmarthen (£6.40, 25 minutes) and Swansea (£4.20, 15 minutes); the centre is a 2.5-mile walk from the station.

gardens of Aberglasney House, 4 miles west of Llandeilo, feels a bit like walking into a Jane Austen novel. The gardens date from the 17th century and contain a unique cloister built solely as a garden decoration. You'll also find a pool garden, a 250-year-old yew tunnel and a 'wild' garden in the bluebell woods to the west. Several derelict rooms in the central courtyard of the house have been converted into a glass-roofed atrium garden full of subtropical plants such as orchids, palms and cycads.

Inside the gardens, a whitewashed and flagstoned **cafe** with an outside terrace sells coffee, cakes and snacks.

Aberglasney is in the village of Llangathen, just off the A40. Bus 280 between Carmarthen and Llandeilo stops on the A40, 500m north of the gardens.

🛏 Sleeping

★**Fronlas**   B&B **££**
(☑ 01558-824733; www.fronlas.com; 7 Thomas St; s/d from £55/65; ℗ 🛜) A Victorian town house given a chic makeover, Fronlas has three rooms dressed in fresh tones, designer wallpaper and travertine marble tiles. A similarly well-attired guest lounge has an honesty bar and a DVD library.

Plough   HOTEL **££**
(☑ 01558-823431; www.ploughrhosmaen.com; s/d from £70/90; ℗ 🛜) On the A40, just north of Llandeilo, this baby-blue inn offers hip, contemporary rooms, some with countryside views. The standard rooms are spacious

enough but the corner-hogging executives have cat-swinging space and then some.

🍴 Eating

★**Heavenly**   PATISSERIE **£**
(☑ 01558-22800; www.heavenlychoc.co.uk; 60 Rhosmaen St; ⊗ 9.30am-5pm Mon-Sat) Believe the name and enter an Aladdin's cave stacked with handcrafted chocolates, artisanal ice cream and enticing pastries and cakes. Grab something yummy and head to the benches by the churchyard for a taste of sweet paradise.

Olive Branch   DELI **£**
(☑ 01558-82303; www.olivebranchdeli.co.uk; Market St; ⊗ 9am-5pm Mon-Sat) This little deli has a whitewashed interior where they'll make you up a quality baguette with organic bread and local cheese. They serve a soup of the day, plus they sell all sorts of Welsh honey, ales and cheeses, plus quiches and cakes.

Y Capel Bach Bistro at the Angel   BISTRO **££**
(☑ 01558-822765; 62 Rhosmaen St; lunch £5-10; ⊗ 11.30am-3pm & 6-11pm Mon-Sat) A lively blackboard menu, hung between an unusual display of historical wedding photos, announces fresh daily specials at this popular gastropub. Thursday nights are devoted to ethnically themed buffets (£10), while a set-price menu is offered otherwise (two/three courses £12.95/14.95).

🛍 Shopping

Fountain Fine Art   ARTS, CRAFTS

(📞 01558-824244; www.fountainfineart.com; 115 Rhosmaen St; ⏱10.30am-5pm Tue-Sat) This fountain overflows with excellent local art, including many recognisable landmarks and landscapes – making for excellent, if rather pricey, holiday mementos.

🛈 Getting There & Away

Buses 280 and 281 between Carmarthen (40 minutes) and Llandovery (37 minutes) stop here, along with bus X13 from Swansea (1½ hours).

Llandeilo is on the Heart of Wales Line, with direct services to Swansea (£5.60, 57 minutes), Llandovery (£2.50, 19 minutes), Llanwrtyd Wells (£3.90, 45 minutes), Llandrindod Wells (£6.10, 1¼ hours), Knighton (£8.60, two hours) and Shrewsbury (£11, three hours).

Llandovery (Llanymddyfri)

POP 2600

Lovely Llandovery is an attractive market town that makes a good base for exploring the western fringes of the Brecon Beacons National Park. The name means 'the church among the waters', and the town is indeed surrounded by rivers, sitting at the meeting place of three valleys: the Tywi, the Bran and the Gwydderig.

It was once an important assembly point for drovers taking their cattle towards the English markets. The Bank of the Black Ox – one of the first independent Welsh banks – was established here by a wealthy cattle merchant.

⊙ Sights

Heritage Centre   INTERPRETATION CENTRE

(📞 01550-720693; www.llandovery.org.uk; Kings Rd; ⏱10am-5pm Easter-Oct; 10am-4pm Mon-Sat, 11am-1pm Sun Nov-Easter) FREE Doubling as the tourist office, this centre has displays about the drovers, the Black Ox bank, local legends and the Heart of Wales railway. Cleverly, faces are projected onto life-sized statues of important identities to bring to life the history of the town. The helpful staff can sort you out with information on walks in Brecon Beacons National Park, to the south, and the moorlands and valleys of Mynydd Epynt, to the east.

Llandovery Castle   CASTLE

Across the car park from the heritage centre rises the shattered ruin of the motte-and-bailey Llandovery Castle, which was built in 1116. The castle changed hands many times between the Normans and the Welsh, and between one Welsh prince and another, taking a severe beating in the process; it was finally left to decay after Owain Glyndŵr had a go at it in 1403. It's fronted by an eerie disembodied stainless-steel statue commemorating Llewellyn ap Gruffydd Fychan, who was gruesomely hung, drawn and quartered by Henry IV for refusing to lead him to Owain Glyndŵr's base.

Dinefwr Craft Centre   MARKET

The town's Victorian market hall now has a cafe and a couple of shops selling local handicrafts of varying descriptions, including lovespoons.

🛏 Sleeping

★Drovers   B&B ££

(📞 01550-721115; www.droversllandovery.co.uk; 9 Market Sq; s/d from £45/65; 🅿🛜) This attractive Georgian house on the town's main square has a comfortably old-fashioned feel with its ancient stone hearth, antique furniture and simply decorated bedrooms. You can take breakfast in front of a roaring fire in winter.

★New White Lion   BOUTIQUE HOTEL £££

(📞 01550-720685; www.newwhitelion.co.uk; 43 Stone St; s/d from £70/100; 🅿🛜) With its exterior an inviting chocolate-milkshake colour and its opulent interiors just shy of over-the-top, this boutique hotel is a stylish proposition indeed. There are only seven rooms, so book ahead.

🍴 Eating

Castle Hotel   PUB ££

(📞 01550-720343; www.castle-hotel-llandovery.co.uk; Kings Rd; mains £9-25; ⏱7am-11pm) A hugely successful makeover of a traditional handsome pub, it eschews the prevalent boutique style and goes for something more simple and authentic: a rambling sequence of low-ceilinged rooms with log fires. As far as food goes, try the Carmarthenshire dry-aged beef, cooked in a charcoal oven, or opt for a Welsh afternoon tea, complete with Welsh cakes and Bara Birth. The Red Giraffe Studio, selling Welsh blankets and cushions and African artefacts, is an unexpected bonus.

> **DON'T MISS**
>
> ## NATIONAL BOTANIC GARDEN OF WALES
>
> Concealed in the rolling Tywi valley countryside, the lavish **National Botanic Garden of Wales** (www.gardenofwales.org.uk; Llanarthne; adult/child £8.50/4.50; ☺10am-6pm Apr-Oct, 10am-4.30pm Nov-Mar) is twice the size of London's Kew Gardens, though it isn't as mature. Opened in 2000, the garden is still a work in progress, with new features being added every year.
>
> Formerly an aristocratic estate, the garden has a broad range of plant habitats, from lakes and bogs to woodland and heath, and has lots of decorative areas too – a walled garden, a Japanese garden and an apothecaries' garden – and educational exhibits on plant medicine and organic farming. The centrepiece is the Norman Foster–designed Great Glasshouse, an arresting glass dome that's sunk into the earth and houses endangered plants from Mediterranean climes all over the world.
>
> The garden is east of Carmarthen; take the A48 out of town (signposted Swansea and the M4) and after 8 miles take the B4310 on the left (signposted Nantgaredig), then follow the signs to the garden.

❶ Getting There & Away

Buses 280 and 281 head to Llandeilo (37 minutes) and Carmarthen (one hour 23 minutes), and bus 64 heads to Brecon (45 minutes).

By train, Llandovery is on the Heart of Wales Line, with direct services to Swansea (£8, 93 minutes), Llandeilo (£3.20, 19 minutes), Llanwrtyd Wells (£2.90, 23 minutes), Llandrindod Wells (£4.70, 58 minutes) and Knighton (£8.40, 96 minutes).

North Carmarthenshire

Pumsaint

Set in a beautiful wooded estate near Pumsaint, the **Dolaucothi Gold Mines** (☎01558-650177;www.nationaltrust.org.uk;adult/child £5.45/2.60; ☺11am-5pm mid-Mar–Oct) are on the site of the only known Roman gold mine in the UK. The Romans left around AD 120, but the locals carried on for a couple of hundred more years.

Mining recommenced with the Victorians and by the time the mine was finally closed down in 1938 the works employed more than 200 men.

The exhibition and the mining machinery above ground are interesting, but the main attraction is the chance to go underground on a guided tour of the old mine workings. Back at the surface, there's a sediment-filled water trough where you can try your hand at panning for gold.

The mines are 10 miles northwest of Llandovery, off the A482.

Dre-fach Felindre

The Cambrian Mills factory, world famous for its high-quality woollen products, closed in 1984 and the **National Wool Museum** (☎01559-370929; www.museumwales.ac.uk; ☺daily Apr-Sep, 10am-5pm Tue-Sat Oct-Mar) **FREE** has taken its place. Former mill workers are often on hand to get the machines clickety-clacking, but there's also a working commercial mill next door where you can watch the operations from a viewing platform. A cafe is on site, as is a gift shop selling snugly woollen blankets.

The museum is positioned in verdant countryside at Dre-fach Felindre, 14 miles north of Carmarthen and 14 miles southeast of Cardigan, signposted from the A484.

Henllan

Pocket-sized steam locomotives puff their way along the wonderful little **Teifi Valley Railway** (☎01559-371077; www.teifivalleyrailway.org; adult/child £7.50/5; ☺Apr-Oct), a 2-mile stretch of narrow-gauge line at Henllan (14 miles southeast of Cardigan). They run to a complicated timetable, so check on the website or with the Cardigan tourist office before making the trip.

Cenarth

The village of Cenarth occupies a picturesque spot by an old stone bridge over the River Teifi, at the foot of a stretch of rapids. It's home to the **National Coracle Centre** (☎01239-710980; www.coracle-centre.co.uk; adult/child £2.50/1.50; ☺10.30am-5.30pm Easter-

Oct), which comprises a 17th-century flour mill and a collection of coracles (small boats made of hide and wicker) from all over the world, along with exhibits and demonstrations showing how these fragile craft were made and used. If you're wondering what one looks like but don't fancy paying the admission, there's one attached to the wall of the 16th-century White Hart Tavern across the road.

Near the south side of the bridge is **Ffynnon Llawddog**, a holy well linked to an early Celtic saint. It's one of many such sites throughout Wales that were popular during medieval times for their supposedly curative powers, although many have ancient pre-Christian origins.

Cenarth is 8 miles southeast of Cardigan and can be reached by bus 460, which runs between Cardigan (14 minutes) and Carmarthen (one hour 12 minutes). There are some free parking spots by the river on the southern side.

St Davids & Pembrokeshire

Best Places to Eat

➡ Cwtch (p166)

➡ Llys Meddyg (p174)

➡ Stackpole Inn (p151)

➡ Shed (p169)

➡ Refectory at St Davids (p164)

Best Places to Stay

➡ Crug Glas (p164)

➡ The Grove (p156)

➡ King Street Rooms (p173)

➡ Tregenna (p153)

➡ Hill Fort Tipis (p170)

Why Go?

The Pembrokeshire coast is what you imagine the world would look like if God were a geology teacher. Knobbly hills of volcanic rock, long thin inlets scoured by glacial melt-waters, stratified limestone eroded into arches, blowholes and sea stacks, and towering red and grey cliffs that scatter the shore. While in between lie perfect sandy beaches. This wild and incredibly beautiful landscape is the region's greatest asset and in summer people flock here to enjoy the spectacular walking, surfing, coasteering and sea kayaking, as well as the glorious beaches and abundant marine life. On top of its natural assets, Pembrokeshire offers a wealth of Celtic and pre-Celtic sites, forbidding castles, fascinating islands and little St Davids – the magical mini-city with its chilled vibe, spectacular cathedral and abiding association with Wales' patron saint.

When to Go

A good time to be in St Davids is 1 March, when the whole country celebrates its patron saint. Fishguard serenades summer with some serious sessions at its Folk Festival in late May/early June. It's peak season with hoards of holi-daymakers from June to August, but also the best time for walking the coast path and hitting the beach.

The kids go back to school but Tenby bursts into life all over again for its annual arts festival in September. Surfers will catch the best swells between September and February on Pembrokeshire's rugged beaches.

SOUTH PEMBROKESHIRE

South Pembrokeshire boasts some of Wales' best sandy beaches and most spectacular limestone formations and makes an impressive starting point for the Pembrokeshire Coast Path (PCP). Once known as Little England Beyond Wales, it was divided from the north by the Landsker Line – a physical and then a linguistic barrier roughly following the old Norman frontier. The divide is less pronounced now, but there's a noticeable English feel to places like Tenby, especially in summer, when the masses descend with their buckets and spades, building miniature replicas of the castles their ancestors once used to keep the Welsh at bay. Those sturdy fortifications are still visible in Tenby, Manorbier, Carew and Haverfordwest, reaching their apotheosis at Pembroke Castle.

Tenby (Dinbych Y Pysgod)

POP 4700

Perched on a headland with sandy beaches either side, Tenby is a postcard-maker's dream. Houses are painted from the pastel palette of a classic fishing village, interspersed with the white elegance of Georgian mansions. The main part of town is still constrained by its Norman-built walls, funnelling holidaymakers through medieval streets lined with pubs, ice-cream parlours and gift shops. In the low season, without the tackiness of the promenade-and-pier beach towns, it tastefully returns to being a sleepy little place. In summer it has a boisterous, boozy holiday-resort feel, with packed pubs seemingly all blasting out Status Quo simultaneously.

Tenby flourished in the 15th century as a centre for the textile trade, exporting cloth in exchange for salt and wine. Clothmaking declined in the 18th century, but the town soon reinvented itself as a fashionable watering place. The arrival of the railway in the 19th century sealed its future as a resort, and William Paxton (owner of the Middleton estate in Carmarthenshire, now home to the National Botanic Garden of Wales) developed a saltwater spa here. Anxiety over a possible French invasion of the Milford Haven waterway led to the construction in 1869 of a fort on St Catherine's Island.

Among those who have taken inspiration or rest here are Horatio Nelson, Jane Austen, George Eliot, JMW Turner, Beatrix Potter and Roald Dahl. The artist Augustus John was born here, and he and his sister Gwen lived here during their early life.

◉ Sights

St Mary's Church   CHURCH

(High St) The graceful arched roof of 13th-century St Mary's Church is studded with fascinating wooden bosses, mainly dating from the 15th century and carved into flowers, cheeky faces, mythical beasts, fish, and even a mermaid holding a comb and mirror. The young Henry Tudor was hidden here before fleeing to Brittany. It's thought he left via a tunnel into the cellars under Mayor Thomas White's house across the road (where Boots is now). There's also a memorial here to Robert Recorde, the 16th-century writer and mathematician who invented the 'equals' sign, and an eerie cadaver-topped tomb intended to remind the viewer of their own mortality.

Tudor Merchant's House   HISTORIC BUILDING

(Quay Hill; adult/child £3.40/1.70; ⊙11am-5pm Easter-Oct, closed Tue) Tenby's oldest buildings are found on steep Quay Hill. This handsome townhouse was once the dwelling of a late-15th-century merchant and has been restored as it would have been in 1500. Period furnishings and the remains of early frescoes can be seen on the interior walls. The merchant's shop, kitchen, bedchamber and the latrine tower can all be explored.

Tenby Museum & Art Gallery   MUSEUM

(www.tenbymuseum.org.uk; Castle Hill; adult/child £4/2; ⊙10am-5pm) Housed within the ruins of a Norman castle, this museum covers the town's development from a fishing village into a 19th-century seaside resort bigger than Blackpool, with interesting exhibits ranging from delicate Roman vases to a Victorian antiquarian's study. There's also a re-created pirate's cell and a gallery including paintings by Augustus and Gwen John.

Castle Hill   HILL

This hilly headland separates North Beach from Castle Beach and the scanty remains of Tenby's Norman castle adorn its summit. Walk along the path from the harbour past **Laston House** (1 Castle Sq), the site of William Paxton's late 18th-century saltwater baths. The Greek writing on the pediment translates as the optimistic 'The sea will wash away all the evils of man'. Beyond here, a path leads out past the old and new Royal National Lifeboat Institution (RNLI)

ST DAVIDS & PEMBROKESHIRE TENBY (DINBYCH Y PYSGOD)

Pembrokeshire Highlights

1 Exploring laid-back **St Davids** (p161) with its mellow vibe and spectacular cathedral

2 Tracing the breathtaking collision of rock and sea along the **Pembrokeshire Coast Path** (p149)

3 Joining the summer fun in **Tenby**, (p143) a colourful seaside resort with velvety-sand beaches

4 Discovering the joys of **Newport** (p173), a little gem surrounded by beaches and hill walks, but devoted to food

5 Braving the waves and taking on some **water sports**, Pembrokeshire has some of the best surfing, sea kayaking and coasteering in the country

6 Observing the locals on **Skomer, Skokholm & Grassholm Islands** (p158), some of the richest wildlife habitats in Britain

7 Heading back in time at **Castell Henllys** (p176) Iron Age Fort

8 Soaking up the view at **Pentre Ifan** (p175), a dolmen formed from the same rock as Stonehenge

lifeboat stations and around the Castle Hill headland. On top of the hill are a memorial to **Prince Albert** and the Tenby Museum & Art Gallery. You'll also get a fine view over the coast.

RNLI Lifeboat Stations NOTABLE BUILDING

(www.tenbyrnli.co.uk; Castle Hill; ⊗ 8.30am-5.30pm) **FREE** It's well worth popping into this swanky new lifeboat station to see the boats, watch footage of them launching and learn a little about one of the UK's busiest lifeboat crews. Planned training launches are posted on noticeboards, a spectacle well worth seeing if you happen to be in town.

St Catherine's Island ISLAND

At low tide you can walk across the sand to little St Catherine's Island, but it's a long, cold wait if you get trapped by the tide – check tide tables in *Coast to Coast*, at any newsagent or ask at the tourist office. The Victorian fort on the island is closed to the public.

☞ Tours

Town Trails Tenby WALKING TOUR

(☑ 01834-845841; www.guidedtourswales.co.uk; adult/child £4.50/3.50; ⊗ Mon-Sat mid-Jun–mid-Sep) Marion Davies brings Tenby's history to life with a variety of guided town tours. Adults with an interest in history will get a great insight into the town's past from the Story of Tenby walk, while families will enjoy the tales of smugglers and shipwrecks on the Pirates tour, and those of fairies, apparitions and witches on the Ghost Walk. Tours depart from various locations.

✦ Festivals & Events

Tenby Arts Festival ARTS

(☑ 01834-845277; www.tenbyartsfest.co.uk; ⊗ late Sep) A week-long celebration in a variety of venues around town, the annual arts fest features everything from poetry readings by Caldey Island monks to sandcastle competitions. Expect classical concerts, talks about seaweed, piano recitals and Tenby's fine male voice choir in between.

⌂ Sleeping

Trevayne Farm CAMPGROUND £

(☑ 01834-813402; www.trevaynefarm.co.uk; Monkstone, Saundersfoot; sites from £15; ☻) This large clifftop-field site on the Pembrokeshire Coast Path has beautiful sea views and segregated areas so back to basics tenters can

avoid the looming motorhomes. The campsite is 3 miles north of Tenby just off the A48.

Penally Abbey HOTEL ££

(☑ 01834-843033; www.penally-abbey.com; Penally; r from £120; ℗) Set on a hillside overlooking Carmarthen Bay, this country-house hotel is built on the site of an ancient monastery and offers beautiful sea views. Expect high ceilings, huge windows, roaring fires and leather Chesterfields in the main house where the bedrooms have four-poster beds and floral carpets. Rooms in the Coach House have a more cottagey feel, while St Deiniol's Lodge is decked out in far more contemporary style. The restaurant serves an understated but impressive French-style menu. The hotel is 2 miles southwest of Tenby along the A4139. Bus 349 plies the route.

Bay House B&B ££

(☑ 01834-849015; www.tenbybandb.co.uk; 5 Picton Rd; r £80-90; ⊗ Apr-Oct; ☎) Lovely rooms, lovely food and lovely people. Bay House is the pick of Tenby's B&Bs offering a modern take on the seaside staple with a relaxed, friendly atmosphere and stylish, contemporary rooms with king-size beds, flat-screen TVs and DVDs. Breakfasts are monumental and prepared with local, organic produce whenever possible. It only has three rooms so book well in advance.

St Lawrence Country Guesthouse B&B ££

(☑ 01834-849727; www.stlawrencecountryguest house.co.uk; Gumfreston; s/d £55/75; ℗☎) Set in 7.5 hectares of gardens, pasture and woodland, this tranquil B&B offers spacious rooms, refined elegance and wonderful sea views. 'Our girls', the free-range hens roaming outside, provide eggs for breakfast, there's bread fresh from the oven, and fruit and tomatoes from the garden. On top of all this there's a wonderfully warm welcome and great attention to detail throughout. The guesthouse is 1.5 miles from Tenby, just off the B4318 west of town.

Ivy Bank B&B ££

(☑ 01834-842311; www.ivybanktenby.co.uk; Harding St; s/d from £40/60; ☻) Subtle swagged curtains, tasselled lampshades and bold floral wallpapers are the order of the day in this Victorian B&B close to the train station. Rooms sizes vary – some are very small – but all are cosy and comfortable, and children are very welcome.

Tenby

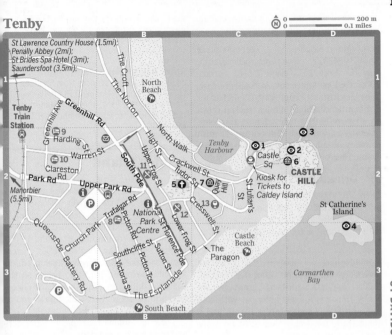

Langdon Villa Guest House B&B **££**
(☑ 01834-849467; www.langdonguesthousetenby.
co.uk; 3 Warren St; s/d £50/70) A traditional
and very comfortable B&B with a variety
of rooms, Langdon Villa has tasteful decor,
great breakfasts, and incredibly friendly and
accommodating owners.

St Brides Spa Hotel HOTEL **£££**
(☑ 01834-812304; www.stbridesspahotel.com; St
Brides Hill, Saundersfoot; s/d from £140/155;
🅿🛜🌊) Pembrokeshire's premier spa hotel
offers the chance to relax in the infinity-edge
pool overlooking the beach and indulge in a
massage before dining in the candlelit Cliff
restaurant (mains £17 to £22). The bedrooms are stylish and modern, in colours
that evoke the seaside. It's 3 miles north of
Tenby along the A48. Take bus 351.

🍴 Eating

D Fecci & Sons FISH & CHIPS **£**
(Lower Frog St; mains £6-8; ⊙ 11.30am-11.30pm
Sun-Thu, 11.30-2.30am Fri & Sat) Eating fish and
chips on the beach is a British tradition, and
D Fecci & Sons is a Tenby institution, having
been in business since 1935. Not only is the
fish locally sourced, so are the potatoes. The
same family run the traditional **Fecci's Ice
Cream Parlour** on St George's St.

Blue Ball Restaurant INTERNATIONAL **££**
(☑ 01834-843038; www.theblueballrestaurant.
co.uk; Upper Frog St; mains £10-24; ⊙ 6-9pm Tue-
Sat, 12.30-2.30pm Sun) 🍴 Polished wood, old
timber beams and exposed brickwork create
a cosy, rustic atmosphere in what is probably
Tenby's best restaurant. The menu makes

good use of local produce, notably seafood. Pork Wellington is the signature dish.

Plantagenet House   MODERN WELSH **£££**
(☑ 01834-842350; www.plantagenettenby.co.uk; Quay Hill; lunch £7-13, dinner £15-40; ☺ noon-2.30pm & 6-10pm high season) Atmosphere-wise, this place instantly impresses; it's perfect for a romantic, candle-lit dinner. Tucked down an alley in Tenby's oldest house, it's dominated by an immense 12th-century Flemish chimney hearth. The menu ranges from acclaimed seafood to organic beef.

Drinking & Nightlife

There are about two dozen pubs crammed into the area around Tudor Sq, and the place can get pretty riotous on summer nights with big groups of lads and ladettes heading between them.

Tenby House   PUB
(www.tenbyhousehotel.com; Tudor Sq; ☺ 11am-12.30am Mon-Thu & Sat, to 1am Fri, to midnight Sun) Tenby House is a lively hotel bar with cool tunes on Friday and Saturday nights, and a sunny, flower-bedecked courtyard for summer afternoon sessions.

Information

National Park Centre (☑ 01834-845040; www.pembrokeshirecoast.org.uk; South Pde; ☺ 9.30am-5pm daily Apr-Sep, 10am-4.30pm Mon-Sat Oct-Mar)

Police Station (Warren St)

Tourist Office (☑ 01834-842402; Upper Park Rd; ☺ 10am-4pm Easter-Oct, Mon-Sat Nov-Easter)

Getting There & Around

If you're coming in high season, expect to pay for parking.

BIKE

Tenby Cycles (☑ 01834-845573; www.tenby-cycles.co.uk; The Norton; ☺ 9.30am-5pm Mon-Sat Easter-Sep) Rents bikes for £12 a day.

BUS

The bus station is next to the tourist office on Upper Park Rd. Routes include 349 to Manorbier (18 minutes), Pembroke (43 minutes) and Pembroke Dock (one hour); 351 to Saundersfoot (15 minutes) and Amroth (40 minutes); 360 to Carew (13 minutes); and 381 to Haverfordwest (one hour).

National Express (www.nationalexpress.com) Coach destinations include London (£27, 8½ hours), Chepstow (£17.50, 3½ hours), Swan-sea (£6.80, 1½ hours), Carmarthen (£5.10, 45 minutes), Pembroke (£3, 25 minutes) and Haverfordwest (£4.50, 50 minutes).

TRAIN

Arriva Trains Wales (www.arrivatrainswales.co.uk) Offers direct services from Swansea (£13.70, 1½ hours), Llanelli (£13.40, 1¼ hours), Carmarthen (£8.70, 43 minutes), Manorbier (£2.90, nine minutes) and Pembroke (£5.10, 28 minutes).

Caldey Island

Boat trips run from Tenby Harbour to Caldey Island (☑ 01834-844453; www.caldey-island.co.uk; adult/child £11/6; ☺ Mon-Sat Apr-Oct), home to lots of grey seals and sea birds, and a red-topped, whitewashed monastery that houses a community of around 15 Cistercian monks. The monks live an austere life but make various luxurious products for sale, including perfume (based on the island's wildflowers), shortbread and chocolate, and do so well that they now employ people from the mainland.

There are guided tours of the monastery and great walks around the island, with good views from the lighthouse. Make sure you visit the old priory and St Illtyd's Church, with its oddly shaped steeple. Inside is a stone with inscriptions in ogham (an ancient Celtic script).

Little St Margaret's Island at the western tip of Caldey is a nature reserve (landings are prohibited); it's home to grey seals and Wales' biggest colony of cormorants.

From Tenby, boats to Caldey Island depart half-hourly from about 10.30am, from the harbour at high tide and from Castle Beach at low tide. Tickets are sold from a kiosk at the harbour slipway.

Manorbier

Manorbier (man-er-*beer*) is a little village of leafy, twisting lanes with an impressive castle nestled above a lovely sandy beach. If the beach at Manorbier gets busy, it's worth walking west along the coast path to remote and tranquil Swanlake Bay where there is a fine stretch of sand at low tide.

☉ Sights

Manorbier Castle   CASTLE
(www.manorbiercastle.co.uk; adult/child £5/3; ☺ 10am-6pm Easter-Sep) Craggy, lichen-spotted Manorbier Castle was the birthplace of

PEMBROKESHIRE COAST PATH

Straddling the line where Pembrokeshire drops suddenly into the sea, the Pembrokeshire Coast Path (PCP) is one of the most spectacular long-distance routes in Britain. Established in 1970, it meanders along 186 miles of Britain's most dramatic coastal scenery running from Amroth to St Dogmaels, passing knobbly hills of volcanic rock, long thin harbours formed from glacial melts, and stratified limestone pushed up vertically and then eroded to form natural arches, blowholes and pillars. Again and again along its route stretches of towering cliff quickly give way to perfect sandy beaches, only to resume around the headland.

The route takes you from popular holiday spots to long stretches where the only evidence of human existence are the ditches of numerous Celtic forts. Marine life is plentiful, and rare birds make the most of the remote cliffs, with peregrine falcons, red kites, buzzards, choughs, puffins and gannets to be spotted.

If you don't have the time or the stamina for the full route, it can easily be split into smaller chunks. You can walk the trail in either direction, but a south–north route allows an easy start in populated areas and builds up to longer, more isolated stretches. Skip from Angle to Dale by bus to avoid two days of industrial landscapes around Milford Haven.

Some sections look deceptively short but expect endless steep ascents and descents where the trail crosses harbours and beaches. Referring to a tide table is essential if you want to avoid lengthy delays in places.

The weather can be quite changeable and mobile phone coverage is unreliable; come prepared, bring wet weather gear and something warm, even in summer. You'll find a wealth of information and tips on the National Trails (www.pcnpa.org.uk) website.

Maps

The route is covered by Ordnance Survey (OS) Explorer 1:25,000 maps No 35 (North Pembrokeshire) and No 36 (South Pembrokeshire). The official national trail guide, *Pembrokeshire Coast Path* by Brian John has detailed route descriptions. Ten single-sheet Trail Cards with basic maps also cover the route and are available from tourist offices and National Park Centres.

When to Walk

Spring and early summer are good times to walk when wildflowers litter the hills, birdlife is abundant and the school holidays are yet to begin in earnest. Late summer tends to be drier and you might spot migrating whales out to sea, but it can be busy and hard to find a bed for a single night. In autumn the crowds die down and seals come ashore to give birth to their pups. Many hostels and campgrounds close from October to Easter and buses are far less frequent. Although walking in winter may be exhilarating, in the wind, rain and cold it may not be the most enjoyable (or safest) experience.

Our Favourite Sections

➡ **Marloes Sands to Broad Haven** (4½ to six hours, 13 miles) A wonderful walk along dramatic clifftops ending in an impressive beach. Many access points and regular public transport make it good for short circular walks too.

➡ **Whitesands to Porthgain** (four to five hours, 10 miles) A beautiful but taxing section worth tackling if your time is limited. Within easy reach of St Davids and offers the reward of some excellent nosh at the end of your day.

➡ **Porthgain to Pwll Deri** (four to six hours, 12 miles) An exhilarating section with sheer cliffs, rock buttresses, pinnacles, islets, bays and beaches but some steep ascents and descents in between. Magnificent views of St Davids and Strumble Head.

➡ **Newport to St Dogmaels** (six to eight hours, 15.5 miles) A tough, rollercoaster section with frequent steep hills but spectacular views of the wild and rugged coast and its numerous rock formations, sheer cliffs and caves.

Giraldus Cambrensis (Gerald of Wales, 1146–1223), one of the country's greatest scholars and patriots. 'In all the broad lands of Wales, Manorbier is the best place by far', he wrote. The 12th- to 19th-century castle buildings are grouped around a pretty garden. Medieval music plays in the Great Hall and there's a murky dungeon, a smugglers' secret passage and a tableau of wax figures in period costume. Look out for the figure that was originally Prince Philip, now sporting a coat of chain mail. The castle starred in the 2003 film *I Capture the Castle*.

King's Quoit   ARCHAEOLOGICAL SITE
This simple neolithic dolmen (burial chamber) fashioned from slabs of rock sits overlooking the shell-shaped Manorbier Bay. The chamber is partially below ground and the enormous capstone is supported by an earth bank and two small sidestones. To get here head down to the beach at Manorbier and turn left onto the coast path. You will see the dolmen before you round the headland.

🛏 Sleeping & Eating

Manorbier YHA   HOSTEL £
(☏ 0845 371 9031; www.yha.org.uk; dm/d from £19/35; P ⛺) Looking like a cross between a space station and a motorway diner, this futuristic ex–Ministry of Defence building is 1.5 miles east of the village centre, close to the beach at Skrinkle Haven. It's a terrific, remote spot and the facilities are good.

Castle Inn   PUB ££
(☏ 01834-871268; mains £7-11) This classic village pub has a rhododendron-shaded beer garden, a jukebox and live music on Saturday nights, as well as a decent range of pub grub.

❶ Getting There & Away

Manorbier is 5½ miles southwest of Tenby. It's served by bus 349 to Tenby (18 minutes), Pembroke (20 minutes), Pembroke Dock (40 minutes) and Haverfordwest (1½ hours). There's also a train station, a mile north of the village, with direct services to Swansea (£13.70, 1¾ hours), Carmarthen (£8.10, one hour), Tenby (£2.90, nine minutes) and Pembroke (£4, 25 minutes).

Stackpole Estate

Run by the National Trust (NT), **Stackpole Estate** (NT; ☏ 01646-661359; admission free; www.nationaltrust.org.uk; ⊙ dawn-dusk) takes in 8 miles of coast, including two fine beaches, a wooded valley and a system of artificial ponds famous for their spectacular display of water lilies.

◉ Sights

Stackpole Elidor Church   CHURCH
This pretty little church with its tall, slender tower is nestled in a wooded valley. The earliest parts of the church date back to the 12th century, with 14th-century vaulting in the transepts. Stackpole was the seat of the Campbells, earls of Cawdor, and the church contains elaborate effigies of Elidor de Stackpole and his wife, and Lord Cawdor, who featured in the French invasion of Fishguard.

Stackpole Quay   HARBOUR
The tiny picturesque harbour of Stackpole Quay marks the point where pink and purple sandstone gives way to the massive grey limestone that dominates the South Pembrokeshire coast from here to Freshwater West. There's an NT car park with information leaflets, and a good tearoom.

Barafundle Bay   BEACH
Regularly voted one of Britain's most beautiful beaches, Barafundle Bay is a scenic 10-minute walk south along the coast path from Stackpole Quay. It is a gorgeous spot but its reputation has put paid to seclusion and on summer weekends it can get pretty crowded despite the lack of road access. Come out of peak season and you may just have the whole place to yourself, though. If you're up for more walking, follow the coast path south of the beach out onto **Stackpole Head** with its impressive cliffs and rock arches.

Bosherston Lily Ponds   OUTDOORS
Criss-crossed by a network of footpaths and wooden bridges, the famous Bosherston Lily Ponds are a wonderfully tranquil spot to stroll. The lilies bloom in June and July but the surrounding woodlands are full of wildlife year-round. The ponds are home to otters, herons and more than 20 species of dragonfly, while the ruins of the manor house are inhabited by the greater horseshoe bat. The ponds can be reached from the car park in Bosherston village, and some of the trails are wheelchair accessible.

Broad Haven   BEACH
A mile southeast of Bosherston village is the beautiful golden beach of Broad Haven,

framed by grey limestone cliffs and pointed sea stacks.

🛏 Sleeping & Eating

Broad Haven YHA HOSTEL £
(☎0845 371 9008; www.yha.org.uk; dm/r from £18/36; 🏠) This excellent purpose-built hostel is close to the beach and has wonderful sea views from its dining room and deck. The hostel is only open on weekends and during school holidays.

★Stackpole Inn INN ££
(☎01646-672324; www.stackpoleinn.co.uk; Jasons Cnr, Stackpole; s/d from £60/90; ⊘restaurant noon-2.30pm & 6.30-11pm Mon-Fri, noon-11pm Sat, noon-3.30pm Sun; P�🔊) This wonderful country inn manages to retain its local charm yet look bang up-to-date. The simple but incredibly stylish bedrooms have white panelled walls, stripped floors and crisp white linens doused with a splash of marine blue. The pub itself is a cosy place on a wet day with a wood burner, beamed ceilings and whitewashed walls, while the garden is perfect for a summer's pint. The food, though, is what really draws locals and in-the-know passersby. Hearty, rustic dishes (mains £9 to £18) just bursting with flavour flow from the busy kitchen where local, seasonal produce is always the key.

St Govan's Country Inn PUB ££
(☎01646-661311; www.stgovanscountryinn.webeden.co.uk; Bosherton; s/d £50/80; P🔊) This friendly village pub in sleepy Bosherton has simple, bright B&B accommodation above a convivial bar decorated with hair-raising photos of rock climbs on the local sea cliffs.

Ye Olde Worlde Cafe CAFE £
(Bosherston; snacks £2.50-5.50; ⊘9am-5.30pm, to 9pm Jul & Aug) Better known as Auntie Vi's, this appealing little cafe is a local institution. Housed in the front room of an old, ivy covered coastguard cottage, it has been serving tea and cake since 1921. Its octogenarian guardian, who took over the business from her parents, was made a Member of the British Empire (MBE) in 2009 to acknowledge her decades of service to the stomachs of coast path walkers.

ℹ Getting There & Away
Bosherston is 5 miles south of Pembroke. The Coastal Cruiser stops at Stackpole Quay, Stackpole, Bosherston and Broad Haven.

St Govan's Head & Stack Rocks

The southern coast of Pembrokeshire around St Govan's Head boasts some of the most harshly beautiful coastline in the country, with sheer cliffs dropping 50m into churning, thrashing surf. Unfortunately, much of this coastline lies within the army's Castlemartin firing range and is off limits to the public.

◎ Sights

St Govan's Chapel CHURCH
From the car park at the end of the St Govan's Head road, steps hacked into the rock lead down to tiny St Govan's Chapel, wedged into a slot in the cliffs just out of reach of the sea. The chapel dates from the 5th or 6th century, and is named for an itinerant 6th-century Irish preacher. The story goes that one day, when he was set upon by thieves, the cliff conveniently opened and enfolded him, protecting him from his attackers; in gratitude he built this chapel on the spot. The waters from St Govan's Well (now dried out), just below the chapel, were reputed to cure skin and eye complaints.

Huntsman's Leap OUTDOORS
A spectacular gash in the cliffs with near vertical walls, Huntsman's Leap is famed as one of Britain's best sea-cliff climbing locations. The sheer sides are often dotted with rock climbers and it makes a good short walk if you're in the area. Park at the end of St Govan's Head road and walk west along the coast path for about 10 minutes to get here.

Stack Rocks OUTDOORS
Some of Pembrokeshire's most spectacular cliff scenery can be seen along this stretch of coast at Stack Rocks where two isolated pillars of rock rise steeply from the sea. The rocks are an important nesting site for guillemots and kittiwakes, which can be seen throughout spring and early summer. Nearby is the **Green Bridge of Wales**, the biggest natural arch in the country. There's a car park close to Stack Rocks, 3 miles to the west of St Govan's Head road.

ℹ Getting There & Away
The Coastal Cruiser stops at St Govan's Head and Stack Rocks car parks.

Two minor roads run south to the coast at St Govan's Head and Stack Rocks; when the range is in use these roads are closed. You can check whether the roads, and the section of coast path that links them, are open by calling ☑ 01646-662367, or by checking the notices posted in Bosherston.

Freshwater West

Wild and windblown Freshwater West, a 2-mile strand of golden sand and silver shingle backed by acres of dunes, is Wales' best surf beach, sitting wide open to the Atlantic rollers. But beware – although it's great for surfing, big waves, powerful rips and quicksand make it dangerous for swimming; several people have drowned here and the beach has year-round red-flag status.

In 2009 scenes from Ridley Scott's *Robin Hood* and *Harry Potter and the Deathly Hallows* were filmed here.

The Coastal Cruiser stops at the car park.

Angle

At the southern head of the Milford Haven waterway, the village of Angle feels a long way off the beaten track. The main attraction is the tiny beach in **West Angle Bay**, which has great views across the mouth of Milford Haven to St Ann's Head, and offers good coastal walks with lots of rock pools to explore.

If you're walking the coast path, consider catching the Coastal Cruiser from Angle to Dale and skip two grim days passing the giant oil refineries lining Milford Haven.

🛏 Sleeping & Eating

Old Point House   INN **££**

(☑ 01646-641205; Angle Point; s/d from £43/75; ⊙ closed Nov-Feb, Mon & Tue Mar & Oct; P) Warm and welcoming but rough around the edges, this 15th-century cottage pub, partly built with shipwreck timbers, is as authentic as it gets. Set at the end of a rutted track looking out over the water and marooned by spring tides, its battered furniture, ancient navigational charts and roaring fire lend it plenty of charm. The home-cooked food is hearty and filling (mains £8 to £18), but the rooms are basic and overpriced.

Pembroke (Penfro)

POP 7550

Pembroke is not much more than a single street of neat Georgian and Victorian houses sitting beneath a whopping great castle – the oldest in West Wales and birthplace of Henry VII, the first Tudor king.

In 1154 local traders scored a coup when a Royal Act of Incorporation made it illegal to land goods anywhere in the Milford Haven waterway except at Pembroke (now Pembroke Dock). In 1648, during the English Civil War, the castle was besieged for 48 days before it fell, after which Cromwell had the town walls demolished.

⊙ Sights

★ **Pembroke Castle**   CASTLE

(☑ 01646-684585; www.pembrokecastle.co.uk; Main St; adult/child £5/4; ⊙ 10am-5pm) Spectacular and forbidding Pembroke Castle was the home of the earls of Pembroke for over 300 years. A fort was established here in 1093 by Arnulph de Montgomery, but most

---

PEMBROKESHIRE COAST NATIONAL PARK

Established in 1952, the Pembrokeshire Coast National Park (Parc Cenedlaethol Arfordir Sir Benfro) takes in almost the entire coast and its offshore islands, as well as the moorland hills of Mynydd Preseli in the north. Pembrokeshire's sea cliffs and islands support huge breeding populations of sea birds, while seals, dolphins, porpoises and whales are frequently spotted in coastal waters.

There are three national park information centres (in Tenby, St Davids and Newport) and the local tourist offices scattered across Pembrokeshire are well stocked with park paraphernalia. The free annual publication *Coast to Coast* (online at www.pcnpa.org.uk) has lots of information on park attractions, a calendar of events and details of park-organised activities, including guided walks, themed tours, cycling trips, pony treks, island cruises, canoe trips and minibus tours. It's worth picking it up for the tide tables alone – they're a necessity for many legs of the coast path.

Pembroke

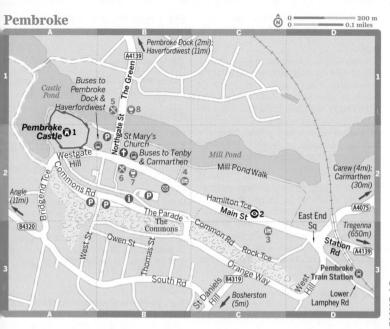

Pembroke

◎ Top Sights
1 Pembroke Castle A2

◉ Sights
2 Pembroke Antiques Centre C2

⊟ Sleeping
3 Penfro C3
4 Woodbine B2

⊗ Eating
5 Cornstore Cafe B1
6 Old King's Arms Hotel B2

⊜ Drinking & Nightlife
7 Castle Inn B2
8 Waterman's Arms B1

of the present buildings date from the 12th and 13th centuries. The sinister, looming keep, built in 1200, is the oldest part. One hundred steps lead to the top, where there are great views over the town.

Next to the keep is the **Dungeon Tower**, where you can peer into the dank, dark prison cell. Nearby, with access through the Northern Hall, are steps to the creepy **Wogan Cavern**, a large natural cave that was partially walled in by the Normans and probably used as a store and boathouse.

The castle is a great place for kids to explore – wall walks and passages run from tower to tower, and there are vivid exhibitions detailing the castle's history. A tableau commemorates Henry Tudor (Harri Tudur), who defeated Richard III at the Battle of Bosworth Field in 1485 to become King Henry VII, in the room in which he is believed to have been born, in 1456.

Guided tours are available from May to August (adult/child £1.50/1). Falconry displays and costumed re-enactments are held in summer.

Pembroke Antiques Centre ANTIQUES
(☑ 01646-687017; Main St; ⊙ 10am-5pm Mon-Sat; P) A wonderful old neoclassical Methodist chapel stocked to the impressively high rafters with antiques, Pembroke Antiques

Centre is a good place to search for a quirky souvenir with a bit of history to it.

⊨ Sleeping

Tregenna B&B ££
(☑ 01646-621525; www.tregennapembroke.co.uk; 7 Upper Lamphey Rd; s/d £40/65; P 🛜) When the treats in the room include a sewing kit, shaving kit, mini toothbrush and toothpaste, bottled water and Welsh cakes, you know you're

somewhere special. It's a newly built house, so everything's modern, shiny and crisp.

Penfro B&B **££**
(📞 01646-682753; www.penfro.co.uk; 111 Main St; s/d from £60/70) Austerely elegant from the outside, this large Georgian town house is a delight inside, retaining many of its original 18th-century features, including 250-year-old glass, Georgian wood panelling, moulded plaster ceilings and period fireplaces. Rooms do not have en suites, as the owner has chosen not to destroy original features.

Woodbine B&B **££**
(📞 01646-686338; www.woodbinebedandbreakfast.co.uk; 84 Main St; s/d £50/60; 🛜 🐾) With three pretty rooms, two of which offer oodles of space, this central B&B is great value. It's an extremely friendly place set in a Georgian town house with fireplaces in the bedrooms, subtle floral wallpapers and tasteful furnishings.

✖ Eating

Cornstore Cafe CAFE **£**
(The Green; mains £4-6.50; ⊙ 10am-5pm Mon-Sat) Housed in an 18th-century granary on the Mill Pond, this cafe conjures up delicious lunches – daily specials include homemade soups and simple hot meals. Choose from the extensive range of speciality teas for the perfect cuppa to accompany one of the luscious cakes. It's worth checking out the homeware shop upstairs for interesting souvenirs.

Old King's Arms Hotel PUB **££**
(www.oldkingsarmshotel.co.uk; Main St; mains £15-22) Dark timber beams, ochre walls and polished copperware lend a country kitchen atmosphere to the restaurant here. The locally sourced protein (black beef, Carmarthen ham, daily seafood specials) comes accompanied with enough potatoes and vegetables to fill even a Tudor king. Simpler bar meals (mains £8 to £9) are also available.

🍷 Drinking & Nightlife

Castle Inn PUB
(📞 01646-682883; 17 Main St; ⊙ 10am-11pm) This snug local pub, all bare stone and horse brasses, is good for a quiet afternoon pint, but it fairly livens up in the evenings as a youngish crowd gathers for a night on the town.

Waterman's Arms PUB
(📞 01646-682718; 2 The Green; ⊙ noon-11pm Sun-Thu, noon-midnight Fri & Sat) The outdoor terrace is a suntrap on a summer afternoon, with fine views across the Mill Pond to the castle.

ℹ Information

Tourist Office (📞 01437-776499; Commons Rd; ⊙ 10am-4pm Mon-Fri, 10am-1pm Sat)

ℹ Getting There & Around

BUS

Bus 349 heads to Tenby (43 minutes), Manorbier (25 minutes), Pembroke Dock (10 minutes) and Haverfordwest (48 minutes); and bus 356 to Pembroke Dock (12 minutes). The Coastal Cruiser loops in both directions between Pembroke, Angle, Freshwater West, Bosherston and Stackpole, terminating at Pembroke Dock.

National Express destinations include London (£27, seven hours), Chepstow (£18, 3¾ hours), Swansea (£8.60, 1¾ hours), Carmarthen (£5.70, one hour), Tenby (£3, 25 minutes) and Haverfordwest (£4.70, 30 minutes).

TRAIN

There are direct trains to Swansea (£13.70, 2¼ hours), Llanelli (£13.40, 1¾ hours), Carmarthen (£8.70, 1¼ hours), Manorbier (£4, 20 minutes) and Tenby (£5.10, 28 minutes).

Pembroke Dock

Between 1814 and 1926 more than 260 Royal Navy ships were built at Pembroke Dock, which was then a Royal Dockyard. It also served as a Royal Air Force (RAF) base for flying boats during WWII and after. Today it's a sprawling expanse of suburbia with a ferry terminal and commercial port.

◉ Sights

Gun Tower Museum HISTORIC BUILDING
(📞 01646-622246; www.guntowermuseum.org. uk; Front St) Some of Pembroke's history survives in the Gun Tower Museum, housed in a 19th-century Martello tower that was built to defend the harbour from possible attack by French invaders. There was rather an unfair distribution of space here – 33 men slept in hammocks in one room, while the officer got to have the other room all to himself. A walkway now runs from the shore, but when the tower was in use the men had to lower a rope ladder for supplies. The tower was closed for refurbishment at the time of writing but due to reopen soon after this book's publication.

ℹ Getting There & Away

BOAT

Irish Ferries (☑08717-300 500; www.irish-ferries.com) Offers two sailings a day on the four-hour route between Pembroke Dock and Rosslare in the southeast of Ireland (car and driver from £89, additional adult £28, foot passenger from £28).

BUS

There are frequent bus services between Pembroke and Pembroke Dock.

Carew

This pretty little village is dominated by its imposing castle and is home to a number of historic sights. In summer it is overrun by tourists; arrive early to beat the crowds.

◎ Sights

Carew Castle   CASTLE
(www.carewcastle.com; adult/child £4.75/3.50; ◎10am-5pm Apr-Oct) Looming romantically over the River Carew with its gaping windows reflected in the glassy water, craggy Carew Castle is an impressive sight. These rambling limestone ruins range from functional 12th-century fortification (built by Gerald de Windsor, Henry I's constable of Pembroke) to Elizabethan country house.

Abandoned in 1690, the castle is now inhabited by a large number of bats, including the protected greater horseshoe bat. A summer program of events includes battle re-enactments and open-air theatre. The castle ticket also gives you admission to

Carew Tidal Mill, the only intact tidal mill in Wales. The Elizabethan mill has a causeway that once trapped the incoming tide in a pond, then released water through sluice gates to turn the millwheels. For 400 years until 1937, the mill ground corn for the castle community.

Near the castle entrance is the 11th-century **Carew Cross**, one of the grandest of its kind – around 4m tall and covered in intricate Celtic carvings.

Visitors arriving by public transport or bicycle can get free admission.

✗ Eating

Carew Inn   INN **££**
(www.carewinn.co.uk; mains £9-14; ◎pub 11am-11pm, meals served noon-2.30pm & 6-9pm; ☑ 🐕) Opposite Carew Castle this cosy traditional inn has a wood-panelled bar with a roaring fire, darts and an old-fashioned 'snug'. The restaurant is small and homey, serves good quality pub grub at lunch and dinner, and has a beer garden with fine views of the castle.

ℹ Getting There & Away

Carew is 4 miles northeast of Pembroke and 6 miles northwest of Tenby. Bus 360 heads here from Tenby (13 minutes) and bus 361 from Pembroke (10 minutes).

Narberth

POP 2490

An arty little town full of independent shops, cafes, restaurants and galleries, Narberth is a gem. Despite being light on specific sights,

CYCLING THE CELTIC TRAIL

From the laid-back joys of St Davids through the glorious Pembrokeshire Coast National Park and past the imposing castles in Haverfordwest, Pembroke and Kidwelly, the **Celtic Trail** (www.routes2ride.org.uk/wales) covers some of the best cycling routes in south Wales.

Starting in Fishguard, the trail follows a mixture of off-road coastal paths, riverside trails, old railway lines and quiet lanes on its way to Chepstow, 220 miles away. From the magnificent traffic-free Llanelli Millennium Coastal Park and sweeping Swansea Bay, the trail splits into two and riders can choose National Route 47, a high level route that climbs almost 600m through the forests around Neath and Pontypridd, or low level National Route 4, which sticks closer to the coast.

From Trelewis, north of Abercynon, there's more traffic-free cycling through Sirhowy Valley Country Park and along the Monmouthshire and Brecon Canal into Newport, where the novel Transporter Bridge will take you across the River Usk. From here it's just a few easy miles to the end of the trail.

The route is best ridden from west to east to make use of the prevailing westerly winds and is generally broken into between five and seven days' riding.

it's well worth a stop en route west for its lively vibe, passion for food and thriving retail scene. Somehow managing to beat the economic odds, butchers and delis, antique shops and boutiques line the streets, there's a friendly food festival in September, a ruined Norman castle and an interesting town hall with a double stairway.

◉ Sights

Narberth Museum MUSEUM
(www.narberthmuseum.co.uk; Church St; adult/child £3.50/2.50; ◷ 10am-5pm Mon-Sat, 11am-4pm Sun) Shortlisted for the prestigious Museum of the Year prize in 2013, this small, local museum packs a punch way above its weight. Rescued by keen volunteers and now in a new home in some wonderfully atmospheric restored bonded stores, it celebrates the rich history of Narberth and the surrounding area. You can learn about medieval siege warfare and Narberth Castle through models and interactive games, walk historic streets and visit the shops, or listen to Welsh folk stories in the storytelling chair. There are lots of hands-on activities and dressing up for children, as well as a well-stocked museum shop with interesting local crafts.

✦ Festivals & Events

Narberth Food Festival FOOD
(www.narberthfoodfestival.com; admission £3.50; ◷ late Sep) A wonderful celebration of Welsh produce, fine food, good wine and the joy of cooking, this small but incredibly friendly festival offers everything from master classes and tutored tastings to free cookery demonstrations, workshops and talks, alongside a host of food stalls and live entertainment, music, street theatre and children's activities. If you're in the area in late September, don't miss it.

⊨ Sleeping & Eating

Canaston Oaks B&B ££
(☎ 01437-541254; www.canastonoaks.co.uk; Canaston Bridge; s/d from £100/110; @⊕) Set amid 81 hectares of working farm, this luxurious B&B has four en suite rooms positioned around a Celtic cross–shaped garden. Earl Grey tea and Welsh cakes on arrival, and a Welsh dresser groaning under the weight of homemade muesli and fresh fruit for breakfast, testify to the warmth of the hospitality. Canaston Oaks is 3 miles from Narberth. Head west along the A40 then south along the A4075 to get here.

★ The Grove HOTEL £££
(☎ 01834-860915; www.thegrove-narberth.co.uk; Molleston; d from £180-290; P ☎ ⊕) ✦ This small, luxury hotel is hidden in the countryside just outside Narberth and has sumptuous rooms featuring period character and contemporary but classical styling. Open fires, luxurious fabrics, cast iron baths and oodles of space combine with the latest in technology to create a truly magical place to stay. The hotel's renowned restaurant is worth a trip in itself, serving a creative modern Welsh menu (three-course dinner £49) featuring many ingredients from the hotel's own kitchen garden. Surrounded by manicured lawns, mature trees and wildflower meadows, The Grove is a magnificent place to relax. To get here, head south from Narberth on the A478 and take the first right, immediately after the bridge.

Ultracomida SPANISH £
(www.ultracomida.co.uk; 7 High St; tapas £5-5.50; ◷ 10am-6pm Mon-Sat) The aroma of cured meats, fine cheeses, olives and freshly baked bread greets you as walk in the door of this wonderful little deli and cafe. Stock up on supplies for a gourmet picnic, enjoy some of the best coffee for miles or tuck in to the delicious tapas. A set menu (two-/three-course £11/13) is also available at lunchtime.

Plum Vanilla CAFE £
(www.plumvanilla.com; 2A St James' St; mains £7-9; ◷ 9am-5pm Mon-Sat; ⊘⊕) Named after the two sisters that run this little boho cafe, this popular local haunt has a loyal following who flock here for the hearty selection of homemade soups, interesting salads, quiches, luscious desserts and daily specials. Be prepared to wait for a table at lunchtime.

ⓘ Getting There & Away

➡ Bus routes include bus 322 to Carmarthen (37 minutes) and Haverfordwest (20 minutes); and bus 430 to Cardigan (one hour).

➡ There are direct trains to Tenby (£4.50, 19 minutes) and Carmarthen (£7.50, 26 minutes).

Haverfordwest (Hwlffordd)

POP 12,000

A workaday town rather than a tourist hot spot, Haverfordwest is Pembrokeshire's main transport and shopping hub. Though it retains some fine Georgian buildings, many are in dire need of repair and it lacks the prettiness and historic atmosphere of many of its neighbours.

Founded as a fortified Flemish settlement by the Norman lord Gilbert de Clare in about 1110, its castle became the nucleus for a thriving market and its port remained important until the railway arrived in the mid-19th century.

Today the Riverside Shopping Centre is the main focus of activity and home to an excellent farmers market with organic and local produce stalls every Friday from 9am to 3pm.

Sights

Haverfordwest Castle   CASTLE

(Castle St) The meagre ruins of Haverfordwest Castle consist of little more than three walls. The castle survived an onslaught by Owain Glyndŵr in 1405, but according to one local story it was abandoned by its Royalist garrison during the English Civil War, when its soldiers mistook a herd of cows for Roundheads.

Town Museum   MUSEUM

(01437-763087; www.haverfordwest-town-museum.org.uk; Castle House; adult/child £1/free; 10am-4pm Mon-Sat Apr-Oct) The museum is housed in the residence of the governor of the prison, which once stood in Haverfordwest Castle's outer ward – it was here that the unsuccessful French invasion force was incarcerated in 1797. It covers the town's history, complete with a boil-ridden plague victim and an interesting section on local nicknames – a study has recorded 700 evocative endearments, such as Arse and Pockets, Drips and Stinko.

Sleeping & Eating

Crundale House   B&B ££

(01437-779749; www.crundalehouse.co.uk; Dingle Lane, Crundale; r from £85;) Out of town but well worth the effort to get to, this gorgeous country house set in large gardens has three bright, spacious rooms decked out in refined period style. Expect stripped floors, sash windows, antique furniture, crisp linens and roll-top baths. You may never want to leave. To get here follow the Cardigan Rd (B4329) out of Haverfordwest for 2 miles, turning right onto Chapel Rd, then right again onto Dingle Lane.

Georges   CAFE ££

(01437-766683; www.thegeorges.uk.com; 24 Market St; lunch £9-14, dinner £10-20; 10am-5.30pm Tue-Sat, 6-9.30pm Fri & Sat;) Gargoyles on leashes guard the door of this trippy, hippy gift shop that doubles as an offbeat cafe. The Georges has cosy nooks of stained glass and candlelight, lanterns and fairy lights, along with a simple menu of home-cooked food ranging from steak to pasta to curry.

Casa Maria   CAFE ££

(2 Castle Sq; dishes £4-10; noon-4pm Mon-Sat) This friendly little cafe attached to a glorious deli serves excellent tapas, sandwiches, and platters of the best artisan foods from both Spain and Wales. Follow it up with a slice of one of its superb cakes and a rich, silky espresso.

Information

Police Station (Merlin's Hill)

Tourist Office (01437-763110; 19 Old Bridge St; 10am-4pm Mon-Sat)

Withybush General Hospital (01437-764545; Fishguard Rd)

Getting There & Away

Bus routes include 322 to Carmarthen (one hour); 349 to Pembroke Dock (35 minutes), Pembroke (45 minutes), Manorbier (1¼ hours) and Tenby (1½ hours); 411 to Newgale Sands (20 minutes), Solva (36 minutes) and St Davids (45 minutes); 412 to Fishguard (41 minutes), Dinas Cross (46 minutes), Newport (52 minutes), Castell Henllys (one hour) and Cardigan (1¼ hours); and the Puffin Shuttle.

National Express destinations include Chepstow (£22.70, 4¼ hours), Swansea (£9.20, 2½ hours), Carmarthen (£7.40, 1½ hours), Tenby (£4.50, 50 minutes) and Pembroke (£4.70, 30 minutes).

There are direct trains to Newport (£27.30, three hours), Cardiff (£23.20, 2½ hours), Swansea (£14.10, 1½ hours), Llanelli (£13.80, one hour) and Carmarthen (£8.80, 37 minutes).

Dale & Around

The fishing village of Dale sits on a rugged and remote peninsula, forming the northern head of the Milford Haven waterway. As you round beautiful St Ann's Head, all vestiges of heavy industry and, indeed, human habitation disappear from view. Little Westdale Bay follows and then the impressive sweep of Marloes Sands, with views over Gateholm Island – a major Iron Age Celtic settlement where the remains of 130 hut circles have been found.

Around Wooltack Point is Martin's Haven, the tiny harbour that is the jumping-

ℹ️ PUFFIN SHUTTLE

Between May and September walkers can make use of the Puffin Shuttle (315/400; fares less than £5), which crawls around the coast three times daily in each direction from Haverfordwest to St Davids. Stops include Milford Haven, Dale, Marloes, Martin's Haven, Little Haven, Broad Haven, Newgale Sands and Solva. For the rest of the year the route is split, with 315 heading from Haverfordwest to Marloes (no Sunday service) and 400 covering all stops from St Davids to Haverfordwest and on to Fishguard (Monday, Thursday and Saturday only).

off point for boat trips to Skomer and Skokholm Islands. An unstaffed information room here has displays on the marine environment, including touch-screen displays of wildlife activity around Skomer. Look for a 7th-century **Celtic cross** set into the wall outside.

Further around the headland the cliffs change from red to black and **Musselwick Sands** comes into view: a large, sandy beach with plenty of craggy inlets to explore.

🏃 Activities

West Wales Watersports   ADVENTURE SPORTS
(☑ 01646-692132; www.surfdale.co.uk; Dale) The rugged coast around Dale is a great place to try out some water sports. West Wales Watersports offers instruction for adults and children. Windsurfing and sailing lessons cost £65/85 per half-/full day for adults and £55/75 for children. Surfing and kayaking lessons cost £35/55 per half-/full day. It also rents wetsuits per half-/full day (£12/24), kayaks (£20/30) and windsurfing rigs (from £35/50).

🛏️ Sleeping

Marloes Sands YHA   HOSTEL £
(☑ 0845 371 9333; www.yha.org.uk; Runwayskiln, Marloes; dm/tw from £18/49; ⊙ Easter-Oct; P 🚗) Housed in a group of National Trust–owned farm buildings near the coast path above Marloes Sands, this hostel offers a mixture of dorms and private rooms.

ℹ️ Getting There & Away

The Puffin Shuttle stops at Dale, Marloes and Martin's Haven.

Skomer, Skokholm & Grassholm Islands

The rocky islands that lie in the turbulent tide-ripped waters at the south end of St Brides Bay are one of the richest wildlife environments in Britain. In the nesting season Skomer and Skokholm Islands are home to more than half a million sea birds, including guillemots, razorbills, puffins, storm petrels and a significant colony of Manx shearwaters. These unusual birds nest in burrows and after a day spent feeding at sea return to their nests under the cover of darkness. Grey seals are also plentiful on Skomer, especially in the pupping season (September).

Eleven miles offshore, Grassholm Island has one of the largest gannet colonies in the northern hemisphere, with 39,000 breeding pairs. Landing is not permitted.

👉 Tours

Dale Sailing Company   BOAT TOUR
(☑ 01646-603123; www.pembrokeshire-islands.co.uk; ⊙ 10am, 11am & noon Tue-Sun Apr-Oct) Dale Sailing Company runs boats to Skomer (adult/child £11/7) on a first-come, first-served basis, departing from Martin's Haven. If you go ashore, there's an additional landing fee of £10 for adults (children under 16 years are free). Other cruises include one-hour round-the-island trips (adult/child £11/7) and, around sunset, an evening cruise (£14/8) that offers the opportunity to see (and hear – the noise can be deafening) the huge flocks of Manx shearwaters returning to their nests. Some boats depart from Dale.

The company also runs three-hour round-the-island trips to Grassholm (£30) departing from Martin's Haven at 1pm on Mondays from April to mid-August. Seals, porpoises and dolphins are often spotted en route; book ahead.

🛏️ Sleeping

Skomer Bunkhouse   CABIN ££
(☑ 01239-621600; www.welshwildlife.org; dm/s from £30/45) For avid birdwatchers, there is basic but comfortable bunkhouse accommodation on Skomer. It's a great way to enjoy the isolation and tranquility of the island after the day-trippers have left. Duvets are provided but you need to bring your own covers and sheets. Book well ahead.

Information

Royal Society for the Protection of Birds
(RSPB; www.rspb.org.uk) Grassholm is owned by the RSPB.

Wildlife Trust of South and West Wales
(www.welshwildlife.org) Skomer and Skokholm Islands are nature reserves run by the Wildlife Trust of South and West Wales, while the surrounding waters are protected by a marine nature reserve.

Getting There & Away

The Puffin Shuttle heads to Martin's Haven.

Little & Broad Havens

Tucked into the southern corner of St Brides Bay, these two bays are joined at low tide but separated by a rocky headland otherwise. Little Haven is the upmarket neighbour, with a tiny shingle beach and a village vibe formed by a cluster of pastel-painted holiday cottages and some nice pubs. The beach is both bigger and better at Broad Haven, backed by tearooms, gift shops, and places selling rubber rings, water wings and body boards.

Activities

Diving, surfing and sea kayaking are all popular in the area.

West Wales Dive Centre DIVING
(☑ 01437-781457; www.westwalesdivers.co.uk; Little Haven) The West Wales Dive Centre offers a one-day Discover Scuba Diving course (£125) and boat dives for certified divers (£50 per person per day).

Haven Sports WATER SPORTS
(☑ 01437-781354; www.havensports.co.uk; Marine Rd, Broad Haven) Haven Sports, at the south end of the prom behind the Galleon Inn, rents wetsuits (per hour/day £3/15), body boards (£3/15), surfboards (£5/20) and kayaks (£6/30).

Sleeping & Eating

The village's pubs all serve good quality food with an emphasis on local seafood

Mill Haven Place CAMPGROUND £
(☑ 01437-781633; www.millhavenplace.co.uk; Talbenny; site/adult/child £20/8/3; ☺ Mar-Oct; ♿) This charming campground is decked out with pretty bunting, brightly coloured tablecloths, solar-powerd fairy lights and paper lanterns. There's a small beach and

plenty of rockpools nearby, a small number of tranquil pitches for tents and five well-equipped yurts (£595 per week) sleeping four. The owner runs bushcraft courses, so you can perfect your fire-lighting technique in order to cook the catch of the day. There are also some self-catering cottages on-site.

Nest Bistro SEAFOOD ££
(☑ 01437-781728; 12 Grove Pl; mains £14-19; ☺ 6.30-9.30pm Tue-Sat Apr-Oct) This informal little restaurant turns out perfectly cooked lobster, crab, sea bass, turbot and plaice. Book ahead in summer as it's very popular.

Getting There & Away

Both the Puffin Shuttle and bus 311 to Haverfordwest (20 minutes) stop here.

Newgale Sands

As you pass over the bridge by the pub near the north end of Newgale, you're officially crossing the Landsker Line into North Pembrokeshire. Newgale is the biggest beach in St Brides Bay, stretching for 2.5 miles.

Activities

Newsurf Hire Centre SURFING
(☑ 01437-721398; www.newsurf.co.uk) Newgale is one of the best beaches in South Wales for beginning surfers; you can hire surfboards (£5/15 per hour/day), body boards (£4/10) and wetsuits (£4/12) from Newsurf Hire Centre, which also offers surfing lessons (£35 per session).

Getting There & Away

Both the Puffin Shuttle and bus 411 between Haverfordwest and St Davids stop here.

NORTH PEMBROKESHIRE

The Welsh language may not be as ubiquitous in North Pembrokeshire as it once was, but there's no escaping the essential Welshness of the region. It's a land of Iron Age hill forts, holy wells and Celtic saints – including the nation's patron, Dewi Sant (St David). Predating even the ancient Celts are the remnants of an older people, who left behind them dolmens and stone circles – the same people who may have transported their sacred bluestones all the way from

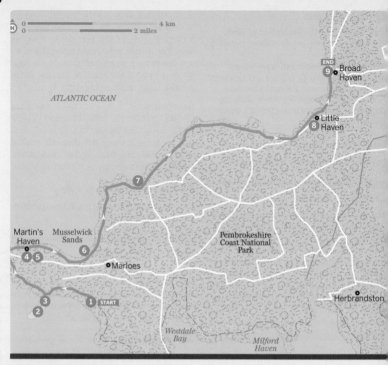

0 ___ 4 km
0 ___ 2 miles

ATLANTIC OCEAN

END Broad Haven

9

Little Haven
8

7

Martin's Haven   Musselwick Sands

Pembrokeshire Coast National Park

4 5   6

Marloes

3   1 START

2

Herbrandston

Westdale Bay

Milford Haven

Walking Tour
PCP: Marloes Sands to Broad Haven

START MARLOES SANDS
END BROAD HAVEN
LENGTH 13 MILES; 4½ TO SIX HOURS

A wonderful but not too challenging walk along dramatic clifftops, this section of the Pembrokeshire Coast Path is close to villages, bus routes and road access points, making it ideal for more leisurely walking but, particularly in mid-summer, potentially busier than more remote sections of the path.

Start out from the long curving stretch of beach at ❶ **Marloes Sands**, where you'll get great views of Skokholm Island. At the end of the beach you pass ❷ **Gateholm Island**, a major Iron Age Celtic settlement where the remains of 130 hut circles have been found. Although the island appears accessible at low tide, it is surrounded by slippery jagged rocks and steep cliffs. Walk on, though, and you'll soon pass the earthwork ramparts of a grand ❸ **promontory fort**. Atlantic storms batter this section of coast and active erosion threatens the sheer red cliffs streaked with

yellow algae. Continue on, enjoying the views over Skomer and Skokholm to the tip of the peninsula to ❹ **Martin's Haven**. This tiny village is the base for Skomer Island boat trips and the office of the Skomer Marine Nature Reserve, which has an interesting display on the underwater environment. Set into the wall next to the office is a ❺ **Celtic cross**, which may date from the 7th century. Around the headland the cliffs change from red to black, and after an hour you'll reach the lovely beach at ❻ **Musselwick Sands**. There are fine views over St Bride's Bay and across to St Davids and Ramsey Island. ❼ **St Brides Haven** is a further 2 miles down the track, with the headland dominated by a Victorian faux-castle, once owned by the Barons of Kensington. A reasonably easy 5-mile stretch leads to ❽ **Little Haven**, separated by rocks from ❾ **Broad Haven**. From the path you'll be able to assess the tide and decide whether to follow the busy road or cross via the beach. Little Haven is a pretty village with restaurants and several B&Bs.

the Preseli Hills to form the giant edifice at Stonehenge. Much of the coastline from St Davids onwards is inaccessible by car. If you're only going to walk part of the Pembrokeshire Coast Path (PCP), this is an excellent section to tackle.

Solva

With its colourfully painted cottages, art galleries, inviting pubs and beautiful L-shaped harbour, Solva is a North Pembrokeshire gem. Clifftop walks provide wonderful views over the village and surrounding coastline, and there's a great B&B in town if you want to make Solva your base for exploring St Davids Peninsula.

◉ Sights & Activities

Solva Woollen Mill MILL
(☑ 01437-721112; www.solvawoollenmill.co.uk; Middle Mill; ⊘ 9.30am-5.30pm Mon-Fri, Sat & Sun Jul-Sep) It's a pleasant walk of just over a mile upriver from Solva to Middle Mill where you'll find the Solva Woollen Mill, the oldest working woollen mill in Pembrokeshire. You can see the weavers at work, browse in the shop, or enjoy tea and cake in the cafe.

Solva Sailboats SAILING
(☑ 01437-720972; www.solva.net/solvasailboats; 1 Maes-y-Forwen) If sailing takes your fancy, you can enjoy a three-hour/full-day cruise aboard a 24ft yacht for £80/160 (up to three passengers) with Solva Sailboats. It also runs official Royal Yachting Association sailing courses.

⊨ Sleeping & Eating

Haroldston House B&B ££
(☑ 01437-721404; www.haroldstonhouse.co.uk; 29 High St; s/d £35/65; ℗) ✔ Set in a lovely old Georgian merchant's house, this wonderful new B&B offers excellent value and chic modern style. The simple but tastefully decorated rooms feature artworks by owner Ian as well as pieces from around the world. There's a free electric-car charging point, discounts for guests arriving by public transport, and tasty, inventive breakfast options.

Cambrian Inn INN ££
(☑ 01437-721210; www.thecambrianinn.co.uk; 6 Main St; mains £8-15; ⊘ 9am-9.30pm, bar 9am-11pm) The Cambrian Inn blends old and new with exposed stonework and original beams but a decidedly contemporary style. It serves an interesting menu of upmarket pub grub and also has three bright and colourful guest rooms (single/double £60/80).

❶ Getting There & Away

Both the Puffin Shuttle and bus 411 between Haverfordwest and St Davids stop here. Alternatively, you can walk along the coast path from St Davids and then bus it back. Join the coast path at Caerfai Bay (signposted from Oriel y Parc), then pick up the eastbound path. It's about 5 miles in total.

St Davids (Tyddewi)

POP 1840

Charismatic St Davids is Britain's smallest 'city', its status ensured by the magnificent 12th-century cathedral that marks Wales' holiest site. The birth and burial place of the nation's patron saint, St Davids has been a place of pilgrimage for more than 1500 years.

The setting itself has a mystical presence. The sea is just beyond the horizon on three sides, so you're constantly surprised by glimpses of it at the ends of streets. Then there are those strangely shaped hills in the distance, which seem to sprout from a particularly ancient landscape.

Dewi Sant (St David) founded a monastic community here in the 6th century, only a short walk from where he was born at St Non's Bay. In 1124 Pope Callistus II declared that two pilgrimages to St Davids were the equivalent of one to Rome, and three were equal to one to Jerusalem. The cathedral has seen a constant stream of visitors ever since.

Today St Davids attracts hordes of non-religious pilgrims too, drawn by the town's laid-back vibe and the excellent hiking, surfing and wildlife-watching in the surrounding area.

◉ Sights

★ **St Davids Cathedral** CHURCH
(www.stdavidscathedral.org.uk; suggested donation £4; ⊘ 8.30am-5.30pm Mon-Sat, 12.45-5.30pm Sun) Hidden in a hollow and behind high walls, St Davids Cathedral is intentionally unassuming. The valley site was chosen in the vain hope that the church would be overlooked by Viking raiders, but it was ransacked at least seven times. Yet once you pass through the gatehouse separating it from the town and its stone walls come into view, it's as imposing as any of its contemporaries.

St Davids

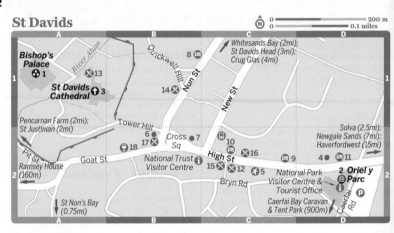

St Davids

Built on the site of a 6th-century chapel, the building dates mainly from the 12th to the 14th centuries. Extensive works were carried out in the 19th century by Sir George Gilbert Scott (architect of the Albert Memorial and St Pancras in London) to stabilise the building and repair damage caused by an earthquake in 1248 and the sloping, boggy ground on which it sits. The distinctive **west front**, with its four pointed towers of purple stone, dates from this period.

The atmosphere inside is one of great antiquity. As you enter the **nave**, the oldest surviving part of the cathedral, the first things you notice are the sloping floor and the outward lean of the massive, purplish-grey pillars linked by semicircular Norman Romanesque arches, a result of subsidence. Above is a richly carved 16th-century oak ceiling, adorned with pendants and bosses.

At the far end of the nave is a delicately carved 14th-century Gothic **pulpitum** (the screen wall between nave and choir), which bears a statue of St David dressed as a medieval bishop, and contains the tomb of Bishop Henry de Gower (died 1347), for whom the Bishop's Palace was built.

Beyond the pulpitum is the magnificent **choir**; check out the mischievous carved figures on the 16th-century misericords (under the seats), one of which depicts pilgrims being seasick over the side of a boat. Don't forget to look up at the colourfully painted lantern tower above (those steel tie rods around the walls were installed in the 19th century to hold the structure together).

In a recess in the **Holy Trinity Chapel** at the east end of the cathedral is the object of all those religious pilgrimages: a simple oak casket that contains the bones of St David and St Justinian. The chapel ceiling is distinguished by superb fan vaulting dating from the early 16th century.

Accessed from the north wall of the nave, the **Treasury** displays vestments and religious paraphernalia crafted from precious metals and stones. Just as valuable are the treasures in the neighbouring **Library**, the oldest of which dates to 1505.

Lord Rhys ap Gruffydd, the greatest of the princes of South Wales, and his son Rhys Gryg are known to be buried in the cathedral, although their effigies in the south choir aisle date only from the 14th century. Gerald of Wales, an early rector of the cathedral, has a gravestone here, but scholars suggest he is actually buried at Lincolnshire Cathedral.

In August there are hour-long **guided tours** at 11.30am Monday and 2.30pm Friday; at other times, tours can be arranged in advance.

★ **Bishop's Palace**   RUIN
(www.cadw.wales.gov.uk; adult/child £3.20/2.80; ☉9.30am-5pm) Across the river from the cathedral, this atmospheric ruined palace, run by Cadw (the Welsh historic monuments agency), was begun at the same time as the cathedral, but its final, imposing form owes most to Henry de Gower, bishop from 1327 to 1347.

Its most distinctive feature is the arcaded parapet that runs around the courtyard, decorated with a chequerboard pattern of purple and yellow stone blocks. The corbels that support the arches are richly adorned with a menagerie of carved figures – lions, monkeys, dogs and birds, as well as grotesque mythical creatures and human heads. The distinctive purple sandstone, also used in the cathedral, comes from Caerbwdy Bay, a mile southeast of St Davids.

The palace courtyard provides a spectacular setting for open-air plays in summer.

★ **Oriel y Parc**   GALLERY
(☑01437-720392; www.orielyparc.co.uk; High St; ☉9.30am-5pm) Occupying a bold, semi-circular, environmentally friendly building on the edge of town, Oriel y Parc is a winning collaboration between the Pembrokeshire Coast National Park Authority and the National Museum Wales. Not only does it function as a tourist office and national park visitor centre, it houses changing exhibitions from the museum's art collection. The focus is on landscapes, particularly Pembrokeshire scenes.

🏃 **Activities**

Ma Sime's Surf Hut   WATER SPORTS
(☑01437-720433; www.masimes.co.uk; 28 High St) Ma Sime's Surf Hut rents wetsuits, surfboards and body boards, and can arrange surf lessons with Whitesands Surf School.

☞ **Tours**

Thousand Islands Expeditions   BOAT TOUR
(☑01437-721721; www.thousandislands.co.uk; Cross Sq) The only operator permitted by the RSPB to land day-trippers on Ramsay Island (adult/child £15/7.50); bookings advised. It has a range of other boat trips, including hour-long blasts in a high-speed inflatable boat (£24/12), 2½-hour whale- and dolphin-spotting cruises around Grassholm Island (£60/30), and one-hour jet-boat trips (£25/12). Book in advance.

Voyages of Discovery   BOAT TOUR
(☑01437-721911; www.ramseyisland.co.uk; 1 High St) Offers trips to Ramsey Island (adult/child £25/12), as well as three-hour whale- and dolphin-watching trips (adult/child £60/30) and evening birdwatching trips (£30/17).

Aquaphobia   BOAT TOUR
(☑01437-720471; www.aquaphobiaramseyisland. co.uk; Grove Hotel, High St) Runs boats to Ramsey Island (adult/child £320/10), Grassholm (£40/20) and three-hour whale- and dolphin-watching trips (£40/20)

🎊 **Festivals**

St Davids Cathedral Festival   MUSIC
(www.stdavidscathedral.org.uk; St Davids Cathedral; ☉May) The St Davids Cathedral Festival is 10 days of classical-music performances, starting on the Spring Bank Holiday weekend at the end of May. The Irish-oak ceiling gives it fine acoustics, so if you're not here for the festival it's well worth checking out one of the many other concerts performed at the cathedral throughout the year.

🛏 **Sleeping**

Caerfai Bay Caravan
& Tent Park   CAMPGROUND £
(☑01437-720274; www.caerfaibay.co.uk; site/adult/ child £15/5/3.50; ☉Mar-Nov) A 15-minute walk south of St Davids, this large campground is on an organic dairy farm practically right on the coast path. There's a small farm shop, fresh croissants in the morning, good facilities and great coastal views across St Brides Bay.

Pencarnan Farm
CAMPGROUND £

(☑ 01437-720580; www.pencarnanfarm.co.uk; sites per adult/child £16/6) Set on a large working farm with a miniature-horse stud, this campground is the most westerly in Wales. There are 60 level pitches within walking distance of the beach. The site is 2 miles from St Davids. Head in the direction of St Justinians and follow the signs.

★ Crug Glas
GUESTHOUSE ££

(☑ 01348-831302; www.crug-glas.co.uk; Abereiddy; r £100-180; ℗) Crug Glas is a very special place to stay. This opulent country house set on a big working farm offers rooms decked out in a grand manner with pastel hues, rich fabrics, ornate beds, enormous bathrooms and elegant period grandeur. But don't worry chaps, the 21st century does exist here and you'll find a TV and CD player to play with. In keeping with the style, the evening meals are exquisite. From St Davids follow the A487 towards Fishguard for 4 miles to get here.

Ramsey House
B&B ££

(☑ 01437-720321; www.ramseyhouse.co.uk; Lower Moor; r £115; ℗ 🛜) The young owners have created a fashionable boutique-style B&B from their new house on the outskirts of St Davids, which is still only a short stroll from the town centre. The six rooms are all different but feature bold wallpapers, contemporary chandeliers, silky throws and goose down duvets, as well as stylish bathrooms.

Coach House
B&B ££

(☑ 01437-720632; www.thecoachhouse.biz; 15 High St; s/d £65/90; 🛜🍴) The bright, simple rooms at the Coach House are just part of its appeal. Friendly and helpful hosts, excellent breakfasts and its central location all conspire to make it one of St Davids' better options. There's also a small cottage at the back sleeping up to five people, which makes a good base for families.

Bryn Awel
B&B ££

(☑ 01437-720082; www.brynawel-bb.co.uk; 45 High St; s/d £70/85) A pretty little terraced house on the main street, Bryn Awel has small but cosy rooms (all en suite). The owners are keen outdoors enthusiasts, and can advise on the best local spots for walking and bird-watching.

Alandale
B&B ££

(☑ 01437-720404; www.stdavids.co.uk/guesthouse/ alandale.htm; 43 Nun St; s/d £36/90; 🛜) A neat terraced house built in the 1880s for coastguard officers, Alandale has a bright, cheerful atmosphere and comfortable, tastefully decorated rooms. Ask for one at the back, which are quieter and have sweeping countryside views.

Grove
INN ££

(☑ 01437-720341; www.grovestdavids.com; High St; r/ste £90/115; ℗ 🛜 🍴) Offering upmarket pub accommodation, the Grove's rooms have been given a fresh, up-to-the-moment look in a recent refurbishment. Expect a bit of noise from the drinkers downstairs – pack earplugs or join in.

✖ Eating & Drinking

Refectory at St Davids
CAFE £

(St Davids Cathedral; mains £5-9; ⊙ 10am-5pm; 🛜) Part of the ongoing restoration of the cathedral cloister, the new refectory is a triumph of design. Medieval St Mary's Hall has been given an ultramodern facelift, with blonde wood contrasting with the exposed stone walls and a shiny mezzanine supported on slanted legs. Take a seat upstairs for better views. On Sundays there's a traditional carvery.

Sampler
CAFE £

(www.sampler-tearoom.co.uk; 17 Nun St; mains £5-9; ⊙ 10.30am-5pm Mon-Thu) Named after the embroidery samples blanketing the walls, this may be the perfect exemplar of the traditional Welsh tearoom. Pembrokeshire Clotted Cream Tea comes served with freshly baked scones and *bara brith* (a rich, fruit tea loaf), and there are Welsh cheese platters, jacket potatoes, soups and sandwiches.

St Davids Food & Wine
DELI £

(www.stdavidsfoodandwine.co.uk; High St; ⊙ 8.30am-5.30pm Mon-Sat) Stock up on picnic supplies at this delicatessen, which specialises in local organic produce.

Sound Cafe
CAFE ££

(18 High St; meals £4-10; ⊙ 9am-4pm Mon & Tue, 9am-9pm Wed-Sun) This chilled out, quirky cafe is renowned for its great breakfasts, but is a welcoming place all day with hearty lunch specials, and gourmet burgers and tapas in the evenings. It's fully licensed so it's equally good for quenching your thirst after a day's walking.

The Bishops
PUB ££

(www.thebish.co.uk; 22-23 Cross Sq; mains £9-13; ⊙ meals noon-9.30pm; 🛜) A friendly, ram-

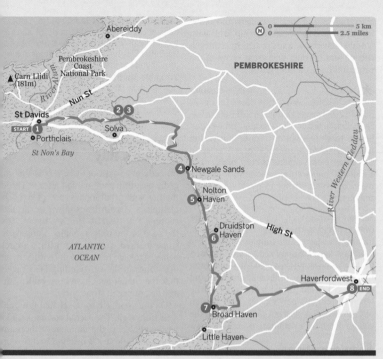

Cycling Tour
The Celtic Trail: St David's to Haverfordwest

START ST DAVIDS
END HAVERFORDWEST
LENGTH 22 MILES; TWO TO FOUR HOURS

The wonderful Celtic Trail (p155) makes a fantastic long-distance ride for cycling enthusiasts, but you don't have to have buns of steel to get a glimpse of the action. Tackling a section of the trail on a hired bike is a great way to explore Pembrokeshire at a slower pace. This route from St Davids to Haverfordwest is mostly on quiet roads and passes some glorious stretches of coast. Don't be fooled by the short distance though, there are some proper hills en route.

Set off from the cathedral in ❶ **St Davids**, heading out of town along the A487 in the direction of Solva. At the edge of town, turn left following the sign for National Cycle Route 4. Flat, rural roads lead you through agricultural land to little ❷ **Middle Mill**. Cross over the stone bridge and veer right. If you're in need of a break or interested in local history, the ❸ **Solva Woollen Mill** (p161)

makes a good stop. Continue east along quiet lanes to a T-junction where the route goes right, and then right again at the second T-junction. Next you'll hit the busier A487 and you need to turn left along this road for a brief spell down to the coast at ❹ **Newgale Sands**, where there's a long sand and pebble beach. When the road forks, veer right along the quiet coast road. From here it's a feast for the eyes but hard work for the legs along a stunning stretch of coast featuring a series of picturesque bays. The road undulates up and down some short but tough hills past ❺ **Nolton Haven** and ❻ **Druidston Haven** to ❼ **Broad Haven**. Catch your breath at this busy seaside village before turning inland along the A48. As you cycle out of the village, the road forks. Veer left along Long Lane and then right at the next T-junction. You'll soon rejoin the A48 towards ❽ **Haverfordwest**, but there is a dedicated cycle path. From here it's an easy 3.5 miles into town.

bling pub full of locals, walkers and blow-ins, this place serves hearty pub grub with a smile. There's a roaring fire in winter, a decent pint on offer and great views of the cathedral from the beer garden.

★Cwtch   MODERN WELSH £££
(☑01437-720491; www.cwtchrestaurant.co.uk; 22 High St; 2-/3-courses £24/30; ⊙5.30-9.30pm Tue-Sat, daily high season) Stone walls and wooden beams mark this out as a sense of occasion place, yet there's a snugness that lives up to its name (*cwtch* means 'a cosy place' or 'a cuddle'). There's an emphasis on local produce, so expect plenty of fresh seafood on the menu.

Farmer's Arms   PUB
(www.farmersstdavids.co.uk; 14 Goat St; ⊙11am-midnight Mon-Sun) Even though St Davids is a bit of a tourist trap, you'd be hard-pressed finding a more authentic country pub than the Farmer's Arms. There's real ale and Guinness on tap, and it's the place to be when the rugby's playing. The beer garden out the back is a pleasant place to watch the sun go down on a summer's evening.

❶ Information

National Park Visitor Centre & Tourist Office
(☑01437-720392; www.orielyparc.co.uk; High St; ⊙9.30am-5pm) In a striking landscaped building 350m east of Cross Sq.
National Trust Visitor Centre (☑01437-720385; High St; ⊙10am-5.30pm Mon-Sat, 10am-4pm Sun) Sells local-interest books and guides to NT properties in Pembrokeshire.

❶ Getting There & Around

The Celtic Way cycling route passes through St Davids. There's pleasant cycling on minor roads around the peninsula but no off-road action (the coast path is for walkers only).

St Davids and the surrounding area suffers from parking problems and congestion in summer. Consider walking or taking the bus if you can.

Tony's Taxis (☑01437-720931; www.tonys-taxis.net) provides a luggage transfer service for Pembrokeshire Coast Path walkers, covering the area from Little Haven to Fishguard.

BUS

Bus routes include 411 and the Puffin Shuttle to Solva (nine minutes), Newgale Sands (20 minutes) and Haverfordwest (46 minutes), and 413 to Trefin (20 minutes), Goodwick (45 minutes) and Fishguard (47 minutes).

Celtic Coaster (403; ⊙Apr-Sep) The Celtic Coaster circles between St Davids, St Non's Bay, St Justinian and Whitesands Bay. See als the Puffin Shuttle. The main bus stops are in New St and the Oriel y Parc car park.
Strumble Shuttle (404; ⊙Mon, Thu & Sat Oct-Apr, daily May-Sep) The Strumble Shuttle follows the coast between St Davids and Fishguard, calling at Porthgain, Trefin, Strumble Head and Goodwick.

St Non's Bay

Immediately south of St Davids is this ru gedly beautiful spot, named after St David mother and traditionally accepted as h birthplace. A path leads down to the 13t century ruins of **St Non's Chapel**. On the base of the walls remains, along with stone marked with a cross within a circ believed to date from the 7th century. Stan ing stones in the surrounding field sugge that the chapel may have been built with an ancient pagan stone circle.

On the approach to the chapel is a pret little **holy well**. The sacred spring is said have emerged at the moment of the sain birth and the water is believed to have cur tive powers. Although pilgrimages were c ficially banned following the suppression Catholicism in the 16th century, people co tinued to make furtive visits.

The site has now come full circle. In 19: a local Catholic, Cecil Morgan-Griffiths, bu the **Chapel of Our Lady & St Non** out the stones of ruined religious buildings th once stood nearby. Its dimensions ech those of the original chapel. The Cathol Church repaired the stone vaulting over th well in 1951, and Morgan-Griffith's house now used by the Passionist Fathers as a r treat centre.

Ramsey Island

Ramsey Island lies off the headland to th west of St Davids, ringed by dramatic s cliffs and an offshore armada of rocky lets and reefs. The island is a Royal Socie for the Protection of Birds (RSPB) reser famous for its large breeding populatic of choughs – members of the crow fami with glossy black feathers and distincti red bills and legs – and for its grey seals. you're here between late August and mi November, you will also see seal pups.

PEMBROKESHIRE ADVENTURES

With all that wild, rugged coastline it's no surprise that water sports are a big deal in Pembrokeshire. All across the region you'll find sailing, surfing, windsurfing, kite surfing, diving and kayaking operators, as well as Pembrokeshire's very own home-grown invention, **coasteering**. A combination of rock climbing, gully scrambling, cave exploration, wave riding and cliff jumping, this demanding activity is the mainstay of the local adventure-sports scene.

The notorious **Bitches** in Ramsey Sound are known as one of Britain's best white-water play spots. This tidal race offers massive whirlpools, eddies, big wave trains and stoppers, and standing waves on higher tides. It's a dangerous place to play, however, so consider hiring a guide for your first attempt. You'll find more information and safety advice on www.canoewales.com/the-bitches.aspx and www.the-bitches.co.uk.

➜ **Celtic Quest** (☏ 01348-881530; www.celticquest.co.uk; per person from £39) Coasteering specialists, taking to the cliffs near Abereiddy.

➜ **Dive in2 Pembrokeshire** (☏ 01646-636684; www.dive-in2-pembrokeshire.com) A long-established dive operator offering guided dives around the islands, Solva and Little Haven.

➜ **Mike Mayberry Kayaking** (☏ 01348-874699; www.mayberrykayaking.co.uk) Offers instruction courses and guided kayaking tours for more experienced paddlers.

➜ **Outer Reef Surf School** (☏ 01646-680070; www.outerreefsurfschool.com) Learn to surf at Newgale Sands or Manorbier before hitting the big breaks at Freshwater West.

➜ **Pembrokeshire Adventure Centre** (☏ 01646-622013; www.princes-trust.org.uk/adventure; Cleddau Reach, Pembroke Dock) Offers coasteering, kayaking, surfing, climbing, sailing and canoeing from its base in Pembroke Dock.

➜ **Preseli Venture** (☏ 01348-837709; www.preseliventure.co.uk) Has its own lodge near Abermawr, on the coast between St Davids and Fishguard. Activities include coasteering, sea kayaking, mountain biking, surfing and coastal hiking.

➜ **Sea Kayak Guides** (☏ 01437-720859; www.seakayakguides.co.uk) Runs single and multiday sea- and surf-kayaking instruction and expeditions as well as guided trips to the Bitches.

➜ **TYF Adventure** (☏ 01437-721611; www.tyf.com; 1 High St, St David's) Organises coasteering, surfing, sea-kayaking and rock-climbing trips, and rents equipment from its St Davids base.

You can reach the island by boat from the tiny harbour at St Justinian, 2 miles west of St Davids. Longer boat trips run up to 20 miles offshore, to the edge of the Celtic Deep, to spot whales, porpoises and dolphins. What you'll see depends on the weather and the time of year; July to September are the best months. Porpoises are seen on most trips, dolphins on four out of five, and there's a 40% chance of seeing whales. The most common species is the minke, but pilot whales, fin whales and orcas have also been spotted.

❶ Getting There & Away

From St Davids the Celtic Coaster heads to St Justinian, from where boats travel daily to Ramsay Island. For further details, see p166.

Whitesands Bay

The mile-long strand of Whitesands Bay (Porth Mawr) is a popular surfing spot. At extremely low tide you can see the wreck of a paddle tugboat that went aground here in 1882, and the fossil remains of a prehistoric forest. If Whitesands is really busy – and it often is – you can escape the worst of the crowds by walking north along the coastal path for 10 to 15 minutes to the smaller, more secluded beach at **Porthmelgan**.

🏃 Activities

Whitesands Surf School   SURFING
(☏ 01437-720433; www.whitesandssurfschool.co.uk) Runs surfing lessons; a 2½-hour beginner's session costs £35, including equipment. You can book at Ma Sime's Surf Hut in St Davids.

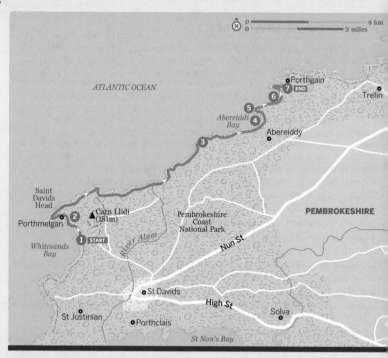

🏃 Walking Tour
PCP: Whitesands to Porthgain

START WHITESANDS
END PORTHGAIN
LENGTH 10 MILES; FOUR TO SIX HOURS

Covering a beautiful but remote stretch of coast from popular Whitesands Bay near St Davids to the historic port of Porthgain, this rewarding walk takes you over rugged headlands and past dramatic cliffs, pretty coves and flooded quarries. It's a taxing route with several steep descents and ascents but it's well worth the effort. Bring provisions, as it's a long way between villages.

Start out at busy ❶ **Whitesands Bay** and head west onto wild and rocky St Davids Head. The start of the route is fairly easy with a good path, wide open views and craggy volcanic outcrops to admire. The only signs of human habitation here are ancient, with the simple ❷ **neolithic burial chamber** on the headline predating the surrounding remnants of Celtic forts. The path soon becomes more rugged with a rock scramble down to and up from the lovely little cove at ❸ **Aber-pwll**. Continue on

past crumbling cliffs to ❹ **Abereiddi**, looking out for seals in the coves, gannets and possibly porpoises diving for fish out at sea. The beach at Abereiddi is famous for its black sand full of tiny fossils. Ruined quarry buildings and slate workers' cottages flank the path beyond the beach that leads to the ❺ **Blue Lagoon**, a deep turquoise flooded slate quarry now popular with coasteerers and, in early September, cliff divers from all over the world who compete here diving 27m into the icy water below. The half-hour walk from Abereiddi to Porthgain is one of the best stretches along the entire coast path, following a cliff-top plateau past the often deserted beach at ❻ **Traeth Llyfn**. A long flight of steep metal stairs leads down to the golden sand, but beware of strong undercurrents and the tide, which can cut off parts of the beach from the steps. Continue on for the last descent into the tiny harbour of ❼ **Porthgain**, where you can reward yourself with some superb seafood at ❽ **Shed** (p169) or some top-notch pub grub at the welcoming ❾ **Sloop Inn** (p169).

🛏 Sleeping

⭐ **St Davids YHA**   HOSTEL **£**
(📞 0845 371 9141; www.yha.org.uk; Llaethdy; dm/r £18/49; 🅿 🛜 ♿) Set in an atmospheric former farmhouse tucked beneath Carn Llidi, this hostel offers excellent views, quick access to Whitesands Beach and endless opportunities for walking and exploring. The snug dorms are in the former cow shed. The hostel is 2 miles northwest of St Davids.

ℹ Getting There & Away

Expect to pay for parking. The Celtic Coaster leads to Whitesands Bay from St Davids or you can walk here, but you will need a decent map to find the twisting paths that make up the route.

St Davids Head

This atmospheric heather-wreathed promontory was fortified by the ancient Celts. The jumbled stones and ditch of an Iron Age rampart are still visible, as are rock circles, which once formed the foundations of huts. The tip of the headland is a series of rock and turf ledges, a great place for a picnic or wildlife-spotting – in summer you can see gannets diving into the sea and choughs soaring on the breeze. Adding to the ancient ambience, wild ponies can often be spotted.

Further along the grassy path through the heather, an even older structure stands. The simple burial chamber known as **Coetan Arthur** (Arthur's Quoit) consists of a capstone supported by a rock at one end and dates to about 3500 BC.

The rocky summit of **Carn Llidi** (181m) rises behind, offering panoramic views that take in Whitesands Bay, Ramsey and Skomer Islands and, on a clear day, the coast of Ireland on the horizon.

Porthgain

For centuries the tiny harbour of Porthgain consisted of little more than a few sturdy cottages wedged into a rocky cove. In the mid-19th century it began to prosper as the port for shipping out slate quarried just down the coast at Abereiddy, and by the 1870s its own deposits of granite and fine clay had put it on the map as a source of building stone.

The post-WWI slump burst the bubble, and the sturdy stone quays and overgrown brick storage 'bins' are all that remain.

Despite having been an industrial harbour, Porthgain is surprisingly picturesque and today it is home to a couple of art galleries and restaurants.

🍴 Eating

⭐ **Shed**   SEAFOOD **££**
(📞 01348-831518; www.theshedporthgain.co.uk; mains £7.50-21.50; ⊙ daily Apr-Oct, call for hours Nov-Mar) Housed in a beautifully converted machine shop right by the little harbour, this simple little 'Fish and Chip Bistro' is renowned as one of Pembrokeshire's finest seafood restaurants. The new simplified menu offers upmarket fish and chips in all guises as well as a short list of daily specials, many of which have been caught by the owners that morning.

Sloop Inn   PUB **££**
(📞 01348-831449; www.sloop.co.uk; mains £9-20; 🛜 📞) With wooden tables worn smooth by many a bended elbow, old photos of Porthgain in its industrial heyday, and interesting nautical clutter all over the place, the Sloop is a cosy and deservedly popular pub. It dishes up breakfast (until 11am) and hearty, home-cooked meals to hungry walkers. Book ahead for dinner.

Porthgain to Fishguard

The section of coast between Porthgain and Fishguard shelters ancient monuments, dramatic cliffs and rocky coves. Seals, dolphins and sharks can often be seen in the water below.

The approach to the little cove of **Pwll Deri** follows cliffs that reach 137m in height and offer expansive views over the sometimes turbulent Irish Sea. The rocky summit of **Garn Fawr** (213m), topped by an Iron Age fort, rises above Pwll Deri.

Further along, on wild and rocky **Strumble Head**, a lighthouse beams out its signal as high-speed ferries thunder past on their way to Ireland. The headland makes a good vantage point for spotting dolphins, seals, sharks and sunfish; below the parking area is a WWII lookout that now serves as a shelter for observing wildlife.

◉ Sights

Carreg Samson   DOLMEN

Sitting in a farmer's field, with terrific views of Strumble Head, this dolmen is quite remarkable. The massive capstone seems to be only just touching the stones that it is balanced on. It's signposted off the minor road between Trefin and Abercastle.

St Gwyndaf's Church   CHURCH

(Llanwnda) At the heart of the tiny village of Llanwnda, St Gwyndaf's Church showcases its antiquity in the carved stones, inscribed with crosses and Celtic designs, set into the outside walls. Inside, look up at the timber roof beams; at the far end of the third beam from the west (door) end, facing the altar, is a 15th-century carving of a tonsured monk's head.

Across the lane from the church, a wooden gate with a yellow waymark indicates the start of the mile-long track to **Carregwastad Point**, the site of the infamous 1797 invasion.

Melin Tregwynt   MILL

(☑ 01348-891288; www.melintregwynt.co.uk; ⊙ 9.30am-5pm Mon-Fri, 10am-5pm Sat, 11.30am-4pm Sun) For over 100 years the same family has run Melin Tregwynt, a traditional woollen mill which churns out some of Wales' best blankets, cushions and upholstery fabrics. New designs have brought the traditional weaves bang up to date and they are some of the most fashionable home accessories around. The full range includes clothing, bags, lampshades and ceramics, all of which are on display in the mill shop. You can watch the looms in action from 9am to 4.30pm Monday to Friday and see just how these gorgeous double-fronted fabrics are created. There's also a small cafe and two self-catering cottages on-site.

⌂ Sleeping

★**Hill Fort Tipis**   CAMPGROUND £

(☑ 01348-891409; www.hillfort-tipis.co.uk; Penparc; sites adult/child £10/5, tipis per night/week £65/395; ♿) ✎ A staggering panorama greets you from this hill-top campground where the views over Strumble Head and the Irish Sea are a knockout. There's an Iron Age hill fort on-site, a children's play area, fresh milk and eggs up for grabs, and traditional campsites as well as cosy tipis sleeping four or six.

Pwll Deri YHA   HOSTEL £

(☑ 0845 371 9536; www.yha.org.uk; Castell Mawr Trefasser; dm/r from £18/36) Perched atop a 120m-high cliff overlooking the sea, this hostel has one of the finest locations in Britain. The views from the dining room would rival those from any top hotel and the sunsets are spectacular.

Old School Hostel   HOSTEL £

(☑ 01348-831800; www.theoldschoolhostel.co.uk; Ffordd-yr-Afon, Trefin; dm/s/d £16/25/42; 🛜📶) ✎ Set in a rambling old school building, this is one of the new breed of independent, brightly painted, personably run backpackers. The six rooms offer flexible accommodation and can be used as dorms or private rooms. Add on a hearty local organic breakfast for an extra £5 before hitting the coast path, which is less than a mile away.

Fishguard (Abergwaun)

POP 5400

Perched on a headland between its modern ferry port and former fishing harbour, Fishguard is often overlooked by travellers, most of them passing through on their way to or from Ireland. It doesn't have any sights as such, but it's an appealing little town with some good eating and drinking options.

The picturesque Lower Town (Y Cwm), next to the old fishing harbour, was used as a setting for the 1971 film version of *Under Milk Wood* with Richard Burton, Peter O'Toole and Elizabeth Taylor. It also featured (for all of two minutes) in the classic *Moby Dick,* starring Gregory Peck.

Around the other side of the headland, Goodwick (Wdig; *oo*-dig) was the site of the 1078 battle between northern and southern Celtic lords (as if they didn't have enough to worry about from the encroaching Normans), culminating in a bloody massacre of the southerners. Fishguard also has the quirky distinction of being the setting for the last foreign invasion of Britain.

The Marine Walk, which follows the coast from the car park on the Parrog around to the Lower Town, offers great views over the old harbour and along the coast to Dinas Head.

Much that goes on in Fishguard happens in the central **Town Hall** on Market Sq. The tourist office is here, as is the library (handy or free internet access) and the **market all**. It hosts a market on Thursday and a armers market on Saturday.

◉ Sights

ast Invasion Gallery EXHIBITION

☑ 01437-776122; ⊙ 9.30am-5pm Mon-Sat) `FREE`

'pstairs in the Town Hall is the Last Invaion Gallery, which displays the *Fishguard apestry*. Inspired by the *Bayeux Tapestry*, vhich recorded the 1066 Norman invasion t Hastings, it was commissioned in 1997 to ommemorate the bicentenary of the failed ishguard invasion. It uses a similar carponish style as the *Bayeux Tapestry* (albeit vith less rude bits) and tells the story in the ourse of 37 frames and 30m of cloth. A film bout its making demonstrates what a huge ndertaking it was.

✯ Festivals & Events

ishguard Folk Festival FOLK FESTIVAL

www.pembrokeshire-folk-music.co.uk; ⊙ late May r early Jun) A four-day festival of music, song nd dance, with mostly free performances nd events, this is a wonderful way to exerience Welsh musical traditions as well as nodern-day interpretations of this ancient raft. With pub sessions, dance displays, pen-mic sessions, workshops and a ripoaring festival *twmpath* (traditional comnunity dance) it's hard not to jump on in.

⌂ Sleeping

Manor Town House B&B ££

☑ 01348-873260; www.manortownhouse.com; 11 Main St; s £65-75, d £75-105; 🛜) This graceful Georgian house has a lovely garden terrace where you can sit and gaze over the harbour. The young owners are charm personified and there's a generally upmarket ambience, although the decor doesn't always hit the spot.

Pentower B&B ££

(☑ 01348-874462; www.pentower.co.uk; Tower Hill; s £50, d £80-85; P) Built by Sir Evan Jones, the architect who designed the harbour, this rambling turreted home is perched on a hill at the edge of town, overlooking his creation. The bright, spacious rooms are decked out in classical B&B style and the hosts are incredibly welcoming. You'd be well advised to book ahead as there are only two guest rooms.

✖ Eating & Drinking

The Lounge@Number3 ITALIAN ££

(☑ 01348-871845; www.theloungerestaurant.co.uk; 3 Main St; mains £8-20; ⊙ 6-10pm Wed-Sat) This simple Italian with stripped floors, leather chairs and a mellow vibe is turning out to be Fishguard's best restaurant. An excellent menu of pasta, pizza, meat and fish combined with a well chosen wine list make it the pick of the crop.

Royal Oak Inn PUB

(☑ 01348-872514; Market Sq; mains £5-15; ⊙ 10am-11pm) Suffused with character, this old inn was the site of the French surrender in 1797, and the table on which it was signed takes pride of place at the back of the dining room. The pub has turned into something of an invasion museum, filled with memorabilia. Not only does the Royal Oak have an important place in Fishguard's

---

THE LAST INVASION OF BRITAIN

While Hastings in 1066 may get all the press, the last invasion of Britain was actually at Carregwastad Point, northwest of Fishguard, on 22 February 1797. The ragtag collection of 1400 French mercenaries and bailed convicts, led by an Irish-American named Colonel Tate, had intended to land at Bristol and march to Liverpool, keeping English troops occupied while France mounted an invasion of Ireland. But bad weather blew them ashore at Carregwastad where, after scrambling up a steep cliff, they set about looting the Pencaer peninsula for food and drink.

The invaders had hoped that the Welsh peasants would rise up to join them in revolutionary fervour but, not surprisingly, their drunken pillaging didn't endear them to the locals. The French were quickly seen off by volunteer 'yeoman' soldiers, with help from the people of Fishguard including, most famously, one Jemima Nicholas who, armed with nothing more than a pitchfork, single-handedly captured 12 mercenaries.

The beleaguered Tate surrendered and a mere two days after their arrival the invaders laid down their weapons at Goodwick and were sent off to the jail at Haverfordwest.

history, it also hosts a popular live folk night on Tuesdays, when musicians are welcome to join in.

Ship Inn
PUB

(☑ 01348-874033; Old Newport Rd, Lower Town; ⊙ 11.30am-11pm) This is a lovely little pub with an open fire in winter and lots of memorabilia on the walls, including photos of Richard Burton filming *Under Milk Wood* outside (the street and nearby quay have not changed a bit).

🛈 Information

Fishguard Tourist Office (☑ 01437-776636; Market Sq, Town Hall; ⊙ 9.30am-5pm Mon-Fri, 9.30am-4pm Sat)

🛈 Getting There & Away

BOAT

Stena Line (☑ 08447 707070; www.stenaline.co.uk) Has two regular ferries a day, year-round (car and driver from £79, additional adult/child £28/15, foot passenger £29, bike £10), and a 'Fastcraft' most days in July and August (car and driver from £94, other fares the same), between Rosslare in the southeast of Ireland and Fishguard Harbour.

BUS

Buses include 412 to Haverfordwest (31 minutes), Dinas Cross (13 minutes), Newport (16 minutes), Castell Henllys (22 minutes) and Cardigan (40 minutes), and 413 to Goodwick (two minutes), Trefin (18 minutes) and St Davids (46 minutes). See also the Strumble Shuttle and Poppit Rocket.

TRAIN

There's a daily direct train to Fishguard Harbour from Cardiff (£24, 2½ hours) via Llanelli (£14, 1½ hours) and Carmarthen (£8.60, 52 minutes). On Sunday there's a slower service via Swansea (£14, two hours).

Cwm Gwaun

Running inland to the southeast of Fishguard is **Cwm Gwaun** (*cum*-gwine), the valley of the River Gwaun. This narrow, wooded cleft, best explored on foot or bicycle, feels strangely remote and mysterious. Numerous ancient sites, cairns, stone circles and standing stones litter the valley and, famously, the inhabitants retain a soft spot for the Julian calendar (abandoned by the rest of Britain in 1752), which means that they celebrate New Year on 13 January. Local children walk from house to house singing traditional Welsh songs on this day and are rewarded with sweets and money.

In tiny Pontfaen meander up the laneway that crosses the river and goes up the hill to **St Brynach's Church**, a wonderfully restored chapel which originally dates back to 540AD. Ruined and then rescued in the late 19th century, it has two 9th-century stone crosses in the graveyard.

🍷 Drinking

Dyffryn Arms
PU

(☑ 01348-881305; Pontfaen; ⊙ 11am-midnight Mon-Sat, noon-10.30pm Sun) It would be a shame to pass through Pontfaen without stopping for a pint at the Dyffryn Arms, better known as Bessie's, a rare old-fashioned pub in the front room of the octogenarian landlady's house. Beer is served from jugs filled straight from the barrel; no hand pumps here!

🛈 Getting There & Away

➤ There is no public transport along this route.

➤ The back roads around the Preseli Hills and Cwm Gwaun offer some of the best on-road cycling in southwest Wales. You can rent a bike from Newport Bike Hire (p175) in Newport .

Dinas Island

The great wedge-shaped profile of Dinas Island juts out from the coast between Fishguard and Newport. It's not really an island as it's attached to the mainland by a neck of land, framed on either side by picturesque coves – the sandy strand of **Pwllgwaelod** to the west, and the rocky inlet of **Cwm-yr-Eglwys** to the east, where you can see the ruin of 12th-century St Brynach's Church, destroyed by the great storm of 1859.

The circuit of the headland (3 miles) makes an excellent walk, with the chance of spotting seals and dolphins from the 142m-high cliffs at Dinas Head, the northernmost point; a path across the neck between Pwllgwaelod and Cwm-yr-Eglwys allows you to return to your starting point.

🍴 Eating

Old Sailors
SEAFOOD £$

(☑ 01348-811491; Pwllgwaelod; mains £7-12; ⊙ Wed-Sat) The Old Sailors in Pwllgwaelod, a remote and rustic place serving locals for the last 500 years, is a great place to break a coast walk and stop for lunch. Its reputation for fine food and stunning sunsets from the beer garden overlooking the beach means it's well worth seeking out. There's a warm welcome for walkers, dogs and children, and some excellent lobster, crab and mussels to reward your effort.

ⓘ Getting There & Away

Bus 412 (Haverfordwest–Fishguard–Cardigan) stops at Dinas Cross, just over a mile from Pwllgwaelod. See also the Poppit Rocket.

Newport (Trefdraeth)

POP 1160

In stark contrast to the industrial city of Newport near Cardiff, the Pembrokeshire Newport is a pretty cluster of flower-bedecked cottages huddled beneath a small Norman castle. It sits at the foot of Mynydd Carningli, a large bump on the seaward side of the Preseli Hills, and in recent years has gained a reputation for the quality of its restaurants and guesthouses.

Newport makes a pleasant base for walks along the coastal path or south into the Preseli Hills, but it does get crowded in summer. At the northwest corner of the town is little Parrog Beach, dwarfed by Newport Sands (Traeth Mawr) across the river.

Newport Castle (now a private residence) was founded by a Norman nobleman called William FitzMartin – who was married to a daughter of Lord Rhys ap Gruffydd – after his father-in-law drove him out of nearby Nevern in 1191. Newport grew up around the castle, initially as a garrison town.

⊙ Sights

There's a little dolmen, **Carreg Coetan**, right in town, well signposted from the main road just past the Golden Lion. At first glance it looks like the capstone is securely supported by the four standing stones. A closer inspection suggests that some old magic has held it together all these thousands of years, as it's balanced on only two of them.

If you keep walking past Carreg Coetan, you come to an iron bridge over the **Nevern Estuary**, a haven for birdlife, especially in winter. Cross the bridge and turn left for an easy walk along the shoreline to the sandy beach of **Newport Sands**.

It's said that in the 6th century, St Brynach of Nevern used to head up **Mynydd Carningli** (347m) to commune with angels, which is the likely derivation of the name. You can climb to the summit from town

ⓘ POPPIT ROCKET

Between May and September, the Poppit Rocket (405) heads three times daily in each direction from Fishguard to Cardigan. Stops include Pwllgwaelod, Newport, Moylgrove, Poppit Sands and St Dogmaels. For the rest of the year it only covers the stops between Newport and Cardigan (Monday, Thursday and Saturday only).

(a 3.5-mile round trip) via Market St then Church St, keeping the castle on your right. At a fork in the lane called College Sq, go right (uphill), following narrow tracks past a couple of farms and houses to reach a gate leading onto the open hillside. Work your way up on grassy paths to the summit, the site of an Iron Age hill fort, with great views of Newport Bay and Dinas Head. On a fine day you might spot Ireland.

� Sleeping

Newport YHA　　　　　　HOSTEL **£**
(☑ 0845 371 9543; www.yha.org.uk; Lower St Mary's St; dm/r from £18/48; ☷) Set in a converted Victorian school, this central hostel has a lovely common room under the vaulted ceiling and a variety of bunkrooms of different sizes.

★ **King Street Rooms**　　　　B&B **££**
(☑ 01239-820225; www.kingstreetrooms.co.uk; 4 King St; s/d from £50/75) There are just two bright, simple rooms in this wonderful new guesthouse where country cool meets urban minimalist chic. Uncluttered yet quirky, warm and cosy, it's the kind of place where you feel immediately at home. There's a terrace with fine views at the front and a large, rambling garden to the rear.

Llys Meddyg　　　　　　B&B **££**
(☑ 01239-820008; www.llysmeddyg.com; East St; s/d from £80/100; ☏☷) This converted doctor's residence takes contemporary big-city cool and plonks it firmly by the seaside. Bedrooms are large and bright and decked out in an unassuming but very stylish manner. Original artworks adorn the walls, locally woven blankets and cushions add a splash of colour, and the bathrooms are spacious. The lounge boasts leather sofas and a period fireplace, and there's a secluded garden at the back.

A COTTAGE OF YOUR OWN

Pembrokeshire is blessed with a wealth of self-catering cottages that make a good base for a longer stay in the area.

Asheston Eco Barns (www.eco-barns.co.uk) A collection of five stylishly converted barns sleeping four to seven people.

Coastal Cottages (www.coastalcottages.co.uk) Something to suit everyone in this huge range of Pembrokeshire cottages.

Holiday Lettings (www.holiday-lettings.co.uk) A vast array of cottages all across the country from simple and cosy to modern and minimalist.

National Trust Cottages (www.nationaltrustcottages.co.uk) Offers 20 quaint and historic cottages in the region.

Welsh Cottages (www.welsh-cottages.co.uk) Holiday accommodation in well-kept cottages throughout the area.

Welsh Country Cottages (www.welsh-country-cottages.co.uk) A collection of mostly rural cottages across Pembrokeshire.

Cnapan
B&B **££**

(☎ 01239-820575; www.cnapan.co.uk; East St; s/d £62.50/95; ☎) Light-filled rooms and a flower-filled garden are offered at this listed Georgian town house above a popular restaurant. If you're man enough for the floral wallpaper, ask for room 4: it's bigger.

Golden Lion Hotel
HOTEL **££**

(☎ 01239-820321; www.goldenlionpembrokeshire.co.uk; East St; s/d £70/90; P ☎ ☕) This warm and cosy country inn has 13 bright, clutter-free rooms with simple but contemporary decor in restful pale and neutral colours. They vary in size from snug doubles to more spacious family rooms. Downstairs there's a good restaurant and a roaring fire in the popular traditional bar, which serves real ales.

Eating

Lou Lous
CAFE **£**

(☎ 01239-820777; Market St; mains £4.50-10; ☉ 10am-5pm Mon-Sat) This friendly little cafe is quickly gaining a reputation as one of the finest in town. The menu features a range of organic soups and tarts, baguettes and crepes, proper coffee and the obligatory indulgent cakes. It's a wonderfully relaxed place with cheerful service.

Wholefoods of Newport
DELI **£**

(☎ 01239-820773; www.wholefoodsofnewport.co.uk; East St; ☉ 8.30am-5.30pm Mon-Sat) The place to go to stock up on picnic supplies and planet-friendly provisions.

★ Llys Meddyg
MODERN WELSH **££**

(☎ 01239-820008; www.llysmeddyg.com; East St; mains £14.50-24; ☕) From the slate floor and leather armchairs in the bar to the modern art in the elegant dining room, this place oozes style. The food is superb – the seasonal menu reflects the best of local produce, combined with an international palate of flavours. There are three dining options, the formal but quirky restaurant, the Cellar Bar and the wonderful Kitchen Garden, which offers al fresco dining in summer as well as beanbags, gaint games and toddler bikes to entertain smaller diners.

Golden Lion Hotel
RESTAURANT **££**

(☎ 01329-820321; www.goldenlionpembrokeshire.co.uk; East St; mains £11-21; P ☎) The recently refurbished restaurant at the town's hotel serves high quality pub grub in comfortable surroundings. It has a relaxed and friendly atmosphere, and is a good bet with children.

Cnapan
MODERN WELSH **£££**

(☎ 01239-820575; East St; 2-/3-course dinner £24/32; ☉ 6.30-8.45pm Wed-Mon) The somewhat formal dining room offers candlelight and crisp white-linen tablecloths, but the service is friendly and relaxed. Local seafood (Penclawdd mussels and the fresh catch of the day) features on the set menu, alongside Welsh black beef and a tempting array of desserts.

ℹ Information

National Park Information Centre & Tourist Office (☎ 01239-820912; Long St; ☉ 10am-6pm Mon-Sat Easter-Oct)

❶ Getting There & Away

Most visitors arrive by car. Expect to pay for, and possibly fight for, parking from April to September.

BICYCLE

Newport Bike Hire (☑01239-820724; www.newportbikehire.com; East St; per half-/full day £14/20; ⏰10am-5.30pm Mon-Sat) Offers bike rental and also stocks cycling guides and books on outdoor pursuits.

BUS

Services include bus 412 to Haverfordwest (one hour), Dinas Cross (six minutes), Fishguard (16 minutes), Castell Henllys (nine minutes) and Cardigan (30 minutes), and the Poppit Rocket.

Nevern (Nanhyfer)

With its overgrown castle and atmospheric church, this little village 2 miles east of Newport makes a good objective for an easy walk. You approach the **Church of St Brynach** along a supremely gloomy alley of yew trees, estimated to be six to seven centuries old; second on the right as you enter is the so-called **bleeding yew**, named after the curious reddish-brown sap that oozes from it. The beautifully melancholy churchyard dates from around the 6th century, predating the church.

Among the gravestones is a tall **Celtic cross**, one of Wales' finest, dating from the 10th or 11th century. According to tradition, the first cuckoo that sings each year in Pembrokeshire does so from atop this cross on St Brynach's Day (7 April).

Inside the church, the **Maglocunus Stone**, thought to date from the 5th century, forms a windowsill in the south transept. It is one of the few carved stones that bears an inscription in both Latin and ogham, and was instrumental in deciphering the meaning of ogham, an ancient Celtic script.

Pentre Ifan

The largest dolmen in Wales, Pentre Ifan is a 4500-year-old neolithic burial chamber set on a remote hillside with superb views across the Preseli Hills and out to sea. The huge, 5m-long capstone, weighing more than 16 tonnes, is delicately poised on three tall, pointed, upright stones, made of the same bluestone that was used for the menhirs at Stonehenge.

The site is about 3 miles southeast of Newport, on a minor road south of the A487; it's signposted.

Preseli Hills

The only upland area in the Pembrokeshire Coast National Park is the Preseli Hills (Mynydd Preseli), rising to 536m at Foel Cwmcerwyn. These hills are at the centre of a fascinating prehistoric landscape, scattered with hill forts, standing stones and burial chambers, and are famous as the source of the mysterious bluestones of Stonehenge.

An ancient track called the **Golden Road**, once part of a 5000-year-old trade

MYSTERY OF THE BLUESTONES

There are 31 bluestone monoliths (plus 12 'stumps') at the centre of Stonehenge, each weighing around 4 tonnes. Geochemical analysis shows that the Stonehenge bluestones originated from outcrops around Carnmenyn and Carn Goedog at the eastern end of the Preseli Hills (Mynydd Preseli). Stonehenge scholars have long been of the opinion that Preseli and the bluestones held some religious significance for the builders of Stonehenge, and that they laboriously dragged these monoliths down to the River Cleddau, then carried them by barge from Milford Haven, along the Bristol Channel and up the River Avon, then overland again to Salisbury Plain – a distance of 240 miles.

In 2000 a group of volunteers tried to re-enact this journey, using primitive technology to transport a single, 3-tonne bluestone from Preseli to Stonehenge. They failed – having already resorted to the use of a lorry, a crane and modern roads, the stone slipped from its raft and sank just a few miles into the sea journey.

An alternative theory is that the bluestones were actually transported by ice age glaciers, and dumped around 40 miles to the west of the Stonehenge site some 12,000 years ago.

route between Wessex and Ireland, runs along the crest of the hills, passing prehistoric cairns and the stone circle of **Bedd Arthur**.

Bus 430 from Cardigan heads to Crymych (30 minutes; no service Sunday), at the eastern end of hills. From here you can hike along the Golden Road to the car park at Bwlch Gwynt on the B4329 (7.5 miles).

Castell Henllys

From 600 BC and through the Roman occupation there was a thriving Celtic settlement at Castell Henllys (Castle of the Prince's Court). For 27 years students from around the world, supervised by the University of York archaeology department, spent their summers digging at the site and learned enough to build a re-creation of the settlement on its original foundations, complete with educated guesses about the clothing, tools, ceremonies and life of that time.

◎ Sights

Castell Henllys   HISTORIC SITE
(www.castellhenllys.com; Felindre Farchog; adult/child £4.75/3.50; ⊗10am-5pm) A visit to Castell Henllys Iron Age Fort is like travelling back in time. There are reconstructions of the settlement's buildings – four thatched roundhouses, animal pens, a smithy and a grain store – which you can enter and touch. Costumed staff, craft demonstrations, Celtic festivals and other events bring the settlement to life.

❶ Getting There & Away

Castell Henllys is 4 miles east of Newport. Bus 412 from Cardigan (20 minutes) to Haverfordwest (1¼ hours), via Newport (nine minutes) and Fishguard (25 minutes) stops at Castell Henllys junction hourly.

Ceibwr Bay

Most of the 15 miles of coast between Newport and Cardigan is accessible only on foot. The one spot where a car or bike can get close is at the scenic, seal-haunted inlet of Ceibwr Bay, near the hamlet of Moylgrove, reached via narrow roads. A grassy platform near the road end, carpeted with

sea pinks in summer, makes a great picnic spot.

The coastal scenery here is spectacular, with contorted cliffs to the north and a couple of sea stacks to the south. A half-mile walk south along the coast path leads to the **Witches' Cauldron**, a large cliff-ringed, sea-filled hole caused by a cavern collapse.

The Poppit Rocket stops at Moylgrove.

St Dogmaels

Across the River Teifi from Cardigan, this village marks the end of the Pembrokeshire Coast Path. From as early as the 5th or 6th century there was a Celtic monastic community here, which the Normans replaced with French Tironian monks in 1115. The remains of the beautiful abbey still stand.

◎ Sights

St Dogmaels Abbey   RUIN
(☑01239-615389;www.welshabbey.org.uk;⊗10am-4pm) FREE St Dogmaels Abbey was dissolved along with all of Britain's monasteries by Henry VIII in 1536, but you can wander around its remains with an audio guide. The visitor centre in the Coach House tells the abbey's story and includes a museum with relics from the abbey, a cafe and gallery. Medieval fun days are run and there's a **produce market** (⊗9am-1pm Tue).

St Thomas the Martyr   CHURCH
The parish church of St Thomas the Martyr houses several ancient stones relating to the first St Dogmael's monastery, including the Sagranus Stone, inscribed in Latin and ogham. The stone was instrumental in deciphering the ancient ogham script in the 19th century. The church's altar was from the monastery and is one of Britain's oldest.

Y Felin   MILL
(☑01239-613999; www.yfelin.co.uk; tours adult/child £2.50/1; ⊗10am-5.30pm Mon-Sat, 2-5.30pm Sun) A working watermill dating from the 1640s, Y Felin is still used to make flour, which you can purchase, along with bread.

🛏 Sleeping

Poppit Sands YHA   HOSTEL £
(☑0845 371 9037; www.yha.org.uk; dm/r from £18/36; ☒) Tucked into a hillside overlooking the beach, this newly renovated hostel offers superb views. Two hectares of grounds

surround the building and there are plenty of activities in the area. There's a flight of 50 steps down to the hostel.

❶ Getting There & Away

The Poppit Rocket stops here, as does the 407 (Poppit Sands–Cardigan; no Sunday service).

Teifi Marshes Nature Reserve

Bordering the River Teifi southeast of Cardigan, Teifi Marshes Nature Reserve is a haven for birds, otters, badgers and butterflies.

The centre is about a mile from Cardigan along a riverside path, or 4 miles by road.

◉ Sights

Welsh Wildlife Centre   WILDLIFE RESERVE
(☑ 01239-621600; www.welshwildlife.org; Cilgerran; parking £3; ☺ 10.30am-5pm Easter-Nov) **FREE**
Find out more about the surrounding river, marsh and woodland habitats at this centre, around which are several short waymarked trails, most of them wheelchair accessible. The centre has live feeds from remote cameras on the reserve and on Skomer Island so you can watch nesting birds without causing disturbance. There's also a shop and cafe.

Aberystwyth & Mid-Wales

Best Places to Eat

➡ The 25 Mile (p183)
➡ Checkers (p198)
➡ Drawing Room (p205)
➡ Ultracomida (p188)
➡ Carlton Riverside (p206)

Best Places to Stay

➡ Harbour Master (p184)
➡ Beudy Banc (p193)
➡ Glandyfi Castle (p193)
➡ Ynyshir Hall (p193)
➡ Gwesty Cymru (p188)

Why Go?

Bordered by the dramatic landscapes of two national parks, Mid-Wales is often overlooked but this region of lustrous green fields, wooded river valleys and small market towns is something of a well-kept secret. This is Wales at its most rural, a sweep of undulating hills that the Industrial Revolution bypassed, and there's a wonderful, unhurried charm to discovering its winding back roads. Criss-crossed with country lanes and dedicated cycling and walking routes, it's an excellent area to explore under your own steam. Apart from exuberant, student-populated Aberystwyth, you won't find much excitement in the urban areas, it's the places in between, and the people who live in them, that are far more interesting. From struggling farmers to pioneers of sustainable development and the weird and wacky minds of Britain's smallest town, Llandrindod Wells, the region reveals more about the Welsh than you may ever have imagined.

When to Go

Long days and the promise of fine weather make June to September the best time to tackle long-distance walking routes such as Offa's Dyke Path, while the wonderful foliage colours make autumn perfect for walking or cycling the wooded trails around the Elan Valley.

Festivals abound in the summer months with oddballs taking part in some of the weirdest sporting events on the planet in Llanwrtyd Wells in May, June and July; a massive celebration of rural life at the Royal Welsh Agricultural Show at the beginning of July; and a look back in time at the Victorian Festival in Llandrindod Wells in late August.

CEREDIGION

Bordered by the vast expanse of Cardigan Bay on one side and the sparsely populated Cambrian Mountains on the other, Ceredigion (pronounced with a *dig* not a *didge*) is an ancient Welsh kingdom founded by a chieftain called Ceredig. The rural communities here escaped the massive population influxes of the coal-mining valleys of the south and the slate-mining towns of the north and, consequently, the Welsh language is stronger here than in any other part of the country except Gwynedd and Anglesea, with over 50% of the local population claiming they speak Welsh.

The lack of heavy industry also left Ceredigion with some of Britain's cleanest beaches, and with no train access south of Aberystwyth, they tend to be less crowded. Adding to the isolation is the natural barrier known as the Desert of Wales, consisting of the barren uplands of the Cambrian Mountains, which separate Ceredigion from Powys. The sandy coves, sea cliffs, wooded river valleys and arid mountains here are as off the beaten track as Wales gets.

Cardigan (Aberteifi)

POP 4180

Small, historically sleepy Cardigan has the feel of a town on the cusp of change. Hip craft shops, trendy home-grown fashion labels, gourmet food stores and stylish B&Bs are creeping up the high street at a steady pace. Dynamic creative types seem to have been drawn here in recent years and although Cardigan hasn't quite shaken off its lacklustre image, it's well on its way. The castle is being restored, the town's reputation for its alternative arts scene is growing and the jumble of historical architecture that lines its streets and lanes has been given a new lease of life thanks to a local heritage initiative.

There's plenty of great walking in the surrounding countryside, lots of outdoor activities and some interesting places to visit such as the Welsh Wildlife Centre (WWC), St Dogmaels and Poppit Sands just across the river in Pembrokeshire. For walkers, Cardigan is the closest town to the end of the Pembrokeshire Coast Path (PCP) and the first town at the beginning of the new Ceredigion Coast Path (CCP), so it sees plenty of hikers coming and going.

Cardigan is an Anglicisation of Ceredigion, 'the place of Ceredig', but the Welsh name, Aberteifi, refers to its location at the mouth of the River Teifi. In Elizabethan times this was Wales' second-most important port and, by the 18th century, one of Britain's busiest seafaring centres. By the late 19th century, however, the railway was displacing sea transport and the river began silting up, relegating the town to an altogether quieter future.

◉ Sights

★ Cardigan Castle   CASTLE

(☏ 01239-615131; www.cardigancastle.com; 2 Green St) Cardigan Castle holds an important place in Welsh culture, having been the venue for the first competitive National Eisteddfod, held in 1176 under the aegis of Lord Rhys ap Gruffydd. However, after years of neglect by its private owner when the shored up, overgrown and rapidly crumbling castle turned into little more than a shameful eyesore, the site is now in public hands and a hive of activity. Grand restoration plans are afoot and the castle should eventually reopen in spring 2014 as a community, recreational and education centre. The complex will include a heritage centre, restored gardens, open-air concert area, wet-weather dome, restaurant and self-catering accommodation. Check the website for the latest update.

Guildhall   MARKET

(www.guildhall-cardigan.co.uk; High St) The neo-Gothic Guildhall dates from 1860 and is home to a variety of community meeting spaces, a thriving gallery and Cardigan's Indoor Market which features stalls selling everything from antiques to local cheeses and handicrafts (Monday to Saturday). The field cannon outside commemorates the Charge of the Light Brigade in 1854, which was led by Lord Cardigan (after whom the button-up woollen sweater was named).

Pendre Art   GALLERY

(☏ 01239-615151; www.pendreart.com; 35 Pendre; ◷ 10am-5pm Mon-Sat) Not only a great place to buy local art, Pendre has an excellent coffee shop serving sandwiches, wraps, baguettes and home-baked scones. Bring your laptop to take advantage of the free wireless connection.

ABERYSTWYTH & MID-WALES CARDIGAN (ABERTEIFI)

N

0 — 20 km
0 — 10 miles

Irish Sea

Penmaenpool
Barmouth
Dolg
Cader
Idris ▲
(893m)
Fairbourne

Abergynolwyn
Dolgoch
Centr
Alterna
Techno
Tywyn
Machyr
A493
Fo
Aberdovey
Derv
*Ynyshir
Hall*

Borth
*Nant-y-
Rese
B
Na
A*

Aberystwyth ❹ *River Rheidol* **A44**
Ysbyty
3
**Vale of
Rheidol
Railway** *Rheidol
Falls*

A485
Llanrhystud

Llanon
Pontrhydfendig
Tregaron
New Quay
North
Aberaeron
⊙ *Llanerchaeron*
New Quay ●●Little Quay
Llanina
A482
Cwmtydu
A485

Penbryn
Manorafon
Synod
Inn
Temple
Bar
Cam
Mou

Mwnt
*Poppit
Sands*
Aberporth
Tresaith

River Teifi

Poppit
Sands
A487
Blaenannerch
A486
Lampeter
Cardigan
A475
Cenarth
Llanybydder
Henllan
Llandysul
River Teifi

*Cardigan
Bay*

Aberystwyth & Mid-Wales Highlights

❶ Trying your hand at bog snorkelling or mountain-bike chariot racing in the capital of crazy, **Llanwrtyd Wells** (p202)

❷ Enjoying the splendid isolation and utter tranquillity of the deserted moorlands of the **Cambrian Mountains** (p207)

❸ Reliving the age of steam with a scenic ride to Devil's Bridge aboard the **Vale of Rheidol Railway** (p188)

Snowdonia National Park

oss
xes Inn

Dyfi
Forest

Mallwyd

River Twrch

Llanwddyn

River Vyrnwy

Meifod

Pontrobert

Glyndŵr's Way

A458

Welshpool

Llanbrynmair

River Vyrnwy

Llanfair
Caereinion

6 Powis Castle

A470

Berriew

Stiperstones

ENGLAND

Carno

Gregynog
Hall

A483

River Severn

Montgomery

A490

A488

Church
Stoke

Dylife

Caersws

Newtown

A489

Llyn
Clywedog

Eaton

Glan-y-Nant

Llanidloes

A488

terwyd

Llangurig

Felindre

Clun Clunbury

Elan
Valley

B4518

Abbey-
cwm-hir

B4355

Brampton
Bryan

brian Mountains

2

Rhayader

Gigrin Farm
Red Kite
Feeding Station

Knighton

A4113

Spaceguard
Centre

Claerwen
Reservoir

Llanwrthwl

Crossgates

A488

Pilleth

Norton

Presteigne

Kinsham

**Llandrindod
Wells**

Newbridge-
on-Wye

Titley

B4358

A481

Kington

Abergwesyn

Cilmery

Llanelwedd

ENGLAND

lyn
nne

**Llanwrtyd
Wells**

1

Builth
Wells

Llangamarch
Wells

A483

Mynydd
Epynt

---

4 Experiencing a collision
of high culture and student-
inspired high jinks in
Aberystwyth (p185), a
colourful seaside university
town

5 Watching the birds of prey
swoop down for a lakeside
feast at **Bwlch Nant yr Arian**
(p190)

6 Discovering the
magnificent gardens and
ornate interiors of **Powis
Castle** (p199)

🏃 Activities

Set between the Pembrokeshire Coast Path and the Ceredigion Coast Path, Cardigan offers plenty of options for walkers as well as anyone keen to try out some adventure sports.

Walking

For a challenging but spectacular day's walk, head to St Dogmaels (p176) and tackle the last leg of the PCP in reverse, catching the bus back from Newport. In the other direction, the first day of the CCP is shorter, ending up in Aberporth where you can catch the 550 bus back.

If you don't fancy a full-day's trek, you can walk or cycle from Cardigan through the **Teifi Marshes** to the Welsh Wildlife Centre (WWC). From the High St head downhill to the river, cross over the footbridge to Castle St and then cross the road. Take the pedestrian walkway leading onto the riverbank and follow it out of town past the reed beds and along a wooded trail the wildlife centre. The walk is about 1 mile long, but it's 4 miles by road.

The tourist office stocks the *Walking the Teifi Estuary* brochure, outlining five other graded walks in the area. including a 10-mile circular walk to the gorgeous hidden cove at **Mwnt**. Here a small arc of golden sand sits between folds of the cliffs, and a simple white-washed church overlooks the sea where you'll often spot dolphins, seals and porpoises.

Adventure Sports

Fforest Outdoor　　　ADVENTURE SPORTS
(☑ 01239-612133; www.coldatnight.co.uk; 1 Cambrian Quay) Cardigan's main outdoor-activity company, Fforest Outdoor, has a cafe and shop by the south end of the bridge and a flash set of camping options near the WWC.

If you fancy splashing along the River Teifi, Fforest offers guided canoe or kayak trips through Cilgerran Gorge as well as climbing, sea kayaking, coasteering, surfing and white-water rafting expeditions and bushcraft trips.

🛏 Sleeping

Caernant　　　　　　　　　B&B **££**
(☑ 01239-612932; www.caernant.co.uk; Gwbert Rd; s/d £40/60; P 🤶) Big, bright, spacious rooms are on offer at Caernant, a delightful modern B&B just outside Cardigan. More than the rooms however, the wonderfully warm welcome will stay with you long after you've left. With tea and scones on arrival and incredible breakfasts it's well worth the short trip from town. Caernant is less than a mile from the centre of Cardigan on the B4548.

Llety Teifi　　　　　　　　B&B **££**
(☑ 01239-615566; www.lletyteifi-guesthouse.co.uk; Pendre; s/d from £45/70; P 🤶) New and stylish, this place set in a large Victorian house has plenty of period character but is kitted out in tasteful modern style. Expect bold patterned fabrics and wallpapers, giant windows and spacious bathrooms, altogether a very good deal. Breakfast is served next door.

Fforest Camp　　　　　CAMPGROUND **££**
(☑ 01239-623633; www.coldatnight.co.uk; Cilgerran; 3-night stay from £300) On the edge of Teifi Marshes Nature Reserve, Fforest challenges the notion that camping means roughing it. Stay in large tents, tepees or geodesic domes and enjoy the country air. Simple, wholesome breakfasts are served at the lodge. If Fforest Camp is full the owners run a second site further up the coast at Manorafon. There's a three-night minimum stay in summer.

CEREDIGION COAST PATH

Not to be outdone by its showy neighbour across the Teifi in Pembrokeshire, Ceredigion has opened up its own shoreline to the relentless march of coastal walkers. You can now walk 63 miles along a waymarked path between mouths of the Rivers Teifi and Dovey.

A sensible six-day itinerary would see you stopping overnight in Aberporth (12 miles from Cardigan), New Quay (14 miles), Aberaeron (6.5 miles), Llanrhystud (7.5 miles), Aberystwyth (11 miles) and Borth (12 miles); each has its own sandy beach to relax on at the end of the day. The truly hardcore enthusiast could tack this on to the end of the 13- to 15-day PCP – a total of 249 continuous coastal miles.

For more information, visit www.walkcardiganbay.co.uk. The **Cardi Bach bus** (⊙ Thu-Tue Jul-Oct, Mon, Thu & Sat Nov-Jul) covers the coast between Cardigan and New Quay year-round, making it easy to split this stretch into day-long walks.

Cardigan

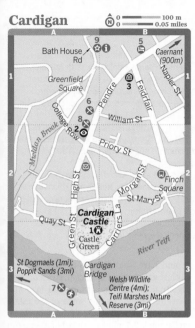

N 0 — 100 m
0 — 0.05 miles

✕ Eating

Fforest Pizzatipi PIZZERIA £

(☏ 01239-623751; www.pizzatipi.co.uk; 1 Cambrian Quay; pizza £6-7; ◷ Fri & Sat 5-10pm Jul-Aug) Brought to you by the hip folks at Cardigan's Fforest empire, this seasonal pop-up venue is the hottest ticket in town on summer nights. Pizza, booze, music and a buzzing atmosphere all set under a candle-lit tepee in a hidden riverside courtyard, what more could you ask for? There's only one oven so order as soon as you arrive to avoid a long wait for food.

Cafe Food for Thought CAFE

(☏ 01239-621863; 13 Pendre; mains £6-8; ◷ 9am-5pm Mon-Sat; ☕) A consistent local favourite, this simple cafe defies expectations with an interesting menu of top-notch dishes ranging from light bites to Welsh lamb, gourmet burgers and local seafood. There are plenty of options for vegetarians and some excellent desserts. Arrive early or be prepared to wait for a table at lunchtime.

★ The 25 Mile MODERN WELSH ££

(☏ 01239-623625; www.the25mile.com; 1 Pendre; mains £9-22; ◷ 10am-10pm Mon-Sat; ☕) 🖋 A blackboard naming its suppliers and graphically displaying their distance from the restaurant proudly explains the philosophy at this 'local eating house'. Practically all ingredients come from within a 25 mile radius and the menu uses seasonal produce in simple, honest dishes that make your palate sing. There's no great gastro fanfare here but a warm, cosy atmosphere, a real passion for food and the best nosh in town.

☆ Entertainment

Theatr Mwldan THEATRE

(☏ 01239-621200; www.mwldan.co.uk; Bath House Rd) Located in the former slaughterhouse, Theatr Mwldan stages comedy, drama, dance, music, films and has an art gallery and a good cafe. In summer there are open-air productions.

ℹ Information

Cardigan Hospital (☏ 01239-612214; Pont-y-Cleifion)

Police Station (☏ 101; Priory St)

Tourist Office (☏ 01239-613230; www.discoverceredigion.co.uk; Bath House Rd; ◷ 10am-5pm) In the lobby of the Theatr Mwldan.

ℹ Getting There & Around

BIKE

New Image Bicycles (☏ 01239-621275; www.bikebikebike.co.uk; 29-30 Pendre; per half-/full day £12/18; ◷ 10am-5pm Mon-Sat)

BUS

Routes include X50 to Aberystwyth (two hours); 407 to St Dogmaels (eight minutes) and Pop-

CARDIGAN BAY'S DOLPHINS

Cardigan Bay is home to an amazingly rich variety of marine animals and plants, but the star attraction is Europe's largest population of bottlenose dolphins. With reliable sightings from May to September, there are few places where these sociable creatures are more easily seen in the wild. Along with the dolphins, harbour porpoises, Atlantic grey seals and a variety of bird life are regularly seen, as well as seasonal visitors such as sunfish, basking sharks and leatherback turtles.

Some of the best places to spot bottlenose dolphins from the shore are the beaches around New Quay at **New Quay North**, **Little Quay**, **Cwmtydu** and **Llanina**, as are the beautiful sandy beaches at **Penbryn** and **Tresaith** north of Cardigan. **Aberystwyth**, **Aberporth** and **Mwnt** also have regular sightings.

You can learn more about Cardigan Bay's marine life at the **Cardigan Bay Marine Wildlife Centre** (☑01545-560032; www.cbmwc.org; Glanmore Tce, New Quay; ⊘9am-4pm Apr-Nov) **FREE** where you can also join a dolphin survey boat trip as researchers collect data on the bottlenose dolphins and other local marine mammals. Choose from four different trips: one-hour (adult/child £12/6), two-hour (adult/child £18/10), four-hour (adult/child £35/20) and full day trips (£55). Check the website for dates.

pit Sands (15 minutes); 412 to Castell Henllys (15 minutes), Newport (22 minutes), Dinas (28 minutes), Fishguard (40 minutes) and Haverfordwest (1¼ hours); 460 to Carmarthen (90 minutes) and the Poppit Rocket.

Aberaeron

POP 1420

The elegant harbourside village of Aberaeron with its brightly painted Georgian houses was once a busy port and ship-building centre, its genteel architecture the result of planned expansion in the early 19th century. Heavy industry is long gone but today Aberaeron is quietly bucking the trends of economic decline and its stylish streets are lined with independent shops and cafes, chic B&Bs and boutique hotels and a glut of excellent restaurants.

⊙ Sights & Activities

Llanerchaeron   HISTORIC BUILDING
(NT; ☑01545-570200; www.nationaltrust.org.uk; adult/child £7.10/3.60; ⊘10.30am-5pm) This lovingly restored 18th-century country estate offers a fascinating insight into the life of the Welsh gentry and their staff 200 years ago. The villa itself was designed by John Nash and is one of his most complete early works and features curved walls, false windows and ornate cornices. The estate was self-sufficient and remains virtually unchanged in that respect with staff in period dress tending to the fruit, veg and herbs in the walled garden and looking after the Welsh Black cattle, Llanwenog sheep and rare Welsh pigs. You can join

in and have a go at beating rugs, washing clothes and baking Georgian style, or simply stroll around the ornamental lake and pleasure gardens or buy some of the estate produce at the well-stocked farm shop. Llanerchaeron is 2.5 miles southeast of Aberaeron along the A482. You can also walk or cycle here from Aberaeron along a disused railway.

SeaMôr Boat Trips   BOAT TOUR
(☑07795-242445; www.seamor.org; Pen Cei; adult/child £20/15; ⊘May-Sep) SeaMôr runs two-hour boat trips into Cardigan Bay past the dolphin feeding sites of Llanina Reef and New Quay Bay. Grey seals, bottlenose dolphins and harbour porpoises are commonly seen and there are occasional sightings of sunfish, basking sharks, minke whales and even humpback whales. Trips leave from in front of the Harbour Master Hotel.

🛏 Sleeping & Eating

3 Pen Cei   B&B ££
(☑01545-571147; www.pen-cei-guest-house.co.uk; 3 Pen Cei; d £100-140; 🐾) The five spacious, modern rooms in this grand Georgian house are beautifully kitted out with crisp linens, bold colour schemes and fresh flowers. The larger rooms have super-king beds and free-standing baths and the incredibly friendly owners go out of their way to make guests feel welcome.

★**Harbour Master**   HOTEL £££
(☑01545-570755; www.harbour-master.com; Pen Cei; s/d from £65/145; 🐾) Reason enough to come to Aberaeron, this small, hip hotel of-

fers food and accommodation worthy of any chic city bolthole. The 13 quirky rooms are housed in three historic buildings on the waterfront and feature Frette linens, vintage Welsh blankets, bold colour schemes and high-tech bathrooms. The spacious rooms in the newly restored grain warehouse have the same cool, contemporary styling with excellent harbour views. Downstairs the renowned restaurant (2-/3-course dinner £25/30) champions local ingredients with lobster and crab, and Welsh beef, lamb and cheeses whisked into imaginative and extremely satisfying dishes. The lively bar offers more casual dining (mains from £9.50) but the same outstanding food.

Hive   MODERN BRITISH **££**
(☑ 01545-570445;   www.thehiveaberaeron.com; Cadgwan Pl; mains £8.50-14; ☺ 9am-11pm) Slick and contemporary, the Hive is set in a converted wharf building and has a large courtyard with outdoor seating overlooking the waterfront. Inside there are whitewashed or exposed stone walls, painted concrete and a friendly, lively vibe. The menu features a good selection of interesting dishes with local seafood commanding a prime position. It's renowned for its incredible honey ice cream – don't leave without trying it!

❶ Getting There & Away

Bus X50 goes regularly to Aberystwyth (45 minutes) and Cardigan (55 minutes); bus 552 runs to Cardigan (two hours) once daily on Tuesday, Wednesday and Friday.

Aberystwyth

POP 13,000

Sweeping around the curving shore of Cardigan Bay, the lively university town of Aberystwyth (aber-*ist*-with) has a stunning location but a bit of an identity crisis. Student bars and cheap restaurants line the streets, the flashing lights of traditional amusements twinkle from the pier and tucked away in the side streets are a handful of chichi boutiques and organic, wholefood cafes. During term time the bars are buzzing and students play football on the promenade, while in summer the bucket-and-spade brigade invade and enjoy the beach. Meanwhile the trappings of this once-stately seaside resort remain in the terrace of grand Georgian houses painted in subtle pastel hues that line the promenade.

The town's now mainly ruined castle was erected in 1277; like many other castles in Wales it was captured by Owain Glyndŵr at the start of the 15th century and wrecked by Oliver Cromwell's forces during the Civil War. By the beginning of the 19th century, the town's walls and gates had completely disappeared.

Aberystwyth developed a fishing industry, and silver and lead mining were also important here. With the arrival of the railway in 1864, the town reinvented itself as a fashionable seaside destination. In 1872 Aberystwyth was chosen as the site of the first college of the University of Wales (Aberystwyth University now has over 7000 students) and in 1907 it became home to the National Library of Wales.

Welsh is widely spoken here and locals are proud of their heritage. Catching a show at the Arts Centre, hearing the male voice choir perform or simply soaking up the sunset over Cardigan Bay are quintessential local experiences.

◉ Sights

◉ The Waterfront

Marine Tce, with its impressive sweep of imposing pastel-hued houses overlooking North Beach harks back to the town's halcyon days as a fashionable resort. When you reach the bottom of the 1.5-mile prom, it's customary to kick the white bar, although the locals can't seem to explain the rationale behind this ritual.

North Beach is lined by somewhat shabby Georgian hotels, albeit with a couple of notable exceptions. The top-heavy **Royal Pier** lumbers out to sea under the weight of its cheerfully tacky amusement arcade, offering a stark contrast to the grand **Old College** building a little further along. Reminiscent of a French chateau, this Gothic revival building with castellated towers, conical spires and flamboyant gargoyles was originally built as a hotel but was sold to the university's founders before it ever opened. Next to it, the enigmatic, sparse ruins of **Aberystwyth Castle** sit looking out to sea from the southern end of the beach, offering views along the Llŷn Peninsula all the way to Bardsey Island. A stone circle planted in the centre of the castle is a relic of a 1915 eisteddfod, while the large war memorial in front of it features a surprisingly raunchy nude.

Aberystwyth

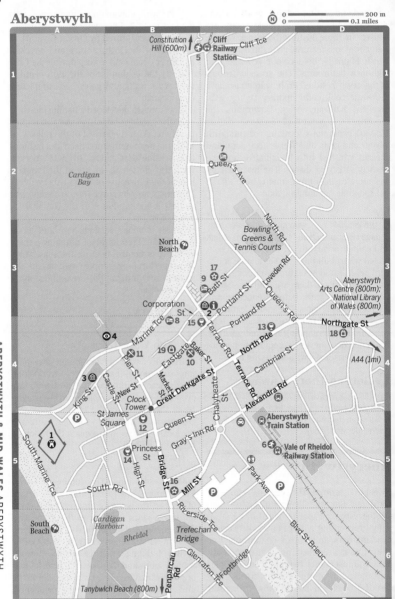

ABERYSTWYTH & MID-WALES ABERYSTWYTH

The prom pivots before leading along **South Beach** – a more desolate but still attractive seafront. Many locals prefer the stony but emptier **Tanybwlch Beach**, just south of the harbour, where the Rivers Rheidol and Ystwyth meet.

⊙ Constitution Hill

At the northern end of North Beach, Constitution Hill rises abruptly from the shore. From the wind-blown balding hilltop there are tremendous, long coastal views –

Aberystwyth

60 miles from the Llŷn to Strumble Head – and you can spot 26 mountain peaks including Snowdon. The site has been redeveloped in recent years with new children's attractions, while the erstwhile Victorian tearooms have been rebuilt.

Camera Obscura LOOKOUT
(☑ 01970-617642; www.aberystwythcliffrailway. co.uk; admission £1; ⏰ 11am-4pm Apr-Oct) One relic of the Victorian era is a camera obscura, an immense pinhole camera or projecting telescope that allows you to see practically into the windows of the houses below and spy on friends on the beach.

Other Sights

National Library of Wales LIBRARY
(☑ 01970-623800; www.llgc.org.uk; ⏰ 9.30am-6pm Mon-Fri, to 5pm Sat) Sitting proudly on a hilltop half a mile east of town, the National Library is a cultural powerhouse. Founded in 1911, it holds millions of books in many languages – it's a copyright library so it has copies of every book published in the UK.

The **Hengwrt Room** is where the library displays all of the really important stuff, such as the 12th-century Black Book of Carmarthen (the oldest existing Welsh text), the 13th-century Tintern Abbey Bible, 15th-century Albert Dürer engravings, a first edition of Milton's *Paradise Lost* from 1668 and early editions by Shakespeare and Newton. Other galleries display an ever-stimulating set of changing exhibitions.

A fire in April 2013 resulted in water damage to some items in the historic collection; these are currently being treated and should soon be back on display.

The entrance to the library is off Penglais Rd; take a right just past the hospital.

Ceredigion Museum MUSEUM
(☑ 01970-633088; http://museum.ceredigion.gov. uk; Terrace Rd; ⏰ 10am-5pm Mon-Sat Apr-Sep, noon-4.30pm Oct-Mar) **FREE** This museum is in the Coliseum, which opened in 1905 as a theatre and served as a cinema from 1932 onwards. The elegant interior still has its stage and the artfully arranged displays include entertaining exhibitions on Aberystwyth's history – everything from old chemist furnishings and hand-knitted woollen knickers to a wall devoted to the *Little Britain* TV series.

🏃 Activities

Cycling & Walking

Sticking mainly to designated cycle paths and quiet country lanes, the 18-mile **Rheidol Cycle Trail** heads from Aberystwyth Harbour to Devil's Bridge through the beautiful Rheidol Valley. Along the way it passes the Woodland Trust's Coed Geufron, and side routes lead to Bwlch Nant yr Arian (p190), Rheidol Power Station and Rheidol Mines.

The **Ystwyth Trail**, for cyclists and walkers, is a 20-mile waymarked route following a train line from Aberystwyth to Tregaron, at the foot of the Cambrian Mountains. For the first 12 miles it shadows the Ystwyth, while at the end it enters the Teifi Valley. At the Aberystwyth end you can pick up the trail from the footbridge on Riverside Tce, but you'll get more downhills from Tregaron.

Heritage Railway Rides

Vale of Rheidol Railway HERITAGE RAILWAY

(☑01970-625819; www.rheidolrailway.co.uk; Park Ave; adult/child return £16/4; ⊙Feb-Oct, check online timetable) One of Aberystwyth's most popular attractions is the one-hour ride (each way) on this narrow-gauge railway. Old steam locomotives built between 1923 and 1938 have been lovingly restored by volunteers and chug for almost 12 miles up the beautiful wooded valley of the River Rheidol to Devil's Bridge. The line opened in 1902 to bring lead and timber out of the valley.

Cliff Railway HERITAGE RAILWAY

(☑01970-617642; www.aberystwythcliffrailway.co.uk; Cliff Tce; adult/child £3/2; ⊙10am-5pm Apr-Oct, shorter hours Nov-Mar) If your legs aren't up to the climb of Constitution Hill (135m), you can catch a lift on the trundling little Cliff Railway, the UK's longest electric funicular (1896) and possibly the slowest, too, at a G-force-busting 4 mph.

🛏 Sleeping

Aberystwyth has a glut of hotels and B&Bs of widely varying standards, many refusing to give up on their old-fashioned decor and attitudes. Thankfully things have improved a little in recent years.

Maes-y-Môr GUESTHOUSE £

(☑01970-639270; www.maesymor.co.uk; 25 Bath St; s/d £35/55; 🐾) Yes, that is a laundrette. But don't be fooled: venture upstairs from the drying machine and you will find clean, bright, inviting rooms and a warm welcome. Breakfast is not included but there's a kitchen for guest use and a locked shed for bicycles.

LÔN TEIFI & LÔN CAMBRIA

Two long-distance cycling routes that are part of the **Sustrans** (☑0845 113 0065; www.sustrans.org.uk) National Cycle Network cut clear through Mid-Wales. The Lôn Teifi (Rte 82) heads 98 miles from Fishguard through Cardigan, Lampeter and Tregaron to Aberystwyth. From here the 113-mile Lôn Cambria (Rte 81) kicks in, passing through Rhayader, Newtown and Welshpool en route to Shrewsbury. Sustrans is a charity devoted to promoting sustainable transport modes. You can buy maps of the routes through its website.

★Gwesty Cymru HOTEL ££

(☑01970-612252; www.gwestycymru.com; 19 Marine Tce; s/d from £67/87; 🐾) A real gem, the Wales Hotel is a characterful boutique property with a strong sense of Welsh identity right on the waterfront. Local slate features throughout, paired with rich aubergine carpets and contemporary styling. The hotel's small restaurant (mains £12.95 to £18.95) has an enviable reputation and serves a good choice of local produce as well as international dishes. Meat lovers should try out the succulent Welsh steak or lamb shank. Book ahead.

Bodalwyn B&B ££

(☑01970-612578; www.bodalwyn.co.uk; Queen's Ave; s/d £55/76; 🐾) Simultaneously upmarket and homey, this handsome Edwardian B&B offers tasteful rooms with sparkling new bathrooms and a hearty cooked breakfast (with vegetarian options). Ask for room 3, with the bay window.

🍴 Eating

★Ultracomida TAPAS, DELI ££

(☑01970-630686; www.ultracomida.co.uk; 31 Pier St; tapas £5-5.50; ⊙10am-5pm Mon, 10am-9pm Tue-Sat, noon-4pm Sun) With its blend of Spanish, French and Welsh produce, this is a foodie's idea of nirvana: a delicatessen out front with a cheese counter to die for and communal tables out the back for tapas and wine. The deli platters are excellent, coming in a choice of meat, mixed fish or cheese (£8.95). There's a set menu (two/three-course £11/13) available at lunchtime and large plates of tapas on offer in the evenings.

Treehouse ORGANIC ££

(☑01970-615791; www.treehousewales.co.uk; 14 Baker St; mains £5-10; ⊙10am-5pm Mon-Fri, 9am-5pm Sat; 🍴) Located upstairs from an inviting food shop in an attractive Victorian house, this excellent restaurant uses organic, locally-grown produce in its wide range of tempting dishes. Vegetarians and vegans are well catered for here as well as meat lovers. Expect everything from buckwheat rissoles and pumpkin pancakes to beef goulash with German bread dumplings. It's certainly one of the best places for lunch in town.

🚫 Drinking & Nightlife

Thanks to its large student population, during term time Aberystwyth has a livelier nightlife than anywhere else in the northern half of the country.

Academy
BAR

(Great Darkgate St; ☺noon-1am Sun-Fri, noon-2am Sat) An incongruous setting for a booze palace, perhaps, but an incredibly beautiful one. This former chapel has Victorian tiles on the floor, a mezzanine supported by slender cast-iron columns, red lights illuminating a wooden staircase leading to an eagle-fronted pulpit and organ pipes behind the bar.

Harry's
PUB

(☎01970-612647; www.harrysaberystwyth.com; 40-46 North Pde; ☺bistro 5-9pm Mon-Fri, noon-9pm Sat, noon-8pm Sun, bar noon-11pm Mon-Thu, noon-midnight Fri & Sat) Although it describes itself as an Irish bar, Harry's is a little more sophisticated with a candlelit bistro section serving up well-presented meals (mains £6.50 to £12). Elsewhere, a series of rooms wraps itself around the central bar, ranging from a large sports bar to a small clubby lounge.

Ship & Castle
PUB

(www.shipandcastle.co.uk; 1 High St; ☺2pm-midnight Sun-Fri, 2pm-1am Sat) A sympathetic renovation has left this 1830 pub as cosy and welcoming as ever, while adding big screens to watch the rugger on. It is the place to come for real ales, with a large selection on tap, along with a few ciders.

The Varsity
PUB

(www.varsitybars.com; Portland St; ☺9am-midnight Sun-Thu, 9am-1am Fri & Sat; ☏) Spacious, simple and student-friendly, The Varsity has huge pipes running around the ceiling and big windows for watching activity on the street. It's packed on weekend nights and relaxing during the daytime when you can make the most of the free wi-fi.

☆ Entertainment

Aberystwyth Arts Centre
THEATRE

(☎01970-623232; www.aberystwythartscentre.co.uk; Penglais Rd) One of the largest arts centres in Wales, this happening place hosts excellent opera, drama, dance and concerts, plus it has a bookshop, an art gallery, a bar and a cafe. The cinema shows a good range of world and foreign-language movies. The centre is on the Penglais campus of the university, half a mile east of the town.

Aberystwyth Male Voice Choir
TRADITIONAL MUSIC

(www.aberchoir.co.uk; Bridge St) Rehearses at the RAFA Club from 7pm to 8.30pm most Thursdays.

A CLASSIC VILLAGE PUB

A village pub par excellence, unassuming little **Y Ffarmers** (☎01974-261275; www.yffarmers.co.uk; Llanfihangel y Creuddyn; mains £8 -18; ☺6-11pm Tue, noon-2pm & 6-11pm Wed-Sat, noon-3pm Sun) is tucked away in the undulating hills south of Aberystwyth. It's the kind of down-to-earth pub every village should have, except this one is also renowed for its incredible food. The short, simple menu features pub classics given a modern overhaul, and every one is a feast for the senses. Seasonal local produce defines what's on offer and you can wash it all down with some proper ale and local beers.

The pub is about 8 miles southeast of Aberystwyth. Take the A4340 out of town to the village of New Cross and follow the signs.

Commodore Cinema
CINEMA

(☎01970-612421; www.commodorecinema.co.uk; Bath St) Shows current mainstream releases and there's a bar here for a preflick beer.

🛍 Shopping

Andy's Records
MUSIC

(☎01970-624581; 16 Northgate St; ☺11.30am-6pm Mon, Tue & Thu-Sat) A handy indie record shop that also sells gig tickets for bands at the university.

Treehouse
HOMEWARES

(☎01970-625116; www.treehousewales.co.uk; 3 Eastgate St; ☺9.30am-5.30pm Mon-Sat; ✔) This little boutique specialises in organic and fair-trade homewares, cosmetics and baby goods.

ℹ Information

Bronglais Hospital (☎01970-623131; Caradoc Rd)

Police Station (☎101; Blvd St Brieuc)

Tourist Office (☎01970-612125; www.tourism.ceredigion.gov.uk; Terrace Rd ; ☺10am-5pm Mon-Sat, daily school holidays; ☏) Below the Ceredigion Museum, this office stocks maps and books on local history, has free wi-fi and the helpful staff can arrange accommodation.

ℹ Getting There & Away

Routes include X18 to Rhayader (one hour), Llandrindod Wells (1½ hours) and Llanwrtyd

Wells (2½ hours); X28 to Machynlleth (45 minutes), T2 to Dolgellau (1¼ hours), Porthmadog (2¼ hours), Caernarfon (three hours) and Bangor (3½ hours); 701 to Carmarthen (two hours), Swansea (2¾ hours) and Cardiff (4¼ hours); and X50 to Aberaeron (35 minutes) and Cardigan (1½ hours).

A daily **National Express** (www.nationalexpress. com) coach heads to/from Newtown (£10, 80 minutes), Welshpool (£11.70, 1¾ hours), Shrewsbury (£14.80, 2¼ hours), Birmingham (£28, four hours) and London (£16.50, seven hours).

Aberystwyth is the terminus of the **Arriva Trains Wales** (www.arrivatrainswales.co.uk) Cambrian Line, which crosses Mid-Wales every two hours en route to Birmingham (£24, three hours) via Machynlleth (£6, 33 minutes), Newtown (£12, 1¼ hours), Welshpool (£13.60, 1½ hours) and Shrewsbury (£18.40, two hours).

Around Aberystwyth

Bwlch Nant yr Arian

Part of Natural Resources Wales, **Bwlch Nant yr Arian** (☑ 01970-890453; www.forestry. gov.uk/bwlchnantyrarian; parking 2hrs £1.50), pronounced *bull*-kheh nant ear *arr*-ee-en, is a picturesque piece of woodland set around a lake, ringed with mountain-biking and walking tracks. The main drawcard, however, is the red kite feeding which takes place at 2pm daily (3pm daylight saving time). Even outside of mealtime you'll quite often see the majestic birds of prey circling around. You can watch all the action from the terrace of the attractive turf-roofed visitor centre and cafe (open 10am to 5pm).

It's 9 miles east of Aberystwyth on the A44.

Ysbyty Cynfyn

Just 2 miles up the A4120 from Devil's Bridge, Ysbyty Cynfyn (es-*bet*-ty *kun*-vin) is a fascinating example of the grafting of the Christian onto the pagan, which is evident in many ancient religious sites throughout

MOVING ON?

For tips, recommendations and reviews, head to shop.lonelyplanet.com to purchase a downloadable PDF of the Birmingham, the West Midlands & the Marches chapter from Lonely Planet's *England* guide.

Wales. Here the remains of a stone circle are clearly visible within the churchyard walls. The church once belonged to the Knight Hospitaller, the precursor of the Order of St John, which runs the St John Ambulance service. The order ran a pilgrims' hospice here to care for invalids making their way to St Davids.

Devil's Bridge & Rheidol Falls

The beautiful wooded hills of the Rheidol Valley head inland from Aberystwyth to the lush western slopes of 752m Plynlimon (Pumlumon Fawr), source of the Rivers Wye and Severn. Here the Rivers Mynach and Rheidol tumble together in a narrow gorge.

Just above the confluence of the rivers the Rheidol drops 90m in a series of spectacular waterfalls. **Devil's Bridge** (www.devilsbridgefalls.co.uk; adult/child £3.50/2) is itself a famous crossing-point where three bridges are stacked above each other. The lowest was supposedly built by the Knights Templar before 1188, the middle one in 1753 and the uppermost road-bridge in 1901.

It's one of many bridges associated with an arcane legend that involves the devil building the bridge on the condition that he gets the first thing to cross it. An old lady then outwits the devil by throwing some food over, which her dog chases and everybody's happy – except the devil and, presumably, the dog.

Access to the waterfalls and the old bridges is from beside the top-most bridge. There are two possible walks: one, just to view the three bridges, takes only 10 minutes (£1); the other, a half-hour walk, descends 100 steps (Jacob's Ladder), crosses the Mynach and ascends the other side, passing what is said to have been a robbers' cave. It's a beautiful walk but it's very steep and can be muddy; wear sensible footwear. Unfortunately there's no way to avoid the charge – you don't cough up, you won't see a sausage.

The Vale of Rheidol Railway (p188) heads to Devil's Bridge from Aberystwyth, as does the Rheidol Cycle Trail.

Strata Florida Abbey

On an isolated, peaceful site southeast of Aberystwyth lies this ruined Cistercian **abbey** (www.cadw.wales.gov.uk; adult/child £3.50/2.60; ☺10am-5pm Apr-Oct, unattended & free in other months) run by Cadw (the Welsh history monuments agency). The best preserved emnant is a simple, complete arched doorway, decorated with lines like thick rope. At the rear of the site a roof has been added to protect two chapels, which still have some of their 14th-century tiling, including one depicting a man admiring himself in a mirror.

The Cistercians were a monastic order with roots in France and the community at Strata Florida (Ystrad Fflur or 'Valley of the Flowers') was founded in 1164 by a Norman lord named Robert FitzStephen. After Welsh resurgence in the southwest, however, the independent, self-sufficient Cistercians won the support of the Welsh princes. Their abbeys also became a focus for literary activity and influence. The present site was established under Lord Rhys ap Gruffydd, and a number of princes of Deheubarth, as well as the great 14th-century poet Dafydd ap Gwilym, are buried here.

The site is a mile down a rural road from the village of Pontrhydfendigaid (pont-reed-en-dee-guide) on the B4343; the village is 15 miles from Aberystwyth or 9 miles south of Devil's Bridge. Bus T21 has limited services from Monday to Saturday from Aberystwyth (35 minutes).

POWYS

Small villages, quiet market towns and an abundance of sheep litter the undulating hills and moorland of rural Powys, by far Wales' biggest county. Named after an ancient Welsh kingdom, this modern entity was formed in 1974 from the historic counties of Montgomeryshire, Radnorshire and Brecknockshire. It's an overwhelmingly rural place ideal for walking and cycling but this county isn't just green in a literal sense – Machynlleth has become a focal point for the nation's environmentally friendly aspirations and all over the county, efforts to restore the threatened red kite have been met with outstanding success. The bird is now the very symbol of Powys, the county at Wales' green heart.

Machynlleth

POP 2200

Little Machynlleth (ma-hun-khleth) punches well above its weight. The town is saturated in historical significance, as it was here that nationalist hero Owain Glyndŵr established the country's first parliament in 1404. But even that legacy is close to being trumped by Machynlleth's reinvention as the green capital of Wales – thanks primarily to the Centre for Alternative Technology (CAT), 3 miles north of town.

The centre has given Machynlleth an eco-magneticism that attracts alternative lifestylers from far and wide. If you want to get your runes read, take up yoga or explore holistic dancing, Machynlleth is the ideal place for you. Unfortunately, it hasn't been enough to protect the town from failing fortunes though with some much-loved shops and cafes succumbing to economic pressures in recent years. Despite this, Machynlleth is still the most cosmopolitan of local towns and is surrounded by serene countryside, particularly suited to mountain biking.

☉ Sights

★ Centre for
Alternative Technology   ECO CENTRE
(CAT; ☑ 01654-705950; www.cat.org.uk; Pantperthog; adult/child £8.50/4; ☉10am-5pm) A small but dedicated band of enthusiasts have spent 40 years practising sustainability at the thought-provoking CAT, set in a beautiful wooded valley 3 miles north of Machynlleth.

Founded in 1974 (well ahead of its time), CAT is an education and visitor centre that demonstrates practical solutions for sustainability. There are more than 3 hectares of displays dealing with topics such as composting, organic gardening, environmentally friendly construction, renewable energy sources and sewage treatment and recycling. To explore the whole site takes about two hours – take rainwear as it's primarily outdoors. Kids love the interactive displays and adventure playground and there's a great organic wholefood restaurant.

The visit starts with a 60m ride up the side of an old quarry in an ingenious water-balanced cable car (closed in winter to save water). A drum beneath the top car fills with stored rainwater and is then drawn down while the bottom car is hauled up. At the top you disembark by a small lake with great views across the Dyfi Valley.

There are workshops and games for children during the main school holidays and an extensive program of residential courses for adults throughout the year (day courses start from around £50). A new purpose-built education centre also offers postgraduate programmes on sustainability, renewable

Machynlleth

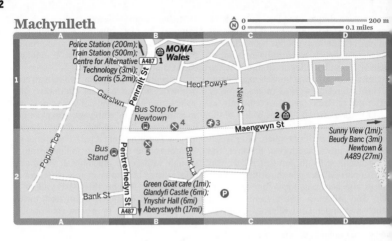

energy and sustainable architecture. Volunteer helpers are welcome, but you'll need to apply.

Look out for information on a range of special events to celebrate the centre's 40th anniversary in 2014.

To get to the CAT from Machynlleth (seven minutes) you can take the 34 bus. Buses T2 and X27 go to the village of Pantperthog, a 10-minute walk away. Arriving by bus or bicycle gets you a discount of £1. Arrive with a valid train ticket and you'll get your entrance ticket for half price.

★ MOMA Wales   GALLERY
(☎01654-703355; www.momawales.org.uk; Penrallt St; ⊘10am-4pm Mon-Sat) FREE Housed partly in the Tabernacle, a neoclassical former Methodist chapel (1880), the Museum of Modern Art exhibits work by contemporary Welsh artists as well as an annual international competition (mid-July to late August). The small permanent collection is supplemented by a continuous roster of temporary exhibitions. The chapel itself has the feel of a courtroom but the acoustics are good – it's used for concerts, theatre and talks.

Owain Glyndŵr Centre   MUSEUM
(☎01654-702932; www.canolfanglyndwr.org; Maengwyn St; adult/child £2.50/1; ⊘10am-5pm Tue-Sat Mar-Sep) Housed in a rare example of a late-medieval Welsh town house, the Owain Glyndŵr Centre has somewhat dry displays but nevertheless tells a rip-roaring story of the Welsh hero's fight for independence. Although it's called the Old Parliament Building it was probably built around 1460, some 50 years after Glyndŵr instituted his parliament on this site, but it's believed to closely resemble the former venue.

🏃 Activities

The rolling wooded hills that surround Machynlleth shelter some of the best mountain biking in the country with numerous tracks and bridleways criss-crossing the hills and four excellent trails to follow.

There is, in addition, a walking and cycling trail that leads off the A487 (just north of the train station) and follows a countryside path, crossing the Millennium Bridge and leading you towards the CAT by the greenest possible forms of transport.

Dyfi Mountain Biking   MOUNTAIN BIKING
(www.dyfimountainbiking.org.uk) Maintaining three waymarked mountain-bike routes from Machynlleth, Dyfi Mountain Biking offers the Mach 1 (10 miles), 2 (14 miles) and

3 (19 miles), each more challenging than the one before. The Mach 3's certainly not for beginners. In the Dyfi Forest, near Corris, is the custom-built, 9-mile Cli-machx loop trail. In May the same crew run the **Dyfi Enduro**, a noncompetitive, long-distance mountain-bike challenge, limited to 650 riders.

Holey Trail MOUNTAIN BIKING
(☎ 01654-700411; www.theholeytrail.co.uk; 31 Maengwyn St; ☺ 10am-6pm Mon-Fri, 9.30am-5pm Sat) Hires mountain bikes (per day £25), performs repairs and is a mine of information on the local trails.

🎪 Festivals & Events

Machynlleth Comedy Festival COMEDY
(www.machcomedyfest.co.uk; ☺ May) A long weekend of laughs.

Gŵyl Machynlleth MUSIC
(Machynlleth Festival; www.momawales.org.uk) Takes place during the third week of August, with music ranging from kids' stuff to cabaret, plus a lively fringe festival.

🛏 Sleeping

★ Beudy Banc CAMPGROUND £
(☎ 01650-511495; www.beudybanc.co.uk; Abercegir; sites £20) 🚳 Set on a working sheep farm nestled in the folds of the Dyfi Valley, this wonderful place offers back-to-basics camping in grassy meadows with glorious views. There are hot showers and composting toilets, campfires are allowed and, with a limited number of pitches, it never feels too crowded. If you feel like a little more comfort you can choose from excellent-value fully furnished bell tents sleeping four (£40 per night), a simple but quirky cabin (£75 per night) or a gorgeous converted barn powered by the wind and sun. The barn can sleep up to eight with prices starting from £100 per night for two people. A walking trail across the farm links up with Glyndŵr's Way but the real joy here are the two excellent mountain bike descents and the network of tracks and bridleways around the farm. Beudy Banc is about 3 miles northeast of Machynlleth off the A489.

★ Glandyfi Castle HOTEL ££
(☎ 01654-781238; www.glandyficastle.co.uk; Glandyfi; r £90-£250; 🅿 🖥) Built in 1820 as a fashionable statement of wealth, this quirky Regency Gothic castle has been brought back to life as a gloriously indulgent small hotel. There's no stuffy attitude here, just eight excellent-value rooms that blend classical styling with modern sensibilities. The cheaper rooms are smaller but no less comfortable and the turrets, towers, octagonal rooms and superb views over the vast grounds make it feel like an incredibly special place to stay. A three-course set menu (from £30) is served in the evening.

The castle is 6 miles south of Machynlleth off the A487.

Sunny View B&B ££
(☎ 01654-700387; www.sunnyviewbandb.weebly.com; Forge; s/d £45/70) Set in a quiet village 1 mile from Machynlleth, this bungalow has immaculate rooms decorated in unfussy modern style. The bathrooms are new, breakfasts are good and there's a very warm welcome. It's a great option for cyclists as all three of the Mach cycle trails pass through the village.

To get here head out of Machynlleth on the A489 towards Newtown and turn right onto the Forge Rd just opposite the hospital. If you arrive by train the owners are happy to pick you up at the station.

★ Ynyshir Hall HOTEL £££
(☎ 01654-781209; www.ynyshirhall.co.uk; Eglwysfach; s/d from £150/205; 🖥) Tucked away to the south of the River Dovey (Afon Dyfi) estuary, just off the main Aberystwyth–Machynlleth road (A487), this grand manor house was once kept as a hunting lodge by Queen Victoria. It's now a quietly opulent boutique hotel and its restaurant (two-/three-course lunch £25/29.50, set dinner £72.50) is one of Wales' finest. The house's Victorian purpose is reflected in a menu that includes game birds such as quail, partridge and pheasant, as well as local seafood and the finest Welsh lamb, beef and pork. The friendly (rather than fawning) staff are never less than professional.

A little ironically, given the fowl-bothering menu, immediately behind the house is the 550-hectare **Ynys-hir Royal Society for the Protection of Birds Reserve**, complete with hides and a small visitor centre.

🍴 Eating

The town's Wednesday **farmers market** (Maengwyn St) has been going on for over seven centuries and remains a lively affair.

Green Goat Cafe CAFE £
(mains £4-5; ☺ 8am-4pm Mon-Fri, 9am-2pm Sat) A roadside cafe with a difference, this bright

green caravan in a layby is not your average greasy spoon but a bastion of home-smoked meats, luscious cakes and daily specials that are worth a trip even if you're not passing this way. Expect the likes of lamb cawl with rosemary and cranberry bread, chorizo salchichas with fried rice and platain and chickpea burgers all cooked to perfection. Find them on the A487 between Machynlleth and Derwenlas.

Number Twenty One   MODERN WELSH **££**
(☑ 01654-703382;   www.numbertwentyone.co.uk; 21 Maengwyn St; mains £8-15; ☺ Tue-Sat; ✍ 📶) A much needed addition to the Mach food scene, this new bistro has been packed full of happy customers since the day it opened. The food is imaginative without being fussy, the service is friendly but professional, children are welcome and nothing seems too much trouble. Space is limited so book ahead.

Wynnstay Hotel   PUB **££**
(☑ 01654-702941;   www.wynnstay-hotel.com; Maengwyn St; mains £11-17) Flying in the face of Machynlleth's vegie-warrior image, the Wynnstay's menu revels in meatiness with just a token nod to the town's vegetarians. In this 1780 coaching inn the reliable country grub is matched by a country pub feel, with roaring fires in winter and dining areas scattered around the ground floor.

ℹ Information

Dyfi Craft & Clothing (☑ 01654-703369; Owain Glyndŵr Centre, Maengwyn St; ☺ 10am-4pm Mon-Sat) Following the demise of the official tourist office, this little store stocks brochures, maps and accommodation information.

Police Station (☑ 101; Doll St)

ℹ Getting There & Around

If you're on a bike, Lôn Las Cymru passes through Machynlleth, heading north to Corris, south to Llanwrtyd Wells and southeast to Rhayader.

Bus routes include X28 to Aberystwyth (40 minutes); T2 to Dolgellau (35 minutes), Porthmadog (90 minutes), Caernarfon (2¼ hours) and Bangor (2¾ hours); X85 to Newtown (51 minutes); and 34 to the Centre for Alternative Technology (7 minutes) and Corris (15 minutes).

By train, Machynlleth is on the Cambrian and Cambrian Coast Lines. Destinations include Aberystwyth (£6, 37 minutes), Porthmadog (£13.20, 1¾ hours), Pwllheli (£15.30, 2½ hours),

Newtown (£9.10, 38 minutes) and Birmingham (£20.90, 2¼ hours).

Around Machynlleth

Corris

POP 720

Set within a commercial pine forest on the edge of Snowdonia National Park, Corris is a peaceful former slate village, 5 miles north of Machynlleth. With a steam railway, craft centre, theatre and two subterranean tours in the village's old slate mine and caves, it's well worth a stop.

🏃 Activities

Corris Craft Centre   CRAFT

(☑ 01654-761584;   www.corriscraftcentre.co.uk; ☺ 10am-5.30pm Apr-Oct) A virtual hive of interconnected hexagonal workshops for potters, glassblowers, leatherworkers, wood turners, candle-makers and quilters, along with a cafe to keep everyone productive, the Corris Craft Centre is an excellent place to see artists and craftspeople at work, join a short workshop or pick up some souvenirs. The centre is just outside the village of Corris on the A487.

Corris Mine Explorers   MINE, GUIDED TOUR
(☑ 01654-761244;   www.corrismineexplorers.co.uk; Corris) The harsh working conditions and sometimes tragic consequences of working in the mines are brought vividly to life at Corris Mine Explorers, where you can discover the dark, cramped depths of the old Corris slate mine. The mine was abandoned about 40 years ago but everything is left just as it was when the miners last walked out. There are three tour options: a one-hour taster (adult/child £10/7; minimum age eight), a two-hour explorer (£20; minimum age 10) and a four-hour expedition (£38; minimum age 13). A reasonable level of fitness and a willingness to get wet and dirty is required. Bookings essential.

Corris Railway   HERITAGE RAILWAY
(☑ 01654-761303;   www.corris.co.uk; Station Yard; adult/child £6/3; ☺ Apr-Sep, see website for timetable) Built in the 1850s to transport slate, the narrow-gauge Corris Railway now offers 50-minute trips, which include a guided tour of the sheds.

King Arthur's Labyrinth GUIDED TOUR

(☎ 01654-761584; www.kingarthurslabyrinth. com; Corris; adult/child £8.95/5.95; ⊗10am-5pm Easter-Oct) Child-focused King Arthur's Labyrinth is an underground boat ride and walking tour through caves and tunnels where a sound-and-light show, manikins and a hooded guide bring old Celtic tales and Arthurian legends to life.

🛏️ Sleeping

Eco Retreats CAMPGROUND £££

(☎ 01654-781375; www.ecoretreats.co.uk; Furnace; d for 2 nights tepee/yurt from £225/245) 🧭 For the ultimate get-away-from-it-all break with a green conscience, Eco Retreats offers chilled accommodation in beautifully furnished tepees and yurts. It's a low-tech experience, with wood burners, compost toilets and outdoor showers set in a remote location up a rough forest track. The tents are well spaced and the views are glorious, making it an incredibly tranquil place to unwind. Reiki, meditation, kinesiology and elemental medicine sessions are also available on site. It's tricky to find; the owners will give you directions to the campground when you make your booking.

❶ Getting There & Away

Bus 30 and 34 from Machynlleth (15 minutes) stop in Corris.

Newtown (Y Drenewydd)

POP 11,400

Newtown's a former mill town with lots of history but, as a destination, it's a sleepy place – absolutely soporific on a Sunday, but waking up for the Tuesday and Saturday markets. Its big claim to fame is that Robert Owen, the factory reformer, founder of the cooperative movement and 'father of Socialism', was born here in 1771, though he left at the age of 10 and only returned just before his death in 1858. Monuments to his esteemed memory abound in the town centre.

Newtown was also once the home of Welsh flannel and a major UK textile centre. When competition began driving wages down, Wales' first Chartist meeting was held here in October 1838. Pryce Jones, the world's first-ever mail-order firm, got its start here, on the back of the textile trade. By the end of the 19th century, Newtown's boom days were over – and they've never

been back. There are several small museums devoted to those long-gone salad days.

Newtown is almost the home of Laura Ashley (she opened her first shop in Carno, 10 miles west of the centre).

◉ Sights

Robert Owen Museum MUSEUM

(☎ 01686-622510; www.robert-owen-museum.org. uk; The Cross; ⊗11am-3pm Tue, Thu & Sat May-Aug) FREE If you're not aware of Robert Owen's legacy, you're best to start here. The displays on Owen's life are broken up with mementoes and pictures; it's quite text-heavy but it makes fascinating reading. Owen was the son of a saddler who became a successful cotton-mill owner. His then-radical reforms included reducing working hours from 14 to 16 hours per day to 10 to 12, setting a minimum working age of 10 and funding schools for his employees' children, which included music and dancing alongside academic instruction. He's considered a founding father of the co-operative and the trade union movements. At the corner of Gas and Short Bridge Sts a statue and garden herald him as a 'pioneer, social reformer and philanthropist'.

The museum is in the town-council building and also serves as the de facto tourist office.

St Mary's Old Parish Church RUIN

(Old Church St) Owen's well-tended grave is in the grounds of St Mary's Old Parish Church. Dating from at least 1253, the church was allowed to fall into ruin after a bigger church was built in 1856 and it's now a public garden, thanks to the local co-operative union. There's also a memorial here to Thomas Powell, a disciple of Owen who became a Chartist leader, part of the movement demanding a vote for all men, not just the rich.

Oriel Davies GALLERY

(☎ 01686-625041; www.orieldavies.org; The Park; ⊗10am-5pm Mon-Sat) FREE One of Wales' leading contemporary spaces hosting often edgy national and international exhibitions, Oriel Davies is the largest visual-arts venue in the region and offers a range of talks, courses and workshops. Its sunny, glassed-in **cafe** (open 10am to 4pm) is the best place for a light meal, such as homemade soup, quiche or baked potatoes. In summer you can eat overlooking the leafy riverside **park** that contains a mound that is all that

LOCAL KNOWLEDGE

GLYNDŴR'S WAY NATIONAL TRAIL

Named after the renowned Welsh leader, Glyndŵr's Way cuts an arc through Powys, taking in many sites connected with him. The persistence of a strong Welsh identity, clear at every stop along the trail, is one of the unique pleasures of walking it.

The landscape is predominantly low moorland and farmland, with lakes, gentle hills and beautiful valleys. A particular highlight is the impressive range of bird life, including buzzards, kingfishers, woodpeckers, red kites, peregrine falcons, flycatchers and wrens.

Most people take nine days to complete the 132-mile walk. Starting from Knighton, we'd suggest making Felindre (15 miles) your first stop, followed by Abbey-cwm-hir (14 miles), Llanidloes (15.5 miles), Dylife (16 miles), Machynlleth (14.5 miles), Llanbrynmair (14 miles), Llanwddyn (17.5 miles), Pontrobert (12 miles) and Welshpool (13.5 miles). Accommodation is scarce along the route, so book ahead. On some of the more remote sections you'll need to pack a lunch and carry enough water for the day.

The hilly terrain and difficulty of route-finding, due to a multitude of paths crossing the trail, can make for pretty slow going, so it's wise to allow a little more time than you would for more established trails. It's essential to carry a compass and a good set of maps. Your best bet is to pick up the *Glyndŵr's Way* official National Trail Guide by David Perrott, which includes extracts from the relevant Ordnance Survey 1:25,000 Explorer maps.

Becky Ohlsen

remains of Newtown's 13th-century **castle** and a Gorsedd (Druidic) **stone circle** dating from the Royal National Eisteddfod of 1965.

Textile Museum　　　　　　　MUSEUM
(☑ 01686-622024; 5-7 Commercial St; adult/child £1/50p; ☺ 2-5pm Mon, Tue & Thu-Sat Jul & Aug) In former weavers' cottages and workshops, just north of the river, the Textile Museum has impressively re-created rooms to show what living conditions were like in the 1820s. Above the cottages are the workshops with depictions of the workers, both adults and children.

WH Smith Museum　　　　　　MUSEUM
(☑ 01686-626280; 24 High St; ☺ 9am-5.30pm Mon-Sat) Newtown's WH Smith bookshop has been lovingly restored to its original 1929 look, complete with wooden furniture, mirrors, signage and skylights. Upstairs is a free little company museum telling the history of one of Britain's biggest household names.

🛏 Sleeping & Eating

Old Vicarage Dolfor　　　　　　B&B ££
(☑ 01686-629051; www.theoldvicaragedolfor.co.uk; Dolfor; s/d from £65/95; P 🛜) A handsome Victorian house set in a quiet rural location, the Old Vicarage offers extremely pretty rooms with muted colour schemes, subtle floral wallpapers, claw-foot bathtubs and an incredibly warm welcome. You can also

dine here and the accomplished two-course dinner menu (£25) features plenty of local produce. Advance booking for dinner is essential. The Old Vicarage is 4 miles south of Newtown by the busy A483.

Highgate　　　　　　　　　B&B ££
(☑ 01686-623763; www.highgatebandb.co.uk; Bettws Cedewain; s/d from £45/75; P 🛜) Fields still surround this heritage-listed half-timbered farmhouse (1651), making it a particularly bucolic retreat. The decor is understated, keeping the focus on the original oak beams and other period features. From Newtown, cross the bridge at the northern end of the main street, turn right, veer left at All Saints Church and continue for 2.5 miles.

Mirrens　　　　　　　　STEAKHOUSE ££
(☑ 01686-621120; www.mirrenssteakandtapasbar. co.uk; 17 Parkers La; mains £8-37; ☺ Mon-Sat) The hot rock steaks here are sourced from local farmers who feed their Japanese Wagu cattle with beer and treat them to the odd massage, so it's no surprise the meat is top quality. The menu includes a bit of everything from Welsh lamb to kangaroo, wildebeest, springbok and zebra. Tapas are another specialty and the £10 set tapas lunch is good value.

ℹ Getting There & Away

Bus routes include X75 to Welshpool (32 minutes) and Shrewsbury (1¼ hours); X85 to

Machynlleth (51 minutes) and T4 to Llandrindod Wells (47 minutes), Builth Wells (1¼ hours) and Brecon (two hours).

The daily **National Express** (www.nationalexpress.com) coach from Aberystwyth (£12.20, 1¼ hours) to London (£32.30, 5½ hours), via Welshpool (£4.60, 25 minutes), Shrewsbury (£8.10, 55 minutes) and Birmingham (£10.80, 2½ hours) stops here.

By train, Newtown is on the Cambrian Line, which crosses from Aberystwyth (£12, 1¼ hours) to Birmingham (£18.20, 1¾ hours) every two hours, via Machynlleth (£9.10, 42 minutes), Welshpool (£4.80, 15 minutes) and Shrewsbury (£6.90, 40 minutes).

Newtown to Welshpool

Gregynog Hall

Dating from the 19th-century in its current mock-Tudor incarnation, **Gregynog Hall** (☑ 01686-650224; www.gregynog.wales.ac.uk; Tregynon; formal garden admission £3; ⊙ dawn to dusk) has been here in some form for 800 years. From 1924 it was the home of the Davies sisters, Gwendoline and Margaret, who are known for the extraordinary collection of paintings they bequeathed to the National Museum. Their grandfather was David Davies (a sawyer turned miner) who, when prevented by the Bute family from exporting his coal from Cardiff, built his own docks at Barry and made a fortune.

The sisters intended to make the house an arts centre, founding a fine-arts press in the stables and holding an annual Festival of Music and Poetry. In the 1960s the estate was given to the University of Wales, which uses it as a conference centre. Successor to the sisters' festival is the week-long **Gwyl** (☑ 01686-207100; www.gwylgregynogfestival.org) held annually in mid-June, with operatic, choral, orchestral and instrumental music performed in the grounds of the house. The house, its interior largely unchanged since Margaret's death in 1963, opens for group tours by appointment and you'll find a cafe and shop (open 11am to 4pm from March to December).

However, the main drawcard is the 300 hectares of Grade 1-listed garden, which are estimated to date from at least the 16th century. There are avenues of sculpted yews, impressive rhododendrons and azaleas, 300-year-old oaks and bird-filled beech woodlands, all accessible on a series of walking tracks. Admission to the grounds is unrestricted, although there is a small charge (£2.50) for parking.

Gregynog Hall is situated about 5 miles north of Newtown and is signposted from the B4389.

Berriew

POP 1300

Shortly before the River Rhiw empties into the Severn it gurgles through this pretty village of black-and-white houses, grouped around an ancient oval churchyard. Tiny Berriew is the unlikely location for the Andrew Logan Museum of Sculpture when the museum is closed there's not much to do here except stroll around and take in the scenery.

◉ Sights

Andrew Logan Museum of Sculpture   GALLERY
(☑ 01686-640689; www.andrewloganmuseum.org; adult/child £3/1.50; ⊙ noon-4pm Sat & Sun Jun-Sep) The supremely flouncy and fascinating Andrew Logan Museum of Sculpture is a surprise discovery in this tiny village well off the beaten track. The building is actually a former squash court but it has played host to a very different display of physical prowess since Logan took it over in 1991. Today, it's a glorious celebration of sequins and camp, with beautiful, frivolous, humorous artworks, including a huge cosmic egg made of fibreglass and a larger-than-life portrayal of fashion designer Zandra Rhodes. Logan has been running the Alternative Miss World contest since 1972 ('a parade of freaks, fops, show-offs and drag queens') and the museum contains many relics of the shows.

✗ Eating

Lychgate Cottage   CAFE £
(☑ 01686-640750; mains £5-7; ⊙ 9am-4.30pm Mon-Sat) This little tearoom and delicatessen by the village church serves delicious Welsh cheese and pate platters, Ludlow olives, sandwiches, baguettes and cakes.

❶ Getting There & Away

Berriew is situated 6 miles south of Welshpool, just off the A483; take bus X75 from Newtown (20 minutes) or Welshpool (12 minutes).

Montgomery

POP 1300

Set around a market square lined with august houses in stone and brick, and overlooked by the ruins of a Norman castle, genteel Montgomery is one of the prettiest small towns in the country. A charming mixture of Georgian, Victorian and timber-framed houses line the streets and a choice of excellent places to eat combine to make it an unexpectedly rewarding place to stop. Near the town is one of the best preserved sections of Offa's Dyke with 6m-high ditches flanking the B4386 a mile east of town.

◎ Sights

Montgomery Castle   RUIN

FREE Rising from the craggy outcrop above the town are the ruins of Norman Montgomery Castle. Work on the castle began in 1233 and in 1267 during treaty negotiations at the castle, King Henry III granted Llewelyn ap Gruffydd the title of Prince of Wales. Little remains of the once great fortress but the views over the chequerboard countryside that surround it are beautiful.

St Nicholas' Church   CHURCH

(Church Bank; ◎9am-dusk) Sturdy Norman St Nicholas' Church dates from 1226 and boasts a vaulted ceiling decorated with intricate coloured bosses, a beautifully carved prereformation rood screen and striking mid-19th-century stained-glass windows. Look out for the elaborate canopied tomb of local landowner Sir Richard Herbert and his wife Magdalen, parents of Elizabethan poet George Herbert. In the churchyard is the Robber's Grave, the final resting place of John Davies of Wrexham who was sentenced to death by hanging in 1821 for highway robbery. He vehemently protested his innocence and declared that grass would not grow on his grave for 100 years. It remained bare for at least a century.

Old Bell Museum   MUSEUM

(✎01686-668313; www.oldbellmuseum.org.uk; Arthur St; adult/child £1/50p; ◎1.30-5pm Wed-Fri & Sun, 10.30am-5pm Sat Easter-Sep) Set in a 16th-century inn, this local history museum sheds light on the town's long history (Montgomery was granted a Royal Charter in 1227, making it the oldest borough in Wales) and features scale models of the castle, artefacts from excavations, and exhibits on the Cambrian Railway, the local work-

house and construction of half-timbered buildings.

⊨ Sleeping & Eating

Castle Kitchen   CAFE £

(✎01686-668795; www.castlekitchen.org; 8 Broad St; mains £4-8; ◎9am-4.30pm Mon-Sat, 11am-4.30pm Sun) This lovely little deli cafe is perfect for stocking up on picnic supplies for a walk along Offa's Dyke or a more substantial takeaway to enjoy in the hills. If you have the time, just sit and relax in the simple cafe over a wonderful selection of soups, breads, sandwiches, daily specials and, of course, some luscious cakes.

Ivy House Cafe   CAFE £

(✎01686-668746; Church Bank; mains £5-7; ◎10am-5pm Mon-Sat; ☎✐) A warm, homey place with local art on the walls and a fine line in home baking, Ivy House offers a good selection of hearty and wholesome classic cafe fare with plenty of choice for vegetarians and not a chip or sausage in sight.

★Checkers   HOTEL, RESTAURANT £££

(✎01686-669822; www.thecheckersmontgomery.co.uk; Broad St; mains £15-26, r from £125; ◎lunch Wed-Sat, dinner Thu-Sat; ☎) It's no exaggeration to say that one of the main drawcards of Montgomery is this truly excellent restaurant-with-rooms. Contemporary style and tastes are underpinned by the best of tradition in both the decor and the food and you'll find modern art below the old crooked beams and top notch but unfussy classic French cooking on the menu. With a Michelin star and first-rate service, this place has a loyal fan base so book ahead. Upstairs, the rooms are simple but luxurious, with extra-comfy beds, L'Occitane products and blissful bathrooms.

❶ Getting There & Away

Bus X71 runs to Welshpool (17 minutes) and Newtown (21 minutes).

Welshpool (Y Trallwng)

POP 6700

The English originally called this place Pool, after the 'pills' – boggy, marshy ground (long since drained) along the nearby River Severn. It was changed in 1835 to Welshpool, so nobody would get confused with Poole in Dorset. Set below a steeply wooded hill, it's a handsome market town with a mixture f Tudor, Georgian and Victorian buildings long its main streets but few other distactions in the town centre and a dearth f places to stay or eat. More compelling, owever, are the peripheral sights such as lorious Powis Castle and the narrow-gauge Velshpool and Llanfair Light Railway.

Sights & Activities

Powis Castle   CASTLE

01938-551944; www.nationaltrust.org.uk; adult/ iild castle & gardens £13/6.50, garden only £9.60/ 80; 12.30-5pm) Surrounded by magnifient gardens, the red-brick Powis Castle ses up from its terraces as if floating on cloud of massive, manicured yew trees. It as originally built in the 13th-century by ruffydd ap Gwenwynwyn, prince of Powys, nd was subsequently enriched by generaons of the Herbert and Clive families.

The extravagant mural-covered, woodanelled interior contains one of Wales' nest collections of furniture and paintgs, including works by Gainsborough and ubens and curios such as Mary, Queen of cot's rosary beads. The **Clive Museum**, in ie former ballroom, holds a fascinating nd exquisite cache of jade, ivory, armour, xtiles and other treasures brought back om India by Baron Clive (British conquerr of Bengal at the Battle of Plassey in 1757), lowing a rare insight into the lifestyle of arly colonialists.

The baroque garden is peerless, dotted ith ornamental lead statues and an orangry, formal gardens, wilderness, terraces and rchards.

The castle is just over a mile south of Velshpool, off Berriew Rd.

owysland Museum & 1ontgomery Canal   MUSEUM

01938-554656; www.powys.gov.uk; Severn Rd; dult/child £1/free; 11am-5pm Mon, Tue, Thu & ri May-Sep, also Sat & Sun Jun-Aug) The Montomery Canal originally ran for 35 miles tarting at Newtown and ending at Frankon Junction in Shropshire, where it joined he Llangollen Canal. After sections of its anks burst in 1936 it lay abandoned until group of volunteers and the British Waterays Board began repairing it in 1969.

Beside the canal wharf is the Powysland 1useum, marked outside by a big blue andbag (an Andy Hancock sculpture to ommemorate the Queen's Jubilee) and illars painted by local schoolchildren and opped by carved birds. Inside, the museum tells the story of the county, with great details – such as the Roman recipe for stuffed dormouse.

Welshpool & Llanfair Light Railway   HERITAGE RAILWAY

(01938-810441; www.wllr.org.uk; Raven Sq; adult/child £12.80/3.50; Apr-Oct, check times online) This sturdy narrow-gauge railway was completed in 1902 to help people bring their sheep and cattle to market. It runs up steep inclines and through the pretty Banwy Valley. The line was closed in 1956 but was reopened seven years later by enthusiastic volunteers.

Trains make the 8-mile journey from Raven Square Station to Llanfair Caereinion in 50 minutes and according to a complex timetable. There are also courses on offer to learn how to drive your very own steam engine.

Festivals & Events

Country & Western Music Festival   MUSIC

(www.countrywestern.org.uk; weekend ticket £25) On the third Sunday in July, the county showground near Powis Castle becomes the unlikely venue for a weekend hoedown with spit roasts and line dancing; proceeds benefit disabled children through the Heulwen Trust.

Sleeping & Eating

Long Mountain   B&B ££

(01938-553456; www.longmountainbandb.co.uk; Hope; s/d £50/75;) A purpose-built B&B 2 miles from town, Long Mountain is a modern extension to a 400-year-old timber frame house. The three guest rooms have top-quality fittings with solid oak furniture, king-sized beds with Egyptian cotton bed linen and marble bathrooms, yet somehow lack a little soul. The welcome is incredibly warm, however, and there are wonderful views. No children under 16.

To get here head east on the B4381 turning left onto the B388 and then right onto the Hope Rd.

Bistro 7   ITALIAN ££

(01938-552879; 7 Hall St; mains £7-10; 11.30am-11pm Mon-Sat) By far the best bet for food in town, Bistro 7 serves up good-value and well executed largely Italian food to the happy masses. Seafood platters, pastas and pizza are firm favourites with a lighter menu of panini, jacket potatoes and sand-

LOCAL KNOWLEDGE

OFFA'S DYKE PATH

They say that good fences make good neighbours, but King Offa may have taken the idea a bit far. The 8th-century Mercian king built Offa's Dyke, Britain's longest archaeological monument, to mark the boundary between his kingdom and that of the Welsh princes, and even today, though only 80 miles of the dyke remains, the modern Wales–England border roughly follows the line it defined.

The Offa's Dyke Path National Trail criss-crosses that border around 30 times in its journey from the Severn Estuary near Chepstow, through the beautiful Wye Valley and Shropshire Hills, to the coast at Prestatyn in North Wales. The dyke itself usually takes the form of a bank next to a ditch, although it's overgrown in some places and built over in others. The trail often strays from the dyke, covering an astonishing range of scenery and vegetation, including river valleys, hill country, oak forests, heathland and bracken, conifer forest, green fields, high moors and the mountainous terrain of the Clwydian Ranges in the north.

While it can be walked in either direction, it's best done south to north, with the wind and sun mainly on your back. Most people take 12 days to complete the 177-mile walk, though it's wise to allow at least two rest days, bringing your adventure to an even two weeks.

The Offa's Dyke Centre (p202) in Knighton is the best source of information about the route, stocking maps, guidebooks and pamphlets.

Becky Ohlsen

---

wiches for lunch. Look out for the local cask ales behind the bar.

ℹ️ Information

Police Station (☑101; Severn St)

Tourist Office (☑01938-552043; Church St, Vicarage Gardens; ☺9.30am-5pm Mon-Sat, 10am-4pm Sun)

Victoria Memorial Hospital (☑01938-553133; Salop Rd)

ℹ️ Getting There & Around

Bus X75 runs to Newtown (32 minutes) and Shrewsbury (46 minutes).

The daily **National Express** (www.nationalexpress.com) coach from Aberystwyth (£11.70, 1¾ hours) to London (£32.80, five hours), via Newtown (£4.50, 25 minutes), Shrewsbury (£4.90, 30 minutes) and Birmingham (£10.30, 2¼ hours) stops in front of the tourist office.

Welshpool is on the Cambrian Line, which crosses from Aberystwyth (£13.60, 1½ hours) to Birmingham (£13, 1½ hours) every two hours, via Machynlleth (£11.70, 57 minutes), Newtown (£4.80, 15 minutes) and Shrewsbury (£5.70, 25 minutes).

Knighton (Tref-Y-Clawdd)

POP 3000

Hilly Knighton (the town on the dyke) is a lively, handsome town of winding streets and half-timbered houses midway along the Offa's Dyke Path National Trail and at or end of the Glyndŵr's Way National Trail. popular stopover for walkers, it is so clos to the border that its train station is actual in England.

The coming of the railway in 1861 and th growth of livestock farming saw Knighton fortunes rise, but they fell again with th decline in population post WWII and faile attempts to turn it into a spa town. One di turbing piece of local folklore suggests tha it was possible for a man to obtain a divorc by 'selling' his wife at the square where th 1872 clock tower now stands. Husband would bring their spouse to the square a the end of a rope; the last wife was sold i 1842.

🅾️ Sights & Activities

St Edward's Church CHUR(
(Church St) All that remains of medieval S Edward's Church is its 14-th-century be tower, the rest of the building was rebui in early Decorated style in the 19th century

Spaceguard Centre PLANETARII
(☑01547-520247; www.spaceguarduk.com; Lla shay La; adult/child £6/3; ☺tours 10.30am, 2pm 4pm Wed-Sun May-Sep) The hilltop Spacegua Centre, in the former Powys Observator is a centre for research into asteroids an comets. Tours take in the telescopes, camer obscura and planetarium shows.

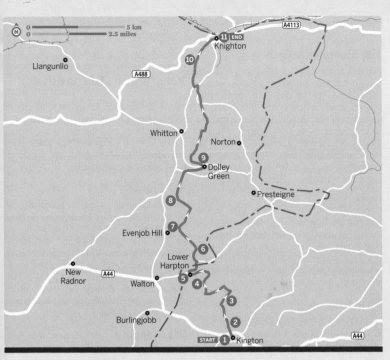

🏃 Walking Tour
Offa's Dyke Path: Kington to Knighton

START KINGTON
FINISH KNIGHTON
DISTANCE 13.5 MILES; FIVE TO SEVEN HOURS

One of the most rewarding sections of Offa's Dyke Path, this route offers glorious views of the surrounding hills and passes some particularly well-preserved sections of the 8th-century defensive earthwork. The walk begins across the border in Herefordshire and weaves between the two countries crossing remote hills to Knighton (Tref-y-Clawdd, the town on the dyke).

From ❶ **Kington Museum** head towards the clock tower, turning left onto Church St and then right onto Doctor's Lane, which soon becomes Prospect Rd. Follow the narrowing road around until you cross a footbridge over a stream. Continue straight across the busy A44 and start your first ascent towards ❷ **Bradnor Green**. Skirt the edge of the golf course and continue the climb along the edge of Bradnor Hill and then ❸ **Rushock Hill** enjoying wonderful views

across the undulating landscape. Follow the path as it runs along a section of the dyke round a field edge to reveal another impressive vista southwest to the Hergest Ridge and East Radnor Hills. Here the dyke heads up near the summit of ❹ **Herrock Hill** but the path runs down the side of the hill to ❺ **Lower Harpton** where you cross back into Wales over an old packhorse bridge. Follow the leafy lane uphill past the scant remains of ❻ **Burfa Camp**, an ancient hillfort. The path then heads up ❼ **Evenjob Hill** where the dyke remains in remarkable condition with wonderful westerly views. As you head up and over ❽ **Pen Offa** the easterly hills are revealed. It's downhill from here to the Lugg Valley past magnificent, towering sections of the dyke. Cross the field to the River Lugg, a small but beautiful river with deep pools and plenty of shade. From nearby ❾ **Dolley Green** it's a steep but short climb up ❿ **Furrow Hill** where you'll get great views to the west. The dyke here is little more than a raised mound of earth. From here on it's a gentle stroll down into ⓫ **Knighton**.

The centre is 1.5 miles east of town, sign-posted off the A4113.

🛏 Sleeping & Eating

Horse & Jockey Inn　　　　B&B **££**
(📞 01547-520062; www.thehorseandjockeyinn.co.uk; Station Rd; s/d from £49/65) This former 14th-century coaching inn is still in the eating-drinking-sleeping game. The six upmarket en suite rooms in the hayloft have flat-screen TVs, modern fittings, ancient exposed stone walls and flash bathrooms. The restaurant (mains £7 to £15) serves hearty traditional fare along with a good selection of pizzas.

Fleece House　　　　B&B **££**
(📞 01547-520168; www.fleecehouse.co.uk; Market St; d £80; 🅿) This 18th-century coaching inn situated at the top of the Narrows has two cosy rooms with cheery quilts and cushions. The facilities are simple but the welcome here is legendary, with nothing too much trouble and a mountain of local knowledge to mine.

ℹ Information

Tourist Office & Offa's Dyke Centre (📞 01547-528753; www.offasdyke.demon.co.uk; West St; ⊙10am-5pm Apr-Oct, 10am-4pm Mon-Sat Nov-Mar) The two-in-one tourist office and Offa's Dyke Centre is full of information for walkers with interactive displays about the dyke, a section of which runs behind the centre.

ℹ Getting There & Away

Knighton is one of the stops on the lovely Heart of Wales Line; destinations include Swansea (£15, 3¼ hours), Llandeilo (£10.30, two hours), Llanwrtyd Wells (£6.70, 1¼ hours), Llandrindod Wells (£4.30, 38 minutes) and Shrewsbury (£9.10, 50 minutes). Bus 41 heads to Presteigne (20 minutes).

Pilleth

At tiny Pilleth a whitewashed church on a hill overlooks the peaceful valley where 800 men were killed in the 1402 victory by Owain Glyndŵr over Edmund Mortimer (Mortimer was captured, switched sides and married Glyndŵr's daughter). Most of them were buried in mass graves in the churchyard.

While the current church dates from the 13th century, it's built on the site of an outpost of St Cynllo (died 460) and its idyllic location speaks of the close relationship of the early Celtic church to nature. Behind the church, steps lead into a well-preserved holy well, which was believed to have had healing

powers, particularly for eye complaints. It's now home to a rowdy family of far-sighted frogs.

Presteigne (Llanandras)
POP 2700

At the far west of the vanished county of Radnorshire, pressed right up against the English border, is Presteigne – its former county town. It's a quaint little place, lined with attractive old buildings and surrounded by beautiful countryside.

⊙ Sights

Judge's Lodging　　　HISTORIC BUILDING
(📞 01544-260650; www.judgeslodging.org.uk; Broad St; adult/child £6.75/3.50; ⊙10am-5pm Tue-Sun Mar-Oct) The Judge's Lodging offers an intriguing glimpse into Victorian times through an audio-guided wander through the town's 19th-century courthouse, lock-up and judge's apartments. The commentary does tend to ramble on but the displays are fascinating. The local tourist office is based here.

🛏 Sleeping

Old Vicarage　　　　B&B **££**
(📞 01544-260038; www.oldvicarage-nortonrads.co.uk; Norton; s/d from £78/112 ; 🅿) A real treat in the lesser-known Welsh Marches region, this three-room gay-friendly boutique B&B features Victorian fittings, all rescued and recycled from auctions and scrapyards. It boasts an almost womblike ambience of opulent, rich colours and perfect calm, the latter only interrupted by the chiming of antique clocks. A three-course dinner (£34.50) is also available if booked in advance. Norton is 2.5 miles north of Presteigne on the B4355.

ℹ Getting There & Away

Bus 41 heads to Knighton (20 minutes).

Llandrindod Wells
POP 5300

This spa town struck gold in Victorian times by touting its waters to the well-to-do gentry who rolled in for rest and recuperation. However, the allure of stinky water gradually diminished and it closed in 1972. The grand architecture of the era remains, but now it's the town that's sleepy – you'd need to prod it with a sharp stick to rouse it on a Wednesday afternoon, when most of the shops close.

Roman remains at nearby Castell Collen show that it wasn't the Victorians who first discovered the healthy effects of the local spring waters, but it was the arrival of the Central Wales railway (now the Heart of Wales Line) in 1865 that brought visitors en masse.

◉ Sights & Activities

Rock Park   PARK
Rock Park, the site of the earliest spa development, is a serene forested, landscaped oasis at the centre of the town. The bath house is now a complementary health centre and the pump room a conference centre. Just southeast of the centre is a sedately pretty, tree-encircled lake, built at the end of the 19th century to allow Victorians to take their exercise without appearing to do so. The original boathouse is now a private residence, but you can still rent a boat, fish for carp or take lunch at the cafe. The centrepiece of the lake is a sculpture of a Welsh dragon.

National Cycle Collection   MUSEUM
(☑ 01597-825531; www.cyclemuseum.org.uk; Temple St; adult/child £4/2; ☺10am-4pm Mon-Fri Apr-Oct) Housed in the art nouveau Automobile Palace, the National Cycle Collection comprises more than 250 bikes. The exhibits show the progression from clunky boneshakers and circus-reminiscent penny-farthings to bamboo bikes from the 1890s and the vertiginous 'Eiffel Tower' of 1899 (used to display billboards), as well as slicker, modern-day versions. Great effort has been made to put the bikes in context, with recreated Victorian and Edwardian cycle shops, photos and signboards – it's run with infectious enthusiasm. The building was constructed by Tom Norton, a local entrepreneur who started as a bicycle dealer and became the main Austin distributor. The trike on which Norton used to ride to work is here, with a picture of him on it.

Radnorshire Museum   MUSEUM
(☑ 01597-824513; www.powys.gov.uk/radnorshire-museum; Temple St; adult/child £1/50p; ☺10am-4pm Tue-Sat) Small and low-key, rather like the town itself, this museum offers a taste of local social history, archaeology and palaeontology. Radnorshire was a historic county, which was incorporated into Powys in 1974.

Llandrindod Wells

Rock Park Health Centre   HEALTH & FITNESS
(☑ 01597-824102; www.actionteam.org.uk; Winter Gardens Pavillion; ☺9am-5pm Mon-Fri) In the former bath house in the serene Rock Park, this small complementary health centre offers therapies such as massage, hypnotherapy, homeopathy and osteopathy. Fill your bottle at the rusty-looking and -tasting Chalybeate Spring (donated to the public by the Lord of the Manor in 1879) beside the Arlais Brook – apparently the water is good for treating gout, rheumatism, anaemia and more (chalybeate refers to its iron salts).

✪ Festivals

Victorian Festival VICTORIANA
(www.victorianfestival.co.uk) In the middle of August Llandrindod Wells indulges in nine days of 19th-century costumes and shenanigans.

🛏 Sleeping

The Cottage B&B ££
(☑ 01597-825435; www.thecottagebandb.co.uk; Spa Rd; s/d £43/65) This large, appealing Edwardian house, set in a flower-adorned garden, has comfortable rooms decorated in period style with heavy wooden furniture and lots of original features. Not all are en suite and the only TV is in the guest lounge.

Metropole Hotel HOTEL £££
(☑ 01597-823700; www.metropole.co.uk; Temple St; s/d from £98/126; P 🔊 🏊) Dating from the town's Victorian heyday, this grand turreted inn has spacious, corporate-style rooms and an excellent leisure complex with a swimming pool, sauna and gym. The Rock Spa offers a full range of treatments and **Spencer's Brasserie** (☑ 01597-823700; Temple St; mains £11-22) serves classic Welsh dishes alongside fairly predictable Thai and Italian choices.

🍴 Eating

Herb Garden Cafe CAFE £
(☑ 01597-823082; www.herbgardencafe.co.uk; 5 Spa Centre; mains £4-7; ⊗ 9.30am-5pm Mon-Sat; 🔊 🍴) 🌿 Tucked down an alley by the Co-op supermarket, the Herb Garden Cafe serves tasty light meals made from organic and wholefood produce. While not strictly vegetarian the cafe makes an effort to cater for various dietary requirements. It gets busy at lunchtime, so book ahead.

Van's Good Food Shop DELI £
(www.organisfoodpowys.co.uk; Middleton St; ⊗ 9am-5.30pm Mon-Sat; 🍴) 🌿 This excellent vegetarian deli features the best of local produce, including organic fruit, cheese and wine, plus ecofriendly cleaning products and other ethically selected goods.

Jules INTERNATIONAL ££
(☑ 01597-824642; www.julesrestaurant.blogspot. co.uk; Temple St; mains £9-15; ⊗ 11.30am-2.30pm & 5.30-10pm Tue-Sat, noon-2pm Sun) A restaurant and wine bar serving dishes from around the globe, Jules is an unexpected find. Expect to see traditional Welsh favourites such as slow-braised lamb or gammon

steaks alongside Kerala-style curries and East African fish dishes.

ℹ Information

Llandrindod Wells Memorial Hospital
(☑ 01597-822951; Temple St)
Police Station (☑ 101; High St)
Tourist Office (☑ 01597-822600; www. llandrindod.co.uk; Temple St; ⊗ 10am-5.30pm Mon-Sat) The tourist office is in the old town hall in the Memorial Gardens.

ℹ Getting There & Away

Bus routes include T4 to Builth Wells (22 minutes), Newtown (46 minutes) and Brecon (one hour), and the X47 to Rhayader (24 minutes) and Aberystwyth (1½ hours).

By train, Llandrindod is on the Heart of Wales Line, with direct services to Swansea (£11.70, 2½ hours), Llandeilo (£7.10, 1¼ hours), Llanwrtyd Wells (£3.90, 28 minutes), Knighton (£4.30, 34 minutes) and Shrewsbury (£10.80, 1½ hours).

Procabs (☑ 01597-736766; www.procabs llandrindodwells.co.uk) If you need a taxi call Procabs.

Builth Wells & Around

Cilmery

Two miles before Builth Wells on the A483 is the place where Llywelyn ap Gruffydd, the last Welsh Prince of Wales, was killed in a chance encounter with a lone English soldier in 1282. The spot is marked with a sad obelisk of Caernarfon granite. The site is often strewn with nationalist banners and pamphlets.

Builth Wells (Llanfair-Ym-Muallt)

POP 2350

Builth (pronounced bilth) Wells is by far the liveliest of the former spa towns, with a bustling, workaday feel. Once the playground of the Welsh working classes, it has a pretty location on the River Wye. While there are no attractions per se, it's a handy base for walkers or cyclists tackling any of the long-distance paths that pass through.

✪ Festivals & Events

Royal Welsh AGRICULTURAL
(☑ 01982-554419; www.rwas.co.uk; Llanelwedd) Builth Wells fills to bursting at the beginning of July, when 230,000 people descend for the show (founded in 1904), which in-

volves everything from livestock judging to lumberjack competitions. The Royal Welsh Showgrounds play host to numerous other events throughout the year from antiques fairs and garden shows to endurance horse-riding tournaments.

🛌 Sleeping

Bronwye   B&B £
(☑ 01982-553587; www.bronwye.co.uk; Church St; s/d from £35/50; 🅿 🛜) Overlooking the River Wye, this imposing 19th-century house has five comfortable, modern rooms with good beds and bathrooms. Unfortunately it retains little of its period character in the guest rooms but there's a warm welcome and excellent breakfasts, which at these rates makes it a bargain.

Caer Beris Manor   HOTEL £££
(☑ 01982-552601; www.caerberis.com; Garth Rd; s/d from £79/138) Once the grand home of Lord Swansea, this half-timbered country manor lies at the end of a long driveway winding through vast parklands overlooking the River Irfon. Classic styling, log fires and spacious rooms with swag curtains, heavy fabrics and tassled lamps await. The oak-panelled restaurant serves a fine menu of seasonally changing dishes featuring plenty of local meats (three-courses £25).

The hotel is on the west side of Builth Wells on the A483.

🍴 Eating

Cosy Corner   CAFE £
(☑ 01982-551700; 55 High St; mains £4-7; ⊙ 10am-4pm Mon-Sat) An atmospheric and, yes, cosy tearoom, offering homemade cakes, sandwiches and jacket potatoes in an 18th-century building.

★ Drawing Room   MODERN WELSH ££
(☑ 01982-552493; www.the-drawing-room.co.uk; 3-courses £40; ⊙ from 7pm, last orders 8.30pm) Set in a Georgian country house, this is one of the region's top restaurants. Prime Welsh Black beef and succulent local lamb are headline acts on a seasonally changing menu featuring simple but innovative dishes made with the finest of local ingredients. It's well worth indulging in the atmosphere here and booking in to one of the beautiful rooms (£90 to £100 including dinner). To get here head north from Builth Wells on the A470 for 3 miles.

⭐ Entertainment

Builth Male Voice Choir   PERFORMING ARTS
(www.builthmalechoir.org.uk) You can catch a rehearsal from 7.30pm on Monday nights in the upper room of the Greyhound Hotel on Garth Rd, which is also one of the best of the town's pubs. The choir formed in 1968 as a rugby choir and now sing internationally.

Wyeside Arts Centre   PERFORMING ARTS
(☑ 01982-552555; www.wyeside.co.uk; Castle St) A great little venue with a bar, exhibition space, cinema and live shows.

ℹ Information

Curio & Welsh Craft (☑ 01982-552253; 24 High St; ⊙ 9am-6pm Mon-Sat) There's no tourist office any more, but maps and brochures are available here.

ℹ Getting There & Away

Buses stopping here include T4 to Llandrindod Wells (22 minutes), Brecon (43 minutes), Rhyader (49 minutes), Newtown (one hour) and Aberystwyth (2½ hours); and the 48 to Llanwrtyd Wells (27 minutes).

Llanwrtyd Wells (Llanwrtud)

POP 850

Llanwrtyd (khlan-*oor*-tid) Wells is an odd town: mostly deserted except during one of its unconventional festivals when it's packed to the rafters with an influx of crazy contestants and their merrymaking supporters.

Apart from its newfound status as the capital of wacky Wales, Llanwrtyd Wells is surrounded by beautiful walking, cycling and riding country, with the Cambrian Mountains to the northwest and the Mynydd Epynt to the southeast.

Theophilus Evans, the local vicar, first discovered the healing properties of the Ffynon Droellwyd (Stinking Well) in 1732 when he found it cured his scurvy. The popularity of the waters grew and Llanwrtyd became a spa town. Nowadays, however, its wells have been capped and, outside of the festivals, it's hard to find much by way of vital signs.

🔎 Sights

Neuadd Arms Hotel   HOTEL
(☑ 01591-610236; www.neuaddarmshotel.co.uk; Y Sgwar; ⊙ 8.30am-midnight Sun-Thu, 8.30am-1am Fri & Sat) Like any good village pub should

be, the Neuadd Arms is a focal point for the community. It was here that former landlord Gordon Green and his punters cooked up many of the kooky events that have put Llanwrtyd Wells on the tourist trail. Today its thick net curtains, peeling paint and friendly staff give it the charm of a bygone era long lost in most parts of the country. If you want to find out anything about mountain biking, pony trekking or hiking in the area, it's the place to come. During winter you might join one of the farmers' dogs on the couch in front of the fire.

There's also a surprisingly interesting menu (mains £7 to £11) and the chance to sample some of the excellent beers brewed in the stables at the back of the hotel.

🛏 Sleeping & Eating

Ardwyn House
B&B ££

(☏ 01591-610768; www.ardwynhouse.co.uk; Station Rd; s/d £60/80; P 🛜) The young owners have been busy restoring the art nouveau grandeur of this once derelict house. Some rooms have claw-foot baths and rural views, and there is parquet flooring, period wallpaper and furnishings, and an oak-panelled guest lounge with a pool table and bar.

★ Carlton Riverside
RESTAURANT, B&B ££

(☏ 01591-610248; www.carltonriverside.com; Irfon Cres; mains £12.50-23; ⏰ 7-8.30pm Tue-Sat) This upscale restaurant with rooms has a boutique feel and a mantelpiece that positively groans under the strain of its foodie awards. The rooms (single/double from £50/£75) are modern, simple and tasteful, and with late breakfasts and checkouts, it's well catered to bon vivants. There's a bar (open Tuesday to Sunday evenings) tucked away in the basement but the real star here is the restaurant and its superb menu which features plenty of local produce cooked up in imaginative guises as well as some more international dishes. Ask about all-inclusive foodie breaks.

Drovers Rest
RESTAURANT ££

(☏ 01591-610264; www.food-food-food.co.uk; Y Sgwar; mains £16-20; ⏰ 10.30am-3.30pm & 7.30-9.30pm Tue & Thu-Sat, 12.30-2.30pm Sun) 🍴 This snug little restaurant serves up the best of local produce and lots of fresh fish mains. The owners also run regular one-day cooking courses (£150 to £185) including a Welsh cooking day and a big Welsh game course featuring venison, pheasant and wild game. There are also a few simple but cosy rooms (single/double £30/60), though not all are en suite.

❶ Getting There & Around

➤ Lôn Las Cymru, the Welsh National Cycle Route (Sustrans Rte 8), passes through Llanwrtyd Wells, heading north to Machynlleth and

---

LLANWRTYD'S TWISTED EVENTS

While mulling over how to encourage tourism in Llanwrtyd in the dark winter months, some citizens started an inspired roll call of unconventionality. There's something on each month (see www.green-events.co.uk for more details) but these are some of the wackiest.

Saturnalia Beer Festival & Mountain Bike Chariot Racing Roman-themed festival in mid-January including a 'best dressed Roman' competition, the devouring of stuffed bulls' testicles and the chariot race.

Man vs Horse Marathon The event that kicked all the craziness off, it has been held every year since 1980 and has resulted in some tense finishes. Two-legged runners have won only twice, the first in 2004. Held mid-June.

World Bog Snorkelling Championships The most famous event of all, held every August bank holiday. Competitors are allowed wetsuits, snorkels and flippers to traverse a trench cut out of a peat bog, using no recognisable swimming stroke and surfacing only to navigate. Spin-off events include Mountain Bike Bog snorkelling ('like trying to ride through treacle') and the Bog Snorkelling Triathlon; both held in July.

Real Ale Wobble & Ramble In conjunction with the **Mid-Wales Beer Festival**, every November cyclists and walkers follow waymarked routes (15 or 25 miles, or 35 miles for the wobblers), supping real ales at the 'pint-stops' along the way.

Mari Llwyd A revival of the ancient practice of parading a horse's skull from house to house on New Year's Eve while reciting Welsh poetry.

east to Builth Wells. There's excellent mountain biking in the surrounding hills; enquire at the Drovers Rest.

◆ Bus 48 heads to Builth Wells (27 minutes).

◆ Llanwrtyd is on the Heart of Wales Line, with direct services to Swansea (£10.10, two hours), Llandeilo (£4.80, 45 minutes), Llandrindod Wells (£3.90, 31 minutes) and Shrewsbury (£12.80, two hours).

Rhayader (Rhaeadr Gwy)

POP 2090

Rhayader is a handsome small and fairly uneventful livestock-market town revolving around a central crossroads marked by a war-memorial clock. It's a place that appeals to walkers visiting the nearby Elan Valley and tackling the 136-mile Wye Valley Walk. Rhayader is deserted on Thursdays when businesses trade for only half a day, but market day on Wednesdays attracts a crowd.

◎ Sights & Activities

Rhayader Museum & Gallery MUSEUM
(☑ 01597-810561; www.carad.org.uk; East St; adult/child £4/free; ☺ 10am-4pm Tue-Sun) Focusing on local identity, social history and life in Rhayader and the surrounding area, this small museum uses historic artefacts, films and oral histories to explore everything from folk tales to sheep farming.

Gigrin Farm Red Kite Feeding Station BIRDWATCHING
(☑ 01597-810 243; www.gigrin.co.uk; South St; adult/child £4.50/2; ☺ 2pm Nov-Mar, 3pm Apr-Oct) There's been a dramatic Mid-Wales resurgence in the UK's threatened population of red kites. A feeding program continues at the Gigrin Farm Red Kite Feeding Station, a working farm on the A470 half a mile south of Rhayader town centre (or 1 mile from the Wye Valley Walk). At 2pm (3pm during summer daylight-saving time) meat scraps from local butchers and a local abattoir are spread on a field. Altogether anywhere from 12 to 500 kites may partake, though it's usually less than 20 at any one time. First come crows, then ravens, then the acrobatically swooping kites – often mugging the crows to get the meat – and later buzzards. You can watch from a wheelchair-accessible hide.

There's an interpretive centre with information on red kites and other local wildlife, recorded night-time footage of badgers, a camera overlooking the feeding site and marked nature trails.

OFF THE BEATEN TRACK

CAMBRIAN MOUNTAINS

The Cambrian Mountains are a rather desolate but starkly beautiful area of uplands covering the region roughly between Snowdonia and the Brecon Beacons. Largely unpopulated and undeveloped, this wild, empty plateau of high moorland is the source of both the Rivers Severn and Wye. Hidden in the folds of the hills are lakes, waterfalls and deserted valleys as well as hill farms home to thousands of sheep. The region sees relatively few visitors except for around the Elan Valley and if you wish to get away from it all there is no finer place in Wales in which to hike or bike in utter solitude and tranquility. Many tracks criss-cross the area including the long-distance Cambrian Way; you can find details of routes on www.walkingbritain.co.uk or more information about the region on www.cambrian-mountains.co.uk.

Clive Powell Mountain Bike Centre MOUNTAIN BIKING
(☑ 01597-811343; www.clivepowell-mtb.co.uk; West St; ☺ 9am-5.30pm, closed Thu) This centre is operated by a former cycling champion and coach. You can hire a mountain/off-road bike here (£20/15 per day, including helmet and puncture kit), and Powell runs a regular program of 'Dirty Weekends', all-inclusive mountain-biking weekends hitting trails around the Elan Valley (from £176, minimum of five people).

⨃ Sleeping

Wyeside CAMPGROUND £
(☑ 01597-810183; www.wyesidecamping.co.uk; Llangurig Rd; site/adult/child £3/7/2.50; ☺ Mar-Oct) A short walk from the centre of Rhayader, this relaxed, grassy site has river views and lots of trees.

Horseshoe B&B ££
(☑ 01597-810982; www.rhayader-horseshoe.co.uk; Church St; s/d £44/68; ℗) This 18th-century former inn offers comfortable modern rooms and plenty of communal space in the large dining room, garden, conservatory and walled courtyard.

Eating

Wild Swan   DELI £

(☑ 01597-811632; West St; mains £4-5; ⊙ 9am-5pm
Mon-Sat) ✐ Set in a restored 17th-century
building on the main street, this organic deli
and wholefood shop is a great place to pick
up picnic supplies and stocks everything
from home-cooked quiches to lavender biscuits and fair-trade clothing.

Tŷ Morgans   BISTRO ££

(☑ 01597-811666; www.tymorgans.co.uk; East St;
mains £6-15; 🍽) This relaxed bar and bistro
serves a good selection of food all day ranging from basic sandwiches to pub classics
and grilled Welsh steaks. There is also a selection of tastefully decorated rooms (from
£60) upstairs but those above the lively bar
can be noisy, especially on weekends.

Drinking

Triangle Inn   PUB

(☑ 01597-810537; www.triangleinn.co.uk; Cwm-
dauddwr; mains £7-13) This tiny 16th-century
inn, just over the bridge from the town centre, is the pick of the local places to drink for
its unique sense of character and history. It's
so small that the toilets are across the road
and the ceiling is so low that there's a trap-
door in the floor so that darts players can
stand in a hole to throw their arrows. Hearty
pub classics make up the menu.

❶ Getting There & Away

Bus X16 goes to Builth Wells (30 minutes) and
the X47 to Llandrindod Wells (30 minutes).

Elan Valley

The Elan Valley is filled with strikingly
beautiful countryside, split by impressive
Edwardian impositions of grey stone on the
landscape. In the early 19th century, dams
were built on the River Elan (pronounced
ellen), west of Rhayader, mainly to provide
a reliable water supply for the English city
of Birmingham. Around 100 people had to
move, but only landowners received com-
pensation. In 1952 a fourth large dam was
inaugurated on the tributary River Claerwen. Together their reservoirs now provide
over 70 million gallons of water daily for
Birmingham and parts of South and Mid-
Wales.

Though not a project to warm Welsh
hearts, the need to protect the 70-sq-mile
watershed (called the Elan Valley Estate) has
turned it and adjacent areas into an important wildlife conservation area. The dams
and associated projects also produce some
4.2 megawatts of hydroelectric power.

☉ Sights & Activities

Elan Valley Visitor Centre   NATURE RESERVE

(☑ 01597-810880; www.elanvalley.org.uk; ⊙ 10am-
5pm Mar-Oct) **FREE** Just downstream of the
lowest dam, 3 miles from Rhayader on the
B4518, is Welsh Water's Elan Valley Visitor Centre with interesting exhibits on the
water scheme, complete with photos of
houses being swallowed up by the waters,
native wildlife and local history. It also provides leaflets on the estate's 80 miles of nature trails and footpaths. Check the website
for details of the frequent guided walks and
birdwatching trips, which are mostly free.

The **Elan Valley Trail** is an 8-mile traffic-
free walking, horse-riding and cycling path
that mostly follows the line of the long-
gone Birmingham Corporation Railway
alongside the River Elan and its reservoirs.
It starts just west of Rhayader at Cwm-
dauddwr.

Snowdonia & the Llŷn

Best Places to Eat

➡ Manorhaus (p218)

➡ Castle Restaurant & Armoury Bar (p234)

➡ Bistro Bermo (p233)

➡ Tyddyn Llan (p219)

➡ Gallt-y-Glyn (p243)

Best Places to Stay

➡ Beech Bank (p243)

➡ Coed-y-Celyn Hall (p238)

➡ Old Rectory on the Lake (p225)

➡ Natural Retreats (p258)

➡ Ffynnon (p223)

Why Go?

This part of Wales really packs it in, from rugged mountain trails and coastal paths to industrial sites and historic train lines. It's dominated by Snowdonia National Park, where the mightiest peaks south of Scotland scrape moody skies. With such a formidable mountain shield, it's little wonder that the northwestern county of Gwynedd has held tightly to its language and culture. Over 64% speak the ancient mother tongue here, which is the highest proportion in the country.

Along with the mountains there's the sea – battering the rocks at Braich-y-Pwll, producing surfer-friendly swells at Porth Neigwl and cooling the bathers at Barmouth. All those bracing sea breezes seem to have blown any shreds of stuffiness or British reserve from the local populace. In many ways, this slice of the country distills the very essence of Welshness – just don't mention that to the folks in Cardiff!

When to Go

April to July are the driest months, while July and August are the warmest. The very best months to hit the mountains are June and July for their combination of higher temperatures and lower wind and rain.

In June the Three Peaks Yacht Race hits Barmouth and the national Catholic pilgrimage descends on Holywell. In July Llangollen holds its International Musical Eisteddfod and Fringe Festival, while Wakestock rocks the Llŷn.

September is the big month for events, with Bala's triathlon, Barmouth's arts and walking festivals, Portmeirion's Festival No 6 and Abersoch's Jazz Festival. Snow starts to fall in the mountains in October and lingers on the paths until May.

Snowdonia & the Llŷn Highlights

1 Climbing **Snowdon** (p244), Wales' highest peak... or cheating by taking the rack-and-pinion train to the top

2 Floating through the air across **Pontcysyllte**

Aqueduct (p215), Britain's latest World Heritage Site

3 Disappearing underground into the slate caverns of **Blaenau Ffestiniog** (p234)

4 Taking an unforgettable coast-to-coast journey on the narrow-gauge **Welsh Highland Railway** (p250)

5 Gazing towards the magical island of Bardsey from

end-of-the-world headland
Braich-y-Pwll (p256)

6 Walking through a
postcard of stone cottages
and dancing rivers at **Betws-y-Coed** (p236)

7 Hearing the stories of
the people who dissected a
mountain at the engaging
National Slate Museum in
Llanberis (p241)

8 Enjoying the cliff-edge views
from the parapets of Harlech
Castle in **Harlech** (p233)

9 Soaking up the countryside
vibe of the historic market town
of **Ruthin** (p213)

NORTH WALES BORDERLANDS

The northeastern counties of Denbighshire, Wrexham and Flintshire are a baffling jumble of the gritty and the gorgeous. From 1974 to 1996 they were all part of the county of Clwyd, before being broken up and reverting to their far older names. Surprisingly, the best bits are further from the coast, particularly in the wild hills and lush farmland of Denbighshire's southern reaches. It's well worth pausing here as you make your way towards Snowdonia.

Holywell (Treffynnon)

POP 8890

Billed as Wales' answer to Lourdes, the market town of Holywell (www.holywell-town.gov.uk) in Flintshire has been a revered site of pilgrimage for over 1300 years. It's the only such site to have survived the Reformation largely intact, and it's now once again administered by the Catholic Church.

Named after a 7th-century Welsh woman venerated as a saint, **St Winefride's Well** (✆01352-713054; www.saintwinefrideswell.com; adult/child 80/20p; ⊙9am-5pm Apr-Sep, 9am-4pm Oct-Mar; P) marks the site of her gruesome decapitation and the place where her head was miraculously reattached by her uncle, St Bueno. Curative bathing in the holy waters started in the 12th century. Henry V made the pilgrimage in 1416 to take the waters after his victory at Agincourt, and Princess Victoria visited in 1828. The vaulted stone shrine and star-shaped well basin were built sometime before 1509.

WORTH A TRIP

CLWYD THEATR CYMRU

The unfortunately named town of Mold, 10 miles east of Ruthin, is the unlikely home of Wales' leading theatre company. **Clwyd Theatr Cymru** (✆0845 330 3565; www.clwyd-theatr-cymru.co.uk) stages a year-round program of new works, mainly in English, including theatre for children and young people. It also hosts opera, live music, dance, comedy, poetry and films.

Modern-day pilgrims still take the waters today, bathing in the holy well at designated times before visiting the adjoining museum, attending one of the pilgrims' Masses and stocking up on vials of holy water. The site is packed in June for the National Catholic Pilgrimage.

There's accommodation just up the road, courtesy of the Bridgettine Sisters, at **St Winefride's Guesthouse** (✆01352-714073; www.bridgettine.org; 20 New Rd; s/d £29/50; P), where the simple but cosy rooms offer an evening of quiet contemplation after a home-cooked meal.

❶ Getting There & Away

Buses head to/from Rhyl (11G; one hour), Prestatyn (11G; 40 minutes), Mold (126; 24 minutes), Flint (11/20; 14 minutes) and Chester (11; one hour).

Clwydian Range

Designated an Area of Outstanding National Beauty (AONB), the 62-sq-mile Clwydian Range stretches from the coast at Prestatyn to within 10 miles of Llangollen. Most walkers rush past the Clwydian Range in their haste to get to Snowdonia, and while it's lesser known, it's a no less attractive an area for family walking and more strenuous hiking. The waymarked paths are easily accessed from Ruthin, Mold and Prestatyn, with some of the day walks criss-crossing the Offa's Dyke Path national trail.

As many as 500 wild goats live in these hills, putting on an impressive show when they lock horns during the autumn rut. The range's highest point is Moel Famau (554m), marked by the ruined Jubilee Tower which was built in 1810 for the 50th jubilee of King George III. The original monument, a 35m obelisk, was to have been the first Egyptian-style monument to be built in Britain but funds ran out and it was never completed. The summit offers a spectacular view across the northwest from Liverpool to the Cheshire Plains.

The trailhead for many of the most popular day walks is the **Clwydian Range Centre** (✆01352-810614; www.clwydianrangeaonb.org.uk; ⊙10am-4pm) in Loggerheads Country Park, on the A494 Mold to Ruthin road (car park £3 per day). A popular day walk is the 6-mile circular route from Loggerheads via Moel Famau and along the Clwydian Way (allow 4½ hours). This and other waymarked trails are outlined in a brochure available from the centre.

Denbigh (Dinbych)

POP 8990

Set on a hill surrounded by farmland, Denbigh is one of several historic market towns scattered around the fertile Vale of Clywd. Although there was a Welsh settlement here before the invasion (the Welsh name means 'Little Fortress'), Denbigh came into its own as a 'planted borough', a small English colony founded to support the garrison stationed at the castle built by Edward I between 1282 and 1311. The remains of the walled town and castle sit above the current town centre.

A steep walk up from the High St leads to the Burgess Gate, where there are displays on the town's history. Inside the remnants of the old walls, the road continues past St Hillary's Tower, which is all that remains of a 14th-century chapel, and on to Denbigh Castle (Cadw; www.cadw.wales.gov.uk; adult/child £3.50/2.65; ⊙10am-5pm Apr-Oct). During the Civil War, it was a Royalist stronghold (Charles I once stayed here) and owes its ruined state to the Parliamentarians who destroyed it in 1660. There's not a lot to see, but a section of wall offers great views over the countryside.

❶ Getting There & Away

Buses head here from Ruthin (X50; 20 minutes), Mold (14; 45 minutes), Rhyl (51; 45 minutes) and Wrexham (X50; 1¼ hours).

Ruthin (Rhuthun)

POP 5500

Tucked away in the quiet Clwyd valley, well off any tourist route, Ruthin (rith-in) is an attractive lost-in-time hilltop town and the administrative hub of Denbighshire. In the Middle Ages it was an important market town and textile producer. There are still livestock markets held three times a week, as well as a produce market on Friday mornings, and a general market on Thursdays.

The heart of Ruthin is St Peter's Sq, lined with an impressive collection of heritage buildings, including a 1401 half-timbered courthouse (now a bank) and St Peter's Collegiate Church, the oldest parts of which date from 1310.

◉ Sights

Nantclwyd y Dre HISTORIC BUILDING
(www.denbighshire.gov.uk/heritage; Castle St; adult/child £3.90/2.50; ⊙10.30am-5pm Fri-Sun Apr-Jun & Sep, Fri-Tue Jul & Aug) Dating from 1435, half-timbered Nantclwyd y Dre is thought to be the oldest town house in Wales. It originally belonged to a family of weavers and despite being extended several times, it retains a palpable sense of antiquity. The rooms have been restored and furnished to reflect the era of each addition, offering a window into the world of the various families that lived in them.

A 'batcam' invades the privacy of the colony of lesser horseshoe bats that reside in the attic – they're the smallest (with bodies about the size of a plum) and rarest bat species in Britain.

Ruthin Gaol HISTORIC BUILDING
(www.ruthingaol.co.uk; 46 Clwyd St; adult/child £3.90/2.50; ⊙10am-5pm Wed-Mon Apr-Oct) This sombre building is the only Pentonville-style Victorian prison that is open to visitors. A 90-minute audio-guide tour will fill you in on all the fascinating and grisly details.

Ruthin Craft Centre ARTS CENTRE
(www.ruthincraftcentre.org.uk; Park Rd; ⊙10am-5.30pm; Ⓟ) FREE The town's flash arts hub has an interesting gallery, artist studios and shops, and a decent cafe.

⌸ Sleeping

Manorhaus BOUTIQUE HOTEL ££
(☎01824-704830; www.manorhaus.com; 10 Well St; s/d from £83/115; ❀) This boutique restaurant-with-rooms contains eight gorgeously styled bedrooms, each showcasing the works of different local and national artists. As well as being Ruthin's best accommodation, it's also one of its best eateries, offering a high-quality selection of contemporary dishes every night (two/three courses £26/33).

Ruthin Castle Hotel HOTEL ££
(☎01824-702664; www.ruthincastle.co.uk; Castle St; r/ste from £115/195; Ⓟ@❀) For a good knight's sleep (sorry, we couldn't resist), try this large rambling hotel built on the ruins of a castle founded by Edward I. Peacocks roam the grounds and there's a spa centre in the old moat. It's a fascinating place to stay, even if the attempts at grandeur

SNOWDONIA & THE LLŶN LLANGOLLEN

sometimes miss the mark (we question the romantic efficacy of the photos of Charles in the over-the-top Prince of Wales bridal suite).

Eating

Leonardo's DELI £
(4 Well St; pies £3; ⊘9am-4.30pm Mon-Sat) This drool-inducing deli is well stocked with local cheeses, preserves and top-notch pies (its beef-and-ale was a 2013 British Pie Award winner).

★ **On The Hill** MODERN BRITISH ££
(☑01824-707736; www.onthehillrestaurant.co.uk; 1 Upper Clwyd St; mains £13-17, 1-/2-/3-course lunch £10/13/16; ⊘6.30-9pm Tue, noon-2pm & 6.30-9pm Wed-Sat) The low ceilings and exposed beams of this 16th-century house near the square make a memorable setting for sophisticated country cooking. Rustic classics such as beef bourguignon sit alongside more contemporary creations, but they all hit the mark.

Myddelton Grill on the Square GASTROPUB ££
(☑01824-707842; St Peter's Sq; mains £11-19; ⊘noon-9pm Wed-Sat, to 6pm Sun) If you're after a good grilling, this is the place to come. Various meats, fish, vegies and kebabs are sizzled up and served with a choice of tasty sides. It occupies a wonderful Tudor building known as 'the Seven Eyes' due its multiple dormer windows.

🛍 Shopping

Ruthin Book Shop BOOKS
(☑01824-703840; 3 Upper Clwyd St; ⊘10am-5pm Tue-Sat) A fabulously old-fashioned place for maps, local history and antiquarian tomes.

❶ Getting There & Away

Bus X50 heads to/from Denbigh (20 minutes) and Wrexham (50 minutes).

Llangollen

POP 3700

Huddled around the banks of the tumbling River Dee (Afon Dyfrdwy) and with the mysterious hilltop ruins of Castell Dinas Brân as a constant backdrop, the picturesque little town of Llangollen has long been recognised as a scenic gem. The riverside walk, heading west from the bridge, has been a popular promenading spot since Victorian times.

In summer Llangollen (khlan-*goth*-len) is the hub of a burgeoning walking and whitewater rafting scene, while in winter, under a thick blanket of snow, it just sits there and looks pretty. Two major arts festivals boost tourist numbers, as does the area's industrial legacy, which attracts railway and engineering enthusiasts.

The town takes its name from St Collen, a 7th-century monk who founded a religious community *(llan)* here. Centuries later it became an important stop on the London to

---

DON'T MISS

ERDDIG MANOR HOUSE

It might be a little out of the way, but the stately home of **Erddig** (NT; ☑01978-355314; www.nationaltrust.org.uk; adult/child £11/5.15, grounds only £6.60/3.30; ⊘house 12.30-4.30pm Mar-Oct, 11am-3.30pm Nov-Feb, last admission 1hr before closing; Ⓟ) is absolutely worth seeking out. This splendid National Trust (NT) property, sitting in the middle of a 485-hectare country park, offers an illuminating glimpse into 18th-century upper-class life. It was the Yorke family's ancestral home for over two centuries (until 1973). Original artwork and furniture is displayed in the fine rooms, while a formal, walled garden has been restored in Victorian style.

The house, the earliest parts of which date from 1680, has hardly been altered since the early 20th century; there's no electricity and it still has extensive outbuildings. It provides a unique insight into the 'upstairs-downstairs' relationship that existed between masters and their servants, with the best archive of servant material of any house in Britain. There are even oil paintings and poems in honour of some of the favourites.

There's plenty to keep both kids and adults busy, with history trails, shire horses and a full program of family-friendly events.

Erddig lies 10 miles northeast of Llangollen, signposted from the A483 on the way to Wrexham.

Llangollen

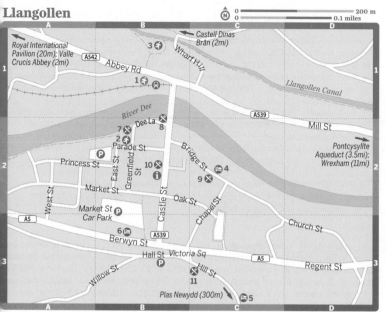

Holyhead stagecoach route, linking the British capital to Ireland.

◉ Sights

★ Pontcysyllte Aqueduct & Canal World Heritage Site

CANAL

(✆ 01978-822 912; www.pontcysyllte-aqueduct. co.uk; guided tours £3; ⊙ visitor centre 10am-4pm Mar-Oct) **FREE** In the 18th century the horse-drawn canal barge was the most efficient way of hauling goods over long distances but, with the advent of the railway, most of them fell into disrepair. The Llangollen Canal fared better than most because it was used, for years more, to carry drinking water from the River Dee to the Hurleston Reservoir in Cheshire. Today it's again in use, carrying visitors up and down the Vale of Llangollen. In addition, the old towpaths offer miles of peaceful, traffic-free walking. And the canal itself is part of the attraction, thanks to the work of the great civil engineer Thomas Telford (1757–1834).

Telford's goal was to connect up the haulage routes between the Rivers Dee, Severn and Mersey. To collect water for the canal from the River Dee, Telford designed an elegant curving weir called Horseshoe Falls. The adjacent riverbank is a tranquil picnic spot.

However, Thomas Telford's real masterpiece is the Pontcysyllte Aqueduct, completed in 1805 to carry the canal over the River Dee. At 307m long, 3.6m wide, 1.7m deep and 38m high, it is the most spectacular piece of engineering on the entire UK canal system and the highest canal aqueduct ever built. In recognition of this, the aqueduct and an 11-mile stretch of the canal have been declared a Unesco World Heritage Site.

The small visitor centre at the aqueduct runs guided tours (call ahead for times),

THE LADIES OF LLANGOLLEN

Lady Eleanor Butler and Miss Sarah Ponsonby, the 'Ladies of Llangollen', lived in Plas Newydd from 1780 to 1829 with their maid, Mary Carryl. They had fallen in love in Ireland but their aristocratic Anglo-Irish families discouraged the relationship. In a desperate bid to be allowed to live together the women eloped to Wales, disguised as men, and set up home in Llangollen to devote themselves to 'friendship, celibacy and the knitting of stockings'.

Their romantic friendship became well known yet respected, and they were visited by many national figures of the day, including the Duke of Wellington, William Wordsworth and Sir Walter Scott. Wordsworth was even suitably moved to pen the following words: 'Sisters in love, a love allowed to climb, even on this earth above the reach of time'.

The ladies' relationship with their maid, Mary, was also close. Mary managed to buy the freehold of Plas Newydd and left it to the 'sisters' when she died. They erected a large monument to her in the graveyard at St Collen's Parish Church in Llangollen, where they are also buried. Lady Eleanor died in 1829; Sarah Ponsonby was reunited with her soulmate just two years later.

---

while canal boats offer trips along the 'stream in the sky' from the nearby quay and from Llangollen wharf. Otherwise you can simply stroll across, free of charge. Whichever way you choose, you'll need a head for heights.

Horseshoe Falls is about 2 miles west of Llangollen (take the A5 west and after about 1.5 miles turn right across the river), while the aqueduct is 4 miles east near the village of Trevor (on the A539 Ruabon road). Both are easily reached by walking along the canal towpath.

Castell Dinas Brân   CASTLE
FREE The ever-visible ragged arches and tumbledown walls of Dinas Brân mark the remnants of a short-lived 13th-century castle of which it was said 'there was not a mightier in Wales nor a better in England'. It was burnt by Edward I after it was surrendered to him in advance of his invasion.

Its fabulous 360-degree views are well worth the 1½-hour return walk up the steep track (turn uphill at the taxidermist, cut up the steps on the other side of the canal, then follow the Offa's Dyke Path arrows).

Valle Crucis Abbey   RUINS
(Cadw; www.cadw.wales.gov.uk; A542; adult/child Apr-Oct £3.50/2.65, Nov-Mar free; ⊙10am-5pm Apr-Oct, 10am-4pm Nov-Mar) The dignified ruins of this Cistercian abbey are a 2-mile walk north of Llangollen. Founded in 1201 by Madog ap Gruffydd, ruler of northern Powys, its largely Gothic form predates its more famous sibling at Tintern. A small interpretation centre brings the monks' daily routines to life.

Plas Newydd   HISTORIC BUILDING
(www.denbighshire.gov.uk/heritage; Hill St; adult/child £5.50/4.50; ⊙house 10am-5pm Wed-Sun Apr-Oct, gardens 8am-9pm Apr-Oct, 8am-6pm Nov-Mar) The 18th-century home of the Ladies of Llangollen, Plas Newydd is an atmospheric step back in time. The celebrated couple transformed the house into a hybrid of Gothic and Tudor styles, complete with stained-glass windows, carved-oak panels and formal gardens. Admission to the house includes a good self-guided audio tour of the house. The tranquil gardens are free to explore.

🏃 Activities

Llangollen Railway   HERITAGE RAILWAY
(☑01978-860979; www.llangollen-railway.co.uk; Abbey Rd; adult/child return £12/6; ⊙daily Apr-Sep, reduced services Feb, Mar, Oct & Nov) The 7.5-mile jaunt through the Dee Valley via Berwyn (near Horseshoe Falls) and Carrog on the former Ruabon to Barmouth Line is a superb day out for rail fans, families and heritage lovers alike. There are regular *Thomas the Tank Engine* theme days for children, and murder-mystery excursions are also popular. At the time of writing, work was continuing to extend the line to Corwen.

Welsh Canal Holiday Craft   BOAT TOUR
(☑01978-860702; www.horsedrawnboats.co.uk; Llangollen Wharf; ⊙mid-Mar–Oct) Peace and quiet are the hallmarks of the horse-drawn boat excursions along the canal from Llangollen Wharf. The 45-minute trips depart half-hourly during the school holidays and hourly otherwise (adult/child £6.50/3.50).

Two-hour journeys head to the Horseshoe Falls and back (adult/child £11/9).

If you want to experience the Pontcysyllte Aqueduct there are motorised boats that will take you there in two hours, with the return journey by coach (adult/child £13/11). If you'd rather drive yourself, you can hire a boat for a day (weekdays/weekend £120/165).

Jones the Boats
BOAT TOUR

(🕿 01978-824166; www.canaltrip.co.uk; Old Wharf, Trevor; adult/child £5/3; ☉ Apr-Oct) Runs 45-minute canal boat trips with a live commentary across the aqueduct and back. If it's a sunny day, try to grab the outside seats up front.

AngloWelsh Waterway Holidays
BOATING

(🕿 0117 304 1122; www.anglowelsh.co.uk; Old Wharf, Trevor; 1-day hire weekday/weekend £110/140) Hires self-drive narrowboats for up to 10 people for a day trip, or for multiday live-in canal touring.

ProAdventure Activity Centre
OUTDOORS

(🕿 01978-861912; www.proadventure.co.uk; Parade St) This not-for-profit company runs canyoning, canoeing, rock climbing, rafting and bushcraft tasters and trips; prices start from £45 per person. Most activities only run from April to October, but bushcraft is offered year-round.

White Water Tubing UK
TUBING, RAFTING

(🕿 07928 278036; www.whitewatertubing.co.uk; tubing/rafting £59/69) Hurtle down the River Dee, either on a seven-person raft or solo on a donut-like inflatable. Prices include all gear.

Festivals & Events

Llangollen International Musical Eisteddfod
MUSIC

(http://international-eisteddfod.co.uk; ☉ Jul) Staged at the Royal International Pavilion during the second week in July, this multicultural competition is held in the spirit of building peace through music. It starts on a Tuesday with Children's Day and a street parade, and culminates with a gala concert the following Sunday. Past performers have included the likes of Luciano Pavarotti, Kiri Te Kanawa, José Carreras, Joan Baez and Ladysmith Black Mambazo. It's a very big deal.

Llangollen Fringe Festival
PERFORMING ARTS

(www.llangollenfringe.co.uk; ☉ Jul) This small-town, volunteer-run arts festival, held over 11 days from mid-July, manages to attract some surprisingly big names: 2012's line-up included Charlotte Church and Poet Laureate Carol Ann Duffy.

Sleeping

Llangollen Hostel
HOSTEL £

(🕿 01978-861773; www.llangollenhostel.co.uk; Berwyn St; dm/d £18/40; P🖥) This excellent independent hostel, based in a former family home, has friendly owners and a cared-for feel. It offers various rooms, from private en suite doubles to a six-bed dorm, as well as an orderly kitchen and cosy lounge. It actively welcomes cyclists and canoeists, with laundry facilities and bike/boat storage. Prices include a self-service cereal-and-toast breakfast.

Cornerstones Guesthouse
B&B ££

(🕿 01978-861569; www.cornerstones-guesthouse.co.uk; 15 Bridge St; s £50, d £80-100; P🖥🛁) All sloping floorboards and oak beams, this converted 16th-century house has charm and history in spades. The river-facing rooms are the quietest; on weekends the front rooms can suffer from street noise. There's also a self-contained town house next door.

Hillcrest Guesthouse
B&B ££

(🕿 01978-860208; www.hillcrest-guesthouse.com; Hill St; s/d £40/60; P🖥) Hillcrest is a traditional little B&B, tucked away from town on the way to Plas Newydd. It's a simple but homey place that gets consistently good reports from visitors for its cosy rooms, hearty breakfast and warm welcome. On a chilly day, settle down by the open fire in the residents' lounge with a good book.

Eating & Drinking

James A Bailey
DELI £

(🕿 01978-860617; 14 Castle St; filled rolls £3; ☉ 9am-4pm Mon-Sat, 10.30am-4pm Sun) If you're planning a picnic or lunch on the run, drop in here for filled baguettes and paninis, gourmet sausage rolls, homemade pies (try a Welsh Oggie – a meat, potato and onion pasty), Welsh ales and ice cream.

Dee Side Caffe Bistro
CAFE £

(Castle St; mains £4-14; ☉ 9am-9pm) Serving a crowd-pleasing menu of burgers, baked potatoes, pies and pasta, this cheap-and-cheerful little riverside eatery is as traditional as they come.

OFF THE BEATEN TRACK

BRIDGE END INN

If you're prepared to make a pilgrimage for a good pub, seek ye out Ruabon's **Bridge End Inn** (www.mcgivernales. co.uk; 5 Bridge St; ⊘ 5-11pm Mon-Fri, noon-11pm Sat & Sun). In 2012 this unassuming little place became the first Welsh pub to win the coveted Campaign For Real Ale (CAMRA) pub of the year award. It's the home of the McGivern Ales microbrewery and alongside its own brews, it showcases craft beers from around the nation.

Ruabon is 6 miles east of Llangollen, on the way to Wrexham.

Gales of Llangollen　　　EUROPEAN ££
(www.galesofllangollen.co.uk; 18 Bridge St; mains £11-15; ⊘ noon-2pm & 6-9.30pm Mon-Sat, 11am-3pm Sun) Deliciously informal, Gales is equal parts wine bar and bistro, and something of a Llangollen institution. It boasts an ever-changing seasonal menu best enjoyed with a good glass of wine from the extensive wine list. Turn up early, as it's not possible to reserve a table. The owners also run the wine shop next door.

Corn Mill　　　GASTROPUB ££
(☑ 01978-869555; www.brunningandprice.co.uk/cornmill; Dee Lane; light meals £7-10, mains £10-14; ⊘ noon-11pm) The water wheel still turns at the heart of this converted mill, now a cheerful, bustling pub and all-day eatery. The deck is the best spot in town for an unfussy alfresco lunch, with views over the River Dee to the steam railway.

★ Manorhaus　　　MODERN BRITISH £££
(☑ 01978-860775; www.manorhaus.com; Hill St; 2-/3-course meal £26/33; ⊘ 6-11pm; 🐾) A sister to the well-established Ruthin Manorhaus, this restaurant-with-rooms brought whole new stratospheres of swish to Llangollen when it opened in 2012. Thankfully the inventive food lives up to the impressive packaging, with a similar approach to quality and detail. For the complete experience, book one of the six stylish rooms upstairs (from £115).

ℹ Information

Llangollen Tourist Office (☑ 01978-860828; www.northwalesborderlands.co.uk; The Chapel, Castle St; ⊘ 9.30am-5pm) Helpful tourist office, well-stocked with maps, books and gifts. It doubles as an art gallery. Pick up the *Llangollen History Trail* brochure, which details a 9.5km walking circuit taking in Valle Crucis and Dinas Brân.

ℹ Getting There & Away

➡ Bus X94 heads to Wrexham (35 minutes), Llandrillo (26 minutes), Bala (48 minutes), Dolgellau (1½ hours) and Barmouth (1¾ hours).

➡ National Express coaches head to Wrexham (£2.80, 25 minutes), Shrewsbury (£4.70, one hour) and Birmingham (£12, 2½ hours).

➡ Parking is at a premium in Llangollen. If your accommodation doesn't have its own, check whether it can provide a pass for the council car parks.

SNOWDONIA NATIONAL PARK (PARC CENEDLAETHOL ERYRI)

Wales' best-known and most heavily used slice of nature became the country's first national park in 1951. The most popular part is Snowdon itself. Around 350,000 people walk, climb or take the train to the 1085m summit each year, and all those sturdy shoes make trail maintenance a never-ending task for park staff. Yet the park is so much more than just Snowdon, stretching some 35 miles east to west and over 50 miles north to south, it incorporates coastal areas, rivers and Wales' biggest natural lake.

Like Wales' other national parks, this one is very lived-in, with sizeable towns at Bala, Dolgellau, Harlech and Betws-y-Coed. Two-thirds of the park is privately owned, with over three-quarters used for raising sheep and cattle.

The Welsh name for Snowdonia, is Eryri (eh-*ruh*-ree) meaning highlands. Snowdon is called Yr Wyddfa (uhr-*with*-vuh), meaning Great Tomb – according to legend a giant called Rita Gawr was slain here by King Arthur and is buried at the summit.

The park is the only home to two endangered species, an alpine plant called the Snowdon lily as well as the rainbow-coloured Snowdon beetle. The *gwyniad* is a species of whitefish found only in Llyn Tegid (Bala Lake), which also has probably the UK's only colony of glutinous snails.

The park authority publishes a free annual visitor newspaper, which includes information on getting around, park-organised walks and other activities.

Bala (Y Bala)

POP 2000

Kayakers, canoeists, windsurfers, sailors, rafters and hikers will appreciate the quiet Welsh-speaking town of Bala. Here you'll find Wales' largest natural lake, Llyn Tegid (Bala Lake), as well as the River Tryweryn, hallowed in white-water kayaking circles.

Bala was a centre for the Welsh wool industry during the 18th century but today it's better known as a gateway to Snowdonia National Park and the park's main watersports hub. The main street is dotted with adventure sports and outdoors shops, and bustles with visitors in summer.

The Romans had a camp here, the remains of which have been found on private land near the river. Just behind the high street is a Norman motte (castle mound) that would once have supported a wooden castle.

Welsh remains the language of everyday commerce and conversation for 76% of its residents. Local hero and MP Thomas Edward Ellis (1859–99), a prominent contemporary of Lloyd George, was a key advocate for a self-governing Wales; he's remembered with a prominent statue on the main street. One of Ellis' friends was Michael D Jones, founder of the Welsh colony in Patagonia.

◎ Sights

Llyn Tegid LAKE

(Bala Lake) Llyn Tegid was formed during the last ice age when glaciers blocked the valley of the River Dee with debris. The resulting rectangular lake is 4 miles long, three-quarters of a mile wide and, in places, over 42m deep.

Local folk tales record an alternative to the glacial version of events. Once upon a time the valley was home to a cruel and dissolute prince named Tegid Foel. One night the harpist at a banquet thrown by the prince kept hearing a small bird urging him to flee the palace. He did so, fell asleep on a hilltop, and awoke at dawn to find the palace and principality drowned beneath the lake.

🏃 Activities

National Whitewater Centre RAFTING

(☑ 01678-521083; www.ukrafting.co.uk; Frongoch, 3.5 miles northwest of Bala on A4212; 1-/2-hr trip £32/60) Due to the damming of the River Tryweryn in the 1960s, this and the River Dee are among the few Welsh rivers with fairly reliable white water year-round. This centre runs rafting, kayaking and canoeing trips on a 1.5-mile stretch of the Tryweryn that is almost continuous class-III white water with class IV sections.

Bookings are best made at least two days in advance and are subject to cancellation in the event of insufficient releases from the dam – call to check the day before.

The centre's Adventure Breaks schedule marries rafting with another activity, such as rock climbing, mountain biking, pony trekking, high ropes, 4WD off-road driving, canyoning, clay-pigeon shooting or quad biking; prices start at £135 and include accommodation.

Bala Adventure & Watersports Centre WATER SPORTS

(☑ 01678-521059; www.balawatersports.com; Pensarn Rd) This one-stop activity and hire centre, behind the leisure centre by the lakeshore, offers windsurfing, sailing, canoeing, kayaking, white-water rafting, mountain biking, rock climbing and abseiling courses (most courses cost £38/75 per half-/full day). Rental gear includes kayaks (£12), canoes (£25), rowboats (£27), pedaloes (£15), windsurfers (£19) and sailing boats (from £28); all prices are per hour.

Bala Lake Railway HERITAGE RAILWAY

(☑ 01678-540666; www.bala-lake-railway.co.uk; adult/child return £10/3; ☉ Apr-Sep) This narrow-gauge trainline was opened in 1868 to link mainline stations at Bala and Dolgellau. In 1965 the entire route from Barmouth

---

WORTH A TRIP

TYDDYN LLAN

Set among gardens near the pretty Georgian village of Llandrillo (located on the secondary B4401 route between Llangollen and Bala), the rural restaurant-with-rooms **Tyddyn Llan** (2-/3-course lunch £19.50/25.50, dinner £45/55; ☉ lunch Fri-Sun, dinner daily) is the only North Wales restaurant to hold a Michelin star. The food, as you'd expect, is both spectacular and spectacularly priced; the most affordable option is the set lunch, served Friday to Sunday. The 12 rooms each boast their own individual style, some frou-frou romantic, some shabby-chic modern.

to Llangollen was shut down. Volunteers reopened the 4.5-mile stretch from Bala to Llanuwchllyn in 1971, with vintage locomotives departing from a little station at Penybont, half a mile from Bala town centre, off the B4391. There are now up to four daily services skirting the lake for a scenic 90-minute return journey.

Roberts Cycles BICYCLE RENTAL
(☑ 01678-520252; rhrcycles@uk2.net; High St; per day £13) Grab a *Bike Routes Around Bala* pamphlet from the tourist office, then head here to get pedalling.

✯ Festivals & Events

Bala Triathlons SPORT
(www.wrecsamtri.org.uk) Bala gets booked up during the middle distance triathlon in June and the standard version in September.

🛏 Sleeping

Bala Backpackers HOSTEL £
(☑ 01678-521700; www.bala-backpackers.co.uk; 32 Tegid St; dm/tw from £20/47) A leap up in comfort from most of Wales' hostels, Bala Backpackers has brightly painted dorms with a maximum of four single beds (it's a bunk-free zone), and a renovated kitchen and bathrooms. It does, however, have many more rules than your average hostel, including a midnight lockout.

★ Abercelyn Country House B&B ££
(☑ 01678-521109; www.abercelyn.co.uk; Llanycil; s £60, d £90-100; P 🛜) Luxurious rooms, excellent breakfasts and a lovely setting in gardens with a gurgling brook make this former rectory (1729) a great option. The owner is a mountain guide and white-water enthusiast. It's located on the A494, a mile along the lake from the town.

🍴 Eating & Drinking

Eagles Inn (Tafarn Yr Eryod) PUB £
(☑ 01678-540278; www.yr-eagles.co.uk; Llanuwchllyn; mains £8-15; ⏱ 6-11pm Mon-Fri, 11am-midnight Sat, noon-3pm & 6-11pm Sun; 🅿) Right down the other end of the lake from the town, this may be your consummate Welsh-speaking village pub but the food is a step above. Most of the vegetables and some of the meat comes from its own garden, and for dessert there's a delicious array of homemade pies and puddings.

Plas-yn-Dre PUB ££
(☑ 01678-521256; 23 High St; lunch £5-14, dinner £9-14; ⏱ 11am-10pm) With a pub on one side and a large country-style dining room on the other, this is the best eating option on the main strip. The menu is unadventurous but hearty, with daily roasts, jacket potatoes, fresh seafood and that British staple, chicken tikka masala.

ⓘ Information

Bala Tourist Office (☑ 01678-521021; www.visitbala.org; Penllyn Leisure Centre, Pensarn Rd; ⏱ 10am-4pm Fri-Tue Easter-Sep; @ 🛜) Located inside a large leisure centre by the

---

THE LEGEND OF TEGGIE

Sightings of the beast of Llyn Tegid have been reported since at least the 1920s and it has been variously likened to a crocodile or a small dinosaur. Affectionately known as Teggie, this Welsh answer to the Loch Ness monster prompted a three-day search by a Japanese film crew in 1995, but their mini-submarine failed to find any sign of the elusive beast.

One man who claims to have seen the beastie from the deep, however, is local farmer Rhodri Jones, whose sheep farm extends to the lake's foreshore. 'One night in the summer of 2006 I was heading home from the fields when I saw something making concentric ripples. The lake was very still, pretty spooky in the dusk and the water was very calm. That's when I saw the top of a creature about the size of a crocodile moving through the water.'

Since then Jones has spoken to other local farmers and found that many of them have stories of mysterious sightings and evidence they have collected dating back over 60 years.

'Bala is a landlocked, volcanic lake and there are species of fish living there that are only to be found in the lake,' says Jones. 'I think there's something special about the waters, but we live in a narrow-minded world where people are afraid of the unexplained. Still, humanity always needs a mystery.'

lake, where there's also a cafe and an indoor pool with waterslides.

❶ Getting There & Around

Buses stop on the High St. Bus X94 heads to/from Barmouth (one hour), Dolgellau (35 minutes), Llangollen (48 minutes) and Wrexham (1½ hours); and bus X6 heads to Betws-y-Coed (1¼ hours).

Dolgellau

POP 2690

Dolgellau (dol-*ge*-khlye) is a charming little market town, steeped in history and boasting the highest concentration of listed buildings in Wales (over 200). It was a regional centre for Wales' prosperous wool industry in the 18th and early 19th centuries, and many of its finest buildings, sturdy and unadorned, were built at that time. Local mills failed to keep pace with mass mechanisation, however, and decline set in – preserving the town centre much as it was then. Pick up the *Dolgellau Town Trail* (£1) brochure from the tourist office to explore the unusual architecture in detail.

The region bounced back when the Romantic Revival made Wales' wild landscapes popular with genteel travellers. There was also, surprisingly, a minor gold rush here in the 19th century. Dolgellau gold, famous for its pink tinge, became associated with royalty (the gold for the the wedding rings of the current crop of senior royals was mined here). The mine has recently reopened, despite having been closed since 1988.

Today the town relies heavily on tourism. One of Snowdonia's premier peaks, bulky Cader Idris, rises to the south, the lovely Mawddach Estuary lies to the west and, to the north, the Coed y Brenin Forest offers glorious mountain biking. Most of Dolgellau's accommodation is plush and boutique, making it an appealing (if pricey) base from which to explore the national park.

◎ Sights

Mawddach Estuary   ESTUARY
The Mawddach Estuary is a striking sight, flanked by woodlands, wetlands and the romantic mountains of southern Snowdonia. There are two Royal Society for the Protection of Birds (RSPB) nature reserves in the estuary valley. On the south side, **Arthog Bog** is a small wetland reserve favoured by cuckoos, grasshopper warblers, lesser red-polls, reed buntings and siskins. Set in oak woodlands along the northern side, **Coed Garth Gell** has two circular walking trails; one 1.25 miles, the other 1.5 miles. Spring visitors include redstarts, wood warblers and pied flycatchers, while in summer you might spot dippers and in winter, woodcocks.

The estuary is easily reached on foot or by bike from Dolgellau or Barmouth via the Mawddach Trail. Arthog Bog is 8 miles west of Dolgellau on the access road to Morfa Mawddach station, off the A493, while Coed Garth Gell is 2 miles west of Dolgellau on the A496.

Cymer Abbey   RUINS
FREE This Cistercian abbey, founded in 1198, was never especially grand but the ruined walls and arches are still picturesque, especially when the daffodils are in bloom. There are walks in the vicinity and nice picnic spots near the river. It's 2 miles northwest of Dolgellau, signposted from the A470.

⭐ Activities

Precipice Walk   WALKING
If you're not up to scaling Cader Idris, this 3.5-mile circular walk through the private Nannau estate is surprisingly varied and offers plenty of beautiful scenery. It leads you through woodland, along the side of a steeply sloped mountain (the precipice in question; keep an eye on the kids) and beside a lake. Walk the loop anticlockwise for the best views of Cader Idris, Snowdon and the Mawddach Estuary. The walk starts from Saith Groesffordd car park, Llanfachreth, around 2.5 miles from Dolgellau (it's well signposted).

Mawddach Trail   WALKING
(www.mawddachtrail.co.uk) The 9.5-mile Mawddach Trail is a flat (and in places wheelchair-accessible) walking and cycling path that follows an old train line through woods and past wetlands on the southern side of the Mawddach Estuary, before crossing over the train viaduct to Barmouth (where you can catch the bus back). The trail starts in the car park beside the bridge.

Mawddach Way   WALKING
(www.mawddachway.co.uk) Mawddach Way is a 30-mile, two- to three-day track looping through the hills on either side of the Mawddach Estuary. Although the highest point is 346m, by the end of the undulating

Dolgellau

path you'll have climbed 2226m. The official guide splits the route into three legs: Barmouth–Taicynhaeaf (10 miles, five to six hours), Taicynhaeaf–Penmaenpool (9 miles, four to five hours) and Penmaenpool–Barmouth (11 miles, six to seven hours). Fit walkers should be able to do it in two days, with pit stops at Barmouth and Dolgellau. An A5 booklet can be ordered or downloaded online (booklet/download £10/5); GPS route data can be downloaded for free.

SnowBikers   MOUNTAIN BIKING
(☎ 01341-430628; www.snowbikers.com) Learn to mountain bike or take a guided ride around the Mawddach Estuary (up to four people, half-/full day £90/165).

Dolgellau Cycles   BICYCLE RENTAL
(☎ 01341-423332; www.dolgellaucycles.co.uk; Smithfield St) Rents bikes, performs repairs and offers advice on local cycle routes. Lôn Las Cymru, the Welsh National Cycle Route (Sustrans route 8), passes through Dolgellau, heading north to Porthmadog and south to Machynlleth.

🛏 Sleeping

HYB Bunkhouse   HOSTEL £
(☎ 01341-421755; www.medi-gifts.com; 2 Bridge St; dm/r £20/80, bedding £5 extra; P 🛜) Lo-

cated above a gift shop, this bunkhouse has a series of oak-beamed rooms with handy kitchenettes, each sleeping four people (in bunkbeds). Only one has an en suite; the rest share bathrooms. During busy periods it's charged by the room rather than by the bed.

Bryn Mair House   B&B ££
(☎ 01341-422640; www.brynmairbedandbreakfast. co.uk; Love Lane; s £75-85, d £95-105; P 🛜) This impressive stone house – a former Georgian rectory no less – sits among gardens on wistfully monikered Love Lane. Its three luxurious B&B rooms are kitted out with Egyptian cotton sheets, DVD players and iPod docks; Room 1 has sublime mountain views.

Pandy Isaf   B&B ££
(☎ 01341-423949; www.pandyisaf-accommodation.co.uk; s/d £50/80; P) You wouldn't think to look at it, but this country house, set alongside a gurgling stream where otters frolic, started life as a 16th-century fulling mill. It's now a peaceful retreat straight out of the pages of *Country Living* offering spotless bedrooms, a large guest lounge full of books and DVDs, and amazing breakfasts. It's located 2 miles northeast of Dolgellau off the A494; turn left after the petrol station.

Y Meirionnydd   HOTEL ££
(☎ 01341-422554; www.themeirionnydd.com Smithfield Sq; s £60-75, d £89-135; 🛜) Slap bang in the centre of town, this listed Georgian town house has been thoroughly refurbished, with a hip new look complementing the roughly hewn stone walls. Special

touches include bathrobes, slippers and bottled water.

★ Ffynnon
B&B £££

(☑ 01341-421774; www.ffynnontownhouse.com; Love Lane; s £100, d £145-200; P ☎) With a keen eye for contemporary design and a super-friendly welcome, this first-rate boutique B&B feels both homey and stylish. French antiques are mixed in with modern chandeliers, claw-foot tubs and electronic gadgets, and each room has a seating area so you can admire the views in comfort. There's even an outdoor hot tub.

Penmaenuchaf Hall
HOTEL £££

(☑ 01341-422129; www.penhall.co.uk; s £115-180, d £170-260; P ☎ ☀) With imposing furnishings and elaborate gardens, this stately country-house hotel is the former pile of Bolton cotton magnate, James Leigh. The 14 rooms have a lavish old-world air but also CD players and satellite TV. It's located 2 miles west of Dolgellau, off the A493.

✗ Eating

TH Roberts
CAFE £

(Parliament House, Glyndŵr St; mains £4-6; ☺9.30am-5.30pm Mon-Sat; ☎) It's easy to walk past this atmospheric Grade II–listed cafe as it still looks exactly like the ironmonger's shop that it once was, with its original counter, glass cabinets, wooden drawers and other fittings. It's a favourite with locals, with jolly, if haphazard, service, light meals (soup, rarebit, sandwiches, cakes), newspapers and books to browse, and a good wi-fi connection.

Mawddach Restaurant & Bar
MODERN WELSH ££

(☑ 01341-424020; www.mawddach.com; Llanelltyd; mains £13-16; ☺noon-2.30pm & 6-9.30pm Wed-Sat, noon-3.30pm Sun) Located 2 miles west of Dolgellau on the A496, Mawddach brings a touch of urban style to what was once a barn. Slate floors, leather seats and panoramic views across to Cader Idris set the scene. The food is equally impressive: meat straight from nearby farms, fresh local fish specials and traditional Sunday roasts (two/three courses £18/20).

Dylanwad Da
TAPAS, WELSH ££

(☑ 01341-422870; www.dylanwad.co.uk; 2 Smithfield St; mains £18; ☺10am-3pm & 7-9pm Thu-Sat) Informal cafe, wine shop and tapas bar by day, contemporary restaurant by night, this well-run, low-lit eatery has been serving high-quality food for 25 years. A long-standing favourite on the Snowdonia scene, it has a healthy wine list and an imaginative menu.

Y Sospan
CAFE, BISTRO ££

(☑ 01341-423174; Queen's Sq; breakfast & lunch £3-7, dinner £11-15; ☺9am-9.30pm; ☎) In a book-lined and woody 1606 building that once served as a prison, this relaxed eatery serves fry-up breakfasts, sandwiches, jacket potatoes and light cooked meals during the day. At night, it switches to a heavier bistro menu, where lamb and beef play a starring role and most of the desserts have been on the booze.

Y Meirionnydd
MODERN WELSH £££

(☑ 01341-422554; www.themeirionnydd.com; Smithfield Sq; 2/3 courses £22/25; ☺7-10pm Mon-Sat) Although it's located in the medieval cellar of what was once the county gaol, there's nothing remotely gloomy about this sophisticated restaurant or its lively kitchen. The menu is short but well thought out.

☆ Entertainment

Tŷ Siamas
LIVE MUSIC

(☑ 01341-421800; www.tysiamas.com; Eldon Sq) Dolgellau has been an important hub for Welsh folk music ever since it held the first Welsh folk festival in 1952. The town's former market hall now houses the volunteer-run National Centre for Welsh Folk Music, named after Dolgellau-born Elis Sîon Siamas who was the royal harpist to Queen Anne and the first Welshman to build a triple harp (now commonly known as a 'Welsh

---

THE DOLGELLAU QUAKERS

The Dolgellau area has historical links with the Society of Friends (the Quakers). After George Fox visited in 1657, preaching his philosophy of direct communication with God, free from creeds, rites and clergy, a Quaker community was founded here. Converts, from simple farmers to local gentry, were persecuted with vigour because their refusal to swear oaths – in particular to the king – was considered treasonous. Many eventually emigrated to William Penn's Quaker community in America. There's an interesting display about the Dolgellau Quakers upstairs in the tourist office.

harp'). The centre has a recording studio, stages workshops, and offers lessons on traditional instruments. Check the website for upcoming performances.

ⓘ Information

Dolgellau Tourist Office (☏01341-422888; www.eryri-npa.gov.uk; Eldon Sq; ☉9.30am-5pm Easter-Oct, 9.30am-4.30pm Thu-Mon Nov-Easter) Sells maps, local history books and trail leaflets for climbing Cader Idris. Downstairs there's a free video about the national park, while upstairs there's a permanent exhibition on the region's Quaker heritage.

ⓘ Getting There & Around

Buses stop on Eldon Sq in the heart of town. Destinations include Machynlleth (route T2/X27; 32 minutes), Betws-y-Coed (X1; 1¼ hours), Llangollen (X94; 1¼ hours), Porthmadog (T2; 50 minutes) and Caernarfon (T2; 1½ hours).

Cader Idris (Cadair Idris)

Cader Idris (893m), or the 'Seat of Idris' (a legendary giant), is a hulking, menacing-looking mountain with an appropriate mythology attached. It's said that hounds of the underworld fly around its peaks, and that strange light effects are often sighted in the area. It's also said that anyone who spends the night on the summit will awake either mad or a poet – although perhaps you'd have to be a little mad or romantic to attempt it in the first place. Regardless of its reputation,

it's popular with walkers and it's the park's favourite locale for rock climbers.

The usual route to the summit is the 'Dolgellau' or **Pony Path** (6 miles return, five hours), which begins from the Tŷ Nant car park, 3 miles southwest of Dolgellau. It's a rocky but safe, straightforward route.

The easiest but longest route is the 'Tywyn' or **Llanfihangel y Pennant Path** (10 miles return, six hours), a gentle pony track that heads northeast from the hamlet of Llanfihangel y Pennant, joining the Tŷ Nant Path at the latter's midpoint. Llanfihangel is 1.5 miles from the terminus of the Talyllyn Railway at Abergynolwyn.

The shortest but steepest route is the **Minffordd Path** (6 miles return, five hours), which begins from the Dol Idris car park (four hours/day £2/4), 6 miles south of Dolgellau at the junction of the A487 and the B4405. This route requires the most caution, especially on the way back down, but there's the added incentive of a hot beverage awaiting at the tearoom, near the car park.

Whichever route you choose, wear stout shoes, carry protective clothing and check the weather conditions, either online (www.metoffice.gov.uk/loutdoor/mountainsafety) or at the Dolgellau tourist office, which also stocks a trail booklet (£1.50).

Near the Minffordd trailhead is **Tal-y-llyn**, a tranquil lake hemmed in by the encroaching mountains. It's stocked with trout and popular with both anglers and otters.

WORTH A TRIP

COED Y BRENIN FOREST PARK

Covering 14 sq miles, this woodland park (8 miles north of Dolgellau off the A470) is the premier location for mountain biking in Wales. It's laced with 70 miles of purpose-built cycle trails, divided into eight graded routes to suit beginners or guns, and impressively presented by way of old-fashioned waterproof trail cards or downloadable geocaches and MP3 audio files. Wildlife includes fallow deer; they're hard to spot but you're most likely to see them early in the morning.

The park's impressive environmentally friendly **visitor centre** (☏01341-440747; www.naturalresourceswales.gov.uk; car park per hr/day £1/4; ☉9.30am-4.30pm) has a cafe, toilets, showers and a children's play area, while downstairs you can hire bikes from **Beics Brenin** (☏01341-440728; www.beicsbrenin.co.uk; per day £25-45).

If you prefer to monkey about in the treetops, the park also contains the **Go Ape** (☏0845 094 2634; www.goape.co.uk; adult/child from £30/24; ☉weekends & school holidays Easter-Oct) high-wires course; book ahead.

Accommodation is available 3.5 miles north of the park at the **Transfynydd Holiday Village** (☏01766-540219; www.logcabinswales.co.uk; A470, Bronaber; cabin from £108; [P][🛜][🐾]), a massive complex of around 350 log cabins, with its own pub, shop and laundrette.

🛌 Sleeping

While Dolgellau is the usual base for walkers, there are a couple of other options tucked around the mountain.

Kings YHA   HOSTEL £

📞 0845 371 9327; www.yha.org.uk; dm/r from £14/54; P) It's slightly creepy and a little rundown, but this remote woodland hostel has a gorgeous setting beside a stream, 2 miles from the Pony Path trailhead. Follow the signposts from the A493, west of Penmaenpool.

⭐ **Old Rectory on the Lake**   B&B ££

📞 01654-782225; www.rectoryonthelake.co.uk; r £60-90 d £90-120, apt £120; P 🐾) If you think you might need a little pampering after your Cader Idris ascent – perhaps a gourmet meal, a complimentary glass of sherry or a soak in a hot tub – this wonderful B&B could be just the ticket. It's located on the shores of Tal-y-llyn, less than 2 miles from the Minffordd trailhead.

Tywyn
POP 3260

While the town falls just outside the national park, Tywyn's long sandy blue-flagged beach is one of the most popular in the region. Its other major drawcard is the narrow-gauge **Talyllyn Railway** (📞 01654-710472; www.talyllyn.co.uk; Wharf Station; adult/child £15/7.25; ⏱ Easter-Oct), famous as the inspiration for Rev W Awdry's *Thomas the Tank Engine* stories. It opened in 1865 to carry slate from the Bryn Eglwys quarries near Abergynolwyn. In 1950 the line was saved from closure by the world's first railway preservation society. It's one of Wales' most enchanting little railways and puffs for 7.3 scenic, steam-powered miles up the Fathew Valley to Nant Gwernol. There are five stations along the way, each with waymarked walking trails (and waterfalls at Dolgoch and Nant Gwernol); trail leaflets are available at the stations. Your ticket entitles you to all-day travel; check online for train timetables.

At Tywyn's Wharf Station, the **Narrow Gauge Railway Museum** (www.ngrm.org.uk; admission free) is one for the history buffs, with shiny narrow-gauge steam locomotives and the story of the volunteers who preserved the railway. Opening hours are coordinated with the train timetable.

WORTH A TRIP

ABERDOVEY & AROUND

From Dolgellau, an interesting drive is the 50-mile circuit of the southern slice of the former kingdom/county of Meirionnydd, bound by the estuaries of the Rivers Mawddach and Dovey (Dyfi). When the A493 reaches the broad estuary of the River Dovey it curves east through Aberdovey (Aberdyfi), a pretty town lined with pastel Georgian town houses. Further east in the village of Pennal, the **Riverside Hotel** (Gwesty Glan Yr Afon; 📞 01654-791285; www.riversidehotel-pennal.co.uk; mains £10-15; ⏱ noon-2pm & 6-9pm; 🐾) is a great place to stop for upmarket gastropub grub and Purple Moose ale.

ℹ Getting There & Away

➡ Tywyn is on the Cambrian Coast Line, with direct trains to/from Machynlleth (£5.50, 30 minutes), Fairbourne (£3.80, 17 minutes), Barmouth (£4.60, 29 minutes), Porthmadog (£11, 1½ hours) and Pwllheli (£12.50, two hours).
➡ Buses head to/from Dolgellau (route 28/30; 40 minutes), Fairbourne (28; 29 minutes) and Machynlleth (X29; 35 minutes).

Fairbourne
POP 1040

Fairbourne has a lovely long beach but little else to recommend it, except for the steam-hauled **Fairbourne Miniature Railway** (📞 01341-250362; www.fairbournerailway. com; Beach Rd; adult/child £9/1; ⏱ Easter-Oct), Wales' only seaside narrow-gauge railway. It was built in 1895 to move materials for the construction of the village. The line heads north along the coast for 2.5 miles to Penrhyn Point, where there are ferries across the mouth of the Mawddach to Barmouth, timed to meet the trains.

There's a restaurant at Penrhyn Point, while Fairbourne station has a cafe and a model railway.

🍴 Eating

Indiana Cuisine   INDIAN £

(📞 01341-250891; www.indianacuisine.co.uk; 3 Beach Rd; mains £5-10; ⏱ 6.30-10pm Mon, Wed & Thu, noon-3pm & 6.30-10pm Fri-Sun; 🐾) Right opposite the train station, this pink-hued

(Continued on page 232)

GRAHAM LAWRENCE / GETTY IMAGES ©

erystwyth &
d-Wales

orld Bog Snorkelling
mpionships (p206)
ts, snorkels and flippers are donned to
e a trench cut out of a peat bog.

erystwyth (p185)
university town that curves around
an Bay.

ntre for Alternative Technology
)
mental sustainability is the centre of
on at the thought-provoking CAT.

wis Castle (p199)
nded by magnificent gardens, this red-brick
was built in the 13th century.

VISITBRITAIN/BRITAIN ON VIEW / GETTY IMAGES ©

JAMES OSMOND / GETTY IMAGES ©

owdonia & Llŷn

owdon (p244)
085m-tall mountain is the highest
it in Wales.

ational Slate Museum
1)
.Lanberis, this fascinating museum
es elements on the tile-making
ss.

wallow Falls (p236)
rrent of water weaves through the
ce and into a green pool below.

elsh Highland Railway
0)
opular heritage railway runs
h 25 miles of Snowdonian
yside.

JOHN HAY / GETTY IMAGES ©

1

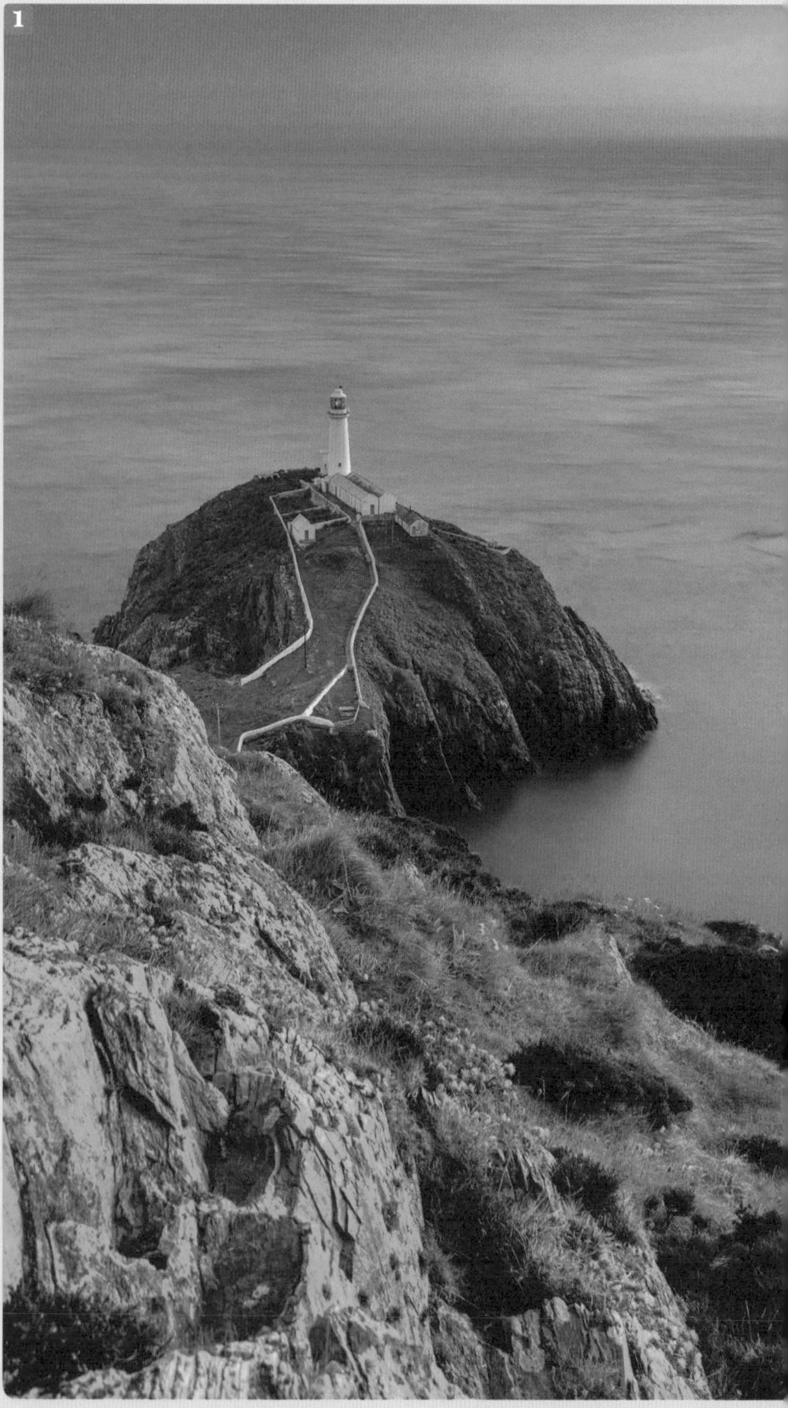

MARK YOULDEN / GETTY IMAGES ©

VISITBRITAIN/BRITAIN ON VIEW / GETTY IMAGES ©

lesey & the
th Coast

th Stack Lighthouse (p288)
:house on Holy Island has an end-
:arth feel.

2. Holy Island (p288)
Sweeping views dominate this rugged island.

3. Beaumaris Castle (p283)
Every sandcastle maker aspires to produce something similar to this 1295 masterpiece.

(Continued from page 225)

restaurant is suprising on a number of fronts: it has nothing to do with the midwest of the USA; it serves authentic Indian cuisine; it's run by a former Bollywood actor and his wife; and, well, it's in Fairbourne. And perhaps most surprising of all, it's very good.

❶ Getting There & Away

➡ Fairbourne is on the Cambrian Coast Line, with direct trains to Machynlleth (£7.80, 55 minutes), Tywyn (£3.80, 17 minutes), Barmouth (£2.50, 11 minutes), Porthmadog (£7.70, 1¼ hours) and Pwllheli (£11, 1¾ hours).

➡ Bus 28 from Dolgellau (route 28; 25 minutes) to Tywyn (28; 29 minutes) stops here.

Barmouth (Abermaw)

POP 2530

Despite a Blue Flag beach and the beautiful Mawddach Estuary on its doorstep, the seaside resort of Barmouth has a faded feel to it. In summer it becomes a typical seaside resort – all chip shops and dodgem cars – catering to the trainloads arriving in their thousands from England's West Midlands. Outside of the brash neon of high summer it's considerably mellower, but it still has its rough edges.

The main commercial strip is spread out along the A496; as it passes through town it's known as Church St, High St and King Edward's St. The oldest part of Barmouth is around the quay. The unusual round building, Tŷ Crwn, was once a jail where drunk and disorderly sailors could cool off until morning. In the 15th century, supporters of Henry Tudor met in nearby Tŷ Gwyn to plot his ascension to the throne (the building now houses Davy Jones' Locker) .

◉ Sights & Activities

Wales' only surviving wooden rail viaduct spans the estuary and has a handy pedestrian walkway attached that forms part of the Mawddach Trail (p221) and Mawddach Way (p221).

Dinas Oleu HILL
Rising behind Barmouth, rocky Dinas Oleu (258m) made history in 1895 by becoming the first property ever bequeathed to the National Trust, kick-starting a movement dedicated to preserving Britain's best landscapes and buildings. A network of trails covers the site, including the popular Panorama Walk (signposted from the A496 on the eastern edge of town), which has the best of the estuary views. Otherwise scramble up any one of several alleys running off the main street, where you'll find the town gets more and more vertical, with better and better views, until the old houses are nearly on top of one another.

✦ Festivals & Events

Three Peaks Yacht Race YACHTING
(www.threepeaksyachtrace.co.uk; ⊘ Jun) Held in late June, the arduous Three Peaks Yacht Race has been attracting international crews for over 35 years. Contestants set sail from Barmouth for Caernarfon, where two crew members run to the summit of Snowdon (Wales' highest peak). They then sail to Whitehaven and run up Scafell Pike (England's highest peak); and finally to Fort William for an ascent of Ben Nevis (Scotland's highest peak) – in all, 389 nautical miles of sailing, 29 miles of cycling and 59 miles of fell running. The record time for the race thus far is two days, 14 hours and four minutes, achieved in 2002.

Barmouth Arts Festival PERFORMING ARTS
(www.barmouthartsfestival.co.uk; ⊘ Sep) A week-long festival of theatre and live music held at the Dragon Theatre in September.

Barmouth Walking Festival WALKING
(www.barmouthwalkingfestival.co.uk; ⊘ Sep) If you fancy a hike but would prefer some companions, this festival takes place over 10 days in September.

⫘ Sleeping

**Hendre Mynach
Caravan Park** CAMPGROUND £
(☏ 01341-280262; www.hendremynach.co.uk; sites from £24; ℗ ▓) Right beside the beach, this well-kept park has caravan sites marked out between manicured hedges and a couple of flat camping fields protected by windbreaks. It's just off the A496, immediately north of Barmouth.

Richmond House B&B ££
(☏ 01341-281366; www.barmouthbedandbreakfast. co.uk; High St; s/d £65/80; ℗ 🛜) This handsome town house has big, contemporary rooms (two with sea views) and an attractive garden area for summer lounging on chunky wooden furniture. It's very handy for both the town centre and the beach.

✖ Eating & Drinking

★ Bistro Bermo MODERN WELSH **££**
(☑ 01341-281284; www.bistrobarmouth.co.uk; 6
Church St; mains £13-22; ⊙ 6-10pm Tue-Sun, plus
noon-2pm Wed-Sat Apr-Oct) Discreetly hidden
behind a forest-green shopfront as if it's
embarrassed about showing up the other
Barmouth eateries, this intimate restaurant
delivers a sophisticated menu chock-full of
Welsh farm produce and fresh fish. There
are only half a dozen tables, so it pays to
book ahead.

Last Inn PUB
(☑ 01341-280530; www.lastinn-barmouth.co.uk;
Church St) Dating from the 15th century and
full of old ship timber, this is easily the most
characterful pub in Barmouth. Most unusually, the mountain forms the rear wall, with
a spring emerging right inside the building.
Kids are welcome and the menu's full of
crowd-pleasers, including a traditional Sunday roast. There's also live music on Tuesday
and Friday nights.

☆ Entertainment

Dragon Theatre THEATRE, CINEMA
(Theatr y Ddraig; ☑ 01341-281697; www.dragon-
theatre.co.uk; Jubilee Rd) The cultural life of the
town is centred on this 1890s chapel and its
year-round schedule of live performances,
cinema and exhibitions.

ℹ Information

Barmouth Tourist Office (☑ 01341-280787;
www.visitsnowdonia.info; Station Rd; ⊙ 10am-
5pm Apr-Oct, 10am-3.30pm Mon-Sat Nov-Mar;
🖥️) Sells leaflets on local walks, and train and
coach tickets, and offers an accommodation
booking service.

ℹ Getting There & Away

➡ Barmouth is on the Cambrian Coast Line,
with direct trains to Machynlleth (£8.80, one
hour), Fairbourne (£2.50, 11 minutes), Harlech
(£4.60, 23 minutes), Porthmadog (£6.90, one
hour) and Pwllheli (£11, 1½ hours).

➡ Buses stop on Jubilee Rd, across Beach Rd
from the train station. Destinations include
Harlech (route 38; 30 minutes), Dolgellau (38/
X94; 20 minutes), Bala (X94; one hour), Llandrillo (X94; 1½ hours) and Llangollen (X94; 1¾
hours).

➡ Cycle path Lôn Las Cymru passes through
Barmouth, heading north to Harlech and south
to Dolgellau.

Harlech

POP 1450

Hilly Harlech is best known for the mighty,
grey stone towers of its castle, framed
by gleaming Tremadog Bay and with the
mountains of Snowdonia as a backdrop.
Some sort of fortified structure has probably
surmounted the rock since Iron Age times,
but Edward I removed all traces when he
commissioned the construction of his castle. Finished in 1289, Harlech Castle is the
southernmost of four fortifications included
in the Castles & Town Walls of King Edward
in Gwynedd Unesco World Heritage Site.

Harlech is such a thoroughly pleasant
place that it has become one of the more
gentrified destinations in Snowdonia – every
other shop seems to sell antiques or tea.
While it's bustling in summer, it can be deliciously sleepy otherwise. It makes a great
base for a beach holiday or for day trips into
the national park – and those views never
get boring.

◉ Sights & Activities

★ Harlech Castle CASTLE
(Cadw; www.cadw.wales.gov.uk; adult/child £4.25/
3.20; ⊙ 9.30am-5pm Mar-Oct, 10am-4pm Nov-Feb)
Edward I finished this intimidating yet spectacular building in 1289, the southernmost
of his 'iron ring' of fortresses designed to
keep the Welsh beneath his boot. Despite
its might, this fortress has been called the
'Castle of Lost Causes' because it has been
lucklessly defended so many times. Owain Glyndŵr captured it after a long siege
in 1404. He is said to have been crowned
Prince of Wales in the presence of envoys
from Scotland, France and Spain during one
of his parliaments in the town. He was, in
turn, besieged here by the future Henry V.

During the Wars of the Roses the castle
is said to have held out against a siege for
seven years and was the last Lancastrian
stronghold to fall. The siege inspired the
popular Welsh hymn *Men of Harlech,* which
is still played today in regimental marches
and sung with patriotic gusto at rugby
matches. The castle was also the last to fall
in the English Civil War, finally giving in to
Cromwell's forces in 1647.

The grey sandstone castle's massive, twin-
towered gatehouse and outer walls are still
intact and give the illusion of impregnabil-
ity even now. A drawbridge leads through
the gatehouse to the compact inner ward,

where four gloomy round towers guard the corners. Some of the ramparts are partly ruined and closed off, but you can climb up other sections for views in all directions. The fortress' great natural defence is the seaward cliff face. When it was built, ships could sail supplies right to the base.

The finest exterior view of the castle (with Snowdon as a backdrop) is from a craggy outcrop on Ffordd Isaf, opposite Maelgwyn House.

Snowdonia Adventure Activities OUTDOORS
(☑ 01341-241511; www.snowdoniaadventureactivi-ties.co.uk; adult/child £70/35) A young couple offering customised adventures within the national park, including rock climbing, abseiling, canyoning, gorge scrambling, canoeing, kayaking, mountain biking and guided hiking. A full day's program combines two activities.

🛌 Sleeping & Eating

Maelgwyn House B&B ££
(☑ 01766-780087; www.maelgwynharlech.co.uk; Ffordd Isaf; r £65-89; P🐾) A model B&B, Maelgwyn has interesting hosts, delicious breakfasts and a small set of elegant rooms with tremendous views across the bay, stocked with DVD players and tea-making facilities. Bridget and Derek can also help arrange birdwatching trips and fungus forays. Full marks.

Castle Cottage HOTEL £££
(☑ 01766-780479; www.castlecottageharlech.co.uk; Ffordd Pen Llech; s £85-125, d £130-175; P🐾) Within arrow's reach of the castle, this 16th-century cottage has spacious bedrooms in a contemporary style, with exposed beams, in-room DVD players and a bowl of fresh fruit for each guest. The award-winning fine-dining restaurant (three-course dinner £40) serves a deliciously patriotic menu, revelling in local produce and traditional dishes executed in classical French style.

Cemlyn Tea Shop TEAROOM £
(www.cemlynteashop.co.uk; High St; snacks around £5; ⊙ 10.30am-4.30pm Wed-Sun Easter-Oct, Sat & Sun Nov-Easter; 🐾) The Coles (Jan and Geoff) may be merry old souls but it's tea that's king here. There are over 30 varieties on offer, along with a simple range of snacks to accompany them and a slew of Tea Guild Awards of Excellence on the walls. Best of all are the views from the terrace.

★ Castle Restaurant & Armoury Bar CARIBBEAN ££
(☑ 01766-780416; www.caribbeancrabharlech.com; Castle Sq; mains £14-18; ⊙ 6.30-10.30pm Mon-Sat) If this place were transported to London it would have queues out the door, so one has to admire the gumption of opening such a wonderful Caribbean restaurant in Wales, let alone sleepy Harlech. Downstairs is the coolest cocktail bar in North Wales, while upstairs, the locals are switching on to the spicy delights of goat curry, jerk chicken and blackened salmon.

☆ Entertainment

Theatr Harlech THEATRE, CINEMA
(☑ 01766-780667; www.theatrharlech.com; Ffordd Newydd) Quite an impressive theatre for a town of this size, Theatr Harlech is a lively local arts centre that stages dance, theatre and music, and screens a well-considered assortment of Hollywood blockbusters and artier, higher-brow films.

❶ Information

Harlech Tourist Office (☑ 01766-780658; www.eryri-npa.gov.uk; High St; ⊙ 9.30am-5.30pm Easter-Oct) At the time of writing, plans were afoot to convert the Castle Hotel (opposite the castle) into a new visitor centre and cafe.

❶ Getting There & Around

➡ Harlech is on the Cambrian Coast Line, with direct trains to Machynlleth (£12, 1½ hours), Fairbourne (£5.60, 37 minutes), Barmouth (£4.60, 23 minutes), Porthmadog (£3.80, 24 minutes) and Pwllheli (£7.80, 47 minutes). The station is at the base of the rocks, below the castle; it's a strenuous 20-minute climb on one of several stepped tracks up to High St, or about half a mile by road.

➡ Bus 38 to Barmouth (30 minutes) stops on High St; some buses continue on to Dolgellau (one hour).

➡ Cycle path Lôn Las Cymru passes through Harlech, heading north to Porthmadog and south to Barmouth.

Blaenau Ffestiniog

POP 4880

Most of the slate used to roof 19th-century Britain came from Wales, and much of that came from the mines of Blaenau Ffestiniog. However, only about 10% of mined slate is usable, so for every tonne that goes to the factory, 9 tonnes are left as rubble. Despite being in the very centre of Snowdonia National Park, the grey mountains of mine waste that surround Blaenau (*blay*-nye) prevented it from being officially included in the park – a slap in the face for this close-knit but impoverished town in the days before Wales' industrial sites were recognised as part of its heritage.

Today, although slate mining continues on a small scale, Blaenau has a mournful feel to it, not helped by famously miserable weather. It's an interesting place to stop but it's unlikely you'll be tempted to stay. That said, the town centre is currently being smartened up and a smattering of new attractions have opened of late. It makes a great day trip from Porthmadog via the historic Ffestiniog Railway.

◎ Sights & Activities

★ **Llechwedd Slate Caverns**   MINE
(☑ 01766-830306; www.llechwedd-slate-caverns.co.uk; single tour adult/child £11/8.50, both tours £17/13) Blaenau's main attraction offers a chance to descend into a real slate mine. Of the two tours offered, the more evocative Deep Mine tour includes a descent on the UK's steepest mining cable railway and re-creates the harsh working conditions of the 19th-century miners – be prepared to duck and scramble around dark tunnels. If you can't manage a lot of steps, go for the Miner's Tramway Tour, a ride through the huge 1846 network of tunnels and caverns. Tours take place throughout the day; call ahead for times.

Cellb   ARTS CENTRE
(☑ 01766-832001; www.cellb.org; Park Sq; ⏰ cafebar 10am-2pm Thu-Sat, 6-11.45pm Fri & Sat, noon-3pm Sun) Recently opened in the Edwardian era police station, this multifunction centre hosts everything from yoga and Welsh language classes, to live bands and film screenings. It's also the town's most appealing dining and drinking space, with a cafe-bar and a cocktail bar.

Antur Stiniog   MOUNTAIN BIKING
(☑ 01766-832214; www.anturstiniog.com; single uplift/day pass £3/26; ⏰ 10am-4pm Thu-Sun) If you're a serious mountain biker and don't know the meaning of fear (being a little bonkers would probably help too), check out these new runs down the mountainside near the slate caverns. Two are graded black and two red; a minibus uplift service is included in the price. The same crew organ-

ises tailored activity-based holidays including walking, kayaking, climbing and wild camping. Big things are afoot here, with a new visitor centre being built and plans to introduce a 'velorail' (a pedal-powered vehicle that runs along train tracks) to an abandoned line leading to Llan Festiniog.

❶ Getting There & Away

➡ Both the Conwy Valley Line from Betws-y-Coed (£4.80, 27 minutes) and Llandudno (£8.10, 1¼ hours), and the steam-powered Ffestiniog Railway (p250) from Porthmadog terminate here.

➡ Buses head to/from Porthmadog (route 1B; 30 minutes), Dolgellau (X1; 47 minutes), Betws-y-Coed (X1; 20 minutes) and Llandudno (X1; 1¼ hours).

Penmachno

POP 617

Tucked away in the valley of the River Machno, the picturesque village of Penmachno dates to at least Roman times, but it's a sleepy place these days. It's edged by the Gwydyr Forest, a leafy paradise for mountain bikers and horse riders.

◎ Sights & Activites

St Tudclud's Church   CHURCH
(www.churchinwales.org.uk/bangor) After 12 years of closure, little St Tudclud's reopened in 2009 after the community rallied around to save it. It isn't particularly old (1859), but inside are five Latin-inscribed stones dating from the 5th century, a 12th-century font, and a 13th-century gravestone which may have belonged to the father of Llywelyn the Great. It's usually open; call in and help yourself to a cup of coffee.

Penmachno Trails   MOUNTAIN BIKING
(www.penmachnobiketrails.org.uk) The southern part of the Gwydyr Forest (p236) has two red-graded mountain biking loops – the 12-mile Dolen Machno (1½ to three hours) and the 7-mile Dolen Eryri (one to two hours) – which can be combined into the 19-mile Penmachno Trail. They offer a good mix of descents and forest climbs, with some sections of boardwalk.

Gwydyr Stables   HORSE RIDING
(☑ 01690-760248; www.horse-riding-wales.co.uk; per hr/half-day/day £22/40/70) Arranges rides through the forest for novice and regular riders alike. It also offers a pub ride for £50,

lasting around four hours and stopping off for a pint at a couple of local pubs along the way. To find the stables, turn right at the Eagles Inn and follow the signs towards Tŷ Mawr.

🛏 Sleeping & Eating

The Eagles   HOSTEL, PUB £
(☑01960-760177; www.eaglespenmachno.co.uk; dm £17; ⊘pub 7pm-late Wed-Fri, 2pm-late Sat & Sun; ⊛) A hand-painted sign of three black eagles hangs above the door of the village's pub, popular for its cask-conditioned ales and local banter. Upstairs there's simple bunkhouse accommodation in nine rooms, sleeping two or four people; there's no sharing, each party gets its own private room. It's well suited to mountain bikers, with a drying room and secure bike storage.

Penmachno Hall   B&B ££
(☑01690-760140; www.penmachnohall.co.uk; s £75, d £90-95; P⊛) Just past the village on the way to Tŷ Mawr, this ivy-draped 1860s stone house has three vibrant colour-coded guest rooms and a separate coach-house cottage for longer stays. 'Yellow' has a sleigh bed but 'Orange' has the best views; they both have claw-foot tubs. Meals are available on request.

ℹ Getting There & Away
➡ Penmachno is 5 miles south of Betws-y-Coed; take the A5 and then turn right onto the B4406.
➡ From Monday to Saturday, bus 64 heads to/from Betws-y-Coed (10 minutes).

Betws-y-Coed
POP 564

If you're looking for a base with an alpine feel from which to explore Snowdonia National Park, the bustling little stone village of Betws-y-Coed *(bet-*us-ee-*koyd)* stands out as a natural option. It boasts a postcard-perfect setting above an inky river, engulfed in the verdant leafiness of the Gwydyr Forest and near the junction of three river valleys: the Llugwy, the Conwy and the Lledr.

The town has been Wales' most popular inland resort since Victorian times when a group of countryside painters founded an artistic community to record the diversity of the landscape. The arrival of the railway in 1868 cemented its popularity, and today

Betws-y-Coed is as busy with families and coach parties as it is with walkers.

One of the joys of Betws is wandering along its riverbanks and criss-crossing over its historic bridges. The main road crosses the Conwy at the 32m-wide **Waterloo Bridge**. Known locally as the 'iron bridge', it bears a large inscription celebrating its construction in the year the battle was fought (1815). Behind the information centre a pleasant path leads around the tongue of land framed by the convergence of the Rivers Conwy and Llugwy, and back past St Michael's Church. Nearby, **Sapper's Bridge** is a white suspension footbridge (1930), which crosses the Conwy and leads through the fields up to the A470.

At the other end of the village, the 15th-century stone **Pont-y-Pair** (Bridge of the Cauldron) crosses a set of rapids on the Llugwy. A riverside path leads to the **Miners' Bridge**, about a mile downstream, so called as this was the route miners took on their way to work in nearby lead mines. This was the oldest crossing of the Llugwy, but the original bridge is long gone.

⊙ Sights

★**Gwydyr Forest**   FOREST
The 28-sq-mile Gwydyr Forest, planted since the 1920s with oak, beech and larch, encircles Betws-y-Coed and is scattered with the remnants of lead and zinc mine workings. It's ideal for a day's walking, though it gets very muddy in wet weather. *Walks Around Betws-y-Coyd* (£5), available from the National Park Information Centre, details several circular forest walks.

The northern section of the park is home to the Marin Trail, a challenging 15.5-mile mountain-biking loop, starting immediately southwest of Llanrwst, 3.5 miles north of Betws. For more on mountain biking and horse riding in the southern part of the park, see Penmachno.

Swallow Falls   WATERFALL
(adult/child £1.50/50p) Betws-y-Coed's main natural tourist trap is 2 miles west of town alongside the A5. It's a beautiful spot, with the torrent weaving through the rocks into a green pool below. Outside of seasonal opening hours, bring a £1 coin for the turnstile.

Ugly House   HISTORIC BUILDING
(Tŷ Hyll; www.theuglyhouse.co.uk; ⊘10.30am-5pm Easter-Oct, 10.30am-4pm Fri-Mon Nov-Easter) The Ugly House isn't actually ugly at all. This un-

Betws-y-Coed

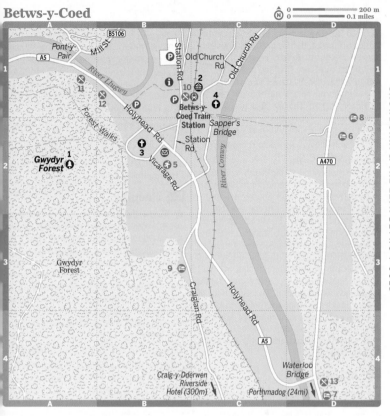

usual cottage is constructed from huge boulders and is home to a characterful tearoom and, upstairs, the Honeybee Room, with displays devoted to the beleaguered insect. Visitors can wander through the grounds and gardens, even when the house is closed.

The origins of the house are steeped in folklore. One yarn suggests it was built in 1475 by two local bandits as their hideout; according to another, there was a Welsh law that allowed any man who built on common land after sunset and had smoke coming out of the chimney by daybreak to stake a claim for the freehold as far as he could throw an axe around the property.

The Snowdonia Society, a charity working to protect and enhance Snowdonia's heritage and wildlife, rescued the property from dereliction and turned it into its headquarters in 1988 following painstaking renovations by a team of dedicated volunteers. It's located half a mile past Swallow Falls on the A5.

Conwy Valley Railway Museum
MUSEUM

(☑ 01690-710568; www.conwyrailwaymuseum.co.uk; Old Church Rd; adult/child £1.50/80p; ☺ 10am-5pm) If you're the sort that's fascinated by dioramas and model train sets, this tiny museum is for you. In which case the model shop you have to pass through in order to enter might pose an unfair temptation. The big attraction for kids is the miniature steam-train ride (the 1-mile round trip costs £1.50) and there's a cafe in a full-sized carriage.

St Michael's Church
CHURCH

(www.stmichaelsbyc.org.uk; Old Church Rd; ☺ 10am-5pm Sun Easter-Sep) The name Betws is thought to be derived from 'bead house', meaning a place of prayer (*y coed* – in the woods). It's likely that 14th-century St Michael's Church, the town's oldest building, stands on the site of that early sanctuary. In 1873 it was replaced as the parish church by the much larger **St Mary's Church** (Holyhead Rd), but it's still used on St Michael's Day (29 September) and for the occasional funeral. The main item of interest inside is a stone effigy of Gruffydd ap Dafydd Goch, the grandnephew of Llywelyn ap Gruffydd, the last native Prince of Wales. If the church is locked, ask for the key at the Railway Museum.

🏃 Activities

The Rivers Conwy and Llugwy are rich with salmon in autumn. Outdoor shops are strung out along Holyhead Rd, selling equipment and specialist references for walkers, climbers and cyclists.

Tree Top Adventures
EXTREME SPORTS

(☑ 01690-710914; www.ttadventure.co.uk; A470; ☺ 9am-4pm) Operates a high-ropes course (adult/child £25/20), a junior trail for four- to eight-year-olds (£12), a 25m-high giant swing (£20) and the 31m-high 'powerfan plummet' parachute simulator (£20). It also offers kayaking, canoeing, rafting, climbing, abseiling, coasteering, gorge-scrambling, orienteering, skiing, tobogganing and mine explorations.

Beics Betws
BICYCLE RENTAL

(☑ 01690-710766; www.bikewales.co.uk; Vicarage Rd; ☺ 9am-5pm Mar-Sep, call ahead at other times) Advises on local cycling trails, sells Marin Trail maps (£1.50), performs repairs and hires mountain bikes (including helmet and tool bag) from £28 per day.

Tours

Go Below Underground Adventures
ADVENTURE TOUR

(☑ 01690-710108; www.go-below.co.uk; adult/child from £49/39) Head into the depths of an old slate mine and try your hand zip-lining across lakes and abseiling down shafts. It's based on the A5 south of Betws at the turn-off to Penmachno.

Snowdonia Safaris
TOUR

(☑ 01690-710910; www.snowdoniasafaris.co.uk; half-day from £70; ☺ Apr-Nov) Offers personalised 4WD tours to 'hidden gems' within a 6-mile radius of Betws.

🛏 Sleeping

★ Coed-y-Celyn Hall
APARTMENT £

(☑ 07821 099595; www.snowdonia-self-catering. co.uk; A470, Coed-y-Celyn; apt from £55; P 🛜) Built in the 1850s for a mining magnate, this grand pile was auctioned off in the 1950s and half of it has been converted into apartments. They're all different, but they're all huge – and terrifically good value. We particularly love Apartment 4 for its moulded ceilings, grand windows and views over the front lawns.

Vagabond
HOSTEL £

(☑ 01690-710850; www.thevagabond.co.uk; Craiglan Rd; dm from £18; P 🛜 🍽) Sitting on the slopes below a forested crag, the Vagabond is Betws' best hostel – and the only one within the town itself. It's a simple set-up, with freshly decorated dorm rooms, shared bathrooms, and an appealing bar, kitchen and common room downstairs. The £23 weekend rate includes a cooked breakfast.

Betws-y-Coed YHA
HOSTEL, CAMPGROUND £

(☑ 01690-710796; www.swallowfallshotel.co.uk; Holyhead Rd, Swallow Falls; dm/tw £17/40, site per adult/child £7/3; P 🛜 🍽) Part of the Swallow Falls Complex – a bustling traveller hub that includes a hotel, tavern, fudge shop and a campground – this no-frills hostel occupies an unattractive building plonked in the middle of the car park. We prefer the terraced camping area at the rear.

Tyn-y-Fron
B&B ££

(☑ 01690-710449; www.snowdoniabedandbreakfast.co.uk; Lon Muriau, off A470; s £55-65, d £70-100; P 🛜) 🌱 The best of a clump of B&Bs over the fields from the town on the Llanrwst road, this gracious old stone house has five guest rooms, all of which have been given a plush, modern makeover. The friendly, rugby-mad owners serve an excellent breakfast, including award-winning sausages and bacon from the local butcher.

Bod Gwynedd
B&B **££**

(☑01690-710717; www.bodgwynedd.com; Holyhead Rd; s/d from £55/70; P☎) On the western edge of town, this friendly B&B offers tastefully furnished bedrooms in an 1895 stone house. The friendly owners keep everything spick-and-span and have plenty of local knowledge to impart.

Maes-y-Garth
B&B **££**

(☑01690-710441; www.maes-y-garth.co.uk; Lon Muriau, off A470; r £60-85; P☎) Just across the river and a field from the township, this newly built home has earned itself a legion of fans. Inside you'll find a warm welcome and three quietly stylish guest rooms with gorgeous views; perhaps the nicest is Room 4, which has its own balcony.

Afon Gwyn
B&B **££**

(☑01690-710442; www.guest-house-betws-y-coed.com; A470, Coed-y-Celyn; r £80-118; P☎) Down in the valley, this old stone house has been skilfully converted into a grand boutique guesthouse. The decor is faultlessly tasteful, with hushed tones, white-painted wood panelling, glittering chandeliers, and bathrooms bedecked in Italian tiles and marble. While all the rooms are spacious, the Alice Suite is massive.

Tŷ Gwyn Hotel
HISTORIC HOTEL **££**

(☑01690-710383; www.tygwynhotel.co.uk; A5; r £56-130; P☎) This atmospheric ex–coaching house has been welcoming guests since 1636, its venerable age borne out by misshapen rooms, low ceilings and exposed beams. Predictably, not all rooms have en suites, but all are attractively decorated; one has a four-poster.

Craig-y-Dderwen Riverside Hotel
HOTEL **££**

(☑01690-710293; www.snowdoniahotel.com; Holyhead Rd; s/d from £105/120; P@☎) There's a slightly frumpy feel to this large fauxTudor hotel, yet all the rooms have been freshened up and the setting is idyllic, right by the river near the Waterloo Bridge. Don't be surprised if your standard room is massive or has a four-poster bed; premium prices are reserved for river-view rooms.

Eating

Alpine Coffee Shop
CAFE **£**

(☑01690-710747; www.alpinecoffeeshop.com; Station Rd; mains £6-9; ☺8.30am-5.30pm; P☎) Stuffed monkeys hang from the counter, chimps grin from photos and there's a gorilla statue outside: this cosy cafe has not quite gone ape, but it has gone palm oilfree – meaning you can tuck into your salad, rarebit or wrap, safe in the knowledge that no orangutan has been harmed in the making of it. There's a gargantuan selection of teas available.

Bistro Betws-y-Coed
WELSH **££**

(☑01690-710328; www.bistrobetws-y-coed.com; Holyhead Rd; lunch £5-9, dinner £12-20; ☺noon-3pm & 6.30-9.30pm Wed-Sun Easter-May, daily Jun-Sep, 6-9pm Wed-Sun Oct-Easter) This cottage style eatery's statement of intent is 'modern and traditional Welsh', and the menu features some interesting adaptations of Welsh recipes from the 18th and 19th centuries. It gets absolutely packed in summer; book ahead.

Tŷ Gwyn Hotel
INTERNATIONAL **££**

(☑01690-710383; www.tygwynhotel.co.uk; A5; mains £8-18; ☺noon-3pm & 6-10pm; ☎) This 400-year-old coaching inn oozes character from every one of its numerous exposed beams. The menu is full of intriguing modern takes on age-old local ingredients (wood pigeon, slow-braised goat with juniper, guinea fowl, lamb wrapped in Carmarthen ham). In the midst all this meatiness, the separate vegetarian menu doesn't disappoint. Book ahead.

Plas Derwen
INTERNATIONAL **££**

(☑01690-710388; www.plasderwen.com; Holyhead Rd; lunch £6-8, dinner £9-11; ☺noon-8pm) A few tables overlook the main street for an al fresco coffee and cake. The mains meander from Thailand to Morocco but linger mainly in Wales; it's a good fallback for when the other places are full.

Information

National Park Information Centre (☑01690-710426; www.eryri-npa.gov.uk; Royal Oak Stables; ☺9.30am-4.30pm) Sells books, maps and local craft, and is a good source of information about walking trails and mountain conditions.

❶ Getting There & Around

➜ Betws-y-Coed is on the Conwy Valley Line, with six daily trains (none on Sunday) to Llandudno (£5.90, 48 minutes) and Blaenau Ffestiniog (£4.80, 27 minutes).

➜ Snowdown Sherpa bus services head to Swallow Falls (route S2/S3; five minutes), Capel Curig (S2/S3/S6; 10 minutes), Pen-y-Pass (S2/S3; 20 minutes), Llanberis (S2/S3; 45 minutes) and Bangor (S6; 50 minutes); all trips are £1.

➜ Other buses head to Llandudno (X1/X6/19; one hour), Conwy (19; one hour), Blaenau Ffestiniog (X1; 20 minutes), Bala (X6; 1¼ hours) and Dolgellau (X1; 1¼ hours).

Capel Curig

POP 206

Tiny Capel Curig, 5 miles west of Betws-y-Coed, is one of Snowdonia's oldest hill stations, and has long been a magnet for walkers, climbers and other outdoor junkies. It's a heady setting, ringed by looming mountains. A popular track heads south from Plas y Brenin to the summit of Moel Siabod (872m). Capel Curig village spreads out along the A5 but the main clump of activity is at the intersection of the A4086.

🏃 Activities

Plas y Brenin National Mountain Sport Centre   OUTDOORS
(☑ 01690-720214; www.pyb.co.uk; A4086) At the western edge of the village, this multi-activity centre has excellent facilities and a huge array of residential, year-round courses, ranging from basic rock climbing to summer and winter mountaineering, and professional development and teaching qualifications. Kayaking and canoeing courses are also offered. Taster days operate throughout the school holidays with an introduction to two activities for £35; advance bookings are required.

🛏 Sleeping & Eating

★**Plas Curig**   HOSTEL £
(☑ 01690-720225;   www.snowdoniahostel.co.uk; A5; dm/r from £23/50; ⓟ🛜🐾) You don't find too many hostels that have paid as much attention to the soft furnishings and decor as this one, but Plas Curig is exceptional in many ways. Most of the built-in bunks have curtains (a simple but effective concession to privacy) and there's a large well-equipped kitchen.

Bryn Tyrch Inn   HOTEL ££
(☑ 01690-720223; www.bryntyrchinn.co.uk; A5; s/d from £60/90; ⓟ🛜) Downstairs there's a restaurant and bar with a roaring fire – Capel Curig's liveliest spot after dark (mains £15 to £18). Upstairs, the rooms have all been prettied up, with feature wallpaper, exposed stonework and modern bathrooms.

❶ Getting There & Away

Snowdown Sherpa buses S2 and S3 head to/from Betws-y-Coed (10 minutes), Pen-y-Pass (15 minutes) and Llanberis (35 minutes); all trips are £1.

Llanberis

POP 2030

While not the most instantly attractive town in the area, Llanberis is a mecca for walkers and climbers, attracting a steady flow of rugged, polar-fleece wearers year-round but especially in July and August when accommodation is at a premium. It's actually positioned just outside the national park but functions as a hub, partly because the Snowdon Mountain Railway leaves from here.

The town was originally built to house workers from the Dinorwig slate quarry; the massive waste tips are hard to miss. While tourism is the cornerstone of Llanberis life these days, the town proudly wears its industrial heritage on its sleeve. Dinorwig, which once boasted the largest artificial cavern in the world, has now become part of Europe's biggest pumped-storage power sta-

---

OFF THE BEATEN TRACK

LLYN OGWEN & LLYN IDWAL

Despite the A5 being the main road to Anglesey, the section of the national park west of Capel Curig is often overlooked. It's a gorgeous drive, with the slate-hued shore of Llyn Ogwen on one side and the Glyderau mountains on the other. You couldn't ask for a more beautiful setting for the **Idwal Cottage YHA** (☑ 0845 371 9744; www.yha.org.uk; Nant Ffrancon; dm/s/d £20/26/40; ☺ daily Mar-Oct, Fri & Sat Nov, Dec & Feb), near the western end of the lake. From here a track leads up to Cwm Idwal, an amphitheatre-shaped hanging valley sheltering another lake, Llyn Idwal.

tion. Some of the old quarry workshops have been reincarnated as a museum of the slate industry, and the narrow-gauge railway that once hauled slate to the coast now transports excited toddlers along Llyn Padarn.

◎ Sights

★ National Slate Museum
MUSEUM
(www.museumwales.ac.uk/en/slate; ⊙10am-5pm Easter-Oct, to 4pm Sun-Fri Nov-Easter) FREE Even if you're not all that fussed by industrial museums, this one's well worth checking out. At Llanberis much of the slate was carved out of the open mountainside – leaving behind a jagged, sculptural cliff-face that's fascinating if not quite beautiful. The museum occupies the Victorian workshops beside Llyn Padarn. It features video clips, a huge working water wheel, workers' cottages (each furnished in a progression from 1861 until 1969, when the quarries closed) and demonstrations on elements of the tile-making process.

The turn-off is along the A4086 between the Electric Mountain exhibition centre and the Snowdon Mountain Railway station.

Electric Mountain
INTERPRETATION CENTRE
(☑01286-870636; www.electricmountain.co.uk; tour adult/child £7.75/3.95; ⊙10am-4.30pm) More than just Dinorwig Power Station's public interface, Electric Mountain is a tourist hub incorporating a gallery, cafe, children's playground, souvenir shop and Llanberis' tourist office. It also has interactive exhibits on hydropower and it's the starting point for an interesting guided tour into the power station's guts, under the mountain.

The Dinorwig pumped-storage power station is the largest scheme of its kind in Europe. Located deep below Elidir mountain, its construction required 1 million tonnes of concrete, 200,000 tonnes of cement and 4500 tonnes of steel. The power station uses surplus energy to pump water from Llyn Peris up to Marchlyn Reservoir. When half the population switches on their kettles for tea during a TV ad break, the water is released to fall through underground turbines. Dinorwig's reversible turbine pumps are capable of reaching maximum generation in less than 16 seconds.

The centre is by the lakeside on the A4086, near the south end of High St. Tours run daily from Easter to October and more sporadically in the low season; call ahead for times.

Dolbadarn Castle
CASTLE
(⊙10am-4pm) FREE Wales is so spoilt with castles that this one gets little attention. Built before 1230 by the Princes of Gwynedd, the keep rises like a perfect chessboard rook from a green hilltop between the two lakes, Llyn Padarn and Llyn Peris. It's a brief stroll from town, rewarded by wonderful views of the lakes, quarries and Snowdon itself.

☆ Activities

Llanberis Lake Railway
HERITAGE RAILWAY
(☑01286-870549; www.lake-railway.co.uk; adult/child £7.50/4.50; ⊙Easter-Oct) If you need something to placate the kids on days that the Snowdonia Mountain Railway isn't operating, this little steam train might be just the ticket. It departs on a 5-mile return jaunt along the route used from 1843 to 1961 to haul slate to the port on the Menai Strait. The tame but scenic one-hour return trip heads alongside Llyn Padarn, past the National Slate Museum and through Padarn Country Park to the terminus at Penllyn.

The starting point is across the A4086 from the Snowdon Mountain Railway station.

Snowdon Star
CRUISE
(☑07974-716418; www.snowdonstar.co.uk; Padarn Country Park jetty; adult/child £6/4; ⊙May-Oct) Float beneath the carved cliffs on a 45-minute Llyn Padarn cruise. The boat departs from the jetty near the National Slate Museum car park on the hour from noon until 4pm, with additional sailings at 11am and 5pm in July and August; call ahead to confirm. The lake is home to the most southerly population of Arctic char, a type of fish that's survived in the depths since the last ice age.

Vivian Diving Centre
DIVING
(☑01286-870889; www.vivianwatersports.com; Padarn Country Park; per day £6; ⊙10am-4pm Mon-Fri, 9am-5.30pm Sat & Sun) Tucked underneath the cliffs near the slate museum, this 18m-deep water-filled quarry offers diving year-round. Beneath the inky-looking but largely sediment-free waters are two boats, a quarryman's house and plenty of fish.

Ropes & Ladders
ADVENTURE SPORTS
(☑01286-872310; www.ropesandladders.co.uk; Padarn Country Park; adult/child £25/20) Right by the slate museum, this high ropes course is aimed at ages 'eight to infinity', but there's a special low course for four to eight year olds.

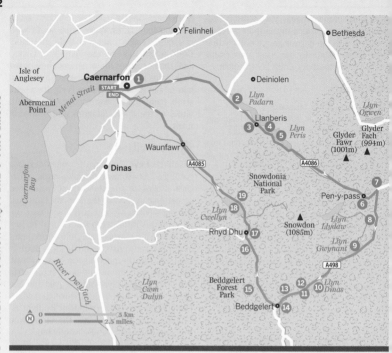

Driving Tour
Circling Snowdon

START CAERNARFON
END CAERNARFON
LENGTH 34.5 MILES, 1¼ HOURS DRIVING

The roads circumnavigating Snowdon make for a memorable drive. You could cruise this loop in about an hour nonstop, but you're better to make a day of it – stopping to enjoy a few of the many sights along the way.

From Caernarfon, the A4086 heads past **1 Segontium Roman Fort** before leaving the houses behind. It eventually reaches **2 Llyn Padarn** and follows the lakeshore to **3 Llanberis**, in the shadow of the carved rockface of the old slateworks. Stop here for food and for the excellent National Slate Museum. As you leave Llanberis, look for **4 Dolbadarn Castle** (p241), perched between the two lakes.

The road then follows the shore of **5 Llyn Peris** and enters Snowdonia National Park proper, making a spectacular ascent along the very edge of Snowdon to **6 Pen-y-Pass**. The road descends to a junction by the

7 Pen-y-Gwryd hotel (p245), the training base for the 1953 Everest conquerors. Turn right onto the A498 for a particularly picturesque stretch following Snowdon's southern slopes. Arguably the best views of the mountain are from the viewpoint at **8 Gueastadanas**. The road then edges past the lakes **9 Llyn Gwynant** and **10 Llyn Dinas** before passing the **11 Sygun Copper Mine** (p247). The hill on the other side of the road is **12 Dinas Emrys** (p247), the legendary home of the red dragon. Look out for **13 Craflwyn Hall** on the right, a little further on.

At **14 Beddgelert** turn right onto the A4085. To the left of the road the **15 Beddgelert Forest** comes into view, followed by the small lake **16 Llyn-y-Gader**. Next up is the village **17 Rhyd Ddu** and then a larger lake, **18 Llyn Cwellyn**, and the **19 Snowdon Ranger YHA** (p245). Shortly afterwards the road leaves the national park and turns its back on the mountain for the return journey to Caernarfon.

A session lasts two hours; call ahead for opening times. The same outfit also offers guided climbs and walks under the name Snowdonia Outdoor.

Boulder Adventures
OUTDOORS

(☑ 01286-870556; www.boulderadventures.co.uk; Bryn Du Mountain Centre, Ty Du Rd; session/full day £40/60) Small groups and families can work with Boulder to devise their own adventure from a list including rock climbing, abseiling, gorge walking, coasteering, orienteering, kayaking, canoeing, raft building, mountain walking, bouldering and canyoning. It also offers hostel-style accommodation within a spacious Victorian house on the slopes above Llanberis.

🛏 Sleeping

Brynteg
HOLIDAY PARK £

(☑ 01286-871374; www.brynteg.co.uk; Llanrug; caravan/lodge from £57/233, minimum 3 nights; P ☎ ☒) Tucked away near a privately owned castle, halfway between Llanberis and Caernarfon, this large complex rents out static caravans (some with central heating and double-glazing) and lodges with hot tubs. Facilities include a swimming pool, climbing wall, adventure playground and a golf course.

Llanberis YHA
HOSTEL £

(☑ 0845 371 9645; www.yha.org.uk; Llwyn Celyn; dm/r from £15/36; P) Originally a quarry manager's house, this no-frills hostel offers great views, a self-catering kitchen and a drying room. It's located on the slopes above the town, signposted from the High St.

★ Beech Bank
B&B ££

(☑ 01286-871085; www.beech-bank.co.uk; 2 High St; r £70; P ☎) First impressions of this double-gabled, wrought iron–trimmed stone house are great, but step inside and it just gets better. A stylish renovation has left beautiful bathrooms and exuberant decor, which matches the gregarious nature of the host well. Highly recommended.

Plas Coch Guest House
HOTEL ££

(☑ 01286-872122; www.plascochsnowdonia.co.uk; High St; s £50-55, d £70-80; P ☎) More like a little hotel than a B&B, this large ivy-draped 1865 house is operated by a friendly couple with lots of local knowledge to impart. Aside from the starkly utilitarian fireproof doors, the rooms are stylishly renovated and very comfortable.

Glyn Afon
B&B ££

(☑ 01286-872528; www.glyn-afon.co.uk; 72 High St; s/d from £40/65; P ☎) Rooms are clean, warm and homey at this midrange guesthouse, and breakfast will set you up well for a day of mountain striding. The owners are happy to help with information on walks and will even lend you a compass or rucksack if you haven't brought one with you.

✖ Eating

★ Gallt-y-Glyn
PIZZERIA £

(www.gallt-y-glyn.co.uk; mains £7-9; ⊘ 6-9pm Wed-Sat Nov-Easter, daily Easter-Oct; 🖩) Sure, it serves pasta, pies and salads too, but almost everyone comes for the pizza-and-pint deal. Simply tick the toppings you want on the paper menu and hand it over at the bar. You'll find Gallt-y-Glyn on the A4086, half a mile towards Caernarfon. It's a bit shabby, slightly chaotic, very family-friendly and utterly brilliant.

Pete's Eats
CAFE £

(☑ 01286-870117; www.petes-eats.co.uk; 40 High St; meals £3-7; ⊘ 9am-6.30pm Mon-Fri, 8am-8pm Sat & Sun; ☎) Pete's Eats is a local institution, a busy, bright cafe where hikers and climbers swap tips over monster portions in a hostel-like environment. There's bunkhouse accommodation upstairs, a huge noticeboard full of travellers' information, a book exchange, a map and guidebook room, and computers for internet access.

Snowdon Honey Farm & Winery
CAFE £

(www.snowdonhoneyfarmandwinery.co.uk; High St; cakes £3-5; ⊘ 10am-4pm) All manner of honey-related goodies are sold here, including a range of mead, graded Roman, Celtic or Medieval, depending on sweetness. There are also homemade fudges, preserves and fruit wine, and if you ask nicely the engaging owner may let you sip before you commit. It also functions as a cafe, serving ice cream and cakes.

★ Peak Restaurant
INTERNATIONAL ££

(Bwyty'r Copa; ☑ 01286-872777; www.peakrestaurant.co.uk; 86 High St; lunch £4-7, dinner £13-17; ⊘ 12.30-2pm & 7-10pm Wed-Fri, 7-10pm Sat) Charming owners and imaginative menus underpin this restaurant's popularity and longevity, and the open kitchen allows you to see the masters at work. Fine local ingredients form the basis of the internationally inspired dishes.

ⓘ Information

Joe Brown (☎01286-870327; 63 High St; ⊗9am-5.30pm) A climbing shop that sells all things outdoors; its noticeboard includes weather forecasts and lots of information and advice for walkers.

Tourist Office (☎01286-870765; www.visit-snowdonia.info; Electric Mountain; ⊗10am-4pm Fri-Tue Easter-Sep)

ⓘ Getting There & Around

➡ Snowdon Sherpa buses stop by Joe Brown's on the High St. S1 heads to Pen-y-Pass (15 minutes), while S2/S3 continues on to Capel Curig (35 minutes) and Betws-y-Coed (45 minutes).

➡ Other buses head to Caernarfon (route 88/89; 23 minutes) and Bangor (41/85/86; 44 minutes).

Snowdon (Yr Wyddfa)

No Snowdonia experience is complete without coming face-to-face with Snowdon (1085m), one of Britain's most awe-inspiring mountains and the highest summit in Wales (it's actually the 61st highest in Britain, with the higher 60 all in Scotland). On a clear day the views stretch to Ireland and the Isle of Man over Snowdon's fine jagged ridges, which drop away in great swoops to sheltered *cwms* (valleys) and deep lakes. Even on a gloomy day you could find yourself above the clouds. Thanks to the Snowdon Mountain Railway it's extremely accessible – the summit and some of the tracks can get frustratingly crowded.

Just below the cairn that marks the summit is **Hafod Eryri**, a striking piece of architecture that opened in 2009 to replace the dilapidated 1930s visitor centre that Prince Charles famously labelled 'the highest slum in Europe'. Clad in granite and curved to blend into the mountain, it's a wonderful building, housing a cafe that serves snacks and light lunches, toilets, and ambient interpretative elements built into the structure itself. A wall of picture windows gazes down towards the west, while a small row faces the cairn. The centre (including the toilets) closes in winter or if the weather's terrible; it's open whenever the train is running.

🏃 Activities

⭐ **Snowdon Trails**   HIKING
Six paths of varying length and difficulty lead to the summit, all taking around six hours return. Just because Snowdon has a train station and a cafe on its summit, doesn't mean you should underestimate it. No route is completely safe, especially in winter. People regularly come unstuck here and many have died over the years, including experienced climbers.

The most straightforward route to the summit is the **Llanberis Path** (9 miles return) running beside the train line. The two paths starting from Pen-y-Pass require the least amount of ascent but are nevertheless tougher walks: the **Miner's Track** (8 miles return) starts off wide and gentle but gets steep beyond Llyn Llydaw; and the more interesting **Pyg Track** (7 miles return) is more rugged still.

Two tracks start from the Caernarfon–Beddgelert road (A4085): the **Snowdon Ranger Path** (8 miles return) is the safest route in winter, while the **Rhyd Ddu Path** (8 miles return) is the least-used route and boasts spectacular views. The most challenging route is the **Watkin Path** (8 miles return), involving an ascent of more than 1000m on its southerly approach from Nantgwynant, and finishing with a scramble across a steep-sided scree-covered slope.

The classic **Snowdon Horseshoe** (7.5 miles, six to seven hours) branches off from the Pyg Track to follow the precipitous ridge of Crib Goch (one of the most dangerous routes on the mountains and only recommended for the very experienced) with a descent over the peak of Y Lliwedd and a final section down the Miner's Track.

For more information about the Snowdon Ranger and Rhyd Ddu paths, refer to our Snowdon Mountain Walk.

⭐ **Snowdon Mountain Railway**   HERITAGE RAILWAY
(☎0844 493 8120; www.snowdonrailway.co.uk; return diesel adult/child £27/18, steam £35/25; ⊗9am-5pm mid-Mar–Oct) If you're not physically able to climb a mountain, short on time or just plain lazy, those industrious, railway obsessed Victorians have gifted you an alternative. Opened in 1896, the Snowdon Mountain Railway is the UK's highest and its only public rack-and-pinion railway. Vintage steam and modern diesel locomotives haul carriages from Llanberis up to Snowdon's very summit in an hour.

Return trips involve a scant half-hour at the top before heading back down again. Single tickets can only be booked for the journey up (adult/child £20/15). Tens of thousands of people take the train to the summit each season: make sure you book well in advance or you may miss out. The frequency of departures is dependent on customer demand. Departures are weather dependent, and from March to May the trains can only head as far Clogwyn Station (adult/child £18/14) – an altitude of 779m.

🛌 Sleeping & Eating

Bryn Gwynant YHA HOSTEL £
(☎ 0845 371 9108; www.yha.org.uk; Nantgwynant; dm/tw £22/50; ⊙ Mar-Oct; P) Of all of the park's youth hostels, Bryn Gwynant has the most impressive building and the most idyllic setting, occupying a grand Victorian mansion facing over a lake to Snowdon – although it's certainly not flash inside. It's located 4 miles east of Beddgelert, near the start of the Watkin Path.

Pen-y-Pass YHA HOSTEL £
(☎ 0845 371 9534; www.yha.org.uk; dm £20, r with/without bathroom £54/52; ⊙ Mar-Dec) Superbly situated on the slopes of Snowdon, 5.5 miles up the A4086 from Llanberis, this hostel has two of the trails literally on its doorstep. The newer wing has the best rooms of any of the park's YHAs; some even have en suites.

Snowdon Ranger YHA HOSTEL £
(☎ 0845 371 9659; www.yha.org.uk; dm/q £18/72; P) On the A4085, 5 miles north of Beddgelert at the trailhead for the Snowdon Ranger Path, this former inn has its own adjoining lakeside beach. Accommodation is basic.

Pen-y-Gwryd HOTEL ££
(☎ 01286-870211; www.pyg.co.uk; Nant Gwynant; r with/without bathroom £100/84; P 🐾) Eccentric but full of atmosphere, Pen-y-Gwryd was used as a training base by the 1953 Everest team, and memorabilia from their stay includes signatures on the restaurant ceiling. TV, wi-fi and mobile phone signals don't penetrate here. Instead, there's a comfy games room, sauna and a lake for bathing. You'll find the hotel below Pen-y-Pass, at the junction of the A498 and A4086.

ℹ️ Getting There & Away

➡ It's worth considering public transport, car parks can fill up quickly, and Pen-y-Pass costs £10 per day.
➡ Before you decide which route you'll take to the summit, study the bus and train timetables. If you're based in Llanberis, you'll find it easiest to get to and from the Llanberis, Pyg and Miner's paths. The Snowdon Ranger and Rhyd

Ddu paths are better connected to Beddgelert and Caernarfon.
➡ The Welsh Highland Railway stops at the trailhead of the Rhyd Ddu Path, and there is a request stop (Snowdon Ranger Halt) where you can alight for the Snowdon Ranger Path.
➡ Snowdon Sherpa buses (£1 on buses S1, S2, S6; adult/child day ticket £4/2) stop at all of the trailheads.
➡ Another option is to take the Snowdon Mountain Railway to the top and walk back down. It's more difficult to do this the other way around as the train will only take on new passengers at the top if there is space.

> ### ℹ️ MOUNTAIN SAFETY
>
> In mountainous areas you need to be prepared to deal with hostile conditions at any time of the year. The sudden appearance of low cloud and mist is common, even on days that start out clear and sunny. Check the weather forecast before setting out, and make sure you're well prepared with warm and waterproof clothing, sturdy footwear, food and drink, the appropriate scale map for the area and a compass (and make sure you know how to use it).
>
> Even some walks described as easy may follow paths that go near very steep slopes and over loose scree. In icy conditions they can be extremely dangerous. In winter you'll need to take crampons, an ice axe, spare clothing, extra food and drink, and a torch, as it gets dark early.
>
> The Met Office keeps the weather conditions constantly updated on its website (www.metoffice.gov.uk/loutdoor/mountainsafety).

Beddgelert

POP 455

Charming little Beddgelert is a conservation village of rough stone buildings overlooking the trickling River Glaslyn with its ivy-covered bridge. Flowers festoon the village in spring and the surrounding hills are covered in a purple blaze of heather in summer, reminiscent of a Scottish glen. Scenes from Mark Robson's 1958 film, *The Inn of the Sixth Happiness,* set in China and starring Ingrid Bergman, were shot here.

The name, meaning 'Gelert's Grave', is said to refer to a shaggy dog tale concerning

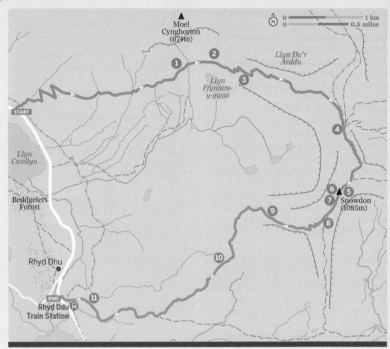

Mountain Walk
Up Snowdon Ranger, Down Rhyd Ddu

START SNOWDON RANGER YHA
END RHYD DDU TRAIN STATION
LENGTH 8 MILES, SIX HOURS

After agonising over which Snowdon route to highlight, we settled on this one for three main reasons. Firstly, it's reasonably straightforward and doesn't involve any difficult scrambles (that said, in snowy and icy conditions, the descent on the Rhyd Ddu Path should only be undertaken by experienced mountaineers equipped with crampons and ice picks; everyone else should double back on the Snowdon Ranger Path). Secondly, both trailheads are connected by buses and trains to accommodation in Caernarfon, Beddgelert and Porthmadog. Finally, and perhaps most importantly, this is the quietest route.

The original 'Snowdon Ranger' was an English mountain guide who built an inn on the site of the current YHA in the early 1800s, and led guests to the summit along this track. The path climbs gently along the lower slopes of ❶ **Moel Cynghorion** to ❷ **Bwlch Cwm Brwynog**, before it steepens and heads above ❸ **Clogwyn Du'r Arddu**. Eventually it draws parallel with the Snowdon Mountain Railway. The path crosses the tracks at a ❹ **standing stone**, turns right, and merges with the Llanberis Path for the final approach to the ❺ **summit**.

When you're ready to descend, pick up the Rhyd Ddu Path below the ❻ **Hafod Eryri** visitor centre. After 200m a ❼ **standing stone** marks the point where the Watkin Path veers off; continue straight ahead. The next section, along ❽ **Bwlch Main** (meaning 'Slender Path') is a narrow track with steep slopes on either side: if there's ice and snow, this is the dangerous bit. Near the end of this stretch the path splits into two; keep on the right-hand track. From here the path broadens as it zigzags down and then edges along ❾ **Llechog ridge**. It starts to flatten out after it passes the ❿ **ruins** of an old refreshment hut. The final stretch continues alongside the abandoned ⓫ **Ffridd Slate Quarry** before terminating near the Rhyd Ddu train station.

13th-century Llywelyn the Great, Prince of Gwynedd. Believing that his dog Gelert had savaged his baby son, Llywelyn slaughtered the dog, only to discover that Gelert had fought off the wolf that had attacked the baby. More likely, the name Beddgelert is derived from a 5th-century Irish preacher, Celert, who is believed to have founded a church here. Regardless, the 'grave' of Gelert the dog is a popular attraction, reached by a pretty riverside trail. It's believed to have been constructed by an unscrupulous 18th-century hotelier in an attempt to boost business.

◉ Sights & Activities

Sygun Copper Mine   MINE
(www.syguncoppermine.co.uk; adult/child £8.95/6.95; ⊙9.30am-5pm Mar-Oct) This mine dates from Roman times, although extraction was stepped up in the 19th century. Abandoned in 1903, it has since been converted into a museum, with a short self-guided underground tour containing dioramas that evoke the life of Victorian miners. You can also try your hand at metal detecting (£2.50) or panning for gold (£2). It's located a mile northeast of Beddgelert, along the A498.

Craflwyn & Dinas Emrys   WALKING
(NT; ☑01766-510120; www.craflwyn.org) A mile northeast of Beddgelert, near the southern end of Llyn Dinas, National Trust–owned Craflwyn Farm is the starting point for several short walks, including a path to one of the most signficant yet largely unheralded sites in Welsh mythology.

According to legend, Dinas Emrys was the hill where King Vortigern – son-in-law of Britain's last Roman ruler, Magnus Maximus – tried to build a castle. It kept collapsing until the young wizard Merlin (Myrddin Emrys) liberated two dragons in a cavern under the hill, a white one representing the Saxons (the Germanic ancestors of the English) and a red one representing the Britons, and prophesied that they'd fight until the red dragon was triumphant. The two dragons have been at each other's throats ever since.

It takes about half an hour to walk through fields, alongside a stream, past a waterfall and through woods to the summit. At the top there are the remains of ancient fortifications and wonderful views over the lake.

The National Trust leases out pretty yellow Craflwyn Hall, near the car park, where there are B&B rooms and a cafe.

Beddgelert Forest   MOUNTAIN BIKING
Within this forestry commission block (2 miles northwest of Beddgelert along the A4805) is a popular campground and two mountain-bike trails: the 6-mile Hir Trail and the easier 2.5-mile Byr Trail.

Beics Beddgelert   BICYCLE RENTAL
(☑01766-890434; www.beddgelertbikes.co.uk; per 2/4/8hr £15/21/28) Rents out mountain bikes, tandems and child seats; you'll find this outfit by the train station.

🛏 Sleeping & Eating

Beddgelert Campsite   CAMPGROUND £
(☑01766-890288; www.campingintheforest.co.uk/wales/beddgelert-campsite; sites £22-31; P ⊠) 🚲 Well equipped and well situated within Beddgelert Forest.

Sygun Fawr Country House   HOTEL ££
(☑01766-890258; www.sygunfawr.co.uk; s £41-74, d £82-107; P �ᐣ) A warm welcome awaits at this sturdy stone house, tucked away at the end of an exceptionally narrow lane. Bits have been grafted on to the 1660s core over the centuries (including a conservatory), so each of the 12 comfortable bedrooms is quite different; some have spectacular mountain views. It's well signposted from the A498, immediately northeast of the village.

Plas Tan y Graig   B&B ££
(☑01766-890310; www.plas-tanygraig.co.uk; Smith St; s £54-78, d £88; ⊙mid-Feb–Oct; ᐣ) This bright, friendly place is the best B&B in the heart of the village. It has seven uncluttered, recently refurbished rooms (each has its own bathroom, but only five are en suite), and a lounge full of maps and books.

Tanronnen Inn   HOTEL, PUB ££
(☑01766-890347; www.tanronnen.co.uk; s/d £55/100; P ᐣ) Right at the centre of things, this attractive stone coaching inn offers a hearty pub menu (mains £9 to £12), ranging from sausages and chips to chicken tikka masala. Upstairs, busy carpets lead to rooms that are comfortable, if a little dated.

Glaslyn Ices & Cafe Glandwr   ICE CREAM £
(www.glaslynices.co.uk; mains £4-10; ⊙10am-5pm Sun-Fri, 9.30am-8.30pm Sat Easter-Oct) In summer this excellent ice-cream parlour is the busiest place in the village. It serves a huge

array of homemade flavours and is attached to a family restaurant offering simple meals, especially pizza.

Lyn's Cafe
CAFE £

(Church St; lunch £4-9, dinner £11; ⊘10am-5pm Feb-Oct, plus dinner high season; 🖼) A family-friendly all-rounder (with a separate children's menu) serving big breakfasts, light lunches, Sunday roasts and cooked dinners in summer. The riverside seats are a prime tea-supping spot.

Beddgelert Bistro & Antiques
CAFE ££

(📞01766-890543; www.beddgelert-bistro.co.uk; Smith St; lunch £4-9, dinner £12-15; ⊘9am-5pm & 6.30-9pm; 🛜📶) You don't see many bistros that double as antique stores, and you certainly don't see many bistros that serve fondue. This eccentric place does both. By day it's more like a tearoom.

ⓘ Information

Tourist Office & National Park Information Centre (📞01766-890615; www.eryri-npa.gov.uk; Canolfan Hebog; ⊘9.30am-5.30pm daily Easter-Oct, to 4.30pm Fri-Sun Nov-Easter; 📶)

ⓘ Getting There & Away

➡ Snowdon Sherpa bus S4 heads to/from Caernarfon (30 minutes), Snowdon Ranger (11 minutes), Rhyd Ddu (nine minutes) and Pen-y-Pass (17 minutes).

➡ Bus S97 heads to Porthmadog (25 minutes), Tremadog (20 minutes) and Pen-y-Pass (17 minutes).

➡ Beddgelert is a stop on the historic Welsh Highland Railway, which runs between Caernarfon (return £26, 1½ hours) and Porthmadog (£18.50, 40 minutes) from Easter to October, and stops at the Rhyd Ddu and Snowdon Ranger trailheads.

LLŶN PENINSULA

Jutting out into the Irish Sea from the mountains of Snowdonia, the Llŷn (pronounced 'khleen' and sometimes spelt 'Lleyn') is a green finger of land, some 25 miles long and averaging 8 miles in width. It's a peaceful and largely undeveloped region with isolated walking and cycling routes, good beaches, a scattering of small fishing villages and 70 miles of wildlife-rich coastline (much of it in the hands of the National Trust, and almost 80% of it designated an Area of Outstanding Natural Beau-

ty). Over the centuries the heaviest footfalls have been those of pilgrims on their way to Bardsey Island.

Welsh is the language of everyday life here. Indeed, this is about as Welsh as it gets. The Llŷn Peninsula and Anglesey were the last stops on the Roman and Norman itineraries, and both have maintained a separate identity, the Llŷn especially so. Isolated physically and culturally, it's been an incubator of Welsh activism. It was the birthplace of David Lloyd George, the first Welsh prime minister of the UK, and of Plaid Cymru (the Party of Wales), which was founded in Pwllheli in 1925 and now holds 18% of the seats in the Welsh Assembly.

Porthmadog
POP 4190

Despite a few rough edges, busy little Porthmadog (port-*mad*-uk) has an attractive estuarine setting and a conspicuously friendly, mainly Welsh-speaking populace. It straddles both the Llŷn Peninsula and Snowdonia National Park, and has the fantastical village of Portmeirion at its doorstep. Throw in abundant transport connections, and you've got a handy place to base yourself for a couple of days.

Both Porthmadog and the neighbouring village of Tremadog (the latter now virtually a suburb of the former) were founded by and named after reforming landowner William Alexander Madocks. In the early 19th century he laid down the mile-long Cob causeway, drained the 400 hectares of wetlands that lay behind it, and created a brand-new harbour. After his death, the Cob became the route for the Ffestiniog Railway: at its 1873 peak, it transported over 116,000 tonnes of slate from the mines of Blaenau Ffestiniog to the harbour. In 1888 TE Lawrence (Lawrence of Arabia) was born in Tremadog, although the Lawrence family moved to Oxford 12 years later; look for his family home (marked with a plaque) near the church.

Today Porthmadog is a mecca for railway buffs. There are 'little trains' all over Wales, a legacy of Victorian industry, but Porthmadog is triply blessed. It forms the southern terminus for two of Wales' finest narrow-gauge train journeys, and has a third steam-train line connected to a rail heritage centre.

Mullet abound in the shallow Traeth Bach estuary, which in turn attract ospreys. Keep an eye out for these large birds of prey as you walk around the cliffs of Borth-y-Gest and Porthmeirion.

⊙ Sights & Activities

Portmeirion Village ARCHITECTURE
(www.portmeirion-village.com; adult/child £10/6; ⊙9.30am-7.30pm; 🅿) Set on its own tranquil peninsula reaching into the estuary, Portmeirion Village is an oddball, gingerbread collection of colourful buildings with a heavy Italian influence, masterminded by the Welsh architect Sir Clough Williams-Ellis. Starting in 1925, Clough collected bits and pieces from disintegrating stately mansions and set them alongside his own creations to create this weird and wonderful seaside utopia. Fifty years later, and at the ripe old age of 90, Sir Clough deemed the village to be complete. Today the buildings are all heritage-listed and the site is a conservation area.

It's really more like a stage set than an actual village and, indeed, it formed the ideally surreal set for cult TV series, *The Prisoner,* which was filmed here from 1966 to 1967. It still draws fans of the show in droves, with rival Prisoner conventions held annually in March and April. The giant plaster of Paris Buddha, just off the piazza, also featured in the 1958 film, *The Inn of the Sixth Happiness,* starring Ingrid Bergman.

A documentary on Williams-Ellis and Portmeirion screens on the hour in a building just above the central piazza. Sir Clough's lifelong concern was with the whimsical and intriguing nature of architecture, his *raison d'être* to demonstrate how a naturally beautiful site could be developed without defiling it. His life's work now stands as a testament to beauty, something he described as 'that strange necessity'. He died in 1978, having campaigned for the environment throughout his life. He was a founding member of the Council for the Protection of Rural Wales in 1928 and served as its president for 20 years.

Most of the kooky cottages and scaled-down mansions scattered about the site are available for holiday lets, while other buildings contain cafes, restaurants and gift shops. Portmeirion pottery (the famously florid tableware designed by Susan, Sir Clough's daughter) is available, even though these days it's made in Stoke-on-Trent (England). A network of walking paths thread

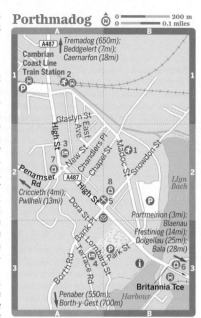

Porthmadog Ⓝ 0 ——— 200 m / 0 ——— 0.1 miles

Porthmadog

⊕ Activities, Courses & Tours
1 Purple Moose B2
2 Welsh Highland Heritage Railway A1

⊝ Sleeping
3 Royal Sportsman Hotel.........................A2
4 Yr Hen Fecws...A3

⊗ Eating
5 Big Rock Cafe B2

⊕ Shopping
6 Cob Records..B3
7 Kerfoots A2
8 Rob Piercy Gallery B2

along the coast and through the private forested peninsula, which includes the ruins of a castle (a real one, not one of Sir Clough's creations). Free guided tours of the village are held most days, and from April to October the 'forest train' tours the woodlands.

Portmeirion is 2 miles east of Porthmadog; public transport isn't great, so if you don't fancy the walk, you're best to catch a taxi. Half-price admission is offered after 3.30pm.

IS AMERICA REALLY NEW WEST WALES?

Porthmadog may be named after William Alexander Madocks, but there's another legendary namesake associated with the area. The story goes that in 1170 Madog ab Owain Gwynedd, a local prince, set off from here and 'discovered' America. The tale was dusted off during Elizabeth I's reign to justify the English crown's claim on the continent over Spain's; America's indigenous occupants weren't canvassed for their opinion. The story gained further traction during Wales' 18th-century Romantic renaissance when it was deployed to give the Welsh a sense of pride in their past.

Madog and his followers were said to have intermarried with Native Americans and formed their own Welsh-speaking tribe. After America's 're-discovery', explorers returned with stories of meeting Welsh-speaking clans in Virginia and Kentucky. In 1796 John Evans, the leader of a party that helped map the Missouri River, sought and failed to find any evidence of them. Given that many small Native American tribes disappeared soon after colonisation, the Madog story still has some traction among hardcore Welsh patriots.

Borth-y-Gest   VILLAGE

The best views over the estuary are from Terrace Rd, which becomes Garth Rd above the harbour. At its end a path heads down to Borth-y-Gest, a pretty horseshoe of candy-coloured houses overlooking a sandy bay. At the other end of the crescent the path continues around the cliffs; if you look carefully, you should be able to spot Harlech Castle in the distance.

★ Ffestiniog & Welsh Highland Railways   HERITAGE RAILWAY

(📞 01766-516024; www.festrail.co.uk) Run by the oldest independent railway company in the world (established 1832), these two wonderful narrow-gauge lines depart from Harbour Station (near the Cob) in pungent puffs of smoke.

The **Ffestiniog Railway** (adult/child return £21/19) is a fantastic, twisting and precipitous narrow-gauge railway that was built between 1832 and 1836 to haul slate down to Porthmadog from the mines at Blaenau Ffestiniog. Horse-drawn wagons were replaced in the 1860s by steam locomotives and the line became a passenger service. Saved after years of neglect, it is one of Wales' most spectacular and beautiful narrow-gauge journeys. Because it links the Cambrian Coast and Conwy Valley main lines, it also serves as a serious public transport link. Nearly all services are steam-hauled. The 13.5-mile, 75-minute journey heads through fern-fringed valleys and tree-lined passes before entering the soot-saturated darkness of the Moelwyn Tunnel. It then hugs the fringe of Tan-y-Grisiau Reservoir and progresses into a landscape of mist-shrouded mountains and slate-grey cottages.

Its sibling, the **Welsh Highland Railway** (adult/child return £34/31), is an amalgamation of several late-19th-century slate railways that runs through equally lovely Snowdonian landscapes for the full 25 miles between Porthmadog and Caernarfon. Walkers can hop off at either Rhyd Ddu (return £23) station or the Snowdon Ranger request stop to follow paths up Snowdon.

Welsh Highland Heritage Railway   HERITAGE RAILWAY

(📞 01766-513402; www.whr.co.uk; High St; adult/child £7.50/3.75; ⊘ Easter-Oct) Unlike the similarly named heritage railways at the other end of town (why must it be so confusing!), this volunteer-run railway doesn't provide any useful transport link. Steam or diesel trains chug less than a mile up the track before heading back via the rail heritage centre and engine sheds at Gelert's Farm. You can swap to a miniature railway here for a short ride through the woods, before boarding the main train again. Tickets are valid all day.

Purple Moose   BREWERY TOUR

(www.purplemoose.co.uk; Madoc St; ⊘ 9am-5pm Mon-Fri) One of approximately 30 microbreweries across Wales, Purple Moose has grown from humble beginnings to an award-winning company supplying the better North Welsh pubs. Tipples include Snowdonia Ale, Madog's Ale, Glaslyn Ale, Dark Side of the Moose and the newest addition, Ysgawen (an Elderflower beer). Ale aficionados can arrange a brewery tour (£5; 1pm to 3pm Tuesday to Thursday), which includes free tastings.

✨ Festivals & Events

Prisoner Convention   FAN CONVENTION
(www.netreach.net/~sixofone/; ☉ Apr) One to either pencil in or to avoid, the annual gathering of fans of the cult TV show converges on Portmeirion in April for a weekend of dress ups and human chess.

Festival No 6   MUSIC
(www.festivalnumber6.com; ☉ Sep) Despite the name, it's not yet another *Prisoner* convention – although it is held in Portmeirion. Started in 2012, this rock and dance music festival with an arts, culture and comedy component has topped many best festival lists. Headliners have included New Order, Manic Street Preachers and James Blake. It's held over a long weekend in September.

🛏 Sleeping & Eating

Penaber   B&B £
(☑ 01766-512041; www.porthmadog.co.uk/penaber; Morfa Bychan Rd; s/d from £45/50; P ☎) Located half a mile from town and a similar distance above Borth-y-Gest (veer right off Borth Rd before it curves down to the bay), this large modern house offers spacious, comfortable and scrupulously clean rooms. It's a real bargain too.

Yr Hen Fecws   B&B ££
(☑ 01766-514625; www.henfecws.com; 16 Lombard St; s/d from £60/75; P ☎) This stylishly restored stone cottage has seven simply decorated en-suite rooms with exposed-slate walls and fireplaces. Breakfast is served within the marigold walls and exposed beams of the cosy cafe downstairs (mains £4 to £10; open 8am to 4pm Monday to Saturday).

Golden Fleece Inn   PUB ££
(☑ 01766-512421; www.goldenfleeceinn.com; Market Sq, Tremadog; s/d from £45/79; ☎) Hop flowers hang from the ceiling of this inviting and friendly old inn, which offers real ales, pub grub, an open fire on cold nights and live acoustic music on Tuesdays. The rooms above the pub are comfortable and atmospheric; however, be prepared for noise until closing. Enquire about quieter rooms in neighbouring buildings.

Royal Sportsman Hotel   HOTEL ££
(☑ 01766-512015; www.royalsportsman.co.uk; 131 High St; s £63-88, d £90-104; P ☎☎) It's not about to win any awards for its decor but this old charmer (constructed in 1862 as a coaching inn) has clean and comfortable rooms, and a staff that's eager to please. 'Courtyard' rooms open onto an enclosed walkway at the rear.

Hotel Portmeirion & Castell Deudraeth   HOTEL, COTTAGE £££
(☑ 01766-770000; www.portmeirion-village.com; Portmeirion; hotel s/d £199/239, castle & village s/d from £159/199; P ☎) You can live the fantasy and stay within the famous fairy-tale village itself in one of 17 whimsical cottages. Down by the water, the over-the-top Hotel Portmeirion (1926) has elegant rooms with quirky wallpaper. Up the drive, storybook Castell Deudraeth is, perversely, a more modern alternative, despite its Victorian provenance. Prices drop considerably in low season.

Big Rock Cafe   CAFE £
(Y Graig Fawr; ☑ 01766-512098; 71 High St; mains £4-6; ☉ 8.30am-5pm Mon-Sat) Although this cool cafe is church-run, you needn't fear any morals being served with your morning mocha. The menu stretches to cooked breakfasts, soups, sandwiches and sweets, and there are plenty of newspapers to peruse.

Y Sgwâr   BISTRO £££
(www.ysgwar-restaurant.co.uk; 12-16 Market Sq; mains £15-25; ☉ noon-2pm & 6-9pm) On the edge of Tremadog's main square (if you hadn't already guessed from the name), this atmospheric eatery serves French food with a Welsh accent. Get in before 7pm for the early bird set menu (two/three courses £16/19; not offered on Saturday).

🔒 Shopping

Although the High St (Stryd Fawr) has an extravagant number of charity shops and more than a few boarded-up businesses, there are still some independent, local enterprises worth seeking out.

Rob Piercy Gallery   ART
(☑ 01766-513833; www.robpiercy.com; Snowdon St; ☉ 10am-5pm Mon-Sat) This small commercial gallery showcases the work of Piercy, a local artist who specialises in watercolours of local scenes.

Kerfoots   DEPARTMENT STORE
(138-145 High St; ☉ 9.15am-5.30pm Mon-Sat, 10.30am-4.30pm Sun) Established in 1874, this independent store is a local institution. It stocks a limited range of household goods and clothing, but is worth checking out for

its upstairs coffee shop and the stained-glass dome above the staircase.

Cob Records
MUSIC

(☑ 01766-512170; www.cobrecords.com; 1-3 Britannia Tce; ⊘ 9am-5.30pm Mon-Sat, noon-5pm Sun) A great little independent record shop (established in 1962) with a healthy collection of Welsh music, and a large secondhand DVD selection.

ℹ️ Information

Porthmadog Tourist Office (☑ 01766-512981; www.visitsnowdonia.info; High St; ⊘ 9.30am-5pm Easter-Oct, 10am-3.30pm Mon-Sat Nov-Easter; 🛜)

Ysbyty Alltwen (☑ 01766-510010; A487, Tremadog) The local hospital treats minor injuries but doesn't have a full emergency department.

ℹ️ Getting There & Around

BICYCLE

The Lôn Las Cymru cycle trail passes through Porthmadog, heading west to Criccieth and south to Harlech.

BUS

Buses stop on High St and most services pass through Tremadog.

➡ A daily National Express coach heads to/ from Pwllheli (£7.20, 30 minutes) Caernarfon (£7.20, 35 minutes), Bangor (£7.90, one hour), Llandudno (£8.60, 1½ hours) and London (£34, 10 hours).

➡ Other buses head to/from Machynlleth (route T2; 1½ hours), Dolgellau (T2; 50 minutes), Beddgelert (S97; 25 minutes), Pwllheli (3; 35 minutes) and Caernarfon (1/1A; one hour).

TRAIN

➡ Porthmadog is on the Cambrian Coast Line, with direct trains to Machynlleth (£14, two hours), Barmouth (£6.90, one hour), Harlech (£3.80, 24 minutes), Criccieth (£2.50, seven minutes) and Pwllheli (£4.80, 22 minutes).

➡ See also the Ffestiniog & Welsh Highland Railways for steamy services to Blaenau Ffestiniog, the Snowdon trailheads and Caernarfon.

Criccieth

POP 1760

This genteel slow-moving seaside town sits above a sweep of sand-and-stone beach, 5 miles west of Porthmadog. Its main claim to fame is ruined Criccieth Castle, perched up on the clifftop and offering views stretching along the peninsula's southern coast and across Tremadog Bay to Harlech.

◎ Sights

Criccieth Castle
CASTLE

(Cadw; www.cadw.wales.gov.uk; Castle St; adult/ child £3.50/2.65; ⊘ 10am-5pm Apr-Oct, 9.30am-4pm Fri & Sat, 11am-4pm Sun Nov-Mar) Constructed by Welsh prince Llywelyn the Great in 1239, Criccieth Castle was overrun in 1283 by Edward I's forces and recaptured for the Welsh in 1404 by Owain Glyndŵr, who promptly burnt it. Today there is a small but informative exhibition centre at the ticket office.

Lloyd George Museum
MUSEUM

(☑ 01766-522071; www.gwynedd.gov.uk/museums; adult/child £5/4; ⊘ 10.30am-5pm Mon-Fri Apr & May, Mon-Sat Jun, daily Jul-Sep, 11am-4pm Mon-Fri Oct) The village of Llanystumdwy, 1.5 miles west of Criccieth, is the boyhood home and final resting place of David Lloyd George, one of Wales' finest ever political statesmen, and the British prime minister from 1916 to 1922. This small museum gives an impression of the man and to some extent illustrates the tension between his nationality and position, through film footage, photos, posters and personal effects.

Highgate, the house he grew up in, is 50m away, and his grave is about 150m away on the other side of the car park. The memorial is designed by Clough Williams-Ellis, the creator of Portmeirion.

🛏️ Sleeping

Glyn-y-Coed
HOTEL ££

(☑ 01766-522870; www.gychotel.co.uk; Porthmadog Rd; s/d from £59-79; P 🛜) While the name alludes to a wooded glen, this 10-bedroom Victorian house is plonked right on the main road, gazing out to sea. The views through the bay windows in the elegant front rooms encompass the castle, the bay and the mountains of Snowdonia.

Seaspray
B&B ££

(☑ 01766-522373; www.seasprayguesthouse.co.uk; 4 Marine Tce; s £50, d £65-70; 🛜) A narrow lemon slice in a block of pastel four-storey town houses lining the waterfront, this old-fashioned B&B has a set of well-kept rooms, some with unimpeded sea views. Knick-knacks are positioned on the stairs in just the right places to challenge luggage-luggers.

Bron Eifion
HISTORIC HOTEL £££

(☑ 01766-522385; www.broneifion.co.uk; s £95-135, d £135-185; P 🛜) The former palace of a slate magnate, with fabulously formal gardens, grand old Bron Eifion has been refurbished with flat-screen TVs sitting alongside faux-Gothic carvings and wooden panels. The hotel is half a mile west of Criccieth, on the A497.

✖ Eating & Drinking

Tir a Môr   BRASSERIE ££
(☑ 01766-523084; www.tiramor-criccieth.co.uk; 1 Mona Tce; mains £15-20; ⊘ 6-9.30pm Tue-Sat mid-Feb–Nov) The name means 'Land and Sea' but don't worry, it doesn't translate to 'surf and turf' on the plate. The succulent Welsh farm produce and the fresh Welsh seafood stick to their own corners of the largely traditional menu. It's an intimate restaurant, and popular too – bookings are advised.

Poachers Restaurant   INTERNATIONAL ££
(☑ 01766-522512; www.poachersrestaurant.co.uk; 66 High St; mains £12-17; ⊘ 6.30-10pm Wed-Sat, extended hours summer) Look past the paper serviettes and limited wine choice and you'll find tasty Welsh produce married with some flavours of Asia. The two-course set menu (£16) is good value.

ℹ Transport

BIKE

The Lôn Las Cymru cycle route passes through Criccieth, heading north to Caernarfon and east to Porthmadog.

BUS

➡ A daily National Express coach heads to/from Pwllheli (£5.50, 20 minutes), Porthmadog (£5.20, 13 minutes), Caernarfon (£8.10, 48 minutes), Llandudno (£8.60, 1¾ hours) and London (£38, 10¼ hours).

➡ Other buses head to/from Pwllheli (route 3; 23 minutes), Llanystymdwy (3; four minutes), Porthmadog (1 and 3; 17 minutes), Caernarfon (1; 50 minutes) and Bangor (1; 1¼ hours).

TRAIN

Criccieth is on the Cambrian Coast Line, with direct trains to Machynlleth (£15, two hours), Barmouth (£8.10, one hour), Harlech (£5.60, 33 minutes), Porthmadog (£2.50, seven minutes) and Pwllheli (£3.30, 15 minutes).

Pwllheli

POP 4080

The peninsula's main market town and public-transport hub, Pwllheli (poolth-*heh*-lee; meaning 'Salt-Water Pool') has a long

---

OFF THE BEATEN TRACK

PENARTH FAWR MEDIEVAL HOUSE

Surrounded by stone farm buildings that time forgot, Penarth Fawr is a privately owned 1416 house that has somehow survived into the 21st century. It's basically one large hall with a big open hearth. The affable owner is more than happy for you to potter about; keep a third eye open for the resident ghost. The hall sometimes doubles as an arts and craft gallery.

It's reached by a country lane, signposted from the A497 between Criccieth and Pwllheli. There are no set opening hours or admission charges – just turn up and see if it's open.

---

sandy beach (blue-flagged Marian y De), a busy marina and a staunchly Welsh population. It's also home to an unusual colony of herons that has chosen to nest in willows near the town centre; look for them from Cardiff Rd.

🏃 Activities

Clwb Offaxis   WAKEBOARDING, KITESURFING
(☑ 01758-713407; www.offaxis.co.uk; Pwllheli Marina; ⊘ 11am-7pm Sat & Sun Apr-Oct, daily school holidays) The boys from Abersoch's Offaxis run this summertime clubhouse as a base for their wakeboarding and kitesurfing lessons. After a day's exsersions you can unwind with a hot shower, a snack, a beer, a round of pool or a surf movie.

Enlli Charters   BOAT TOUR
(☑ 0845 811 3655; www.enllicharter.co.uk; cruise £35) Boats depart from the marina for Bardsey Island.

🎊 Festivals & Events

Wakestock   MUSIC, SPORT
(www.wakestock.co.uk; ⊘ Jul) Somehow joining the dots between wakeboarding and live music, this weekend in July includes the boarding comp at Pwllheli Marina, and the main festival site at Penrhos between Pwllheli and Llanbedrog. Headliners have included Dizzee Rascal, Ed Sheeran and Moby.

🛏 Sleeping & Eating

★ **Plas Bodegroes**   HOTEL £££
(☑ 01758-612363; www.bodegroes.co.uk; s £117-162, d £130-180; 🅿🛜) Set in a stately 1780

manor house strewn with modern art, this restaurant-with-rooms is a romantic option. The elegant restaurant ups the Welshness by serving its dishes on slabs of slate. Local, organic and sustainable produce features heavily on the menu (four-course dinner £45, Sunday lunch £23; open 7pm to 9.30pm Tuesday to Saturday, 12.30pm to 2.30pm Sunday March to November). It's located amid immaculately coiffured gardens, a mile inland from Pwllheli along the A497.

Pili Palas   CAFE
(☑ 01758-612248; 2-4 Stryd Moch; mains £5-6; ☉ 10am-4.30pm Mon-Sat) Friendly Pili Palas serves light bites such as sandwiches, wraps, salads and hot ciabatta in cosy surrounds. It's licensed too.

Taro Deg   CAFE £
(☑ 01758-701271; www.tarodeg.com; 17 New St; mains £4-8; ☉ 9am-4.30pm Mon-Sat; 🛜🚻) Relaxed and spacious, this centrally located cafe (near the train station) offers newspapers to browse and a tasty selection of cooked breakfasts, sandwiches and cakes.

ⓘ Information

Pwllheli Tourist Office (☑ 01758-613000; www.visitsnowdonia.info; Station Sq; ☉ 9.30am-5pm Apr-Oct)

ⓘ Getting There & Away

BUS
➡ A daily National Express coach heads to/from Porthmadog (£7.20, 30 minutes), Caernarfon (£7.40, one hour), Bangor (£7.60, 1½ hours),

Llandudno (£9.10, two hours) and London (£38, 10½ hours).

➡ Most of the peninsula's services originate or terminate at Pwllheli. Destinations include Aberdaron (route 17; 40 minutes), Morfa Nefyn (8; 20 minutes), Criccieth (3; 23 minutes), Porthmadog (3; 35 minutes) and Caernarfon (12; 45 minutes).

TRAIN
Pwllheli is the terminus of the Cambrian Coast Line, with direct trains to Criccieth (£3.30, 15 minutes), Porthmadog (£4.80, 22 minutes), Harlech (£7.80, 47 minutes), Barmouth (£11, 1½ hours) and Machynlleth (£16, 2¼ hours).

Llanbedrog
POP 1000

The main attraction of this seaside village is the excellent **Oriel Plas Glyn-y-Weddw** (www.oriel.org.uk; admission free; ☉ 10am-5pm Wed-Mon, daily school holidays), featuring a lively collection of work by contemporary Welsh artists, all of which are available for purchase. The gallery is worth visiting just to gape at the flamboyant Victorian Gothic mansion it's housed in, with its flashy exposed beams and stained glass. One room is devoted to the history of the house and a collection of porcelain. Look out for the two carved stones in the foyer, dating from the 5th or 6th century. There's also a nice cafe here, a newly opened outdoor amphitheatre and paths through the wooded grounds, which roll down to National Trust–owned **Llandbedrog beach**.

Up in the village, the **Ship Inn** (☑ 01758-741111; www.theshipinn.org.uk; B4413; mains £10-16; ☉ noon-midnight Easter-Oct, 4-11pm Mon-Wed, noon-11pm Thu-Sun Nov-Easter; 🚻) is a popular, family-friendly pub with garden seating, offering hearty bar meals.

ⓘ Getting There & Away

Buses head to/from Pwllheli (route 17/18; eight minutes), Abersoch (17/18; 13 minutes) and Aberdaron (18; 30 minutes) .

Abersoch
POP 1990

Abersoch comes alive in summer with a 30,000-person influx of boaties, surfers and beach bums. Edged by gentle blue-green hills, the town's main attraction is its beach, one of the most popular on the peninsula.

OFF THE BEATEN TRACK

PLAS YN RHIW

The three Keating sisters came to the rescue of this little decaying 17th-century **manor house** (NT; ☑ 01758-780219; www.nationaltrust.org.uk/plas-yn-rhiw; adult/child £5/2.50; ☉ noon-5pm Thu-Sun Apr, Oct & Nov, Wed-Mon May-Aug, Thu-Mon Sep) in the 1930s and '40s. The lush gardens provide a sharp contrast to the surrounding moorland and the views over Porth Neigwl (Hell's Mouth) to Cardigan Bay are sublime. It's on the heights near the hamlet of Rhiw, 4 miles east of Aberdaron; follow the signposts from the B4413.

Surfers head further south for the Atlantic swell at **Porth Neigwl** (Hell's Mouth) and **Porth Ceiriad**.

Activities

Abersoch Sailing School   SAILING
(☑07917 525 540; www.abersochsailingschool.co.uk; ⊗Sat & Sun & school holidays Mar-Oct) Offers sailing and powerboating lessons from £50) and joy rides (per half-hour £25). It also hires laser funboats (one/two hours £30/40), catamarans (one/two hours £40/60), sea kayaks (per hour single/double £10/20), pedaloes (per hour £20) and skippered yachts (2½ hours per person/boat £50/180).

West Coast Surf Shop   SURFING
(☑01758-713067; www.westcoastsurf.co.uk; Lôn Pen Cei; lessons incl equipment from £30; ⊗10am-5pm Mon, Tue & Thu-Sat, noon-5pm Wed & Sun) Runs the not-at-all-intimidating-sounding Hells Mouth Surf School, and hires out boards (£10) and wetsuits (£8) year-round. Its website features a live surfcam and daily surf reports.

Offaxis   WAKEBOARDING, SURFING
(☑01758-713407; www.offaxis.co.uk; Lôn Engan; lessons incl equipment from £30) This surf shop hires equipment and specialises in wakeboarding, kitesurfing and surfing lessons. Most of the kitesurfing and wakeboarding is run out of Clwb Offaxis at the Pwllheli marina.

Festivals & Events

Abersoch Jazz Festival
(www.abersochjazzfestival.com; ⊗Sep) Hep cats join the surf rats at Abersoch for a weekend of smooth sounds in September.

Sleeping & Eating

★ **Venetia**   HOTEL ££
(☑01758-713354; www.venetiawales.com; Lôn Sarn Bach; r £108-148; P🅿️🛜) No sinking old Venetian palazzo, just five stylish rooms in a grand Victorian house decked out with designer lighting and modern art; cinque has a TV above its bath tub. The restaurant specialises in the traditional tastes of Venice (mains £12 to £19), particularly fish and pasta dishes, and serves them under twinkling modern chandeliers.

Egryn   HOTEL ££
(☑01758-712332; www.egryn.com; Lôn Sarn Bach; s £80, d £100-120; P🛜) With tones as muted

as Venetia's are bright, this Edwardian house has eight comfortable, modern rooms with marbled en suites and sea views. The downstairs restaurant is open for evening meals in summer.

Coconut Kitchen   THAI ££
(☑01758-712250; www.thecoconutkitchen.co.uk; Lôn Pont Morgan; mains £11-16; ⊗5.30-10pm mid-Mar–Dec; 🍴) The fact that Coconut Kitchen has a chef who's actually from Thailand goes a long way to explaining why it has the reputation for being the best Thai restaurant in North Wales. You'll find it by the marina, on the approach to town.

Fresh   BISTRO, BAR ££
(☑01758-710033; www.fresh-abersoch.co.uk; Stryd Fawr; mains £9-18; ⊗6pm-midnight Tue-Sun; 🍴) A popular surfer's hang-out, whether for a beer on the front terrace or dinner, Fresh serves hearty bistro food along the lines of lamb shanks and pork chops.

Drinking

The Vaynol   PUB
(☑01758-712776; www.thevaynol.co.uk; Stryd Fawr; 🛜🍴🎵) The local pub has been given a Hamptons-style bleached-wood makeover. Don't despair: it still plays sports on big TVs and welcomes dogs, only now it's got a better range of craft beers.

Information

Abersoch Tourist Office (☑01758-712929; www.abersochandllyn.co.uk; Stryd Fawr; ⊗10.30am-2pm Fri-Sun Jan-Mar & Oct, daily Apr, Jul & Aug, Thu-Sun May, Thu-Mon Jun & Sep; @)

Getting There & Away

Buses 17 and 18 stop on Stryd Fawr (High St), heading to/from Llanbedrog (13 minutes) and Pwllheli (25 minutes).

Aberdaron

POP 965

Aberdaron is an ends-of-the-earth kind of place with whitewashed, windswept houses contemplating the sands of Aberdaron Bay. It was traditionally the last resting spot before pilgrims made the treacherous crossing to Bardsey Island. The little Gwylan Islands, just offshore, are North Wales' most important puffin-breeding site.

◉ Sights

St Hywyn's Church   CHURCH

(www.st-hywyn.org.uk; ⊘10am-6pm Apr-Oct, to 3pm Nov-Mar) Stoically positioned above the pebbly beach, St Hywyn's Church has lingered here since the days of the pilgrimage. The left half of the church dates from 1100 while the right half was added 400 years later, to cope with the volume of penitents. The church was restored in 2006 and today has lots of information about local history, as well as two 6th-century memorial stones and a medieval font and holy-water stoup. Welsh poet RS Thomas was the minister here from 1967 to 1978 and it seems an appropriate setting for his bleak, impassioned work.

Y Gegin Fawr   HISTORIC BUILDING

(The Big Kitchen; ⊘9am-6pm) With their spiritual needs sorted, the Bardsey-bound saints could claim a meal at Y Gegin Fawr, a little thick-walled building with tiny windows, just over the bridge in the centre of the village. Dating from 1300, it still dishes up meals to hungry visitors.

★ Braich-y-Pwll   OUTDOORS

(NT; Uwchmynydd) While the boats for Bardsey now leave from Porth Meudwy, this rugged headland on the very tip of the Llŷn Peninsula is where the medieval pilgrims set off from – and one glimpse of the surf-pounded rocks will reinforce what a terrifying final voyage that must have been. It's an incredibly dramatic, ancient-looking landscape, with Bardsey rising out of the slate-grey sea like the mystical Avalon. A path leads down past the earthworks that are all that remain of St Mary's Abbey, to a neolithic standing stone known as Maen Melyn, bent like a finger towards the island and suggesting this was a holy place long before the Celts or their saints arrived.

A natural freshwater spring issues from a cleft in the rock below the high-tide mark; called St Mary's Well (Ffynnon Fair), it was held to be holy and pilgrims would sip the water before setting out. There are sheer drops to the sea and high surf, so we don't recommend you attempt it.

Inland are strip fields that preserve many of the patterns of ancient land use. Keep an eye out for choughs, a cheeky red-legged relation of the crow, and the rare spotted rock rose – this is the only place on the British mainland where this yellow bloom is found.

Porth Oer   BEACH

(NT; car park £1.50) This lovely remote scoop of beach, 2.5 miles north of Aberdaron, has sand that squeaks when you walk on it, giving it it's English name, Whispering Sands. From here it's a 2-mile coastal walk southwest via the twin headlands of Dinas Bach and Dinas Fawr to the cove of Porth Orion.

St Gwynhoedl's Church   CHURCH

(Llangwnnadl) Part of the chain of pilgrim's churches leading to Bardsey, pretty St Gwynhoedl's looks like three churches fused together. It still has its 15th- and 16th-century roof timbers, and embedded in one of the walls is a Celtic Cross dating from around AD 600. Check out the carved font; the crowned figure represents Henry VIII. The church is 5 miles north of Aberdaron, off the B4417.

🛏 Sleeping & Eating

Tŷ Newydd   HOTEL ££

(☎01758-760207;   www.gwesty-tynewydd.co.uk; s/d from £65/100; ☎) Right on the beach, this friendly hotel has fully refurbished, light-

---

THE BARDSEY PILGRIMAGE

At a time when journeys from Britain to Italy were long, perilous and beyond the means of most people, the Pope decreed that three pilgrimages to the holy island of Bardsey would have the same spiritual value as one to Rome. Tens of thousands of penitents took advantage of this get-out-of-Purgatory-free (or at least quickly) card and many came here to die. In the 16th century, Henry VIII's ban on pilgrimages put pay to the practice – although a steady trickle of modern-day pilgrims still walk the route.

The traditional path stops at ancient churches and holy wells along the way. It's broken into nine legs on the Edge of Wales Walk (www.edgeofwaleswalk.co.uk) website, run by a cooperative of local residents. They can help to arrange a 47-mile, self-guided walking tour, including five nights' accommodation and baggage transfers (from £280). A similar service is also offered for the 95-mile Llŷn Coastal Path, which circumnavigates the peninsula.

drenched, spacious rooms and some truly wonderful sea views. The tide comes in right under the terrace off the pub restaurant (mains £10 to £16), which seems designed with afternoon gin-and-tonics in mind.

Ship Hotel
PUB **££**

☑ 01758-760204; www.theshiphotelaberdaron.co.uk; from £89; ☎) The rooms above this family-run pub are unremarkable but perfectly acceptable; some have sea views. The bar's commitment to stocking the product of small Welsh breweries has earned it the praise of CAMRA.

ⓘ Getting There & Away

Buses head to/from Nefyn (route 8B; 30 minutes), Llanbedrog (18; 30 minutes) and Pwllheli (17; 40 minutes).

Bardsey Island (Ynys Enlli)

POP 8

This mysterious island, 2 miles long and 2 miles off the tip of the Llŷn, is a magical place. In fact, it's one of many candidates for the Isle of Avalon from the Arthurian legends. It's said that the wizard Merlin still sleeps in a glass castle somewhere on the island.

In the 6th or 7th century the obscure St Cadfan founded a monastery here, giving shelter to Celts fleeing the Saxon invaders, and medieval pilgrims followed in their wake. The island's Welsh name means 'Isle of the Currents', a reference to the treacherous tidal surges in Bardsey Sound, which doubtless convinced medieval visitors that their lives were indeed in God's hands. A Celtic cross amid the abbey ruins commemorates the pilgrims who came here to die and inspired the island's poetic epithet: the Isle of 20,000 Saints. Their bones still periodically emerge from unmarked graves; it's said that in the 1850s they were used as fencing, there were so many of them.

Most modern pilgrims to Bardsey are sea-bird-watchers; during the summer around 7,000 Manx shearwaters nest in burrows here, emerging at night. A colony of Atlantic grey seals lives here year-round; a pile of rocks by the harbour is a popular hang-out. Other sights include 6th-century carved stones, the remains of a 13th-century abbey tower and a candy-striped lighthouse.

The Bardsey Island Trust (☑ 0845 811 2233; www.bardsey.org) is Bardsey's custodian and can arrange holiday lets in cottages on the island. In summer Bardsey Boat Trips (☑ 07971-769895; www.bardseyboattrips. com; adult/child £30/20) sails to Bardsey from Porth Meudwy, a little cove near Aberdaron. Enlli Charters (p253) sails from the marina in Pwllheli.

Morfa Nefyn

The diminutive village of Morfa Nefyn sits above a pretty crescent of sand at Porth Dinllaen. It's hard to believe that this was once a busy cargo, shipbuilding and herring port, the only safe haven on the peninsula's north coast. Indeed, it was eyed up by slate magnate William Madocks as a possible home for ferries to Ireland, but in 1839 the House of Commons gave that job to Holyhead. Today it's owned in its entirety by the National Trust, which maintains a small information kiosk in its car park (parking summer/winter £5/1.50).

At the western end of the beach is an isolated cluster of buildings, which includes the legendary Tŷ Coch Inn (☑ 01758-720498; www.tycoch.co.uk; mains £6-10; ☺ noon-4pm Sat & Sun Dec-Feb, 11am-3pm Mon-Thu, 11am-3pm & 6-11pm Fri & Sat, 11am-5pm Sun Mar-May & Sep-Nov, 11am-11pm Mon-Sat, to 5pm Sun Jun-Aug), famous for its views and for pints that you can drink while dabbling your toes in the sea.

Buses head here from Pistyll (route 14; eight minutes) and Pwllheli (8/14; 20 minutes).

Pistyll

One of the main pit-stops on the Bardsey pilgrimage, the ancient hospice church St Beuno's sits peacefully in the middle of its oval churchyard below the village of Pistyll. St Beuno (died 640) was to North Wales what St David was to the south of the country (another St Beuno's Church is further up the coast at Clynnog Fawr, where his religious community was based). This tiny stone church's slate roof would once have been thatched, but original features include a Celtic carved font and a window beside the altar that allowed lepers standing outside to watch Mass being celebrated. On the interior face of this wall there are rare remnants of pre-Reformation frescoes. St Beuno's is at its most atmospheric during the Christmas, Easter and harvest seasons, when the floors are covered in reeds and fragrant herbs – unless, of course, you're a hay-fever sufferer.

East of Pistyll are the 100m sea cliffs of Carreg y Llam, a major seabird site, with huge colonies of razorbills, guillemots and kittiwakes. A 3-mile loop walk starts from the National Trust car park near the church.

🛏 Sleeping

★ **Natural Retreats**   APARTMENT £££

(☑ 0843 249 5042; www.naturalretreats.com; Pistyll Farm; apt from £195; P 🛜 🐾) 🍃 Offering big-city luxury in the middle of nowhere, Natural Retreats has taken an old stone farm complex and converted it into a gorgeous set of one- to three-bedroom apartments, fully equipped with all the mod cons (including that ultimate traveller treat, the clothes washer-dryer). It's peacefully and picturesquely located on the cliffs near St Beuno's Church.

ⓘ Getting There & Away

Pistyll is on the B4417, 1.5 miles northeast of Nefyn. The turn-off to the church and National Trust car park is past the village; look for the Natural Retreats sign.

Nant Gwrtheyrn

The village of Nant Gwrtheyrn was built for quarry workers in the 19th century, when granite was dug out of the surrounding mountains and shipped to Liverpool, Manchester and elsewhere to be used in building roads. The quarries closed after WWII and the village was gradually abandoned. In 1982 it was given a new lease of life when the Welsh Language & Heritage Centre (☑ 01758-750334; www.nantgwrtheyrn.org; weekend course from £240; ⊙ call ahead for times) opened in the restored buildings. Its main focus is offering residential Welsh-language courses to suit all levels of ability, including B&B accommodation in homey little grey-stone cottages and meals at the on-site restaurant. Holidaymakers can also rent the self-contained cottages.

Even if you don't take a course, Nant Gwrtheyrn's a magical place – eerily quiet and ideal for a tranquil walk along world's-end cliffs. According to tradition it's the burial place of the 6th-century Celtic King Vortigern (Gwrtheyrn in Welsh), who features in many of the Arthurian legends. The old chapel has a small but compelling exhibition on the history of the village and the founding of the centre. A 10-minute film on life in the village is shown in one of the worker's cottages, which has been decked out in period furnishings. There's also a marked 3-mile loop walk heading past the pebbly beach, various quarries and the ruins of earlier farms.

Nant Gwrtheyrn has an isolated and dramatic setting, reached by a preposterously steep road down into the valley, accessed from the village of Llithfaen (on the B4417). If you're driving, take it very slowly and be extremely careful; we managed it in a small car but we wouldn't attempt it if it were raining. Otherwise it's a 25-minute walk from the car park at the top of the hill.

The top car park is also the start of the 30- to 50-minute track to striking Tre'r Ceiri, one of the best preserved Iron Age hillforts in Europe, where the remains of 150 stone huts have been discovered.

Anglesey & the North Coast

Best Places to Eat

➡ Cennin (p285)

➡ Bishopsgate Restaurant (p285)

➡ Bodnant Welsh Food (p273)

➡ Watson's Bistro (p272)

➡ Y Gegin Fach (p265)

Best Places to Stay

➡ Victoria House (p265)

➡ Cleifiog (p284)

➡ Totters (p265)

➡ Bodysgallen Hall (p278)

➡ Plas Rhianfa (p282)

Why Go?

The essence of this compact region can be boiled down to two things: castles and coast. Yes, there are look-at-me castles all over Wales, but few attract more admiring stares than the glamorous trio of Caernarfon, Conwy and Beaumaris, which is why they're recognised as World Heritage Sites today. As for the coast, there's a reason that Llandudno has been crowned 'the Queen of Welsh Resorts'. Its genteel appeal stands in stark contrast to the altogether more wild edges of the Isle of Anglesey, where the echoes of the ancients can be heard in the waves that batter South Stack and the breezes that eddy around clifftop barrows. Beyond the sands and stones, this part of Wales offers munificent opportunities for surfing, sailing, windsurfing, kayaking, kitesurfing, powerboating, paddleboarding, walking and birdwatching. You certainly won't be bored.

When to Go

May is both the sunniest and the driest month, and Llandudno celebrates the warming weather with much Victorian merriment. Walkers will find it a good time to hit the coastal paths. Temperatures are highest in July and August, which are the best beach months, although average highs are rarely above 20°C.

In October, Gwledd Conwy Feast gives foodies an excuse to start working on a warming layer of winter fat. The winter months give student musicians plenty of incentive to stay inside and practise for the Bangor New Music Festival in March.

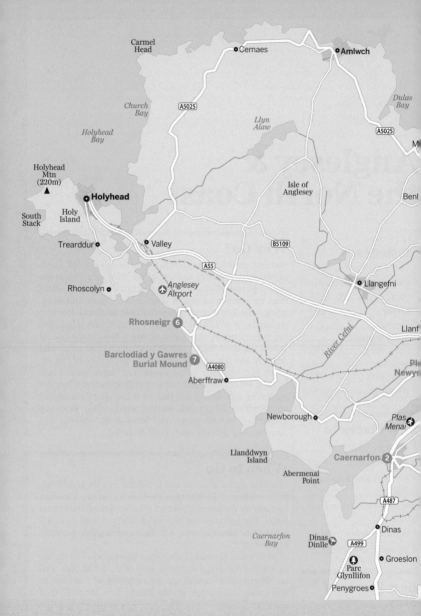

Anglesey & the North Coast Highlights

① Falling for the Georgian charms of **Beaumaris** (p282), Anglesey's finest town

② Witnessing the Byzantine beauty and strength of

Caernarfon Castle (p262) in Caernarfon

③ Revelling in all things Victorian – pier, promenade and Mr Punch – at the seaside resort of **Llandudno** (p274)

④ Savouring the sense of history within the medieval town walls of **Conwy** (p269), under the shadow of its mighty castle

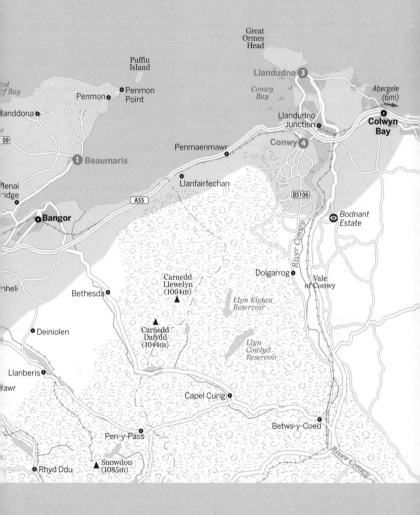

N 0 ——————————— 10 km
0 ——————————— 5 miles

IRISH SEA

Puffin Island

Great Ormes Head

Llandudno ❸

Conwy Bay

Abergele (6mi) →

Penmon ⊙ ⊙ Penmon Point

ed f Bay

⊙ 09

nddona ⊙

Llandudno Junction

Colwyn Bay

❶ Beaumaris

Penmaenmawr

Conwy ❹

Menai idge

Llanfairfechan

B5106

Bangor

A55

⊙ *Bodnant Estate*

River Conwy

Carnedd Llewelyn (1064m) ▲

Dolgarrog ⊙

Vale of Conwy

Bethesda ⊙

Llyn Eigiau Reservoir

heli

⊙ Deiniolen

Carnedd Dafydd (1044m) ▲

Llyn Cowlyd Reservoir

Llanberis ⊙

awr

Capel Curig ⊙

Betws-y-Coed ⊙

Pen-y-Pass ⊙

River Conwy

⊙ Rhyd Ddu

Snowdon ▲ (1085m)

---

❺ Musing over the perspective-changing Rex Whistler painting in the dining room of gracious **Plas Newydd** (p281)

❻ Strolling along the long sandy beach at **Rhosneigr** (p290) and watching the surfers at play

❼ Communing with the ancients in their tomb with a view at **Barclodiad y Gawres Burial Mound** (p290)

THE NORTH COAST

The North Wales coast has both perennial charms and cultural black spots in equal measure. The section west of Colwyn Bay includes glorious Unesco World Heritage-listed castles at Caernarfon and Conwy and the Victorian resort of Llandudno, a favourite family holiday hub. The sands continue further east but the associated towns are shabbier, duller and quite a lot rougher – which is why we haven't included them in this book.

Caernarfon

POP 9700

Wedged between the gleaming Menai Strait and the deep-purple mountains of Snowdonia, Caernarfon's main claim to fame is its fantastical castle. Given the town's crucial historical importance, its proximity to Snowdonia National Park and its reputation as a centre of Welsh culture (it has the highest percentage of Welsh speakers of anywhere), parts of the town centre are surprisingly down at heel. Still, there's a lot of charm in its untouristy air, despite the many boarded-up buildings, and a tangible sense of history in the streets around the castle. Within the cobbled lanes of the old walled town are some fine Georgian buildings, while the waterfront has started on the inevitable march towards gentrification.

Caernarfon Castle was built by Edward I as the last link in his 'iron ring' and it's now part of the 'Castles and Town Walls of King Edward in Gwynedd' Unesco World Heritage site. In an attempt by the then-prime minister, David Lloyd George (himself a Welshman), to bring the royals closer to their Welsh constituency, the castle was designated as the venue for the 1911 investiture of the Prince of Wales. In retrospect, linking the modern royals to such a powerful symbol of Welsh subjugation may not have been the best idea. It incensed fervent nationalists, and at the next crowning, that of Prince Charles in 1969, the sentiment climaxed with an attempt to blow up his train.

◉ Sights

★ **Caernarfon Castle** CASTLE, MUSEUM
(Cadw; adult/child £6/4.50; ⊙9.30am-5pm Mar-Oct, 10am-4pm Mon-Sat, 11am-4pm Sun Nov-Feb)
Majestic Caernarfon Castle was built between 1283 and 1330 as a military stronghold, a seat of government and a royal palace. Like the other royal strongholds of the time, it was designed and mainly supervised by Master James of St George, from Savoy but the brief and scale were extraordinary. Inspired by the dream of Macsen Wledig recounted in the *Mabinogion* (p290), Caer

Caernarfon

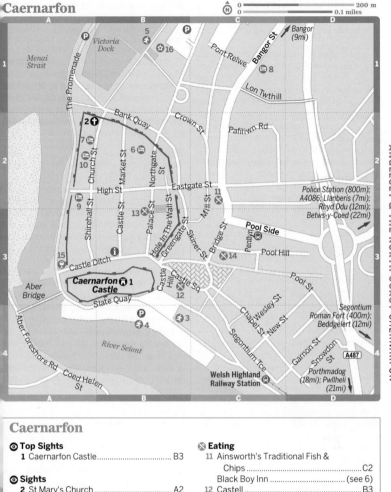

Caernarfon

narfon echoes the 5th-century walls of Constantinople, with colour-banded masonry and polygonal towers, instead of the traditional round towers and turrets.

Despite its fairy-tale aspect it is thoroughly fortified with a series of murder holes and a sophisticated arrangement of multiple arrow slits. It repelled Owain Glyndŵr's army in 1404 with a garrison of only 28 men, and resisted three sieges during the English Civil War before surrender to Cromwell's army in 1646.

A year after construction began, Edward I's second son was born here, becoming heir to the throne four months later when his elder brother died. To consolidate Edward junior's power he was made Prince of Wales in 1301, thus creating the tradition of English kings conferring that title on their heirs. As King Edward II he came to a very nasty end, possibly via a red-hot poker; his much-eroded statue is over the King's Gate. However, the first investiture that actually took place here (rather than in London) was that of his namesake, Edward VIII, in 1911 (co-incidentally his reign was also cut short, albeit less violently).

Caernarfon Castle is a large, relatively intact structure. You can walk on and through the interconnected walls and towers gathered around the central green, most of which are well preserved but empty.

Start at the **Eagle Tower**, the one with the flagpoles to the right of the entrance. On the turrets you can spot the weathered eagle from which it gets its name, alongside stone-helmeted figures intended to swell the garrison's numbers (they're easier to spot from the quay). Inside there are displays on Edward I and the construction of the castle, as well as a short film, *The Eagle & The Dragon*, which screens on the half-hour.

There is an exhibition on the Princes of Wales in the **North East Tower**, including video footage of the 1969 investiture of Prince Charles in that role. In the **Queen's Tower** (named after Edward I's wife Elean-or) is the **Regimental Museum of the Royal Welch Fusiliers**, which is filled with medals, uniforms, weapons and historical displays.

St Mary's Church   CHURCH

(Church St) Built in 1307 at the same time that the castle was going up, this pretty Gothic church once ministered to the castle's garrison. Its most unusual feature is that it's built directly into the old town wall; head outside the walls for a better look.

Segontium Roman Fort   RUINS

(Cadw; www.cadw.wales.gov.uk; Ffordd Cwstenin; ⊙10am-4pm) FREE Just east of the town centre, these low stone foundations represent the westernmost legionary fort of the Roman Empire. The fort dates back to AD 77, when General Gnaeus Julius Agricola completed the Roman conquest of Wales by capturing the Isle of Anglesey. It was designed to accommodate a force of up to 1000 infantrymen, and coins recovered from the site indicate that it was an active garrison until AD 394 – a reflection of its crucial strategic position. Caernarfon's name is a reference to this site, meaning 'fort opposite Anglesey'.

Sadly the on-site museum is closed for the foreseeable future and the only interpretive sign is on the side of the building. The site is about half a mile along the A4085 (to Beddgelert), which crosses through the middle of it.

Dinas Dinlle   BEACH

Dolphins and porpoises can sometime be spotted from this long, sandy Blue Flag beach, 6 miles southwest of Caernarfon. The flatness of the surrounding land stands in contrast to the dramatically sculpted Llŷn Peninsula, visible in the distance. The exception is a solitary hill, with a path leading up to the remains of an Iron Age fort.

Activities

Plas Menai   WATER SPORTS

(☎01248-670964; www.plasmenai.co.uk) The excellent National Watersports Centre offers year-round water-based courses for all interests and ability levels (sailing, power boating, kayaking, windsurfing, stand-up paddleboarding). Advance reservations are necessary. On-site accommodation includes B&B rooms (singles/doubles £45/70) and a bunkhouse (dorms £25).

WORTH A TRIP

GREENWOOD FOREST PARK

This 7-hectare adventure park (www.greenwoodforestpark.co.uk; Y Felinheli; admission £11; ⊙11am-5pm mid-Mar–Oct) makes a brilliant family day out, with a slew of activities for younger kids, all underpinned by a strong green ethos. You'll find mazes, a sledge run, archery, a tree-top playground, den-building, paddle boats, a forest theatre and the world's first people-powered roller-coaster, the Green Dragon. It's sign-posted from the A487 near Y Felinheli, 4 miles northeast of Caernarfon.

It's located 3 miles along the A487 towards Bangor. Bus 1A (Caernarfon to Bangor) stops here.

Menai Strait Pleasure Cruises CRUISE
(☑ 01286-672772; www.menaicruises.co.uk; adult/child 40min £6/4, 2hr £12/7; ☺ May-Oct) The 1937 ferry *Queen of the Sea* offers 40-minute cruises, with a full commentary, to the southwest entrance of the Menai Strait, and two-hour cruises in the other direction as far as the Menai Suspension Bridge. They leave from Slate Quay, beside the castle.

RibRide BOAT TOUR
(☑ 0333 1234 303; www.ribride.co.uk; Victoria Dock; adult/child £24/16) For an adrenaline kick take a blast out to sea on a one-hour rigid inflatable boat (RIB) ride through the Menai Strait and along sandy Llanddwyn Bay.

Beics Menai BICYCLE RENTAL
(☑ 01286-676804; www.beicsmenai.co.uk; 1 Slate Quay; per 2/4/6/8hr £15/17/19/22; ☺ 9.30am-4pm Tue-Sat) Hires bikes (including tandems, children's bikes and child seats) and can advise on local cycle routes. Recreational cycle routes include the 12.5-mile **Lôn Eifion** (starting near the Welsh Highland Railway station and running south to Bryncir) and the 4.5-mile **Lôn Las Menai** (following the Menai Strait to the village of Y Felinheli).

Beacon Climbing Centre ROCK CLIMBING
(☑ 0845 450 8222; www.beaconclimbing.com; Cibyn Estate, Lôn Cae Ffynnon; climbs £7.50; ☺ 10am-10pm Mon-Fri, 10am-8pm Sat & Sun) This large indoor climbing centre offers 1½-hour taster sessions for beginners (from £20) and plenty of challenging faces for experienced climbers to hone their skills on. It's located in an industrial estate off the Llanberis Rd (A4086), about a mile east of town.

🛏 Sleeping

★ Totters HOSTEL £
(☑ 01286-672963; www.totters.co.uk; 2 High St; dm/d £17/47) Modern, clean and very welcoming, this excellent independent hostel is the best-value place to stay in town. The 14th-century arched basement gives a sense of history to guests' free breakfasts (cereal, toast and hot beverages are included in the price). In addition to dorms, there's a two-bed attic apartment.

Caer Menai B&B £
(☑ 01286-672612; www.caermenai.co.uk; 15 Church St; s £45, d £57-67; @ 🛜) A former county school (1894), this elegant building is on a quiet street nestling against the western town wall. The seven renovated rooms are fresh, clean and snug; number seven has sunset sea views.

★ Victoria House B&B ££
(☑ 01286-678263; www.thevictoriahouse.co.uk; Church St; r £75-80; @ 🛜) Victoria House is an exceptional four-bedroom guesthouse with a homey feel, spacious modern rooms and some nice touches, such as an impressive selection of free toiletries and a DVD on the town's history in each room. Breakfast is a joy.

Plas Dinas Country House B&B ££
(☑ 01286-830214; www.plasdinas.co.uk; Bontnewydd; r from £99; P 🛜) Until the 1980s this large 17th-century house belonged to Lord Snowdon's family; his wife, Princess Margaret, often stayed here. Despite the ancestral photos in the hallway and the grand drawing room, the overall impression is surprisingly homey. The nine bedrooms are filled with antiques and thoughtful touches (Moulton Brown toiletries, fluffy bathrobes). It's set amid extensive grounds off the A487, 2 miles south of Caernarfon.

Black Boy Inn PUB ££
(☑ 01286-673604; www.black-boy-inn.com; Northgate St; s/d from £59/73; P 🛜♿) 🏳 Dating from 1522, this is one of the oldest pubs in Wales and one of the most atmospheric – it's even said to be haunted. The creaky but comfortable rooms have original wooden beams and panelling but a modern sensibility .

Celtic Royal Hotel HOTEL £££
(☑ 01286-674477; www.celtic-royal.co.uk; Bangor St; s/d £105/145; P 🛜🏊) This grand old Georgian building resembles a stately home with its impressive entrance hall and wood-panelled corridors. At 110 rooms it's hardly intimate, but it has all the advantages of a large hotel, including an indoor pool, sauna, steam room, Jacuzzi, gym, restaurant and bar.

🍴 Eating & Drinking

★ Y Gegin Fach CAFE, WELSH £
(www.facebook.com/YGeginFach; 5-9 Pool Hill; mains £4-7; ☺ 9.30am-3pm) 'The Little Kitchen' is a proper old-fashioned Welsh-speaking *caffi*, right down to the floral drapes and net

curtains. It's a great spot to tuck into traditional faves (like rarebit, faggots and Welsh cakes) and wish you had a Welsh granny.

Ainsworth's Traditional
Fish & Chips
FISH & CHIPS **£**

(41 Bridge St; mains £3-6; ⊙11.30am-9pm Mon-Sat) Our favourite North Wales chippie offers a choice of crispy cod, plaice and haddock, along with burgers, pies and fried chicken. It's mainly a takeaway operation, but there are four stools by the window counter if you want to tuck straight in.

Doc
CAFE **£**

(☑01286-685200; www.galericaernarfon.com/doc; Galeri Caernarfon, Victoria Dock; mains £6-10; ⊙10am-8.30pm; ☑) Split between a glassed-in dining area with views over the marina and a lounge bar in the arts centre lobby, Doc is an attractive spot for a bite or a beer. Sandwiches and baguettes are served at lunchtime, alongside a globetrotting set of hot dishes (fish and chips, Moroccan meatballs, burgers, satay).

Black Boy Inn
PUB **££**

(☑01286-673604; www.black-boy-inn.com; Northgate St; mains £8-18; ⊙noon-10pm; ☎🐾) 🐾 Packed with original 16th-century features, this cosy pub is divided into a series of snug rooms, with low ceilings, open fires and Welsh beer on tap. The menu highlights local meats and seafood, including hearty pub-grub staples such as roasts, pies, burgers, scampi and grilled fish.

Wal
ITALIAN **££**

(☑01286-674383; www.walrestaurant.co.uk; Palace St; mains £8-20; ⊙9.30am-3pm Sun-Tue, 9.30am-9pm Wed-Sat) We fell for this convivial little place, firstly for the cosy interior, bisected by the arches of an ancient wall and packed with merry people; secondly for its charming staff; and finally for the big, well-presented plates of tasty food. It has become a firm town favourite – book ahead for weekend nights.

Castell
BRITISH **££**

(☑01286-678895; www.castellcaernarfon.co.uk; 33 Castle Sq; mains £9-20; ⊙noon-3pm & 6-9.15pm) Caernarfon's glitziest bar looks on to Castle Sq from behind a grand Georgian facade. Inside it's all black furniture and pink trim – which isn't anywhere near as much of a 1980s nightmare as it sounds. Drop in for soup or a sandwich at lunchtime (£4 to £8) or a more substantial evening meal.

Anglesey Arms
PUB

(www.theangleseyarms.co.uk; The Promenade; ⊙noon-midnight; ☎) If you're after a pint, this converted 18th-century waterfront customs house is your best bet. In summer, grab a seat outside; it's a great spot for watching the sunset.

☆ Entertainment

Galeri Caernarfon
THEATRE, CINEMA

(☑01286-685222; www.galericaernarfon.com; Victoria Dock) This excellent multipurpose arts centre hosts exhibitions, theatre, films and events; check online for details.

❶ Information

Tourist Office (☑01286-672232; www.visit-snowdonia.info; Castle St; ⊙9.30am-4.30pm Apr-Oct, 10am-3.30pm Mon-Sat Nov-Mar; ☎) Opposite the castle's main entrance. It incorporates the Pendeitsh Gallery, which hosts art exhibitions and a permanent display on Caernarfon's history.

❶ Getting There & Away

BUS

Buses and coaches depart from the **bus station** (Pool Side).

➡ A daily **National Express** (www.nationalexpress.com) coach stops en route to Pwllheli (£7.40, one hour) and London (£34, 9½ hours), via Bangor (£6.40, 25 minutes), Llandudno (£7.90, one hour) and Birmingham (£29, six hours).

➡ Buses include 1/1A to Bangor (22 minutes), Plas Menai (three minutes), Criccieth (50 minutes), Tremadog (56 minutes) and Porthmadog (one hour); 5/X5 to Bangor (30 minutes), Conwy (1¼ hours) and Llandudno (1½ hours); 12 to Parc Glynllifon (12 minutes) and Pwllheli (45 minutes); and 87/88/89 to Llanberis (30 minutes).

➡ Snowdon Sherpa bus S4 heads to Beddgelert (30 minutes) via the Snowdon Ranger (19 minutes) and Rhyd Ddu (21 minutes) trailheads.

CAR & MOTORCYCLE

Free street parking is at a premium but you might snatch a park in the walled town (try Church St) and there are highly contested free parks by the water on the south embankment of Victoria Dock.

TRAIN

Caernarfon is the northern terminus of the **Welsh Highland Railway** (☑01766-516024; www.festrail.co.uk) tourist train, which runs to Porthmadog (£34 return, 2½ hours) via Rhd Ddu (£21 return, one hour) and Beddgelert (£26 eturn, 1½ hours) from April to October. The station is near the river on St Helen's Rd.

Bangor

POP 16,400

Like the jaunty one-hit wonder from 1980 suggests, a *Day Trip to Bangor* is plenty of time to see this unassuming little city's sights, and even that is enhanced by drinking cider. Dominated by its university and some rather large shopping centres, Bangor is the largest city in Gwynedd and a major transport hub for North Wales, with plenty of onward connections to Anglesey and Snowdonia.

St Deiniol established a monastery here in the 6th century, which grew up into Bangor's sweet little cathedral. The main university building sits above it on a ridge, it's contours aping those of the cathedral. Bangor University was founded in 1884, and it is now rated as the best university in Wales and one of the top 15 in the UK. During term time 10,000 students swell the city's population.

◎ Sights

Penrhyn Castle

CASTLE

(NT; www.nationaltrust.org.uk/penrhyn-castle; off Llandegai Rd; adult/child £10/5; ⊙ noon-5pm Wed-Mon Mar-Jun, 11am-5pm daily Jul-Oct) Edward I's medieval masterpieces get the glory in these parts, but this fantasy take on a Norman castle should not be missed. Designed by Thomas Hopper for the wealthy Pennant family, it was built between 1820 and 1845 on the spoils of Welsh slate and Jamaican sugar.

The extravagant rooms are a faux-Gothic wonder, complete with intricately carved ceilings, stained-glass windows, hand-painted wallpaper, opulent furniture and even early flushing toilets. There's a great hall modelled on Durham Cathedral, a lofty staircase which took 10 years to construct, and a 1-tonne slate bed built for Queen Victoria. The adjacent stable blocks are home to several galleries and mini-museums, including a railway musuem. The beautiful grounds offer epic views of Snowdonia and include a Victorian walled garden and a bog garden.

The castle is 1.5 miles east of Bangor. Buses to Llandudno stop at the gate.

Bangor Cathedral

CHURCH

(www.churchinwales.org.uk/bangor; Glanrafon; ⊙ 9am-4.30pm Mon-Fri, 10.30am-1pm Sat) More formally known as the Cathedral Church of St Deiniol, this building occupies one of the oldest ecclesiastical sites in Britain, dating from AD 525 when the saint founded his community here. The earliest part of today's stone church dates to the 12th century, although that building was largely destroyed in 1211 during a raid by England's King John, whose men also burned the city. Further ravages took place in the 13th century, during Edward I's invasion, and in 1402, during the Glyndŵr uprising. Two centuries later Cromwell's men used the cathedral as stables.

Much of the architecture seen today is thanks to the work of the eminent architect Sir George Gilbert Scott between 1870 and 1880. More recently, Aled Jones (choirboy turned TV and radio presenter) trained his adolescent vocal chords here.

The cathedral has a small shop and an exhibition about its history. An artistic highlight is the late-15th-century, almost life-sized, oak carving of Christ, seated and shackled in the moments before his crucifixion. A stroll in the adjoining bible gardens, supposedly containing every plant mentioned in the bible, makes for a tranquil counterpoint to the city's bawdy pub scene.

Gwynedd Museum & Art Gallery

MUSEUM

(www.gwynedd.gov.uk/museums; Gwynedd Rd; ⊙ 12.30-4.30pm Tue-Fri, 10.30am-4.30pm Sat) **FREE** In between the archaeological relics and beautifully crafted furniture typical of similar small collections, this museum has some interesting displays on the nature of Welshness and the battles for its survival. Downstairs there's a gallery devoted to temporary art exhibitions (most works are for sale), and a tourist information terminal (Bangor doesn't have a tourist office).

Garth Pier

LANDMARK

(adult/child 50/20p; ⊙ 8am-6pm Mon-Sat, 10am-5pm Sun) Given the large expanse of mud-flats exposed at high tide (a paradise for all manner of wading birds), it's surprising that the Victorians chose to build one of Britain's longest pleasure piers here. Built in 1896, Garth Pier stretches 460m into the Menai Strait, reaching most of the way to Anglesey. Kiosks with fanciful oriental rooves are scattered along its length and there's a tearoom at the very end. In the distance you catch the sun glinting off Thomas Telford's handsome Menai Suspension Bridge.

Bangor

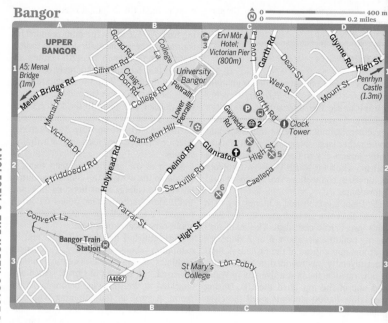

🎆 Festivals & Events

Bangor New Music Festival   MUSIC
(www.bnmf.co.uk; ⊙ Mar) Run in collaboration
with Bangor University's School of Music,
this six-day festival is devoted to new works
by contemporary composers, ranging from
chamber music to 'electroacoustic' and experimental music.

🛏 Sleeping

Management Centre   HOTEL ££
(☎ 01248-365912; www.themanagementcentre.
co.uk; College Rd; s £70-80, d £90; P ⑨) Bangor

isn't exactly blessed with accommodation
options, but this university business centre
has 57 en suite rooms and makes for a comfortable (if slightly unusual) stay. There's an
on-site restaurant and bar if you don't fancy
the steep walk down into town and back.

🍴 Eating & Drinking

Blue Sky   CAFE £
(☎ 01248-355444; www.blueskybangor.co.uk; Ambassador Hall, 236 High St; mains £4-9; ⊙ 9.30am-
5.30pm Mon-Sat) Easy to miss, the Blue Sky
Cafe hides itself down an alleyway off the
high street. Locally sourced ingredients go
into its breakfasts, soups, sandwiches, burgers and salads, and rich wood and restful-
red walls make for a cosy ambience. Check
the website for details of upcoming gigs.

1815   CAFE £
(☎ 01248-355969; www.1815bangor.co.uk; 2 Waterloo St; mains £4-9; ⊙ 9.30am-6pm Mon-Sat; ⑭)
Fresh local produce, lovingly presented,
and a strong Spanish influence are the key
themes of this friendly cafe-bar. It's a buzzy
lunch spot, or call in for an afternoon vino
and tasty tapas (three plates for £9).

Kyffin   CAFE £
(☎ 01248-355161; 129 High St; mains £7; ⊙ 10am-
5pm Mon-Sat; ⑦) Kyffin is a true gem at the

less salubrious end of the main street: a fair-trade, vegetarian and vegan cafe with antique-shop fittings and a deli counter crammed with organic goodies. As well as serving excellent coffee, it has a large selection of teas – or you can sink into a sofa with a glass of wine while the jazz music plays.

☆ Entertainment

Pontio   ARTS CENTRE
(www.pontio.co.uk; Deiniol Rd) By the time you're reading this, the university's ambitious new multimillion-pound arts and innovation centre should have opened. The 450-seat main theatre, 120-seat studio theatre and cinema are expected to stage all manner of performing arts events.

❶ Information

Police (☏121; www.north-wales.police.uk; Deiniol Rd)

Ystyby Gwynedd (☏01248-384384; www. bcu.wales.nhs.uk; Penrhos Rd) Located 2 miles southwest of the city centre; this is the regional hub for accident and emergency (A&E) treatment.

❶ Getting There & Around

BUS

The **bus station** is located behind the Deiniol Shopping Centre.

➜ National Express coaches head to/from Porthmadog (£7.90, one hour), Caernarfon (£6.40, 25 minutes), Holyhead (£20, 50 minutes), Birmingham (£27, 5½ hours) and London (£34, nine hours).

➜ Bus routes include 5/X5 to Caernarfon (30 minutes), Conwy (35 minutes) and Llandudno (56 minutes); 53-58 to Menai Bridge (11 minutes) and Beaumaris (30 minutes); 85/86 to Llanberis (27 minutes); T2 to Caernarfon (25 minutes), Porthmadog (one hour), Dolgellau (two hours), Machynlleth (2½ hours) and Aberystwyth (3¼ hours); and X4 to Menai Bridge (12 minutes), Llanfair PG (18 minutes), Llangefni (36 minutes) and Holyhead (50 minutes).

➜ Snowdon Sherpa S6 has a morning service to Capel Curig (33 minutes) and Betws-y-Coed (45 minutes).

TRAIN

Bangor's train station is on Holyhead Rd, just off the southwest end of the High St. Direct services head to/from Holyhead (£8.70, 30 minutes), Rhosneigr (£6.10, 24 minutes), Llanfair PG (£2.80, six minutes), Conwy (£6.30, 17 minutes) and London Euston (£86, 3¼ hours).

Conwy

POP 4100

A visit to Britain's most complete walled town should be high on the itinerary for anyone with even a mild crush on things historic. The World Heritage–listed castle continues to dominate the town, as it's done ever since Edward I first planted it here.

Approaching from the east, the scene is given another theatrical flourish by a tightly grouped trio of bridges crossing the River Conwy, including Thomas Telford's 1826 suspension bridge (one of the first of its kind in the world) and Robert Stephenson's 1848 wrought-iron railway bridge (the first ever tubular bridge).

◉ Sights

★ Conwy Castle

(Cadw; ☏01492-592358; www.cadw.wales.gov.uk; adult/child £5.75/4.35; ◷9.30am-5pm Apr-Oct, 10am-4pm Mon-Sat, 11am-4pm Sun Nov-Feb; ℗) Caernarfon is more complete, Harlech more dramatically positioned and Beaumaris more technically perfect, yet out of the four castles that comprise the Unesco World Heritage site, Conwy is the prettiest to gaze upon. At around £15,000 (over £10 million in today's money), it was certainly the most costly to build. If its crenellated turrets and towers call to mind romance and fairy tales rather than subjugation and oppression, it certainly wasn't the intention of its builders.

Constructed between 1283 and 1287, Conwy rises from a rocky outcrop with commanding views across the mountains of Snowdonia and the mouth of the River Conwy. With two barbicans (fortified gateways), eight fierce, slightly tapered towers of coarse dark stone and a great bow-shaped hall all within the elongated complex, it's very solid indeed.

After the Civil War in the 17th century, the castle fell into some disrepair and the Council of State ordered it to be partially pulled down. But today it lives on, a slightly more tumbledown sister to its Unesco partner at

> ### ❶ CADW JOINT TICKET
>
> Cadw (the Welsh historic monuments agency) offers combined tickets (adult/child £8.05/6.10) for the two historic properties it manages in Conwy: Conwy Castle and Plas Mawr.

Caernarfon, and a must visit for anyone with an interest in Welsh history.

Exploring the castle's nooks and crannies makes for a superb, living-history visit, but best of all, head to the battlements for panoramic views and an overview of Conwy's majestic complexity.

Town Wall FORTIFICATIONS

FREE The survival of most of its 1300m-long town wall, built concurrently with the castle, makes Conwy one of the UK's prime medieval sites. It was erected to protect the English colonists from the Welsh, who were forbidden from living in the town and were even cleared from the surrounding countryside.

You can enter the town walls at several points and walk along the battlements. Perhaps the easiest place to start is the short section that runs alongside the castle car park to the **Mill Gate**. Head through this gate for great views of the wall's exterior.

To find the other accessible section, follow the path under the train tracks, turn right and head through the wall onto the train station platform. The entrance to the largest section of wall starts here and heads up to the **Upper Gate** (where there are great views over the town to the castle), before continuing all the way to the quay.

To get down to the quay you'll need to double back and exit the wall on Berry St, and head through the **Lower Gate**. One of the quayside houses, built hard up against the wall, bills itself as the **Smallest House In Great Britain** (Lower Gate St; adult/child £1/50p; ◷ 10am-5.30pm Mon-Sat, 11am-4pm Sun Apr-Oct), and at a minuscule 3m by 1.8m, they're probably not exaggerating.

Plas Mawr HISTORIC BUILDING

(Cadw; www.cadw.wales.gov.uk; High St; adult/child £5.75/4.35; ◷ 9am-5pm Tue-Sun Easter-Oct) Completed in 1585 for the merchant and courtier Robert Wynn, Plas Mawr is one of Britain's finest surviving Elizabethan town houses. The tall, whitewashed exterior is an indication of the owner's status, but gives no clue to the vivid interior, with its colourful friezes and plasterwork ceilings. The admission price includes a helpful audio guide.

Aberconwy House HISTORIC BUILDING

(NT; www.nationaltrust.org.uk/aberconwy-house; Castle St; adult/child £3.40/1.70; ◷ 11am-5pm daily Jul & Aug, 11am-4pm Wed-Mon Sep, Oct & Mar-Jun, noon-3pm Sat & Sun Nov-Feb) Timber-and-plaster Aberconwy House is the town's oldest medieval merchant's house, dating from around 1300. Over the years it has been a coffee house, temperance hotel, bakery and antique shop, but it remains surprisingly well preserved. An audiovisual presentation shows daily life from different periods of history. The National Trust shop downstairs has a good range of souvenirs and gifts.

Royal Cambrian Academy GALLERY

(www.rcaconwy.org; Crown Lane; ◷ 11am-5pm Tue-Sat Mar-Oct, 11am-4pm Wed-Sat Nov-Feb) **FREE** Founded in 1881 and still going strong, the academy runs a full calendar of exhibitions by its members in its twin white-walled galleries, plus visiting shows from the National Museum Wales and elsewhere. It also hosts the excellent Annual Summer Exhibition from August to September, featuring the cream of contemporary fine art in Wales under one roof.

🏃 Activities

With all that history, it's easy to forget that Conwy benefits from a superb natural location. One of the best ways to appreciate the simple country pleasures of Conwy life is by taking a stroll along the quay and the beach towards the marina, hugging the headland with views across the River Conwy en route. It's a short and leisurely stroll with fine views of boats bobbing gently in the water, birdlife fluttering around and wildflowers peeking through the grassy banks.

🎭 Festivals & Events

Gwledd Conwy Feast FOOD

(www.gwleddconwyfeast.co.uk; ◷ Oct) Held over a weekend in late October, this food festival, spiced up with performances and a lantern parade, is the highlight of the Conwy calendar. It incorporates the Blinc digital art festival, with images projected onto the castle walls at night. Around 25,000 people attend, so book accommodation well in advance. If you're out of luck, nearby Llandudno has more options.

🛏 Sleeping

⭐ **Conwy YHA** HOSTEL £

(✆ 0845 371 9732; www.yha.org.uk; Larkhill, Sychnant Pass Rd; dm/r £23/49; P 🛜 🖨) Perched on a hill above the town, this former hotel has been converted into a top-notch hostel – the best in North Wales. Dorms have either two or four beds, and many of the private rooms have en suites. Head up to the large dining room for awesome views of the

Conwy

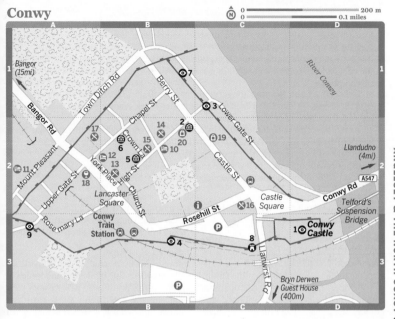

Conwy

⊙ Top Sights

⊙ Sights

🛏 Sleeping

⊗ Eating

⊙ Drinking & Nightlife

🛍 Shopping

mountains and the sea. To get here, continue from Upper Gate St onto Sychnant Pass Rd; the hostel's up a long drive to the left.

Bryn Derwen Guest House   B&B **£**
(☑01492-596134; www.conwybrynderwen.co.uk; Woodlands, Llanwrst Rd; s/d from £40/57; [P][☎]) Sitting behind steep lawns, this six-bedroom Victorian town house B&B is barely a five-minute walk south of the walled town. The rear rooms are small, with tiny bathrooms, but they're priced accordingly.

★**Gwynfryn**   B&B **££**
(☑01492-576733; www.gwynfrynbandb.co.uk; 4 York Pl; r £60-85; [☎]) Although it seems in danger of being engulfed by butterfly ornaments and dangling mobiles, this very friendly five-bedroom B&B – set in a refurbished Victorian property just off the main square – is a great place to stay. The clean, bright rooms are filled with thoughtful extras such as small fridges, biscuits, chocolates and earplugs. When we last stayed it

THE KINMEL ARMS

If you've ever had the urge to hole yourself up in a comfortable pub in a small village, this one's for you. Located in the countryside near Abergele, 15 miles east of Conwy, the village of St George is a sleepy little place consisting of little more than a scattering of houses, a parish church, a privately owned Victorian manor house, a primary school and, of course, a pub. However, the **Kinmel Arms** (☑01745-832207; www.thekinmelarms. co.uk; St George; ste from £135-175; ☺Tue-Sat; ℗🎅) isn't your average country pub – it's a top-notch enclave of fine food, real ales and boutique accommodation. The four Alpine-style units are totally self-contained, with high-end features, beautiful bathrooms and lots of rustic touches. Cooked breakfasts aren't offered, but room fridges are stocked with brekkie fare the night before – which is great if you fancy a lie-in.

To get here from Conwy, take the A55 to junction 24 and exit on to the A547 (Rhuddlan Rd). After 1.6 miles look for the signpost pointing to St George on your right.

was in the process of creating an annexe out of the neighbouring chapel.

Castlebank Hotel   HOTEL ££

(☑01492-593888; www.castlebankhotel.co.uk; Mount Pleasant; s £40-85, d £75-90; ℗🎅💻) The stepped roofline gives this friendly, family-run Victorian town-house hotel a distinctly Dutch look. Inside, it's old-fashioned and homey. Being just outside the walled town offers the distinct advantage of dedicated parking spaces.

Castle Hotel   HOTEL £££

(☑01492-582800; www.castlewales.co.uk; High St; s/d/ste from £85/140/240; ℗🎅) A major refit has loosened the tie on the once-stuffy ambience of this stately coaching inn. The new-look bedrooms feature contemporary decor and Bose sound systems, while higher-priced rooms boast castle views and free-standing baths.

Quay Hotel & Spa   HOTEL £££

(☑01492-564100; www.quayhotel.co.uk; Deganwy Quay, Deganwy; s/d from £155/165; ℗🎅💻) Located across the river at Deganwy Quay (and offering superb views of Conwy Castle illuminated by night), this modern hotel can feel a bit corporate during the week but lets its hair down on weekends with weddings and private parties. There's a popular day spa, along with a gym, indoor pool, restaurant and grill bar.

✗ Eating & Drinking

Press Room   CAFE £

(☑01492-592242; 3 Rosehill St; mains £6-9; ☺10.30am-3.30pm; 💻🍴) Located right next to the castle entrance, this arty cafe serves a tasty selection of meals, including rarebit and 'vegetarian haggis' (surely an

oxymoron), and a good choice of cakes to finish with. There's terrace seating for an al fresco lunch and a craft shop downstairs.

Edwards of Conwy   DELI £

(www.edwardsofconwy.co.uk; 18 High St; snacks £3; ☺9am-5pm Mon-Sat) While first and foremost a butcher's, Edwards also sells savoury pies, local cheeses, and freshly filled baps and sandwiches. Awards are continually piled on them, for everything from their sausages to their pork pies.

★ Watson's Bistro   MODERN WELSH ££

(☑01492-596326; www.watsonsbistroconwy.co.uk; Bishop's Yard, Chapel St; mains £16-18, 2-course lunch £10; ☺5.30-8pm Tue, noon-2pm & 5.30-8.30pm Wed-Sat, noon-2pm Sun) Hidden in a garden-like setting, right up against the town wall, Watson's marries classic French bistro cooking with a modern Welsh sensibility and quality local ingredients. Everything on the menu is homemade, from the chicken-liver paté at the start of the meal to the ice cream at the end. Book to arrive before 6.30pm for the early-bird set menu (three courses £18).

Dawson's   INTERNATIONAL ££

(☑01492-582800; www.castlewales.co.uk; Castle Hotel, High St; mains £15-19; ☺noon-9.30pm) For Conwy's most rarefied dining experience, the Castle Hotel's over-the-top restaurant can't be beaten. Flocked wallpaper and gilt-framed orientalist scenes cover the walls, while daperly dressed staff glide about delivering tasty brasserie-style meals. The adjoining bar offers a good selection of wine and hand-pulled ales in similarly upmarket surrounds.

Amelie's   FRENCH **££**

(☑ 01492-583142; 10 High St; lunch £6-8, dinner £13-16; ⊗ 11am-2pm & 6-9pm Tue-Sat) Named after the Audrey Tautou film, Amelie's is a welcoming French-influenced bistro with wooden floors and flowers on the tables. It's a relaxed place for an easygoing lunch or a more hefty evening meal – make sure you leave room for dessert.

Alfredo's   ITALIAN **££**

(☑ 01492-592381; Lancaster Sq; mains £9-24; ⊗ 6-10pm; ☑ ⓦ) There's something tremendously appealing about the stereotypical Italian-ness of Alfredo's (chequerboard tablecloths, fake ivy, fairy lights draped from the ceiling, shabby carpets, and a giant menu of pasta, pizza and traditional grills) that could only be enhanced with comedy moustaches and

DON'T MISS

BODNANT ESTATE

Whether you're a lover of gardens or fine food, the publicly accessible attractions on this privately owned agricultural estate (www.bodnant-estate.co.uk) should not be missed. While many large country estates fell on hard times in the 20th century, the McLaren family (holders of the title Baron Aberconway) have managed to keep hold of theirs. The 2nd Baron Aberconway, a keen horticulturist, donated Bodnant Garden (NT; www.nationaltrust.org.uk/bodnant-garden; adult/child £5/2.50 Jan & Feb, £8.45/4.22 Mar-Oct; ⊗ 11am-3pm Jan & Feb, 10am-5pm Mar-Oct; ℗) to the National Trust in 1949, although the family continue to maintain it on the trust's behalf.

Bodnant is one of Wales's most beautiful gardens. Laid out in 1875, its 32 lush hectares unfurl around picturesque Bodnant Hall, the McLaren's gracious late-18th-century pile, which the family continue to own and live in. Formal Italianate terraces and rectangular ponds creep down from the house into orderly disorder, transforming themselves into a picturesque wooded valley and wild garden, complete with rushing stream. Key features are the 55m laburnum tunnel, a hair-raising howl of yellow when it blooms in late May/early June; fragrant rose gardens; great banks of azaleas and rhododendrons; and some of the tallest giant redwoods in Britain. Spring is probably the best time to visit but there's something to see in every season.

On the other side of the vast estate, a disused collection of 18th-century stone farm buildings has been painstakingly restored (at a cost of £6 million) and opened in 2012 as Bodnant Welsh Food (☑ 01492-651100; www.bodnant-welshfood.co.uk; Furnace Farm, Tal-y-Cafn; admission free; ⊗ farm shop 10am-6pm Mon-Sat, 10am-4pm Sun; ℗). One of the big attractions here is the wonderful Farm Shop, which includes a deli counter laden with Welsh cheese, a bakery, fresh produce, chocolate, ale and the kind of butchery that practically knows the names of each animal that passes over the counter. The estate even bottles and sells its own water. At present 75% of the shop's wares are made in Wales, but the plan is to increase that to 100%.

However, this is only part of Bodnant's gastronomic offering. There's also the Furnace Tea Room (mains £5-9; ⊗ 9am-5.30pm) in the former cowsheds, the Hayloft Restaurant (☑ 01492-651102; mains £9-10; ⊗ noon-3pm Sun-Wed, to 9pm Thu-Sat) above the shop, and a cookery school (lessons from £50) with an impressive group kitchen classroom – all of which make the most of the farm's homegrown and homemade products. On Thursday nights the restaurant hosts live Welsh folk music and harpists.

The centre is also home to the National Beekeeping Centre Wales (www.beeswales.co.uk; tours adult/child £7/3.50; ⊗ 10am-4pm Wed-Sun), a nonprofit organisation dedicated to encouraging people to take up beekeeping. Its corner of the complex has interesting displays about the plight of the honey bee, a live hive-cam, and lots of bee-produced products to sample and purchase. In warm weather it runs apiary tours (minimum two people).

If you want to settle in to gorge yourself to the point of immobility, there are five attractive little B&B rooms available in the farmhouse (s/d from £50/80; 🕾). The estate also rents self-contained cottages.

The estate is located east of the River Conwy, 4 miles south of Conwy. Bodnant Welsh Food is on the A470, while the garden is accessed by a well-signposted side road.

loud exclamations of 'mamma mia'. The pizza is excellent.

★ **Albion Ale House**　　　　　PUB
(www.albionalehouse.weebly.com; 1-4 Upper Gate St; ⊘noon-11pm) Born out of a collaboration of four Welsh craft breweries (Purple Moose, Conwy, Nant and Great Orme), this heritage-listed 1920s boozer is a serious beer-drinker's nirvana. Of the 10 hand pulls, eight are loaded with real ale and two with cider. Wine and whisky drinkers are well looked after, too. There's no TV or background music – just the crackle of the fire, the gentle hum of conversation and the odd contented slurp.

Shopping

The Potter's Gallery　　　ARTS & CRAFTS
(☑01492-593590; www.thepottersgallery.co.uk; 1 High St; ⊘10am-5pm daily Apr-Sep, Thu-Tue Oct-Mar) Run by a cooperative of North Wales–based potters and designers, this gallery showcases the latest works from its members and is a mine of information about the local arts scene.

Conwy Outdoor Shop　　OUTDOOR EQUIPMENT
(☑01492-593390; www.conwyoutdoor.com; 9 Castle St; ⊘9am-6pm) Well stocked with waterproofs, fleeces, guides and lots of other kit for indulging in outdoor adventures, this is also a great stop for practical advice on making the best of the local activities. The mountain weather forecast is posted outside.

ℹ Information

Conwy Tourist Office (☑01492-577566; www.visitllandudno.org.uk; Rosehill St; ⊘9.30am-5pm daily Apr-Oct, 9.30am-4pm Mon-Sat, 11am-4pm Sun Nov-Mar) Extremely busy office, well stocked with pamphlets and souvenirs. There's an interesting interactive exhibition on the Princes of Gwynedd in the adjoining room.

ℹ Getting There & Away

BUS

Most buses stop by the train station. Bus routes include 5/X5 to Caernarfon (1¼ hours), Bangor (30 minutes) and Llandudno (22 minutes); 15 to Llandudno (21 minutes); and 19 to Llandudno (22 minutes) and Betws-y-Coed (one hour).

CAR & MOTORCYCLE

Through-traffic bypasses Conwy on the A55 via a tunnel under the river. The main road into town from Bangor skirts the outside of the town walls before cutting inside the walls, crawling along Berry and Castle Sts, and heading across the road bridge. The rest of the narrow grid within the walls has a one-way system and restricted parking during the day.

There are pay-and-display car parks on Mount Pleasant, and by the castle. If you're after a free park and don't mind a 10-minute walk, turn right off Bangor Rd on the second to last street before you reach the town walls, cross the narrow rail bridge and park on residential Cadnant Park.

TRAIN

Conwy's train station is just inside the town walls, on Rosemary Lane. Direct services head to/from Holyhead (£13.50, one hour), Rhosneigr (£13.50, 44 minutes), Llanfair PG (£7.60, 26 minutes), Bangor (£6.30, 17 minutes) and Shrewsbury (£20, 2¼ hours).

Llandudno

POP 20,700

Wales' biggest seaside resort straddles a flat peninsula, with long sandy beaches on either side. The twin humps of ancient mountains, the Great Orme and Little Orme, loom over the graceful Victorian wedding-cake architecture of the seafront buildings that line the sweeping 2-mile prom for half its length. Developed as an upmarket holiday town, Llandudno still retains much of its 19th-century grandeur today. Innumerable B&Bs and small private hotels cater to mainly mature-aged travellers in the low season, while young families descend with their buckets and spades in summer.

Alongside the lost-in-time charms of the British seaside (pier, promenade, Punch and Judy shows), Llandudno's main attraction is the near-wilderness of the Great Orme on its doorstep. Old-school tram and cable-car rides head to the summit of this striking limestone headland where there are breathtaking views of the Snowdonia range and miles of trails to explore.

A very tenuous link to *Alice In Wonderland* (Alice Liddell, the real inspiration for Lewis Carroll's fictional Alice, used to holiday here with her family) has seen statues of the characters sprout around the town, along with gift shops full of Alice memorabilia.

◎ Sights

Great Orme　　　　　　HEADLAND
From sea level it's difficult to gauge the sheer scale of the Great Orme (Y Gogarth), yet it stretches for around 2 miles and rises to a height of 207m. Named after a Norse word

Llandudno

Llandudno

◎ Sights
1 Llandudno Pier	C1
2 Mostyn Gallery	C3

✦ Activities, Courses & Tours
3 Cable Car	B1
4 City Sightseeing	B2
5 Great Orme Tramway	A1

🛏 Sleeping
6 Abbey Lodge	A2
7 Adcote House	A3
8 Burleigh House	B1
9 Can-y-Bae	D3
10 Cliffbury	B4
11 Escape B&B	A2
12 Lauriston Court	B2
13 Llandudno Hostel	C3
14 Lynton House	B1
15 Osborne House	B1
16 Plas Madoc	A1
17 St Tudno Hotel	B2

✘ Eating
18 Badgers	B3
19 Candles	B3
20 Characters	A2
21 Cottage Loaf	B3
22 Fish Tram Chips	A1
23 Ham Bone Food Hall & Brasserie	B2
24 Orient-Express	B2
Osborne's Cafe Grill	(see 15)
25 Seahorse	B1

☕ Drinking & Nightlife
26 King's Head	A1

✪ Entertainment
27 Professor Codman's Punch & Judy Show	B1
28 St John's Methodist Church	C3
29 Venue Cymru	D3

LOCAL KNOWLEDGE

LLANDUDNO YESTERDAY & TODAY

Jacqueline Millband Codman's family have staged Punch and Judy shows (p266) in Llandudno for over 150 years. Her great-grandfather started the show outside the Empire Hotel in 1860, which moved to its present spot on the Promenade in 1864. We asked her to share some tips about the town.

Llandudno Today

It's very much a year-round place these days, always bustling and definitely moving with the times. A lot of EU money was invested in updating the Promenade in 2000 and lots of smart new places opened up. Llandudno always did cater for top-end clientele with private jazz clubs and cafes in its post-war heyday. Unlike some resorts on the North Wales coast, Llandudno is definitely not rough and ready. We work hard to maintain the Victorian ambience of the town and to preserve its natural beauty. I can honestly say that much of the Promenade and many of the hotels along the seafront haven't changed much since I was a girl growing up in Llandudno in the 1950s.

What to Do

Take a picnic to Happy Valley, or head to West Shore to feed the swans on the boating pool. Walking around the Great Orme is good for sea views, and taking the Great Orme Tramway is perfect for nostalgia. We're also very lucky that we're so close to the mountains of Snowdonia. After a couple of days exploring the resort itself, take the train to Betws-y-Coed. From Llandudno, you're just 20 minutes from the heart of Snowdonia National Park.

Best Eats

I don't get out as much as I used to but Seahorse (p279) is still superb for fresh fish and Fish Tram Chips (p279) remains perennially popular for a simple but good-value supper.

for worm or sea serpent, this gentle giant looms benevolently over the town. Designated a Site of Special Scientific Interest (SSSI), the headland is home to a cornucopia of flowers, butterflies and sea birds; a herd of around 150 wild Kashmir mountain goats; three waymarked summit trails (of which the Haulfre Gardens Trail is the easiest to negotiate); a neolithic burial chamber; a Bronze Age mine, the remains of an Iron Age fort; and an ancient church dedicated to Llandudno's namesake, St Tudno. At the summit there's a cafe, bar, gift shop and various amusements, as well as the Great Orme Country Park Visitor Centre (www.conwy.gov.uk/greatorme; ⏲10am-5.30pm Easter-Oct), which has lots of fascinating displays including a 15-minute video.

Great Orme Ancient Mines   MINE
(www.greatormemines.info; adult/child £6.75/4.75; ⏲10am-5pm mid-Mar–Oct) Archaeology and industrial history buffs should stop halfway up the Great Orme to explore this, the largest prehistoric mine in the world. A 45-minute self-guided tour explains how the ancients turned rock into copper at the smelting site and heads underground for about 200m into 3500-year-old tunnels, dug by people using tools of stone and bone. The site continued to be worked by the Romans, and then from the 17th to 19th centuries, and the entire tunnel network extends for around 4 miles.

Llandudno Pier   LANDMARK
(⏲9am-6pm) A trip to Llandudno isn't complete until you've strolled along the Victorian pier, eating ice cream and shooing away seagulls. At 670m it's the longest pier in Wales. When it opened in 1878 its main use was as a disembarkation point for passengers from the Isle of Man steamers. Those days are long gone, and candyfloss, slot machines and views of the offshore wind farm are now the order of the day. High art it ain't, but the kids will love it.

West Shore   BEACH
When the main beach gets too frantic, go west to this considerably less built-up stretch on Conwy Bay. The views over Anglesey and the mountains of Snowdonia make a magnificent backdrop to sandy strolls, and there's a model boating pool at the Orme end. It's just a shame that the water quality on this side is substandard.

Mostyn Gallery

GALLERY

(www.mostyn.org; 12 Vaughan St; ⊙10.30am-5pm Tue-Sun) FREE A listed 1901 terracotta and brick exterior hides the sharply angled innards of North Wales' leading contemporary art gallery. Its five galleries house changing and often challenging exhibitions. Call in to explore the shop or grab a coffee upstairs even if you find the art perplexing.

🏃 Activities

Great Orme Tramway

TRAM

(🖉01492-577877; www.greatormetramway.co.uk; Church Walks; adult/child return £6/4.20; ⊙10am-6pm Easter-Oct) Head to the top of the Great Orme without breaking a sweat in an original 1902 tramcar. It's one of only three cable-operated trams in the world (the other two are in equally glamorous Lisbon and San Francisco). Trips head up the steep incline every 20 minutes, weather permitting.

Cable Car

CABLE CAR

(🖉01492-877205; adult/child return £8/6; ⊙10am-6pm Easter-Oct)   Britain's longest cable car runs from the Happy Valley Gardens above the pier (subject to the somewhat changeable weather, of course) and completes the journey up the Great Orme in just 18 minutes, with superb sea views en route.

👉 Tours

City Sightseeing

BUS TOUR

(🖉01492-879133; www.city-sightseeing.com; adult/child £8/4; ⊙Mar-Sep) Departs from the pier for a hop-on/hop-off double-decker bus tour of Llandudno and Conwy; tickets are valid for 24 hours.

Llandudno Land Train

BUS TOUR

(one way £1.50) During the school holidays this colourful trackless 'train' runs a regular shuttle from the pier to the West Shore and back.

🎎 Festivals & Events

Victorian Extravaganza

PERFORMING ARTS

(www.victorian-extravaganza.com; ⊙May) Llandudno plays dress up for this annual event, held over the early-May bank holiday weekend. It's the social event of the year, with parades, bands, funfairs – and grossly over-inflated accommodation prices.

🛏 Sleeping

Burleigh House

B&B £

(🖉01492-875946; www.burleighhouse.co.uk; 74 Church Walks; s/d from £35/58; 📶) Levitate up from the New Age shop downstairs to Burleigh's eight fresh and contemporary rooms. Some of them are quite large, particularly the sunny corner ones, and there's a room with a four-poster at the rear with a giant bathroom.

Llandudno Hostel

HOSTEL £

(🖉01492-877430; www.llandudnohostel.co.uk; 14 Charlton St; dm £20, tw £48-52, f £69-156; 🅿🛜🛏) 🛈 Staking out the middle ground between hostel and budget B&B, this powder-blue Victorian town house offers tidy rooms, bike storage and a free continental breakfast. It's family run and very family friendly – not the kind of place for booze hounds, but then neither is Llandudno. Kitchen facilities are limited to a microwave and kettle.

Escape B&B

BOUTIQUE HOTEL ££

(🖉01492-877776; www.escapebandb.co.uk; 48 Church Walks; r £89-140; 🅿🛜) Escape brought a style revolution to Llandudno with its boutique-chic ambience and magazine-spread design. It recently upped the ante again, with a major, design-led makeover to include a host of energy-saving and trendsetting features. Even if you're not a *Wallpaper** subscriber, you'll still love the honesty-bar lounge, the DVD library, the tasty breakfasts and the atmosphere of indulgence. Unique.

Lauriston Court

HOTEL ££

(🖉01492-877751; www.lauristoncourt.com; 11 North Pde; s/d from £60/70; 🅿🛜) Sorry Ritz, Savoy and Hilton, if you believe Trip Advisor's 2013 rankings, this is the best hotel for service in the entire world. It's a mighty big call for a small family-run hotel with no restaurant, room service or dedicated reception staff, but the personable couple who run this little place makes sure that it does what it does well – and that's providing clean, reasonably priced rooms and a warm welcome.

Cliffbury

B&B ££

(🖉01492-877224; www.thecliffbury.co.uk; 34 St David's Rd; r £66-80; 🅿🛜) Set on a quiet back street, this attractive corner house has six individually styled B&B rooms, some of which are almost suite-like in their proportions. The friendly youngish owners tactfully describe the place as 'mainly catering for over 25s'.

Can-y-Bae
HOTEL ££

(☑ 01492-874188; www.can-y-baehotel.com; 10 Mostyn Cres; s/d from £40/80; 🛜🐾) Just down the road from Venue Cymru, this welcoming, gay-friendly hotel accommodates many a visiting thespian among its mainly older clientele. Signed memorabilia blankets the walls of the little residents' bar, and there's a piano, if anyone wants to start a sing along. The carpets are at war with the wallpaper in the rear-facing singles, but the sea-view rooms have been freshened up.

Adcote House
B&B ££

(☑ 01492-871100; www.adcotehouse.co.uk; 10 Deganwy Ave; s £40, d £60-66, ste £76; P 🛜) Deganwy Ave isn't Llandudno's most charming street (all of the gardens have been paved over for parking), but Adcote's owners have more than enough charm to go round. Its six tidy rooms are 'exclusively for adults'.

Lynton House
B&B ££

(☑ 01492-875057; www.lyntonhousellandudno.co.uk; 80 Church Walks; s £42, d £64-80; P 🛜) Occupying a doubled-sized town house close to the pier and the tramway, Lynton House is almost like a little midrange hotel. All but the cheaper rooms have newly renovated bathrooms. The sunny front patio is an appealing place for book reading and tea supping.

Plas Madoc
B&B ££

(☑ 01492-876514; www.plasmadocguesthouse.co.uk; 60 Church Walks; s £43, d £68-73; P 🛜🍴) It's not Llandudno's flashest B&B but Plas Madoc distinguishes itself by catering to vegetarians, vegans and the gluten adverse just as well as it does lovers of flesh and grain. Although it's set back from the water, its elevated position affords views from the front rooms and plenty of peace and quiet. No children under 10 years.

St Tudno Hotel
HOTEL ££

(☑ 01492-874411; www.st-tudno.co.uk; 16 North Pde; s/d from £85/104; P 🛜🐾) Alice Liddell used to stay in this seafront town house when she wasn't in Wonderland. Nowadays it's a smart albeit old-fashioned 18-room hotel with an inviting front parlour, a well-regarded terrace restaurant and a heated indoor swimming pool

Abbey Lodge
B&B ££

(☑ 01492-878042; www.abbeylodgeuk.com; 14 Abbey Rd; s/d £45/80; P 🛜) The owners of this well-run four-room guesthouse keep everything fresh and clean, and provide some homey touches, such as a small collection of local-interest books in each room. Hang out in the garden on a sunny day or read in the cosy lounge.

★ Bodysgallen Hall
HISTORIC HOTEL £££

(NT; ☑ 01492-584466; www.bodysgallen.com; s/d from £159/179; P 🛜🐾) The National Trust has taken over this magnificent pink-stone 1620 country house and its spectacular French-style formal gardens. Lose yourself in the wood-panelled world of the Jacobean gentry and justify the expense as your contribution towards saving Britain's heritage. The rooms, split between the main hall and outlying cottages, are traditional with a nod to mod cons, and there's a well-regarded restaurant and spa centre in the grounds. It's located 3 miles south of Llandudno on the A470.

Osborne House
HOTEL £££

(☑ 01492-860330; www.osbornehouse.co.uk; 17 North Pde; ste £155-175; P @) All marble, antique furniture and fancy drapes, the lavish Osborne House takes a classical approach to aesthetics and the results are impressive. The best suites are on the 1st floor with Victorian-style sitting rooms and sea views. Guests have use of the spa and swimming pools at nearby sister property, the Empire Hotel.

✖ Eating

Characters
CAFE £

(www.charactersllandudno.com; 11 Llewelyn Ave; lunch £4-6, dinner £14-16; ⊙11am-5pm Mon-Thu, 11am-8.30pm Fri & Sat) If you're wondering whether it's the place that's full of character or the people running it, it's both. Llandudno's hippest tearoom serves wonderful cream teas (£4) and three-tiered high teas (£7), along with light lunches of sandwiches, soup and jacket potatoes; avoid the coffee. Weekends sizzle with hot-stone dinners.

Orient-Express
CAFE, TURKISH £

(8 Gloddaeth St; mains £4-8; ⊙8am-4pm; 🚻) Brown leather, dark wood, chandeliers and tight confines conjure a faint impression of train travel's golden age, but above all this is simply a welcoming, child-friendly cafe. The Turkish influence is equally subtle, limited to haloumi, grilled chicken and baklava among the familiar British cafe fare.

Ham Bone Food Hall & Brasserie
DELI, CAFE **£**

(www.hambone.co.uk; 3 Lloyd St; mains £7-9; ☺8am-5pm Mon-Sat, 10am-4pm Sun; 🐾) The best deli-cafe in Llandudno serves a huge range of freshly made sandwiches, perfect for a picnic on the promenade. Breakfast is served until 11.30am, or come in at lunchtime for burgers, fishcakes, steak-and-ale pies, huge pizzas and an everchanging selection of specials.

Fish Tram Chips
FISH & CHIPS **£**

(www.fishtramchipsllandudno.co.uk; 22-24 Old Rd; mains £6-9; ☺noon-2pm & 5-7pm Tue-Sat, noon-2.30pm Sun, extended hours summer) Low on thrills but big on tasty, fresh fish and homemade side dishes, this is where the locals head for good-value fish meals. It's probably the best bargain in the resort town.

Badgers
CAFE **£**

(www.badgerstearooms.co.uk; Victoria Shopping Centre, Mostyn St; mains £4-7; ☺9.30am-5pm Mon-Sat Jan & Feb, plus 11am-4pm Sun Mar-Dec) Something of a local institution, this traditional tearoom is best known for its creamy afternoon teas, *bara brith* (a rich, fruit tealoaf) and gooey cakes, but it's the Edwardian attire of the staff that adds a frisson of genteel nostalgia to the experience.

Mamma Rosa
ITALIAN **££**

(☑01492-870070; www.italian-restaurant-llandudno.co.uk; 11 Mostyn Ave; mains £7-21; ☺5-9pm Mon-Sat; 🖉) The front parlour setting of this family-run restaurant only emphasises the Italian home cooking on offer. The lengthy menu is full of pasta, risotto, pizza and traditional grills, although the chef gets to show off on a specials page crammed with lobster and crayfish.

Cottage Loaf
PUB **££**

(☑01492-870762; www.the-cottageloaf.co.uk; Market St; mains £9-16; ☺11am-11pm; 🐾) Tucked down an alleyway off Mostyn St, this homey pub makes staunchly traditional meals using high-quality local ingredients: Menai mussels, slow-roasted pork belly, beef-and-ale pie (vegetarian options exist, but are tame in comparison). Good beer, smiling service and a flower-filled beer garden enhance the experience.

Candles
EUROPEAN **££**

(☑01492-874422; www.candlesllandudno.com; 29 Lloyd St; mains £15-24, 3-/4-course menu £18/20; ☺5.30-10pm; 🖉) Popular with locals for celebration meals, this cosy family-run cellar restaurant serves a hearty selection of British, French and Italian dishes. Staff are friendly, the set menus are good value, and there's even a three-course vegetarian alternative available.

Osborne's Cafe Grill
EUROPEAN **££**

(☑01492-860330; www.osbornehouse.co.uk; 17 North Tce; mains £10-14; ☺10.30am-9.30pm) If you really want to live the grand Victorian fantasy, starch your shirt and head to Osbourne House, where military types peer out of gilt frames from black walls offset with white columns and candle-powered chandeliers. Even the seafood-heavy menu values tradition over contemporary tomfoolery. The prices are very reasonable given the ambience.

Seahorse
SEAFOOD **£££**

(☑01492-875315; 7 Church Walks; mains £18-23; ☺4.30pm-late Tue-Sat) Puzzlingly for a coastal resort, this is Llandudno's only proper seafood restaurant. Thankfully it's a good 'un! The chef is a keen fisherman, and the menu reflects his passion for the local catch (although there are meat and veggie options too). The restaurant is a split-level affair: upstairs is decorated with large murals, while the more intimate cellar room has a cosier feel.

🍷 Drinking & Nightlife

Upper Mostyn St is the place to head to get a taste for Llandudno's nightlife with a group of fashion-conscious bars lining the strip. Cottage Loaf is the best pub for real ale and live music.

King's Head
PUB

(www.kingsheadllandudno.co.uk; Old Rd; ☺noon-11pm) Dating from the late 18th century, Llandudno's oldest pub is a great place for a quiet pint or a hearty meal. There's a music quiz on Tuesday and a general knowledge quiz on Wednesday.

☆ Entertainment

Venue Cymru
THEATRE, MUSIC

(☑01472-872000; www.venuecymru.co.uk; Penrhyn Cres; ☺box office 10am-7pm Mon-Sat, plus 1 hour before performances) Having undergone a major expansion, Venue Cymru is one of North Wales' leading event and performance venues. The line-up covers all bases from big rock gigs to high-brow classical performances via shows for children.

**Professor Codman's
Punch & Judy Show** THEATRE
(The Promenade; ◷2pm & 4pm Sat & Sun plus
school holidays Easter–mid-Sep) Queen Victoria herself watched this show, performed
by the same family with the same puppets
since 1860. Mr Punch's iconic red-and-white-
striped tent sits near the entrance to the
pier. If you're not familiar with the Punch
and Judy tradition, you might be surprised
by the violence – but the kids don't seem to
mind.

St John's Methodist Church LIVE MUSIC
(www.stjohnsllandudno.org; 53 Mostyn St) Hosts
a summer season of performances, with
choirs on Tuesday and Thursday, and brass
bands on most weekends.

ⓘ Information

Llandudno General Hospital (📞01492-
860066; www.bcu.wales.nhs.uk; Hospital Rd)
One mile south of the town centre, off the
A546. The nearest A&E department is at Ysbyty
Gwynedd in Bangor.
Llandudno Tourist Office (📞01492-577577;
www.visitllandudno.org.uk; Mostyn St; ◷9am-
5.30pm Apr-Oct, 9am-5pm Mon-Sat Nov-Mar)
In the library building, with helpful staff and an
accommodation booking service.

ⓘ Getting There & Away

BUS

Buses stop on the corner of Upper Mostyn St
and Gloddaeth St.
➡ National Express coaches head to/from
Liverpool (£13, 2½ hours), Manchester (£16,
3½ hours), Birmingham (£35, five hours) and
London (£35, 8½ hours).
➡ Bus routes include 5/X5 to Caernarfon (1½
hours), Bangor (56 minutes) and Conwy (22
minutes); 15 to Conwy (21 minutes); and 19 to
Conwy (22 minutes) and Betws-y-Coed (one
hour).

CAR & MOTORCYCLE

Parking is metered during the day on the main
part of the Promenade, but it's free once you get
past the roundabout east of Venue Cymru.

TRAIN

Llandudno's train station is centrally located on
Augusta St. Direct services head to/from Betws-
y-Coed (£5.90, 48 minutes), Blaenau Ffestiniog
(£8.10, 1¼ hours), Chester (£18, one hour) and
Manchester Piccadilly (£30, 2¼ hours); for other
destinations you'll need to change at Llandudno
Junction (£2.60, eight minutes).

ISLE OF ANGLESEY (YNYS MÔN)

At 276 sq miles, the Isle of Anglesey is Wales'
largest island and bigger than any in England. It's a popular destination for visitors
with miles of inspiring coastline, hidden
beaches, chocolate-box villages and Wales'
greatest concentration of ancient sites. A
brush with royalty has given Anglesey an
added caché in recent years, with the Duke
and Duchess of Cambridge setting up home
here while Prince William serves at the Royal
Air Force base in Valley.

From prehistoric times, Anglesey's fertile land was settled by small communities
of farmers. The island was holy to the Celts
and, in AD 60, it was the last part of Wales
to fall to the Romans. Given its outpost status and singular character, Anglesey stakes
a fair claim to being the Welsh heartland.
Gerald of Wales quoted the ancient name
for the island in declaring it 'Môn mam
Cymru' (Mother of Wales) at the end of the
12th century.

Almost all of the Anglesey coast has
been designated as an Area of Outstanding
Natural Beauty. The little town of Beaumaris makes an attractive base due to its
excellent accommodation and eateries, but
there are hidden gems scattered all over
the island.

Llanfairpwllgwyngyllgo-gerychwyrndrobwllllan-tysiliogogogoch (Llanfair PG)

POP 3110
The small town with the absurdly long,
consonant-mangling name is an unlikely
hot spot for visitors, yet coaches stop by frequently, waiting while their passengers jostle for a photo opportunity on the train station platform (go on, you know you want to).
The name (which means St Mary's Church in
the Hollow of the White Hazel near a Rapid
Whirlpool and the Church of St Tysilio near
the Red Cave) was dreamt up in the 19th
century to get the tourists in. And it worked.
The previous name Llanfairpwllgwyngyll
would have been hard enough; most locals
call it Llanfairpwll but you'll more often see
it written as Llanfair PG.

⊙ Sights & Activities

Marquess of Anglesey's Column LOOKOUT
(adult/child £1.50/75p; ☉9am-5pm; P) Visible from across the Menai Strait, this monument commemorates Wellington's right-hand man at the 1815 Battle of Waterloo, Henry William Paget, who lived at nearby Plas Newydd. Climb the 115 steps up to the base of the statue for great views across the island.

★ Plas Newydd HISTORIC BUILDING
(NT; www.nationaltrust.org.uk/plas-newydd; adult/child £8.90/4.45, garden only £7/3.50; ☉house noon-4.30pm Sat-Wed Mar-Oct, garden 10am-5.30pm Sat-Wed Mar-Oct, 11am-4pm Sat-Wed Nov-Feb; P) When you pull up into the car park, don't get too excited by the impressive building you can see in front of you – that's just the stables! The grand manor house of the Marquesses of Anglesey is set well back from the road surrounded by tranquil gardens, gazing out across the Menai Strait to the heights of Snowdonia. The earliest parts date from the early 15th century, but most of the Gothic masterpiece that stands today took shape in the 1790s.

Inside, the walls are hung with gilt-framed portraits of worthy ancestors of the Paget family (William Paget was secretary of state to Henry VIII), who owned the house until 1976. A highlight is a giant painting by Rex Whistler filling an entire wall of the dining room, which magically changes perspective as you walk around the room. In the grounds there's a tearoom, a cafe, an adventure playground and a well-established rhododendron garden.

The house is 2 miles southwest of Llanfair PG, along the A4080.

Bryn Celli Ddu Burial Chamber ARCHAEOLOGICAL SITE
FREE There are neolithic burial mounds scattered all around Wales, but many have been completely stripped of their earthen covering by over-enthusiastic archaeologists and left as a stone shell. What makes Bryn Celli Ddu fascinating is that it's relatively intact; you can enter the barrow and pass into a stone-lined burial chamber that was used as a communal grave 5000 years ago.

'The Mound in the Dark Grove' now sits on farmland southwest of Llanfair PG. To find it, continue on the A4080 past Plas Newydd, look for the signpost on the right

MOVING ON?

For tips, recommendations and reviews, head to shop.lonelyplanet.com to purchase a downloadable PDF of the Manchester, Liverpool & the Northwest chapter from Lonely Planet's *England* guide.

ANGLESEY & THE NORTH COAST LLANFAIR PG

THE DRUIDS

The magical mystique that the ancient druids enjoy today is assisted by a lack of evidence – they wrote down nothing about their beliefs. It is known that they had charge of Celtic religion and ritual, and were educators and healers as well as political advisors, and so were vastly influential. However, the main sources of information about this spiritual aristocracy are Roman scholars, whose accounts are seen through an adversarial glass. The Romans are coloured as a civilising force, and the Celts and druids as bloodthirsty and keen on human sacrifice.

Resistance to the Romans was powered by druidic influence in Britain. Anglesey was a major seat of druidic learning because of its strategic placement between Wales, Ireland and France. According to the Roman historian Tacitus, when the Romans attacked Anglesey in AD 60, they were terrified by the resident wild women and holy fanatics who greeted them with howls and prayers, and found the altars there covered in the blood of prisoners. The conquerors set about destroying the druids' shrines and sacred groves, and did all they could to impress their culture on the locals, but the result was inevitably a mix of new and old beliefs.

Druidism became a fashionable interest in the 18th century, and the Welsh poetic tradition is believed to stem from the druids. In 1820 Edward Williams created druidic ceremonies to be performed during the annual Eisteddfod, which accounts for many of the long beards and solemn ceremonies still in evidence at this festival of poetry and literature today.

ORIEL YNYS MÔN

As Anglesey's county town, Llangefni holds claim to the island's main gallery and museum. **Oriel Ynys Môn** (www.orielynysmon.info; ⊙10.30am-5pm) FREE is the lynchpin of the island's cultural scene, playing host to a busy calendar of exhibitions and events. The main draw is the Oriel Kyffin Williams, dedicated to Wales' most celebrated artist. The art in this hall changes regularly but always features some of the over 400 Williams works that the gallery holds. His portraits and landscapes provide a unique window into Welsh culture.

For an island with such a fascinating history, the attached museum is strangely disjointed but it's still a good place to top up your knowledge of the Roman invasion. The complex also has an excellent shop and cafe. It's located immediately north of Llangefni, well signposted from the B5111.

and follow the country lane to the marked car park. From there a footpath follows a stream, skirting the fields for five minutes.

ℹ Information

Llanfair PG Tourist Office (☏01248-713177; www.visitanglesey.co.uk; ⊙9.30am-5pm; 🛜) Located across the car park from the train station this is the island's only permanently staffed tourist office. Call in to stock up on information, maps and souvenirs.

ℹ Getting There & Away

➡ Buses head to/from Holyhead (X4; one hour), Llangefni (4A/41/44A/X4; 19 minutes), Menai Bridge (4A/41/43/44A/X4; five minutes), Bangor (4A/41/43/44A/X4; 18 minutes) and Llanberis (41; 39 minutes).

➡ Direct trains head to/from Holyhead (£7.70, 38 minutes), Rhosneigr (£5.80, 18 minutes), Bangor (£2.80, six minutes), Conwy (£7.60, 26 minutes) and Shrewsbury (£36, 2¾ hours).

Menai Bridge

POP 3380

It's a testimony to his genius that not only does engineer extraordinaire Thomas Telford have a large town in Shropshire named after him, this small town is named after one of his creations. The industrial age arrived in Anglesey in 1826 when Telford established the first permanent link to the mainland with his innovative 174m Menai Suspension Bridge across the Menai Strait – the first bridge of its kind in the world. The central span is 30m high, allowing for the passage of tall ships. It was joined in 1850 by Robert Stephenson's Britannia Bridge, further south, which carried the newly laid railway.

To learn more about these feats of Victorian engineering and about the ecology of the Menai Straits, visit the **Thomas Telford Centre** (www.menaibridges.co.uk; Mona Rd; adult/child £3/free; ⊙10am-5pm Sun-Thu Jul-Sep). The friendly volunteers regularly arrange talks, tours and family activities.

🛏 Sleeping

⭐**Plas Rhianfa** HOTEL £££
(☏01248-713656; www.plasrhianfa.com; Beaumaris Rd, Glyngarth; r from £155; 🅿🛜) Would-be Prince Charmings can indulge their fantasies in this remarkable turreted Victorian mansion, styled after a French renaissance chateau. Some rooms are chic and contemporary, while others are old-fashioned and romantic. The Duchess Suite – a massive room with a sleigh bed and a freestanding bath on a dais by the window – is popular with princess brides.

ℹ Getting There & Away

Menai Bridge is Anglesey's bus hub. Destinations include Holyhead (X4; 1¼ hours), Llanfair PG (4A/41/43/44A/X4; five minutes), Beaumaris (53-58; 17 minutes), Bangor (4A/41/43/44A/53-58/X4; 11 minutes) and Llanberis (41; 35 minutes).

Beaumaris (Biwmares)

POP 1940

Anglesey's prettiest town offers a winning combination of a waterfront location, ever-present views of the mountains, a romantic castle lording it over en elegant collection of mainly Georgian buildings, and a burgeoning number of boutiques, galleries, smart hotels and chic eateries. Many of the houses are extremely old; the local real estate agent occupies a half-timbered house dating from 1400 – one of the oldest in Britain (look for it on Castle St near the bottom of Church St).

The town's romantic name dates back to the time of French-speaking Edward I, who built the castle. It's a corruption of *beau marais* (meaning 'beautiful marsh') rather than *beau maris* (meaning 'good husbands') – although, unlike in French, the final 's' is sounded.

◉ Sights

★ Beaumaris Castle · CASTLE
(Cadw; www.cadw.wales.gov.uk; adult/child £4.50/3.40; ⊘ 9.30am-5pm Mar-Oct, 10am-4pm Mon-Sat, 11am-4pm Sun Nov-Feb) Started in 1295, Beaumaris was the last of Edward I's great castles of North Wales and today it's deservedly a World Heritage site. With swans gliding on its water-filled moat, it's definitely got the wow factor. This is what every sandcastle maker unknowingly aspires to. The four successive lines of fortifications and concentric 'walls within walls' make it the most technically perfect castle in Great Britain, even though it was never fully completed.

The overall effect may seem more fairy tale than horror story, but the massive gates with their murder holes (used to pour boiling oil on invaders), hint at its dark past. The walk along the top of part of the inner wall gives super views of the castle layout and the breathtaking scenery that surrounds it. Look out for the old latrines (only marginally less unpleasant than the murder holes for those walking below) and the arrow slits in the wall for picking off those unwelcome visitors.

Beaumaris Courthouse & Gaol · HISTORIC BUILDINGS
(combined ticket adult/child £7.50/6; ⊘ 10.30am-5pm Sat-Thu Easter-Sep, Sat & Sun Oct) The grim business of crime and punishment is brought into stark relief by a visit to this twin set of civic buildings on opposite sides of the town. Start as the prisoners did, at the courthouse; dating from 1614, it's the oldest in Wales. Built at the tail end of the Georgian period, the jail (1829) is an altogether more eerie environment. It contains the last-surviving treadwheel in Britain; this punishment for hard-labour prisoners is a forbidding witness to the harshness of Victorian law and order.

Admission includes excellent audio guides that really bring both places to life. The courthouse is opposite the castle, and the jail is on Steeple Lane behind the parish church.

Penmon Priory · CHURCH
(Cadw; www.cadw.wales.gov.uk; Penmon; parking £2.50; ⊘ 10am-4pm; 🅿) Penmon, 4 miles north of Beaumaris at the eastern extremity of the island, is Anglesey at its most numinous. An early Celtic monastery was established here in the 6th century by St Seiriol; the basin of the holy well, tucked behind the current church, is thought to date from that time.

Vikings looted and burned the original church in AD 971. The current simple stone church has elements from shortly after that time, including two 10th-century Celtic crosses, a font from around the turn of the millennia, and some wonderful decorated Romanesque arches from around 1160.

In the 13th century an Augustinian Priory took over the site, which survived until 1536 when it was dissolved. After this the buildings fell into ruins, with the exception of the church, which was converted into a parish church and remains in use to this day. Once the monks were turfed out, the land was taken over by Beaumaris' leading family, the Bulkeleys, who in 1600 built the gigantic dovecote that stands nearby. Pigeons, used for their meat and their eggs, would enter through the cupola and roost in the 930 holes.

The extortionate car-parking charge includes access to a toll road leading to Penmon Point, where there's a cafe and fantastic views of the lighthouse, Puffin Island and the Great Orme.

🏃 Activities

Puffin Island Cruises · BOAT TOUR
(📞 01248-810746; www.beaumarismarine.com; adult/child £9/7; ⊘ Apr-Oct) Off Anglesey's eastern point, Puffin Island is a hotbed of bird and marine life, designated a Special Protection Area. The cliffs are alive with puffins, cormorants and kittiwakes, while seals, porpoises and dolphins call the waters around the 28-hectare island home. The weather-dependent boat trips cruise alongside the island; book at the kiosk at the entrance to the pier, or by phone.

RibRide · BOAT TOUR
(📞 0333 1234 303; www.ribride.co.uk; adult/child £24/16) Runs hour-long blasts in a rigid inflatable as far as Plas Newydd, giving a different perspective on the bridges and the posh homes lining the Menai Strait.

THE ISLE OF ANGLESEY COASTAL PATH

Anglesey is a big draw for walkers thanks to the Isle of Anglesey Coastal Path (www. angleseycoastalpath.co.uk), a 125-mile route passing through a watery landscape of coastal heath, salt marsh, clifftops and beaches. It's well waymarked and not particularly gruelling, especially if you stick to the leisurely 12-day itinerary that's suggested (strong walkers could easily slice off a few days).

The official trailhead is at St Cybi's Church in Holyhead but the 12 stages can be tackled as individual day hikes, ranging from seven to 13 miles per day. Some of the stages, particularly the far northern legs from Church Bay to Cemaes, make for bracing strolls against a dramatic backdrop of wild, wind-swept scenery. A highly recommended section passes from Red Wharf Bay to Beaumaris, via the beach at Llanddona and the ancient priory at Penmon. We've outlined another favourite section, from Trearddur Bay to Holyhead (p273).

Ordnance Survey (OS) *Explorer Maps 262 (west coast)* and *263 (east coast)* are useful (£8 each), as is the *Isle of Anglesey Coastal Path – Official Guide* by Carl Rogers (£11 from the Llanfair PG tourist office).

Anglesey Walking Holidays (www.angleseywalkingholidays.com; per person from £450) offers self-guided walking and cycling packages, including accommodation, breakfast, luggage transfers and transport between trailheads.

🛏 Sleeping

Kingsbridge
CAMPGROUND £

(☑ 01248-490636; www.kingsbridgecaravanpark. co.uk; Llanfaes; sites s/d £17/30; ⊞ 🐕) 🦮 This well-equipped camping and caravanning site is also a haven for local wildlife and wildflowers, earning it a David Bellamy Conservation Award. It's located 2 miles north of Beaumaris, signposted from the B5109.

★ Cleifiog
B&B ££

(☑ 01248-811507; www.cleifiogbandb.co.uk; Townsend; s £60-80, d £90-110; 🛜) A charming little gem, this art-filled town house oozes character and history, and boasts superb views over the Menai Strait. The front bedrooms have their original 18th-century wood panelling, while the rear room sports a 16th-century barrel ceiling; all three are stylishly decorated.

Churchbank
B&B ££

(☑ 01248-810353; www.bedandbreakfastanglesey. co.uk; 28 Church St; s/d from £60/80; 🛜) Friendly former farmer Richard has done a great job transforming this heritage-listed early-Georgian house into an upmarket B&B, retaining the period atmosphere without scrimping on comfort. Each of the three antique-strewn bedrooms has a private bathroom, but only one is en suite.

Victoria Cottage
B&B ££

(☑ 01248-810807; www.victoriacottage.net; Castle Sq; r/ste £90/110; 🛜 ⊞) Behind the bright yellow door of this 1833 terrace house are three well-appointed B&B rooms and an extremely cute Westie terrier, whose portrait graces many a wall. Two of the rooms have claw-foot tubs, while all have Egyptian cotton sheets and goose-down duvets.

Ye Olde Bulls Head Inn & Townhouse
HOTEL ££

(☑ 01248-810329; www.bullsheadinn.co.uk; Castle St; s/d from £80/100; 🛜) These sister properties, located just across the road from each other, provide quite a contrast. Where the Bulls Head accommodation is historic and elegant, the Townhouse is contemporary, high tech and design driven. Breakfast for both is served at the former.

Bishopsgate House
HOTEL ££

(☑ 01248-810302; www.bishopsgatehotel.co.uk; 54 Castle St; s £60-70, d £99-111; P 🛜 ⊞) The nine bedrooms in this fine pale-green Georgian town house are all very different: some have Jacuzzis, others have four-poster beds; some have an antique sensibility, others have quirky modern wallpaper. Heavenly mattresses are a constant throughout.

🍴 Eating & Drinking

Red Boat Ice Cream Parlour
ICE CREAM £

(www.redboatgelato.com; 34 Castle St; scoop £2; ⊙10am-5pm) This popular parlour whips up authentic Italian gelato in a range of flavours, from the exotic (strawberry, mascarpone and balsamic vinegar) to the very extremely Welsh *(bara brith)*.

★ **Bishopsgate Restaurant** EUROPEAN ££

(☑ 01248-810302; www.bishopsgatehotel.co.uk; 54 Castle St; mains £15-20, 3-course menu £23; ☺ 6-10pm) While its unlikely to be accused of being innovative, Bishopsgate's formal restaurant serves beautifully executed, hearty French-influenced dishes. Get in before 7pm to take advantage of the early-bird menu (£15 for two courses).

★ **Cennin** MODERN WELSH £££

(☑ 01248-811230; www.restaurantcennin.com; 13 Castle St; mains £18-22; ☺ 6.30-9pm Fri & Sat) 🍴 Having worked with the likes of Gordon Ramsay and Heston Blumenthal, local lad Aled Williams has returned home to front this upmarket restaurant, attached to a wonderful butchers, which in turn is attached to a local farm. Settle in beneath the centuries-old beams and tuck into the best quality local black beef, lamb and sea bass.

Loft MODERN WELSH £££

(☑ 01248-810329; www.bullsheadinn.co.uk; Castle St; 3 courses £41; ☺ 7-9.30pm Tue-Sat) Climb the stairs to the top of Ye Olde Bulls Head Inn for elegant decor, a refined ambience and lovingly crafted food, focusing on seasonal Anglesey produce. The buzzy brasserie downstairs will certainly be kinder on your wallet (mains £11 to £15), but the food can be hit and miss. Finish up beside the roaring fire in the downstairs bar, one of the most atmospheric drinking spots in Beaumaris.

George & Dragon PUB

(Church St) For over 600 years drinkers have been sipping their ales within these walls and beneath these low ceilings. Join this venerable throng and while you're at it, keep an eye out for the horse brasses and 400-year-old wall paintings. Test your smarts at the weekly general knowledge and music-themed quiz nights.

ℹ Information

Tourist Information Point (www.visitbeaumaris.co.uk; Town Hall, Castle St; ☺ 10am-2pm Mon-Fri) This information point is only staffed for limited hours; at other times, it's a handy spot to pick up brochures.

ℹ Getting There & Around

➤ Buses stop on Church St. Routes include 53-58 to Menai Bridge (17 minutes) and Bangor

(30 minutes); 57 and 58 continue on to Penmon (11 minutes).

➤ There's a large pay-and-display car park on the waterfront, by the castle. If you're prepared to walk, there are often free parks on the Menai Bridge approach to town.

Benllech

Benllech is a small holiday town with a Blue Flag beach and an even better Blue Flag beach at nearby Llanddona. In between is Red Wharf Bay, apparently named after a Viking battle which drenched the beach in blood. Perhaps Benllech's main claim to fame is that Lemmy from the heavy metal band Motörhead grew up here.

✕ Eating & Drinking

Bay Cafe CAFE ££

(Beach Rd; mains £9-13; ☺ 9.30am-9pm Easter-Sep, 10am-4pm Sun, Mon, Wed & Thu, 10am-9pm Fri & Sat Oct-Easter) It doesn't look like much from the outside, but inside you'll find a cosy pistachio-walled cafe, serving delicious cakes along with sandwiches, burgers and Sunday roasts.

Ship Inn PUB

(☑ 01248-852568; www.shipinnredwharfbay.co.uk; Red Wharf Bay; mains £5-16; ☺ noon-2.30pm & 6-9pm Mon-Fri, noon-9pm Sat & Sun) Toby jugs line the walls of this atmospheric white-washed pub (1740), which serves hearty pub grub, local ales and over 50 different types of whisky.

ℹ Getting There & Away

Bus routes include 62 to Amlwch (26 minutes), Moelfre (six minutes), Menai Bridge (18 minutes) and Bangor (29 minutes); and 50 to Beaumaris (20 minutes).

Moelfre

POP 1070

Moelfre is the prettiest harbour village on the east coast. A stream splashes between the old stone houses before cascading down a waterfall and exiting onto the stony beach.

◉ Sights

Seawatch Centre MUSEUM

(☑ 01248-410300; ☺ 10.30am-4.30pm daily mid-Feb–Oct , Sat & Sun Nov) **FREE** Anglesey's treacherous east coast has claimed numerous ships over the centuries, perhaps most famously the *Royal Charter* in 1859, which claimed 460 lives and £360,000 of gold. This little centre is devoted to the brave souls of the Royal National Lifeboat Institute (RNLI), including Richard Evans (1905–2001), who rescued 281 people in his 49 years stationed here; his statue stands outside.

Lligwy Burial Chamber
ARCHAEOLOGICAL SITE

FREE Sometime before 3000 BC the local people raised Lligwy's 25-tonne capstone into place, forming a stone chamber which they covered with an earthen mound. When the barrow was excavated in 1908, the bones of about 30 people were found buried within. To find it, look for the country lane marked 'Ancient Monument' near the roundabout on the approach to Moelfre. Park at the marked car park and walk back along the road; the chamber is on the right, although the sign is partly obscured by an overgrown hedge.

Din Lligwy
RUINS

FREE In the 4th century, during the relative stability of the lengthy Roman occupation, local farmers built a small fortified settlement here consisting of stone buildings behind a large stone wall. All that remains are the foundations, but it's enough to give a good sense of the layout of the site. Nearby, across the fields, stands the photogenic remains of a 12th-century chapel. The small crypt beneath appears vampire-free.

Din Lligwy sits on the same farm as the Lligwy burial chamber and shares the same car park.

OFF THE BEATEN TRACK

LASTRA FARM HOTEL

For a dose of country air, head to this converted 16th-century farmhouse, located inland from the beach town of Amlwch. There are five bedrooms in the main building, but we prefer the three in the cute little coach house, 100m away. Both the **hotel** (☑ 01407-830906; www.lastra-hotel.com; Penrhyd; s £67-75, d £75-95; ℗ 🛜) and its restaurant have won local tourism awards; it's a popular place, so book ahead.

🛏️ Sleeping & Eating

Tyddyn Isaf Camping & Caravan Park
CAMPGROUND £

(☑ 01248-410203; www.tyddynisaf.co.uk; Lligwy Bay, Dulas; sites from £27; 🛜 🚻 🎱) 🏊 With sandy, undeveloped Lligwy Bay close at hand, this large, well-established campground makes a great base for family holidays. Facilities include a restaurant, bar and children's playground with a very cool lighthouse slide.

Ann's Pantry
CAFE £

(☑ 01248-410386; www.annspantry.co.uk; lunch £5-11, dinner £11-16; ⊙ 11am-4pm Thu-Sun, 6-9pm Fri mid-Feb–Apr & Oct–mid-Nov, 11am-5pm Sun-Fri 11am-9pm Sat May-Sep) With a pretty garden setting and a funky beach-hut-meets-stone-cottage interior, Ann's is a gem. The lunch menu includes deli rolls, burgers, salads and local fish.

Derimôn Smokery & Shop
DELI

(☑ 01248-410536; www.derimonsmokery.co.uk; Dulas; ⊙ 9am-4.30pm Mon-Sat) Go straight to the supplier and stock up the picnic hamper at this traditional farmhouse smokery. They smoke and sell a lot of what you'd expect (fish, poultry, meat and cheese) and quite a few surprises (sea salt, paprika, eggs, rice, salted popcorn). Look for the sign pointing off the A5025 on the way to Amlwch.

ℹ️ Getting There & Away

Bus routes include 62 to Cemaes (32 minutes), Amlwch (20 minutes), Benllech (six minutes), Menai Bridge (25 minutes) and Bangor (28 minutes).

Cemaes

A wooded river cuts through this picturesque little fishing village to a scooped sandy beach. The pastel-coloured terrace houses on the narrow high street make for a pretty sight, despite the many empty shops. If you're keen to soak up village life further, the **Woburn Hill Hotel** (☑ 01407-711388; www.woburnhillhotel.co.uk; High St; s/d £35/70; ℗ 🛜) has pleasantly decorated rooms and an old-fashioned charm.

Bus routes include 61 to Holyhead (44 minutes); and 62 to Moelfre (32 minutes), Benllech (36 minutes), Menai Bridge (54 minutes) and Bangor (one hour).

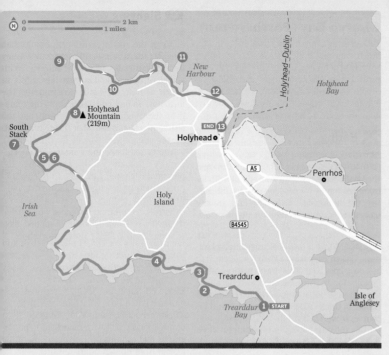

Coastal Walk
Trearddur Bay to Holyhead

START TREARDDUR BEACH CAR PARK
END ST CYBI'S CHURCH
LENGTH 12 MILES; FIVE TO SIX HOURS

This walk takes in one of the most interesting sections of the Isle of Anglesey Coastal Path, circling the northern half of Holy Island. It's also part of the Wales Coastal Path; look for the blue-and-yellow disks that point the way. To reach the start, catch bus 4 from Holyhead; services run hourly, Monday to Saturday.

Pretty scallop-shaped **1 Trearddur Bay** has a sandy beach edged by rocks. Head right and continue along the path as it passes a succession of rocky coves. For the most part, the waymarked route hugs the road but it does cut a few corners. At **2 Porth y Pwll**, a tiny bay with a scrap of sand, it leaves the road and rounds a headland before reaching the larger beach at **3 Porth y Post**.

The route then follows the road before heading to the cliffs and arching back to picturesque **4 Porth Dafarch**. From here the path takes a long amble along the cliffs, before eventually coming back to the road, crossing it and continuing parallel to it. It then joins the narrow road heading to **5 Ellin's Tower** and the **6 RSPB Visitor Centre** (p289). There's a cafe and toilet here, making it the perfect pitstop. If you're making good time and feeling energetic, stop to explore **7 South Stack Lighthouse** (p288), but beware: it's a very steep walk back up.

Pick up the track again for the most remote section of the walk, edging alongside **8 Holyhead Mountain** (219m) towards **9 North Stack**. Here the path loops back and passes **10 Breakwater Country Park** (another handy toilet and coffee stop) and then skirts the base of the **11 breakwater** before reaching Holyhead. Walk along the promenade past the **12 Maritime Museum** (p288) and then follow the road towards the port. Turn right onto Victoria Rd and follow it until you see the gate of **13 St Cybi's Church** (p288) on your right.

Church Bay (Porth Swtan)

Tucked away Church Bay has a fine grin of a beach, smirking at the Irish Sea. There's only a scattering of houses, one of which is 17th-century **Swtan** (www.swtan.co.uk; adult/child £3/1; ⊙noon-4pm Tue-Sun Easter-Sep), the last surviving thatched cottage on Anglesey. Surprisingly, there are a couple of excellent eateries.

✗ Eating

★**Wavecrest Cafe**   CAFE £
(☑01407-730650; snacks £3-9; ⊙10.30am-4pm Thu-Mon Easter-Sep) A cosy, relaxed cafe with local photography for sale, great snack lunches (try the homemade fish pie), and creamy scones and gigantic sponges for afternoon tea.

Lobster Pot   SEAFOOD £££
(☑01407-730241; www.thelobsterpotrestaurant. co.uk; Church Bay; mains £14-26; ⊙6-10pm Thu-Sat, noon-2pm Sun) This local institution is famous for its fresh seafood and decadent three-course set menus, which come in a choice of duck (£17), sea bass (£20) and, of course, lobster (£28).

❶ Getting There & Away

The nearest buses stop a little over a mile away at Rhydwyn. Bus 61 heads to Holyhead (24 minutes), Cemaes (12 minutes) and Amlwch (25 minutes).

Holyhead (Caergybi)

POP 11,500

In the heyday of the mail coaches, Holyhead (confusingly pronounced 'holly head') was the vital terminus of the London road and the main hub for onward boats to Ireland. The coming of the railway increased the flow of people through the town, but the rise of cheap flights reduced the demand for ferries and Holyhead has fallen on hard times. Regeneration funding allowed the impressive Celtic Gateway bridge to be built (linking the train station and ferry terminal to the main shopping street) and a waterfront redevelopment has been promised; but for now, the centre remains a moribund affair.

Holyhead isn't actually on Anglesey at all. Holy Island is divided from the west coast of Anglesey by a narrow channel, although the various bridges obstruct the views these days, and you might not realise that you're crossing onto another island.

◉ Sights

St Cybi's Church   CHURCH
St Cybi, the son of a 6th-century Cornish king, became a priest and eventually washed up in North Wales, where the King of Gwynedd gave him an old Roman naval fort in which to base a religious community. The fort came to be known as Cybi's Fort (Caergybi: the Welsh name for Holyhead) and the island on which it stood became Cybi's Island (Ynys Gybi: the Welsh name for Holy Island).

You can still see the remains of the 4th-century Roman walls surrounding the present-day church yard. The Gothic church came much later, with the oldest parts built in the 13th century. Interesting medieval carvings peer out from the walls, while inside the light is softened by beautiful stained-glass windows from William Morris' workshop.

Holyhead Maritime Museum   MUSEUM
(www.holyheadmaritimemuseum.co.uk; Newry Beach; adult/child £3.50/2; ⊙10am-4pm Tue-Sun Easter-Oct) Small but lovingly restored, this museum is housed in what is believed to be the oldest lifeboat house in Wales (c 1858). It's a family-friendly visit with model ships, photographs and exhibits on Holyhead's maritime history from Roman times onwards.

Ucheldre Centre   ARTS CENTRE
(☑01407-763361; www.ucheldre.org; Millbank; ⊙10am-5pm Mon-Sat, 2-5pm Sun) Housed in a former convent chapel, Ucheldre is the town's artistic hub. Call in to view the latest exhibition and to find out what's coming up in the way of films, live music, drama and dance.

South Stack Lighthouse   LIGHTHOUSE
(☑01407-763900; www.trinityhouse.co.uk; South Stack Rd; adult/child £4.90/2.80; ⊙11am-4.30pm Easter-Sep) The rocky islet of South Stack has an end-of-the-earth feel, with waves crashing around the base of the cliffs and birds nesting overhead. The trail to the old bridge anchoring it to Holy Island is not for the faint-hearted, with 400 slippery steps and a steep return climb. Admission includes a tour of the still-operating 1809 lighthouse. On a blustery day, spare a thought for model Jerry Hall who had to crawl semi-naked on the rocks below dressed as a mermaid for the cover of Roxy Music's *Siren* album.

South Stack is 3 miles west of Holyhead along narrow South Stack Rd. Otherwise, head to Trearddur Bay and follow the coastal road.

Holyhead

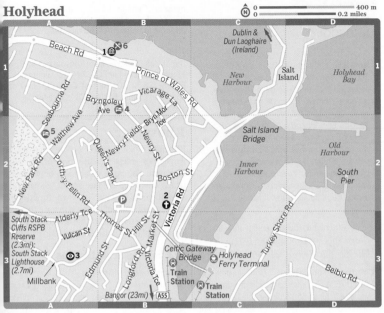

South Stack Cliffs
RSPB Reserve
WILDLIFE RESERVE

(☏ 01407-762100; www.rspb.org.uk/wales; South Stack Rd; ⊘ visitor centre 10am-5pm) **FREE** Between May and June around 12,000 guillemots, 1200 razorbills and 15 loved-up puffin couples congregate here – and that's not to mention the choughs, fulmars, peregrine falcons and other species that can be spotted throughout the year. For a sheltered view, head to Ellin's Tower, a cutesy crenulated structure built in 1868 and now stocked by the Royal Society for the Protection of Birds with binoculars and telescopes. There's also a TV with a live feed from cameras on the cliffs. The tower is open from April to September, but the nearby visitor centre runs year-round. It incorporates a cafe and a gift shop, and has information on local walks.

While you're here, follow the path opposite the car park to the remains of Celtic round houses on the lower slopes of Holyhead Mountain.

🛏 Sleeping

Dublin Ferry Guest House
B&B £

(☏ 01407-762000; www.dublin-ferry.com; 85 Newry St; s/d £39/59; 🛜) In springtime this tidy three-storey house, occupying a corner site near the maritime museum, is garlanded with hanging

flowers and daffodils in jugs. If your ferry's cancelled, it could prove a godsend.

Yr Hendre
B&B ££

(☏ 01407-762929; www.yr-hendre.net; Porth-y-Felin Rd; s/d £40/60; 🅿 @) Facing a park on the quiet edge of town, Yr Hendre is the best place to stay. Professionally managed and homey, the three bedrooms have a feminine touch and one has sea views. Walkers are welcomed, and bicycle storage is available.

🍴 Eating

Ucheldre Kitchen
CAFE £

(www.ucheldre.org; Millbank; mains £3-5; ⊘ 10am-4.30pm Mon-Sat, 2-4.30pm Sun) Avoid the greasy spoons around the high street and head up to

WORTH A TRIP

THE WHITE EAGLE, RHOSCOLYN

Tucked away in the southwest corner of Holy Island, the White Eagle (☑ 01407-860267; www.white-eagle.co.uk; Rhoscolyn; mains £11-15; ⊗ noon-3pm & 6-11pm Mon-Fri, noon-11pm Sat & Sun; ☻) has been zooshed up and transformed from a past-its-best village pub into a snazzy eatery. The menu is more inventive but the portions remain pub-sized and the service is friendly, if not always completely polished. There's also a good selection of beer, perfect for downing on the back deck on a sunny day.

the cafe attached to the arts centre instead. It's a relaxed spot for light lunches (wraps, toasted sandwiches, paninis, soup) or tea and cake.

★ **Harbourfront Bistro**   INTERNATIONAL ££
(☑ 01407-763433; www.harbourfrontbistro.co.uk; Newry Beach; lunch £5-12, dinner £10-14; ⊗ noon-2.30pm & 6-9pm Thu-Sat, noon-2.30pm Sun) For good food and sea views, this cosy bistro adjoining the maritime museum is hard to beat. Sandwiches and baguettes are served alongside cooked lunches, along with coffee and pastries outside meal times.

ⓘ Information

Holyhead doesn't have a tourist information centre but some of the local stores stock brochures. The South Stack Cliffs RSPB Reserve (p289) visitor centre is a good for advice about local walks.

ⓘ Getting There & Away

BOAT

When the weather's poor, it pays to check with the ferry companies before heading to the **ferry terminal**, as services are sometimes cancelled.
Irish Ferries (☑ 08717 300 200; www.irishferries.com) Two daily slow ferries (3¼ hours) and two fast services (1¾ hours) head to Dublin daily.
Stena Line (☑ 08447 70 707; www.stenaline.co.uk) Four daily services to Dublin (3¼ hours) and one service to Dun Laoghaire (2¼ hours).

BUS

➜ National Express coaches stop at the ferry terminal, heading to/from Bangor (£20, 50 minutes), Liverpool (£28, 2¾ hours), Manchester (£36, 4¾ hours), Birmingham (£45, four hours) and London (£29, 7¼ hours).
➜ The main bus stops are on Summer Hill. Destinations include Trearddur (route 4; 10

minutes), Cemaes (61; 44 minutes), Llanfair PG (X4/758; one hour), Menai Bridge (X4; 1¼ hours) and Bangor (X4; 50 minutes).

TRAIN

Direct trains head to/from Rhosneigr (£4.10, 12 minutes), Llanfair PG (£7.70, 29 minutes), Bangor (£8.70, 30 minutes), Conwy (£13.50, one hour) and London Euston (£89, 3¾ hours).

Rhosneigr

Rhosneigr's long sandy beach may not be Anglesey's safest but it's one of its most beautiful. The large village sits between the beach and a small lake, and it has the rare advantage of having its own functioning train station – all of which conspire to make it one of the most desirable addresses in Anglesey. It's also the island's best surfing spot.

◉ Sights & Activities

★ **Barclodiad y Gawres
Burial Mound**   ARCHAEOLOGICAL SITE
(☑ 01407-810153; ⊗ noon-4pm Sat & Sun Apr-Oct)
FREE Squatting on a headland above Trecastle Bay, 2 miles south of the village, Barclodiad y Gawres (The Giantess' Apronful) is the largest neolithic tomb in Wales. When it was excavated in the 1950s, archaeologists were excited to find five standing stones inside, decorated in spirals and zigzags similar to those found in Ireland's Boyne Valley.

Due to problems with vandalism the entrance to the mound is now blocked by an iron gate, but you can still peer into the murky space. If you're keen to get inside, call ahead to the staff at Wayside Stores (1 mile up the road) to make an appointment during the allotted opening times.

Funsport   WATER SPORTS
(☑ 01407-810899; www.funsportonline.co.uk; 1 Beach Tce; ⊗ 9am-5pm) Right by the beach at the bottom of town, this is the hub for the shaggy-haired brigade, renting out boards and wetsuits, and then providing a bragging venue with the Surf Cafe upstairs. It also offers two-hour taster courses in surfing, windsurfing and kitesurfing (£35).

ⓘ Getting There & Away

➜ Direct trains head to/from Holyhead (£4.10, 12 minutes), Llanfair PG (£5.80, 18 minutes), Bangor (£6.10, 24 minutes), Conwy (£13.50, 44 minutes) and Shrewsbury (£42, three hours).
➜ Bus routes include 25 to Holyhead (30 minutes) and 45 to Llangefni (35 minutes).

Understand
Wales

Wales Today

Wales stormed into the new millennium with a renewed sense of optimism, buoyed by its freshly minted National Assembly, with its newly devolved powers, and the major rejuvenation of its capital city. The world has changed considerably since then, and Wales hasn't been immune to financial meltdowns and other global catastrophes. The optimism hasn't completely disappeared, but it has certainly taken a few knocks.

Best on Film

How Green Was My Valley (1941) Acclaimed adaptation of Richard Llewellyn's novel.
Sleep Furiously (2008) Award-winning documentary about life in a Mid-Wales village.
Human Traffic (1999) An edgy romp through Cardiff's clubland.
Edge of Love (2008) Dylan Thomas biopic starring Sienna Miller, Keira Knightley and Matthew Rhys.
Under Milk Wood (1972) Thomas' play about life in a fictional Welsh fishing village, adapted into a film starring Wales' most iconic actor, Richard Burton.

Best in Print

How Green Was My Valley (Richard Llewellyn; 1939) Life in a Welsh mining community laid bare.
Collected Poems 1934-1953 (Dylan Thomas; 2003) Worth it for *Do Not Go Gentle into That Good Night* alone.
Rape of the Fair Country (Alexander Cordell; 1959) Powerful family tale.
A History of Wales (John Davies; revised 2007) Comprehensive and fascinating.
Wales: Epic Views of a Small Country (Jan Morris, 1998) Lovingly written travelogue.

Cohesion Despite Difficulties

Though not as badly affected as other countries, the UK still suffered considerably with recession and increased unemployment over the last few years. And compared with the rest of the UK, Wales comes out at the bottom of most economic indicators, making the people on its margins particularly susceptible to downturns and government austerity moves.

In April 2013, 8.2% of the population (120,000 people) were out of work – a higher rate than the UK-wide figure of 7.6%. On top of that, average gross incomes are low: £521 per week, compared with £814 in London. Even the earnings in Wales' highest paid county, the Vale of Glamorgan, only just equals the Scottish average .

Yet when disaffected young people rioted across English cities in 2011, Welsh cities were almost completely unaffected. In fact, a 2013 report by the Institute of Economics & Peace ranked Cardiff and Swansea (combined) as the most peaceful major urban area in the UK. The same report placed Wales as by far the least violent part of the UK, with the lowest rates of homicide and violent crime, and an overall violence ranking less than half that of Scotland (which, by the way, is a fraction of that of the USA). Some commentators have suggested that despite high levels of poverty and deprivation, these figures speak favourably to the relative cohesion of Welsh society.

Welsh Language Woes

Although support for the Welsh language has strengthened in recent years and other minority cultures look to Wales as a shining example, in reality the threat to the language is acute. These days more people are learning Welsh as a second language and all school children are required to study Welsh up to the age of 16, but pressure on Welsh as a living first language remains.

It's thought that right up until the 1870s, more people in Wales could speak Welsh than could speak English. Between the 2001 and 2011 censuses, the proportion of the population who could speak Welsh dropped from 20.5% to 18.6%.

Economic hardship in Welsh-speaking rural areas in Mid, West and North Wales has resulted in a drift to urban centres. At the same time, large numbers of non-Welsh speakers have been moving in, changing the cultural dynamic of rural Wales in a very short time. Historically, few of these migrants have learnt the Welsh language or become involved in local traditions, and their presence inflates house prices and forces local people out.

During the rise of nationalism from the 1960s to 1980s, opposition to the English 'invaders' rose steadily and anti-English slogans and graffiti were common. A radical underground organisation, the Sons of Glyndŵr, went even further, firebombing English-owned holiday homes. Today, with the advent of the Welsh Assembly, the focus has shifted towards education and the strengthening of the language's official status.

Yet for the first time in the 2011 census, the number of Welsh speakers in Ceredigion fell below 50%, leaving Gwynedd and the Isle of Anglesey as the only counties where a majority of people can still speak the ancient mother tongue.

The United Kingdom?

Scotland's decision to hold an independence referendum poses interesting questions for Wales and its own status within the UK. While there is no immediate likelihood of Wales following suit, Plaid Cymru (which holds 17% of the seats in the Welsh Assembly) has independence as one of its key goals. In the run-up to the Scottish referendum, Plaid Cymru leader Leanne Wood has called on the UK Government to fast-track further devolution of powers to the Assembly, such as the ability to vary income tax, in the event of a Scottish exit. She also speculated that a UK without Scotland would always be dominated by Conservative governments. The Conservatives have never won more than a third of the popular vote in Wales.

POPULATION: **3,070,000**

AREA: **8022 SQ MILES**

UNEMPLOYMENT: **8.2%**

HIGH STREET SHOP
VACANCIES: **17%**

if Wales were 100 people

58 class themselves as Welsh only
7 class themselves as Welsh and British
1 class themselves as Welsh and another nationality
34 don't class themselves as Welsh

Welsh speaking
(% of population)

74
Don't understand
Welsh at all

19
Speak
Welsh

5
Understand but
can't speak Welsh

2
Read but don't
speak Welsh

population per sq km

WALES   UK   USA

 ≈ 3 people

History

Everywhere you go in Wales you'll see the nation's history written large. The landscape is littered with ancient burial mounds, standing stones, earthworks, rusting machinery, sculpted mountainsides, great mounds of slag, sturdy churches, dour chapels and evocative graveyards – and everywhere castles, castles and more castles. Travel through Wales with its history in mind and you'll find it easier to understand Welsh resentment and Welsh pride.

Perhaps the most intriguing glimpse into Wales' early history is the 33,000-year-old ochre-stained skeleton of the Red Lady of Paviland, the earliest known formal burial in Western Europe, found in a cave in Gower's Rhossili Bay.

Early History

Little is known of Britain's earliest peoples, but by 3500 BC the cromlechs, standing stones and stone circles that are evident throughout Britain today started to be raised. This is evidence of the presence of fairly large communities; for instance, it is estimated that it would have taken 200 men to raise the giant capstone at Tinkinswood, near Cardiff, into place.

It was much later, around 600 BC, that the first wave of Celts arrived on Brtiain's shores and with them their poets and priests – the druids – who were revered as much for their knowledge as for their spiritual power. By the 3rd century BC they were the dominant force in Europe, with Celtic tribes ranging from Turkey to Ireland. The Celts had a defining role in Britain, making enormous technical and artistic advances and introducing a new social hierarchy, belief system and language. The British variant on the Celtic language became known as Brythonic, which later developed into modern Welsh.

The Romans

When Julius Caesar arrived in Britain in 55 BC with 10,000 Roman legionnaires, the Celtic tribes who had occupied the island for over half a millennia put up a staunch resistance. In AD 43 the Romans returned with 40,000 men and proceeded to advance through Britain. Mona (Anglesey) was the centre of Druidic power and resistance to Rome. After the druids' last stand on Anglesey in AD 60, the Romans eventually took control of present-day Wales and England. They cemented their rule by

TIMELINE	250,000 BC	600 BC	AD 60
	Someone loses a tooth in a cave in Denbighshire, not realising what excitement it will cause a quarter of a million years later, when it becomes the earliest evidence of a human presence in Wales.	The Celtic people begin to settle in Britain. It's unclear whether they displaced the indigenous people or whether the indigenous people adopted the Celtic culture and language.	The Druids' last stand on Anglesey unleashes the brute force of the Roman army, who set about destroying the island's sacred groves and shrines.

uilding a series of military forts, the remains of which can still be seen n Cardiff Castle, Caernarfon and, most impressively, at the 'city of the egion', Caerleon. In true Imperial fashion they gradually Romanised the ocal population, while allowing them to maintain their own language, ustoms and gods – at least until Christianity became the official state eligion in 391.

Wales is Born

n the wake of the fall of the Western Roman Empire in the 5th century, arious kingdoms arose across Britain and a new threat surfaced in the orm of Germanic tribes such as the Saxons and the Angles. This era is hrouded in legend but it is quite possible that there was a figure such s King Arthur who briefly held the Saxon invaders at bay, inspiring ro-nantic fables in the process.

Eventually the Anglo-Saxons conquered most of present-day Eng-and, with native Brythonic-speakers holding on in remote places such s Wales and Cornwall. To this day, the Welsh word for the English is *'aeson* (Saxon); the English word for the Welsh derives from the old Anglo-Saxon word for foreigner. For their part, the Welsh started to re-er to themselves as *Cymry,* a word meaning 'fellow countrymen', and a eparate Welsh identity was born – distinct for the first time from the est of Britain.

Religion was a point of difference between the Christian Welsh and the pagan Saxons. In the 6th century, religious communities were founded all ver Wales. Many of these *llan* were associated with charismatic leaders, ushering in the so-called 'Age of Saints', and bequeathing Wales with a fair hare of its current place names (Llandudno – St Tudno's community; Llandeilo – St Teilo's community etc). St David became a key figure, estab-ishing his eponymous town as a centre of religion and learning.

During the 9th and 10th centuries savage coastal attacks in the south y Danish and Norse pirates forced the small kingdoms of Wales to co-perate. Rhodri Mawr (Rhodri the Great), a charismatic leader, managed o unite most of the kingdoms, only for them to be split among his sons.

His grandson, Hywel Dda (Hywel the Good), reunified the country and hen went on to consolidate its laws, decreeing communal agricultural practices and affording women and children greater rights than other egal systems of the time.

Enter the Normans

When the Normans claimed England in 1066, William the Conqueror set up feudal barons, the Marcher Lords, along the Welsh border to secure his kingdom. Under sustained attack, the Welsh rulers were pushed back and it was not until Llywelyn ap Gruffydd (Llywelyn the Last) that a

A present-day reminder of the tensions between the Anglo-Saxons (in the form of the Kingdom of Mercia, under King Offa) and the Welsh is Offa's Dyke, the 8th-century forti-fication marking the boundary between the two. The Offa's Dyke Path National Trail traces this border, which still largely aligns with the border of Wales today.

383	c 410	5th century	6th century
Magnus Maximus, commander of Britain, becomes emperor of the Western Roman Empire. He enters Welsh mythology as Macsen Wledig, whose 'dream' inspires the architecture of Caernarfon Castle.	The Romans pull out of Britain and the empire starts to crumble. A number of disparate kingdoms emerge in Wales, including Morgannwg (Glamor-gan), Gwent, Dyfed, Gwynedd and Powys.	The Saxons and other Germanic tribes arrive in Britain, eventu-ally overrunning all of England. The Celtic Britons hold fast in the west where a separate Welsh identity starts to form.	Wales enters the 'Age of Saints'. Religious communities spring up all over the country, including the one founded in Pembroke-shire by Wales' patron saint, David.

pan-Welsh leader again emerged. He adopted the title 'Prince of Wales' and by 1267 had forced England's Henry III to recognise him as such. But Llywelyn's triumph was short-lived and by 1277 he had lost much of what he had achieved.

Edward I fought to control the Welsh upstart and eventually killed both Llywelyn and his brother Dafydd. He then set up his 'Iron Ring' of castles to prevent further Welsh revolt. Of these, Caernarfon is the ultimate expression of military and royal authority, and it was here that his infant son, the future Edward II, was born. The younger Edward was later invested with the title Prince of Wales, a title bestowed, to this day, on the eldest son of the reigning monarch.

Curiously, against this troubled backdrop Welsh storytelling and literature flourished. In 1176 Rhys ap Gruffydd (Lord Rhys), one of Wales' great leaders, convened the first bardic tournament – the original eisteddfod. The 13th-century Black Book of Carmarthen, the oldest surviving Welsh-language manuscript, also dates from this period and is today held at the National Library of Wales in Aberystwyth.

Owain Glyndŵr

Anti-English feeling was rife throughout Wales by 1400 and Owain ap Gruffydd (better known as Owain Glyndŵr), a descendant of the royal

> The Marcher Lordships had a degree of autonomy from the English crown and maintained a separate legal status right up until the time of Henry VIII. Eventually the Marches came to cover much of the south and east of Wales, and some of the neighbouring English counties.

WHO WAS ST DAVID?

St David (Dewi Sant) is the only truly native patron saint of his country in the British Isles. He was born in the 6th century on a clifftop near present-day St Davids. Like many young men of noble birth, David was educated by monks and went on to found churches across South and East Wales. In company with Saints Teilo and Padarn he made a pilgrimage to the Holy Land, eventually returning to West Wales. Fellow churchmen acclaimed his spiritual stature when he preached at the Synod of Brefi (Ceredigion). The ground rose under him and a dove, representing the Holy Spirit, landed on his shoulder. He performed many miracles of healing.

David established his monastery beside Pembrokeshire's River Alyn, where the cathedral now stands. His claim to the site was disputed by Boia, a local chieftain, whose scheming wife made her maidens dance naked in the river to tempt the monks. But David and his fellow monks led a spartan life dedicated to manual labour, care for the poor and prayer. He subdued the appetites of the flesh by standing up to his neck in cold water and reciting the psalms.

David died on 1 March, in the late 6th century. In 1123, Pope Callistus II recognised his sainthood and he has since become a focus for Welsh identity.

Nona Rees is the author of St David of Dewisland

1066 >	1134 >	13th century >	1301
The Normans invade England. By 1086 the Kingdom of Gwent has fallen and there are Norman castles in Chepstow, Monmouth and Caerleon, controlled by the powerful Marcher Lords.	Robert, the eldest son of William the Conqueror, dies in Cardiff Castle, where he had been imprisoned for many years by his brother, Henry II of England.	Llywelyn ap Gruffydd emerges as a unifying Welsh leader but is trounced by Edward I, who builds a ring of castles to suppress the Welsh uprising.	Edward I formally invests his son Edward with the title Prince of Wales, starting the tradition where the heir-apparent to the English throne is granted that title.

house of Powys, became the uprising's leader, declaring himself Prince of Wales and attacking neighbouring Marcher Lords.

Henry IV reacted harshly and passed a series of penal laws imposing severe restrictions on the Welsh. This only increased support for the rebellion and by 1404 Glyndŵr controlled most of Wales, capturing Harlech and Aberystwyth castles, and summoning a parliament at Machynlleth and at Harlech. But Glyndŵr met his match in Prince Henry, son of Henry IV and hero of the Battle of Agincourt. After a series of defeats, his allies deserted him and after 1406 Glyndŵr faded into myth-shrouded obscurity. Glyndŵr remains a great hero to the Welsh; he is memorialised in the Owain Glyndŵr Centre in Machynlleth, devoted to his life story, and the Glyndŵr's Way National Trail, a multiday walking track connecting places associated with him.

The Acts of Union & their Aftermath

By the later part of the 15th century the Welsh and English had learnt to coexist uneasily. With the Wars of the Roses raging, the Welsh cast their hopes on Harri Tudur (in English, Henry Tudor), viewing him as the prophesied ruler who would restore their fortunes. Born in Pembroke Castle, his claim to the English throne was through his Lancastrian mother, but his father was descended from a noble Welsh family from Anglesey. After years of exile in Brittany, Henry defeated Richard III in the Battle of Bosworth Field in 1485 and ascended the throne as Henry VII. This began the Tudor dynasty, which would reign until the death of Elizabeth I in 1603.

But it was Henry VIII who brought real change with the Tudor Acts of Union in 1536 and 1543 to establish English sovereignty over the country. Although the Welsh became equal citizens and were granted parliamentary representation for the first time, Welsh law was abolished and English was declared the official language of law and administration. The glory years of the Cistercian abbeys as centres of learning also came to an end when Henry VIII declared the independence of the Church of England in 1534 and dissolved the abbeys in 1536.

Protestantism was initially slow to catch on in Wales and for many years places such as Monmouthshire and the Llŷn Peninsula had a determined Catholic underground. Under the reign of Elizabeth I, several Welsh priests were caught and executed; they're now recognised as saints by the Catholic Church. Acceptance of the Church of England was greatly assisted by the translation of the Bible into Welsh and the commencement of services in the native tongue.

The effect of the Acts of Union was to make Wales a constituent part of England. Later, when Scotland and Ireland were brought into the fold to form the United Kingdom, Wales wasn't even represented on the

1400	1536 & 1543	1563	1642–49
Welsh nationalist hero Owain Glyndŵr leads the Welsh in rebellion and is declared 'Prince of Wales' by his followers, but his rebellion is short-lived and victory fleeting.	The Tudor Acts of Union introduced by Henry VIII unite Wales and England, granting equal rights and parliamentary representation, but make English the main language.	Church services begin to be held in Welsh. Before then the Reformation had seen services move from one little understood foreign language (Latin) to another (English). Protestantism starts to catch on.	Major battles are fought at St Fagans and Pembroke during the English Civil War between the forces of King Charles I and the Parliamentarians led by Oliver Cromwell.

MORALS

Union Flag. Throughout the next two centuries, the Welsh gentry became increasingly anglicised, while the majority of the ordinary people continued to speak Welsh.

The Nonconformist Protestant churches – particularly the Methodists – started to make great inroads into the Welsh-speaking population and eventually Wales became a land of chapels. Until very recently the chapel was one of the defining symbols of Welsh life, with Sundays being bookended by lengthy services accompanied by hearty hymn-singing. Wherever you go in Wales, even in quite small villages, you'll see multiple chapels – although these days many are abandoned, or have been converted into museums, apartments or even bars.

Romantic Wales

Towards the end of the 18th century the influence of the Romantic revival made the wild landscapes of Wales fashionable with genteel travellers. The works of landscape painters such as Richard Wilson did much to popularise the rugged mountains and ruined castles, and the rediscovery of Celtic and Druidic traditions fuelled a growing cultural revival and sense of Welsh identity.

Scholars were increasingly concerned about the need to preserve the culture and heritage of their country and efforts were made to collect and publish literature. Edward Williams (Iolo Morganwg to use his bardic name) went on to revive ancient bardic competitions and held the first 'modern' eisteddfod in Carmarthen in 1819.

Industrialisation & Unrest

In 1847 the Commission on Education published a damning report on the state of education in Wales. It questioned Welsh morality and blamed the influences of religious nonconformity and the Welsh language for allegedly lax morals. The introduction of the 'Welsh Not', a ban on speaking Welsh in schools, created a tide of anger.

The iron industry had been growing steadily across Wales since the mid-18th century with an explosion of ironworks around Merthyr Tydfil. Industrialists constructed roads, canals and tramways, changing the face of the valleys forever. Major engineering developments from this period include Thomas Telford's spectacular Pontcysyllte Aqueduct and his graceful suspension bridge at Conwy.

As the Industrial Revolution gathered pace, workers were increasingly dissatisfied with the appalling conditions and low rates of pay. Trade unions emerged and the first half of the 19th century was characterised by calls for a universal right to vote. In 1839 the Chartist Riots broke out in towns such as Newport when a petition of more than one million signatures was rejected by Westminster. Between 1839 and 1843 the Rebecca Riots broke out in the rural southwest. The name 'Rebecca' refers to a biblical verse: 'Rebecca... let thy seed possess the gate of those who hate them'. The 'Daughters of Rebecca' (men dressed in women's clothes) attacked the hated turnpike tollgates that charged hefty tolls for those using the roads.

1759–82	1865	1900	1916
With the Industrial Revolution gripping the South Wales valleys, Dowlais and Merthyr Tydfil ironworks start production and Bethesda's slate quarry opens for business.	A Welsh colony is set up in Patagonia, Argentina. Welsh is the language of the courts, schools, chapels and newspapers until 1896.	James Keir Hardie, a Scotsman, becomes the first Labour MP to enter parliament, after winning a seat in the Welsh mining town of Merthyr Tydfil.	With WWI in progress, David Lloyd George becomes prime minister, the only Welshman to have ever held the role. Welsh was his first language, English his second.

Reform & the Depression

By the second half of the 19th century, coal had superseded iron, and the population of Wales exploded. In 1867 industrial workers and small tenant farmers were given the right to vote, and elections in 1868 were a turning point for Wales. Henry Richard was elected as Liberal MP for Merthyr Tydfil, and brought ideas of land reform and native language to parliament for the first time.

The Secret Ballot Act of 1872 and the Reform Act of 1884 broadened suffrage and gave a voice to the rising tide of resentment over the hardships of the valleys and the payment of tithes (taxes) to the church. In 1900 Merthyr Tydfil returned James Keir Hardie as Wales' first Labour MP.

National sentiment grew and education improved substantially. During WWI, Wales boomed and living standards rose as Welsh coal and agriculture fed the economy.

Between the world wars the country suffered the results of economic depression and thousands were driven to emigrate in search of employment. The Labour Party weathered the storm and, as the 20th century progressed, became the dominant political force in Wales. In 1925 six young champions of Welsh nationalism founded Plaid Cenedlaethol Cymru (the Welsh Nationalist Party; later shortened to Plaid Cymru) in Pwllheli and began a campaign for self-government.

> A quarter of a million people were employed in Wales' coal industry in the 1920s. Remnants of this heyday can be seen in World Heritage–listed Blaenavon and dozens of other communities in the valleys.

Postwar Wales & Industrial Decline

The postwar years were not kind to Wales. The coal industry went into steep decline, forcing the closure of mines and a bitter struggle as unemployment levels rose to twice the UK average. The Welsh language was suffering and national pride was at an all-time low.

The final blow came in 1957 when the North Wales village of Capel Celyn, near Bala, and the surrounding valley were flooded to provide water for the city of Liverpool, despite vigorous campaigning across Wales. There were too few Welsh MPs in the House of Commons to oppose the project and resentment lingers over the issue even today, intensified in dry summers by the appearance of the chapel, school and farms above the waters of Llyn Celyn.

The 1960s became a decade of protest in Wales, and Plaid Cymru gained ground. Welsh pop music began to flourish and Welsh publishing houses and record labels were set up. In 1962 Cymdeithas yr Iaith Gymraeg (the Welsh Language Society) was founded. Further electoral successes by Plaid Cymru in the 1970s started people thinking about a measure of Welsh self-government. In 1976 the Welsh Development Agency (WDA) was established to foster new business opportunities across Wales in the face of the decline in traditional industry.

1939–1945	1955	1959	1962
WWII rages across Europe and much of Africa, Asia and the Pacific. Parts of Wales are bombed by the Germans, notably Swansea, Cardiff and the Rhondda Valley.	After a ballot of members of the Welsh local authorities, Cardiff is declared the first-ever Welsh capital, garnering three times as many votes as nearest contender, Caernarfon.	Wales adopts the red dragon on a white and green background as its official flag. Henry VII, the first Tudor king, used this banner at the Battle of Bosworth Field in 1485.	Cymdeithas yr Iaith Gymraeg (the Welsh Language Society) is founded to campaign for legal status for the language and for Welsh-speaking radio and TV.

Margaret Thatcher's Conservative Party initiated a sweeping campaign of privatisation during the 1980s, leading to severe cuts in the coal, manufacturing and steel industries. Agriculture, too, was in a state of disarray and unemployment began to soar. Welsh living standards lagged far behind the rest of Britain, and with the collapse of the UK Miners Strike (1984–85) Welsh morale hit another low point. Many mines were subsequently shut down and whole communities destroyed. Some have since reopened purely as tourist attractions, notably Big Pit at Blaenavon and the Rhondda Heritage Park.

Something good did come out of the '80s, however, with the 1982 establishment of S4C (Sianel Pedwar Cymru), the Welsh-language TV channel. Support and enthusiasm for the Welsh language increased, night courses popped up all over the country, Welsh-speaking nurseries and schools opened, university courses were established and the number of Welsh speakers started to stabilise at around 20% of the population.

DAVID LLOYD GEORGE (1863–1945)

David Lloyd George began his career as the champion of Welsh populist democracy and a critic of society and its institutions. A talented and witty orator, in 1890 he won his first seat as Liberal MP for Caernarfon Boroughs and, at 27, became the youngest member of the House of Commons.

As Chancellor of the Exchequer he launched a broad but controversial agenda of social reform, including the introduction of old-age pensions, a 1909 budget that taxed the wealthy to fund services for the poor, and the 1911 National Insurance Act to provide health and unemployment insurance. Elected prime minister in 1916 after a divisive alliance with the Conservatives, Lloyd George went on to become an energetic war leader. He excelled at a time when strong leadership was needed, dismissing red tape and forcing his opinion when necessary.

Postwar industrial unrest and economic reconstruction dogged the country, however, and he eventually agreed to Irish independence to end civil war, a solution the Conservative alliance never forgave. Accusations of corruption, financial greed and the selling of honours began to ruin his reputation. Radicals, Welsh nationalists and campaigners for women's rights all felt betrayed. In 1922 the Conservatives staged a party revolt and broke up the shaky coalition. Lloyd George resigned immediately.

His popularity faded, the Liberal Party was in disarray, political allies had abandoned him, and both the Welsh and the British working class felt thoroughly deceived. Lloyd George's political career had reached a sad anticlimax.

He died in 1945 at Llanystumdwy, where there is now a small museum devoted to his life.

1966	1984	1997	1999
A colliery spoil tip collapses on the village of Aberfan, near Merthyr Tydfil, killing 116 children and 28 adults. An enquiry blames the National Coal Board for extreme negligence.	Margaret Thatcher's Conservative government announces the closure of 20 coal mines. The ensuing Miner's Strike ends in 1985 with the workers defeated. Further pit closures follow.	A referendum asking whether a Welsh Assembly should be formed narrowly passes. The 'yes' vote is strongest in the west (except Pembrokeshire); the majority of people in the border counties vote 'no'.	The first National Assembly For Wales is elected, with limited powers devolved from the UK Parliament. The Assembly is led by a coalition between the Welsh Labour Party and the Liberal Democrats.

Devolution

The 1997 general election brought Tony Blair's 'New Labour' to power in the UK and the devolution process got off the ground once again. In September of that year a referendum on the establishment of the Welsh Assembly scraped through by the narrowest of margins.

Lacking the powers granted to the Scottish Parliament, the Assembly was always going to have a hard time convincing the world, including Wales, of its merit. The unveiling of the new National Assembly building in Cardiff Bay and the passing of the Government of Wales Act in 2006, creating a new legislature and executive, gave the Assembly more teeth and helped the new seat of government to become part of the fabric of daily Welsh life.

A further referendum in 2011, asking whether the Assembly should be able to create laws in its own right, rather than having to have them rubber-stamped by the UK Parliament, passed with a much stronger affirmative vote. These law-making powers are still limited in scope, but include such important areas as housing, health, social welfare, tourism, culture and the Welsh language.

2008	2011
Wales' last deep coal mine closes. The Tower Colliery in Hirwuan had been bought and operated successfully by a workers' collective since the National Coal Board had deemed it uneconomic in 1994.	A further referendum is held asking whether the Welsh Assembly should be able to make laws without the approval of the UK Parliament; 64% of the population vote 'yes'.

Culture

Cultural debate in Wales often centres on one theme: identity. What is the identity of Wales in the 21st century? What are the defining elements of Welsh culture? Historically Wales struggled to overcome negative stereotypes about its lack of sophistication. But Welsh pride has been buoyed by the success of its pop and rock stars, actors and film-makers, writers and thinkers. To be Welsh today is a complex blend of historical association, ingrained defiance and Celtic spirit.

Literature

Dylan Thomas' reputation for hard drinking almost over-shadows the impact of his literary works, but he is acclaimed for writing half a dozen of the greatest poems in the English language, including such timeless works as *Fern Hill* and *Do Not Go Gentle into That Good Night.*

Wales has an incredibly rich literary history, with storytelling firmly embedded in the national psyche. The Welsh language is also a defining characteristic, its lyrical nature and descriptive quality heavily influencing the style of Welsh writers. Caradoc Evans' (1883–1945) controversial collection of short stories, *My People,* was one of the first works of fiction to bring Welsh literature to a worldwide audience. Its publication in 1915 saw a move away from established nostalgic themes and instead exposed a darker side of Welsh life.

In an international sense, however, it was the bad-boy genius of Welsh literature, Dylan Thomas (1914–53), who was Wales' most notable export. He is probably best known for his comic play for voices, *Under Milk Wood,* describing a day in the life of an insular Welsh community. You can visit his boathouse home in Laugharne.

Welsh literature also matured with home-grown heroes taking on the clichés of valley life and developing more realistic, socially rooted works. Among the leading figures, poet and painter David Jones (1895–1974) began the trend with his epic of war, *In Parenthesis,* published in 1937. Kate Roberts (1891–1985) explored the experiences of working men and women in rural Wales, often evoking qualities of a time since past with *Feet in Chains.* The elegant *On the Black Hill,* by Bruce Chatwin (1940–89), also evokes the joys and hardships of small-town life, exploring Welsh spirit and cross-border antipathy through the lives of torpid twin-brother farmers.

Poetry

In terms of poetry, the loss of the referendum for devolution in March 1979 was a catharsis for modern Welsh literature. It heralded a flood of political and engaged writing and poetry, most notably the left-wing historian Gwyn Alf Williams' re-evaluation of Welsh history in his masterpiece *When Was Wales?*

This renaissance of Welsh poetry among a younger generation of poets, such as Menna Elfyn, Myrddin ap Dafydd, Ifor ap Glyn and Iwan Llwyd, took poetry out of the chapel, study and lecture room to be performed in pubs, clubs and cloisters. This led to a series of poetry tours, making Welsh-language poetry once again a popular medium of protest and performance. Recent years have also seen an increasing crossover between Welsh and English poetry and literature with poets and musicians, such as Twm Morys and Gwyneth Glyn, establishing new audiences with their blend of words and music.

Myths & Legends

Considering Wales' lyrical language, complex history, fairy-tale landscape and wealth of mysterious ancient sites, it's hardly surprising that Welsh culture is rich in legend and mythology. Embellished by generations of storytellers, musicians and poets, these tales of supernatural strength, magic, grotesque beasts and heroic adventurers offer an insight into the pagan Celtic world.

The Red Dragon

One of the first mythical beasts in British heraldry, the red dragon is a powerful symbol in ancient legends. It was apparently used on the banners of British soldiers on their way to Rome in the 4th century, and was then adopted by Welsh kings in the 5th century to demonstrate their authority after the Roman withdrawal. The Anglo-Saxon King Harold, and Cadwaladr, the 7th-century king of Gwynedd, liked it so much they used it for their standards in battle, forever associating the symbol with Wales. In the 14th century Welsh archers used the red dragon as their emblem, and Owain Glyndwr used it as a standard in his revolt against the English crown. A century later, Henry Tudor (later King Henry VII) made the dragon part of the Welsh flag, though it was only in 1959 that Queen Elizabeth II commanded that the red dragon, on a green-and-white field, be recognised as the official flag of Wales.

King Arthur

King Arthur has inspired more legends and folk tales, and given his name to more features of the landscape in Wales, than any other historical figure. He is mentioned in the oldest surviving Welsh manuscripts but his true identity remains unknown. Depicted as a giant with superhuman strength, a dwarf king who rode a goat and as a Celtic god, it is most likely he was a 5th- or 6th-century cavalry leader who led early Britons against Saxon invaders. By the 9th century, Arthur was famous as a fighter throughout the British Isles and in the centuries that followed, other writers – most recently and perhaps most famously the Victorian poet Alfred Lord Tennyson – climbed on the bandwagon, weaving in love stories, Christian symbolism and medieval pageantry to create the romance that surrounds Arthur today.

CULTURE MYTHS & LEGENDS

Literary Events

Laugharne Weekend, April

Hay Festival, late May

Beyond the Border, July

National Eisteddfod, August

Dylan Thomas Festival, late Oct

THE POETRY OF RS THOMAS

One of Wales' most passionate and most reclusive modern writers, the priest-turned-poet RS Thomas (1913–2000), was an outspoken critic of the so-called Welsh 'cultural suicide' and a staunch supporter of unpopular causes. Nominated for the Nobel Prize in Literature in 1996, his uncompromising work has a pure, sparse style, which he used to explore his profound spirituality and the natural world.

RS Thomas was also more politically controversial than any other Welsh writer, becoming the Welsh conscience and campaigning fervently on behalf of indigenous language and culture. His unflinching support of Welsh issues did not always extend to his compatriots, however, with him proclaiming at one point that they were 'an impotent people/sick with inbreeding/worrying the carcass of an old song'. In the late 1980s and early 1990s he was at the centre of a highly public row when he publicly praised the arsonists who firebombed English-owned holiday homes in Wales.

You can follow sites closely associated with Thomas around the Llŷn Peninsula, including the Aberdaron church where he was the local vicar from 1967 to 1978.

Merlin the Magician

This great Welsh wizard is probably modelled upon Myrddin Emrys (Ambrosius), a 6th-century holy man who became famous for his prophecies. It was probably Geoffrey of Monmouth who changed Myrddin's name to Merlin and presented him as the wise, wizardly advisor to Arthur's father King Uther Pendragon. One of Merlin's seminal acts was to disguise Uther as Duke Gorlois, allowing him to spend the night with the duke's wife, Ygerna, who duly conceived Arthur. Merlin also predicted that Uther's true heir would draw a sword from a stone and acquired the sword Excalibur from a Lady of the Lake. Merlin's own end appears to have come courtesy of this same lady when she trapped the wizard in a cave on Bryn Myrddin (Merlin's Hill), east of Carmarthenshire, where wind-carried groans and clanking chains are part of local lore even today.

Few of Wales ancient myths and legends were written down and consequently many were lost. *The Mabinogion* (Tales of Hero's Youth), a translation of two remarkable 14th-century folk-tale compendiums, remains the key source of Welsh legends.

Music

According to a Welsh proverb, 'to be born Welsh is to be born with music in your blood and poetry in your soul'. Hence, Wales is officially known as the land of song. But where does this close association between Wales and music actually originate?

There are references to the Celts as a musical race as early as the 1st century BC when ancient scholars wrote of bards (poets who sing songs of eulogy and satire) and Druids (philosophers or theologians who are held in extreme honour). There are traditional Welsh songs with harp accompaniment from the early 19th century and unaccompanied folks songs that tell a story in the form of verse.

Today the diversity of music in Wales is huge, yet united by a common factor – music remains at the heart of this nation. In just the last few years the Cory Band from the Rhondda Valley has won the European Brass Band Championships twice. Child star Charlotte Church swapped her classical beginnings for perky pop before evolving into a more mature experimental sound. And the Welsh National Opera has gone from strength to strength since launching the career of opera singer Bryn Terfel, plucked from a North Wales sheep farm to become a national champion for the Welsh voice.

Folk

Today it is traditional folk and the emerging nu-folk that is the keeper of the flame of traditional Welsh music. Catch a live session at local pubs, folk clubs or smaller festivals, and look out for bands such as 9Bach and Calan, which blend traditional and contemporary Welsh sounds with international influences. Welsh folk music even has a permanent home at

Tŷ Siamas (National Centre for Welsh Folk Music) in Dolgellau. Events at the centre are an ideal way to keep abreast of new acts and influences.

Rock

The late 1990s marked the high tide of the Cool Cymru movement and it was rock music that really put Wales on the map. A series of Welsh groups, including Manic Street Preachers, Catatonia, Stereophonics and Super Furry Animals, made headlines with their innovative sounds, clever lyrics, rabble-rousing rock sound and poignant ballads packed with pathos. They changed the staid image of Wales as a nation of melodious harpists and male voice choirs forever.

Today the Welsh music scene may not be as hyped as it once was, but its true substance has come to the fore with an important network of artists, labels and agencies. The Manics are still going strong, while their contemporary Gruff Rhys, former lead singer with the Super Furry Animals, won the Welsh Music Prize for his solo album *Hotel Shampoo* in 2011. Multi-award-winning singer Duffy, who released the album *Rockferry* to global and critical acclaim, and won a Grammy award in 2009, has all but retired from the music scene, while a host of new names is gaining ground. Look out for Future of the Left, who won the Welsh Music Prize in 2012 for their third album, *The Plot Against Common Sense*, alternative rockers Joy Formidable, singer-songwriter Cate le Bon, and indie popsters Los Campesinos!.

The Welsh metal scene meanwhile has Bullet For My Valentine and hardcore Funeral for a Friend, while comic rappers Goldie Lookin' Chain from Newport fly the flag for Welsh hip-hop. Those with a more sophisticated hip-hop style should take a look at Akira the Don, the political and electronic rapper from Anglesey.

For more, see www.walesonline.co.uk/showbiz-and-lifestyle/music-in-wales.

Cinema

The first genuinely Welsh film was Karl Francis' *Above Us the Earth* in 1977. Based on the true story of a colliery closure, it featured an amateur cast in real valley locations. More recently, the Welsh film industry has matured considerably with a growth in high-quality independent productions.

CULTURE CINEMA

FESTIVAL

Wales' biggest music festival, the Green Man Festival, features over 400 acts on 10 stages as well as a fringe event featuring holistic therapies, talks, comedy, workshops and youth events.

THE EISTEDDFOD

Nothing encapsulates Welsh culture like the eisteddfod (ey-steth-vot; literally a gathering or session). Infused with a sense of Celtic history and drawing heavily on the Bardic tradition of verbal storytelling, this uniquely Welsh celebration is the descendant of ancient tournaments in which poets and musicians competed for a seat of honour in the households of noblemen.

The first recorded tournament dates from 1176 but the tradition slowly waned following the Tudor Acts of Union in the mid-16th century. In the late 18th century Edward Williams (better known by his bardic name of Iolo Morganwg) reinvented the eisteddfod as a modern Welsh festival. Today the **National Eisteddfod** (www.eisteddfod.org.uk) of Wales is one of Europe's largest cultural events and a barometer of contemporary Welsh culture with aspiring bands and emerging artists often making their debut there. The whole event takes place in Welsh, but there's loads of help on hand for non-Welsh speakers. The festival is held during the first week of August, alternately in North and South Wales. Another event to watch out for is the International Musical Eisteddfod (p217), which is held in Llangollen each July. Acts from over 40 countries compete with folk tunes, choral harmony and recitals. Competitions take place daily and famous names take to the stage for gala concerts every night.

One of the most successful recent releases is *The Edge of Love* (2008), the biopic about the life and loves of Dylan Thomas, which starred Keira Knightley, Sienna Miller and Matthew Rhys in the role of Thomas. Another cult success was a low-budget documentary about life in a Mid-Wales village. *Sleep Furiously* (2008), described as an elegy for the landscape and population of Trefeurig, Ceredigion. The film was directed by Gideon Koppel, who himself was brought up in Trefeurig – where his family sought refuge from Nazi Germany. Welsh director Justin Kerrigan has enjoyed considerable commercial success with a series of films including Cardiff-based *Human Traffic* (1999), the story of drug-fuelled hedonistic youth that captured the late-90s zeitgeist. Another exploration of urban decline, *Twin Town* (1997), set in Swansea, was a funny but clichéd comedy which launched the career of Rhys Ifans. More recently the BAFTA nominated comedy drama *Submarine* (2010) was critically acclaimed and enjoyed a highly successful global release. Based in Swansea, it was an incredible debut performance by director Richard Ayoade.

For more information about Welsh film, visit the website of the **Film Agency for Wales** (www.filmagencywales.com).

Film Locations

Freshwater West
(Harry Potter & the
Deathly Hallows)

Snowdonia (Tomb
Raider II & Quantum of Solace)

Tenby
(Edge of Love)

Caerwent
(Captain America)

Television

The Welsh-language TV channel S4C has been instrumental in supporting emerging talent and promoting Welsh culture to the outside world. A fantastic success story for S4C was the Welsh-language docudrama *Solomon a Gaenor*, nominated for an Oscar for Best Foreign Language Film in 1999. Another S4C production *Eldra*, a coming-of-age tale about a young Romany girl growing up in a slate-quarrying community in North Wales, won the 2003 Spirit of Moondance award at the Sundance Film Festival.

S4C and BBC Wales have also provided a springboard for small-screen success, challenging preconceptions and fuelling independent production, while the BAFTA Cymru awards are promoting the work of Welsh actors, directors and camera crew to a far wider audience.

The revival of BBC TV series *Doctor Who*, and its spin-off, *Torchwood*, have reintroduced sci-fi fans to Cardiff as the centre of alien activity. Both are filmed around Cardiff Bay.

Theatre & Dance

Theatre is thriving in Wales. The leading English-language professional company is the Clwyd Theatr Cymru, based in northeast Wales and attracting top-name performers such as Sir Anthony Hopkins. Cardiff's acclaimed theatrical organisation, Sherman Cymru, produces a wide range of productions each year, including theatre for young people and inventive adaptations of classic dramas. The highly acclaimed Music Theatre Wales, a pioneering force in contemporary opera, has a growing international reputation. Dance lovers should look out for Earthfall, Wales'

MALE VOICE CHOIRS

Born out of the Temperance Movement in the mid-19th century, the male voice choir (*cor meibion*) became an institution in the coal-mining towns of the southern valleys. With the collapse of the former coal-mining communities, the choirs struggled to keep numbers up and some even allowed women to join their ranks.

But they have enjoyed a renaissance of late with younger people signing up to their local choir to flex their vocal chords. The latest incarnation made their name as winners of a BBC TV reality show, *Last Choir Standing*. Only Men Aloud!, an 18-strong Cardiff-based choir of part-timers, beat off stiff competition to take the title and went on to sign a multimillion pound, five-record contract and record an album.

Local choirs still practise in the back rooms of pubs and church halls each week. Most are happy to have visitors sit in on rehearsals.

leading dance-theatre company and one of the most sought-after companies across Europe.

The biggest recent theatre event in Wales was a 72-hour live production by the National Theatre Wales. The *Passion in Port Talbot* was a hard-hitting secular retelling of the Passion of Christ, which included a 'last supper' of beer and sandwiches at a local social club.

For more, visit the website of the **Arts Council of Wales** (www.artswales.org.uk).

Castles & Architecture

Castles are Wales' most famous historical and architectural attraction and the country is covered with them – 'The magnificent badge of our subjection', as the writer Thomas Pennant put it. They are a living-history statement on Wales' past and a symbol of its complex social heritage. The most impressive castles are those built by Edward I in North Wales. Among them, Caernarfon Castle, built between 1283 and 1330, has retained all of its original strength and beauty, and Harlech Castle is a great example of a perfectly concentric castle, whereby one line of defence is enclosed by another. Conwy Castle is considered to be one of the greatest fortresses of medieval Europe, and the medieval city walls are among the most complete in the world.

Apart from castles, Welsh architecture is most commonly associated with the country's industrial heritage and its contemporary, post-millennium transformation. Among the former, Blaenavon's ironworks, quarries and workers' houses received Unesco World Heritage status at the turn of the millennium. And the town was recently joined on the Unesco World Heritage list by the Pontcysyllte Aqueduct in Llangollen.

For a taste of modern architecture, Richard Rogers' Senedd, the National Assembly debating chamber in Cardiff Bay, is a stunning mix of slate and Welsh Oak, while the Millennium Stadium has a striking design of stacked Welsh slate topped with a bronzed-steel shell. Also worth a look is the award-winning Royal Welsh College of Music and Drama's new purpose-built facility in Cardiff Castle's grounds.

Rugby

The Welsh and rugby go hand in hand. Wales is known as one of the world's biggest exponents of the sport, joint-hosting the rugby union World Cup in 2013. The national side has recently restored Welsh pride after a lengthy period spent in the wilderness, culminating in grand-slam successes in 2005, 2008 and 2012 at the Six Nations tournaments, and they were winners of the tournament in 2013. Tickets for international matches are guaranteed to sell out, while recent success on the pitch has elevated the team's star players, such as Shane Williams (now retired), Stephen Jones and Gethin Jenkins, into national sporting heroes.

Rugby union is equally well supported at club level, with four teams representing different regions of South Wales. The Swansea Ospreys, one of the league's most competitive teams in recent years, won the championship in 2010 and 2012. From 2012 Welsh clubs began operating under a self-imposed salary cap, which has resulted in some high-profile defections to other teams. The rugby season takes place between September and Easter; for more information, check the **Welsh Rugby Union** (www.wru.co.uk) website.

For more on Welsh sport, see www.walesonline.co.uk/sports.

CULTURE CASTLES & ARCHITECTURE

A number of Hollywood stars, including Charlie Chaplin, Christian Bale and Catherine Zeta-Jones, first trod the boards at regional theatres in Wales. The highest-profile performances are found at the Wales Millennium Centre in Cardiff Bay, while the city's Chapter arts centre is an important venue for fringe events.

The equivalent of the National Trust in Wales is Cadw, the division within the National Assembly government charged with the protection, conservation and promotion of the historic environment.

Food & Drink

A quiet revolution has been taking place across the kitchens of Wales. Boosted by the abundance of fresh, local produce and a new generation of young masterchefs with an innovative, modern take on traditional Welsh recipes, the food scene is buzzing.

Local Treats

Bara brith

Cawl

Faggots

Laver bread

Perl Las

Sewin

Welsh cakes

Welsh Specialities

Traditionally, Welsh food was based on what could be grown locally and cheaply. This meant that oats, root vegetables, dairy products, honey and meat featured highly in most recipes. Food was functional and needed to satisfy the needs of labourers on the farm or workers down the mine. It was hearty and wholesome but not exactly haute cuisine. The food revolution in Wales has changed that, but traditional staples, such as Welsh lamb, Welsh Black beef, sewin (wild sea trout), Penclawdd cockles, Conwy mussels, laver bread and farmhouse cheeses, still have their place in the kitchens of any decent eating place in Wales – albeit the recipes have a contemporary twist.

Most menus will feature Welsh lamb or Welsh Black beef and you rarely go wrong with these. On the coast try some sewin or cockles. The most traditional Welsh dish remains *cawl,* the hearty, one-pot meal of bacon, lamb, cabbage, swede and potato. It's one of those warm, cosy dishes that you long for when you're walking in the hills. Another traditional favourite is Welsh rarebit, a kind of sophisticated cheese on toast, generously drizzled with a secret ingredient tasting suspiciously like beer. For breakfast, try laver bread, not bread at all, but boiled seaweed mixed with oatmeal and served with bacon or cockles.

A top tip is to finish your meal with some great Welsh cheese, notably Caws Cenarth, Celtic Blue or Perl Las. The real cheese cognoscenti head to the award-winning Blaenavon Cheddar Co, located in the industrial town of Blaenavon, where handmade cheeses are matured down the mineshaft of the Big Pit: National Coal Museum.

Regional Treats

Our pick of the specialist food outlets in Wales.

Albert Rees Ltd (www.carmarthenham.co.uk) Delicious ham produced the farmhouse way; Carmarthen Market.

E Ashton's (www.ashtonfishmongers.co.uk) Fantastically fresh sea trout; Cardiff Central Market.

PRICE GUIDE

Eating listings in Lonely Planet reviews are categorised according to the following scale, based on the cost of a main course at dinner.

£ below £9

££ £9 to £18

£££ over £18

COOKING CLASSES

Cooking with Angela Gray (www.angelagray.co.uk) Tailored courses from the Welsh TV chef.

Drovers Rest (www.food-food-food.co.uk/courses.htm; Y Sgwar) Private and group classes from dinner parties to Welsh game held at a charming Mid-Wales restaurant.

Dryad Bushcraft (www.dryadbushcraft.co.uk) One-day Wilderness Gourmet course combines bushcraft with wild camping.

Fungi Forays (www.fungiforays.co.uk) Mushroom hunting, preparation and cooking in Mid-Wales as part of weekend breaks in October.

The Culinary Cottage (p84) One- to five-day themed courses, plus the option to stay on-site near Abergavenny.

Penarth Vineyard (www.penarthwines.co.uk) Fruity Welsh wines – try the Pinot Noir; Welshpool.
Rhug Estate Farm Shop (www.rhug.co.uk) Slow-grown and grass-fed Welsh beef; Corwen.
Trealy Farm Charcuterie (www.trealy.co.uk) Sausages made from traditional-breed pigs; Monmouthshire.

Where to Eat & Drink

Pub grub remains the most convenient and affordable option with most pubs serving food between noon and 2pm, and 5pm and 9pm. It can be hit-and-miss, but mostly you get a perfectly reasonable lunch or dinner. An increasing number of places are championing local produce and bringing the concept of the gastropub to Wales. The trend for talented chefs to abandon their urban stomping grounds, wind down a peg or two and get closer to their ingredients is making waves in rural Wales, and could turn your quick pit-stop lunch into a long, lingering affair.

In larger towns and cities you'll find switched-on bistros and restaurants serving anything from decent to superbly inspired food. An increasingly popular extension of the restaurant business is the concept of the restaurant with rooms, whereby fine dining and a cosy bed are generally only a staircase apart. Most of these places combine gourmet food with a small number of lovingly decorated rooms.

For most restaurants you'll need to book ahead, particularly on weekends, and a 10% to 15% tip is expected on top of the bill. In smaller towns, the only food available on Sunday may be the popular roast dinner served at pubs and hotel restaurants.

Continental-style cafe society is blooming all over Wales, though aesthetics vary between towns from the more twee tea-and-cake teashops to the hip hang-out coffee shops for loafers looking for free wi-fi connections. Most places across Wales can serve up both a decent, European-style frothy coffee and an old-fashioned bacon sandwich, dripping in brown sauce. That is, of course, the best of both worlds. And practically every eating place, including pubs, has at least one token vegetarian dish, though don't expect it to always be inspired.

When it comes to drinking in Wales, the local pub is still the social hub of the community – despite increasing concerns about the number of pubs closing in rural locations. You'll miss out on a great part of Welsh culture if you never make it through the swinging doors and onto the sticky carpet of the village local. However, Welsh pubs vary enormously, from cosy watering holes with big fires and an inviting atmosphere to tough inner-city bars where solo women travellers may feel decidedly ill at ease.

First Catch Your Peacock by Bobby Freeman is a classic guide to Welsh food, combining proven recipes with cultural and social history.

FOOD & DRINK GLOSSARY

BASICS

bara	*bara*	bread
cawl	*kaool*	soup
caws	*kaoos*	cheese
halen	*halen*	salt
llefrith	*llevrith*	milk
siwgr	*shoogoor*	sugar

DRINKS

coffi	*kophee*	coffee
coffi gyda llefrith	*kophee guhda llevrith*	coffee with milk
cwrw	*kooroo*	beer
dŵr	*door*	water
sudd oren	*seedh o·ren*	orange juice
te	*te*	tea

FISH & SEAFOOD

brithyll	*brithill*	trout
eog	*eog*	salmon
penllwyd	*penllooeed*	sewin
pysgodyn	*puhsgodin*	fish

MEAT

cig	*keeg*	meat
cig oen	*keeg oeen*	lamb
cig eidion	*keeg e-eedyon*	beef
cig moch	*keeg moch*	bacon
cyw iâr	*kioo yar*	chicken
selsig	*selseeg*	sausage

FRUIT & VEGETABLES

afal	*aval*	apple
blodfresychen	*blodvresuhchen*	cauliflower
ffa pob	*pha pob*	beans
ffrwyth	*phrooeeth*	fruit
llysiau	*llushayaee*	vegetables
madarchen	*madarchen*	mushroom
moronen	*moronen*	carrot
nionyn	*neeonin*	onion
oren	*oren*	orange
pys	*pis*	peas
taten	*taten*	potato

DESSERTS

pwdinau	*poodinau*	desserts
tarten ffrwyth	*tarten phrooeeth*	fruit pie
teisen	*te-eesen*	cake

DON'T MISS EXPERIENCES
· ·

➡ Farmers markets – Sniff out a local market such as Cardiff's Riverside Real Food Market for the pick of organic produce.

➡ Distillery tours – The return of Welsh whisky is celebrated with tours and tastings at the Penderyn Distillery (p104).

➡ Real ale – Stock up on Snowdonia Ale at the Purple Moose (p250) brewery, one of Wales' growing band of microbreweries.

➡ Cafe culture – Catch the sun, indulge in some people-watching and sip espresso at Cardiff's fashionable Mermaid Quay.

➡ Michelin stars – Wales now boasts three Michelin-starred eateries for fine dining Welsh style; book ahead.

Local Tipples

Village life in Wales traditionally revolved around the local pub. It was part of the social fabric of the community and a focal point of village life. The new breed of Welsh drinking den, however, offers a far more modern spin on the traditional cocktail hours, bar food and live music *de rigueur* in urban Wales. Pubs are closing across the UK as their community element is eroded, but the traditional boozer still lives on in Wales with some fine historic examples to be found in Swansea and Cardiff. Meanwhile a new generation of local microbreweries is creating an artisan range of tasty real ales, supplying local bars and selling direct to the consumer via their websites.

Among the places to look out for, Cardiff's Zerodegrees (p57) is a specialist microbrewery with a great selection of artisan beers with a flavoursome twist. Across town, the Brewery Quarter, located on the site of the old Brains Brewery dating from 1713, has a slew of modern bars for a drop of Brains Gold. In North Wales, the town of Porthmadog, located on the fringes of the Snowdonia National Park, is home to the Purple Moose (p250) brewery, one of Wales' most successful microbreweries, supplying pubs from Anglesey to Harlech. The Snowdonia Ale was voted CAMRA Champion Beer of Wales 2009, while the Dark Side of the Moose, a hoppy and fruity brew for winter, was named the Gold Medal winner at the International Beer Challenge 2009: the beers have also been lauded in the discerning Great Taste Awards.

Welsh whisky is also enjoying a renaissance with the Penderyn Distillery (p104), located in the southern reaches of the Brecon Beacons National Park, boasting a new high-tech visitors centre. The independently owned distillery released its first whisky in 2004 and remains, unlike Scottish and Irish whisky, a single-distilled malt.

COOKBOOK

The Welsh Table by Christine Smeeth contains simple, traditional Welsh dishes, kitchen anecdotes and words of wisdom.

The Natural Environment

No other country in Europe is as densely packed with nature conservation sites as Wales, and the natural environment here is protected with a near visionary zeal. The craggy peaks, rugged coastlines and patchwork fields harbour numerous historic, cultural and economic treasures and the Welsh people are fiercely proud of them. Thankfully, the National Assembly is now equally passionate about Wales' diverse landscapes, enshrining sustainable development into the statute books.

Fossilised marine life on Snowdon's summit reveals that Snowdonia's peaks and valleys are remnants of a continental collision that occurred 520 million years ago, swallowing the ancient Iapetus Ocean that divided Britain.

Geology

Wales can claim one of the richest and most diverse geological heritages in the world; and it is geology, more than anything else, that has helped shape the destiny of Wales in modern times. Since the 17th century, geologists have pondered the mysteries of Wales' rippled rocks, puzzling fossils and ice-moulded valleys. In contrast with Wales' relatively young evolutionary age of just 200 million years, some of the oldest rocks in the world lie exposed at St Davids Head on the Pembrokeshire coast.

The flat-topped Brecon Beacons in South Wales are the product of extreme, rock-shattering temperatures. The mountains were eroded to form the red-sandstone moorland, and the porous limestone cliffs were perforated with waterfalls, creating massive cave systems. Rich deposits of coal south of the Brecon Beacons and the slate mountains of Snowdonia altered the face of Wales, sparking an industrial revolution that attracted hordes of fortune-hungry workers.

But the natural wonder of Wales is not solely related to geological history. Two of the world's 64 Unesco Geoparks, scenic locations of special geoscientific significance, are found in Wales. Visit Fforest Fawr in the western half of the Brecon Beacons National Park or GeoMôn in Anglesey for a more contemporary take on natural beauty.

Fauna

Offering opportunities for unexpected encounters, Wales is less of a wonderland and more of a wild card when it comes to wildlife. Atlantic grey seals headline the fascinating coastal wildlife, delivering around 1000 fluffy white pups on Pembrokeshire's shores in late September and early October. Twitchers, meanwhile, head for Pembrokeshire's offshore islands, a haven for seabirds from April to mid-August. Grassholm Island, in particular, has one of the world's largest gannet colonies, with 39,000 pairs nesting there during breeding season (April to September). Colonies of guillemots, razorbills, storm petrels, kittiwakes and puffins crowd the rock faces of Skomer and Skokholm Islands and together with nearby Ramsey Island they play host to 50% of the world's Manx shearwater population. Rare red-billed choughs can be seen on Ramsey and at South Stack on Anglesey.

In North Wales numbers of hen harriers and Welsh black grouse are increasing, and otters are re-establishing themselves along the River Teifi and in the border area of northern Powys. Pine martens and polecats – staples of Welsh wildlife – are found almost everywhere.

Flora

Following years of industrialisation, just 14% of the Welsh countryside remains covered by woodland, characterised mostly by non-native Sitka spruce, a fast-growing crop shirked by most wildlife. In many areas erosion caused by cultivation and overgrazing has prevented native species from rooting and reseeding, although native ash is thriving on the Gower Peninsula and in Brecon Beacons; several types of orchid flower in its shade, together with common dog violets, from March to May.

Away from grazing animals, alpine-arctic plants breed in mountainous regions, although hikers and climbers can cause irreparable damage to purple saxifrage and moss campion nestling between the rocks on higher slopes. Rare cotton grass sprouts from inland bogs and soggy peat lands in midsummer, among bog pimpernel and thriving myrtle. Butterwort, one of Britain's few insectivorous plants, traps insects in wet grassland at Cwm Cadlan near Penderyn, in southwest Wales. Evening primrose, sea bindweed and marram grass may be spotted on the coast between the sand dunes, while thrift and samphire grace the Gower Peninsula.

Protected Species

Animals once on the endangered list, such as bottlenose dolphins, Risso's dolphins, minke whales and lesser horseshoe bats are no longer officially endangered per se, but they each are subject to a National Biodiversity Action Plan.

A vestige of the last ice age, the Snowdon lily has survived on the slopes of Snowdon for over 10,000 years, yet warmer climates and overgrazing have drastically reduced its number. It could be mistaken for a grass before its white flowers emerge between May and mid-June. Also on the critical list is the distinctive shrub Ley's whitebeam, which flowers in late May and early June in the Taff Valley. The fen orchid, rare throughout Europe, is protected in the Kenfig National Nature Reserve near Port Talbot.

New Environmental Challenges

When it comes to environmental issues, Wales is hugely ambitious. In part the environmental focus is sharper in Wales because the crucial tourism industry is so closely associated with the country's natural environment.

DOLPHINS

THE NATURAL ENVIRONMENT FLORA

One of only two semiresident bottle-nose dolphin populations in the UK can be found in Cardigan Bay. Sightings occur year-round, although numbers increase in summer, peaking in late September and October. Common and Risso's dolphins are found further out to sea, along with minke whales.

RED KITE COUNTRY

Doggedly fighting its way back from the verge of extinction, the majestic red kite (*Milvus milvus*) is now a common sight in Mid-Wales. This aerobatic bird with its 2m-long wingspan was once common across the UK and was even afforded royal protection in the Middle Ages. However, in the 16th century it was declared vermin and mercilessly hunted until only a few pairs remained.

The red kites owe their reprieve in part to a 100-year-long campaign in the Tywi and Cothi Valleys of Mid-Wales, the longest-running protection scheme for any bird in the world. Despite persistent threats from egg-hunters and poison intended for crows and foxes, more than 400 pairs of red kites navigate the Welsh sky.

An ecotourism initiative, the **Kite Country Project** (www.kitecountry.co.uk) was launched in 1994 to encourage visitors to see the red kite in action without disturbing or endangering the species. It runs five designated information points throughout Mid-Wales, where visitors can watch kites being fed at close range.

ALTERNATIVE ENERGY

Innocuous though they may seem, land-based wind turbines have become one of the most contentious and divisive issues in rural Wales. Nobody disputes the need for sustainable energy and few object to community-based schemes that bring much-needed income to small towns and villages. However, the huge visual impact of commercial schemes and their irregular output has brought both locals and campaigners out in droves. It's an emotive issue, pitting one environmental campaign group against another. Although the focus has turned to offshore wind farms and tidal power as viable alternatives, the battle continues with every new planning application.

More recently, controversy has surrounded the proposal to build a new nuclear power plant on Anglesey by 2020. The existing nuclear plant, Wylfa, will cease generation in 2014, but Wylfa 'B' could become one of the first of the new generation of nuclear power stations planned across the UK. The island's council estimates that the development could bring £8 billion into the local economy but local people are fiercely opposed.

Dogged in this endeavour, the National Assembly sought and received independence from the rest of the UK on environmental legislation.

The 'One Wales: One Planet' manifesto lays down challenges to be achieved by 2025, among them a minimum 80% reduction in carbon-based energy reliance and an electricity supply derived entirely from renewable sources. Bolstering its ambition to eliminate waste production by 2050, Wales already recycles and composts more than 45% of its rubbish.

Although agri-environment schemes such as 'Glastir' remunerate farmers who adopt environmentally sensitive practices and incorporate tree-planting programs aimed at dramatically expanding woodland, the comprehensive 2013 State of Nature study warned that wildlife in Wales was at a crisis point with one in 10 species facing extinction. Farming practices were blamed for loss of habitat, and woodland management policies were under fire for not placing enough emphasis on biodiversity. Upland wading birds such as curlews, lapwings and golden plovers, and wildflowers, butterflies and woodland plants are particularly affected and conservation groups believe the next decade will be crucial to their survival.

The enthusiasm for sustainable lifestyles in Wales can be traced back to St David himself who taught his followers the importance of living in harmony with nature.

Critics also maintain that government policies are not always in line with sustainable development indicators. In 2012 test drilling for shale gas was approved, a decision which could have major implications for the Welsh environment. Campaigners warn of catastrophic consequences if companies are allowed to use fracking (a controversial extraction technique which blasts water, sand and chemicals through rock at extreme pressures) to release gas in the abandoned mines of South Wales. The UK Government maintains that if fracking is approved high standards of safety and environmental protection will be ensured. With an estimated £120 billion's worth of recoverable gas reserves in one layer of rock in one area of South Wales alone, campaigners will have a sizeable battle on their hands.

Survival Guide

Directory

Accommodation

Wales has been attracting tourists in the modern sense for 350 years, so it's fair to say that the country is well prepared for visitors. **Visit Wales** (www.visitwales.com), the national tourist board, operates a grading system based on facilities and quality of service. Participating establishments usually display their star rating (from one to five), although some excellent places don't join the scheme, as it costs to do so. Tourist offices rarely mention good nonparticipating places, or may simply dismiss them as 'not approved'. In practice, there's variability within each classification, and a one-star guesthouse might be better than the three-star hotel around the block.

Bed and breakfast (B&B) accommodation in private homes is plentiful, and is often the only option in smaller towns and villages. Some of the finest and most family-friendly B&Bs are in rural farmhouses, used to the muddy boots and large appetites of walkers, cyclists and climbers. Guesthouses, which are often just large converted houses with half a dozen rooms, are an extension of the B&B idea. In general they're less personal and more like small hotels, but without the same level of service.

Both B&Bs and guesthouses usually have, as a minimum, central heating, TV, tea and coffee making facilities and a wash basin in the bedrooms. They range from boutique establishments with chic decor, en suites and every gadget imaginable to basic places with shared-bathroom facilities. Likewise, the standard of breakfast varies enormously, although the norm is a full Welsh fry-up – bacon and eggs (and often mushrooms, tomatoes and baked beans) on toast – with cereals, yoghurts and fruit also provided.

The term 'hotel' is used with abandon in Wales, and may refer to anything from a pub to a castle. In general, hotels tend to have a reception desk, room service and other extras such as a licensed bar. The very best hotels are magnificent places, often with restaurants to match. In rural areas you'll find country-house hotels set in vast grounds, and castles complete with crenellated battlements, grand staircases, oak panelling and the obligatory rows of stags' heads. A new breed of boutique hotel has emerged, offering individually styled designer rooms, clublike bars, quality restaurants and a range of spa treatments.

A variation is the restaurant with rooms, where the main focus is on gourmet cuisine; the attached rooms sometimes come comparatively cheaply. Such places usually offer dinner, bed and breakfast (DB&B) rates.

Many pubs offer accommodation, though they vary widely in quality. Staying in a pub or inn can be good fun as it places you at the hub of the community, but they can be noisy and aren't always ideal for solo women travellers. Many of the better pubs are former coaching inns (places where horse and coach passengers would stop on long journeys).

For longer stays, self-contained weekly rentals are popular. Options include traditional stone farmhouses, tiny quaint cottages, gracious manor houses and seaside hideaways. For something special, the **National Trust Cottages** (www.nationaltrustcottages.co.uk) has rural properties that are let as holiday cottages. Similarly splendid rentals are offered by the

Landmark Trust (☎01628-825925; www.landmarktrust.co.uk), an architectural charity that rescues unique old buildings and supports the work by renting them out.

Hostels in Wales are generally basic affairs with bunk beds in dormitories. However, they're often spectacularly located, very handy for long-distance walkers and can be a great place to meet fellow travellers.

Free camping is rarely possible in Wales but there are plenty of campgrounds around the country, concentrated in the national parks and along the coast. Most campgrounds have reasonable facilities, though quality can vary widely and some can be tricky to reach without your own transport. Price structures vary widely but will often include a per-person charge, an additional charge for a vehicle or a powered site, and sometimes a minimum site charge at busy times regardless of how many people are staying.

Prices & Booking

Wales is a popular 'weekender' destination for people throughout Britain. Consequently prices shoot up and availability plummets on Friday and Saturday nights, regardless of the season, especially in popular beauty spots such as Pembrokeshire and Snowdonia. In business-orientated establishments in Cardiff, prices sometimes drop over the weekend, depending on what's on in the city. If there's a big rugby game scheduled, you won't get a room in the city or its surrounds for love or money.

It's essential to book ahead for Easter and Christmas. Otherwise, the high season runs from mid-May to mid-September, with the absolute peak (especially in seaside towns) between July and August. Prices are generally cheaper for longer stays and advance bookings.

Outside the high season, room rates are often reduced and special offers may be available – it's always worth enquiring. Some establishments, especially hostels and camping grounds, shut up shop completely from November until Easter.

Most tourist offices will book accommodation for you for a small fee. Almost all B&Bs charge £60 to £100 for a double room; in many places it's hard to find anything cheaper or more expensive.

Business Hours

Wales follows the general UK conventions when it comes to opening hours, but as Great Britain moves closer to a 24-hour society, hours are extending and Sundays are no longer a day of rest.

Where Lonely Planet reviews do not list business hours, it is because they adhere to the standard hours we have identified following.

Business hours are generally 9am to 5.30pm Monday to Friday. Banks are open from 9.30am to 5pm Monday to Friday and 9.30am to 1pm Saturday (main branches). Post offices open from 9am to 5pm Monday to Friday and 9am to 12.30pm Saturday.

Shops generally open from 9am to 5.30pm or 6pm Monday to Saturday, with an increasing number of shops also opening on Sunday from 11am to 4pm. Late-night shopping (to 8pm) is usually on Thursday or Friday nights.

Cafes tend to open from 9am to 5pm Monday to Saturday and from 11am to 4pm Sunday, while restaurants generally open from noon to

---

PRICE GUIDE

We've categorised the Lonely Planet listings according to the following scale, based on the cheapest double on offer in high (but not necessarily peak) season. Unless otherwise stated, prices include private bathrooms.

£	less than £60
£££	£60 to £100
£££	more than £100

PRACTICALITIES

➡ **Weights & Measures** Wales uses the metric system for weights and measures. However, speed and distance are measured in miles, and pubs still pull pints.

➡ **DVD** Wales uses the PAL system.

➡ **Newspapers** The popular *Western Mail* is Wales' only national English-language daily newspaper.

➡ **Magazines** For the low-down on what's happening around the country, try the magazines *Cambria*, *Planet* or *Golwg* (Vision), the latter only available in Welsh.

➡ **Radio** Tune in to BBC Radio Wales (103.9FM) for English-language news and features, or BBC Radio Cymru (a range of frequencies between 103.5FM and 105FM) for the Welsh-language version.

➡ **TV** The national Welsh-language television broadcaster is 4C (Sianel Pedwar Cymru).

ONLINE RESOURCES

Brecon Beacons Holiday Cottages (www.breconcottages.com) Get away from it all in one of the country's national parks. Search categories include Eco, Pets Welcome, Glamping and Close to the Pub.

Bunkhouses in Wales (www.bunkhousesinwales.co.uk) Fairly basic accommodation, often in stunning locations. In some cases you may need to bring a sleeping bag, though many bunkhouses offer a hostel-style service.

Camping & Caravanning Club (www.campingandcaravanningclub.co.uk) A long-established club, where the emphasis is more on caravanning than carefree backpacker-style camping.

Coastal Cottages of Pembrokeshire (www.coastalcottages.co.uk) Cosy cottages in one of the most beautiful regions of Wales. The site includes a section for foodies.

Escape To (www.escape-to.co.uk) Youth Hostel Association (YHA) hostels available for groups; lists some great historic properties at bargain rates.

Freedom Days (www.freedom-days.co.uk) Brief listings on all types of Welsh accommodation.

Home Base Holidays (www.homebase-hols.com) An established holiday home–swap site.

Homelink (www.homelink.org.uk) A holiday home–swap site, with a team of coordinators on hand to help with the process.

Independent Hostel Guide (www.independenthostelguide.co.uk) Includes 70 independent hostels in Wales in its listings.

Quality Cottages (www.qualitycottages.co.uk) Features some wonderful historic properties throughout Wales.

Rural Retreats (www.ruralretreats.co.uk) Click 'Property of the Week' to whet your appetite for a holiday cottage.

Snowdonia Tourist Services (www.sts-holidays.co.uk) Holiday cottages in north Wales.

Stay in Wales (www.stayinwales.co.uk) Comprehensive accommodation-booking service.

UK Campsite (www.ukcampsite.co.uk) Thorough campground listings and user reviews to help you decide where to pitch up.

Venue Masters (www.venuemasters.co.uk) A not-for-profit organisation listing university accommodation.

Visit Wales (www.visitwales.com) Official tourist board accommodation listings.

Wales Directory (www.walesdirectory.co.uk) Accommodation reviews with plenty of pics to illustrate.

Wales Holidays (www.wales-holidays.co.uk) Holiday cottages in North Wales and Snowdonia, West Wales and Pembrokeshire, Gower, Mid Wales and the Brecon Beacons.

Wales in Style (www.walesinstyle.com) Atmospheric accommodation, with an emphasis on luxury and boutique options.

Welsh Rarebits (www.rarebits.co.uk) Independent and unusual accommodation – have a look at its online offer section. It also organises gourmet, golf, castles and culture tours.

Youth Hostel Association (YHA; www.yha.org.uk) The YHA has some wonderful properties in Wales, often in the heart of walking country.

2pm and also 6pm to 10pm. Pubs and bars usually open at around 11am and close at 11pm (10.30pm on Sunday). Many bars in larger towns have a late licence and stay open until 2am from Thursday to Saturday.

Some businesses in small country towns still have a weekly early-closing day – it's different in each region, but is usually Tuesday, Wednesday or Thursday. However, not all shops honour it. Early closing is more common in winter.

If someone tells you a place (eg a shop, cafe or restaurant) opens daily, they nearly always mean 'daily except Sunday'.

Climate

Llandudno

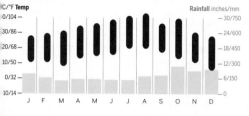

Aberstwyth

Cardiff

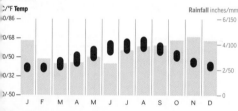

Wales is increasingly cosmopolitan, but outside the main cities the population is still overwhelmingly white, and although racists are a small minority, there have been some unpleasant incidents.

In Wales never assume that just because it's midsummer it will be warm and dry. General wetness aside, it's even more important to treat outdoor adventures in areas such as Brecon Beacons and Snowdonia National Parks with respect. Mist can drop with startling suddenness, leaving you dangerously chilled and disoriented. Never venture onto the heights without checking the weather forecast and without being sensibly clad and equipped with good waterproof gear, and always make sure someone knows where you're heading. Check mountain area forecasts in advance with the **Met Office** (www.metoffice.gov.uk/loutdoor/mountainsafety) website.

Discount Cards

There are several passes available to travellers that offer good value for people keen on castles, stately homes, ruined abbeys and other properties owned by Wales' two heritage trusts, Cadw (*kadoo*; Welsh for 'to keep') and the Welsh arm of the UK-wide National Trust (NT).

Dangers & Annoyances

In general you'll receive a warm welcome all across Wales. The country is, overall, a pretty safe place to travel, but use your common sense when it comes to hitchhiking or walking alone in city centres at night. Traffic issues and car theft are not major concerns.

The obvious things to guard are your passport, travel documents, tickets and money. Don't leave valuables lying around in your hotel or B&B room and never leave valuables in a car, especially overnight, even in more rural locations. Look for secure parking near tourist offices and national-park visitor centres.

If you do encounter a problem, it could be inspired by alcohol. Binge drinking remains a social curse in Wales. If you're unlucky enough to encounter a brawl outside a bar or club at closing time, just give it a wide berth.

HOSTELS

The concept of flashpacking hasn't yet taken hold in Wales and the vast majority of hostels and bunkhouses run the risk of triggering repressed memories of school camps and scout dens. On the upside, many of them are spectacularly located and well set up for walkers, with drying rooms and places for muddy boots.

Britain's **Youth Hostel Association** (YHA; www.yha.org.uk) operates hostels throughout the national parks that may come in handy for filling overnight gaps in your walking or cycling itinerary. Many of the more remote ones close from November to Easter or are only available for groups. A dorm bed costs around £18, unless otherwise stated in the review.

STAYING IN HISTORIC BUILDINGS

Elan Valley Trust (www.elanvalley.org.uk) Has the best-preserved long house in Wales (Llannerch y Cawr), as well as the wonderfully isolated farmhouse of Tynllidiart.

Landmark Trust (☏01628-825925; www.landmarktrust.co.uk) Lets a tower in Caernarfon Castle, a Victorian fort in Pembrokeshire and what is probably Britain's fanciest chicken shed at Leighton.

National Trust Cottages (www.nationaltrustcottages.co.uk) Lets Abermydyr, a Georgian estate cottage near Aberaeron designed by no less an architect than John Nash, as well as the Old Rectory at Rhossili, which is the only building above what is consistently voted as Wales' finest beach.

Portmeirion (www.portmeirion-village.com) Provides the opportunity to stay in Clough's architectural masterpiece in either self-catering cottages, the waterfront hotel or the boutique-chic Castell Deudraeth.

Under the Thatch (www.underthethatch.co.uk) Specialises in traditional thatched cottages but also lets a converted Edwardian railway carriage by the sea at Aberporth and traditional Romany caravans.

A one-year **Cadw** (☏0800 074 3121; cadw.wales.gov.uk) membership costs £34 for individuals and £57 for a family (two adults plus all children under 16 years). Wheelchair users and the visually impaired, together with assisting companions, are admitted free to all Cadw monuments.

A one-year **National Trust** (NT; ☏0844 800 1895; www.nationaltrust.org.uk) membership costs £55 for individuals and £97 for a family (two adults plus all children or grandchildren under 18 years). Children under five get in free at NT properties.

Membership of one, or both, of the trusts is well worth considering, especially if you're going to be in Wales for a couple of weeks or more. Both organisations care for hundreds of spectacular sites and membership allows you to visit them for free. You can join at any staffed Cadw or NT site, by post or phone, or online.

The **Hudson's Explorer Pass** (www.hudsonsexplorerpass.com) gives free access to almost 600 properties under the care of Cadw, NT (and NT Scotland), Historic Scotland and English Heritage. A three- /seven- /15- /28-day adult pass costs £49/79/109/179 irrespective of age, but it's available only to non-British citizens. You can buy the pass online, and in the UK at many international airports and seaports and selected tourist offices.

It's also worth noting that students carrying valid National Union of Students (NUS) cards and people carrying a valid **16–25 Railcard** (www.16-25railcard.co.uk) can get discounted entrance to many attractions across Wales.

Travellers aged 60 and over can get 50% off standard National Express bus fares with a **Senior Coachcard** (http://www.nationalexpress.com/waystosave/senior-coachcard.aspx;

no card required) and 30% off most rail fares with a **Senior Railcard** (www.senior-railcard.co.uk; 1-year card £26). Many attractions have lower admission prices for those aged over 60 or 65 (sometimes 55 years for women); it's always worth asking even if it's not posted.

If you plan to do a lot of travelling by bus or train, there are some good-value travel passes. Most local bus operators also offer day and family passes.

Electricity

230V/50Hz

Gay & Lesbian Travellers

In general, Wales is tolerant of homosexuality. Certainly, it's possible for people to acknowledge their homosexuality in a way that would have been unthinkable 20 years ago or more. But tolerance only goes so far, as a glance at any tabloid newspaper will confirm, and the macho image of rugby-playing Welshmen still prevails in smaller – and smaller-minded – communities.

Cardiff and Swansea both have active gay and lesbian

INTERNATIONAL VISITORS

Entering the Region

No visas are required if you arrive in Wales from within the UK. If you arrive directly from any other country, British regulations apply.

At present, citizens of Australia, Canada, New Zealand, South Africa and the USA are given 'leave to enter' the UK at their point of arrival for up to six months, but are prohibited from working. If you're a citizen of the EU, you don't need a visa to enter the country and may live and work freely. However, visa regulations are always subject to change, so check with your local British embassy, high commission or consulate before leaving home. For more information, visit www.ukvisas.gov.uk.

To extend your stay in the UK, contact the **Home Office, Immigration & Nationality Directorate** (☎0870 606 7766; www.ind.homeoffice.gov.uk; 40 Wellesley Rd, Lunar House, Croydon, London, CR9 2BY) before your existing permit expires. You'll need to send your passport with your application.

Money

The currency in Wales is the pound sterling (£) and Wales has the same major banks as the rest of the UK. There are 1p, 2p, 5p, 10p, 20p, 50p, £1 and £2 coins and £5, £10, £20 and £50 notes.

Most banks and larger post offices can change foreign currency; US dollars and euros are the easiest currencies to change.

Nearly all banks in Wales have ATMs linked to international systems such as Cirrus, Maestro or Plus. However, an increasing number of ATMs, especially the ones you find in small shops and at service stations, will make a charge for withdrawal (at least £1.50). It's best to avoid these and simply seek out a regular ATM that offers free withdrawals.

Various cards, including Visa, MasterCard, American Express (Amex) and Diners Club, are widely accepted in Wales, although some smaller businesses and B&Bs may prefer payment in cash. If your credit card is lost or stolen, contact the relevant provider.

Amex (☎01273-696933)

Diners Club (☎0870 190 0011)

MasterCard (☎0800 964767)

Visa (☎0800 891725)

Telephone

The UK uses the GSM 900/1800 mobile phone network, which covers the rest of Europe, Australia and New Zealand, but isn't compatible with the North American GSM 1900 network (though some North Americans have GSM 1900/900 phones that work in the UK). If you have a GSM phone, check with your service provider about using it in the UK, and beware of calls being routed internationally (very expensive for a 'local' call).

You can also rent a mobile phone – ask at a local tourist office for details – or buy a 'pay-as-you-go' UK SIM card for as little as £10.

To dial a UK number from overseas, dial your country's international access code, then 44 (the country code for the UK), then the local number *without* the initial 0.

Time

All of the UK is on GMT/UTC in winter and GMT/UTC plus one hour during summer. Clocks are set forward by an hour on the last Sunday in March and set back on the last Sunday in October.

scenes, and there are small above-the-parapet gay communities in Newport and in the university towns of Aberystwyth and Bangor, although overt displays of affection may not be wise beyond acknowledged venues. The latter two University of Wales campuses also have limited but regular social events for gay and lesbian students (and visitors), and have lesbian/gay/bisexual student officers who can be contacted for information and help.

Wales' biggest gay/lesbian/bisexual bash is the extravagant **Cardiff Mardi Gras** (www.cardiffmardigras. co.uk) held in late August or early September.

For more information try the following websites.

Diva (www.divamag.co.uk) British lesbian magazine.

Gay Times (www.gaytimes. co.uk) British gay periodical.

Gay Wales (www.gaywales. co.uk) The best Wales-specific resource, with news, events, listings and helplines.

Lesbian & Gay Switchboard (☎0300-330 0630; www.llgs.org.uk; ☉10am-11pm) London resource that can help with most enquiries.

Pink UK (pinkuk.com) UK-wide gay and lesbian resource.

Holidays

Most banks and businesses and a few museums and attractions are closed on public holidays. A 'bank holiday' is a weekday closure of major businesses and tends to fall on the first or last Monday of particular months. These are popular times for British weekend trips, so be sure to book accommodation ahead.

Wales' official public holidays:

New Year's Day 1 January

Good Friday March/April

Easter Monday March/April

May Day Bank Holiday First Monday in May

Spring Bank Holiday Last Monday in May

Summer Bank Holiday Last Monday in August

Christmas Day 25 December

Boxing Day/St Stephen's Day 26 December

If New Year's Day, Christmas Day or Boxing Day falls on a weekend, the following Monday is also a bank holiday. Most museums and attractions in Wales close on Christmas and Boxing Day but stay open for the other holidays. Exceptions are those that normally close on Sunday. Some smaller museums close on Monday and/ or Tuesday.

Peak holiday times in Wales coincide with the school holidays, notably Christmas and New Year, Easter, six weeks in July and August, and two midterm breaks of a week each (one in February and one in October). During these times it's essential to book transport and accommodation in advance, and be prepared for larger crowds at the major attractions. In particular, for B&B accommodation during the August school holidays start looking for vacancies a good six months in advance. You'll be amazed just how fast things get booked up.

Insurance

However you're travelling, make sure you take out a comprehensive travel insurance policy that covers you for medical expenses, luggage theft or loss, and cancellation of (or delays in) your travel arrangements. When choosing a policy, check whether the insurance company will make payments directly to providers or reimburse you later for overseas health expenditures.

The National Health Service (NHS) provides free treatment across the UK, including Wales, and foreign nationals are entitled to register with a local doctor if staying in the UK for an extended period. EU nationals carrying the European Health Insurance Card (EHIC) may receive free treatment. However, the UK notified all European member states in 2008 that their citizens will be expected to show an EHIC in order to access necessary hospital treatment without charge. If overseas visitors are not able to do this, they will be liable for NHS charges. Any prescriptions issued will still be chargeable unless the patient is covered by one of the NHS exemptions. For more details of the scheme and how to apply for an EHIC card, visit www.nhs. uk/NHSEngland/Healthcareabroad/EHIC.

Paying for your flight tickets with a credit card often provides limited travel-accident insurance (ie it covers accidental death, loss of limbs or permanent total disablement). You may be able to reclaim the payment if the operator doesn't deliver the service, but this should not be relied upon instead of a full travel insurance policy.

Finally, it's a good idea to photocopy all of your important documents (including your travel insurance policy) before you leave home. Leave one copy with someone at home and keep another with you, separate from the originals. If something does go wrong, you'll be glad you did.

Internet Access

If you're travelling in Wales with a laptop, or a handheld wireless device such as an iPhone, getting online is easy. Many upmarket hotels, and plenty of midrange B&Bs and even hostels, now offer in-room internet access via an ethernet connection or wi-fi. Increasingly, it's free to guests (sometimes password protected).

If the hotel insists on making a charge, there is an ever-increasing number of wi-fi hot spots around Wales where you can access the internet with a wi-fi-enabled laptop for free.

If you don't have a laptop, the best places to check email and surf the internet are public libraries – almost every town and village in Wales has at least a couple of computer terminals devoted o the internet, and they are mostly free to use.

Internet cafes are also common in cities and larger towns, and generally charge £2 to £5 per hour. Always check the minimum charge, though, before you settle in – it's sometimes not worth the 10 minutes it takes to check your emails.

Many of the larger tourist offices across the country have internet access as well.

Legal Matters

If you are a victim of petty crime, head to the nearest police station to file a crime report. You will need this for your insurance claim. It's a good idea to take some identification with you, such as a passport.

Police have the power to detain anyone suspected of having committed an offence punishable by imprisonment (including drug offences) for up to six hours. They can search you, take photographs and fingerprints, and question you. You are legally required to provide your correct name and address – not doing so, or giving false details, is an offence – but you are not obliged to answer any other questions.

After six hours, the police must either formally charge you or let you go. If you are detained and/or arrested, you have the right to inform a lawyer and one other person, though you have no right to actually see the lawyer or make a telephone call. If you don't know a lawyer, the police will inform the duty solicitor for you.

Possession of a small amount of cannabis is an offence punishable by a fine, but possession of a larger amount of cannabis, or any amount of harder drugs, is much more serious, with a sentence of up to 14 years in prison. Police have the right to search anyone they suspect of possessing drugs.

You're allowed to have a maximum blood alcohol level of 35mg/100mL when driving. Traffic offences (illegal parking, speeding etc) often incur a fine, which you're usually given 30 to 60 days to pay. Speeding incurs a £60 fine and two penalty points if you hold a UK driving licence.

Maps

Two useful countrywide maps, updated annually by **Visit Wales** (☎08708-300306; www.visitwales.co.uk; ⊙9am-5pm Mon-Fri), are available at nearly every tourist office. The *Wales Tourist Map* presents all major roads and major sights, national parks, towns with tourist offices (and a list of those open in winter), several town plans and suggested car tours. The free *Wales Bus, Rail and Tourist Map and Guide* manages to map just about every bus and train route in Wales that has more than three services per week, plus the essentials of bus, train and ferry connections into Wales, as well as tables of frequencies and information numbers. Both maps will come in very handy on the ground.

Free regional transport booklets, with complete maps and timetables, are also available at tourist offices, and train stations stock free timetables provided by each train operator.

For motoring, there is a huge array of maps available. You can pick up a decent road map, such as the *AA Road Atlas Great Britain and Ireland,* at just about any motorway service station you stop at on the way through Wales. Also look for the OS Routemaster series at 1:250,000, while A to Z publishes 1:200,000 *North Wales* and *South Wales* road maps, with useful detailed town indexes.

For walkers and cyclists, it's essential to have a good map before setting off on

any trip. Most tourist offices and local bookshops stock maps produced by the UK's national mapping agency, the **Ordnance Survey** (OS; www.ordnancesurvey.co.uk), which cover its regions, including the useful 1:50,000 Landranger series and the excruciatingly detailed 1:25,000 Explorer series. OS Pathfinder Walking Guides cover short walks in popular areas, and Outdoor Leisure maps cover the national parks, both at 1:25,000.

Maps can be ordered online at the OS website or from www.amazon.co.uk.

Toilets

Public toilets can be a hit-and-miss affair, depending on how much the local council spends on their upkeep, but they are almost always of the sit-down variety and equipped with toilet paper. In major towns and cities, the public toilets are generally clean and free to use. Likewise, toilets at train stations and motorway service stations are regularly maintained and fine on the whole.

For a more luxurious loo off the beaten track, you can always stop off at a local cafe, a village pub or a rural coffee shop to use the facilities. You will be expected to buy a coffee or drink while you're there, but it's a chance to sit down and plan your route at the same time.

If you're particularly concerned about public conveniences, do some advance research at www.loo.co.uk.

Tourist Information

Wales is blessed with a network of superb, government-funded tourist offices in just about every major town and city you could hope to visit, and they are staffed with friendly, knowledgeable staff. Make the tourist office your friend. It will serve you well.

Tourist offices can provide maps and brochures, and often also feature books on Welsh culture, food and mythology, OS maps for walkers, and even local art exhibitions. Staff speak English, often Welsh, and sometimes have a basic grasp of other main European languages. For specialist outdoors information, towns in and around Wales' three national parks also often boast a tourist office run by the park (which can be attached to the regular town tourist office).

Many tourist offices make local hotel and B&B reservations, sometimes for a small fee; you pay a £2 fee and a 10% deposit, which is then deducted from the cost of your accommodation. Some tourist offices now have limited currency-exchange services and internet access, the latter especially in more rural areas.

Visit Wales (☑08708-300306; www.visitwales.co.uk; ⊙9am-5pm Mon-Fri) is the department for tourism within the National (Welsh) Assembly. Its contact centre is your first port of call for information on holidays and short breaks in Wales.

Details of tourist offices appear in each major city, town or area listing.

Travellers with Disabilities

For many disabled travellers, Wales is a strange mix of user-friendliness and unfriendliness. Most new buildings are wheelchair accessible, so large new hotels and modern tourist attractions are usually fine. However, most B&Bs and guesthouses have been converted from hard-to-adapt older buildings. This means that travellers with mobility problems may pay more for accommodation than their able-bodied fellows.

It's a similar story with public transport. Newer buses sometimes have steps that lower for easier access, as do trains, but it's always wise to check before setting out. Most tourist offices, tourist attractions and public buildings reserve parking spaces for the disabled near the entrance. Most tourist offices in Wales are wheelchair accessible, have counter sections at wheelchair height, and provide information on accessibility in their particular area.

Many ticket offices and banks are fitted with hearing loops to assist the hearing impaired; look for the ear logo.

Visit Wales (☑08708-300306; www.visitwales. co.uk; ⊙9am-5pm Mon-Fri) publishes useful information on accommodation for people with disabilities in its *Where to Stay* guide, which is available at tourist offices and online.

The **National Trust** (NT; ☑0844 800 1895; www.nationaltrust.org.uk) has its own *Access Guide* (downloadable as a PDF file) and offers free admission at all sites for companions of the disabled.

Cadw (☑0800 074 3121; cadw.wales.gov.uk), the Welsh historic monument agency, allows wheelchair users and the visually impaired (and their companions) free entry to all monuments under its auspices.

For more information contact the following organisations:

Disability Wales (☑029-2088 7352; www.disabilitywales.org) The national association of disability groups in Wales is a good source of information.

Disability Rights UK (☑020-7250 3222; http://disabilityrightsuk.org) Radar publishes *Holidays in the British Isles*, an annually updated guide to accessible accommodation in the UK and Ireland.

Royal National Institute for the Blind (RNIB; ☑0303-123 9999; www.rnib.org.uk) RNIB's holiday service provides information for the visually impaired. It also produces a guidebook of hotels recommended by visually impaired people, which is available in large print and Braille, and on tape and disc.

Shopmobility (☑0845-644 2446; www.shopmobilityuk.org) UK-wide scheme under which wheelchairs and electric scooters are available in some towns at central points for access to shopping areas. The scheme is run as a charity in Cardiff; in other Welsh towns (including Swansea, Newport, Merthyr Tydfil and Wrexham) it's council-run, with modest rental fees.

Tourism for All (☑0845-124 9971; www.tourismforall.org.uk) A UK-based group that provides tips and information for travellers with disabilities.

Transport

GETTING THERE & AWAY

Airports & Airlines

Although Cardiff has an international airport, most overseas visitors fly into London. Five international airports service the UK's capital but Heathrow is by far the biggest, serving most of the world's major airlines. It is also the closest to Wales. Other options include Manchester, which is handy for North Wales, and Bristol and Birmingham, both close to the Welsh border.

Many of the airlines directly servicing Wales are budget operators, which means you might get a good deal if you're coming from one of the handful of destinations that they fly from.

Airports
ENGLAND

London Heathrow Airport (www.heathrowairport.com) The UK's major hub welcoming flights from all over the world.

Manchester Airport (www.manchesterairport.co.uk) Flights from all over Europe and the Middle East, as well as some destinations in Africa, Asia, North America and Central America.

Bristol Airport (www.bristolairport.co.uk) Flights from all over Europe as well as some popular holidays destinations in North Africa and North America.

Birmingham International Airport (www.birminghamairport.co.uk) Flights from all over the world, but mainly Europe, New York and Dubai.

WALES

Cardiff Airport (www.tbicardiffairport.com) Flights to Anglesey and UK destinations, including Newcastle, Glasgow, Edinburgh, Belfast and Jersey. European destinations include Cork, Dublin, Paris, Amsterdam, Munich, Geneva and Murcia; charter flights service holiday destinations in summer.

Anglesey Airport (☎01407-878056) Flights to Cardiff with **Citywing** (www.citywing.com).

Land
Bus

Buses between England and Wales are generally slower, cheaper and more flexible than trains. Local buses zip across the border from Gloucester, Hereford and Ludlow.

National Express (☎08717 81 81 78; www.nationalexpress.co.uk) operates frequent services between most major cities in the UK. The sample fares in the table on p312 are the cheapest options for next-day travel.

Megabus (www.uk.megabus.com) offers one-way fares from London to Cardiff (via Newport) from as little as £4.

CLIMATE CHANGE & TRAVEL

Every form of transport that relies on carbon-based fuel generates CO_2, the main cause of human-induced climate change. Modern travel is dependent on aeroplanes, which might use less fuel per kilometre per person than most cars but travel much greater distances. The altitude at which aircraft emit gases (including CO_2) and particles also contributes to their climate change impact. Many websites offer 'carbon calculators' that allow people to estimate the carbon emissions generated by their journey and, for those who wish to do so, to offset the impact of the greenhouse gases emitted with contributions to portfolios of climate-friendly initiatives throughout the world. Lonely Planet offsets the carbon footprint of all staff and author travel.

ENGLAND TO WALES BUS DEPARTURES

FROM	TO	COST (£)	TIME (HR)
London Victoria	Cardiff	2	3¼
London Victoria	Aberystwyth	33	16½
London Victoria	Welshpool	32	5½
Bristol	Cardiff	9	1¼
Birmingham	Aberystwyth	28	4
Birmingham	Bangor	27	5
Edinburgh	Wrexham	43	12
Manchester	Llandudno	5	3½

Train

Fast train services run to Cardiff from Bristol, Birmingham and London Paddington. Direct trains from London Paddington also stop in Newport and Swansea. From Chester trains run to Bangor and Holyhead.

Other direct services include the following:

Cambrian Line (www.the-cambrianline.co.uk) Runs from Birmingham to Aberystwyth through Shrewsbury, Welshpool, Newtown and Machynlleth.

Heart of Wales Line (www.heart-of-wales.co.uk) A wonderful scenic route through the heart of Mid-Wales from Shrewsbury to Swansea via Knighton, Llandrindod Wells, Llanwrtyd Wells, Llandovery and Llandeilo.

West Coast Main Line (www.virgintrains.co.uk) Heads from London's Euston station to Bangor and Holyhead.

FARES

Trains in the UK are privatised and expensive in comparison to the rest of Europe. The fare structure is bewildering, but in general the cheapest tickets are those bought well in advance.

Timetables and fares are available from **National Rail** (☑08457 48 49 50; www.nationalrail.co.uk) and **trainline** (www.thetrainline.com). The sample fares in the table on p313 are the cheapest options for next-day travel.

TRAINS TO ENGLAND

All rail connections from Continental Europe to Wales pass through the Channel Tunnel to London. The high-speed passenger service **Eurostar** (☑in France 0892 35 35 39, in the UK 08705 186 186; www.eurostar.com) links London St Pancras International with Paris and Brussels. Like National Rail, the fare structure is baffling but, in short, it pays to book early. Cheaper rail connections can be had by crossing the Channel by ferry.

Sea

Ferries from Ireland operate from Dublin and Dun Laoghaire to Holyhead (1¾ to 3½ hours); Rosslare to Pembroke Dock (four hours) and Rosslare to Fishguard (3½ hours).

Fares vary considerably depending on the season, day, time and length of stay. Typical one-way fares start from £28 for a foot passenger and from £79 for a car and driver. Bikes can be transported for £10.

It's worth keeping an eye out for promotional fares that can reduce the cost considerably. Following are the main ferry services:

Irish Ferries (☑08717 300 400; www.irishferries.com) Ferry and fast-boat services from Dublin to Holyhead, and ferry services from Rosslare to Pembroke Dock.

Stena Line (☑08447 70 70 70; www.stenaline.co.uk) Ferry services from Dublin to Holyhead and Rosslare to Fishguard, and seasonal fast-boat services from Dun Laoghaire to Holyhead.

FERRIES TO ENGLAND

There's a wide array of ferry services to England from Continental Europe, including services from Denmark to Harwich; from the Neth-

SAILRAIL

A little-known option for travelling between the UK and Ireland, SailRail is an absolute bargain. The combined train and ferry service connects all UK and Irish train stations, and by comparison to airlines' restrictive fare rules, it's incredibly flexible. You can make changes to your booking, get a partial refund for some types of unused tickets and you can even rock up to a train station and buy your ticket on the day. And the best bit? Tickets cost from just £31 one way, children aged five to 15 pay half-price and under fives go free (but must have a reservation for the ferry). It's worth checking the main rail routes before booking to avoid unnecessary connections.

rlands to Newcastle, Hull nd Harwich; from Belgium o Hull and Ramsgate; from pain to Plymouth and Portsmouth; and from France to Dover, Newhaven, Portsmouth, Poole, Weymouth and Plymouth. For details check out www.directferries.co.uk or www.ferrybooker.com.

All of these port towns are linked into the train network, allowing you to get to Wales with two or three connecting trains.

GETTING AROUND

When people talk of the north–south divide in Wales, it's not just about language – part of it is physical. The barrier that is created by the Cambrian Mountains, Brecon Beacons and Snowdonia means that it's often quicker to duck in and out of England to get between north and south Wales. The same is true by train: there's a network of lines that slowly zigzag their way throughout the country but the faster trains head through Bristol and Birmingham. That said, both roads and rail lines are extremely scenic. In Wales that old adage about the journey outweighing the destination is aptly demonstrated here.

Wales is one of those places where Brits come to get back to nature, so it's very well set up for walkers and cyclists. With a flexible schedule and a modicum of patience it's quite possible to explore the country by public transport. However, it's worth considering hiring a car for at least part of your trip, especially if you're on a limited time frame and you're not averse to losing yourself in the sort of narrow country lanes that require pulling over when a car approaches from the other direction.

Buses are nearly always the cheapest way to get around but you'll generally get to places quicker by train. For information on services your best bet is the local tourist office where you'll be able to pick up maps and timetables. For up-to-date information on public transport throughout Wales check with **Traveline** (☏0871 200 22 33; www.traveline-cymru.info). Unfortunately the website doesn't list prices but the **Arriva Trains Wales** (www.arrivatrainswales.co.uk) website does, as does the **National Express** (☏08717 81 81 78; www.nationalexpress.co.uk) website.

Bicycle

Rural Wales is a great place for cycling: traffic on back roads is limited; there are loads of multi-use trails and three long-distance cycling routes as part of Sustrans'

National Cycle Network (NCN; www.sustrans.org.uk). For long-distance travel around Wales, though, the hilly and often mountainous terrain is mostly for experienced tourers.

In the larger towns and cities, there are few bike lanes and the usual problems with inconsiderate motorists. Bike theft can also be a major problem in urban areas.

Bikes can be taken on most trains, although there is limited space for them. On most services it's worth making a reservation for your bike at least 24 hours in advance; there is a small charge for this on some routes.

Arriva Trains Wales (www.arrivatrainswales.co.uk), which operates most rail services in Wales, publishes an annual guide called *Cycling by Train*. It's also available for download from the website.

Hire

Most sizeable or tourist towns in Wales have at least one shop where you can hire bikes from £12 to £25 per day for a tourer and £25 to £50 for a full-suspension mountain bike. Many hire outfits will require you to make a deposit of about £50 for a tourer and up to £100 for a top-of-the-line mean machine.

ENGLAND TO WALES TRAIN DEPARTURES

FROM	TO	COST (£)	TIME
Bristol	Cardiff	9	50min
Birmingham	Cardiff	24.50	2hr
London Paddington	Cardiff	34	2hr
London Euston	Bangor	38	3½hr
London Euston	Holyhead	38	4hr
Shrewsbury	Swansea	22	3hr
Shrewsbury	Llandrindod Wells	10.80	1½hr
Birmingham	Aberystwyth	14	3hr
Birmingham	Machynlleth	14	2¼hr
Chester	Holyhead	24.30	1¾hr

TRAVEL PASSES

If you're planning a whirlwind tour of Wales by public transport, getting an Explore Wales pass is a good idea. Passes allow free travel in Wales and adjacent areas of England, on all rail routes and nearly all intercity bus routes and can be bought online, at most staffed train stations and at rail-accredited travel agencies in Wales.

The passes also get you discounts on various sights and activities, on heritage railways and at a variety of accommodation. Full details are in the travel guide provided when you buy your pass.

The passes on offer include the following, which allow eight days of bus travel plus four days of train travel (within that period):

4 in 8 Day All Wales Pass (£94)

Freedom of South Wales Flexi Rover (£64)

North & Mid-Wales Flexi Rover (£64)

Bus

Wales' bus services are operated by dozens of private companies but you'll find centralised information on routes and timetables with **Traveline Cymru** (📞0870 608 2608; www.traveline-cymru.org.uk). Buses are generally reasonably priced and efficient, although some have limited weekend services (or don't run). Generally you'll need to hail the bus with an outstretched arm and pay the driver on board. Some buses, particularly in the cities, don't give change, so it pays to carry coins. Most fares within a region will be less than £5, while those within a city are generally less than £2.

Coaches are mainly run by **National Express** (📞08717 81 81 78; www.nationalexpress.co.uk), and for these you'll need to book and pay in advance.

Long-distance bus services are thin on the ground. Following are the principal cross-regional routes, all of which operate at least Monday to Saturday throughout the year:

National Express 409 London, Birmingham, Shrewsbury, Welshpool, Newtown, Aberystwyth

X32 Bangor, Caernarfon, Dolgellau, Machynlleth, Aberystwyth

X40 Cardiff, Swansea, Carmarthen, Aberystwyth

X50 Cardigan, Aberaeron, Aberystwyth

X94 Wrexham, Llangollen, Bala, Dolgellau, Barmouth

Apart from National Express, these are the biggest bus operators in Wales:

Arriva Cymru (📞0871 200 22 33; www.arrivabus.co.uk) Services in North and West Wales.

First Cymru (📞01792-582233; www.firstcymru.co.uk) Services in Swansea and southwest Wales.

Stagecoach (📞01633-485118; www.stagecoachbus.com/southwales) Services in southeast Wales.

Bus Passes

Apart from the combined bus and rail Explore Wales passes, there are lots of regional and local one-day and one-week passes, but many are only worthwhile if you're planning to do a lot of travel-ling. You can usually buy tickets from the bus driver.

FirstWeek South & West Wales Pass Unlimited travel on all First bus services in South and West Wales for seven days (adult/child £21/13.50).

FirstDay Swansea Bay Pass Unlimited travel on First and Pullman buses in Swansea and the Gower Peninsula for the day of purchase (adult/child £4.50/3.10). You can buy these passes in Swansea bus station, or from the driver on any First bus.

Snowdon Sherpa Day Ticket Covers all buses zipping around Snowdonia National Park (adult/child £4/2).

Red Rover Valid for one day on buses 1 to 99 in Gwynedd and the Isle of Anglesey in northwest Wales, including the Snowdon Sherpas (adult/child £6.40/3.20). You can buy these tickets from the driver; for full details ask at a tourist office.

If you are planning to travel throughout the UK, National Express has a variety of passes and discount cards, including options for senior travellers. More information is available online at www.nationalexpress.com.

National Park Bus Services

Each of Wales' national park authorities runs or organises dedicated bus services aimed at walkers and cyclists travelling around the parks. Many routes include transport for bicycles.

Car & Motorcycle

If you want to see the more remote regions of Wales or cram in as much as possible in a short time, travelling by car or motorcycle is the easiest way to go. There are very few tolls and petrol is expensive – about £1.36 per litre at the time of research.

Getting around North or South Wales is easy, but elsewhere roads are considerably slower, especially in he mountains and through Mid-Wales. To get from the northeast to the southeast, it's quickest to go via England. Rural roads are often single-track affairs with passing places only at intervals, and they can be treacherous in winter. In built-up areas be sure to check the parking restrictions as traffic wardens and clampers can be merciless.

Wales can be a dream for motorcyclists, with good-quality winding roads and stunning scenery. Just make sure your wet-weather gear is up to scratch.

If you're bringing your own vehicle from abroad, make sure you check that your insurance will cover you in the UK; third-party insurance is a minimum requirement. If you're renting a car, check the fine print – policies can vary widely and the cheapest hire rates often include a hefty excess (for which you are liable in the event of an accident).

Automobile Associations

The main motoring organisations provide services such as 24-hour breakdown assistance, maps and touring information – usually for an annual fee of around £30. Others are more like clubs.

Auto-Cycle Union (☑01788-566400; www.acu. org.uk)

Automobile Association (AA; ☑0800 085 2721; www. theaa.co.uk)

British Motorcyclists Federation (☑0116-279 5112; www.bmf.co.uk)

Environmental Transport Association (☑0800 212 810; www.eta.co.uk)

Royal Automobile Club (RAC; ☑0844 891 3111; www. rac.co.uk)

Hire

Hire cars are expensive in the UK and you'll usually get a better rate by booking online in advance. To hire a car, driv-

> ### SPEED LIMITS
> → 30mph (48km/h) in built-up areas
> → 60mph (96km/h) on main roads
> → 70mph (112km/h) on motorways and dual carriageways

ers must usually be between 23 and 65 years of age – outside these limits special conditions or insurance requirements may apply. You will also need a credit card to make an advance booking and act as a deposit.

For a compact car, expect to pay in the region of £140 a week (including insurance etc); most cars are manual; automatic cars are available but they're generally more expensive to hire. If you need a baby chair or booster seat, specify this at the time of booking.

Some agencies in Wales:

Alamo (☑0871 384 1086; www.alamo.co.uk)

Avis (☑0844 581 0147; www. avis.co.uk)

Budget (☑0844 544 3439; www.budget.co.uk)

Europcar (☑0871 384 9900; www.europcar.co.uk)

Hertz (☑0843 309 3099; www.hertz.co.uk)

Holiday Autos (☑0800 093 3111; www.holidayautos.co.uk)

Road Rules

A copy of the Highway Code can be bought in most bookshops or read online at www. gov.uk/highway-code.

The most basic rules:

→ Drive on the left, overtake to the right.

→ When entering a roundabout, give way to the right.

> ### HERITAGE RAILWAYS
>
> To a large extent, trains along Wales' north and south coasts were built to link the English rail network with seaports at Swansea, Pembroke Dock, Fishguard and Holyhead. But there are some fine rail journeys across the middle of the country and a staggering number of 'heritage' railways (mainly steam and narrow-gauge), survivors of an earlier era, worth seeking out for their spectacular scenery and hypnotic, clickety-clack pace.
>
> **Ffestiniog & Welsh Highland Railways** (www.festrail. co.uk) An integral, but incredibly scenic, part of the network heading from Porthmadog (on the Cambrian Coast Line) to Blaenau Ffestiniog and Caernarfon respectively.
>
> **Heart of Wales Line** (www.heart-of-wales.co.uk) One of Wales' most beautiful railway journeys heading from Shrewsbury to Swansea through southern Mid-Wales.
>
> **Cambrian Line** (www.thecambrianline.co.uk) Across northern Mid-Wales from Shrewsbury to Aberystwyth and its spectacular branch line up the coast from Machynlleth to Pwllheli and the Llŷn.
>
> **Conwy Valley Line** (www.conwy.gov.uk/cvr) A little gem heading down through Snowdonia from Llandudno to Blaenau Ffestiniog.

→ Safety belts must be worn by the driver and all passengers.

→ Motorcyclists and their passengers must wear helmets.

→ The legal alcohol limit is 80mg of alcohol per 100ml of blood or 35mg on the breath.

→ It is illegal to use a mobile phone while driving unless you have a hands-free kit.

Taxi

You'll usually find a taxi rank outside the train station in bigger towns. The best place to find the local taxi phone number is in the local pub. In rural areas a 5-mile ride will cost around £12.

Train

Like in the rest of the UK, the Welsh rail network has been privatised. **National**

Rail (☎08457 48 49 50; www. nationalrail.co.uk) provides centralised timetable information for all train operators in the UK, and allows you to buy tickets and make reservations by phone using a credit card. You can also buy tickets online through www. thetrainline.com, though you'll need a UK address to register with the site.

The following train operators provide the main rail services in Wales and on routes between England and Wales:

Train Routes

Arriva Trains Wales (www.arrivatrainswales.co.uk) Operates almost all train services in Wales.

First Great Western (☎08457 000 125; www.firstgreatwestern.co.uk) Operates the London (Paddington)–Cardiff–Swansea route.

Virgin Trains (☎08719 774 222; www.virgintrains.co.uk) Operates the London (Euston)–Chester–Holyhead route.

Classes & Costs

There are two classes of rail travel in the UK: 1st class and 'standard' class. First class costs about 50% more than standard and simply isn't worth the extra money.

You can roll up to a station and buy a standard single (one way) or return ticket, but this is often the dearest way to go. Each train company sets its own fares and has its own discounts, and passengers can only use tickets on services operated by the company that issued the ticket.

You might find that the same journey will have a different fare depending on whether you buy it at the station, over the phone or online. The fare system is so bizarre that in some cases two singles are cheaper than the ticket.

a return ticket, and even a one-way journey can be cheaper if you split it into two (ie if you're going from A to C, it can be cheaper to buy a single from A to B, and another single from B to C; go figure). You can check your options at www.splityourticket.co.uk.

The least expensive fares have advance-purchase and minimum-stay requirements, as well as limited availability. Children under five years travel free; those aged between five and 15 pay half-price for most tickets. When travelling with children, it is almost always worth buying a Family & Friends Railcard.

Main fare classifications:

Advance Has limited availability so must be booked well in advance; can only be used on the specific trains booked.

Anytime Buy any time, travel any time.

Off-peak Buy any time, travel outside peak hours.

Railcards

Railcards are valid for one year and entitle the holder to discounts of up to 30% on most rail (and some ferry) fares in the UK. You can buy a railcard at most train stations or at www.railcard.co.uk, but it must be delivered to a UK

address. Railcards are accepted by all train companies.

16-25 Railcard (£28) For those aged 16 to 25 years, or a full-time UK student of any age.

Disabled Persons Railcard (£20) Applies to its holder and one person accompanying them.

Family & Friends Railcard (£28) Allows discounts for up to four adults travelling together (only one needs to hold a card and you'll need one child in tow), and a 60% discount on children's fares.

Senior Railcard (£28) For anyone aged over 60.

Train Passes

BritRail passes (available only to non-Brits and bought overseas) are not cost effective for a holiday in Wales. The following local passes, both available through National Rail, will be more useful. They allow unlimited one-day rail travel on weekdays after 9am and on all weekends and holidays.

Cambrian Coaster Day Ranger (£10.50) Valid between Pwllheli and Machynlleth or Aberystwyth.

Heart of Wales Circular Day Rover (£34) Circular trip in either direction on the Heart of Wales line from Cardiff to Shrewsbury.

Language

You can get by almost anywhere in Wales these days without speaking Welsh. Nevertheless, anyone who's serious about getting to grips with Welsh culture will find it fun trying to speak basic Welsh.

The Welsh language belongs to the Celtic branch of the Indo-European language family. It's closely related to Breton and Cornish, and more distantly to Irish, Scottish and Manx. It's estimated there are over 700,000 Welsh speakers in Wales.

Pronunciation

All letters in Welsh are pronounced and the stress is usually on the second-last syllable. Letters are pronounced as in English, except for those listed below. If you read our coloured pronunciation guides as if they were English, you will be understood.

Note that vowels can be long or short. Those marked with a circumflex (eg *ê*) are long; those with a grave accent (eg *è*) short.

a	short as in 'map'; long as in 'farm'
e	short as in 'pen'; long as in 'there'
i	short as in 'bit'; long as in 'sleep'
o	short as in 'box'; long as in 'bore'
u	as i (short and long)
w	short as the 'oo' in 'book'; long as the 'oo' in 'spook'
y	as i (short or long); sometimes as the 'a' in 'about', especially in one-syllable words such as y, yr, fy, dy and yn

WANT MORE?

For in-depth language information and handy phrases, check out Lonely Planet's *British Language & Culture*. You'll find it at **shop.lonelyplanet.com**, or you can buy Lonely Planet's iPhone phrasebooks at the Apple App Store.

In words of one syllable, vowels followed by two consonants are short – eg *corff* (body). If a one-syllable word ends in *p, t, c, m* or *ng,* the vowel is short – eg *llong* (ship). If it ends in *b, d, g, f, dd, ff, th, ch* or *s,* the vowel is long – eg *bad* (boat) – as is any vowel at the end of a one-syllable word, eg *pla* (plague). In words of more than one syllable, all unstressed vowels are short, eg *cariadon* (lovers). Stressed vowels can be long or short and in general follow the rules for one-syllable words. Welsh also has several vowel sound combinations:

ae/ai/au	as the 'y' in 'my'
aw	as the 'ow' in 'cow'
ei/eu/ey	as the 'ay' in 'day'
ew	as a short 'e' followed by 'oo'
iw/uw/yw	as the 'ew' in 'few'
oe/oi	as 'oy' in 'boy'
ow	as the 'ow' in 'tow'
wy	as 'uey' (as in 'chop suey') or as the 'wi' in 'wing' (especially after g)

The combinations *ch, dd, ff, ng, ll, ph, rh* and *th* count as single consonants.

c	always as 'k'
ch	as the 'ch' in the Scottish *loch*
dd	as the 'th' in 'this'
ff	as the 'f' in 'fork'
g	always as the 'g' in 'garden'
ng	as the 'ng' in 'sing'
ll	as 'hl' (put the tongue in the position for 'l' and breathe out)
ph	as 'f'
r	rolled
rh	pronounced as 'hr'
s	always as in 'so'
si	as the 'sh' in 'shop'
th	always as the 'th' in 'thin'

BASICS

Hello.
Sut mae. sit mai

Good morning.
Bore da. *bo*·re dah

Good afternoon.
Prynhawn da. *pruhn*·hown dah

Good evening.
Noswaith dda. *nos*·waith thah

Good night.
Nos da. nohs dah

See you (later).
Wela i chi (wedyn). *we*·lah ee khee (*we*·din)

Goodbye.
Hwyl fawr. hueyl vowr

Please.
Os gwelwch in dda. os *gwe*·lookh uhn thah

Thank you (very much).
Diolch (in fawr iawn). dee·*olkh* (uhn vowr yown)

You're welcome.
Croeso. *kroy*·soh

Excuse me.
Esgusodwch fi. es·gi·so·*dookh* vee

Sorry./Forgive me.
Mae'n ddrwg gyda fi. main throog *guh*·da vee

Don't mention it.
Peidiwch â sôn. *pay*·dyookh ah sohn

May I?
Ga i? gah ee

Do you mind?
Oes ots gyda chi? oys ots *gi*·da khee

How are you?
Sut ydych chi? sit *uh*·deekh khee

(Very) well.
(Da) iawn. (dah) yown

Yes & No

How you say 'yes' and 'no' in Welsh depends on the verb used in the question. So, rather than simply 'yes', you might answer 'I do' *(Ydw)* or 'It is' *(Ydy)*. Here are just a few examples:

Yes./No.	*Ie./Nage.*	yeh/*nah*·geh

(general use when the question doesn't start with a verb)

I do./I am.	*Ydw.*	uh·*doo*
I don't./ I'm not.	*Nac ydw.*	nak uh·*doo*
It is.	*Ydy.*	uh·*dee*
It isn't.	*Nac ydy.*	nak uh·*dee*
There is.	*Oes.*	oys
There isn't.	*Nac oes.*	nak oys

What's your name?
Beth yw eich enw chi? beth yu uhkh *e*·noo khee

My name is ...
Fy enw i yw ... vuh *e*·noo ee yu ...

Where are you from?
O ble ydych chi'n dod? oh ble *uh*·deekh kheen dohd

I'm from ...
Dw i'n dod o ... doo een dohd oh ...

I don't understand.
Dw i ddim in deall. doo ee thim uhn *deh*·ahl

How do you say ...?
Sut mae dweud ...? sit mai dwayd ...

What's this called in Welsh?
Beth yw hwn yn Gymraeg? beth yu hoon uhn *guhm*·raig

I don't know.
Wn i ddim. oon ee dhim

EATING & DRINKING

Are you serving food?
Ydych chi'n gweini bwyd? *uh*·deekh kheen *gway*·nee bweed

A table for ..., please.
Bwrdd i ... os gwelwch yn dda. boordh ee ... os *gwe*·lookh uhn thah

Can I see the menu, please?
Ga i weld y fwydlen, os gwelwch yn dda? gah ee weld uh *voo*·eed·len os *gwe*·lookh uhn thah

What's the special of the day?
Beth yw pryd arbennig y dydd? beth yu preed ar·*be*·nig uh deeth

Can I have ...?
Ga i ...? gah ee ...

The bill, please.
Y bil, os gwelwch yn dda. uh bil os *gwe*·lookh uhn thah

Cheers!
Iechyd Da! *ye*·khid dah

I'd like a (half) pint of ...	*Ga i (hanner o) beint o ...*	gah ee (*ha*·ner oh) baynt oh ...
bitter	*chwerw*	*khwe*·roo
cider	*seidr*	*say*·duhr
lager	*lager*	*lah*·guhr

TIME, DATES & NUMBERS

minute	*munud*	*mi*·nid
hour	*awr*	owr
week	*wythnos*	oo·*ith*·nos
month	*mis*	mees
today	*heddiw*	*hedh*·yoo
tomorrow	*yfory*	uh·*voh*·ree

PLACE NAMES

Welsh place names are often based on words that describe a landmark or a feature of the countryside.

bach	bahkh	small
bro	broh	vale
bryn	brin	hill
caer	kair	fort
capel	ka·pl	chapel
carreg	kar·eg	stone
clwn	kloon	meadow
coed	koyd	wood/forest
cwm	koom	valley
dinas	dee·nas	hill fortress
eglwys	eglueys	church
fach	vahkh	small
fawr	vowr	big
ffordd	forth	road
glan	glahn	shore
glyn	glin	valley
isa	issa	lower
llan	hlan	church/enclosure
llyn	hlin	lake
maes	mais	field
mawr	mowr	big
mynydd	muhneeth	mountain
nant	nahnt	valley/stream
ogof	o·gov	cave
pen	pen	head/top/end
plas	plahs	hall/mansion
pont	pont	bridge
rhos	hros	moor/marsh
twr	toor	tower
tŷ	tee	house
uchaf	ikhav	upper
ynys	uh·nis	island/holm

Monday	Dydd Llun	deeth hleen
Tuesday	Dydd Mawrth	deeth mowrrth
Wednesday	Dydd Mercher	deeth merr·kherr
Thursday	Dydd Iau	deeth yigh
Friday	Dydd Gwener	deeth gwe·ner
Saturday	Dydd Sadwrn	deeth sa·doorn
Sunday	Dydd Sul	deeth seel

January	Ionawr	yo·nowr
February	Chwefror	khwev·rohr
March	Mawrth	mowrth
April	Ebrill	ehb·rihl
May	Mai	mai
June	Mehefin	me·he·vin
July	Gorffennaf	gor·fe·nahv
August	Awst	owst
September	Medi	me·dee
October	Hydref	huhd·rev
November	Tachwedd	tahkh·weth
December	Rhagfyr	hrag·vir

0	dim	dim
1	un	een
2	dau (m)	dy
	dwy (f)	duey
3	tri (m)	tree
	tair (f)	tair
4	pedwar (m)	ped·wahr
	pedair (f)	ped·air
5	pump	pimp
6	chwech	khwekh
7	saith	saith
8	wyth	ueyth
9	naw	now
10	deg	dehg

GLOSSARY

AONB – Area of Outstanding Natural Beauty

aber – confluence of water bodies; river mouth

ap – prefix in a Welsh name meaning 'son of' (Welsh)

bridleway – path that can be used by walkers, horse riders and cyclists

byway – secondary or side road

Cadw – Welsh historic monuments agency (Welsh)

castell – castle (Welsh)

coasteering – making your way around the coastline by rock climbing, gully scrambling, caving, wave riding and cliff jumping

Cool Cymru – rise of Welsh bands during the mid- to late 1990s

cromlech – burial chamber (Welsh)

Cymraeg – Welsh language (Welsh)

Cymru – Wales (Welsh)

dolmen – chambered tomb

eisteddfod – literally a gathering or session; festival in which competitions are held in music, poetry, drama and the fine arts; plural eisteddfodau (Welsh)

Gymraeg – Welsh language (Welsh)

hiraeth – sense of longing for the green, green grass of home (Welsh)

Landsker Line – boundary between Welsh-speaking and English-speaking areas in south-west Wales

Mabinogion – key source of Welsh folk legends

menhir – standing stone

merthyr – martyr (Welsh)

mynydd – mountain (Welsh)

National Assembly – National (Welsh) Assembly; devolved regional government of Wales, in power since 1999

newydd – new (Welsh)

NT – National Trust

ogham – ancient Celtic script

oriel – gallery (Welsh)

OS – Ordnance Survey

Plaid Cymru – Party of Wales; originally Plaid Cenedlaethol Cymru (Welsh Nationalist Party)

RSPB – Royal Society for the Protection of Birds

S4C – Sianel Pedwar Cymru; national Welsh-language TV broadcaster

SSSI – Site of Special Scientific Interest

Sustrans – sustainable transport charity encouraging people to walk, cycle and use public transport

towpath – path running beside a river or canal

tre – town (Welsh)

urdd – youth (Welsh)

way – long-distance trail

y, yr – the, of the (Welsh)

YHA – Youth Hostel Association

Behind the Scenes

SEND US YOUR FEEDBACK

We love to hear from travellers – your comments keep us on our toes and help make our books better. Our well-travelled team reads every word on what you loved or loathed about this book. Although we cannot reply individually to postal submissions, we always guarantee that your feedback goes straight to the appropriate authors, in time for the next edition. Each person who sends us information is thanked in the next edition – the most useful submissions are rewarded with a selection of digital PDF chapters.

Visit **lonelyplanet.com/contact** to submit your updates and suggestions or to ask for help. Our award-winning website also features inspirational travel stories, news and discussions.

Note: We may edit, reproduce and incorporate your comments in Lonely Planet products such as guidebooks, websites and digital products, so let us know if you don't want your comments reproduced or your name acknowledged. For a copy of our privacy policy visit lonelyplanet.com/privacy.

OUR READERS

Many thanks to the travellers who used the last edition and wrote to us with helpful hints, useful advice and interesting anecdotes:

Casey Bergman, Joe Brann, Jenni Dixon, Concepcion Dominguez, Frans Groot, Kelvin Hayes, Jane Hydon, Trevor Mazzucchelli, Lorena Mazija, Noel McPherson, Alice Rawstorne, Hugo Rhys, Adrian Short, Ian Tanner, Ruth Williams, Denis Wolff

AUTHOR THANKS

Peter Dragicevich

Many thanks to Jane Bentley and her postgraduate class from the Cardiff School of Journalism, Media & Cultural Studies, who gave me the low-down on all of the coolest places in Cardiff. And thanks to Matt Swaine for setting it up, and for providing feedback about climbing Snowdon. Thanks, too, to Lorraine and James Hedderman, Kerri and Finn Tyler, and Roy Lawford for good times in Anglesey, Harlech and Llangollen.

Etain O'Carroll

Thanks to all the staff in tourist offices across Pembrokeshire and Mid-Wales for their patient answers to my numerous questions, and to all the unwitting helpers along the way who gave me tips on where to go, eat, drink and stay. Particular thanks to Peter for all the tips and assistance, Anja Gebel for the low-down on Aberystwyth, and to Mark and the boys for company on the road and the space to hole up and get writing on return.

Helena Smith

I'm grateful to Grahame and Angela for their insights, and to everyone who helped with food, sights and accommodation along the way, particularly at Llanddeusant hostel. And thanks to the family in Swansea who didn't mind a surprise visit and welcomed me into their home so I could see the room I was born in.

ACKNOWLEDGMENTS

Climate map data adapted from Peel MC, Finlayson BL & McMahon TA (2007) 'Updated World Map of the Köppen-Geiger Climate Classification', *Hydrology and Earth System Sciences*, 11, 163344.

Cover photograph: Cwm Idwal, Glyderau, Justin Foulkes/Getty Images

THIS BOOK

This 5th edition of Lonely Planet's *Wales* guidebook was researched and written by Peter Dragicevich, Etain O'Carroll and Helena Smith. The previous edition was written by Peter Dragicevich and David Atkinson. The guidebook was commissioned in Lonely Planet's London office, and produced by the following:

Commissioning Editor Clifton Wilkinson

Coordinating Editors Kristin Odijk, Justin Flynn
Senior Cartographer Anthony Phelan
Cartographer Julie Dodkins
Coordinating Layout Designer Wendy Wright
Managing Editors Sasha Baskett, Angela Tinson
Senior Editor Karyn Noble
Managing Layout Designer Jane Hart
Assisting Editors Alison Barber, Peter Cruttenden, Kate Daly, Kate Evans, Helen Koehne

Assisting Cartographers Mick Garret, Rachel Imeson
Cover Research Naomi Parker
Internal Image Research Barbara Di Castro
Language Content Annelies Mertens

Thanks to Anita Banh, Ryan Evans, Larissa Frost, Genesys India, Jouve India, Wayne Murphy, Trent Paton, Kerrianne Southway, Gerard Walker

Index

NOTES

NOTES

NOTES

Map Legend

Sights

- Beach
- Buddhist
- Castle
- Christian
- Hindu
- Islamic
- Jewish
- Monument
- Museum/Gallery
- Ruin
- Winery/Vineyard
- Zoo
- Other Sight

Activities, Courses & Tours

- Diving/Snorkelling
- Canoeing/Kayaking
- Skiing
- Surfing
- Swimming/Pool
- Walking
- Windsurfing
- Other Activity/ Course/Tour

Sleeping

- Sleeping
- Camping

Eating

- Eating

Drinking

- Drinking
- Cafe

Entertainment

- Entertainment

Shopping

- Shopping

Information

- Post Office
- Tourist Information

Transport

- Airport
- Border Crossing
- Bus
- Cable Car/ Funicular
- Cycling
- Ferry
- Monorail
- Parking
- S-Bahn
- Taxi
- Train/Railway
- Tram
- Tube Station
- U-Bahn
- Underground Train Station
- Other Transport

Routes

- Tollway
- Freeway
- Primary
- Secondary
- Tertiary
- Lane
- Unsealed Road
- Plaza/Mall
- Steps
- Tunnel
- Pedestrian Overpass
- Walking Tour
- Walking Tour Detour
- Path

Boundaries

- International
- State/Province
- Disputed
- Regional/Suburb
- Marine Park
- Cliff
- Wall

Population

- Capital (National)
- Capital (State/Province)
- City/Large Town
- Town/Village

Geographic

- Hut/Shelter
- Lighthouse
- Lookout
- Mountain/Volcano
- Oasis
- Park
- Pass
- Picnic Area
- Waterfall

Hydrography

- River/Creek
- Intermittent River
- Swamp/Mangrove
- Reef
- Canal
- Water
- Dry/Salt/ Intermittent Lake
- Glacier

Areas

- Beach/Desert
- Cemetery (Christian)
- Cemetery (Other)
- Park/Forest
- Sportsground
- Sight (Building)
- Top Sight (Building)

OUR STORY

A beat-up old car, a few dollars in the pocket and a sense of adventure. In 1972 that's all Tony and Maureen Wheeler needed for the trip of a lifetime – across Europe and Asia overland to Australia. It took several months, and at the end – broke but inspired – they sat at their kitchen table writing and stapling together their first travel guide, *Across Asia on the Cheap*. Within a week they'd sold 1500 copies. Lonely Planet was born.

Today, Lonely Planet has offices in Melbourne, London and Oakland, with more than 600 staff and writers. We share Tony's belief that 'a great guidebook should do three things: inform, educate and amuse'.

OUR WRITERS

Peter Dragicevich

Coordinating Author; Cardiff; Anglesey & the North Coast; Snowdonia & the Llŷn Wales has held a fascination for Peter ever since he was sent to write about Welsh castles for one of his first ever newspaper travel features. Since then he's co-authored dozens of Lonely Planet titles, including the previous edition of this book, three editions of *Great Britain*, and *Walking in Britain*, where he got to trek around the entirety of the beautiful Pembrokeshire coast. By researching and writing the Anglesey & the North Coast chapter of this book, he's now covered every corner of Wales for Lonely Planet. And while his name may not be Welsh, it does at least have over half a dragon in it! Peter also contributed to the Plan Your Trip section, and wrote the Wales Today and History chapters.

Read more about Peter at:
lonelyplanet.com/members/peterdragicevich

Etain O'Carroll

St Davids & Pembrokeshire; Aberystwyth & Mid-Wales Cherished childhood memories of summer holidays spent clambering over castle walls, slipping down rocky waterfalls and digging siblings into the sand have given Etain a lifelong love of Wales. Regular return visits to explore the same winding roads and mountain passes, her own children in tow, have led to the delight in discovering how much the hotels, restaurants and roads have improved. Etain works as a freelance travel writer and photographer (www.etaino.co.uk) and now lives in Oxford. Etain also wrote the Travel with Children, Culture, The Natural Environment and Transport chapters.

Read more about Etain at:
lonelyplanet.com/members/etainocarroll

Helena Smith

Brecon Beacons & Southeast Wales; Swansea, Gower & Carmarthenshire Helena Smith was born in Swansea, and she was very happy to go back to explore the city, the Gower and the Brecon Beacons. She is a travel writer, photographer and editor and blogs about food and community at eathackney.com. Helena also wrote the Outdoor Activities, Food & Drink and Directory chapters.

Published by Lonely Planet Publications Pty Ltd
ABN 36 005 607 983
5th edition – January 2014
ISBN 978 1 74220 134 4
© Lonely Planet 2014   Photographs © as indicated 2014
10 9 8 7 6 5 4 3 2 1
Printed in China

Although the authors and Lonely Planet have taken all reasonable care in preparing this book, we make no warranty about the accuracy or completeness of its content and, to the maximum extent permitted, disclaim all liability arising from its use.